The New International Lesson Annual

2005-2006

September–August

The
New International
Lesson Annual

2005–2006

September–August

Abingdon Press
Nashville

THE NEW INTERNATIONAL LESSON ANNUAL 2005–2006

Copyright © 2005 by Abingdon Press

This book is printed on recycled, acid-free, elemental-chlorine–free paper.

ISBN 0-687-03912-6

ISSN 1084-872X

05 06 07 08 09 10 11 12 13—10 9 8 7 6 5 4 3 2 1

MANUFACTURED IN THE UNITED STATES OF AMERICA

PREFACE

The 2005–2006 edition of *The New International Lesson Annual* is both firmly rooted in the tradition of the International Lesson Series and on the cutting edge of twenty-first century Sunday school curriculum designed for a life-changing relationship with God through Jesus Christ. Each weekly session is designed to give you and your students the knowledge you need to integrate the truth of the Scripture lesson into your own heart and life.

The lessons in this book are based on the work of the Committee on the Uniform Series of the National Council of Churches, a representative ecumenical group of writers, editors, pastors, and Christian educators who work together to develop a framework around which each session is built. Although the International Lesson Series predated the National Council of Churches by decades, this series has always been designed ecumenically by church leaders and teachers who are passionate about their own relationship with God and about sharing God's good news with others.

Although adult learners often use *The New International Lesson Annual,* it is mainly designed for teachers of adults who want a solid biblical basis for each session and a teaching plan that will help them lead their classes. The following features are especially valuable for busy teachers who want to provide in-depth Bible study experiences for their students. Each lesson includes the follow sections:

Previewing the Lesson highlights the background and lesson Scripture, focus of the lesson, three goals for the learners, a pronunciation guide in lessons where you may find unfamiliar words or names, and supplies you will need to teach.

Reading the Scripture includes the Scripture lesson printed in both the *New Revised Standard Version* and the *New International Version.* By printing these two highly respected translations in parallel columns, you can easily compare them for in-depth study. If your own Bible is another version, you will then have three translations to explore as you prepare each lesson.

Understanding the Scripture closely analyzes the background Scripture by looking at each verse. Here you will find help in understanding concepts, ideas, places, and persons pertinent to each week's lesson. You may also find explanations for Greek or Hebrew words that are essential for understanding the text.

Interpreting the Scripture looks at the lesson Scripture and relates it to contemporary life.

Sharing the Scripture provides you with a detailed teaching plan. It is divided into two major sections: Preparing to Teach and Leading the Class.

In the *Preparing to Teach* section you will find a devotional reading related to the lesson for your own spiritual enrichment and a "to do list" to prepare your mind and classroom for the session.

The *Leading the Class* portion begins with "Gather to Learn" activities to welcome the students and draw them into the lesson. Here, the students' stories and experiences are highlighted as preparation for the Bible story. The next three headings of *Leading the Class* are the three main "Goals for the Learners." The first goal always focuses on the

Bible story itself. The second goal relates the Bible story to the lives of the adults in your class. The third goal prompts the students to take action on what they have learned. You will find a variety of activities under each of these goals to help the learners fulfill them. The activities are diverse in nature and may include: listening, reading, writing, speaking, singing, drawing, interacting with others, and meditating. The lesson ends with "Continue the Journey," where you will find closing activities, preparation for the following week, and ideas for students to commit themselves to action during the week, based on what they have learned.

In addition to these weekly features, you will find:

- **Introductions to each quarter** provide you a quick survey of each lesson to be studied in the quarter. This feature is found on the first page of each quarter.
- **Meet Our Writer,** which follows each quarterly introduction, provides biographical information about each writer, including education, pastoral and/or academic teaching experience, previous publications, and family information.
- **Background articles for each quarter,** written by the same writer who authored the lessons, are designed to give you a broader scope of the materials to be covered than is possible in each weekly lesson. You will find these immediately preceding the first lesson in the quarter.
- **Teacher helps,** which in this volume include an article entitled "Saying Hello and Goodbye," which considers greetings and farewells in our weekly lessons and ways the class can be more intentional about bidding welcome and taking leave, and "Possible Chronology of the Life of Paul," which is a chart showing dates, Paul's locations, notable events, and letters he wrote. These helps follow the last session of the year.
- **Index of Background Scriptures** is offered for those of you who keep back copies of *The New International Lesson Annual* so that you can easily locate Scripture passages from previous years.

I love to hear from our readers! If you ever have any questions or comments, please write to me and include your e-mail address and/or phone number. I will respond as soon as your message reaches my home office in Maryland.

Dr. Nan Duerling
Abingdon Press
PO Box 801
Nashville, TN 37202

We thank you for choosing *The New International Lesson Annual* and pray that God will work through this material, as you are guided by the Holy Spirit, to lead your students to the life-changing discipleship that Jesus yearns for in each of us. God's grace and peace be with you!

Nan Duerling, Ph.D.
Editor, *The New International Lesson Annual*

CONTENTS

FIRST QUARTER

You Will Be My Witnesses
September 4–November 27, 2005

UNIT 1: IN JERUSALEM
(September 4-25)

UNIT 2: IN ALL JUDEA AND SAMARIA
(October 2-30)

UNIT 3: TO THE ENDS OF THE EARTH
(November 6-27)

SECOND QUARTER

God's Commitment—Our Response
December 4, 2005–February 26, 2006

UNIT 1: GOD'S REDEEMING LOVE
(December 4-25)

UNIT 2: GOD'S GIFTS OF LEADERSHIP
(January 1-29)

UNIT 3: FAITHFUL FOLLOWERS, FAITHFUL LEADERS
(February 5-26)

THIRD QUARTER

Living in and as God's Creation
March 5–May 28, 2006

UNIT 1: THE GLORY OF GOD'S CREATION
(March 5-26)

UNIT 2: LIVING WITH CREATION'S UNCERTAINTY
(April 2-30)

UNIT 3: LESSONS IN LIVING
(May 7-28)

FOURTH QUARTER

Called to Be a Christian Community
June 4–August 27, 2006

UNIT 1: SERVANTS OF GOD
(June 4-25)

UNIT 2: CALLED TO OBEDIENCE
(July 2-30)

UNIT 3: THE SPIRIT OF GIVING
(August 6-27)

FIRST QUARTER
You Will Be My Witnesses

SEPTEMBER 4, 2005—NOVEMBER 27, 2005

Through a study of the book of Acts we will discern how the early church spread from its roots in Jerusalem to "the ends of the earth." The title for this quarter and the unit titles are all taken from Jesus' last words prior to his ascension: "You will be my witnesses in Jerusalem, in all Judea and Samaria, and to the ends of the earth" (Acts 1:8). Although this book is known as the Acts of the Apostles, it could have been entitled the Acts of the Holy Spirit. As our study progresses we will encounter numerous examples of the Spirit's power.

Unit 1, "In Jerusalem," includes four sessions that focus on the early church in Jerusalem. The session for September 4, "Encountering the Spirit," examines the coming of the Spirit on Pentecost, as recorded in Acts 2:1-42. "Sharing Community," the lesson for September 11, looks at Acts 2:43-47 and 4:32-35 to see what life was like among the earliest church members. Acts 3:1-26, which we will study on September 18 in a lesson entitled "The Gift of Healing," records the story of Peter and John healing a lame man. In "Power to Be Bold," the session for September 25 based on Acts 4:1-31, we overhear Peter and John giving a strong witness before the Sanhedrin.

In Unit 2, "In All Judea and Samaria," we will spend five weeks exploring how the gospel traveled to outlying communities and to people who were considered outsiders. The unit opens on October 2 with "Faithful Servant," a session from Acts 6:8–7:60 concerning the call and execution of the first Christian martyr, Stephen. "Christians Without Borders," the lesson from Acts 8:4-25 for October 9, delves into Philip's ministry with the Samaritans. The account of his ministry to "outsiders" continues on October 16, when we see him "Interpreting the Word" to an Ethiopian official who requests help in understanding a biblical passage. In "Breaking the Gospel Barriers," the lesson for October 23 rooted in Acts 10:1-48, we recognize how Peter is able to overcome obstacles created by his religious beliefs so as to minister to Cornelius, a Gentile. Unit 2 ends on October 30 with "Never Alone," a lesson on Acts 12:1-17 that spotlights Peter's deliverance from prison by an angel of the Lord.

During the four weeks in which we study Unit 3, "To the Ends of the Earth," we will discover how the good news spread even further. We begin on November 6 with "Encountering Truth," a study of how Saul became a follower of Jesus, as recorded in Acts 9:1-31. "Offering of Oneself," the session from Acts 16 on November 13, explores the story of Lydia and the hospitality she made available as a result of her commitment to Christ. On November 20, "Working Together in Ministry" highlights the ministry of Priscilla and Aquila as recounted in Acts 18:1–19:10. The quarter ends on November 27 with "Saying Good-bye," the record in Acts 20:17-38 of Paul's final farewell to the elders in Ephesus.

MEET OUR WRITER

DR. KAY HUGGINS

Someone recently asked me, "Why do you write curriculum for adult Christians?" I discovered I could not answer that question briefly. Instead, I began where I began, in Northern California. There I learned humility naturally; I spent many days and nights in the Redwood forest. There also I learned caution. Floods, forest fires, and earthquakes inspired a sense of awe before God's power and terror. From my earliest years, I humbly desired to know God, even as I wondered if such knowledge were possible. The geography in which I grew up raised insistent spiritual questions in my young soul. Perhaps I write curriculum for adult Christians because those questions still stir my soul.

But geography—even spiritually powerful geography—is not a sufficient response to the question, "Why do you write curriculum for adult Christians?" I would be dishonest if I didn't credit all the teachers and preachers who took this teenage questioner seriously. In the small Methodist church of my childhood, the youth were challenged to sort through Scripture, to struggle through prayer, and to persevere in loving one another. We were given a full dose of Christian education. I credit my desire to study Scripture and to encourage others to do likewise to the faithful teachers, pastors, youth advisors, and camp counselors of my teenage years. Their commitment to Jesus produced in me a thirst for Scripture. During those teenage years my faith was propositional and slightly judgmental; still, I developed an almost magnetic attraction to God's word. Perhaps I write curriculum for adult Christians because I was such a Scripture-thirsty teenager.

Geography and education set my soul on a search, but I was restless until through the blessing of Christian community I experienced the love of Christ. I've been privileged to be a part of several types of communities: wealthy and poor, educated and prosaic, quietist and charismatic, socially engaged and intentionally withdrawn. A particular slice of gospel prompted each community's rhythm. Through this rich mosaic of faith, I met Jesus again and again and again. The encounters continue in congregation after congregation. Surely, one reason I write curriculum materials for adult Christians is the cloud of witnesses I've been blessed to know.

There's one final way to answer my friend's question: I am called to a ministry of words! Although writing was a ministry "in addition to" my pastoral ministry during my first quarter century, I strongly anticipate that Christian writing will be at the center of my ministry for the second quarter century. Why? I believe God called me through all my senses while a child in northern California, inspired my mind to search the Scriptures through the youth ministry of a Methodist congregation, surrounded me with a magnificent, international and intercultural community of saints, and sat me down at a computer to do what I am called to do: minister through words on a printed page. At this point in my life, this challenging, creative, and deadline-persistent ministry is a blessing I'm glad to extend to you.

YOU WILL BE MY WITNESSES

What Is This?

The Acts of the Apostles is well placed in the canon. It follows the Gospels and precedes the Epistles and the final Apocalypse. It is not a gospel, although the good news of Jesus resonates through the chapters. It is not a letter, although directions for church leaders and encouragement for congregations abound. It is not a visionary glimpse into God's future, although without an awareness of the significance of God's future the book makes little sense. The Acts of the Apostles is absolutely unique in our Christian canon. To uncover the meanings embedded in Acts, the reader must exercise caution! This book demands an interpretative style supported by history, softened by nostalgia, and shaped by the gospel of Jesus.

The Acts of the Apostles, like the Gospel of Luke, reads somewhat like a good historical novel. Historical events are evident; some even allow a precise dating. A few datable events, however, do not make a history. History is written to describe, accurately, the development of a flow of events, people, and practices over a specific period of time. The Acts of the Apostles rushes from one event to a random series of people who conduct ministries in a variety of settings and places. The inner coherence of Acts does not come from its historical integrity. Rather, Acts, like the Gospel of Luke, proclaims another coherence: the integrity of God's vision, Jesus' gospel, and the Spirit's activity among humans.

If Acts is not history, but a series of short stories held together by a particular faith, then how are the stories to be read? Certainly, these stories are not all that could be recorded. From other documents of the early church, we know that church growth was not one-sided, but multifaceted. The church grew in orthodoxy and in heresy, in the homeland of Judea and the foreign lands of Africa, India, and Spain, with the rich and the slave as well as the educated elite and the honest laborer. In addition to the stories recorded in Acts, many more tales were told; as with all four Gospels, the ones included led the reader to faith. In Acts, stories begin, but are left dangling; important leaders conduct stunning ministries and then are forgotten; whole regions are evangelized and then not mentioned again. The stories that are told, as well as the historical dates and persons, serve faith's greater goal.

So the Acts of the Apostles is neither history nor story. It is, rather, proclamation. It is the second part of a two-volume set written about A.D. 80–85 by a very literate Hellenistic Jew who looked back, through a variety of sources, on the church of A.D. 30–60. The author, according to ancient tradition from the second century, was a traveling companion of Paul, quite likely "Luke, the beloved physician," who extends a greeting in Colossians 4:14. Since the author does not identify himself in the text, this early tradition may be our best clue to the author's name. Whatever his name or occupation, the author had a singular purpose in the composition of a gospel and a collection of early church stories. The first volume disclosed the powerful good news of God's deed in Jesus; the second continues the impact of that deed through the Spirit's formation and guidance of the church. Whereas the Gospels present all that is necessary for faith in Jesus, the Acts of the Apostles demonstrates how faith in Jesus became rooted in community and grew to a worldwide witness of Jesus as the Messiah (Christ). These two sets of stories testify to one truth: God in Jesus Christ was reconciling the world and granting to the church the ministry of reconciliation.

The Audience: A Closer Look

Every teacher, parent, preacher, or friend knows it is important to listen to your audience before you try to influence them! This is not merely the foundation of successful communication; it is also the foundation of a solid community. The Acts of the Apostles was written from faith for faith. A Christian who knew well the Roman world penned this book; citizens and residents of that same world read it. Before us is a major cultural separation, but here are some steps over the divide of centuries, cultures, and continents.

1. The Acts of the Apostles is an urban document. The Gospel stories began in the country with farmers and fishermen, lingered by the seaside with common folk, walked the trade routes, and concluded the pilgrimage in the holy city, Jerusalem. Acts began with an international gathering in Jerusalem and spread from city to city through many regions. An urban setting replaced the pastoral parables of the Gospels; Christianity was nurtured in homes of wealthy citizens and laborers. As you read, notice the frequent mention of table fellowship; urban Christians lived in close community.
2. The Acts of the Apostles assumes the faith of Jesus and teaches a religion about Jesus. The foundations of economic and ethical behavior are set; the issues of Acts are built upon the teachings of Jesus; however, there is only one quotation from Jesus in the texts selected for our lessons (and that quotation in Acts 20:35 is not found in our Gospels). Without a conviction of Jesus' basic teachings on money, servanthood, mutuality, self-sacrifice, trust, and suffering the Acts of the Apostles makes little sense. This religion of Jesus is deeply rooted in Jesus' teaching. Remember, Jesus taught his disciples by inviting them to "come and see" what he was doing; in Acts, church leaders' lives are models for imitation.
3. The Acts of the Apostles charts the significant transition from a period of apostolic leaders (those who were eyewitnesses to Jesus or, as is the case with Paul, called by the risen Lord) to future generations of church leaders. It is a time when traditions are being established, documents produced, standards set, and authority validated. Every transition has rough edges; Acts includes both the dramatic and the mundane moments of change.
4. The Acts of the Apostles is probably misnamed. It should be titled the Acts of the Holy Spirit. The apostles play only a modest role; Paul's authority as an untimely called apostle is hardly mentioned (unlike his self-defense in the Epistles). Rather, throughout the text the Spirit is authoritative. The Spirit alone gives authority; no individual exercises authority apart from the Holy Spirit.
5. The backdrop of Acts is the growing hostility by the Roman Empire and the culture against the church. The counter-cultural practices of the church provoked strong reactions. An ethic of mutuality, equality among all members, women's leadership, and an international agenda shocked the status quo of Roman rule and polite society. The seriousness of this reaction necessitated a resource for facing difficulties; the Acts of the Apostles is one such resource.
6. Acts' scale is universal. This was not a religion content with a grassy hillside and the re-enactment of Jesus' Sermon on the Mount. This was a religion that had a particular beginning point, Jerusalem, and a particular direction, to Judea, Samaria, and then to the ends of the earth. Christian faith would produce a church able to offer a witness of Jesus to nations and leaders. The vision was as high as heaven, as wide as the word *enemy*, as quick as a tongue of fire, and as persistent as the prayers of the early Christians. The vision would bring suffering and joy, as well as sorrow and expansion because this vision was not derived from human insight. This vision was the gift of the Spirit, and the Spirit knows no boundaries.

The Acts of the Spirit

Beginning in Jerusalem, Acts testified to the power of the Holy Spirit. On Pentecost, the Spirit propelled Peter into the first public proclamation of the good news of Jesus. His text for that sermon came from the prophet Joel. It was a stunning description of the in-breaking of God's season of salvation. That time was distinguished by strange phenomena: Women and men of every status and age were touched by God's Spirit; there were signs in heaven and on earth; and whoever called on the name of the Lord was saved. This is but the first act of the Spirit—but it was interpreted as a true sign of the fulfillment of God's promise. From a theological perspective, this interpretation established a primary connection. The good news of Jesus was anticipated in Israel by the prophets centuries before. The faith of the disciples was nothing more than the recognition of God's promised time of salvation.

Because the initial audience of the apostles was the Jewish community, the first acts of the Spirit demonstrated the continuity of the good news of Jesus with the prophets of Israel. But, more assurance was needed if the apostles were to be trusted as leaders. Jesus had performed signs and wonders; his miracles testified to his status as beloved Child of God, the chosen one, the righteous one, and the Messiah. As Peter and John began to witness to Jesus, they began to offer healing power "in his name." This, too, was an act of the Spirit. Wherever spiritual power existed there was Jesus. Not everyone was gifted with healing powers, but only those whom the Spirit endowed. As the stories of Acts began, two apostles, Peter and John, preformed signs and wonders. But, with each miracle came the proclamation: This deed is done in the name of Jesus. Surely, those who saw and experienced these miracles made the connection—the Spirit that worked through Jesus was now active in the apostles. The acts of the Spirit included the power and presence of Jesus in the ministry of signs and wonders.

A final demonstration was the Spirit among the congregation—spreading out across the empire—unifying the churches into one entity. According to Acts, the distinguishing feature of every congregation was the presence of the Holy Spirit. The Greek word *pneuma*, Spirit, is used seventy times in the Acts of the Apostles; that is equal to about one fifth of the entire New Testament usage of the word. Wherever the church exists (in Acts the word *church* means a local congregation), there is the Spirit; by the Spirit's residence within congregations, the whole church is bound into the one, holy, catholic, and apostolic church that bears witness to Jesus as Lord and Savior.

Therefore, in the Acts of the Apostles the Spirit acts in three ways to demonstrate the continuity of God's whole purpose:

1. The Spirit binds the witness to Jesus with the word of the prophets to Israel; this is not a new religion, but the fulfillment (the filling up) of an ancient promise.
2. The Spirit connects the apostles to their Lord Jesus through mighty signs and wonders; this is not an innovation, but a demonstration of Jesus' presence with the disciples-become-apostles.
3. The Spirit relates the congregations to one another by the confirmation of faith through the baptism of the Holy Spirit. The signs of the Spirit within each congregation varied; however, the spiritual energy was profound. The Spirit was alive whenever enemies were forgiven, widows were fed, repentance was enacted, prayers were ceaseless, and sermons presented Christ's claims. Moreover, by these acts congregations were united in one hope, one Lord, one faith, one baptism, one God.

The Spirit's continuity began with the word of the prophets, settled completely upon Jesus, continued through the apostles' spiritual gift of healing, and enfolded many congregations into one body, the church of Jesus Christ. The apostles did some of this; the deacons contributed their share; countless itinerant preachers offered witness; hundreds of families opened their homes for forming congregations; yet there was only one Spirit. That's why the book might better have been titled the Acts of the Spirit.

Contemporary Directions

The stories from the Acts of the Apostles not only intrigue contemporary readers, but they also inspire. There is a glamorous, almost romantic, notion in Acts that God's purposes are always triumphant. As the words roll on the sentiment increases: Yes! This movement begun in the modesty of an upper room will one day fill the entire universe. Regardless of the obstacles, God will find a way around, over, through, within, between, and out of any and all resistance. As apostles are freed from prison and the recently converted begin to preach, the heady sense of the Acts of the Apostles intensifies: By the Spirit the church will be triumphant. Indeed, when contemporary readers pause to review their own experience of church history, a similar affirmation forms. Whenever error or stupidity threatens the survival of the church, we give thanks and praise because the Spirit is there offering renewal, direction, gifts, and leadership.

The backdrop of early church history painted by the Acts of the Apostles is the color of triumph! Everything Acts describes becomes bigger and better. While this strong assurance was useful for the original audience, as contemporary readers we ought to be somewhat humble and just a little cautious before we apply the upswing of Acts to our congregations. If read in isolation from the whole canon, contemporary congregations may feel perplexed as membership declines, institutions begin to close, and culture turns away from traditional Christian values. But remember, the Acts of the Apostles is one book of the Bible; in other books we read less rosy pictures. For example, the twelve tribes of Israel narrow down to one; the official supports of the faith (monarchy, priesthood, and temple) fail to be faithful to God and thereby to the people; exile brings not only a season of anguish, but also a profound re-evaluation of faith. God's promise is not that growth is inevitable and triumph is sure. God's promise is: I am with you. The places God accompanies us include the heights of a prosperous mission and the depths of a martyr's witness. Although the Spirit guides the church, at times the journey is through the "valley of the shadow of death" rather than steadily on the upward call.

So, realizing the cautionary approach to Acts' triumphal spirit, what contemporary directions can we trace from this study to our witness? Here are a few issues raised by the Acts of the Apostles that still invite the best of our faith's witness:

- The relationship among Christians—ecumenical, international, and intercultural— always deserves our best witness.
- The relationship of Christians to the culture will always cause problems (sometimes leading to suffering) and create opportunities (sometimes leading to the salvation of others), but we must never flag in our zeal to reach out to the nearest neighbor in need.
- The Christian stance toward the state will never stop challenging our witness; while we respect the state's authority, as Christians we are citizens of another kingdom. Like our Lord, if there's a contest between the powers of the kingdoms, we always seek God's kingdom.

- Persistent prayer is the life force of the church. When things are going well, pray; when times are difficult, pray; when God's will is hard, pray; when God seems distant, pray. The early church became triumphant by a spirit nurtured in prayer. What more need be said: pray!
- In every generation, as broadly as possible, the church must teach the faith. There is no inherited faith; there is only Spirit-quickened belief.

As the early church told stories of their heroes and heroines and tales of the amazing spread of the knowledge of Jesus, so the contemporary church continues to be nourished on stories. Enjoy these stories from the Acts of the Apostles. This is not all that can be said about that remarkable moment when our faith was passed from eyewitnesses to the rising generation; but this is enough to make sense of their world, to trace heaven's outline on their community, and to shape a Christian character suitable to the living of these days. Enjoy the stories; let their witness become yours.

UNIT 1: IN JERUSALEM
ENCOUNTERING THE SPIRIT

PREVIEWING THE LESSON

Lesson Scripture: Acts 2:1-8, 38-42
Background Scripture: Acts 2:1-42
Key Verse: Acts 2:38

Focus of the Lesson:
People search for good news that will transform their lives. How does this life-transforming message come to people today? The story of Pentecost shows that God's Spirit helps people hear the message of the risen Christ.

Goals for the Learners:
(1) to read the Pentecost account and explore how the gospel expanded into the world through the transforming power of the Holy Spirit.
(2) to identify examples of the Spirit's presence and role in their own lives.
(3) to identify and give thanks for ways the Holy Spirit works in the church.

Pronunciation Guide:
glossolalia (glos uh lay' lee uh)
xenolalia (zee no lay' lee uh)

Supplies:
Bibles (including some in foreign languages that class members may speak), newsprint and marker, paper and pencils, hymnals

---

READING THE SCRIPTURE

NRSV
Acts 2:1-8, 38-42

¹When the day of Pentecost had come, they were all together in one place. ²And suddenly from heaven there came a sound like the rush of a violent wind, and it filled the entire house where they were sitting. ³Divided tongues, as of fire, appeared among them, and a tongue

NIV
Acts 2:1-8, 38-42

¹When the day of Pentecost came, they were all together in one place. ²Suddenly a sound like the blowing of a violent wind came from heaven and filled the whole house where they were sitting. ³They saw what seemed to be tongues of fire that separated and came to rest on each of them. ⁴All

rested on each of them. [4]All of them were filled with the Holy Spirit and began to speak in other languages, as the Spirit gave them ability.

[5]Now there were devout Jews from every nation under heaven living in Jerusalem. [6]And at this sound the crowd gathered and was bewildered, because each one heard them speaking in the native language of each. [7]Amazed and astonished, they asked, "Are not all these who are speaking Galileans? [8]And how is it that we hear, each of us, in our own native language?"

[38] Peter said to them, **"Repent, and be baptized every one of you in the name of Jesus Christ so that your sins may be forgiven; and you will receive the gift of the Holy Spirit.** [39]For the promise is for you, for your children, and for all who are far away, everyone whom the Lord our God calls to him." [40]And he testified with many other arguments and exhorted them, saying, "Save yourselves from this corrupt generation." [41]So those who welcomed his message were baptized, and that day about three thousand persons were added. [42]They devoted themselves to the apostles' teaching and fellowship, to the breaking of bread and the prayers.

of them were filled with the Holy Spirit and began to speak in other tongues as the Spirit enabled them.

[5]Now there were staying in Jerusalem God-fearing Jews from every nation under heaven. [6]When they heard this sound, a crowd came together in bewilderment, because each one heard them speaking in his own language. [7]Utterly amazed, they asked: "Are not all these men who are speaking Galileans? [8]Then how is it that each of us hears them in his own native language?"

[38]Peter replied, **"Repent and be baptized, every one of you, in the name of Jesus Christ for the forgiveness of your sins. And you will receive the gift of the Holy Spirit.** [39]The promise is for you and your children and for all who are far off—for all whom the Lord our God will call."

[40]With many other words he warned them; and he pleaded with them, "Save yourselves from this corrupt generation." [41]Those who accepted his message were baptized, and about three thousand were added to their number that day.

[42]They devoted themselves to the apostles' teaching and to the fellowship, to the breaking of bread and to prayer.

UNDERSTANDING THE SCRIPTURE

Acts 2:1-4. The Acts of the Apostles might be better titled "The Acts of the Spirit through the Apostles"! As the book opens, Jesus speaks his final words to his disciples (Acts 1:7-8) cautioning a non-anxious approach to "times or periods" and promising them the power to become his witnesses. In the second chapter, that promise is fulfilled. The context is the day of Pentecost. This celebration, also known as the Feast of Weeks, was one of the three annual pilgrimage festivals of Israel. During these festivals the city of Jerusalem swelled by over one hundred thousand pilgrims.

Just seven weeks prior to Pentecost, the Passover festival had brought the faithful to Jerusalem. However, not all the Pentecost pilgrims made a second journey to Jerusalem. Some, particularly those not engaged in agriculture, stayed in Jerusalem for the fifty days between the two festivals. Those who stayed in Jerusalem spent their days in the temple courtyard listening to the many teachers and worshiping at the daily temple services. It was a rich time of personal devotion and of corporate identity for the international Jewish community. Evidently, Jesus' followers—the eleven remaining disciples, the women who assisted Jesus, and those who joined the company during the journey to Jerusalem—stayed together during the fifty days between Passover and Pentecost. On the day of Pentecost they were praying and waiting when a spectacular event took place. Fire and wind, the ancient signs of God's presence, are the metaphors used by the author to convey the majesty of the moment. But the source of this event was not a mystery: The Holy Spirit was the power behind these extraordinary events. Tersely, Luke explained that the Holy Spirit filled them and they "began to speak in other languages." All present in the room were inspired and, strangely, articulate.

Acts 2:5-13. As the story moves forward, the scene shifts from inside a closed room to the street below where representatives of the international Jewish community gathered. The crowd was initially bewildered by the strange event; they heard Galileans, frequently discredited as the least cultured citizens of the nation, speaking in a multitude of languages. In fact, these "devout Jews" explained to one another that they heard in their "own native languages" the testimony to "God's deeds of power." This is the first use of the word "Jews" in Acts; it will be used more than fifty times to distinguish the people of Israel from their religious leaders. The author's point is clear: The disciples were spiritually empowered to witness to devout Jews—to those most likely to hear and respond in faith. This accorded well with Jesus' declaration that the disciples would witness first in Jerusalem, then in Judea and Samaria and, finally, to the ends of the earth (Acts 1:8). But their witness, although precise in appropriate languages, provoked a variety of responses. Some were astonished; theirs was a response of awe before God's presence. Some were perplexed; these responded by seeking a rational understanding of this extraordinary event. Some mocked; theirs was a response to dismiss strange circumstances with a con-

venient explanation: They are drunk. Carefully, Luke describes both sides of the Pentecost event: Those within the house were filled by the Holy Spirit and those outside on the street heard a witness to God's deed in the familiar language of their native tongues. However, the demonstration of power did not provoke faith immediately; faith came only after interpretation.

Acts 2:14-36. Peter, the spokesman, stepped forward to address the crowd. This is the first of many "speeches" in Acts; indeed, nearly one third of the book is devoted to formal speech whether as testimony, sermon, or prayer. Peter begins by appealing to the audience to listen; however, our author uses a unique word that literally means "let me place it [the word of God] into your ears." Dismissing the convenient judgment of drunkenness, Peter began his speech with an interpretation based on the prophet Joel's description of the time when God's Spirit is poured out on all flesh (Joel 2:28-32). The word "all" links the event of the all in the house, the event on the street, and the prophecy; the distinctive characteristic of God's gift of the Holy Spirit is its inclusiveness. All were filled with the Holy Spirit and all heard in their own languages. But the prophecy also explained the strange sounds and sights of the morning; according to Joel, extraordinary manifestations accompany God's Spirit as it is poured out. Moreover, such an experience was more than a divinely devised phenomenon. It also indicated a critical time: the season of salvation when all who called on the name of the Lord were saved. A second time Peter implored the audience to listen; he succinctly set Israel's responsibility for handing over Jesus for crucifixion before the crowd and contrasted their deed with God's resurrection of Jesus. Arguing from Scripture, Peter declared that Jesus was David's true heir—the one to reign forever. Finally, Peter declared the most powerful truth he knew: God made Jesus both Lord (ruler) and Messiah (savior). Peter's speech concluded with a stinging remark: You crucified God's servant. This speech, his first sermon, included Scripture, a recollection of recent events, and personal testimony. The singular point he made was the essence of the first-century gospel proclamation: Jesus is Lord and Messiah.

Acts 2:37-42. The crowd responded in a unified manner; evidently the skeptics and the rationalizers departed while Peter preached! At the conclusion, the crowd was moved to action. They asked what they should do. Peter, speaking for all who were filled by the Holy Spirit, gave the directions. First, Peter instructed the crowd to repent. Then, he invited them to accept Jesus by being baptized in his name. If they did so,

forgiveness and the gift promised of the Holy Spirit was theirs. Peter's last appeal was to dissociate from their corrupt generation—meaning those who refuse to repent. The response was magnificent: about three thousand united with Jesus' followers. The quality of their repentance was indicated by their deeds:

- they were attentive to the apostles' teaching.
- they shared in the community's table fellowship and the prayers.

Thus, a new community of faith in Jesus was drawn together by the power of the Holy Spirit.

INTERPRETING THE SCRIPTURE

(1) A Dramatic Moment

The story of Pentecost is one of the best-known stories of the New Testament. As with the beloved stories of the Gospels—such as the Good Samaritan, the Last Supper, and the Visitation of the Magi—familiarity actually obscures rather than enhances our understanding. This text, however, comes to life when read slowly and thoughtfully. As with other good stories from Scripture, the story of Pentecost has a specific setting: a festival day in Jerusalem. Not only do the place and time set the context, but also there is a sense of anticipation related to this day. The day of Pentecost was fifty days after the festival of Passover. Two dynamics blended to make this a popular holiday. The ancient roots of Pentecost are traced back to an agricultural celebration; the harvest of the first sheaves of barley brought joy to the people. Later, as the liturgical life of the people developed, Pentecost became a remembrance of the events on Mount Sinai, specifically the gift of the law to Moses. This blessed gift of the Ten

Commandments also evoked joy. These two joyful elements increased the significance of the holiday of Pentecost; not only was God dependable, as witnessed in the first sheaves of the barley harvest, but God was also gracious, as attested to by the provision of a divine law.

Every year the nation gathered in gratitude to celebrate and remember God's providence. On this particular year, when the day arrived, all the followers of Jesus were together, attending to their usual tasks of remembering and giving thanks.

Every year the whole nation waited in anticipation for the announcement of the actual day of Pentecost. In this particular year, when the day arrived, all the followers of Jesus were together waiting and praying. Into the quiet of prayer, a sound like a mighty wind shook the room. (Try to imagine the shock and surprise of a prayer meeting blown open!) The sound, however, was only a call to attention. Next came the vision of something like tongues of fire, and with that vision came the peculiar manifestation of foreign speech. The formal name of this phenomenon is xenolalia, the inspired capacity to speak a foreign language. As distinct from glossolalia, the gift of speaking in spiritual tongues requiring interpretation, xenolalia is articulate speech immediately understood by those familiar with the particular language. The wind, vision, and foreign tongues were amazing; however, even more amazing was the inclusivity of God's Spirit. All were included in the event: disciples and followers, young women and old men, as well as strangers from across the known world.

(2) In Our Native Language

Have you ever left a worship service with the comment, "That sermon was meant just for me"? Have you later discovered that several others—some whose lives differ radically from yours—shared the same sentiment? A wide range of experiences and life contexts are present whenever God's word is read and interpreted; yet each individual hears the sermon as if it were prepared specifically to meet a particular need. This is an amazing, yet also dependable, dynamic of preaching: The word is read, interpreted, set free, and the Spirit adjusts the reception of the word perfectly. We are familiar with both aspects of contemporary preaching: the inspiration of the speaker and the inspiration of the hearer. Evidently, this was true for the earliest Christian community.

The crowd that gathered (perhaps because of the sound of the mighty wind) was initially bewildered. Something extraordinary was afoot. No one was able to explain what was occurring, but as individuals in the crowd compared experiences, a common denominator emerged. All who gathered, regardless of their nationality or country of residence, heard their native languages spoken by Galileans. Each heard the testimony to God's mighty deeds in the most intimate and familiar language available to humankind—native language learned at mother's knee and by father's workbench. This fact moved the crowd from bewilderment to a spiritual state of "amazed and astonished." A random assembly, roughly representing international Judaism, intuitively knew that this extraordinary event was God-inspired. Moreover, it was clear that the inspiration was not limited to those who spoke. Those who heard also felt strangely warmed by a testimony offered in intimate cadences and words.

(3) A Preacher's Punch

The experience, while dramatic, sensory, and captivating, was not, however, revelatory of God's purpose. Something more was needed to move the crowd from amazement to commitment. That something was Peter's testimony. The story of Pentecost has four parts: an event, an audience, a sermon, and a response. Peter's sermon (recorded in outline form in Acts 2:14-36) included a variety of rhetorical tactics. He challenged his audience to listen; he interpreted the extraordinary event by a beloved prophecy from Joel about God's promised time of salvation; he explained the events of Passover week, noting in particular the responsibility of the religious authorities for Jesus' crucifixion; he united the purpose of Jesus with the crowd's hope for the heir of David's everlasting reign; he offered his personal testimony; he concluded with an allusion to the crowd's participation in the deadly deed against God's anointed. As Peter preached, the Spirit moved among the crowd. They were "cut to the heart" and asked for more. Peter, with the wisdom of a young seminarian yet to complete Preaching 101, was unaware that conviction was insufficient without a path to repentance. His sermon ended with a punch, but not a push toward a new way of being. Happily, the Spirit worked overtime that Pentecost day. Acknowledging the appeal of the crowd, Peter offered a way out of their spiritual dilemma: repent, be baptized in Jesus' name, and receive forgiveness as well as the gift of the Holy Spirit. Together these Spirit-infused individuals formed a new community, the church of Jesus Christ.

(4) In a New Community

Peter's text for his Pentecost sermon was the prophecy from Joel concerning God's season of salvation. This wonderful salvation was promised to all people: the young and the old, men and women, slave and master. In this season there was only one criterion for salvation: calling on the name of the Lord. An inspired Peter, therefore, announced the name of *Jesus* as the appropriate name of the Lord. Finally, he offered baptism as a means of incorporation into those God was saving. The crowd was able to save themselves from "this corrupt generation" by joining together as a new community of trust and confidence in the Lord Jesus. Many responded. Perhaps the Bible's number is not exactly accurate, but the rapid growth of the early Christian community is widely acknowledged as impressive beyond human calculations. Still, human communities—even Spirit-infused communities—require structure and formation. Therefore, the story of that Pentecost day is concluded not with the roll of those baptized, but with a summary of the structure of their new communal life. This life was characterized by devotion to the apostles' teaching, to fellowship, to common meals, and to community prayer. These four aspects of spiritual formation continue in contemporary churches.

As we study Scripture and listen to teachers who share inspired lessons blessed by the authority of the church, we learn the profound and good news of salvation.

- As we join together in Christian fellowship, the witness and integrity of the saints of the church impress our souls.
- As we break bread, both in the holiness of the sacrament and at the common table of a church supper, the bread of life that satisfies completely nourishes us.
- And as the community gathers for prayer, we are continually aware that the same Spirit that blew open the first circle of disciples may very well blow us into a new faithfulness.

Thanks be to God that when the day of Pentecost came, the Spirit's work did not end but began among all those who were gathered, heard, and responded.

SHARING THE SCRIPTURE

PREPARING TO TEACH

Preparing Our Hearts

This week's devotional reading is found in Psalm 16. Here the psalmist seeks God's protection and instruction, for he trusts that God will take care of him. Are you willing to entrust your entire life to the Lord? Do you place your whole confidence and trust in God? Have you had a life-changing encounter with God that enables you to say yes to these questions? Meditate on your relationship with God.

Pray that you and the adult learners will rely on the Holy Spirit to empower and guide you.

Preparing Our Minds

Study the background Scripture, Acts 2:1-42. Focus your attention especially on verses 1-8, 38-42. Consider ways in which the story of Pentecost helps people to hear the life-changing message of the risen Christ.

Be sure to read the background article for this quarter and introduction to this quarter's sessions as you prepare this week's lesson.

Write on newsprint:

❏ information for next week's lesson, found under "Continue the Journey."

Plan how you will present the suggested information in "Read the Pentecost Account and Explore How the Gospel Expanded into the World through the Transforming Power of the Holy Spirit."

LEADING THE CLASS

(1) Gather to Learn

❖ Welcome the class members and introduce any guests.

❖ Pray that the students will be open to a fresh encounter with the Holy Spirit.

❖ Invite the adults to tell stories of times when they heard really good news. Ask them to state how this news affected them when they first heard it and how it may have changed their lives.

❖ Note that as we study the Acts of the Apostles this quarter, we will explore how people heard and responded through the power of the Holy Spirit to the good news of Jesus.

❖ Read aloud today's focus statement: **People search for good news that will transform their lives. How does this life-transforming message come to people today? The story of Pentecost shows that God's Spirit helps people hear the message of the risen Christ.**

(2) Read the Pentecost Account and Explore How the Gospel Expanded into the World Through the Transforming Power of the Holy Spirit

❖ Explore the Pentecost account found in Acts 2:1-8 by choosing several volunteers to read the story in different languages, if possible, or from different English translations. Then discuss these questions, or use information from Understanding the Scripture to prepare a brief lecture.

(1) **Had you been present on Pentecost, how would you have responded to these uneducated Galileans speaking in your language about God's amazing deeds?**

(2) **What images of God's presence do you see in this story? Where else in the Bible do you recall God being described in these ways?** (Note especially the images of wind and fire.)

(3) **Why do you suppose this event took place in Jerusalem during the Jewish festival of Pentecost?**

❖ Briefly recount Peter's message, which is part of today's background scripture from Acts 2:14-36. Your purpose is to set the stage for the crowd's response. You will not have time to explore the details of this story.

❖ Select a volunteer to be the narrator and someone to read the part of Peter in Acts 2:38-42. Begin the passage by inviting everyone to read 2:37*b*, "Brothers, what should we do?"

■ Discuss the crowd's response to Peter's message and his instructions to them.

■ Identify the actions that members of the crowd took, according to verses 41-42.

■ Point out that churches often work by means of committees today. Discuss how the Pentecost experience makes the church more than just an institution that operates on the basis of "majority rules."

(3) Identify Examples of the Spirit's Presence and Role in the Learners' Lives

❖ Brainstorm with the students answers to this question: **In what ways do you believe people experience the power and presence of the Holy Spirit?** Write their answers on newsprint.

❖ Distribute paper and pencils. Invite the students to choose one or two of the brainstormed ideas and write a specific example of how the Spirit worked in an "up close and personal way" in their own lives.

❖ Encourage the learners to share their stories with a partner or small group.

(4) Identify and Give Thanks for the Ways the Holy Spirit Works in the Church

❖ Invite the students to discuss their beliefs about how the Spirit operates in the church today. (Note that some adults believe that although the Pentecost event is unrepeatable, the power of the Holy Spirit continues to be present and available to the church in amazing ways. Other Christians, however, perceive that the powerful work of the Spirit, along with spiritual gifts, existed only for the early church. Recognize that some class members may raise questions about modern charismatic groups, that is, Christians who exercise the power of the Spirit in remarkable ways.)

❖ Brainstorm with the group answers to this question: **In what ways do you see the Holy Spirit at work in your congregation?** List their ideas on newsprint.

❖ Discuss these questions in light of the list.

(1) **How would you compare the way the Spirit works within your congregation to the way the Spirit worked in the church formed at Pentecost?**

(2) **If you do not believe the Spirit is as active in your church as in the early church, what might be some reasons for the difference?**

(3) **If your list shows evidence of the Spirit moving mightily in your congregation, what might be some of the reasons for this outpouring of spiritual power?**

❖ Wrap up this portion of the lesson by asking the learners to give thanks for the way that God's Spirit is moving among them.

(5) Continue the Journey

❖ Pray that as a result of the touch of the Holy Spirit the lives of the participants and the life of the congregation may be transformed.

❖ Read aloud this preparation for next week's lesson. You may also want to post it on newsprint for the students to copy. **Prepare for next week's session, entitled "Sharing Community," by reading Acts 2:43-47 and 4:32-35. Both of these passages are our background and lesson scriptures. Consider these ideas as you study the lesson: People yearn for true community. What are the marks of a Christian community? Worship, sharing of resources, unity, and spreading the good news made the first Christian community stand out.**

❖ Read aloud the following three ideas. Challenge the students to commit themselves to use these activities as a springboard to spiritual growth.

(1) **Meditate on your own experiences with the Holy Spirit. Would you describe them as "wind and fire" events or as stirrings of the still, small voice within, or in some other way? How does God's Spirit communicate with you?**

(2) **Consider ways in which the Spirit operates in your congregation. Would you describe it in terms such as those used in Acts 2:42? What evidence do you see of the Spirit's working in your community of faith?**

(3) **Talk with someone about the Spirit's presence and activity in your life.**

❖ Sing or read aloud "O Spirit of the Living God."

❖ Lead this benediction to conclude the session: **May the Holy Spirit empower you to be witnesses for Jesus Christ in your community, in your nation, and to the ends of the earth. Amen.**

UNIT 1: IN JERUSALEM
SHARING COMMUNITY

PREVIEWING THE LESSON

Lesson Scripture: Acts 2:43-47; 4:32-35
Background Scripture: Acts 2:43-47; 4:32-35
Key Verse: Acts 2:44

Focus of the Lesson:
People yearn for true community. What are the marks of a Christian community? Worship, sharing of resources, unity, and spreading the good news made the first Christian community stand out.

Goals for the Learners:
(1) to examine how the word, love, and worship of God served as the foundation of true community in the early church.
(2) to compare their faith community with the early church.
(3) to make a commitment to live together faithfully in community.

Pronunciation Guide:
eschatological (es kat uh loj' i kuhl)

Supplies:
Bibles, newsprint and marker, paper and pencils, light snack such as fruit, hymnals

READING THE SCRIPTURE

NRSV
Acts 2:43-47

⁴³Awe came upon everyone, because many wonders and signs were being done by the apostles. **⁴⁴All who believed were together and had all things in common;** ⁴⁵they would sell their possessions and goods and distribute the proceeds to all, as any had need. ⁴⁶Day by day, as they spent much time together in the temple, they broke bread at home and ate their food with glad and generous hearts, ⁴⁷praising God

NIV
Acts 2:43-47

⁴³Everyone was filled with awe, and many wonders and miraculous signs were done by the apostles. **⁴⁴All the believers were together and had everything in common.** ⁴⁵Selling their possessions and goods, they gave to anyone as he had need. ⁴⁶Every day they continued to meet together in the temple courts. They broke bread in their homes and ate together with glad and sincere hearts, ⁴⁷praising God and enjoying the

and having the goodwill of all the people. And day by day the Lord added to their number those who were being saved.

Acts 4:32-35

[32]Now the whole group of those who believed were of one heart and soul, and no one claimed private ownership of any possessions, but everything they owned was held in common. [33]With great power the apostles gave their testimony to the resurrection of the Lord Jesus, and great grace was upon them all. [34]There was not a needy person among them, for as many as owned lands or houses sold them and brought the proceeds of what was sold. [35]They laid it at the apostles' feet, and it was distributed to each as any had need.

favor of all the people. And the Lord added to their number daily those who were being saved.

Acts 4:32-35

[32]All the believers were one in heart and mind. No one claimed that any of his possessions was his own, but they shared everything they had. [33]With great power the apostles continued to testify to the resurrection of the Lord Jesus, and much grace was upon them all. [34]There were no needy persons among them. For from time to time those who owned lands or houses sold them, brought the money from the sales [35]and put it at the apostles' feet, and it was distributed to anyone as he had need.

UNDERSTANDING THE SCRIPTURE

Acts 2:43-45. In Acts 2:1-42, Luke describes the "birth" of the church; in Acts 2:43-47 and Acts 4:32-35 the "baby" is described. Although the church was birthed in drama, the community that developed was composed of ordinary folks. However, there was one striking characteristic of this community: they were filled with awe. Something of "the day of Pentecost" continued among the members as a palpable quality of their common life. Naturally, some of the awe resulted from the "many wonders and signs" performed by the apostles. However, the community had another source of amazement: their commitment to share life and to care for the needs of all. Luke selected a practical and business-oriented word, *koinos*, to describe the community's commitment to sharing and caring. It is the root of a popular New Testament word, *koinonia*, meaning fellowship, communion, and participation. However, before the word carried sacred meaning, it was a secular word describing a business relationship. In the new commu-

nity, this "business relationship" was characterized by a radical sharing of resources—the community had all things in common (in *koinos*). Awe increased as individuals sold personal property and possessions in order to care for needy brothers and sisters; each generous act intensified awareness of God's all-sufficient grace.

Acts 2:46-47. The new community lived by a routine that balanced time apart with time together. Each day those who called on the name of Jesus gathered at the temple. Some of this time was social and included sharing personal testimonies of God's salvation. Quite likely, the apostles taught in the temple courtyard. Of course, everyone wanted to be present for the evening prayer service. (Remember, these who turned their lives toward Jesus were, first and foremost, Jews who believed that in Jesus, God's restoration of Israel and of all creation had begun.) Their community life, however, extended beyond the sacred plot of temple ground. They shared a common meal in someone's home following the evening prayers. However, this common meal, although Jewish by tradition, was nuanced by the memory of Jesus' last meal with his disciples. As they shared bread and remembered Jesus, they subtly began to shape a meal into a liturgical deed.

In addition to their daily routine, there was something special that distinguished this new community from other Jewish communities. Those who joined this community were blessed with a new attitude of heart; Luke describes the new community as having "glad and generous hearts." Obviously, others noticed the joy and generosity, for the text also says that they received "the goodwill of all." The daily routine included time at the temple (social, educational, and devotional time), common meals shared in homes, and the demonstration of gladness and generosity to neighbors and friends. This was a tranquil, peaceful season for the early church; opposition was, briefly, nonexistent. Moreover, the effect of God's mighty deed of salvation expanded as more and more learned the name of the Lord, confessed faith in Jesus, and entered into the community of those being saved.

Acts 4:32. A good storyteller knows the power of a pause. Luke inserts such a pause with this verse. The story of chapter 4 revealed the beginning of controversy between Jesus' followers and the religious establishment of Jerusalem. However, the impact of the controversy on the new community is of even greater significance. Therefore, Luke inserts a pause with the word "Now," a word that breaks into the story and offers another perspective on the community. First, their unity is affirmed. The whole group of believers exhibited one quality of heart (quite possibly, the glad and generous heart attitude of Acts 2:46), and one orientation of soul. They lived as an organic, caring community. The stronger members aided the weaker members; the wealthy assisted the needy; the learned taught and the eager-to-learn joyfully learned; some prayed and some served the meals, and some provided home hospitality. Their life was a careful matching of spiritual, social, educational, emotional, and material needs and resources. Everything was in common; neither any believers nor their possessions were left out. Luke's pause demonstrated how the community radiated the hope of Israel. Indeed, they lived the prophets' promise of blessing for all, especially the eschatological blessing of the poor (Isaiah 61:1-2). Their common life offered the outline of a restored Israel—a community where every member enjoyed the full status of son or daughter of Abraham. There were no intellectual, social, material, or religious distinctions. Rather, having everything in common meant each had whatever was necessary for a blessed life.

Acts 4:33-35. The powerful preaching and teaching of the apostles inspired the common life of the community. It may surprise a modern audience, however, that there was only one preaching theme: the resurrection of Jesus. Interpreted by the promises of Scripture and applied to every aspect of life, the apostles' preaching and teaching on resurrection shaped individual and corporate faith. The resurrection text brought hope to those who feared eternal separation from God; it promised a new beginning to those caught in deadly sins; and it offered a new source of community blessing to those who assumed deprivation was their lot in life. The God who raised Jesus from the dead was able to change life from despairing to joyful, from futile to fruitful, and from dead to living. This great news enabled the community to live a remarkable life. The phrase in verse 34, "there was not a needy person among them," demonstrated that their faith directed ethics. It was wrong that some had more than enough and some had less than enough; therefore, the redistribution of wealth (a sign of God's season of salvation) occurred whenever a need was discovered. Property was sold; the money was given to the apostles; the leaders handled the distribution of resources. Not only did faith direct ethical behavior, but also this trusting community initiated a system to administer the distribution of resources. In other words, they lived by their faith. Material possessions and property did not secure life; righteous deeds and charitable offerings did not ensure blessing; special privileges and religious standing did not guaran-

tee divine favor. Instead, the community received the apostles' testimony to the resurrection, and through that they discovered the great power to live in unity, to meet every need, and to trust their leaders. Surely, the awe that filled the community intensified as more and more participated in the common life of those who confessed Jesus as the Savior and master.

INTERPRETING THE SCRIPTURE

A Common Life

A common meal, a common cup, and a common prayer—the word "common" pops up in our religious vocabulary with surprising frequency. However, rarely does our word "common" stretch to encompass something as profound as the common life described in the first few chapters of Acts. Indeed, as we read the passages for this lesson, it may be difficult to restrain our skepticism. Was there ever such a solidly sweet Christian community? Did the earliest Christian community really have everything in common—or is this a story told to make a point by creating an appropriate past or fashioning the ideal people of God? In truth, we cannot know the actual life of the earliest community of believers. For example, we do not know each member's name. We cannot audit the records of the first church treasurer. Instead, as we listen to Luke's descriptions of the earliest Christians, their compelling and brilliant community life breaks through our questions and doubts. Luke's account is revelatory, even if incomplete. As we ponder these brief passages, we remember that this is a testimony to what mattered most: a common Christian life.

Marks of the Christian Community

Imagine the informational brochure that a media consultant might produce for the first group of Christians. It might begin with a description of the community: Awe comes upon everyone! And then might come an invitation, "Wouldn't you like to be part of something like that?" The brochure might describe the benefits of membership: a common purse, renewed whenever necessary and distributed according to individual need, as well as daily community gatherings at the temple courtyard and in the temple proper for prayers. The brochure might also describe the community meals ("where no one is left hungry") and the joyful evenings of sharing and praising God. The closing lines might stress that everyone (neighbors and community leaders) respected this community, and, best of all, if you became a member you'd be joining a growing, lively group. The brochure would confirm one reality: God was at work in this community.

There were the four distinguishing marks of this earliest community. First, a system of shared resources; the common life clearly had an economic as well as spiritual and social component. Second, a commitment to spend time together; the common life was nurtured through social, educational, spiritual, and recreational events. Third, a pervasive attitude of joy and generosity; the common life chased away all fears and anxiety. And finally, there was numeric growth; the common life continually included the individuals and families God was saving—growth happened with amazing intensity and speed. In our contemporary church vocabulary these marks might be described as: mission or ministry to those in need, comprehensive community formation, personal and corporate witness to God's grace, and church growth that is numerical and spiritual. Indeed, we find ourselves, our brothers and sisters in Christ, and our congregations in the few words describing the earliest community. Their distinctive marks are our aims. Their youthful shape outlines our well-seasoned structures.

United in Heart and Soul

Although the early church is reflected in the contemporary church, there is one phrase that does not fit our context: "Now the whole group of those who believed were of one heart and soul" (4:32). Our contemporary church is composed of a multitude of races, cultures, languages, convictions, liturgical practices, missions, and ministries—and all this can be discovered in the churches of North America before considering the international forms of Christian faith. Not only is there an abundance of variety in the contemporary church, there is also a rich treasury of commitments. Rarely is the contemporary church united about any church direction, pronouncement, aim, or standard. In our day and age, we affirm this diversity as good; it provides the push and pull that keeps contemporary witness to Jesus Christ fresh and new.

However, in the earliest stage of the formation of the church, a spirit of unity was essential—perhaps even mandatory. Believers were filled with awe by one truth: that in Jesus Christ, God's season of salvation had begun. Anxieties, doubts, fears, and turmoil paled before the bright truth offered by the apostles. For years they had hoped for a new, free, joyful life before God; now, in Jesus, the time had arrived. Personal priorities seemed petty when compared to the resurrection of Jesus. Grace washed away class distinctions; slaves and masters saw one another as members of one family. Even gossip and criticism were handled with a light touch. The early community kept the focus on God's amazing deed of salvation—they were all young believers, so confident in God that they innocently ignored problems and issues near at hand. Their unity was strong, but as we study on in Acts, it was short lived.

It Is Enough

How have you learned to measure "enough"? Some learn the dimensions of enough after a frantic race for more and more ends with an empty exhaustion. Some learn through the delight of a baby's first smile. Some learn by visiting a culture steeped in love rather than materialism. Some learn by a natural bent toward simplicity. Some even learn by studying Scripture. The early Christian community learned by doing; they met needs within the community by the simple practice of selling property or goods and allowing the apostles to distribute the resources. In a sense, the whole community engaged in an experiment deeply rooted in the faith of Israel. Leviticus and Deuteronomy include numerous directions for maintaining the economic life of the community. For example, Deuteronomy 15 is a description of the proper conduct of a sabbatical year: debts are forgiven and brothers and sisters who had been sold into slavery are released. Every seventh (sabbatical) year was a time for joy to gain its rightful place in the homes, villages, and hearts of all God's people. This sabbatical renewal of community, economy, and joy, however, was a prelude to a more amazing year to come. After seven sabbatical seasons, the trumpet was to sound over the whole nation to initiate the year of Jubilee. In this year, every Israelite individual was restored to a full status as heir of the covenant. According to Leviticus 25, not only were debts forgiven, but also any inherited land that was sold was returned to the original owner. The whole nation released, redeemed, and renewed itself by honest acts of liberation, forgiveness, and return.

The Jubilee Year is a shining moment within the law; however, it was a law that was most likely never practiced. There is no account of a grand Jubilee season in the life of the nation Israel; rather, like so many passages that imply a radical approach to material possessions and property, this year was treated as a poetic metaphor or a prophetic promise. No one really believed the Year of Jubilee was possible—apart from a mighty deed of God. However, by the gift of the Holy Spirit the earliest Christians began to live Jubilee-styled lives. They softened their hearts, they loosened their grasp, and they gave whenever a need emerged. By the continuing work of the Spirit, each act of generosity added to the depth of understanding about God's salvation. There was nothing abstract or ethereal about the power of God in their common life; it was as simple as need observed, money offered, distribution made, and joy increased.

SHARING THE SCRIPTURE

PREPARING TO TEACH

Preparing Our Hearts

This week's devotional reading is found in Romans 8:9-17. In chapter 8, Paul writes about what it means to live in the Spirit. As the children of God, we have God's Spirit dwelling within us. What difference does that Spirit make in how you interact with God, with other people, and with all of creation? How might your life be different if you were unaware of God's Spirit within? Write answers to these questions in your spiritual journal.

Pray that you and the adult learners will be open to the leading of the Holy Spirit as you seek to live together within the community of faith.

Preparing Our Minds

Study the background and lesson Scriptures, both of which are from Acts 2:43-47 and Acts 4:32-35. As you read, think about how these two passages describe the marks of a Christian community.

Write on newsprint:
❑ information for next week's lesson, found under "Continue the Journey."

Plan the snack you will use for the closing activity. You may wish to contact class members during the week to bring some food.

LEADING THE CLASS

(1) Gather to Learn

❖ Welcome the class members and introduce any guests.

❖ Pray that the participants will be open to the work of the Holy Spirit in their midst today.

❖ Encourage the students to call out the names of organizations to which they belong. Discuss with the students reasons why they choose to be part of these organizations. What are they seeking? List these ideas on newsprint. If not already noted, end the list by adding that many people join groups because they want to find a sense of belonging and community.

❖ Read aloud today's focus statement: **People yearn for true community. What are the marks of a Christian community? Worship, sharing of resources, unity, and spreading the good news made the first Christian community stand out.**

(2) Examine How the Word, Love, and Worship of God Served as the Foundation of True Community in the Early Church

❖ Choose a volunteer to read Acts 2:43-47.

■ Distribute paper and pencils. Invite the students to imagine themselves as members of this first church and write an account, based on these verses, of how they lived with other Christians. You may ask students to work individually or with a group.

■ Encourage volunteers to read or retell their account.

■ Wrap up this portion of the lesson by asking the students to identify the marks of this first Christian community. List their ideas on newsprint.

❖ Select someone to read Acts 4:32-35.

■ Urge the students to add to their list any marks of the community described here.

■ Suggest that the learners talk with a partner or small group about why they would—or would not—want to be part of such a church.

(3) Compare the Learners' Faith Community with the Early Church

❖ Request that the students look over the list of characteristics they have created to describe the early church.

❖ Summarize that list by reading the second paragraph under "Marks of a Christian Community" in Interpreting the Scripture.

❖ Brainstorm with the students a list of characteristics that they believe describe how their own church lives together.

❖ Compare the two lists by checking off attitudes, practices, or other distinguishing marks that describe both the learners' congregation and the early church.

❖ Look at items that are not checked and discuss these questions.

(1) Do the marks that describe our congregation enhance or detract from our ministry in the twenty-first century? Support your answer with reasons or examples.

(2) What have we lost that was valuable in the early Christian church? Is there any way that we can reclaim that which was lost? If so, how?

❖ Read aloud the first paragraph under "Marks of the Christian Community" in Interpreting the Scripture.

❖ Divide the class into groups and distribute paper and pencils or markers. Ask each group to create a brochure listing the activities of their congregation. They may choose to divide it according to categories suggested in Acts 2:43-47, such as: mission, outreach, fellowship, evangelism, spiritual formation, or other words that are familiar to your congregation.

❖ Conclude this section by inviting the groups to swap brochures with one another. The students may be surprised to see events/programs that are unfamiliar to them.

(4) Make a Commitment to Live Together Faithfully in Community

❖ Pass around some light snack food, such as fruit or cheese and crackers. As the class members eat, remind them that the early church fellowshiped together regularly.

❖ Ask each person to state at least one way that he or she is living—or intends to live—faithfully with the church community.

❖ Close this time by asking the students to repeat this affirmation, adapted from "Baptismal Covenant II" of The United Methodist Church: **With God's help we will so order our lives after the example of Christ that each person who participates in our community of faith will be surrounded by steadfast love, established in the faith, and strengthened in the way that leads to life eternal. To that end, we renew** our covenant faithfully to participate in the ministries of the church by our prayers, our presence, our gifts, and our service, that in everything God may be glorified through Jesus Christ.

(5) Continue the Journey

❖ Pray that the participants will recognize the movement of the Holy Spirit in their midst and respond in faith.

❖ Read aloud this preparation for next week's lesson. You may also want to post it on newsprint for the students to copy. **Prepare for next week's session, entitled "The Gift of Healing," by reading Acts 3:1-26, noting especially our lesson scripture, Acts 3:1-16. As you read this story of healing, keep this focus in mind: Many people are wounded physically, emotionally, or spiritually. Where can they find healing? The apostles carried on the healing ministry of Jesus Christ, and we carry it on as the community of faith.**

❖ Read aloud the following three ideas. Challenge the students to commit themselves to use these activities as a springboard to spiritual growth.

(1) Share something of value to you with someone else this week. As you do, recall that the first members of the church shared generously with one another, as each had need.

(2) Ponder this question: What can I do to help my congregation become more like the sharing, caring church depicted in Acts 2:43-47 and 4:32-35? What action will you commit yourself to take?

(3) Invite an unchurched person to join you in worship and Sunday school this week. As you do so, boldly proclaim your belief in the risen Christ and his power to transform lives through the Holy Spirit.

❖ Sing or read aloud "Filled with the Spirit's Power."

❖ Lead this benediction to conclude the session: **May the Holy Spirit empower you to be witnesses for Jesus Christ in your community, in your nation, and to the ends of the earth. Amen.**

UNIT 1: IN JERUSALEM
THE GIFT OF HEALING

PREVIEWING THE LESSON

Lesson Scripture: Acts 3:1-16
Background Scripture: Acts 3:1-26
Key Verse: Acts 3:6

Focus of the Lesson:

Many people are wounded physically, emotionally, or spiritually. Where can they find healing? The apostles carried on the healing ministry of Jesus Christ, and we carry it on as the community of faith.

Goals for the Learners:

(1) to investigate the story of the Holy Spirit's working through Peter and John to heal a crippled beggar.
(2) to identify ways they need to be healed, and invite the Spirit to do so.
(3) to become involved in the church's holistic healing of those who are wounded physically, emotionally, and spiritually.

Pronunciation Guide:

colonnade (ka le nad')
portico (por' ti ko)

Supplies:

Bibles, newsprint and marker, paper and pencils, CD or tape and appropriate player, hymnals

---

READING THE SCRIPTURE

NRSV
Acts 3:1-16

¹One day Peter and John were going up to the temple at the hour of prayer, at three o'clock in the afternoon. ²And a man lame from birth was being carried in. People would lay him daily at the gate of the temple called the Beautiful Gate so that he could ask for alms from those entering the temple.

NIV
Acts 3:1-16

¹One day Peter and John were going up to the temple at the time of prayer—at three in the afternoon. ²Now a man crippled from birth was being carried to the temple gate called Beautiful, where he was put every day to beg from those going into the temple courts. ³When he saw Peter and John about

[3]When he saw Peter and John about to go into the temple, he asked them for alms. [4]Peter looked intently at him, as did John, and said, "Look at us." [5]And he fixed his attention on them, expecting to receive something from them. [6]**But Peter said, "I have no silver or gold, but what I have I give you; in the name of Jesus Christ of Nazareth, stand up and walk."** [7]And he took him by the right hand and raised him up; and immediately his feet and ankles were made strong. [8]Jumping up, he stood and began to walk, and he entered the temple with them, walking and leaping and praising God. [9]All the people saw him walking and praising God, [10]and they recognized him as the one who used to sit and ask for alms at the Beautiful Gate of the temple; and they were filled with wonder and amazement at what had happened to him.

[11]While he clung to Peter and John, all the people ran together to them in the portico called Solomon's Portico, utterly astonished. [12]When Peter saw it, he addressed the people, "You Israelites, why do you wonder at this, or why do you stare at us, as though by our own power or piety we had made him walk? [13]The God of Abraham, the God of Isaac, and the God of Jacob, the God of our ancestors has glorified his servant Jesus, whom you handed over and rejected in the presence of Pilate, though he had decided to release him. [14]But you rejected the Holy and Righteous One and asked to have a murderer given to you, [15]and you killed the Author of life, whom God raised from the dead. To this we are witnesses. [16]And by faith in his name, his name itself has made this man strong, whom you see and know; and the faith that is through Jesus has given him this perfect health in the presence of all of you.

to enter, he asked them for money. [4]Peter looked straight at him, as did John. Then Peter said, "Look at us!" [5]So the man gave them his attention, expecting to get something from them.

[6]**Then Peter said, "Silver or gold I do not have, but what I have I give you. In the name of Jesus Christ of Nazareth, walk."** [7]Taking him by the right hand, he helped him up, and instantly the man's feet and ankles became strong. [8]He jumped to his feet and began to walk. Then he went with them into the temple courts, walking and jumping, and praising God. [9]When all the people saw him walking and praising God, [10]they recognized him as the same man who used to sit begging at the temple gate called Beautiful, and they were filled with wonder and amazement at what had happened to him.

[11]While the beggar held on to Peter and John, all the people were astonished and came running to them in the place called Solomon's Colonnade. [12]When Peter saw this, he said to them: "Men of Israel, why does this surprise you? Why do you stare at us as if by our own power or godliness we had made this man walk? [13]The God of Abraham, Isaac and Jacob, the God of our fathers, has glorified his servant Jesus. You handed him over to be killed, and you disowned him before Pilate, though he had decided to let him go. [14]You disowned the Holy and Righteous One and asked that a murderer be released to you. [15]You killed the author of life, but God raised him from the dead. We are witnesses of this. [16]By faith in the name of Jesus, this man whom you see and know was made strong. It is Jesus' name and the faith that comes through him that has given this complete healing to him, as you can all see.

UNDERSTANDING THE SCRIPTURE

Acts 3:1-3. For this story, time and place are critical: a customary hour of prayer and sacrifice (three in the afternoon) at the temple gate. The notation of time, a rarity in the Acts of the Apostles, is not accidental. The careful reader immediately makes a connection by remembering another three in the afternoon. Jesus died on the cross at this hour (see Luke 23:44-46); moreover, his last words were a prayer. In the days following Pentecost, as pious and faithful Jews, the followers of Jesus went to the temple to join with the whole community of God's people for prayer and praise. Some of the community may have been present for the prayers when animals were ritually sacrificed (Exodus 29:39; Leviticus 6:20). Especially during festival days, long lines of pilgrims waited throughout the day with lambs and doves in order to seal vows, demonstrate gratitude, or affirm devotion to God. But even during "ordinary" time, the temple grounds teemed with activity throughout the day: The money changers ensured that everyone had the proper temple coins to place in the offering boxes and the merchants were ready with approved, ritually pure lambs and doves for sacrifices. In every portico and corner were teachers, healers, preachers, and a few zealots recruiting young revolutionaries. Possibly, the apostles spent whole days in the temple courtyard witnessing and instructing others as their teacher Jesus had done. However, since the day began at dawn and most work was accomplished before the intense heat of the afternoon, the hour of evening prayer was the most likely time for the new community of those who called on the name of Jesus to gather at the temple. Leaving workplaces and homes, these new believers walked through the city and its misery. Outside the temple were the beggars: the poor who had no hope but charity, as well as the blind and lame who were prohibited from entering the temple. Surely, the members of the new community had passed beggars outside the temple hundreds of times before, but now, with Spirit-cleansed eyes and hearts, they saw differently.

Acts 3:4-11. After sketching this ordinary scene, Luke moves the story forward with intensity. The first clue that something powerful is about to happen is the phrase "Peter looked intently at him." Again the careful reader is reminded of the times when Jesus looked intensely at someone; specifically, Luke may be associating Peter's intense look at the beggar with the last look Jesus cast on Peter. After Peter denied Jesus for the third time, Luke simply writes, "The Lord turned and looked at Peter" (Luke 22:61). A look highlighted a personal need for salvation in each story. Peter, by his denial, separated himself from Jesus; he needed a restored relationship with Jesus. The beggar by his status of ritual uncleanness was excluded from the life of God's people; he needed a new path to God. The need for salvation is always unique. But, as is often the case, the intense personal need obscured unexpected possibilities. Here, for example, the beggar expected only charity. Peter and John, by their faith in Jesus, knew God's response was greater than a few coins to ensure a beggar a day of subsistence. Peter declared what could not be given (silver or gold) and gave what could not be imagined (a lame man standing and walking). The gift was given in the name of Jesus Christ of Nazareth. Rather than a puff of air and sound, the name Jesus was an act of confession. This was neither a magical nor a superstitious incantation; rather, Peter pronounced the holy name of Jesus in full accord with God's law (Exodus 20:7 and Deuteronomy 5:11). As the lame man stood, it was clear God had intervened. The lame man praised God and all who saw the miracle "were filled with wonder and amazement" (3:10).

Acts 3:12-16. In the commotion of the moment, Peter and John recognized an opportunity for preaching the gospel. Notice how Luke weaves the story together: First, Peter and John demanded that the beggar look at them and then, they casually questioned why the crowd was staring at them. They would not be misperceived; neither would they allow the crowd to continue in a state of ecstasy. With a careful speech, Peter explained that divine power was not theirs but came directly from God. Peter based his speech on the ancient promise that through Abraham all people would be saved. He declared that this promise to Abraham and all his descendants was fulfilled in God's servant, Jesus. However, these very descendants of Abraham, who moments ago had witnessed the power of Jesus in the healing of a lame man, belonged to the nation whose leaders arranged Jesus' crucifixion.

Embedded in Peter's speech are several titles applied to Jesus. Each title picked up a piece of the distinctive religious vocabulary of Israel. As "servant" of God, Jesus is the one described by Isaiah to initiate God's redemption. As "the Holy and Righteous One," Jesus is associated with God (rather than a merely human priest or ruler). As the "Author of life,"

Jesus' resurrection is the final proof that he is God's anointed one, the Messiah of Israel.

Acts 3:17-26. The punch line of Peter's speech was this: You killed the Author of life! With these words, the speech became a sermon. Peter gently drew his audience into his circle of friendship; he excused their behavior with the words "you acted in ignorance." Moreover, he declared that their deeds actually fulfilled the Scripture that proclaimed the Messiah had to suffer. All this happened; now the people are encouraged to repent and turn to God. They are assured that God will (1) wipe out their sins, (2) send a season of spiritual refreshment and rest, and (3) receive Jesus, who is their Messiah. But there was more than the offer of salvation in this sermon. There was also a division being made. Peter challenged the crowd to think independently. They were ancestors of Abraham; they knew the prophets; they could accept Jesus regardless of the judgment of the religious leaders. Indeed, Peter concluded with the necessity of each individual deciding: "When God raised up his servant, he sent him first to you, to bless you by turning each of you from your wicked ways" (3:26). The message was clear: Salvation is offered to all, but to each individually.

INTERPRETING THE SCRIPTURE

On An Ordinary Day

Consider your ordinary Sunday morning routine: rising, eating breakfast, preparing to leave for church. Think about the drive or walk to the church building. Imagine the streets you pass and the people you see. Is there any place in that routine that the miraculous power of Jesus might emerge? Sadly, many Christians expect nothing more from Sunday morning than a good sermon, uplifting music, the sustaining support of a

community at prayer and, perhaps, a discreet brush by the Holy Spirit within the confines of our church building—but certainly not on the way to church!

The routine of the early Christian community was as ordinary as your Sunday morning routine. First there would be worship; then, a shared meal. After the meal, questions initiated a teaching time. The conversation was insightful and intense; the talk was peppered with testimonials as both the apostles and the newer believers shared their spiritual insights. However, for the earliest Christian community, God's work was obvious everywhere and at all times. Every aspect of life was filled with anticipation: God was busy restoring, reconciling, and redeeming creation. Therefore, with minds and hearts, as well as eyes and ears, attentive to the next outpouring of the Holy Spirit, Peter and John walked across Jerusalem to the temple. Perhaps they were already discussing the God-filled events of the day. Perhaps they were just observing the Holy City. Perhaps they had passed the lame beggar the previous day, or perhaps they were seeing him for the first time.

Suddenly, the reality of the man's life called Peter and John to attention. Here was a man excluded from birth from temple worship and thereby from full participation in God's community of salvation. Friends carried him to the Beautiful Gate in order that he might be near the blessed community and receive from them the alms that sustained his life. He was placed very close to the heart of the community of faith, but he was not permitted entrance. On an ordinary day this sight burned with extraordinary intensity into the hearts of the apostles.

In the Name of Jesus

The beggar asked his usual question: Alms? Apparently, Peter heard more in his request than the man imagined; Peter looked intently at the man. Frequently in Scripture stories the intensity of Jesus is focused through his eyes. Jesus sees people not as lame or blind or sinners or saints or rich or poor or young or old or male or female, but rather as glorious children of God. Jesus responded to all he saw with amazing knowledge of their unique character and true needs. As Peter looked intently at the man, he saw more than a lame man needing strong leg muscles and straight leg bones. Peter saw a man who needed God. Evidently, John saw the same thing. The two claimed the man's attention with a command: "Look at us" (3:4).

Have you ever been approached by a panhandler? Frequently, there is no real connection between the two people. Neither the one asking nor the one responding (or not responding) looks at the other. A crumpled bill passes hands or the tin can is extended to the next passer-by; anonymity maintains separation. By the intensity of their look Peter and John began to break the anonymity; then, they invited the beggar to do the same. Do the apostles realize their boldness? Are they assured that a healing will happen? The pace of the story does not pause for such introspection; instead, the moment becomes a miracle performed in the name of Jesus. Peter, the spokesman, declares his poverty. He, like all the members of his community, had turned personal resources over to the common purse; his words were true: He had neither gold nor silver. He did have, however, something more precious. Peter had confidence in the power of the resurrected Jesus. Calling on the name of Jesus of Nazareth, he commanded the man to stand up and walk. Then, like a gentle parent, Peter reached out his hand to steady the lame man trying to do what he has never done: to stand upright. The lame man was instantaneously healed; just as swiftly he praised God. In the space of a few moments, by the name of Jesus, and with the guidance of an apostle, a man who lived outside the circle of God's people began to shout and jump and praise and dance his way into the temple proper. Naturally, wonder and amazement filled those who saw the extraordinary change.

While He Clung to Peter and John

The miracle stirred a commotion. The spectacle was intensified by the way the healed man clung to Peter and John. It did not take long before an interested crowd of evening worshipers surrounded the apostles. Like the crush of reporters awaiting an update from a hospital spokesperson following a rock star's surgery, the crowd surrounding Peter and John were most likely interested in the "facts" of the healing. Their unrecorded questions are familiar: What has happened? Why? What's the prognosis for the future? Expecting a detailed explanation, the crowd basked in astonishment. But Peter and John recognized this as a moment for conversion, not for explanation.

The reason behind their reluctance to give an explanation may be indicated by the apostles' reluctance to use the word "healed." Throughout the passage the healing is described, but not named as a healing. The apostles demonstrated great wisdom, as well as restraint, by avoiding the Greek word for healing, *soteria*, which has a breadth of meanings, including rescue from danger, restoration of health, survival, and salvation. It is a word used in secular and in religious vocabularies. It is also a word that demonstrates the nature of salvation experienced powerfully by the early Christian community. In this community there was no distinction drawn between a rescue, an economic restoration, a reconciliation between enemies, a healing, or an assurance of divine favor: Each and every powerful event pointed to God's greater salvation. Therefore, as Peter and John testified they moved the audience away from the tangible sign of God's healing/salvation in the man clinging to them and toward the ultimate decision facing each individual.

Through Faith in Jesus

The message was succinct: Salvation comes through faith in Jesus. The presentation, however, was detailed. Respectful of the time and place, Peter addressed the audience as brothers and sisters in faith. He further affirmed his own humanity; he neither welcomed their wonder nor needed their lauds. Moreover, he boldly shared the account of Jesus' crucifixion, but kindly allowed the audience a shield of ignorance even as he attributed the responsibility for Jesus' death to their religious leaders. His words are charged with the power of the prophets and his concepts as joyful as the giddy, dancing, once-lame man. God accomplished the unexpected: Jesus was killed yet raised from the dead; a man who never walked was healed by his name, and by faith in Jesus, God blesses each and every individual who turns in repentance. The healing became an appeal to consider Jesus. The crowd did not have their questions answered that day; rather, they were challenged to rethink their ultimate loyalty, to consider the power released by confessing the name of Jesus and to come to terms with God's healing, restoring, reconciling, rescuing salvation through faith in Jesus. It is ever so!

SHARING THE SCRIPTURE

PREPARING TO TEACH

Preparing Our Hearts

This week's devotional reading is found in Luke 7:18-23. Here we read the report of Jesus' response to the disciples of John the Baptist, who ask whether Jesus is truly the Messiah. Jesus responds by encouraging them to tell John what they have seen Jesus do. Apparently these messengers were eyewitnesses to healings and other amazing deeds of God. What more did they need to know? What firsthand experiences have you had with Jesus the Healer? Commit yourself to telling at least one of your stories to one or more people this week.

Pray that you and the adult learners will recognize the healing power of Jesus, which continues to be active in today's world through the Holy Spirit.

Preparing Our Minds

Study the background Scripture, Acts 3:1-26, and lesson Scripture, verses 1-16. As you read consider how the apostles followed the example of Jesus as healers, and how we too are to follow this example as the community of faith.

Write on newsprint:

❑ information for next week's lesson, found under "Continue the Journey."

Create a brief lecture on the meaning of the details of Acts 3:1-3 in the "Investigate the Story of the Holy Spirit's Working through Peter and John to Heal a Crippled Beggar" section.

Select a meditative compact disk (CD) or tape for use during the "Identify Ways Learners Need to Be Healed, and Invite the Spirit to Do So" portion. Have the appropriate player, along with an electrical adapter and extension cord if needed.

LEADING THE CLASS

(1) Gather to Learn

❖ Welcome the class members and introduce any guests.

❖ Pray that the students will be receptive to the message of God's gracious gift of healing in their own lives.

❖ Read aloud today's devotional reading from Luke 7:18-23, which speaks about Jesus healing those in need.

❖ Invite the students to recount stories that illustrate how they or loved ones were healed. Remember that God can and does work through physicians, medical personnel, and medications, as well as by means that can only be described as miraculous to bring about healing. If the class is large, you may choose to divide into groups to tell these stories.

❖ Read aloud today's focus statement:

Many people are wounded physically, emotionally, or spiritually. Where can they find healing? The apostles carried on the healing ministry of Jesus Christ, and we carry it on as the community of faith.

(2) Investigate the Story of the Holy Spirit's Working Through Peter and John to Heal a Crippled Beggar

❖ Ask a volunteer to read Acts 3:1-3.

■ Encourage the students to note as many details as possible.

■ Use the information for these verses from the Understanding the Scripture portion to explain why each of these details is so important to the story.

❖ Enlist volunteers to pantomime the roles of Peter, John, and the crippled man. The rest of the class is to act as the crowd. Read Acts 3:4-10 aloud yourself for the pantomime. Then choose one of the following options.

■ **Option 1:** Ask the students to envision themselves as the newly healed man. What would you want to ask Peter and John? How might your life be different now that you are no longer economically dependent and separated from the community of faith because of your infirmity?

■ **Option 2:** Ask the students to imagine themselves as part of the crowd of witnesses. Encourage them to voice any questions or observations about the event they have just witnessed.

❖ Select someone to read Acts 3:11-16.

■ Encourage the students to summarize Peter's message in a sentence or two.

■ Discuss Peter's understanding of who Jesus was, the reason for his death, and the role that this crowd did (or did not) play in his death.

■ Ask the class to consider how they would have responded to Peter's message had they been present. How might this event have created and/or shaped a relationship with

Jesus—or would they have remained unconvinced that Jesus was the Messiah?

(3) Identify Ways Learners Need to Be Healed, and Invite the Spirit to Do So

❖ Distribute paper and a pencil to each student. Challenge them to list physical, mental, emotional, or spiritual "wounds" in their lives that need to be healed. Assure them that their lists will not be shared with anyone. As the students work, play a meditative CD or tape, such as the sounds of nature or soothing instrumental selections.

❖ Lead the class in a guided imagery activity.

■ Imagine yourself in a quiet place where you feel safe and at peace. (pause)

■ See Jesus coming toward you, looking intently at you as he reaches out his hands. Envision yourself responding to him. (pause)

■ Tell Jesus about at least one of the "wounds" you have identified and ask him to heal you. (pause)

■ Listen as Jesus speaks words of comfort to you. (pause)

■ Offer thanks and sit quietly as the Spirit works through you. (pause)

■ Open your eyes when you are ready. (pause)

(4) Become Involved in the Church's Holistic Healing of Those Who Are Wounded Physically, Emotionally, and Spiritually

❖ Brainstorm ways that your congregation reaches out to offer healing to those who are sick. Write these ideas on newsprint.

❖ Poll the class to see who is involved in these various ministries. Invite those who participate to speak about the ministry and what it means to them and to those it serves. (One example may be Stephen's Ministry, which you can learn more about at http://www.stephenministries.org.)

❖ Ask students who are willing to make a commitment to explore how they might become involved in the healing ministry of your congregation to raise their hands as a sign of their commitment.

(5) Continue the Journey

❖ Pray that the participants will give thanks for God's gift of healing in their own lives and proclaim the good news of this gift to others.

❖ Read aloud this preparation for next week's lesson. You may also want to post it on newsprint for the students to copy. **Prepare for next week's session, entitled "Power to Be Bold," by reading Acts 4:1-31. The lesson will focus on verses 1-4, 23-31. As you study the Scripture, keep this main idea in mind: Courage and conviction lead people to witness for good. What gives us courage to do the same as Christians? Acts shows that God's Spirit encouraged and emboldened the early Christians, and it can do so with us today.**

❖ Read aloud the following three ideas. Challenge the students to commit themselves to use these activities as a springboard to spiritual growth.

(1) Search the Internet or your local library or a bookstore for information about the connection between health and spirituality. Read a book or an article of interest to you.

(2) Visit, send a card, or make a phone call to someone who is ill. Assure that individual of God's love and healing power.

(3) Attend a healing service. Seek God's healing power for your own physical, mental, emotional, or spiritual ills.

❖ Sing or read aloud "Dear Lord, for All in Pain."

❖ Lead this benediction to conclude the session: **May the Holy Spirit empower you to be witnesses for Jesus Christ in your community, in your nation, and to the ends of the earth. Amen.**

UNIT 1: IN JERUSALEM
POWER TO BE BOLD

PREVIEWING THE LESSON

Lesson Scripture: Acts 4:1-4, 23-31
Background Scripture: Acts 4:1-31
Key Verse: Acts 4:29

Focus of the Lesson:
Courage and conviction lead people to witness for good. What gives us courage to do the same as Christians? Acts shows that God's Spirit encouraged and emboldened the early Christians, and it can do so with us today.

Goals for the Learners:
(1) to explore the story of Peter and John boldly proclaiming the gospel in the face of persecution.
(2) to discern resources they can draw on in challenging circumstances.
(3) to identify and commit to ways they can witness boldly.

Pronunciation Guide:
Caiaphas (kay' uh fuhs)
Sadducee (sad' joo see)
Sanhedrin (san hee' druhn)

Supplies:
Bibles, newsprint and marker, paper and pencils, hymnals

READING THE SCRIPTURE

NRSV
Acts 4:1-4, 23-31

¹While Peter and John were speaking to the people, the priests, the captain of the temple, and the Sadducees came to them, ²much annoyed because they were teaching the people and proclaiming that in Jesus there is the resurrection of the dead. ³So they arrested them and put them in custody until the next day, for it was already evening.

NIV
Acts 4:1-4, 23-31

¹The priests and the captain of the temple guard and the Sadducees came up to Peter and John while they were speaking to the people. ²They were greatly disturbed because the apostles were teaching the people and proclaiming in Jesus the resurrection of the dead. ³They seized Peter and John, and because it was evening, they put them

[4]But many of those who heard the word believed; and they numbered about five thousand.

[23]After they were released, they went to their friends and reported what the chief priests and the elders had said to them. [24]When they heard it, they raised their voices together to God and said, "Sovereign Lord, who made the heaven and the earth, the sea, and everything in them, [25]it is you who said by the Holy Spirit through our ancestor David, your servant:

'Why did the Gentiles rage,
    and the peoples imagine vain things?
[26]The kings of the earth took their stand,
    and the rulers have gathered together
against the Lord and against his Messiah.'

[27]For in this city, in fact, both Herod and Pontius Pilate, with the Gentiles and the peoples of Israel, gathered together against your holy servant Jesus, whom you anointed, [28]to do whatever your hand and your plan had predestined to take place. [29]**And now, Lord, look at their threats, and grant to your servants to speak your word with all boldness,** [30]while you stretch out your hand to heal, and signs and wonders are performed through the name of your holy servant Jesus." [31]When they had prayed, the place in which they were gathered together was shaken; and they were all filled with the Holy Spirit and spoke the word of God with boldness.

in jail until the next day. [4]But many who heard the message believed, and the number of men grew to about five thousand.

[23]On their release, Peter and John went back to their own people and reported all that the chief priests and elders had said to them. [24]When they heard this, they raised their voices together in prayer to God. "Sovereign Lord," they said, "you made the heaven and the earth and the sea, and everything in them. [25]You spoke by the Holy Spirit through the mouth of your servant, our father David:

"'Why do the nations rage
    and the peoples plot in vain?
[26]The kings of the earth take their stand
    and the rulers gather together
against the Lord
    and against his Anointed One.'

[27]Indeed Herod and Pontius Pilate met together with the Gentiles and the people of Israel in this city to conspire against your holy servant Jesus, whom you anointed. [28]They did what your power and will had decided beforehand should happen. [29]**Now, Lord, consider their threats and enable your servants to speak your word with great boldness.** [30]Stretch out your hand to heal and perform miraculous signs and wonders through the name of your holy servant Jesus."

[31]After they prayed, the place where they were meeting was shaken. And they were all filled with the Holy Spirit and spoke the word of God boldly.

UNDERSTANDING THE SCRIPTURE

Acts 4:1-4. In the healing story of the third chapter, the cast of characters consisted of Peter and John, a healed man, and the crowd of worshipers. In chapter 4 three more characters/groups are introduced: the temple priests, the captain of the temple guard, and the Sadducees. All three are described as "much annoyed"; their initial annoyance was with the apostles' teaching on the resurrection. As we examine the social positions of these three, however, other nuances arise. There were two groups within the temple: the clergy and the laity, and each group was divided into a hierarchy of responsibility, privilege, and duties. Two of the three groups introduced, ordinary priests and the captain of the temple, were clergy of lower standing; the Sadducees were the aristocrats of both the laity and the priests. Each group had a reason to be troubled by Peter's preaching on Jesus as the Messiah. The temple guards, under the supervision of the captain of the temple, were responsible for the arrest of Jesus; they were not pleased by the inference that they murdered the "Author of life" (3:15). The priests, who actually commanded the patrols of the guards, undoubtedly feared more disruption to their schedule of services. The Sadducees considered themselves superior to all the uneducated commoners, especially those without property or social status; they were not interested in a messiah from Nazareth. Regardless of their social standings, these three groups colluded together to suppress a religious movement that was growing by leaps and bounds.

Acts 4:5-12. Since the arrest occurred near the day's end, the prisoners were held over until the morning, when the Sanhedrin assembled under the authority of the powerful, upper class of priests: Caiaphas, John (or in some translations, Jonathan), and Alexander. The Sanhedrin functioned as a supreme court for the nation. Because of its mixed composition, however, the Sanhedrin conducted business informally. Those who were most knowledgeable in a given subject crafted court opinions on behalf of the whole; rarely was a vote taken or a consensus sought. If the matter to be considered concerned moral law or ethical conduct, the case was decided by the Pharisees, who excelled in interpretation of the law; however, if the case concerned matters of ritual conduct and purity, the Sadducees, on behalf of the priesthood, rose to make the pronouncement.

Evidently, Peter and John understood the makeup of the court. When they were asked by what power they healed, Peter knew their case was to be decided as a matter of priestly authority. Peter hoped to gain the favor of the Pharisees by arguing his case on moral ground. The healing, after all, was a "good deed." Peter assumed the Pharisees would not contest the righteousness of this healing. However, more than a clever orator, Peter was also a man filled with the Holy Spirit prompting a witness on behalf of Jesus. Though he was untrained and uneducated, Peter stood before the mighty men of his religion and declared Jesus as the source of salvation. It was an impressive moment in the formation of the early Christian defense of faith.

Acts 4:13-23. Peter and John initially impressed the members of the Sanhedrin, but these two followers of Jesus were clearly dangerous. Not only were the apostles filled with spiritual power, but they were also involved in the recent unpleasantness on the temple grounds, the arrest, trial, and execution of Jesus of Nazareth. The Sanhedrin began to realize that their solution with regard to Jesus was not so final. Now they were faced with his former disciples and a wave of enthusiasm at a hazardous level. In executive session, the various members presented pro and con arguments. The common denominator for each proposed action was the impact on "the people." Finally, the judges agreed to silence the disciples. It is an old power play, but one doomed to fail. Rarely does censorship accomplish its goal. Talk may go underground, but truth will not be silenced. The Sanhedrin was about to learn this lesson.

The apostles were escorted back to their judges; the decision was announced; the apostles challenged the judges to judge themselves with regard to Jesus because the apostles had already completed their discernment. Peter and John do not question their newly granted faith: They trust completely in Jesus as the Messiah, in the gift of the Spirit as a sign of the initiation of God's season of redemption, and in their own purpose as witnesses to the truth. Moreover, they publicly proclaim that they will not abide by the court's decision. Instead, they will continue to testify to God's great deeds, the greatest being, of course, the resurrection of Jesus.

Acts 4:24-31. The apostles headed back to their friends; it was time to debrief. They shared their story. They discussed the import of the event. Then, with unanimity, they settled upon the Scripture that clearly interpreted the experience. Their text in verses 25-26 came from Psalm 2:1-2, the prophecy concerning the judgment of the powerful against God's Messiah. This engagement with Scripture led, seamlessly, to prayer. As the company of believers discussed the events of the previous twenty-four hours and as they held these events before the light of Scripture, they saw the impact of their commitment to Jesus in a very personal manner. Their identification with Jesus was risky business; therefore, they prayed! It is humbling to read their petition. They do not pray for protection, but for boldness in their witness. Jesus promised that the Spirit would prompt their speech when they were called before the officials (Mark 13:9-11); his followers prayed for that Spirit. As the prayer ended, a confirmation came in the form of a tremor shaking the home in which they were gathered. The scene echoes the events of the opening of chapter 2: Believers are all together in prayer, there is a dramatic natural occurrence, all are filled with the Holy Spirit, and the testimony to God's great deeds continued. If considered as a whole, these three chapters (Acts 2–4) are a sustained Pentecost experience, initiated and completed in a community gathered in prayer and prompted by the inspiration of the Holy Spirit to testimony.

INTERPRETING THE SCRIPTURE

A Temple Confrontation

In the center of the city, at the heart of the religious institution, sitting precisely on the boundary line between "acceptable and unacceptable," was the lame man. In our contemporary world, we like to think there are no more boundary lines keeping the lame, and the slow of limb or mind away from God. Church signs proclaim: All Are Welcome Here! Community events are publicized as "come as you are" events—the subtext suggests no judgment according to dress or social standing or sin. However, looking closely at our life as the church or analyzing our cities or examining the heart of our "religious institution," we discover boundary lines as distinct as those of Israel in the first century. Although we rarely see friends carrying a lame beggar to the church's threshold, many wonder about whether or not they or their friends are truly accepted inside. This week's lesson is about the apostles' challenge to ancient boundaries, their confidence in the saving grace of Jesus, and the source of their spiritual power. This is not an easy lesson, but it is a necessary one.

This story has a prelude: a lame man healed by the power of the name of Jesus gathered a crowd wanting to understand what happened; following the apostles' interpretation, in the center of the temple courtyard, many were converted. Then, the officials stepped forward and our lesson for today begins. Whenever the power structures decide to quiet the people, be prepared: This is a time when God's Spirit will be active on behalf of "the least of these." Powerful people are preoccupied with their own status and security; this was true for the priests, who understood their function as providing the only approved venue for human/divine relationship. This was also true for the captain of the temple guard, who commanded the men who recently arrested Jesus and turned him over to the Roman authorities. Even the Sadducees, who were wealthy and closely tied to temple politics and commerce, preferred highly regulated religious activities that did not interfere with their everyday conduct. An odd collusion of groups, each with a particular self-interest at heart, sent the apostles to cool down in prison before the morning meeting of the Sanhedrin.

History Is Rewritten

The Sanhedrin was a supreme court for settling disputes impacting the whole community. They were the highest authority for the people of Israel—except, of course, for the higher authority of God. It was to the higher authority that the apostles gave their loyalty. When the Sanhedrin issued their decision intended to silence the apostles' use of the name "Jesus," the apostles continued to appeal to God's higher authority. Turning the tables on their judges, the apostles reminded them that they must judge for themselves what God required. As for the apostles, they vowed to continue their witness to Jesus. They left as free men— unafraid of the highest human authority, but emboldened by God's higher authority.

Returning to their friends, the apostles told the story of their experience and in doing so held their experience up to the light of Scripture. Their text was familiar: Psalm 2. Although verses 1-2, quoted in Acts 4:25-26, were ordinarily applied to the occupation forces of Rome, these verses precisely interpreted the apostles' experience. Indeed, Psalm 2 cast a light on the recent event of Jesus' arrest and crucifixion, as well as illuminating present and future events. The apostles and their friends began to understand the forces against Jesus, and thereby against their new community, as purposeful and, strangely, within the providence of God. Experience combined with Scripture to offer a new understanding. No longer was history a random series of painful events leading to Jesus' death. Suddenly history was God's patient press of reconciliation. Regardless of the plans of the powerful, the community sensed the triumph of God's purpose. This first interaction with the temple power structure frightened neither the apostles nor their friends. Indeed, this encounter, and its aftermath, was inspirational.

A Prayer for Boldness

I wonder if your prayers are like mine. When difficulties arise before my path, I frequently pray to be shown the way out. My tendency is to look for the path of least resistance and to gleefully pursue that course. I am not inclined toward confrontation; I definitely do not like going toe to toe with powerful authorities. Therefore, my prayers in times of danger frequently sound more like pitiful whines than confident petitions. But the apostles did not whine. They didn't even ask God for a convenient escape route. Instead, as the community shared experiences and Scripture, they were inspired to pray for boldness to speak God's word.

It was a beautiful moment as the community realized their purpose within God's purpose. Imagine who was in that prayer circle.

- There were certainly the apostles, the men who were sent by the ascending Jesus to wait on the Holy Spirit and to minister to all the ends of the world.
- There were possibly the other disciples who were in the room on the day of Pentecost when all experienced the power of the Holy Spirit.
- There were perhaps recent converts just beginning to learn the story of Jesus, but aware of the warmth of the Spirit within this community.
- There were possibly others: men and women, the religiously well educated

and the religiously ignorant, as well as the previously pious over-achievers and the previously excluded unacceptable ones.

It was an amazing collection; yet, they all agreed that Psalm 2 perfectly interpreted their experience, and their prayer for boldness was in unison.

Pentecost Power Persists

Signs and wonders are theme words for the first four chapters of the Acts of the Apostles. Yet God's power is demonstrated in a rich variety of ways. There are miraculous healings; however, just as miraculous is the courage of the apostles to speak their convictions to those in power. There are unexplained physical manifestations (a sound like the rush of a violent wind filling a house in 2:2 and a quaking of the house in 4:31); however, just as wonderful is the response of those who hear the apostles' preaching and teaching. In a brief period, a small group that kept to themselves and from the scrutiny of others became a public movement attracting converts. Surely, such activity was greater than human dreams and capacities. God's Spirit was dramatically present and by God's empowerment the ordinary events became extraordinary.

As this first unit, "In Jerusalem," concludes we have experienced the birth and beauty of the earliest Christian community. What characteristics stand out in your mind? Where do you see similar characteristics in the contemporary church—especially in your congregation? I find it inspiring that men and women, those making a bold witness to Jesus, pray for the very gift they already abundantly possess. These are neither fearful nor timid believers; these are courageous and demonstrative witnesses. They stepped across a boundary and, by the power of the Holy Spirit, they intended to live in a new way. Although the precise details concerning the formation of this community are unrecorded, the record we do have shares with believers of all generations the essential source of the church. The church of Jesus Christ began as believers prayed for, opened themselves to, and were emboldened by the power of the Holy Spirit. This is good news of the account of the church in Jerusalem: Pentecost power persists and persists and persists! Because of their experience we are still emboldened to pray: Make us your witnesses, Lord. Amen.

SHARING THE SCRIPTURE

Preparing Our Hearts

This week's devotional reading is found in Ephesians 6:10-20. This familiar passage, which calls us to "put on the whole armor of God," tells us to "stand firm." Paul asks for prayers to enable him to speak boldly the good news of Jesus Christ. This idea is a focal point for today's lesson from Acts 4. Examine your own life. Have you prepared yourself spiritually to act with boldness, even in the face of opposition? What examples can you recall of situations in which you needed to speak boldly and did—or did not—respond as you believe God would have wanted you to?

Pray that you and your students will muster courage, by the power of the Holy Spirit, to speak and act in the name of Jesus.

Preparing Our Minds

Study Acts 4:1-31. Be especially aware of the Holy Spirit's role in emboldening Peter and John, and now us, to witness.

Write on newsprint:

❑ information for next week's lesson, found under "Continue the Journey."

Create a brief lecture as suggested under "Explore the Story of Peter and John Boldly Proclaiming the Gospel in the Face of Persecution."

LEADING THE CLASS

(1) Gather to Learn

❖ Welcome the class members and introduce any guests.

❖ Encourage the participants to recall times when they had to speak with boldness. Perhaps they were shy about giving a report to a school class or co-workers. Maybe they recognized a problem or injustice and needed to muster courage to confront those involved. Invite volunteers to tell the class or a small group how they found the courage to speak and act on their convictions.

❖ Read aloud today's focus statement: **Courage and conviction lead people to witness for good. What gives us courage to do the same as Christians? Acts shows that God's Spirit encouraged and emboldened the early Christians, and it can do so with us today.**

(2) Explore the Story of Peter and John Boldly Proclaiming the Gospel in the Face of Persecution

❖ Choose a volunteer to read Acts 4:1-4.

■ Present a brief lecture to introduce the people mentioned in these verses. You will find information in the Understanding the Scripture portion, Acts 4:1-4.

■ Ask several volunteers to imagine themselves as the religious leaders mentioned in these verses and role-play a discussion among themselves about the teachings of Peter and John and their effect on the crowds who heard them.

❖ Select one person to read the narrator's part of Acts 4:23-31, which is found in verses 23-24a, 31. Invite the rest of the class to read in unison the prayer in verses 24b-30. If the students use different translations, consider assigning different verses to different translations so that everyone can participate.

■ Discuss these questions.

(1) **What resources did the people draw on to offer this prayer for boldness?** (Note their understanding of God and of Jesus. Also note how they related Psalm 2:1-2 to their situation.)

(2) **What was the result of this prayer?** (See verse 31.)

■ List on newsprint current situations that call for prayers for boldness. Provide quiet time for the adults to lift silent prayers for one or more of these situations.

(3) Discern Resources the Learners Can Draw on in Challenging Circumstances

❖ Distribute paper and pencils. Ask the participants to make a list of the resources they can draw on when they need to act with boldness.

❖ Invite the learners to call out ideas from their lists and write them on newsprint. Suggest that the students add any new ideas to their personal lists.

❖ Talk with the group about these ideas. Discern together concrete ways that the Holy Spirit, the Scriptures, prayer, role models, the community of faith, and other resources the class has listed may help them in challenging circumstances.

(4) Identify and Commit to Ways the Learners Can Witness Boldly

❖ Begin this section by noting that the word "witness" and "martyr" are the same in Greek. Those who were willing to stand up and testify on behalf of Jesus faced the real possibility of martyrdom. To be a witness in the early church required a degree of boldness that only the Holy Spirit could provide.

❖ Point out that although contemporary Christians in North America will likely not face martyrdom for their faith in Jesus, believers in other parts of the world are in danger.

❖ Discuss these questions.

(1) **Since our lives are not in danger, what keeps us from making a bolder witness? Are there situations that truly silence us?**

(2) **We have talked earlier in the session about situations that cry out for a bold witness. Which one are you willing to commit yourself to?**

(3) **What are some ways that we can act boldly in the situations to which we feel called to bear witness?**

❖ Conclude this portion of the lesson by inviting each person to tell someone seated near them about the situation that concerns them and what they hope to do about it. Suggest that the partners pray for one another as they make this leap of faith.

(5) Continue the Journey

❖ Pray that the students will be willing to "step up to the plate" and make a bold stand for Jesus as they are led by the power of the Holy Spirit.

❖ Read aloud this preparation for next week's lesson. You may also want to post it on newsprint for the students to copy. **Prepare for next week's session by reading "Faithful Servant," the story of Stephen, found in Acts 6:8–7:60. The lesson, which begins the unit entitled "In All Judea and**

Samaria," will focus on Acts 6:8-15 and 7:53-60. Allow these ideas to shape your thinking as you study: Movements need committed leadership to bring about change. How do strong leaders develop? The example of Stephen and others shows that God's Spirit calls, inspires, and guides strong leaders in the church.

❖ Read aloud the following three ideas. Challenge the students to commit themselves to use these activities as a springboard to spiritual growth.

(1) **Search the Internet for the topic "Christian martyrs." Read stories of some of these bold witnesses, both ancient and contemporary. What common threads do you perceive among these people? How would you compare your willingness to witness to that of these believers who lost their lives because of their steadfast faithfulness?**

(2) **Reread the prayer in Acts 4:24-30 several times this week. What impetus does this prayer give you to witness? Pray this prayer for yourself and for all who want to speak boldly in the name of Jesus.**

(3) **Identify at least one person to whom you feel called to tell how Jesus has acted in your life. Talk with this person and invite him or her to make a response.**

❖ Sing or read aloud "Spirit of God, Descend upon My Heart."

❖ Lead this benediction to conclude the session: **May the Holy Spirit empower you to be witnesses for Jesus Christ in your community, in your nation, and to the ends of the earth. Amen.**

UNIT 2: IN ALL JUDEA AND SAMARIA
FAITHFUL SERVANT

PREVIEWING THE LESSON

Lesson Scripture: Acts 6:8-15; 7:53-60
Background Scripture: Acts 6:8–7:60
Key Verse: Acts 6:8

Focus of the Lesson:
Movements need committed leadership to bring about change. How do strong leaders develop? The example of Stephen shows that God's Spirit calls, inspires, and guides strong leaders in the church.

Goals for the Learners:
(1) to delve into the story of the arrest and stoning of Stephen.
(2) to explore their own call to faithful service.
(3) to name and express gratitude for servants who are called and inspired by God today.

Pronunciation Guide:
Alexandrian (al ig zan' dree uhn)
Cilicia (suh lish'ee uh)
Cyrenian (si ree' nee uhn)

Supplies:
Bibles, newsprint and marker, paper and pencils, hymnals

READING THE SCRIPTURE

NRSV
Acts 6:8-15

8Stephen, full of grace and power, did great wonders and signs among the people. 9Then some of those who belonged to the synagogue of the Freedmen (as it was called), Cyrenians, Alexandrians, and others of those from Cilicia and Asia, stood up and argued with Stephen. 10But they could not withstand the wisdom and the Spirit with which he

NIV
Acts 6:8-15

8Now Stephen, a man full of God's grace and power, did great wonders and miraculous signs among the people. 9Opposition arose, however, from members of the Synagogue of the Freedmen (as it was called)—Jews of Cyrene and Alexandria as well as the provinces of Cilicia and Asia. These men began to argue with Stephen, spoke. [11]Then they secretly instigated some men to say, "We have heard him speak blasphemous words against Moses and God." [12]They stirred up the people as well as the elders and the scribes; then they suddenly confronted him, seized him, and brought him before the council. [13]They set up false witnesses who said, "This man never stops saying things against this holy place and the law; [14]for we have heard him say that this Jesus of Nazareth will destroy this place and will change the customs that Moses handed on to us." [15]And all who sat in the council looked intently at him, and they saw that his face was like the face of an angel.

Acts 7:53-60

[53]You are the ones that received the law as ordained by angels, and yet you have not kept it."

[54]When they heard these things, they became enraged and ground their teeth at Stephen. [55]But filled with the Holy Spirit, he gazed into heaven and saw the glory of God and Jesus standing at the right hand of God. [56]"Look," he said, "I see the heavens opened and the Son of Man standing at the right hand of God!" [57]But they covered their ears, and with a loud shout all rushed together against him. [58]Then they dragged him out of the city and began to stone him; and the witnesses laid their coats at the feet of a young man named Saul. [59]While they were stoning Stephen, he prayed, "Lord Jesus, receive my spirit." [60]Then he knelt down and cried out in a loud voice, "Lord, do not hold this sin against them." When he had said this, he died.

[10]but they could not stand up against his wisdom or the Spirit by whom he spoke.

[11]Then they secretly persuaded some men to say, "We have heard Stephen speak words of blasphemy against Moses and against God."

[12]So they stirred up the people and the elders and the teachers of the law. They seized Stephen and brought him before the Sanhedrin. [13]They produced false witnesses, who testified, "This fellow never stops speaking against this holy place and against the law. [14]For we have heard him say that this Jesus of Nazareth will destroy this place and change the customs Moses handed down to us."

[15]All who were sitting in the Sanhedrin looked intently at Stephen, and they saw that his face was like the face of an angel.

Acts 7:53-60

[53][Y]ou who have received the law that was put into effect through angels but have not obeyed it."

[54]When they heard this, they were furious and gnashed their teeth at him. [55]But Stephen, full of the Holy Spirit, looked up to heaven and saw the glory of God, and Jesus standing at the right hand of God. [56]"Look," he said, "I see heaven open and the Son of Man standing at the right hand of God."

[57]At this they covered their ears and, yelling at the top of their voices, they all rushed at him, [58]dragged him out of the city and began to stone him. Meanwhile, the witnesses laid their clothes at the feet of a young man named Saul.

[59]While they were stoning him, Stephen prayed, "Lord Jesus, receive my spirit." [60]Then he fell on his knees and cried out, "Lord, do not hold this sin against them." When he had said this, he fell asleep.

UNDERSTANDING THE SCRIPTURE

Introduction. The sixth chapter of Acts opens in controversy between two subgroups within the Jerusalem community. One group was composed of the disciples and the women who traveled with Jesus. These men and women, colloquially called "the Hebrews," were traditional in their Jewish upbringing and practices. The second group, "the Hellenists," consisted of converts to Christianity from the Jewish Diaspora. These men and women spoke Greek as their first language and were considered by "the Hebrews" to have a background that culturally compromised the faith of Israel. Although sharing a common faith history and recent conversions, both groups exercised caution with each other. Thus when the distribution of food for the poor, especially the poor widows, seemed unequal, tensions rapidly escalated. The apostles mediated this controversy by suggesting the community designate leaders to oversee the daily distribution of food. This was the beginning of the organized leadership for the community—a second generation of leaders selected on the basis of personal qualities rather than by direct experience with Jesus.

Acts 6:8-15. One of these leaders, Stephen, became known for more than waiting on tables. In this passage from verses 8-15, leaders from a religious movement within Judaism, the Freedmen, first argued with Stephen and then secretly plotted against him. These men, jealous of his preaching and envious of his signs and wonders, stirred up the crowd to accuse Stephen of blasphemy. When outrage reached a shrill pitch, those who opposed Stephen brought him before the Sanhedrin. The scene was a mixture of riotous commotion and momentary revelation. For the first time, the common people opposed the followers of Jesus and, for the first time, the members of the Sanhedrin glimpsed glory on the face of a leader of the new community. Something important was about to happen.

Acts 7:1-50. When the high priest questioned him, Stephen responded with a speech that is the longest and most important speech in Acts. It is unique in style and content. Stephen did not defend himself nor did he testify to Jesus' resurrection; rather, he told the story of Israel's history as a saga of God's providence in spite of Israel's persistent rebellion. Stephen began with the patriarchs; from Abraham to Joseph, he explained, the people held onto God's promise, but never knew a fulfillment of that promise. They were a wandering people, frequently displaced, and yet bound by a spiritual covenant to Yahweh. According to Stephen, during the patriarchal period worship was important, but mobile; there was no one sacred place and no one ritual of worship. Moreover, Stephen asserted that although God providentially provided leaders, the people consistently rejected them. Having established two significant points—(1) God's dealings with Israel were not confined to a particular worship space, and (2) Israel rejected God's chosen leaders—Stephen moved from the tales of the patriarchs to the saga of Moses. Stephen pictured Moses as a prophet rather than as a law-giver, emphasizing Moses' obedience to God's living oracles. This established Stephen's third point: Obedience to God's Spirit is greater than obedience to the literal law. Stephen concluded his speech with negative comments, based on Isaiah 66:1-2, concerning Solomon's construction of the temple. Stephen's speech was a very dangerous, subversive interpretation of Israel's history and Scriptures.

Acts 7:51-53. Although the speech was lengthy, Stephen did not explain that his reinterpretation of Israel's history came through Jesus. In fact, he did not mention Jesus' name at all! Nonetheless, Jesus was clearly the subtext of the speech and everyone in the audience likely knew Stephen was preaching that Jesus was God's Messiah. At the conclusion of his speech, Stephen stunned the audience by indicting them as rebels whose hands were stained with the blood of the prophets. Standing before the highest court in Israel, this newly appointed church leader declared to the leaders of Israel that they had not kept the law. Stephen's point was crystal clear: The people of Israel could be in a right relationship with God not as a result of temple worship or Torah wisdom, but only by obedience to God's word. Because the leaders did not listen for God's Spirit speaking in the Torah and the prophets, they murdered "the Righteous One." If these leaders of Israel had known God's word, especially Isaiah 52:13–53:12, they would have recognized Jesus. Sadly, they knew only proper temple conduct and literal Torah interpretation. Without obedience to God's living Word, the leaders of Israel failed to identify Isaiah's suffering servant as Jesus, God's Messiah.

Acts 7:54-60. The scene shifts from the rarified atmosphere of a courtroom to the rowdy outburst of a crowd. The events tumbled swiftly forward: The crowd erupted; Stephen saw the heavens opened; an enraged mob dragged Stephen outside the city for immediate execution. Luke's account rises and falls as a well-crafted tale. Perhaps he is relying on a well-known (and much beloved) account of the stoning of Stephen. The importance of the tale is in the details.

First, in verse 54, the crowd ground their teeth: In both the Psalms and the Gospels, this phrase describes those who oppose God. Next, the vision of the Son of Man suggested that as the crowd took the law into their own hands, Jesus advocated for Stephen before God's judgment seat. Additionally, the crowd covered their ears in order not to hear blasphemy. Ironically, these are the same men Stephen called "uncircumcised in heart and ears" (7:51) indicating their insensitivity to the Spirit. Moreover, although the Sanhedrin had no authority to issue a death sentence and apparently there was no verdict announced, the stoning proceeded with modest attention to protocol. Stephen was taken outside the Holy City and witnesses were present. However, the crowd pelted Stephen with stones, whereas in an official stoning, the criminal would be kept from escaping, sometimes by being pushed off a cliff of twelve or more feet, or incapacitated in some other way. The witnesses against the condemned person would then cast the first stones. Stoning was a regulated activity ordinarily reserved for blasphemers. Stephen's death, however, was motivated by suspicion and jealousy. His death, oddly, became an enactment of the theme of his sermon: an illustration of Israel's rebellion. Yet, the final glimpse of Stephen provided a gift for his community—a community about to face persecution. Stephen died trusting Jesus and forgiving his enemies.

INTERPRETING THE SCRIPTURE

A Leader Is Called

In the third stanza of a familiar hymn, "Once to Every Man and Nation," are these words: "New occasions teach new duties, Time makes ancient good uncouth; They must upward still and onward, Who would keep abreast of truth." These words capture the challenge faced by the earliest Christians. Living in a community devoted to having all things in common, these Christians constantly faced new duties and evaluated former practices. A new occasion prompted the selection of seven new leaders for the young church. The occasion was a mundane controversy, but the selection of leaders was a spiritual necessity.

Apparently, the daily distribution of food at the common table included a perceived favoritism for the widows of the Hebrews. The Hellenists objected, explaining that their widows were not receiving their fair share of the food. These two groups of widows, both in need and both honored, provided the context for the selection of the first leaders from the community.

The apostles proposed that the community resolve the issue by selecting "seven men of good standing, full of the Spirit and of wisdom" (6:3) to oversee the daily distribution of food. Although the task was simple, the implications were great. The community took its first independent step of organizing; this step, like all to follow, began with prayer. After discernment brought consensus, Stephen was the first of seven leaders selected. Our passage opens with a tribute to the Spirit's power in Stephen through signs and wonders; the passage continues with a demonstration of his ability to argue for the faith. He was selected as a table server (the Greek work is "deacon"), but his leadership went far beyond service at the common meal table. In a similar manner, contemporary Christian leaders often recount their early experiences in leadership. Small tasks, such as greeting, ushering, chaperoning youth, and visiting the elderly, frequently teach the basics of Christian leadership: recognition of each individual as a precious, unique child of God and performance of ministry tasks with equity and cheerfulness. In the early church, those who were faithful in small things proved capable of undertaking more challenging tasks. Stephen began as a humble servant of the widows; he gave his life in witness to Jesus.

New Testament Leadership

As they prayed, so they led: boldly. In the New Testament church the apostles accepted the primary responsibility for teaching and preaching. However, in actual practice every new believer was a teacher and a preacher. Wherever one went and whatever engaged one, whether at home or in the workplace, the good news of Jesus transformed the standards of relationships and ethical behavior. Living in the season of God's salvation refreshed the community; in their refreshment they exuded joy and were renowned in the city. Frequently, these Christians were called upon to explain themselves. From then until now, all Christians share in the teaching and preaching ministry of the church of Jesus Christ. Dietrich Bonhoeffer confirmed this truth in his brief book on Christian fellowship, *Life Together*. He writes, "Where Christians live together the time must inevitably come when in some crisis one person will have to declare God's Word and will to another." The early church understood the unique authority of the apostles, but they also recognized the spiritual gifts of each and every member. Therefore, the movement from informal leadership and conflict resolution, to a set apart (ordained) leadership was first and foremost the recognition of spiritual gifts. Because the community placed a high value on spiritual gifts, leaders also valued their individual spiritual gifts. Evidently, Stephen was wise, articulate, faithful, and bold. He was the first of a new breed of leaders for the church. His ministry, however brief, was brilliant.

A Leader Is Executed

In a tale reminiscent of the twists and turns of the account of Jesus' arrest and trial, Stephen was called before the court of religious leaders known as the Sanhedrin. The charges were inflated (blasphemy against not only God, but also Moses, the temple, and the Torah) and false witnesses were ready to testify. This is the first instance of the common people of Israel opposing the new community of believers. Resistance came from official religious authorities in the first five chapters of Acts; now in two verses everything changed. The people condemned Stephen (6:12); the members of the council saw glory on Stephen's face (6:15); and somewhere behind the scenes, the Freedmen were rubbing their hands in anticipation of a final defeat of Stephen's words and deeds. The mixture of emotions confused the trial's course of conduct.

Two questions arise immediately: Why did the people turn against Stephen? And why did the council fail to manage the crowd? Both questions suggest that the Christians—particularly their leaders—had begun to pose a threat to the Jewish religious institutions. But what was the root of that threat? Taken from the perspective of the Freedmen, the root was envy! Stephen's preaching and miraculous deeds, if left unchecked, would surely advance his popularity. The crowd, spurred on by lies, was determined to root out blasphemers. The council, always concerned with keeping the peace in Jerusalem, worried about the impact of their decision. Evidently, the council members decided this danger must be stopped; however, they did not vote to execute the leader. They merely allowed Stephen to be stoned.

Execution Becomes Testimony

There are two types of tales told to reveal character: stories from birth or infancy and stories of final days or death. This is true in literature, in Scripture, and in everyday life. One story I tell about my daughter describes a toddler's wobbly steps toward a door and her persistent repetition of the word "Go!" The incident captures one aspect of her adventurous spirit. As a pastor I've been privileged to hear stories of the deaths of loved ones. The treasure of these tales is not only the speaker's obvious sense of peace, but also the impression formed in those who receive such an intimate account. After hearing the story, the one who has died is better known. Up to this point in Luke's story of the church, signs and wonders accompany the "birth" of the new community. Now, a significant death taught the community about its character and nature.

The account of Stephen's death must have been widely discussed within the community. Notice how beautifully the tale is balanced: The crowd raged, while Stephen saw Jesus at the throne of God; the crowd became a lynching mob, while Stephen offered his Spirit to Jesus; as the stones fell on Stephen, he knelt to pray; there was no cry of terror, instead the crowd heard Stephen pray for them. At each point in the account, the community received a visual image of faith in Jesus. These few verses were an advanced course on preparation for persecution. It was the most brilliant ministry Stephen offered, precisely because it was the most needed. And remember, the community selected him as their leader to provide equitable service to all the widows. His gifts for ministry, confident faith, and the indwelling of the Holy Spirit developed as he defended the faith, called others to belief, performed signs and wonders, preached before the Sanhedrin, and knelt in prayer as a final act of witness to Jesus. He was bold, gifted, and generous in his living and his dying. See what happens when leaders take their first small tasks of ministry seriously.

SHARING THE SCRIPTURE

PREPARING TO TEACH

Preparing Our Hearts

This week's devotional reading is found in Isaiah 6:1-8, which is the well-known story of the call of the prophet. Isaiah's story relates to Stephen's story in that both were faithful servants of God. What evidence do you see of Isaiah's faithfulness in this passage? Examine your own life. How has God called you? How have you responded?

Pray that you and the adult learners will

be sensitive to the call of God upon your life and willing to respond with utmost eagerness to do God's will.

Preparing Our Minds

Study the background and lesson scripture, Acts 6:8-15 and 7:53-60. As you study the story of Stephen, consider how strong leaders develop within the church.

Write on newsprint:

❑ information for next week's lesson, found under "Continue the Journey."

Use information from the "Introduction" in Understanding the Scripture and "A Leader Is Called" in the Interpreting the Scripture portion to plan a lecture for the "Delve into the Story of the Arrest and Stoning of Stephen" section to introduce the students to Stephen.

Prepare a brief lecture to summarize Acts 7:1-50, which is Stephen's speech before the council.

LEADING THE CLASS

(1) Gather to Learn

❖ Welcome the class members and introduce any guests.

❖ Pray that the class members will be open to God's call on their own lives and willing to respond faithfully so that all people may come to know Jesus.

❖ Post two sheets of newsprint. Brainstorm with the class answers to this question: **What makes a good leader?** Write ideas on one of the sheets of newsprint. Now ask: **What are the traits of good church leaders?** Write ideas on the second sheet of newsprint. Discuss how these lists are similar and different.

❖ Read aloud today's focus statement: **Movements need committed leadership to bring about change. How do strong leaders develop? The example of Stephen and others shows that God's Spirit calls, inspires, and guides strong leaders in the church.**

(2) Delve into the Story of the Arrest and Stoning of Stephen

❖ Give a brief lecture to introduce Stephen to the class.

❖ Choose a volunteer to read Acts 6:8-15.

■ Discuss these questions.

    (1) Who opposed Stephen? (Note that Freedmen were emancipated Jews and their descendants.)

    (2) What prompted their opposition?

    (3) What charges did they try to trump up against Stephen?

    (4) What evidence does this passage offer to support the claim in verse 8 that Stephen was "full of grace and power"?

■ Sum up this section by pointing out that this "trial" before the council of the Sanhedrin bears similarities to the proceedings against Jesus.

❖ Outline the speech Stephen made to the council, known as the Sanhedrin, in Acts 7:1-52. Be concise. The main point you want to make is that Stephen neither defended himself nor testified to Jesus' resurrection; rather, he told the story of Israel's history as a saga of God's providence in spite of Israel's persistent rebellion. Soon, Stephen himself would re-enact the story by being martyred.

❖ Ask someone to read Acts 7:53 as Stephen, and someone else to read verses 54-60.

■ Invite the students to note any similarities they see between the stoning of Stephen and the crucifixion of Jesus. List these ideas on newsprint.

■ Encourage the students to imagine themselves as members of Luke's community reading this story. Consider the effect Stephen's speech and martyrdom might have on them as members of the early Christian church.

■ Distribute paper and pencils. Ask the adults to write a eulogy for Stephen, based on what they know about him from the text. Provide time for several volunteers to share what they have written, as if they were speaking at his funeral.

(3) Explore the Learners' Calls to Faithful Service

❖ Use one of these ideas to help the learners see how they are serving God faithfully.

■ **Option 1:** If the students know each other well, ask them to make brief remarks about how someone in the class (or the congregation at large) has been a faithful servant on their behalf. Be careful to make sure that everyone is included in this affirmation activity.

■ **Option 2:** Distribute paper and pencils. Invite the students to write a description of the servant-leader roles that they have assumed, or would think about assuming. Nudge them to include spiritual characteristics, such as being "full of grace and power" (Acts 6:8), as well as other traits more commonly associated with leadership. Make sure that even those who do not classify themselves as *leaders* do see themselves as *servants* to the body of Christ. Ask the students to put these papers in their Bibles so that they will be reminded of how they are following in Stephen's footsteps as faithful servants.

(4) Name and Express Gratitude for Servants Called and Inspired by God Today

❖ Invite the learners to offer simple prayers of gratitude for contemporary Christians they know, or know of, who are faithfully serving God. Suggest that the students name the individual and one or two traits of his or her service. Here is an example: *Clara, who is always willing to lend a sympathetic ear and a helping hand.* Ask the students to respond to each name with, **Lord, we give thanks for your servant, [name].**

❖ If time permits, the group may wish to talk about how well-known church servants, such as Billy Graham or Mother Teresa, have made an impact on their own faith and practice.

(5) Continue the Journey

❖ Pray that the participants will go forth boldly, willing to take whatever risks necessary to be a faithful servant and witness for Jesus.

❖ Read aloud this preparation for next week's lesson. You may also want to post it on newsprint for the students to copy. **Prepare for next week's session, entitled "Christians Without Borders," by reading Acts 8:4-25. Look especially at our lesson Scripture from Acts 8:4-17. Keep these thoughts in mind as you study next week's lesson: People of all cultures and races need to hear the good news of God's love. How can cultural and racial barriers be overcome? Evangelists like Philip extended the gospel beyond Judea to Samaria, welcoming others as brothers and sisters in Christ and setting an example for us.**

❖ Read aloud the following three ideas. Challenge the students to commit themselves to use these activities as a springboard to spiritual growth.

(1) **Pray for faithful servants who are being persecuted for their faith.**

(2) **Examine the service that you are offering to the people of the church. Write in your journal what you are doing and how you perceive God may feel about your work.**

(3) **Write a thank you note to a servant who has helped you in your own journey of faith.**

❖ Sing or read aloud "Stand Up, Stand Up for Jesus."

❖ Lead this benediction to conclude the session: **May the Holy Spirit empower you to be witnesses for Jesus Christ in your community, in your nation, and to the ends of the earth. Amen.**

UNIT 2: IN ALL JUDEA AND SAMARIA
CHRISTIANS WITHOUT BORDERS

PREVIEWING THE LESSON

Lesson Scripture: Acts 8:4-17
Background Scripture: Acts 8:4-25
Key Verse: Acts 8:14

Focus of the Lesson:

People of all cultures and races need to hear the good news of God's love. How can cultural and racial barriers be overcome? Evangelists like Philip extended the gospel beyond Judea to Samaria, welcoming others as brothers and sisters in Christ and setting an example for us.

Goals for the Learners:

(1) to probe how Philip spread the good news of God's love beyond Judea, bringing healing and joy to new believers.
(2) to identify barriers that keep them from reaching out to others.
(3) to commit to overcoming barriers that keep them from accepting others.

Pronunciation Guide:

Gerizim (ger' uh zim)

Supplies:

Bibles, newsprint and marker, paper and pencils, hymnals

READING THE SCRIPTURE

NRSV
Acts 8:4-17

⁴Now those who were scattered went from place to place, proclaiming the word. ⁵Philip went down to the city of Samaria and proclaimed the Messiah to them. ⁶The crowds with one accord listened eagerly to what was said by Philip, hearing and seeing

NIV
Acts 8:4-17

⁴Those who had been scattered preached the word wherever they went. ⁵Philip went down to a city in Samaria and proclaimed the Christ there. ⁶When the crowds heard Philip and saw the miraculous signs he did, they all paid close attention to what he said.

the signs that he did, [7]for unclean spirits, crying with loud shrieks, came out of many who were possessed; and many others who were paralyzed or lame were cured. [8]So there was great joy in that city.

[9]Now a certain man named Simon had previously practiced magic in the city and amazed the people of Samaria, saying that he was someone great. [10]All of them, from the least to the greatest, listened to him eagerly, saying, "This man is the power of God that is called Great." [11]And they listened eagerly to him because for a long time he had amazed them with his magic. [12]But when they believed Philip, who was proclaiming the good news about the kingdom of God and the name of Jesus Christ, they were baptized, both men and women. [13] Even Simon himself believed. After being baptized, he stayed constantly with Philip and was amazed when he saw the signs and great miracles that took place.

[14]**Now when the apostles at Jerusalem heard that Samaria had accepted the word of God, they sent Peter and John to them**. [15]The two went down and prayed for them that they might receive the Holy Spirit [16] (for as yet the Spirit had not come upon any of them; they had only been baptized in the name of the Lord Jesus). [17]Then Peter and John laid their hands on them, and they received the Holy Spirit.

[7]With shrieks, evil spirits came out of many, and many paralytics and cripples were healed. [8]So there was great joy in that city.

[9]Now for some time a man named Simon had practiced sorcery in the city and amazed all the people of Samaria. He boasted that he was someone great, [10]and all the people, both high and low, gave him their attention and exclaimed, "This man is the divine power known as the Great Power." [11]They followed him because he had amazed them for a long time with his magic. [12]But when they believed Philip as he preached the good news of the kingdom of God and the name of Jesus Christ, they were baptized, both men and women. [13]Simon himself believed and was baptized. And he followed Philip everywhere, astonished by the great signs and miracles he saw.

[14]**When the apostles in Jerusalem heard that Samaria had accepted the word of God, they sent Peter and John to them.** [15]When they arrived, they prayed for them that they might receive the Holy Spirit, [16]because the Holy Spirit had not yet come upon any of them; they had simply been baptized into the name of the Lord Jesus. [17]Then Peter and John placed their hands on them, and they received the Holy Spirit.

UNDERSTANDING THE SCRIPTURE

Acts 8:4-8. A persecution began following the stoning of Stephen; the line between Jewish faith and Christian belief was being drawn. Because of this new reality some Christian leaders moved away from Jerusalem. They did not, however, seek safety. Rather, the Jerusalem persecution spurred the leaders to take the gospel to new people in foreign places by imaginative forms of presentation. Philip went north to the land of Samaria. Whether Samaria was

his ultimate destination, or a safe route to Galilee, is not stated. He was, however, on a mission; his ministry, initiated by serving tables in Jerusalem (6:5), became one of healing and preaching in Samaria. Philip's work in Samaria added a new dimension to the witness to Jesus Christ: He performed exorcisms. While this sign was significant in the gospel ministry of Jesus, it was an innovation in the witness of the young church. The Samaritans were attentive to Philip's deeds and preaching, even though for generations there was animosity between the two groups who were historically tied by common ancestors. As Paul Walaskay in the *Westminster Bible Companion on Acts* points out, to the Jews of Jesus' day, "There was no such thing as a *good* Samaritan." Yet, Jesus instructed his disciples to carry the gospel to Samaria before going to all the ends of the earth (Acts 1:8). Philip, in obedience, stepped over a boundary line of race and religion to welcome into God's kingdom those whom Jews considered outsiders because of their racial impurity due to mixed marriages and their practice of worshiping God on Mount Gerizim.

Acts 8:9-13. In Samaria, there were more obstacles to face than historic animosities. There was also magic. Luke used the story of Simon and Philip to teach the distinction between the phenomenon of magic and the phenomenon of exorcism. Evidently, magicians easily captured the attention of the Samaritans. While Simon practiced his magic, he earned a lofty title "the Great," which literally translated from the Greek means "the power of God." When Philip cast out spirits by the name of Jesus, the source of his power was the Holy Spirit. The actions of each man were superficially similar. However, when examined, each man's core value was distinct. Simon was in the magic business for social, political, and economic success. If there was any doubt about his greatness, Simon was ready to endorse himself. Philip, however, was on a mission to present Jesus Christ. Whenever he cast out an unclean spirit, someone was set free to live life abundantly. The Samaritan community recognized the difference by the palpable joy that accompanied Philip's exorcisms. Luke records that the Samaritans joyfully accepted Philip's message. Their interest led to belief. Simon, however, moved along a different course. Simon believed, was baptized, and became a follower—literally—of Philip. After his baptism, but before his faith matured, Simon

became amazed. This is out of step with Luke's usual pattern of conversion. Ordinarily, amazement comes before, not after, conversion. Simon heard, believed, and then was amazed by Philip's power. This fascination would be his undoing.

Acts 8:14-17. When the news of the mission with the Samaritans reached Jerusalem, a delegation was sent from the mother congregation in Jerusalem to investigate and undergird Philip's work. To ensure cohesion in the expanding faith community, the apostles needed to experience Philip's witness across the boundary lines. Perhaps emerging authority issues prompted their visit, but there was also a sincere interest in the mission to the Samaritans. As soon as Peter and John arrived, however, they knew something was missing. The Samaritan believers knew the truth and teachings of Jesus, but their faith lacked the fire of Pentecost. Therefore, with prayer and the laying on of hands, the apostles ministered to the Samaritans. The text is terse: The Samaritans received the Holy Spirit. There is no explanation of the difference between the baptism in the name of Jesus and the baptism or gift of the Holy Spirit; evidently, the forming community had yet to write the first treatise on the dynamics of the Holy Spirit! However, in order for the apostles to establish a community able to hold "all things in common" (2:44), more was needed than orthodox belief. An active spiritual power guided the church in Jerusalem; that same power was essential for every new Christian community outside of Jerusalem. Before the Samaritans could really live their faith, they required a spiritual bond with the Holy Spirit. This bond established the community and linked it, through the apostles, to the church in Jerusalem. Peter and John took a bold and an essential trip to plant the gospel and bring the Holy Spirit to believers "in Jerusalem, in all Judea and Samaria, and to the ends of the earth" (1:8).

Acts 8:18-25. After the dramatic gift of the Holy Spirit to the Samaritans, Simon's interests shifted. He began to shadow the apostles. Almost immediately his interest led to an economic proposal. Often, when Luke describes the depth of conversion, he uses an illustration related to personal finances (see Acts 5:1-11: Luke 7:36-50; 12:13-21; 16:13, 19-31; 18:18-25; 19:1-10; 20:20-26; 21:1-4). A testimony to the depth of the early community's conversion was their capacity to hold all things in common and to sell property to relieve the needs of others (Acts 4:32-37). The story of Ananias and his wife, Sapphira, illustrated the danger of an unconverted heart and secret treasure (5:1-10). Here, Simon's amazement leads to economic speculation intended to ensure his leadership within the community. Simon offered the apostles money in exchange for the gift of administration of the Holy Spirit. Peter firmly denied his request. Using words similar to Jesus' rebuke of Peter (Matthew 16:23 and Mark 8:33), the apostle declared that Simon had no share in God's gift because his attachment to money (and his own egotistical desires) separated him from God. The message was clear: A divided heart is an unconverted heart. Therefore, Peter offered Simon a way out: Repent, pray, and, if possible, be forgiven. Quietly, Simon requested, "Pray for me." His words became a testimony to the ongoing nature of conversion. His experience was repeated in congregation after congregation, throughout the centuries, and even today is on the lips of those who know their heart's intention is not on the side of God.

INTERPRETING THE SCRIPTURE

Stepping Over the Boundary Line

Some boundaries are physical. I, for example, live in a border state. A Mexican citizen entering New Mexico must show papers and answer questions. The physical boundary is not easily or accidentally crossed. Other boundaries are cultural. Think of an embarrassing moment when cultural ignorance led to insult or worse. Many boundaries are ancient. In the church, old boundaries are maintained by seven well-worn words: "We never did it that way before!" Sadly, we know the ongoing agony of racial boundaries and the perversions of racism; most Americans still live in homogeneous communities, even as our population grows more and more diverse. Yet, in the church of Jesus Christ, we declare that Jesus is the Savior of all and that all believers are brothers and sisters in him. Our affirming words are challenged by our actual deeds. This lesson demonstrates the first step out of Judea and into another land. It is a lesson burdened with unnamed tensions, colored by humor, and possessed of rich wisdom.

Characteristically, Luke began with awe. Philip, one of the seven selected for table duty in Jerusalem, stepped across the border between Judea and Samaria. His journey took him to a people who, like the men and women of faith, worshiped the God of Israel, observed the law of Moses, and anticipated God's arrival. Moreover, the Samaritans traced their somewhat muddled family tree back to Philip's ancestors in faith—to Abraham, Isaac, and Jacob. Yet, as much as these two peoples shared, the Jews and the Samaritans were bitter enemies. The Jews were suspicious of the Samaritans' loyalty; too many times, the people of Samaria supported one powerful ruler, then, switched alliances when power shifted. The Samaritans, for their part, were exhausted by the continual ridicule of the Jews and acted out their disdain in dramatic forms. Once, a few days before a Passover celebration, some Samaritans desecrated the temple in Jerusalem with human bones.

Certainly, such conduct did not endear each to the other.

However thick the enmity, there was a path to a new relationship in the gospel of Jesus Christ. These two nations held opposing ideas on the proper site of worship: Jerusalem or Gerizim (see Jesus' discussion with the Samaritan woman, John 4:19-24). As Philip stepped over the geographic, cultural, and religious boundary into Samaria, he declared that Jesus, not temple worship in Jerusalem or Gerizim, restored one's relationship to God. This was unexpected good news.

Distinguishing Spirits

In every culture the gospel of Jesus Christ encounters points of connection and of confusion. For the Samaritans, a connecting point was Philip's teaching about true worship through Jesus Christ. For Philip, a point of confusion was the Samaritans' interest in magic. To distinguish between the show of the charlatans and the substance of the Holy Spirit, Luke recorded the tale of a magician's conversion. The magician's stage name declares his core value: He is called "Great." Simon walked throughout Samaria practicing his magic art and welcomed the peoples' admiration. But, as people of faith have long known, the great power of God is for service, not for self-aggrandizement. Whenever a person dabbles in God's power for personal reward, failure and frustration are near at hand. The first task in distinguishing spiritual authenticity is the question: What is being served?

The second question is a bit subtler: What happens to the joy (or awe or mystery or peace) produced? For Simon, the awe of his audience gratified his ego and, presumably, filled his treasury. For Philip, an exorcism created an intense hunger for God's word. One outcome was personal gratification; the other outcome was God's sweet salvation. And there was still another distinction to be made: Belief may begin with a powerful spiritual event, but it is lived consistently on an everyday scale. Simon's interest in the spectacular increased as he followed Philip about; the Samaritan community, however, believed in Philip's message, confessed faith in Jesus, received baptism, and began to live their old lives in a new way. A spirituality based only on magnificent moments and mountaintop highs does not work well in the mundane and shadowy valleys of life. Philip preached a gospel the Samaritans could live; he did not whet their appetite for more and more signs and wonders. The word he offered satisfied completely.

Don't Forget the Leaders!

Meanwhile, back in Jerusalem, the young church faced multifaceted challenges. Persecution created sensitivity to danger; leadership scattered; every day brought a new challenge for faithful witnessing. Into the mix came the report that Philip had baptized many residents of a Samaritan city. The news intrigued the apostles. They knew the "wind blows where it chooses" (John 3:8) nature of the Holy Spirit and they granted the possibility that Philip's baptisms signaled something new for the Jerusalem congregation. What would these new converts add to the faith? How would they receive and live the good news of Jesus? Were there resources in Samaria for a new faith community? Would the Samaritans encounter the resistance (perhaps even persecution) faced by the Jerusalem community? With these and many more questions, two of the apostles went to Samaria to see Philip's work and to greet the new community. If the Spirit was moving outward, these leaders did not want to be left behind.

It is easy to imagine the scene in Samaria when Peter and John arrived. Probably, Philip, refreshed by the sight of these beloved apostles, was the perfect host, individually introducing the recent converts. Surely, a banquet was provided. It is likely that the faith sharing was intense. But, something was amiss. The apostles sensed it and, after conversation with Philip, named it: The new believers had not received the Holy Spirit. Suddenly, the apostles' visit had a new dimension. They were there to pray, to lay on hands, and to invite the Holy Spirit among the Samaritan believers. Once again, the Spirit that blew open the circle of disciples on Pentecost initiated a new ministry for the apostles. They were instruments conveying God's Spirit. As they did so not only was the congregation nurtured, but also a remarkable link was forged between former enemies. This time, the leaders were not forgotten; their spiritual leadership was essential.

Growing in God's Grace

Maturing in faith is rarely, if ever, instantaneous. Some spiritual experiences are so powerful that a person is literally able to do the impossible: forgive a horrendous abuse, sacrifice personal standing or wealth for another, witness boldly to evil powers, persist in constant prayer, or endure deprivation while maintaining inner peace.

However, ordinarily, faith grows over time. One of the most puzzling aspects of the Acts of the Apostles is Luke's inattention to time. Infrequently he notes that a month or a few days or a week passed, but on the whole, the book reads as a fast paced novel. Consider the synopsis of these lessons. Several hundred heard Peter preach and were baptized; a lame man was healed; apostles were arrested then miraculously freed; simple fishermen-disciples preached before the highest Jewish authority, the Sanhedrin; ordinary men and women changed their relationship to personal wealth in favor of a wholesome community life. But how many days, weeks, months flew by as these events and changes developed? There is no answer, because Luke was not writing history; he was inspiring faith. His stories offered moments of "ah-ha" and "Yes!" He didn't explain how faith grows, but he testified to the maturing of the early Christian faith. This faith was proclaimed, claimed, and nurtured in Samaria, just as Jesus had instructed (Acts 1:8). The church was moving in the direction of creating a Christian body without borders.

SHARING THE SCRIPTURE

PREPARING TO TEACH

Preparing Our Hearts

This week's devotional reading is found in Acts 19:1-10. Here we see Paul asking disciples in Ephesus whether they had received the Holy Spirit. When they pleaded ignorance of the Spirit, Paul laid hands on them and they experienced the power of the Holy Spirit. We will see similar events in today's lesson. What is your understanding of the Holy Spirit's entrance into and role in the life of a believer? What evidence do you see of the Spirit's work in your life?

Pray that you and the adult learners will recognize the Spirit within yourselves and within all persons, regardless of their race, culture, or other boundaries.

Preparing Our Minds

Study the background from Acts 8:4-25, and lesson Scripture, verses 4-17. As you prepare this week's lesson, keep in mind that all persons, regardless of racial, cultural, or any other boundaries are within the scope of God's loving care.

Write on newsprint:

❑ at the left top, "Philip" and at the right

top, "Simon," for the section entitled "Probe How Philip Spread the Good News of God's Love."

❏ information for next week's lesson, found under "Continue the Journey."

LEADING THE CLASS

(1) Gather to Learn

❖ Welcome the class members and introduce any guests.

❖ Pray that the participants will open their minds to today's study and their hearts to all people who have not yet heard the gospel message.

❖ Invite class members to talk about worship experiences they have had in different countries, in congregations whose racial and ethnic traditions were different from their own, or in denominations different from their own.

❖ Discuss how the rich variety of ways people worship and experience the presence of God remind us that Christianity reaches across all borders and barriers.

❖ Read aloud today's focus statement: **People of all cultures and races need to hear the good news of God's love. How can cultural and racial barriers be overcome? Evangelists like Philip extended the gospel beyond Judea to Samaria, welcoming others as brothers and sisters in Christ and setting an example for us.**

(2) Probe How Philip Spread the Good News of God's Love Beyond Judea

❖ Introduce today's Bible reading by reminding the class members that Philip was one of the seven deacons chosen with Stephen (Acts 6:5). After Stephen was martyred, many Christians, including Philip, fled Jerusalem to avoid "severe persecution" (8:1). Inadvertently, Saul (who would later be known as Paul) created the situation that prompted the spread of the gospel from Jerusalem to Judea and Samaria, and even-

tually into all the world, just as the risen Christ had said would happen (Acts 1:8).

❖ Select a volunteer to read Acts 8:4-13.

■ Encourage the students to talk about Simon. List on the newsprint you have prepared what he did and how the people of Samaria responded to him.

■ Discuss Philip's actions and the crowd's reactions. Add to newsprint.

■ Compare Philip and Simon's actions and their effect on the people of Samaria.

■ Conclude this section with these questions:

(1) What do you think prompted the people, including Simon, to seek baptism in the name of Jesus?

(2) What conclusions can you draw about the differences between Philip and Simon, and their messages?

❖ Ask a student to read Acts 8:14-17.

■ Note that in Samaria the believers received water baptism and then, by the laying on of hands of the apostles, they received the Holy Spirit. If time permits, look with the class at other patterns of baptism found in:

• Acts 2:38-41 (Peter called for repentance, which would be followed by water baptism and reception of the Holy Spirit).

• Acts 10:44-48 (Gentiles received the Spirit first and then water baptism).

• Acts 19:1-6 (people first received John's baptism for repentance; later, water baptism in the name of Jesus and reception of the Holy Spirit at the same time).

■ Discuss these questions:

(1) How do Peter and John, who came from the "mother church" in Jerusalem, support Philip's ministry?

(2) What do their actions suggest about connections among congregations?

(3) Identify Barriers That Keep the Learners from Reaching Out to Others

❖ Note that in today's Bible lesson Philip had to overcome longstanding ethnic prejudices that Jews held toward Samaritans in order to preach effectively to them.

❖ Encourage the students to name barriers that keep them from reaching out to others to tell and enact the gospel. List these ideas on newsprint.

❖ Prod the students to identify the sources of these barriers. For example, some may be longstanding prejudices that they have been taught or "caught" from family or the society at large. Others may be personal biases. Still others, such as unwillingness to engage in a prison ministry, may be motivated by fear. Another set of barriers may have been erected as a result of moral superiority and a refusal to interact with those who "don't measure up."

(4) Commit to Overcoming Barriers That Keep the Students from Accepting Others

❖ Distribute paper and pencils. Provide quiet time for the students to review the list of barriers and the reasons these barriers may exist. Ask them to write two or three barriers that deter them personally from spreading the gospel. Then they are to state in writing how they will attempt to overcome each barrier.

❖ Call on volunteers who are willing to state their intended commitments. Affirm their willingness to destroy barriers so that they can truly become Christians without borders.

(5) Continue the Journey

❖ Pray that the class members will be willing to reach across racial, ethnic, age, gender, socio-economic, and all other barriers to share the love of Christ with others.

❖ Read aloud this preparation for next week's lesson. You may also want to post it on newsprint for the students to copy. **Prepare for next week's session, entitled "Interpreting the Word," by reading Acts 8:26-40, noting especially verses 26-38. Keep these ideas in focus as you study: People need help in understanding and applying the Scriptures. How will they receive the help they need? The Holy Spirit sent Philip to help an African official understand how Jesus Christ fulfilled the prophecies he was reading, and the same Spirit calls Christians today to help explain God's word to others.**

Read aloud the following three ideas. Challenge the students to commit themselves to use these activities as a springboard to spiritual growth.

(1) Reach out to someone whom you consider to be on the opposite side of a cultural, ethnic, or other border. Act with kindness. If the situation permits, say something about the gospel and Christ's love for all humanity.

(2) Check a Bible dictionary, Bible commentary, or other reference book to learn more about the Samaritans and their relationship with the Jews.

(3) Select a missionary whom your church or denomination sponsors. Pledge to give a specific amount or percentage of your income to support this individual. Some missionaries communicate via e-mail, so you may be able to learn directly about how the gospel is being spread in a particular place.

❖ Sing or read aloud "We've a Story to Tell to the Nations."

❖ Lead this benediction to conclude the session: **May the Holy Spirit empower you to be witnesses for Jesus Christ in your community, in your nation, and to the ends of the earth. Amen.**

UNIT 2: IN ALL JUDEA AND SAMARIA
INTERPRETING THE WORD

PREVIEWING THE LESSON

Lesson Scripture: Acts 8:26-36, 38
Background Scripture: Acts 8:26-40
Key Verse: Acts 8:35

Focus of the Lesson:
People need help in understanding and applying the Scriptures. How will they receive the help they need? The Holy Spirit sent Philip to help an African official understand how Jesus Christ fulfilled the prophecies he was reading, and the same Spirit calls Christians today to help explain God's word to others.

Goals for the Learners:
(1) to encounter the story of how the Holy Spirit sent Philip to teach an African official the good news about Jesus.
(2) to consider ways that the Holy Spirit helps them to understand and apply Scripture.
(3) to commit to regular reading of Scripture and listening for God's Spirit to discern how it speaks to their lives.

Pronunciation Guide:
Azotus (uh zoh' tuhs)
Elephantine (el uh fan ti' nee)
Nubia (nyoo' bee ah)

Supplies:
Bibles, newsprint and marker, paper and pencils, hymnals

READING THE SCRIPTURE

NRSV
Acts 8:26-36, 38

   ²⁶Then an angel of the Lord said to Philip, "Get up and go toward the south to the road that goes down from Jerusalem to Gaza." (This is a wilderness road.) ²⁷So he got up and went. Now there was an Ethiopian eunuch, a court official of the Candace,

NIV
Acts 8:26-36, 38

   ²⁶Now an angel of the Lord said to Philip, "Go south to the road—the desert road—that goes down from Jerusalem to Gaza." ²⁷So he started out, and on his way he met an Ethiopian eunuch, an important official in charge of all the treasury of Candace, queen

queen of the Ethiopians, in charge of her entire treasury. He had come to Jerusalem to worship [28]and was returning home; seated in his chariot, he was reading the prophet Isaiah. [29]Then the Spirit said to Philip, "Go over to this chariot and join it." [30]So Philip ran up to it and heard him reading the prophet Isaiah. He asked, "Do you understand what you are reading?" [31]He replied, "How can I, unless someone guides me?" And he invited Philip to get in and sit beside him. [32]Now the passage of the scripture that he was reading was this:

"Like a sheep he was led to the slaughter,
    and like a lamb silent before its shearer,
        so he does not open his mouth.
[33]In his humiliation justice was denied him.

    Who can describe his generation?
    For his life is taken away from the earth."
[34]The eunuch asked Philip, "About whom, may I ask you, does the prophet say this, about himself or about someone else?" [35]Then Philip began to speak, and starting with this scripture, he proclaimed to him the good news about Jesus. [36]As they were going along the road, they came to some water; and the eunuch said, "Look, here is water! What is to prevent me from being baptized?" [38]He commanded the chariot to stop, and both of them, Philip and the eunuch, went down into the water, and Philip baptized him.

of the Ethiopians. This man had gone to Jerusalem to worship, [28]and on his way home was sitting in his chariot reading the book of Isaiah the prophet. [29]The Spirit told Philip, "Go to that chariot and stay near it."

[30]Then Philip ran up to the chariot and heard the man reading Isaiah the prophet. "Do you understand what you are reading?" Philip asked.

[31]"How can I," he said, "unless someone explains it to me?" So he invited Philip to come up and sit with him.

[32]The eunuch was reading this passage of Scripture:

"He was led like a sheep to the slaughter,
    and as a lamb before the shearer is silent,
        so he did not open his mouth.
[33]In his humiliation he was deprived of justice.

    Who can speak of his descendants?
    For his life was taken from the earth."
[34]The eunuch asked Philip, "Tell me, please, who is the prophet talking about, himself or someone else?" [35]Then Philip began with that very passage of Scripture and told him the good news about Jesus.

[36]As they traveled along the road, they came to some water and the eunuch said, "Look, here is water. Why shouldn't I be baptized?" [38]And he gave orders to stop the chariot. Then both Philip and the eunuch went down into the water and Philip baptized him.

UNDERSTANDING THE SCRIPTURE

Acts 8:26-29. Luke employs the term "then" to indicate that this new story is subsequent to the former tale. Philip continued his ministry in Samaria until the Holy Spirit directed him to a specific wilderness road. Heading south Philip traveled on a wilderness road that ran between Jerusalem and Gaza. A wilderness road carried no caravan traffic and was dangerous, but more important such a road was also symbolic. In the

New Testament the wilderness represented a place of spiritual seeking (Jesus tempted in the wilderness, Luke 4:1-13) and of spiritual enlightenment (the two disciples on the deserted road to Emmaus, Luke 24:13-35). The physical setting favored a spiritual encounter between Philip and an unnamed Ethiopian. A servant/slave, this eunuch was a highly trusted official in the court of the Candace, which is the generic Nubian word for "queen." The Ethiopian court treasurer was returning to his home after a season of spiritual refreshment in Jerusalem. His home was Nubia (the contemporary land of Sudan); in the first century, the term "Ethiopian" applied to a vast area of northern Africa beyond Egypt. It may seem remarkable that this foreign official was interested in the faith of Israel; however, as early as the eighth century B.C., a strong Jewish colony existed on the island of Elephantine, at Egypt's southern border with Nubia. This court treasurer was probably a "God-fearer," a Gentile worshiper who accepted the theological and ethical teaching of the Jews. Because this man's profession required castration, he was barred from full membership in Israel and, specifically, from temple worship. He was permitted to enter the court of the Gentiles, but regardless of his piety and understanding, his physical condition forever excluded him from the people of God.

Acts 8:30-33. God directed the entire encounter. First, a messenger (an angel) brought specific instructions to Philip; then, the inner voice of the Spirit indicated that Philip was to join the man. Philip was obedient to both instructions; he undertook his mission without knowing what he was to accomplish. As an act of faith, his wilderness-road trip was another demonstration of the Spirit-responsive character of the early Christian community. The unfolding story defies imagination. A high court official, bouncing along in a chariot on a deserted road, was reading aloud from a scroll. Suddenly, a man on foot beside the chariot overheard a familiar passage from Isaiah and asked the reader about his comprehension. At this point, the story slowed; somehow the bumpy ride quieted and two men intently engaged in conversation about Scripture. Then, the court official, an educated man of power, invited the stranger, a man of modest means covered with dust from walking or running, into his chariot to teach him. Between these two was the prophetic Servant Song, Isaiah 52:13-53:12, a passage that was to become a standard for the early Christian community's interpretation of Jesus' death. This account is Acts' first identification of Jesus as the Suffering Servant. What the court treasurer could not understand, Philip opened in a profound way.

Acts 8:34-38. "About whom does the prophet speak?" The eunuch's question struck the center of the interpretative puzzle. He offered his own thoughts as he wondered if the words applied to the prophet or to someone else. Here is a case where what is not mentioned is as significant as what is mentioned. In first-century orthodox Jewish teaching the most common interpretation of Isaiah's Suffering Servant was the nation Israel. Since the eunuch was forever separated from the nation Israel, this interpretation held little interest for him. By associating the prophet's words with a person, Philip received an interpretive springboard. He jumped right in! Beginning with Isaiah's suffering servant, Philip taught the revelation of Jesus in Scripture. As Philip spoke, literally "opened his mouth" signifying that the speech is Spirit-filled, the eunuch heard good news. He asked a second question: "What is to prevent me from being baptized?" The question signified the eunuch's faith in Jesus and readiness to receive the Spirit. Peter immediately baptized the man; however, this was the first instance of a baptism without the benefit of community. As the two separated, it was unclear what would become of this learned, new disciple. Church history, however, gives us a clue. The treasurer's baptism resulted in more than an individual's new life; it opened the way for the gospel to reach another nation on another continent.

Acts 8:39-40. After the baptism the treasurer left, apparently singing a new song. No longer estranged from God and God's people, the man returned with good news to share. And what became of Philip? Philip's Spirit-led journey continued. Luke tells us that Philip was "deposited" in Azotus and there continued his ministry. Thus the saga concluded as it began with Philip's obedience to the Spirit. In Acts 6 and 8, Luke discussed Philip's activities as the first among the community-selected leaders and the first evangelist beyond Jerusalem. The apostles in Jerusalem did not direct this missionary expansion. Yet Philip, guided by the Spirit, expanded the ministry in bold directions. He crossed the social, ethnic, and religious boundary to bring good news to the Samaritans. He interpreted Scripture to a spiritual seeker prohibited from full inclusion in the community of Israel. The Spirit led the way across these boundaries, and Spirit-discerning believers, both men and women, followed. Moreover, one Ethiopian convert went on his way, unaccompanied yet rejoicing; his impact is spiritually alive today in the church of Ethiopia.

INTERPRETING THE SCRIPTURE

Under Holy Orders

Only a few decades ago, missionary tales captivated children being raised in North American congregations. Sunday school lessons featured accounts of gospel ministry around the world and missionaries on furlough itinerated throughout the country personalizing the distant work. Pennies dropped into coin boxes supplied baby blankets and books, bandages, and Bibles. The church's overseas mission intrigued and eventually called many a young person. In contrast, our contemporary congregations, prompted by limited time and a pervasive cultural biblical illiteracy, focus on the basics of Bible content and discipleship to Jesus in children's educational programs. The exotic tales of the church around the world are seldom told; in their absence our corporate imagination is stunted. Not only did foreign missions captivate, but they also expanded faith at home. The story of Philip's encounter with the Ethiopian eunuch is a missionary tale that provoked deep renewal within the Jerusalem church. These renewal opportunities emerged as church leaders followed the Spirit's direction. The willingness to be "under holy orders" is one characteristic of all missionary work.

After Stephen was executed, the church understood that he would not be the last. The record of martyrs is sketchy, at best, but every execution, exile, imprisonment, and flight was recorded on the community's heart. After community prayer and consensus, Philip, the second of the seven leaders selected from the congregation, left Jerusalem. Because he was solid in his faith and in himself, Philip acted as a man under orders throughout his time in Samaria. His ministry witnessed to the rich renewal that flows from attention to the Spirit's guidance.

With the Word Between

The romantic vision of missionary work pictures a teacher, an audience, and a Bible. This picture is also the practical stuff of evangelism. At the heart of Christian faith is a wonderful story that could be titled *Saved by Jesus*. The full text is long and rich: It is the whole Bible and its interpretation. Many have studied Scripture a lifetime and still discover new depths, fresh inspiration, and radical challenges. Nonetheless, the church of Jesus Christ still grows by a teacher, an audience, and a Bible between them.

The Ethiopian eunuch was a literate man who was also a God-seeker. His spiritual thirst was not sated by the richness of a "spiritual vacation" at the temple. Although on the temple grounds he heard great teaching and observed, from somewhat of a distance, the ritual drama of human/divine reconciliation, something was missing. Therefore, he pondered Scripture on his own. It is not surprising that he read the prophet Isaiah. After all, this is the prophet who declared that when the day of God's salvation came the temple would be a house of prayer for all peoples and even eunuchs would join the ranks of worshipers (see Isaiah 56:4-8). These words hinted at the "something missing"; with his entire mind, heart, and soul the Ethiopian eunuch longed for the season of God's salvation when even a man such as he would be accepted and, indeed, honored among God's people.

Isaiah's words whetted the Ethiopian's thirst for God; Philip's teaching offered him scriptural satisfaction. As Philip answered the first question, the Ethiopian was led deeper and deeper into the mystery of Scripture revealed in Jesus. Beginning with the image of the Suffering Servant, Philip filled out God's purpose in the life and witness of Jesus. He spared no details. Surely he presented Jesus' good deeds and wonders, but just as likely, he alluded to the persistent resistance of the religious leaders of Israel. Philip's witness conformed to the preaching standard of the first century: The crucifixion was tragic, but it was not unexpected. God's power was, however, greater than the people's resistance and this power was set loose in Jesus' resurrection. From that power, the church came into existence. Sealed with the Holy Spirit, all those baptized in the name of Jesus shared this Spirit with one another and lived harmoniously in God's season of salvation. Patiently, Philip surely described the Christian communities where all property was held in common, all who confessed faith were baptized, and no condition excluded one from faith and community.

Down to the Water

The Ethiopian responded with faith and enthusiasm to Philip's interpretation of Scripture. He knew immediately what he wanted to do: confess his faith in Jesus the Messiah, be baptized, and begin living as a fully accepted man of God. Yet, according to Luke's account, no one had baptized a Gentile; if the apostles were sufficiently intrigued by what happened in Samaria to send a delegation, what might they think about this baptism? Philip, however, agreed with the Ethiopian. According to the good news nothing prevented this baptism. So down to the water the evangelist and the convert went.

Mainline Protestant churches always grimace a bit at the mention of a "private baptism." For them, baptism is not only a personal response to Jesus in faith and not only a provision of God's gift of the Holy Spirit, but baptism is also the entrance into the Christian community. By baptism a believer is joined, intimately, structurally, and completely to the church of Jesus Christ. Those who are baptized are never alone; they are provided with a community in which to mature, to use their spiritual gifts and to witness to Jesus. Whenever baptism is bereft of community, there is the possibility of a too small understanding of baptism as a private matter between an individual and God. Contemporary baptism is always personal, but it is not private. The Ethiopian eunuch's baptism, however, happened ages before the church's suspicion of private religion. Moreover, the man who was baptized desired, more than anything else, to be a part of the blessed community of those who called on the name of the Lord and were heard. As Philip interpreted the Scriptures to him, this man saw himself joining that community. He went to the baptismal water to begin a new way of living—and he likely envisioned that this new life included a rich and diverse community.

Renewed in the Spirit

Joy and gladness are sprinkled throughout the first section of Acts. Although difficulties are described and persecutions mentioned, there is lightness to Luke's storytelling that sings. Joy is so tangible in Luke's account of this conversion that one imagines the Ethiopian dancing away from Philip. However, as the characters separate little information follows. The eunuch returns to his home and Philip continues his mission in Samaria. The eunuch is never mentioned again; what became of him resides in the historical consciousness of the Church of Ethiopia. Luke is likewise silent about Philip's work; although his name appears in Acts 21:8, as Paul and a traveling companion stay at Philip's home in Caesarea.

What really came of this encounter is not recorded. Rather, Luke told this story to inspire individuals to recognize the ever-expanding boundaries of Jesus' influence. What began as a small circle of Jesus-followers, shut up in a room to wait and pray, became, by the gift of the Spirit, a series of small communities of faith. Some of these communities were located in the region of Israel, but others were settled in Samaria and beyond. It is likely that each convert, as the story of the rejoicing Ethiopian suggests, carried the good news of Jesus to homes in many places and of various social settings. The refreshment of the waters of baptism commissioned new believers as ambassadors of Jesus. Do the math: The explosive growth of the church is understandable when each baptized believer is also an evangelist attentive to the Spirit's direction.

SHARING THE SCRIPTURE

PREPARING TO TEACH

Preparing Our Hearts

This week's devotional reading is found in Acts 11:19-26. Here we see that Jewish Christians, dispersed due to persecution following the martyrdom of Stephen, are spreading the gospel. Their work fulfills the command of Jesus in Acts 1:8. Verse 26 reports that for the first time those who follow Christ are called "Christians." Where do you see the good news being scattered today? What role are you playing in this important effort?

Pray that you and the adult learners will be open to participating in ministries that will enable them to be ambassadors of the gospel of Christ.

Preparing Our Minds

Study the background, Acts 8:26-40, and lesson scripture, Acts 8:26-38. Focus on how this account demonstrates ways in which people receive help in understanding and applying the Scriptures to their lives.

Write on newsprint:
- ❑ sentences for activity in "Commit to Regular Reading of Scripture and Listening for God's Spirit to Discern How It Speaks to the Learners' Lives."
- ❑ information for next week's lesson, found under "Continue the Journey."

Plan a brief background lecture as suggested under "Encounter the Story of How the Holy Spirit Sent Philip to Teach an African Official the Good News About Jesus."

LEADING THE CLASS

(1) Gather to Learn

❖ Welcome the class members and introduce any guests.

❖ Pray that even as the students grow in their own understanding of God's word they will be eager to help others interpret the word as well.

❖ Encourage the students to talk about an "aha" moment they had in understanding the Bible. Perhaps someone said something that "clicked." Or maybe they suddenly gleaned a new insight from a familiar passage. Consider doing this activity in small groups so that everyone can participate.

❖ Read aloud today's focus statement: **People need help in understanding and applying the Scriptures. How will they receive the help they need? The Holy Spirit sent Philip to help an African official understand how Jesus Christ fulfilled the prophecies he was reading, and the same Spirit calls Christians today to help explain God's word to others.**

(2) Encounter the Story of How the Holy Spirit Sent Philip to Teach an African Official the Good News About Jesus

❖ Choose volunteers to read the parts of the narrator, the Holy Spirit, Philip, the Ethiopian official, and the passage from Isaiah in verses 32-33. Ask them to read Acts 8:26-38 as a drama.

❖ Use information from Acts 8:26-29 in Understanding the Scripture to give the students some background about the Ethiopian eunuch and his relationship to Judaism.

❖ Select students to retell the story from the point of view of the Ethiopian or Philip. Suggest that they imagine the questions, fears, and other emotions he might have experienced.

❖ Look at verses 32-33, quoted from Isaiah 53:7-8. Note that this excerpt is from Isaiah 52:13–53:12, commonly known as the fourth "Servant Song." Discuss these questions.

(1) **What does Philip's interpretation of the fourth "Servant Song" excerpt say about how the early church understood this passage from Isaiah?** (The church already must have applied it to Jesus, and understood him to be the one to

whom this passage referred. It is extremely unlikely that Philip would have been interpreting Isaiah this way on his own.)

(2) **What does Philip's use of the church's interpretation suggest to you about how interpretation is done and who is involved in making such decisions?**

(3) Consider Ways That the Holy Spirit Helps the Learners to Understand and Apply Scripture

❖ Note that although the African man was reading the Scripture on his own, he could not adequately interpret it. He invited Philip to help him. Yet, Philip did not rely on a personal reading but instead shared the community of faith's belief that this prophetic passage was fulfilled in Jesus.

❖ Discuss these questions.

(1) **What implications does this story have for studying the Bible individually?**

(2) **What implications does this story have for studying the Bible as part of a group in the community of faith?**

(3) **What role do you believe the Holy Spirit plays in the interpretation of Scripture?**

(4) **The Ethiopian eunuch immediately responded to Philip's explanation of Scripture by seeking baptism. What are some of the ways that you respond to Scripture?** (You may want to list these ideas on newsprint. Some ways will call forth personal piety; other ways will call forth actions to promote peace and justice.)

❖ Point out that people's stands on "hot button" issues in the church today, such as the place of homosexuals and lesbians or ethical implications of stem cell research, are often based on how they read and interpret the Bible. Some will point to specific chapters and verses, whereas others will look at the broader message of the Bible. Some will accept only interpretations that have been authorized in the church for centuries and are therefore considered "orthodox." Others will read the Bible in the context of today's world and try to hear God speaking to issues that were completely unknown or viewed differently in the context of biblical cultures.

❖ Encourage the students to discuss how they read and interpret the Bible and the roles that they believe the Holy Spirit and church play in helping them discern its meaning and applying its teachings.

(4) Commit to Regular Reading of Scripture and Listening for God's Spirit to Discern How It Speaks to the Learners' Lives

❖ Distribute paper and pencils. Ask the students to write these sentences, which you may want to post on newsprint: **To hear the Spirit speak to me through God's word, I commit myself to encounter the Scriptures regularly. I feel led to study . . . (theme, such as grace), or . . . (book), or . . . (genre of Scripture, such as prophecy). Signed**_____

❖ Suggest that they include on their sheet a question/problem that they need God to respond to. Note that the answer may come as they delve into the Scriptures.

(5) Continue the Journey

❖ Pray that all who have come today will go forth ready and willing to read the Bible, to consider its meaning for their lives, and to encourage others to do the same.

❖ Read aloud this preparation for next week's lesson. You may also want to post it on newsprint for the students to copy. **Prepare for next week's session, entitled**

"Breaking the Gospel Barriers," by reading Acts 10:1-48, paying particular attention to verses 1-20. Keep these ideas in mind as you study: People of all nationalities need to know that God loves them. How can messengers of God's love overcome their resistance to carry the good news to people who are different from themselves? Peter received a vision that helped him overcome his own cultural and religious hesitations to share the good news with all, and God gives us the power to break down our own resistances.

❖ Read aloud the following three ideas. Challenge the students to commit themselves to use these activities as a springboard to spiritual growth.

(1) **Attend a Bible study during the week, perhaps with a friend of another denomination, to see how that group reads and interprets the Bible. How is their method similar to and/or different from the way your class undertakes this task? What new ideas did you glean?**

(2) **Invite at least one person to join you in Sunday school this week so that he or she may experience the value of studying the word of God in community.**

(3) **Peruse at least one commentary on Acts to see how the scholar(s) who wrote that resource read and interpret this important biblical book. Think about points at which you agree or disagree.**

❖ Sing or read aloud "O Word of God Incarnate."

❖ Lead this benediction to conclude the session: **May the Holy Spirit empower you to be witnesses for Jesus Christ in your community, in your nation, and to the ends of the earth. Amen.**

UNIT 2: IN ALL JUDEA AND SAMARIA
BREAKING THE GOSPEL BARRIERS

PREVIEWING THE LESSON

Lesson Scripture: Acts 10:1-20
Background Scripture: Acts 10:1-48
Key Verses: Acts 10:19-20

Focus of the Lesson:
People of all nationalities need to know that God loves them. How can messengers of God's love overcome their resistance to carry the good news to people who are different from themselves? Peter received a vision that helped him overcome his own cultural and religious hesitations to share the good news with all, and God gives us the power to break down our own resistances.

Goals for the Learners:
(1) to encounter the story of the visions of Peter and Cornelius, and the prejudices both men had to overcome.
(2) to identify their personal prejudices.
(3) to commit to overcoming prejudices and reach out to all others in God's name.

Pronunciation Guide:
Caesarea (ses uh ree' uh)
Cornelius (kor neel' yuhs)

Supplies:
Bibles, newsprint and marker, paper and pencils, hymnals

READING THE SCRIPTURE

NRSV
Acts 10:1-20

¹In Caesarea there was a man named Cornelius, a centurion of the Italian Cohort, as it was called. ²He was a devout man who feared God with all his household; he gave

NIV
Acts 10:1-20

¹At Caesarea there was a man named Cornelius, a centurion in what was known as the Italian Regiment. ²He and all his family were devout and God-fearing; he gave

alms generously to the people and prayed constantly to God. [3]One afternoon at about three o'clock he had a vision in which he clearly saw an angel of God coming in and saying to him, "Cornelius." [4]He stared at him in terror and said, "What is it, Lord?" He answered, "Your prayers and your alms have ascended as a memorial before God. [5]Now send men to Joppa for a certain Simon who is called Peter; [6]he is lodging with Simon, a tanner, whose house is by the seaside." [7]When the angel who spoke to him had left, he called two of his slaves and a devout soldier from the ranks of those who served him, [8]and after telling them everything, he sent them to Joppa.

[9]About noon the next day, as they were on their journey and approaching the city, Peter went up on the roof to pray. [10]He became hungry and wanted something to eat; and while it was being prepared, he fell into a trance. [11]He saw the heaven opened and something like a large sheet coming down, being lowered to the ground by its four corners. [12]In it were all kinds of four-footed creatures and reptiles and birds of the air. [13]Then he heard a voice saying, "Get up, Peter; kill and eat." [14]But Peter said, "By no means, Lord; for I have never eaten anything that is profane or unclean." [15]The voice said to him again, a second time, "What God has made clean, you must not call profane." [16]This happened three times, and the thing was suddenly taken up to heaven.

[17]Now while Peter was greatly puzzled about what to make of the vision that he had seen, suddenly the men sent by Cornelius appeared. They were asking for Simon's house and were standing by the gate. [18]They called out to ask whether Simon, who was called Peter, was staying there. **[19]While Peter was still thinking about the vision, the Spirit said to him, "Look, three men are searching for you. [20]Now get up, go down, and go with them without hesitation; for I have sent them."**

generously to those in need and prayed to God regularly. [3]One day at about three in the afternoon he had a vision. He distinctly saw an angel of God, who came to him and said, "Cornelius!"

[4]Cornelius stared at him in fear. "What is it, Lord?" he asked.

The angel answered, "Your prayers and gifts to the poor have come up as a memorial offering before God. [5]Now send men to Joppa to bring back a man named Simon who is called Peter. [6]He is staying with Simon the tanner, whose house is by the sea."

[7]When the angel who spoke to him had gone, Cornelius called two of his servants and a devout soldier who was one of his attendants. [8]He told them everything that had happened and sent them to Joppa.

[9]About noon the following day as they were on their journey and approaching the city, Peter went up on the roof to pray. [10]He became hungry and wanted something to eat, and while the meal was being prepared, he fell into a trance. [11]He saw heaven opened and something like a large sheet being let down to earth by its four corners. [12]It contained all kinds of four-footed animals, as well as reptiles of the earth and birds of the air. [13]Then a voice told him, "Get up, Peter. Kill and eat."

[14]"Surely not, Lord!" Peter replied. "I have never eaten anything impure or unclean."

[15]The voice spoke to him a second time, "Do not call anything impure that God has made clean."

[16]This happened three times, and immediately the sheet was taken back to heaven.

[17]While Peter was wondering about the meaning of the vision, the men sent by Cornelius found out where Simon's house was and stopped at the gate. [18]They called out, asking if Simon who was known as Peter was staying there.

[19]While Peter was still thinking about the vision, the Spirit said to him, "Simon, three men are looking for you. [20]So get up and go downstairs. Do not hesitate to go with them, for I have sent them."

UNDERSTANDING THE SCRIPTURE

Acts 10:1-8. The story of the baptism of the family and friends of the Gentile Cornelius was so rich with social custom, cultural prejudice, distinct characters, and Spirit-influenced guidance that it challenged the best of storytellers. Luke, however, met the challenge with style. In this chapter, Luke subtly filled in the personalities of Cornelius and Peter, foreshadowed the controversy between Jewish and Gentile believers, and presented the Spirit's ample and amusing interventions. Luke began the tale by introducing Cornelius, who has the distinction of being the first person of Roman authority named in Acts. As a centurion, Cornelius was an officer in charge of 100 soldiers. A "cohort" was 600 soldiers (one-tenth of a legion), though some scholars debate the date, location, and role of the Italian Cohort mentioned in Acts 10. Even though he was a commanding officer of an occupation army, Cornelius's spiritual attributes were more important to Luke than his military prowess. Cornelius was a devout God-fearer, one who accepted the Mosaic law and participated in temple worship, but who had not taken the steps of formal preparation and circumcision necessary for full membership in Israel. By reputation, he was generous in his charity and he prayed constantly. One afternoon while Cornelius was at prayer (note the hour of three is mentioned; see comments in the lesson for September 18, Acts 3:1-3), he saw a vision of an angel and heard clear and precise instructions. The angel disclosed no purpose with the instructions, yet Cornelius responded without hesitation. He entrusted the message to two slaves and another devout soldier and sent the men to Joppa in search of Peter. He neither delayed nor kept information to himself; Cornelius followed the inspired directions precisely.

Acts 10:9-16. Having introduced one character and one divine intervention, Luke moved to another character and another intervention. On the following day in the port city of Joppa, the apostle Peter was also in prayer. The text states that he became hungry; this may indicate that Peter was fasting as he prayed. He evidently asked his host for something to eat, and while it was being prepared Peter "fell into a trance." As Luke precisely described Cornelius's encounter with an angel, so Peter's vision was precisely described. However, whereas in Cornelius's encounter the message was plainly stated, Peter initially experienced a dissonance between his vision and his moral sensibility. Peter heard God's voice commanding him to kill and eat animals without regard for the manner of slaughter or the categories of clean and unclean. The issue was deeper than etiquette or even personal piety; the cleanliness laws of Israel established the identity of God's chosen people. The Jewish people ate only meat that was slaughtered according to kosher practice, and they did not eat prohibited meat, such as pork or shellfish. Peter heard a voice that sounded divine yet commanded him to break the law. Moreover, the vision and the message, "What God has made clean, you must not call profane," were repeated three times.

Acts 10:17-33. Peter pondered his experience. Evidently, the vision was so compelling he fell into another trance-like state. As with Cornelius, the Spirit intervened directly to bring together Peter and Cornelius. This time the inner pressure of God's Spirit alerted Peter to the men at the door calling for him. "Get up, go down, and go with them without hesitation," was the direction given to Peter. Peter was almost obedient. He got up; he went down from the roof. However, he hesitated as he interrogated the men about their purpose. The men shared their information. They explained that Cornelius was "directed"—here Luke used a Greek word denoting revelation—to bring Peter to his home to hear what he had to say. Finally, Peter responded appropriately; he offered hospitality and the next day began a very significant journey. Two cultures were about to meet; neither knew what to expect of the other. Cornelius, for his part, was a bit too dramatic as he fell face down worshiping Peter. Peter, for his part, was a bit too rude, as he explained that entering a Gentile house was unlawful, at least without the necessary "objections." But, the urging of the Spirit was greater than Peter's obtuse nature or Cornelius's exuberant expectations. At Cornelius's entry door, Peter blurted out the truth of his vision: "God has shown me that I should not call anyone profane or unclean." Inside the house, a circle of Gentiles awaited good news.

Acts 10:34-48. Peter was invited to preach and preach he did! Luke uses a Greek literary convention—literally, "Peter opened his mouth"—to emphasize that Peter's speech is inspired, not casual. These are the main points of his sermon:

- God is without partiality.
- Jesus is Lord of all.
- By the Holy Spirit the apostles continue Jesus' ministry.

Perhaps, Peter had a conclusion in mind, but something remarkable happened before he reached his final remarks: The Holy Spirit fell on the Gentiles. The interruption of Peter's preaching was similar to the crowd's question following the first Pentecost sermon (see Acts 2:37). Then, Peter, by the Spirit's urging, offered baptism as the appropriate response to his words. Now as a "Gentile Pentecost" began, Peter and his friends observed as the Spirit enacted the sermon Peter preached. The force of the Spirit was undeniable; the believers from Joppa bowed to the spiritual evidence they witnessed. Once again, as with the Ethiopian eunuch, there was no reason to withhold baptism. It was ordered and the teaching/preaching continued for several days.

Considering the story as a whole, one wonders: Did Luke tell this story to explain the conversion of a Gentile or the conversion of an apostle? The Spirit's movement was complementary in the lives of both men (and presumably among their respective circles of family and friends). Both men changed as a result of their visions their belief in Jesus and their experience of the Spirit. Both entered holy space previously uncharted. The Roman soldier, partially converted to the faith of Israel, fully confessed Jesus and was baptized as a believer. Peter, a pious Jew, rejected the Jewish purity laws and began preaching without the restrictive categories of Jew and Gentile. However dramatic the change for each, neither could imagine the profound impact their encounter would have on the church of Jesus Christ. This truly was the beginning of the one, new people of God.

INTERPRETING THE SCRIPTURE

When God Speaks Clearly

Have you ever wanted God to speak directly and clearly to you? Ordinarily, God's direction, intervention, and providential care are gently diffused within our lives. We encounter a person by accident and much later the stranger is a close friend. We think a career choice is rational, but later realize God's hand was in our muddled deciding. We pray for a sign sufficient for an urgent decision and realize in retrospect that the lack of a sign indicated the lack of urgency. Regardless of the intense assurance gained from looking backward, we still want God to speak directly.

In this lesson, an outsider among God's people heard a clear and direct instruction from God. This is not a unique instance of a divine message given, with clarity, to an outsider. In the birth stories of Jesus, the shepherds (ritually unclean by profession) heard the first announcement of Jesus' birth and magi (foreigners from another religious faith) obediently followed a star to greet an infant king unnoticed by the Jewish king. In Scripture as in life, those who stand some distance from the center of faith are, at times, the first to notice change. When God is ready to change human hearts and history, whoever is attentive becomes a channel for something new. Evidently, it was God's time to change the relationship between Jews and Gentiles. This time, the blessed clarity came to Cornelius. An angel appeared to him. Without alluding to the purpose, the angel gave detailed instructions on the place where Peter was temporarily living. Cornelius was blessed, shocked, and obedient. The point of Luke's story was clear: An outsider felt God drawing him into a new community of faith.

When God Speaks in Images

The outsider heard God's clear message; the insider's vision was neither clear nor easily unscrambled. Peter saw a sheet filled with animals gradually descending from heaven. The attending words matched the vision perfectly; even Peter's growling stomach seemed to fit the image. To Peter's credit, he recognized the vision as a divine message. His spiritual sensitivity was honed during his time with Jesus. He saw Jesus transfigured. He witnessed countless miracles. He learned to understand God's mysteries in common things: leaven and lilies, stones and storms at sea. He was humbled by a cock-crowing prophecy. He walked, broke bread with, and learned from the risen Lord. He saw Jesus taken up in glory. Therefore, when "the heaven opened" during his trance-like dream, Peter was prepared for a heaven-sent message. Excusing his growling stomach, Peter responded to the dream as a test of his obedience. His interpretation—"I have never broken the kosher laws"—was corrected by a voice saying, "What God has made clean, you must not call profane" (10:15). The vision repeated itself three times; Peter was greatly puzzled.

How do you work with troubling, yet seemingly divine, messages? After all, those who are steeped in religion know that divine speech is formed from the language of images, symbols, signs, and metaphors. All these have power because they transform the divine into the ordinary, while maintaining the integrity of both the mundane and the mysterious. For example, in Jesus' parable of the leaven hidden within the flour, the characteristic bubbling of yeast during bread making provided a perfect image for God's realm bubbling into human history. The leaven remained leaven, yet as such it signified a spiritual reality. To understand a spiritually charged image, attention to the actual physical characteristics of the image is necessary. In Peter's vision, the challenge was to understand the spiritual reality of the image of the sheet filled with animals. The accompanying words offered an interpretive clue; still Peter was wise to puzzle over what he saw.

When an Outsider Becomes an Insider

Nothing was left to accident in this wonderful account. God directed Cornelius to send for Peter; a vision prepared Peter for a new understanding of God's acceptance; three men traveled from Cornelius's home to Peter's temporary residence to bring the two men face to face. Even when Peter hesitated, his resistance melted before the spiritual intensity of the message and the messengers. After a night of rest (provided by Jews for Gentiles), a traveling company of Peter's colleagues and friends set off for Cornelius's home. The lines separating Jew from Gentile were becoming fuzzy, but the import of Peter's dream was yet to be interpreted, enacted, and confirmed.

First, Peter (the supposed insider with an inherited as well as a faith-inspired connection to God) entered Cornelius's home (an outsider's place where food was not prepared in a kosher manner, where no covenant of circumcision was in effect, and where cultural practices were contrary to Mosaic law). This was not a modest step for Peter; however, the Spirit working with Cornelius and with Peter was greater than either man. It was and is this Spirit that makes such steps possible. Consider the various changes you've witnessed: racial reconciliation, international cooperation, freedom from gender-specific roles, increased opportunities for disabled persons. Although each change is not completed, it is clear that God's message is within these changes. Peter's first step was profound; it also fell short. Something more was needed. That something more was added when the first words of Peter's sermon interpreted his dream: God is, was, and will be impartial. There was no race, no intelligence quotient, no precondition of any sort for divine love; rather God's impartial standard was turning toward God and doing right. Not only did Peter preach this message, but the Holy Spirit also enacted it before the whole company. Suddenly, a room previously made uncomfortable by ancient rules and attitudes of separation became an oasis of divine delight as the distinctions between insiders and outsiders became irrelevant.

When an Insider Receives Hospitality

It is tempting to hear this story as the opening of the "Jewish only" Christian community to the Gentiles. However, when those who were once separated join together, an opening is created on both sides. For Peter, the insider, Cornelius's hospitality was a gift equal with his divine dream. Peter and the company from Joppa stayed several days with Cornelius. Much of that time was spent in teaching, but an equal amount of time was at the table, walking the streets of the town, offering and receiving grace from one another. The usual dance of life went on: eating, sleeping, keeping house, studying, praying, conversing, and holding silence. However, this dance was between two groups with no experience in fellowship together. Only by leaning on the power of the Spirit did these groups begin to form a new entity. It was not sufficient for Peter to cross the threshold; he and his companions had to stay in the home of the outsider. They needed to receive Cornelius's hospitality. In his home, the real change began. Over the span of several days, the nametags of Jew and Gentile faded. Over the span of several weeks, the discomfort at the dinner table lessened. Over the span of several months, the stunning vision of God's impartiality was spiritually imprinted on the expanding church. Luke's story provides the characters, the plot, and the spiritual guidance; it teaches, however, that although change may begin with dreams, it requires an unending commitment of words, deeds, and relationships. Surely, those who first read this tale heard Peter's comment on God's impartiality and wondered about the status of their community of faith. Surely, studying this story nearly 2,000 years later, we puzzle about the same issues. Perhaps it is time to do as "insider" Peter did: to receive hospitality from an "outsider."

SHARING THE SCRIPTURE

PREPARING TO TEACH

Preparing Our Hearts

This week's devotional reading is found in Acts 13:44-49. Here we find Paul and Barnabas ministering in the city of Antioch in Pisidia. They announced that they were turning their attention to the Gentiles, who "were glad and praised the word of the Lord" (13:48) when they heard the good news. Those who previously had been excluded were now invited into the family of God. What groups of people do you believe are currently excluded? What can you do to break down barriers to let others know that God loves and welcomes them?

Pray that you and the adult learners will recognize and work to overcome prejudices that separate you from those who need to experience God's good news.

Preparing Our Minds

Study the background, Acts 10:1-48, and lesson scripture, Acts 10:1-20. As you read this account of Peter and Cornelius, consider how Christians, as messengers of God's love, can overcome their resistance to carry the good news to people who are different from themselves.

Write on newsprint:

❑ the list of questions in the "Encounter the Story of the Visions of Peter and Cornelius, and the Prejudices Both Men Overcome" portion.

❑ information for next week's lesson, found under "Continue the Journey."

LEADING THE CLASS

(1) Gather to Learn

❖ Welcome the class members and introduce any guests.

❖ Pray that the students will be obedient to the Spirit's leading and open to healthy relationships with all persons.

❖ Encourage the class to identify several "great divides" that separate people because of some sort of prejudice. List their ideas on newsprint. Discuss how people of faith could attempt to bridge these divides.

❖ Read aloud today's focus statement: **People of all nationalities need to know that God loves them. How can messengers of God's love overcome their resistance to carry the good news to people who are different from themselves?** Peter received a vision

that helped him overcome his own cultural and religious hesitations to share the good news with all, and God gives us the power to break down our own resistances.

(2) Encounter the Story of the Visions of Peter and Cornelius, and the Prejudices Both Men Overcome

❖ Choose four readers for the parts of the narrator, angel/voice/Holy Spirit, Cornelius, and Peter. Ask them to read Acts 10:1-20 as a drama.

❖ Divide the class in half. Ask each group to answer these questions, which you will write on newsprint prior to the session. One group (or several smaller subgroups) will look at verses 1-8, and the other, verses 9-20.

(1) **What does this passage tell you about Cornelius (or Peter)?**

(2) **How did Cornelius (or Peter) respond to the directions he received?**

(3) **What barriers would you expect to find between these two men?**

(4) **How were these barriers broken?**

❖ Call the groups together to discuss their answers.

(3) Identify the Learners' Personal Prejudices

❖ Distribute paper and pencils. Suggest that the students list groups of people they find difficult to relate to because of some barrier. Assure the adults that they will not be asked to share this list with anyone.

❖ Invite the students to reread silently Acts 10:11-16 and ponder the ways that Peter's vision challenges the prejudices they have listed.

❖ Ask the learners to reflect silently on these questions.

(1) **Are you willing to cross lines of race, ethnicity, language, culture, age, socio-economic class, gender orientation to invite someone else to God? If not, what prevents you from doing so?**

(2) What principles from the story of Peter and Cornelius might help you?

❖ Conclude this portion of the session by pointing out that some students were likely able to identify reasons for their attitudes. For example, they may recall that a parent was prejudiced against a certain group. Note that deeply ingrained attitudes are difficult to root out, but with God's help all things are possible.

(4) Commit to Overcoming Prejudices and Reach Out to All Others in God's Name

❖ Tell the students that the biggest challenge of the early church, composed originally of Jews, was the inclusion of Gentiles. Invite the class to identify groups of people whom the contemporary church seems to exclude or accept only on a second class basis. List their ideas on newsprint.

❖ Discuss why each of these groups is apparently difficult to accept. (Note that just as Peter was challenged to come to a new understanding of Scripture before he could accept Cornelius as a brother in Christ, so we may also be challenged.)

❖ Provide a few moments of quiet time for students who choose to do so to commit themselves to overcoming their prejudices so that they will be able to reach out to all persons in God's name.

(5) Continue the Journey

❖ Break the silence with a prayer that the participants will be able to walk in the Spirit, interacting with all persons without prejudice.

❖ Read aloud this preparation for next week's lesson. You may also want to post it on newsprint for the students to copy. Prepare for next week's session, entitled "Never Alone," by reading Acts 12:1-17. The lesson will focus on the first sixteen verses. Keep these ideas in mind as you study: People need help in times of trouble. Where is the source of help for people who get in trouble because of their beliefs? The account of the angel sent to rescue Peter from prison and possible death shows us that God can help us endure persecution.

❖ Read aloud the following three ideas. Challenge the students to commit themselves to use these activities as a springboard to spiritual growth.

(1) Write in your spiritual journal about dividing walls that have separated you from others. How have these walls hampered your willingness to share—or receive—God's good news? What insights did you gain about yourself, the "other," and your faith when these walls fell?

(2) Approach someone from whom you have felt divided due to a bias. Try to get to know that person as an individual, not a stereotype. As you develop a relationship, begin to witness to your faith.

(3) Research recent examples of religious, racial, or other barriers collapsing. What parallels do you see between these events and those of Acts 10?

❖ Sing or read aloud "Help Us Accept Each Other."

❖ Lead this benediction to conclude the session: **May the Holy Spirit empower you to be witnesses for Jesus Christ in your community, in your nation, and to the ends of the earth. Amen.**

UNIT 2: IN ALL JUDEA AND SAMARIA
NEVER ALONE

PREVIEWING THE LESSON

Lesson Scripture: Acts 12:1-16
Background Scripture: Acts 12:1-17
Key Verse: Acts 12:7

Focus of the Lesson:
People need help in times of trouble. Where is the source of help for people who get in trouble because of their beliefs? The account of the angel sent to rescue Peter from prison and possible death shows us that God can help us endure persecution.

Goals for the Learners:
(1) to study the circumstances that led to Peter's imprisonment and how God freed and protected him in surprising ways.
(2) to compare and contrast God's rescue of Peter with the ways in which God helps them today.
(3) to affirm the constant presence of God.

Pronunciation Guide:
Herod Agrippa (her' uhd   uh grip' uh)

Supplies:
Bibles, newsprint and marker, paper and pencils, hymnals, magazines, photos, markers, glue, scissors, butcher/craft paper

---

READING THE SCRIPTURE

NRSV
Acts 12:1-16

¹About that time King Herod laid violent hands upon some who belonged to the church. ²He had James, the brother of John, killed with the sword. ³After he saw that it pleased the Jews, he proceeded to arrest Peter also. (This was during the festival of Unleavened Bread.) ⁴When he had seized him,

NIV
Acts 12:1-16

¹It was about this time that King Herod arrested some who belonged to the church, intending to persecute them. ²He had James, the brother of John, put to death with the sword. ³When he saw that this pleased the Jews, he proceeded to seize Peter also. This happened during the Feast of Unleavened

he put him in prison and handed him over to four squads of soldiers to guard him, intending to bring him out to the people after the Passover. [5]While Peter was kept in prison, the church prayed fervently to God for him.

[6]The very night before Herod was going to bring him out, Peter, bound with two chains, was sleeping between two soldiers, while guards in front of the door were keeping watch over the prison. **[7]Suddenly an angel of the Lord appeared and a light shone in the cell. He tapped Peter on the side and woke him, saying, "Get up quickly." And the chains fell off his wrists.** [8]The angel said to him, "Fasten your belt and put on your sandals." He did so. Then he said to him, "Wrap your cloak around you and follow me." [9]Peter went out and followed him; he did not realize that what was happening with the angel's help was real; he thought he was seeing a vision. [10]After they had passed the first and the second guard, they came before the iron gate leading into the city. It opened for them of its own accord, and they went outside and walked along a lane, when suddenly the angel left him. [11]Then Peter came to himself and said, "Now I am sure that the Lord has sent his angel and rescued me from the hands of Herod and from all that the Jewish people were expecting."

[12]As soon as he realized this, he went to the house of Mary, the mother of John whose other name was Mark, where many had gathered and were praying. [13]When he knocked at the outer gate, a maid named Rhoda came to answer. [14]On recognizing Peter's voice, she was so overjoyed that, instead of opening the gate, she ran in and announced that Peter was standing at the gate. [15]They said to her, "You are out of your mind!" But she insisted that it was so. They said, "It is his angel." [16]Meanwhile Peter continued knocking; and when they opened the gate, they saw him and were amazed.

Bread. [4]After arresting him, he put him in prison, handing him over to be guarded by four squads of four soldiers each. Herod intended to bring him out for public trial after the Passover.

[5]So Peter was kept in prison, but the church was earnestly praying to God for him.

[6]The night before Herod was to bring him to trial, Peter was sleeping between two soldiers, bound with two chains, and sentries stood guard at the entrance. **[7]Suddenly an angel of the Lord appeared and a light shone in the cell. He struck Peter on the side and woke him up. "Quick, get up!" he said, and the chains fell off Peter's wrists.** [8]Then the angel said to him, "Put on your clothes and sandals." And Peter did so. "Wrap your cloak around you and follow me," the angel told him. [9]Peter followed him out of the prison, but he had no idea that what the angel was doing was really happening; he thought he was seeing a vision. [10]They passed the first and second guards and came to the iron gate leading to the city. It opened for them by itself, and they went through it. When they had walked the length of one street, suddenly the angel left him.

[11]Then Peter came to himself and said, "Now I know without a doubt that the Lord sent his angel and rescued me from Herod's clutches and from everything the Jewish people were anticipating."

[12]When this had dawned on him, he went to the house of Mary the mother of John, also called Mark, where many people had gathered and were praying. [13]Peter knocked at the outer entrance, and a servant girl named Rhoda came to answer the door. [14]When she recognized Peter's voice, she was so overjoyed she ran back without opening it and exclaimed, "Peter is at the door!"

[15]"You're out of your mind," they told her. When she kept insisting that it was so, they said, "It must be his angel."

[16]But Peter kept on knocking, and when they opened the door and saw him, they were astonished.

UNDERSTANDING THE SCRIPTURE

Acts 12:1-4. Attempting to read Acts as history is a persistent temptation, but a constant frustration. Rarely does Luke include a date. However, in Acts 12:1 Luke mentions King Herod, and in 12:23 this same king is struck dead. Working with nonscriptural sources a date for the text emerges: King Herod (Aprippa I) died in A.D. 44. Time and events moved forward, while Luke stated the theologically significant markers along the way. The Jerusalem persecution was such a marker. First, the apostolic leadership was attacked: James, the brother of John and son of Zebedee, was executed and Peter was arrested by order of King Herod. He was a violent and a capricious leader with a strong allegiance to Rome. However, the execution of James obviously won approval for Herod among the Jews. Thereafter, King Herod "staged" the arrest of Peter during Passover. Peter, a leader of the increasingly unpopular Christian movement and a man who posed no threat of violence (although he might be a candidate for flight; see Acts 5:17-21), was placed under the highest level of security. Sixteen guards were assigned in sets of four—two at the door of his cell and one on each side of Peter, who was bound by wrist chains. Each set's guard duty lasted only three hours; then the shift changed to ensure constant wakefulness on the part of the guards and to eliminate any possibility of escape.

Acts 12:5-11. While the king used his power of violence and intimidation, the church used its power of persistent and unceasing prayer. At the last possible moment, a miraculous intervention prevented the execution of Peter. As Luke recorded this well-known tale, Peter was passive throughout the escape; he neither questions nor suggests. Indeed, although the angel of the Lord appeared—with requisite lighting—the angel tapped Peter to awaken him (the Greek word used implies more of a poke or a jab than a gentle touching). The angel was clearly in charge: Orders were issued and obeyed; chains and doors were loosened; Peter was led through dark city streets to freedom. Peter must have reported to the whole community the dream-like quality of his experience, for this detail colored Luke's account. Interestingly, nothing was mentioned about the guards—whether they slept or fretted is not considered worthy of the story's aim. Rather, Luke wanted his audience to experience the absolute power of God in this rescue. It was a sweet taste of grace for Christians who daily shed bitter tears. The persecution began; one leader was lost; one leader was miraculously rescued. If the readers followed the course of events with Peter, eventually, they reached the same conclusion: God really is in charge of the growth and development of the church. Neither ruling powers nor fickle popular sentiment stopped God's new creation.

Acts 12:12-16. Once Peter was alone, he realized the danger of his situation. He was an escaped prisoner, conspicuous on the deserted street and in a hostile city. "Coming to himself" he acted swiftly. There was no time to muddle; he had to find safety and he knew where to find it. He headed directly for the house of Mary, the mother of John Mark, where he knew his community was in prayer for him. After all, if events proceeded as the powers and the people assumed, Peter would die the following day. Up to this point in the story, Luke's content and style alternated between dangerous powers at work against the church and God's miraculous power at work on behalf of the church. As Peter knocked at the outer gate, Luke shifted to a whole new rhetorical tone: humor. Evidently, Luke believed that congregations facing persecution needed to laugh! With a light touch, Luke recounted that the servant girl Rhoda answered Peter's knock, but forgot to open the door. Rather, she ran back to the community with the good news that Peter was standing at the gate. Recalling Luke's account of the women's news of the empty tomb (Luke 24:11), the community assumed the girl was crazy and continued the prayer meeting. However, their explanation, "It is his angel," prepared the community to receive Peter's account of his escape. The stage was set, but the main character, Peter, stood in the street, still knocking at the gate. Finally, the gate was opened and the typical response to God's extraordinary intervention, amazement, spread over the community.

Acts 12:17. Amid the noise from the community's songs of praise and shouts of joy, Peter motioned for silence. Quickly, he told his story. Reminiscent of Jesus' resurrection appearances, Peter gave particular instructions and left the community on their own. Luke offered little further: Peter went to Caesarea and stayed there (see Acts 12:19); much later, Peter offered his support of the mission to the Gentiles (see Acts 15:7-11); but nothing more of his ministry after leaving Jerusalem was mentioned. A leader was rescued, revealed, and removed to another place. The gap in the story suggests a rich (and unrecorded) development of the church. As believers, evangelists, and apostles spread out from Jerusalem, the gospel was planted in community after community. In each place, the challenges were unique and specific, yet a common connection through faith in Jesus and the presence of the Holy Spirit unified the church. There were, as yet, no rules or structures agreed upon by these independent communities. Likewise, the teaching was concise—theology was in its infancy, but the stories about, of, and from Jesus were shared with enthusiasm. Something new was coming into the world. The church was moving ever outward and from the boundaries came the issues that evolved into church order and orthodoxy. However, during these first few precious years, the church was truly Spirit-led and Spirit-filled. That central reality prompted stories such as this tale of Peter's rescue from prison, a bold testimony to God's faithfulness to the church. Individual leaders rose up, led, and were arrested, killed, or moved away; still the church continued to grow.

INTERPRETING THE SCRIPTURE

Persecution Begins

The book of Acts records stories of faith, community practice, and cultural setting. Although the faith of the earliest believers included some emphases that may be unfamiliar to us (for example, ecstatic foreign languages), the confession of Jesus as our Lord and Savior unites one generation of witnesses to other generations of believers. Likewise, we are fascinated by the hints about church organization and structure. We smile in recognition of the Greek word for "deacon" used to designate those selected to serve at table. We applaud their discernment and resonate with their emphasis on prayer and consensus. However, when we touch the culture of the early church, there we discover a great divide.

There is no greater difference between the world of the first-century Christians and our modern world in most of the West than the fact of persecution. While we speak up for the rights of the poor and the voiceless, the first-century Christians *were* the poor and the voiceless. While we manage our personal resources to support missions and ministry, they shared their modest means of living for the survival of the community. While we risk our reputations on a particular justice issue, they experienced economic boycott, community surveillance, arrest, imprisonment, and execution. While we study Scripture to understand the grand sweep of God's will and way, they listened to the stories of missionaries and martyrs as inspiration for their personal witnesses. The difference between their world and our world is vast—longer than the centuries and wider than the oceans. Nevertheless, in studying Acts we are invited to step over that vast separation and take our place beside those who were persecuted. As we investigate this story from the twelfth chapter of Acts, we do so with humble, teachable spirits. This lesson is beyond our experience, yet necessary to our growth in faith.

The Impossible Release

The chapter begins with malicious plotting and desperate circumstances. On one side was Herod Agrippa I, a vicious king who delighted in pleasing the powers-that-be and in dangling disruption before his subjects. For about a decade, the Christians irritated the Jerusalem religious authorities; gradually the irritation touched the ordinary citizens of Israel. King Herod seized this as an opportunity to increase his popularity. Evidently, the beheading of a known leader of the Christians drew unprecedented applause among the Jewish community. On the wave of growing popularity, the king arrested another leader, Peter. Placing him in prison during the festival of Passover was a dramatic gesture not lost on the Jewish and the Christian communities. Everyone anticipated that Peter's end would be as Jesus' was. This well-known script guided the events, and the end of the story was already written. Although hope for Peter's life was slim, the community carried such hope. Their sorrow over James's death did not dampen their prayers for Peter. The first lesson from persecution begins with persistent, hopeful prayer, regardless of the recent experience of defeat and despair.

When forces of violent power meet patient prayer, be prepared for disruption. Sometimes the disruption comes in the form of poignant loss, like the execution by sword of James. Other times the disruption comes as an inconceivable last-minute rescue. This time, while the community prayed, Peter was ferreted out of prison by an angel and sent on his way as a freed man. Once again, the seemingly impossible was just that: seemingly so, not actually so; another lesson necessary for times of persecution.

Necessary Laughter

The astounding release was too wonderful for even Peter to believe. All that happened came as a gift: Peter was amazed by God's escape plan. However, being alone on the street also made him conscious of surrounding dangers. As swiftly as possible, Peter hurried to the house where his community was gathered. At this point, rather than embroidering the tale with pious praise, the author, Luke, employs a wholly other genre: humor! The scene of Peter knocking at the door is the stuff of a Marx Brothers' film. With the lightest touch Luke recounts the imprisoned leader's return to the community. Why the humor? Why the mirth? Why the playful storytelling technique? When faced with grim realities and when granted a momentary suspension of that reality, laughter is a natural response. Praise will always be present as the mighty deeds of God are recounted; occasionally, however, something else is needed. For a community facing persecution, this something else was a good, belly-jiggling laugh. They needed to laugh at their own frightened huddle; they needed to laugh at the tumble of Rome's mighty power; they needed to laugh that a leader was actually spared; they needed to laugh at their own resistance to good news. Laughter cleared their minds, softened their rigidity, chased away their fears, and bound the community to a hope greater than despair.

You may have experienced such oddly timed laughter: After the solemnity of a funeral come the silly stories; after the dangerous hike in the wilderness comes the exaggerated version; after the near fatal car crash comes the recollection of the absurdly appropriate music on the car's radio. Laughter, one of God's most precious gifts, enters unexpectedly, relieving tension and prompting spiritual rest. Luke knew that his audience needed to laugh in the face of the powers that threatened them; he wrote the twelfth chapter of Acts to give them permission to do just that. Perhaps, one day contemporary Christians will also recognize that laughter is necessary.

New Directions

The persecution in Jerusalem not only scattered the leadership of the community, but it also prompted a faith issue with which the church struggled from those early days until the present. The issue was captured in this chapter by the dissonance between the death of James, the rescue of Peter, and the faith of the community. Why was one leader lost and another leader saved? Was the faith of one greater than the faith of the other? Were the prayers of the people more diligent on Peter's behalf than on James's? The text is silent before all such questions; rather, Luke simply says, one man died, one man lived, and you, the community of faith, must continue to seek and do God's will. This is a stunning testimony against those who claim that with faith and prayer, everything will turn out rosy and prosperous. Indeed, the gospel includes both tragedy and triumph. At the center of the gospel of our Lord Jesus is a cross. There our Savior suffered neither because he lacked faith nor because he was a sinner. Jesus suffered for exactly the opposite reasons. He suffered because he would not release his vision of a just and a righteous world. Because he saw a vivid reality soaked with divine insight, Jesus risked his life in trust of God's power to reconcile and redeem—not simply his momentary grief, but the grief of the whole world. His suffering and death disarmed all neat platitudes that faith solves every immediate and urgent problem. Rather, Jesus' death and resurrection displayed the long-range reconciliation of God's coming kingdom. Sometimes faith actually creates problems. By those faith-provoked problems comes an opportunity for deepening conversions and maturing faith. Persecution provided the early Christian community in Jerusalem with a direct route into mature faith. As is the history of human communities, some rose to the challenge, some waffled, and some simply slipped away. But to those who remained hopeful, prayerful, and focused, God granted a vision so amazing that a poor community of believers in Jerusalem trusted the gospel of Jesus would reach the ends of the earth . . . and it did!

SHARING THE SCRIPTURE

PREPARING TO TEACH

Preparing Our Hearts

This week's devotional reading is found in Psalm 46. In this song, the Jewish community confesses its strong faith that God is a "refuge" who can be depended upon to help them in times of trouble. No matter how difficult our circumstances may be, God is there for us. We are never alone. How does Psalm 46 relate to your life? When have you turned to God for strength and help? Do you need a refuge right now because of problems that confront you? Meditate on Psalm 46 in light of these questions.

Pray that you and the adult learners will recognize that God is always present and able to do far more to help than we could ever imagine.

Preparing Our Minds

Study Acts 12:1-17. As you read, be alert for sources of help for Peter, who was in trouble with the authorities because of his beliefs and proclamation about Jesus.

Write on newsprint:

❑ information for next week's lesson, found under "Continue the Journey."

Plan a brief lecture as suggested under "Study the Circumstances That Led to Peter's Imprisonment and How God Freed and Protected Him in Surprising Ways."

Gather art supplies and affix butcher/craft paper to a wall or bulletin board.

LEADING THE CLASS

(1) Gather to Learn

❖ Welcome the class members and introduce any guests.

❖ Pray that the students will open themselves to the presence of God, who is with us everywhere.

❖ Have available on a table magazines, photos, markers, glue, and scissors. Invite the students to select a picture that for them represents a place where they feel God's presence especially near. Ask them to cut and paste that picture onto the butcher/craft paper that you have affixed to the wall or bulletin board in order to create a collage. (You may want to have the students begin to work as they come into the learning area.)

❖ Talk with the students about the reasons for their selections. Likely, many of the selections will be of peaceful places, churches, or family and friends. Discuss the possibility of finding God in the midst of trouble, perhaps in an unlikely place such as a prison.

❖ Read aloud today's focus statement: **People need help in times of trouble. Where is the source of help for people who get in trouble because of their beliefs? The account of the angel sent to rescue Peter from prison and possible death shows us that God can help us endure persecution.**

(2) Study the Circumstances That Led to Peter's Imprisonment and How God Freed and Protected Him in Surprising Ways

❖ Choose a volunteer to read Acts 12:1-5.

◼ Use information in the Understanding the Scripture portion to prepare a brief lecture to help the students understand: who Herod Agrippa I was; James's beheading; how the squads of soldiers worked.

◼ List on newsprint any similarities the class members can identify between Peter and Jesus.

❖ Ask the class members to close their eyes as you read Acts 12:6-16 and try to put themselves into this story. Tell them to be aware of sights, sounds, aromas, tastes, and things they can touch.

◼ Discuss with the class whatever captured their senses in this story.

◼ Suggest that the adults envision themselves as Peter and imagine his feelings about this amazing deliverance. Invite them to talk about these feelings in groups of two to four.

◼ Conclude this portion of the lesson by asking these three questions.

(1) With which person in the story could you most closely identify— Peter, one of the guards, Rhoda, or someone in Mary's home? Why?

(2) What ideas can you glean from this story about your own attitudes, actions, and beliefs?

(3) In what ways does this story demonstrate that we are never alone, even in life-threatening circumstances?

(3) Compare and Contrast God's Rescue of Peter with the Ways in Which God Helps the Learners Today

❖ Distribute paper and pencils. Encourage the students to write an autobiographical account of one or more difficult situations. Suggest that they discuss the circumstances and how they believe God helped them to get through the problem. Recommend that they look for similarities and differences between the way God assisted them and the way in which God worked in Peter's life.

❖ Ask the students to exchanges stories with a partner concerning God's help in their times of need.

❖ Bring the class together. Discuss examples of how they see God at work in trying circumstances around the world. Consider what God's faithfulness to those in need says to the learners about the nature of God.

(4) Affirm the Constant Presence of God

❖ Invite the students to participate in this guided imagery activity.

■ **Imagine yourself in one of the situations that you have just described in writing and talked about with a partner. Notice where you are, who is in the scene, and how you are feeling.** (pause)

■ **Envision Jesus walking into this scene. He approaches you. Feel him give you a hug. Pour out your heart to Jesus about your situation.** (pause)

■ **Hear what he has to say to you.** (pause)

■ **Reflect on how his presence has made a difference in you, even if the situation itself has not changed.** (pause)

■ **Offer a silent prayer of thanksgiving for God's steadfast presence in your life.** (pause)

■ **Open your eyes when you are ready.** (pause)

(5) Continue the Journey

❖ Pray that all of the students will recognize that they are never alone, for God is faithfully present with each person in all times and places.

❖ Read aloud this preparation for next week's lesson. You may also want to post it on newsprint for the students to copy. **Prepare for next week's session, entitled "Encountering Truth," by reading Acts 9:1-31. Pay particular attention to verses 3-18. As you study the lesson, focus on these ideas: Sometimes people need a radical change in the direction of their lives. What kind of intervention can bring that kind of change? Saul was changed from a persecutor to a believer when he directly encountered Jesus Christ, and Christians today still experience the transforming power of an encounter with Jesus.**

❖ Read aloud the following three ideas. Challenge the students to commit themselves to use these activities as a springboard to spiritual growth.

(1) **Write in your spiritual journal about a time when you felt alone. How were you able to experience God's presence? What difference did it make in your attitude once you realized that you were not truly alone?**

(2) **Identify at least one person who seems to feel alone. What steps will you take to support this person and help him or her to know that God is always present?**

(3) **Recall an encounter you had with God. Is there music, art, or poetry that you could create (or already know of) that can describe that experience with the Holy? How will you share your experience with someone else?**

❖ Sing or read aloud "Be Still, My Soul."

❖ Lead this benediction to conclude the session: **May the Holy Spirit empower you to be witnesses for Jesus Christ in your community, in your nation, and to the ends of the earth. Amen.**

UNIT 3: TO THE ENDS OF THE EARTH
ENCOUNTERING TRUTH

PREVIEWING THE LESSON

Lesson Scripture: Acts 9:3-18
Background Scripture: Acts 9:1-31
Key Verse: Acts 9:18

Focus of the Lesson:
Sometimes people need a radical change in the direction of their lives. What kind of intervention can bring that kind of change? Saul was changed from a persecutor to a believer when he directly encountered Jesus Christ, and Christians today still experience the transforming power of an encounter with Jesus.

Goals for the Learners:
(1) to examine the story of Saul's transformation from a persecutor to a believer when he saw a vision of Jesus Christ.
(2) to relate the radical nature of Paul's transformation to their own lives.
(3) to live as those who have been transformed by Christ.

Pronunciation Guide:
Ananias (an uh ni' uhs)

Supplies:
Bibles, newsprint and marker, paper and pencils, hymnals

NOVEMBER 6

READING THE SCRIPTURE

NRSV
Acts 9:3-18

³Now as he was going along and approaching Damascus, suddenly a light from heaven flashed around him. ⁴He fell to the ground and heard a voice saying to him, "Saul, Saul, why do you persecute me?" ⁵He asked, "Who are you, Lord?" The reply came, "I am Jesus, whom you are persecuting. ⁶But get up and enter the city, and you will be told what you are to do." ⁷The men

NIV
Acts 9:3-18

³As he neared Damascus on his journey, suddenly a light from heaven flashed around him. ⁴He fell to the ground and heard a voice say to him, "Saul, Saul, why do you persecute me?"

⁵"Who are you, Lord?" Saul asked.

"I am Jesus, whom you are persecuting," he replied. ⁶"Now get up and go into the city, and you will be told what you must do."

who were traveling with him stood speechless because they heard the voice but saw no one. [8]Saul got up from the ground, and though his eyes were open, he could see nothing; so they led him by the hand and brought him into Damascus. [9]For three days he was without sight, and neither ate nor drank.

[10]Now there was a disciple in Damascus named Ananias. The Lord said to him in a vision, "Ananias." He answered, "Here I am, Lord." [11]The Lord said to him, "Get up and go to the street called Straight, and at the house of Judas look for a man of Tarsus named Saul. At this moment he is praying, [12]and he has seen in a vision a man named Ananias come in and lay his hands on him so that he might regain his sight." [13]But Ananias answered, "Lord, I have heard from many about this man, how much evil he has done to your saints in Jerusalem; [14]and here he has authority from the chief priests to bind all who invoke your name." [15]But the Lord said to him, "Go, for he is an instrument whom I have chosen to bring my name before Gentiles and kings and before the people of Israel; [16]I myself will show him how much he must suffer for the sake of my name." [17]So Ananias went and entered the house. He laid his hands on Saul and said, "Brother Saul, the Lord Jesus, who appeared to you on your way here, has sent me so that you may regain your sight and be filled with the Holy Spirit." **[18]And immediately something like scales fell from his eyes, and his sight was restored. Then he got up and was baptized.**

[7]The men traveling with Saul stood there speechless; they heard the sound but did not see anyone. [8]Saul got up from the ground, but when he opened his eyes he could see nothing. So they led him by the hand into Damascus. [9]For three days he was blind, and did not eat or drink anything.

[10]In Damascus there was a disciple named Ananias. The Lord called to him in a vision, "Ananias!"

"Yes, Lord," he answered.

[11]The Lord told him, "Go to the house of Judas on Straight Street and ask for a man from Tarsus named Saul, for he is praying. [12]In a vision he has seen a man named Ananias come and place his hands on him to restore his sight."

[13]"Lord," Ananias answered, "I have heard many reports about this man and all the harm he has done to your saints in Jerusalem. [14]And he has come here with authority from the chief priests to arrest all who call on your name."

[15]But the Lord said to Ananias, "Go! This man is my chosen instrument to carry my name before the Gentiles and their kings and before the people of Israel. [16]I will show him how much he must suffer for my name."

[17]Then Ananias went to the house and entered it. Placing his hands on Saul, he said, "Brother Saul, the Lord—Jesus, who appeared to you on the road as you were coming here—has sent me so that you may see again and be filled with the Holy Spirit." **[18]Immediately, something like scales fell from Saul's eyes, and he could see again. He got up and was baptized.**

UNDERSTANDING THE SCRIPTURE

Acts 9:1-2. The first glimpse of Saul was as a minor assistant to those stoning Stephen (Acts 7:58–8:1). Saul was an observer, but also one who approved of the execution. In the space of a few weeks (or months) Saul transformed into a persecutor of the Christians. As the ninth chapter opened, Saul was on the road with violence in mind. His determination was to ferret out believers. He obtained letters of introduction from the high priest so that he could inquire into the affairs of the synagogues in

Damascus. Saul had no authority to interfere in synagogue politics other than the authority to return to Jerusalem those of questionable beliefs and practices. Although Luke described him as "breathing threats and murder," he was relatively powerless: a petty officer in a grand inquisition. Luke's intention, however, was to paint this man as an enemy. Saul's violence against the church set the context for divine intervention. What follows is perhaps the most dramatic passage in all of Scripture. Luke sets the parameters of that drama by an exaggeration of Saul's power, by a declaration of believers as followers of "The Way," and by an ominous threat hanging over the text. Those who are on "The Way" know that they are walking with Jesus, who called himself the way and frequently demonstrated choices between deeds leading to life and deeds leading to perdition (see Matthew 7:13-14). These Christians understood that Jesus suffered and that following in his footsteps included personal risk and danger. However, as the disciples could not understand Jesus' message about his suffering prior to the actual event (Luke 18:31-34), those who followed Jesus were only beginning to glimpse the meaning of their personal "way of suffering."

Acts 9:3-9. Luke's story of Saul on the road to Damascus is replete with scriptural clues. If we fail to attend to these clues, we diminish the text's impact. Therefore, let us consider how Scripture interprets Scripture. First, Luke modeled the whole experience as an appearance of God (a theophany) to a prophet; the bright light was the first clue (see Ezekiel 1:4 and following; Daniel 10:6). Saul responded appropriately; when in the presence of God, mortals fall to the ground. Saul was a Pharisee and well-versed in Scripture; he knew the signs of the power of God. Next, Saul heard his name, repeated twice, another indication of a holy calling (see Genesis 22:11, "Abraham, Abraham"; Genesis 46:2, "Jacob, Jacob"' Exodus 3:4, "Moses, Moses"). Thus Saul responded

with the question, "Who are you, Lord?" The intention is unclear: Was Luke emphasizing the irony of the man who would soon understand Jesus as Lord or was he merely demonstrating Saul's cautious approach to the divine? The divine voice explained concisely: "I am Jesus, whom you are persecuting." The message was powerful, for although Saul was not persecuting Jesus, he was searching for his followers. He glimpsed Jesus' identity within his followers. Then the voice gave a specific direction: Saul was to get up and go to the city (Damascus); there he would learn the next steps. Saul's companions on the road were bewildered; they heard the voice, but saw no speaker. Moreover, now Saul was blind and it was necessary to lead him by the hand down the road to Damascus. The impact of the vision and audition was so profound that Saul sat in darkness, neither eating nor drinking for three days—a symbolic reference to Jesus' own three days of darkness.

Acts 9:10-18. Meanwhile, another devout Jew received a vision. Luke continues the allusions to Old Testament accounts of God's call. Ananias, apparently without hesitation, recognized God's voice and responded, "Here I am, Lord" as had Abraham in Genesis 22:1-2; Moses in Exodus 3:4; and Samuel in 1 Samuel 3:4. Four facts were presented: Saul's name, his birth city, the address where he was staying, and his actual circumstance. Ananias questioned God; why go to an enemy of the church? God did not waver; indeed, God explained that Ananias must heal Saul because Saul was God's chosen instrument. The one who previously persecuted the church was God's choice to expand the witness of the church in Jerusalem to the ends of the earth. Ananias's fear and suspicion vanished as a result of God's surprising announcement. Without further questions, Ananias left on his mission. When he entered the house, he addressed the blind man as "Brother." For Ananias, Saul was already accepted, appointed, and approved for ministry. Ananias explained his share in God's mission: He was there to heal according to the will of God, to open the way for the Holy Spirit, and to baptize Saul in the name of Jesus. The real purpose of his visit, however, was to assist Saul into his new ministry. Saul was healed, gifted, and commissioned for ministry in community with those he once persecuted. Like a little child, the blind man was brought to the Lord by a fearless disciple. A change had begun for Saul, for the church, and for the world.

Acts 9:19-31. Luke moves the story forward with the use of the word "immediately," a word usually associated with a believer's response to a miracle. In this case, the miracle was that Saul, who sought out Christians in the synagogues, was now truly able to see God's will and began preaching Christ in the synagogues. As his preaching gained power and persuasiveness, a second reversal transpired. Saul the persecutor become preacher became the preacher persecuted! As the situation in Damascus grew more dangerous, those who formerly feared this man arranged for his escape. Since many homes were built into the wall of the city, a window was the escape route and by a basket Saul was lowered to freedom. This once powerful man, for the third time in this story, was reduced to absolute dependence on others. However, there was still another instance of Saul's dependence on the community; as he arrived in Jerusalem, the church refused him hospitality. They believed neither his conversion nor his call; one member, however, Barnabas, took him in. The witness of Barnabas granted acceptance to Saul within the Jerusalem church. Again, the Jewish leaders plotted against Saul and again, the church arranged for his safety. Throughout this tale, Saul received from the church healing, guidance, education, and security. He offered on their behalf a bold verbal witness to Jesus and modeled humility as he followed the community on "The Way."

INTERPRETING THE SCRIPTURE

The Call of God

The story of the conversion of Saul is dramatic, well known, and inspiring. As such it is also a story that has a "life of its own." Sermons, plays, paintings, and monologues are based on these few verses. Usually, the approach is highly speculative and emphatically personal. Quite likely, Luke told the tale with aims exactly opposite to contemporary use. Luke's interest is in the building up of the church, rather than the character reformation of an individual. Luke's desire is to demonstrate the irresistible progress of the faith, rather than to document the turnabout of one in opposition to the faith. There is a great temptation to focus on Saul to the exclusion of the greater concern of the growth and development of the church. In this session, direct your thoughts first to the church and second to the individual, Saul.

The context for Saul's call is the season of persecution. This was a time when the Christians were tempted to slip into fear. Leaders were arrested, imprisoned, executed, or exiled; the community was harassed by slander and economic boycott. The only secure time was the house meeting for prayer and even there some wondered about the commitments of new believers. Every response was justified, but every fear dampened the fire of the Holy Spirit. Fear and faithfulness cannot live side by side. God's Spirit sought freedom and by the conversion and call of Saul that freedom was granted. Indeed, the relationship between the church in Damascus and Saul was an enactment of Jesus' teaching: love your enemies.

The beginning of this changed relationship occurred on the road to Damascus. By a brilliant light and a divine voice, Saul was prepared to become God's messenger for Jesus. He did not understand what was happening; he only knew, by the brightness of the light and the holy ring of the voice, that he was face to face with God. Saul was a zealous Jew, a Bible-literate Jew, and a man who understood the meaning of being on a mission. God gathered those qualities and reduced them to nothing. The light blinded Saul; he could not see. The voice, silenced Saul; he did not know what to say. The experience left him exhausted. He was led into the city where he lay, neither eating nor drinking for three days. The impact of the call reduced Saul to a shadow of his former self.

The Darkness

Have you ever been in darkness—in the thick, dense darkness of a cave, for example? There you cannot see your hand in front of your face or the shadowy outline of your fellow spelunker. That is the darkness into which Saul sank. He was a man bereft of all that formerly gave him confidence. He was dependent on others to lead him from room to room. He could not check the sun to know the time of day. If he still had the letters of introduction, he could not read them and reassure himself of the importance of his mission. And, he had much to ponder.

In his vision, he heard and saw Jesus. It was an odd, totally unexpected confrontation. Jesus only announced himself as the object of Saul's persecution and gave him directions to go and wait. Enemies usually don't act that way; enemies have zeal for the destruction of the other. Enemies are not interested in a relationship with the other. But this "enemy" was different. Saul pondered that difference. Perhaps you've had the opportunity to ponder your relationship with an enemy. One of the blessings of being in opposition to another is insight.

Frequently, our enemies know us as truly as do our friends. Sometimes the insight of enemies is keener; if we are wise, our enemies teach us about ourselves by their opposition precisely at our points of ignorance, arrogance, and blindness. That's how Jesus worked on Saul in his blindness. He offered Saul an opportunity to know himself apart from all the "props" that usually supported him. In the darkness Saul was no longer a zealous Pharisee on a murderous mission; he was simply a man confronted and called by God who had to prepare his response. For three days, Saul worked on this one issue: Who was he to Jesus?

Another Call of God

Some are called in bursts of light for missions too magnificent to disclose; others are called to undertake small tasks of discreet faithfulness. Saul was called to a missionary's life of danger; Ananias was called to enter one house and offer God's grace to one man. There was a difference of scale in each call, but each call was absolutely necessary. Ananias's response was a demonstration of confident trust in God. Remember, the context of persecution meant that the congregation was pressed by fears. Someone needed to step over the fear; in this story, that someone is Ananias. He already knew about Saul; he knew the trouble he had caused for Christians in Jerusalem; he knew that Saul was coming to Damascus with the intention of seeking out the Christians and returning them to Jerusalem for trial before the Jewish authorities. Ananias had every right and reason to fear Saul, but in the vision God discounted all such fears. Ananias was informed: Saul is my choice and you will help him. Then, God disclosed one more fact to Ananias: Saul was not only God's choice, but Saul's future included suffering. This part of the message rang with Christ-like authenticity. As the community was straining to live faithfully in a season of persecution, so Saul would also suffer in his divinely appointed task. Saul who once was an enemy would become a true brother, but how? By following the Spirit's direction exactly as Ananias followed. Regardless of where the Spirit led, to an enemy's house to heal or to a missionary's journey to preach, the early Christians recognized and supported one another as brothers and sisters of their suffering Lord. Ananias followed without hesitation.

The Light

Ananias is a model disciple. He completed his divinely appointed task with an undivided heart. Notice his obedient actions: He laid his hands on Saul. This was both an act of blessing and the touch of the Holy Spirit; Ananias did not hesitate before his former enemy. Next, he addressed Saul as "Brother." Earlier he had referred to Saul as "this man" in a manner similar to that of the elder son in the parable of the prodigal dissociating himself from his brother with the words "this son of yours" (Luke 15:30). Ananias demonstrated solidarity with the weakness of Saul. Then, Ananias explained the truth of their new relationship: The Lord Jesus appeared to both. Each was called to this particular moment: Saul entered through the darkness of dependence and Ananias through obedience to a difficult (however modest) commission to greet and heal. Ananias was an ordinary man who performed an extraordinary service for the Lord. He stands as a beacon to all who follow Jesus that ministry is more than a calling to an office or status; ministry is an obedient "doing" for the Lord. By Ananias's deed, the light dawned for Saul, for the community in Damascus, and throughout the church.

SHARING THE SCRIPTURE

PREPARING TO TEACH

Preparing Our Hearts

This week's devotional reading is found in Acts 9:23-31, which is part of our background reading. Saul's zealousness in proclaiming Jesus as the Son of God soon prompted those who opposed him to hatch a plot against his life. With the help of friends, Saul escaped from Damascus and went to Jerusalem, where Barnabas befriended him. Once again Saul's life was threatened as a result of his ardent preaching. This time, Saul was sent to Tarsus. Yet, the church was continuing to grow in Judea, Galilee, and Samaria, despite the hardships Jesus' followers endured. Saul paid dearly for his encounter with the Lord on the Damascus road. What has discipleship cost you?

Pray that you and the adult learners will be open to truth as it is revealed to you and be willing to share it with others, no matter what the cost.

Preparing Our Minds

Study the background, Acts 9:1-31, and lesson Scripture, Acts 9:3-18, to discern the kind of intervention that can bring about a radical change in the direction of one's life.

Write on newsprint:
❏ the three options under "Examine the Story of Saul's Transformation from a Persecutor to a Believer When He Saw a Vision of Jesus Christ."
❏ information for next week's lesson, found under "Continue the Journey."

Plan a brief lecture based on the information in Acts 9:1-2, as found in Understanding the Scripture, for "Examine the Story of Saul's Transformation from a Persecutor to a Believer When He Saw a Vision of Jesus Christ."

LEADING THE CLASS

(1) Gather to Learn

❖ Welcome the class members and introduce any guests.

❖ Pray that the students will be changed by an encounter with the risen Christ.

❖ Read aloud this information: **Nicky Cruz left his family's home in Puerto Rico at the age of 15 to live with his brother in New York. Within six months of joining the Mau Maus, a notorious gang on the streets of Brooklyn, Nicky had become their warlord. Priding himself on the gang's senseless violence, Nicky spurned Reverend David Wilkerson when this audacious preacher tried to tell Nicky that God loved him. Going to a church meeting with the intent of disrupting it, Nicky found God in such a powerful way that the next day this feared warlord turned over to the police all of his guns and knives. A changed teen, Nicky studied, eventually became a preacher, and continues to minister through T.R.U.C.E. (To Reach Urban Children Everywhere), an organization he runs that brings the good news to gang members and others who need to know that God loves them.**

❖ Note that Nicky's story is recounted in his own book *Run, Baby, Run* and Wilkerson's book *The Cross and the Switchblade.* Class members who have read either of these books may want to add details to the story you have read.

❖ Provide reflection time for the students to consider how dramatic changes occur in people's lives. Invite volunteers to state their ideas.

❖ Read aloud today's focus statement: **Sometimes people need a radical change in the direction of their lives. What kind of intervention can bring that kind of change? Saul was changed from a persecutor to a believer when he directly encountered Jesus Christ, and Christians today still experience the transforming power of an encounter with Jesus.**

(2) Examine the Story of Saul's Transformation from a Persecutor to a Believer When He Saw a Vision of Jesus Christ

❖ Set the stage for today's Scripture study by giving a brief lecture based on the information in Acts 9:1-2, as found in Understanding the Scripture.

❖ Choose volunteers to read the parts of the narrator, Saul, Jesus/Lord, and Ananias in Acts 9:3-18.

❖ Invite the students to select one of the following options, which you will need to read aloud or post on newsprint.

■ **Option 1:** Distribute paper and pencils. Ask the students to write a news account of the Damascus road experience as if they were one of the men traveling with Paul. What did this man see, hear, or think?

■ **Option 2:** Invite several students to role-play the conversation between God and Ananias. This activity goes beyond what is written in the Bible so that Ananias can question God further about Saul.

■ **Option 3:** Encourage some students to create a liturgical dance/movement demonstrating Saul's response after he was baptized.

Provide an opportunity for students to comment on any insights they gleaned from their experiences with this Scripture.

(3) Relate the Radical Nature of Saul's Transformation to the Learners' Lives

❖ Encourage the students to talk with the class, or a small group, about life-changing experiences they have had that drew them closer to Christ. These experiences need not be "Damascus road" events, but possibly they occurred during some transition point in life, such as an illness, a death in the family, or a financial or career crisis.

❖ Wrap up this time of sharing stories by asking these questions.

(1) **Saul thought he was doing God's will when an experience with the living Christ changed him. In what ways have your own experiences transformed you into a more faithful disciple?**

(2) **Saul truly suffered as a result of his transformation, just as God said he would (Acts 9:16). In what ways have the transforming experiences in your own life led to some kind of suffering?**

(4) To Live as Those Who Have Been Transformed by Christ

Read aloud this quotation found in *Seeking a Purer Christian Life: Sayings and Stories of the Desert Mothers and Fathers.* **Abba Lot went to see Abba Joseph and said to him, "Abba, as far as I can, I say my little office; I fast a little; I pray and meditate; I live in peace; and as far as I can, I purify my thoughts. What else can I do?" Then the old man stood up and stretched his hands toward heaven. His fingers became like ten lamps of fire, and he said to him, "If you will, you can become all flame."**

Encourage those students who are able to stretch their hands upward as you again read the last sentence.

Invite the students to meditate on this question: **If your life were so transformed by Jesus Christ that you were truly on fire for him, how would your actions and attitudes be different than they are today?**

(5) Continue the Journey

❖ Break the silence of meditation by praying that the students will not only encounter Jesus but also open themselves to his transforming power so that the fire in their lives will draw others to our Lord.

❖ Read aloud this preparation for next week's lesson. You may also want to post it on newsprint for the students to copy. **Prepare for next week's session, entitled "Offering of Oneself," by reading Acts 16, particularly verses 6-15. As you study, consider these ideas: People committed to God have a need to offer service to others and to God. How can that commitment be expressed? In Lydia's case, the Lord prompted her to offer hospitality and service to Paul.**

Read aloud the following three ideas. Challenge the students to commit themselves to use these activities as a springboard to spiritual growth.

(1) **Think about the image of scales falling from Saul's eyes (Acts 9:18, key verse). Recall an experience in which your spiritual sight became much keener. How were you transformed as a result of this experience?**

(2) **Ask the Holy Spirit to help you examine your heart and mind. Are there habits, relationships, or attitudes that are not in keeping with God's will? If so, pray that the Holy Spirit will prompt you to make any necessary changes.**

(3) **Identify someone who needs guidance or help in some other way. How can you be like Ananias to this individual? What steps will you take this week?**

❖ Sing or read aloud "Have Thine Own Way, Lord."

❖ Lead this benediction to conclude the session: **May the Holy Spirit empower you to be witnesses for Jesus Christ in your community, in your nation, and to the ends of the earth. Amen.**

UNIT 3: TO THE ENDS OF THE EARTH
OFFERING OF ONESELF

PREVIEWING THE LESSON

Lesson Scripture: Acts 16:6-15
Background Scripture: Acts 16
Key Verse: Acts 16:15

Focus of the Lesson:
People committed to God have a need to offer service to others and to God. How can that commitment be expressed? In Lydia's case, the Lord prompted her to offer hospitality and service to Paul.

Goals for the Learners:
(1) to learn about Lydia, her conversion, and her hospitality.
(2) to identify ways they can offer hospitality and service.
(3) to make a commitment to serve others.

Pronunciation Guides:
Bithynia (bi thin' ee uh)
Derbe (duhr' bee)
Galatia (guh lay' shuh)
Macedonia (mas uh doh' nee uh)
Mysia (mis' ee uh)
Neapolis (nee ap' uh lis)
Phrygia (frij' ee uh)
Samothrace (sam' uh thrays)
Thyatira (thi uh ti' ruh)
Troas (troh' az)

Supplies:
Bibles, newsprint and marker, paper and pencils, hymnals, map, optional magazines (especially news magazines), scissors, glue, paper

---

READING THE SCRIPTURE

NRSV

Acts 16:6-15

⁶They went through the region of Phrygia and Galatia, having been forbidden by the

NIV

Acts 16:6-15

⁶Paul and his companions traveled throughout the region of Phrygia and

Holy Spirit to speak the word in Asia. [7]When they had come opposite Mysia, they attempted to go into Bithynia, but the Spirit of Jesus did not allow them; [8]so, passing by Mysia, they went down to Troas. [9]During the night Paul had a vision: there stood a man of Macedonia pleading with him and saying, "Come over to Macedonia and help us." [10]When he had seen the vision, we immediately tried to cross over to Macedonia, being convinced that God had called us to proclaim the good news to them.

[11]We set sail from Troas and took a straight course to Samothrace, the following day to Neapolis, [12]and from there to Philippi, which is a leading city of the district of Macedonia and a Roman colony. We remained in this city for some days. [13]On the sabbath day we went outside the gate by the river, where we supposed there was a place of prayer; and we sat down and spoke to the women who had gathered there. [14]A certain woman named Lydia, a worshiper of God, was listening to us; she was from the city of Thyatira and a dealer in purple cloth. The Lord opened her heart to listen eagerly to what was said by Paul. [15]When she and her household were baptized, she urged us, saying, **"If you have judged me to be faithful to the Lord, come and stay at my home."** And she prevailed upon us.

Galatia, having been kept by the Holy Spirit from preaching the word in the province of Asia. [7]When they came to the border of Mysia, they tried to enter Bithynia, but the Spirit of Jesus would not allow them to. [8]So they passed by Mysia and went down to Troas. [9]During the night Paul had a vision of a man of Macedonia standing and begging him, "Come over to Macedonia and help us." [10]After Paul had seen the vision, we got ready at once to leave for Macedonia, concluding that God had called us to preach the gospel to them.

[11]From Troas we put out to sea and sailed straight for Samothrace, and the next day on to Neapolis. [12]From there we traveled to Philippi, a Roman colony and the leading city of that district of Macedonia. And we stayed there several days.

[13]On the Sabbath we went outside the city gate to the river, where we expected to find a place of prayer. We sat down and began to speak to the women who had gathered there. [14]One of those listening was a woman named Lydia, a dealer in purple cloth from the city of Thyatira, who was a worshiper of God. The Lord opened her heart to respond to Paul's message. [15]When she and the members of her household were baptized, she invited us to her home. **"If you consider me a believer in the Lord,"** she said, **"come and stay at my house."** And she persuaded us.

UNDERSTANDING THE SCRIPTURE

Acts 16:1-10. In the sixteenth chapter of Acts we find individuals whose lives intersect with the Apostle Paul. The flow of serving and being served, of offering and receiving hospitality, of being safe and in danger provides the spiritual momentum. As the chapter opened, Paul was on a return visit to the churches previously organized. In Derbe, Paul met Timothy, a young man who is the personification of the diversity of the first-century church. His grandmother and

mother were Jewish converts to Christianity; his father was a Gentile who has prohibited Timothy from full membership in the nation Israel by disallowing his circumcision. Therefore, a young man who should have been (but was not) a Jew was converted to Christianity as a Gentile (not a Jew). Paul evidently saw a leader for the whole church in Timothy. But, in order for him to labor side-by-side with Paul, Timothy had to be circumcised. Paul's rationale was practical; circumcision had nothing to do with Timothy's relationship to God. If Timothy were to enter synagogues to preach and to teach, he must do so as a Jew who followed Jesus. Then, as though the reader required a reminder, Luke affirmed Paul's mission was under the direction of the Holy Spirit. First, Paul was prohibited entrance into the western region of Asia Minor; later, he was directed by a personal and intimate vision to come to Macedonia and help. Luke's point was clear: God is in charge of leadership, the destination, and the way church growth occurs.

Acts 16:11-15. Beginning with the tenth verse and continuing through the seventeenth verse, the narrator's voice shifts: The "we passages," ninety-seven verses in all, are found in Acts 16:10-17, 20:5-15, 21:1-18, and 27:1–28:16. Scholars have no explanation for this shift in voice. Suggestions include:

- Luke was Paul's traveling companion for a brief time.
- Luke was using another source, such as a travel diary.
- Luke's rhetorical style was designed to increase interest.

Regardless of the identity of the "we," Paul, Silas, and, probably, Timothy entered Philippi, a Roman colony without a significant Jewish population. Since the first-century missionary pattern began at a synagogue, Paul and Silas followed directions to a place outside the city where Jews and God-fearers worshiped. They left the city to find the prayer place; in a Roman colony proselytizing a religion other than the official Roman cult was illegal. When they found a collection of women (apparently Philippi lacked ten Jewish men to constitute a Sabbath service), Paul sat down, assuming the posture and authority of a visiting rabbi, and taught the women about God's Messiah, Jesus. Lydia, a Gentile God-fearer, was present. She was a homeowner and a businesswoman who likely dealt exclu-

sively with the most privileged class. Although Paul taught all the women, God opened Lydia's heart to the gospel. The scene concluded with a baptism of everyone in Lydia's household and her offer of hospitality to the missionaries. Once again Luke draws the connection between conversion and material resources: Under Lydia's influence, the congregation in Philippi grew close to Paul and was afforded a secure home for worship.

Acts 16:16-24. Paul and Silas continued their mission at a prayer site outside the city. Nothing was hidden from the people of Philippi; the missionaries could be seen coming and going. Indeed, a young slave girl, with a spirit of divination, began to follow Paul and Silas about announcing their status of "slaves of the Most High God." Surely this was confusing; some hearing the girl's announcement thought that Paul and Silas represented Zeus, known as "the Most High God." Hoping to sidetrack a controversy, Paul exorcised the spirit from the slave girl. Silence momentarily ensued; however, the girl's owners calculated their economic loss. Breathing threats against Paul and Silas in particular and the Jewish people in general, these slave owners dragged Paul and Silas before the city magistrates as they held court in the marketplace. They presented these charges to the magistrates:

- Paul and Silas were disturbing the peace;
- they were Jews; and
- they promoted foreign (religious) practices.

Paul and Silas were guilty of only one charge: They were Jews. Otherwise, they were peaceful and respectful in the Roman colony; their teaching occurred outside the city gate, and a noisy slave girl caused the only disturbance. The crowd sided with the slave owners, adding their fists to the flogging and their voices to the humiliation of Paul and Silas. The city magistrates concluded the day by marching the Jews off to prison.

Acts 16:25-40. Confident of God's providence, Paul and Silas, with feet locked in stocks, prayed and sang hymns that evening. At midnight, an earthquake loosened chains and crumbled walls. The jailor, certain to lose his life if he failed to keep the prisoners secure, prepared to commit suicide, but Paul and Silas called out to him. With fear and trembling the jailor fell before the missionaries asking: "What must I do to be saved?" It is likely that his question was prompted by actual fear, rather than theological inquiry. Nonetheless, Paul and Silas responded to him faithfully: They explained the way to life abundant and eternal through faith in Jesus. Their testimony so moved the jailor that he took them to his home, washed their wounds, fed them, and presented them to his entire household. Joy abounded. In response, Paul and Silas baptized the members of the household. The next day, the orders came for the prisoners' release; Paul refused a quiet release. He announced (for the first time we are aware of) his Roman citizenship and insisted upon a formal apology. After this was granted, the two returned to Lydia's house to encourage the newly formed community of faith. Then, they departed. Much transpired in Philippi; there Timothy was exposed to Paul's conduct of ministry; a Gentile woman gave shelter to the believers and eventually became a leader of the house church of Philippi; a slave girl was freed of an oppressive spirit, causing her greedy owners to plot against the missionaries; a jailor and his household converted and showed mercy to prisoners. The church was growing!

INTERPRETING THE SCRIPTURE

Closed Doors, Open Doors

Serving as the organizing pastor for a new congregation was a great adventure in my ministry. The connection to the Holy Spirit was dynamic and challenging. But one disappointment was so great that some despaired of God's providence over the congregation. The land purchased for the development of a church facility was placed under a temporary restriction; we could not build until the restriction was lifted. It was a heavy disappointment prompting this question: Was the Holy Spirit in the decision of the city council? The restriction was in place for nine months; during that time the congregation continued to grow and mature. When the door was opened to develop the church property, the congregation was stronger and the facility constructed supported a greater vision. A closed door allowed a young congregation time to mature; the open door resulted in a wider blessing for the community. Such experiences—whether in personal or church life—resonate with Paul's ministry. He hoped to enter Asia Minor, but was called instead to Macedonia. Being sensitive to the Spirit's guidance includes accepting doors that are closed as well as doors that are open.

Not only did Paul deal with closed and open doors, but leadership issues also were always before him. Wherever he went, he measured the leadership capacities of recent converts. Believers from these new communities needed to be "fast tracked" into leadership. In this lesson, Paul traveled to Philippi, a chief city in Macedonia. With him is his colleague, Silas, an experienced church leader. Likely, these two men were accompanied by a leader-in-training, Timothy. As the stories of the sixteenth chapter of Acts unfold, imagine their impact on the young man Paul had selected as one of the next generation of church leaders.

A Closed City

God opened a door to a closed city. Philippi was not a city with deep roots; when Paul and Silas arrived it was slightly less than four hundred years old. However, being situated on the major trade and military route between Asia and the West, it was an important Roman colony. Philippi boasted a forum, a library, a theater, baths, and two temples. The population of the city was mixed, as were the religious persuasions; residents were indigenous Greeks and relocated Italians. Excavations have revealed significant archeological finds that supply helpful information for our understanding of Paul's missionary work in Philippi.

The text states that Paul and Silas went outside the city, to a place of prayer located beside a river. Archeologists determined that an arch stood on the Via Egnatia in close proximity to the River Gangites. This arch may indicate a boundary line establishing empty space surrounding the city. This buffer zone was actually a prohibition for all foreign religions and strange cults; the space ensured that non-Roman religions would not infect the residents of the city. Thus it may be that the place of prayer where Paul and Silas met the women worshipers was a mile west of the city in the only acceptable area for Jewish worship and teaching. Such was the open door God provided Paul.

Regardless of the restrictions, Paul proceeded through the open door of the closed city of Philippi. His example is the stunning witness of a Spirit-led missionary. Where God directs, Paul goes, even though indications of success are dismal. Imagine, two passionate missionaries walk a mile on a Sabbath morning and find . . . a collection of Gentile women. Is this any way to begin a new congregation? Paul and Silas shrugged their shoulders, accepted God's providence, and sat down to teach the women. It is an amazing scene when viewed closely.

An Open Heart

Luke could have offered details about that first meeting outside the city. He could have narrated the search for the proper group—imagine Paul and Silas dropping in on various prayer circles seeking for the one directing prayers to the God of Israel. Or Luke could have included a list of all the women present or the text of Paul's sermon. Luke chose, however, to share one detail: Lydia was there. Luke described Lydia as a worshiper of God, indicated her status as a God-fearer, and noted that she was from the city of Thyatira in Lydia. Lydia's city of birth is mentioned to assure the audience that this Gentile woman had the opportunity to know the religion of Israel from an authorized source, a Jewish community of the Diaspora. The second fact about Lydia was her occupation: a dealer in purple cloth. Her business required significant capital; purple dyed cloth was the most expensive material available. It was produced in the region of Lydia and exported throughout the Roman world specifically for use by the most wealthy and royal classes. Lydia, as a dealer in purple cloth, related to the most powerful leaders of the Roman colony of Philippi. She herself was probably wealthy, educated, and socially prominent.

The most prominent characteristic of Lydia, according to Luke, was neither her cultural/religious heritage nor her occupation. It was, rather, her eager listening. As is often the case in the stories Luke tells, the one who is eager and listening hears the gospel. As the Ethiopian eunuch, Cornelius's friends and family, and the Samaritans had listened and were turned toward God, so God opened Lydia's heart to the gospel. The power of the Holy Spirit was surely with Paul and Silas as they shared their faith, but it was also with Lydia as she heard and received their testimony. Her open heart initiated a relationship with these men that eventually led to the baptism of her entire household. She was not only the first woman named as a convert, she also was destined to become much, much more to Paul and Silas.

An Open Home

How do you measure the depth of conversion? Is faithful attendance in worship sufficient? What about compassionate service to others? Does conversion ignite a passion for spiritual inquiry and growth? Is the converted heart characterized by joy or peace or hope? Surely, all of these and more are signs of the Spirit's work in recently (and not so recently) converted Christians. Luke, however, has one standard of measurement: How does the convert manage personal resources? Generosity with money, possessions, and place of residence indicated authenticity of conversion. Can you imagine such a standard being applied in our contemporary churches? Imagine, three months after new members are received into membership a church officer arrives with the stated intention of examining financial records dating from prior to and subsequent to a public confession of faith in Jesus Christ. No, it would not happen; moreover, it probably did not happen in the early church. Nonetheless, Christians were characterized by generosity and unofficially, at least, the use of personal possessions and resources bore witness to faith. Lydia's heart was opened; in response, she opened her home to Paul and Silas.

This was a dramatic deed in a city that required foreign religions to practice their faith a mile from the city boundary. However, Lydia had connections. She was known, respected, and trusted by the elite of Philippi; she used her status to offer her home as a sanctuary for the missionary work of Paul and Silas. Their work resulted in a community that reflected the joy and generosity of the original patroness, Lydia. The congregation was a great source of support, financial and emotional, for Paul throughout his ministry. The most intimate of all his letters—and also the most joyful— Paul wrote from prison to the Philippians' congregation. From an open heart and an open home, the Spirit blessed Paul's work as it began in Macedonia.

SHARING THE SCRIPTURE

PREPARING TO TEACH

Preparing Our Hearts

This week's devotional reading is found in Acts 16:25-34, which is part of our background Scripture. This familiar passage recounts the story of Paul and Silas in jail in Philippi when a violent earthquake opened the doors of the prison. Instead of escaping, Paul and Silas used this miraculous moment to minister to the jailer, and later to his family, so that they might become believers. The salvation of the jailer's household would not have occurred had Paul and Silas not been willing to serve others at the expense of their own safety and freedom. What have you—or are you willing—to risk or sacrifice in order to tell the good news to those who need to hear it?

Pray that you and the adult learners will be willing to use even the most difficult circumstances of your own lives to witness for Christ.

Preparing Our Minds

Study the background, which is Acts 16, and lesson scripture, verses 6-15. As you study, be aware of how people can express their commitment to God, especially through service and hospitality.

Write on newsprint:

❑ litany for the "Make a Commitment to Serve Others" portion.

❑ information for next week's lesson, found under "Continue the Journey."

Have the supplies you will need if you plan to do the suggested photo album readily available for use.

LEADING THE CLASS

(1) Gather to Learn

❖ Welcome the class members and introduce any guests.

❖ Pray that the participants will be open to the leading of the Holy Spirit as we consider our commitment to God, as expressed through service to others.

❖ Ask the students to imagine that they have been invited to a dinner party at a friend's home. Encourage them to discuss their expectations regarding the hospitality and service they will receive. They may also want to express how they might feel if such hospitality were not offered.

❖ Read aloud today's focus statement: **People committed to God have a need to offer service to others and to God. How can that commitment be expressed? In Lydia's case, the Lord prompted her to offer hospitality and service to Paul.**

(2) Learn About Lydia, Her Conversion, and Her Hospitality

❖ Read aloud Acts 16:6-10.

■ Use a map to trace the route that Paul, Silas, and Timothy took from Phrygia to Troas. Locate Macedonia, especially the city of Philippi.

■ Invite the students to recount "Macedonia visions" they may have had, that is, times when they had made sound plans but then believed that God was leading them in a different direction. Encourage them to talk about how they knew that God

was calling them to act and how they responded.

❖ Note that the next portion of the lesson, verses 11-15, are one of the sections in Acts known as "we passages." See Understanding the Scripture for Acts 16:11-15 for further information.

❖ Read aloud Acts 16:11-15.

■ Head a sheet of newsprint with two columns: *What we know about Philippi* and *What we know about Lydia*. Invite the students to use the information from the text to flesh out these two columns.

■ Use the information for verses 11-15 in the Understanding the Scripture portion to enlarge the list.

■ Discuss these questions.

(1) **Keeping in mind that Lydia was obviously a prominent businesswoman, what effect do you think her acceptance of Christ and baptism might have had on others?** (Note that she was the first known convert in Europe.)

(2) **What does her urging of Paul and his friends to stay at her home suggest about Lydia?**

(3) **How might Lydia act as a role model for us?**

3) Identify Ways the Learners Can Offer Hospitality and Service

❖ Help the students to think about who needs hospitality or service by using one of the following options.

■ **Option 1:** Set out old magazines, scissors, glue, and paper. Invite each student to select one photo showing persons in need of hospitality/service. Encourage the participants to think globally (for example, refugees, victims of famine), locally (for example, those who do not have adequate food or shelter, those who are sick), and across genders and age levels (children who may be victims of abuse, those who are unemployed, elderly who are lonely). Ask the adults to glue the selected picture onto a sheet of paper. Invite the participants to discuss why they have selected the pictures they have for the class's photo album. You may wish to put all of the pictures in a binder, as an album.

■ **Option 2:** Divide the class into three groups and give each group a marker and sheet of newsprint. Ask one group to brainstorm groups of people who need hospitality/service globally; a second group to think about those who are in need of hospitality/service locally; and a third group to consider needs across genders and age levels. (See Option 1 for ideas.) Provide time for the groups to tell their ideas to the entire class.

❖ Invite the students to work together to name projects within the church or community that they could participate in to offer hospitality and service to some of the people they have already identified.

(4) Make a Commitment to Serve Others

❖ Distribute paper and pencils to each learner. Ask them to complete this sentence using ideas they have gleaned from the previous discussion: **As the Spirit of God leads and empowers me, I will offer myself in service to others by....**

❖ Invite the students to read aloud this litany, which you will have written on newsprint prior to class.

> **GROUP 1:** You have told us, O God, what is good
>
> **GROUP 2:** and what you require of us.
>
> **GROUP 1:** We are to do justice, love kindness,
>
> **GROUP 2:** and to walk humbly with you, our God.
>
> **ALL:** We offer ourselves to you now as we commit ourselves to do that which you have laid upon our

hearts so that your justice and loving kindness will reach to the ends of the earth. Amen.

(5) Continue the Journey

❖ Read aloud this preparation for next week's lesson. You may also want to post it on newsprint for the students to copy. **Prepare for next week's session, entitled "Working Together in Ministry," by reading Acts 18:1–19:10. Our session will focus on Acts 18:1-4, 18-21, 24-28. As you engage the Scripture, keep these ideas in mind: People need to work together to do God's work. What models of team ministry do we have? Acts describes how Aquila and Priscilla, mentored by Paul, learned to minister to others as a team.**

❖ Read aloud the following three ideas. Challenge the students to commit themselves to use these activities as a springboard to spiritual growth.

(1) **Identify someone to whom you could offer a meal, a place to stay, or some other form of hospitality and extend an invitation.**

(2) **Choose a local project that you could participate in, such as cooking for a soup kitchen, acting as a host in a homeless shelter, providing information to travelers at an airport, or working with a hospice. Make a commitment to offer yourself to the project of your choice.**

(3) **Volunteer to perform service in your congregation. Select a committee or project that makes good use of your God-given talents.**

❖ Sing or read aloud "Lord, I Want to Be a Christian."

❖ Lead this benediction to conclude the session: **May the Holy Spirit empower you to be witnesses for Jesus Christ in your community, in your nation, and to the ends of the earth. Amen.**

UNIT 3: TO THE ENDS OF THE EARTH

WORKING TOGETHER
IN MINISTRY

PREVIEWING THE LESSON

Lesson Scripture: Acts 18:1-4, 18-21, 24-28
Background Scripture: Acts 18:1–19:10
Key Verse: Acts 18:3

Focus of the Lesson:
People need to work together to do God's work. What models of team ministry do we have? Acts describes how Aquila and Priscilla, mentored by Paul, learned to minister to others as a team.

Goals for the Learners
(1) to discover how people of various trades, gifts, and skills ministered to others.
(2) to explore modern examples of team ministry.
(3) to develop a plan for engaging in an act of ministry together.

Pronunciation Guide:
Achaia (uh kay' yuh)
Aquila (ak' wi luh)
Cenchreae (sen' kruh ee)

Supplies:
Bibles, newsprint and marker, paper and pencils, map, hymnals

---

READING THE SCRIPTURE

NRSV
Acts 18:1-4, 18-21, 24-28

¹After this Paul left Athens and went to Corinth. ²There he found a Jew named Aquila, a native of Pontus, who had recently come from Italy with his wife Priscilla, because Claudius had ordered all Jews to leave Rome. Paul went to see them,

NIV
Acts 18:1-4, 18-21, 24-28

¹After this, Paul left Athens and went to Corinth. ²There he met a Jew named Aquila, a native of Pontus, who had recently come from Italy with his wife Priscilla, because Claudius had ordered all the Jews to leave Rome. Paul went to see

³and, because he was of the same trade, he stayed with them, and they worked together—by trade they were tentmakers. ⁴Every sabbath he would argue in the synagogue and would try to convince Jews and Greeks.

¹⁸After staying there for a considerable time, Paul said farewell to the believers and sailed for Syria, accompanied by Priscilla and Aquila. At Cenchreae he had his hair cut, for he was under a vow. ¹⁹When they reached Ephesus, he left them there, but first he himself went into the synagogue and had a discussion with the Jews. ²⁰When they asked him to stay longer, he declined; ²¹but on taking leave of them, he said, "I will return to you, if God wills." Then he set sail from Ephesus.

²⁴Now there came to Ephesus a Jew named Apollos, a native of Alexandria. He was an eloquent man, well-versed in the scriptures. ²⁵He had been instructed in the Way of the Lord; and he spoke with burning enthusiasm and taught accurately the things concerning Jesus, though he knew only the baptism of John. ²⁶He began to speak boldly in the synagogue; but when Priscilla and Aquila heard him, they took him aside and explained the Way of God to him more accurately. ²⁷And when he wished to cross over to Achaia, the believers encouraged him and wrote to the disciples to welcome him. On his arrival he greatly helped those who through grace had become believers, ²⁸for he powerfully refuted the Jews in public, showing by the scriptures that the Messiah is Jesus.

them, ³and because he was a tentmaker as they were, he stayed and worked with them. ⁴Every Sabbath he reasoned in the synagogue, trying to persuade Jews and Greeks.

¹⁸Paul stayed on in Corinth for some time. Then he left the brothers and sailed for Syria, accompanied by Priscilla and Aquila. Before he sailed, he had his hair cut off at Cenchrea because of a vow he had taken. ¹⁹They arrived at Ephesus, where Paul left Priscilla and Aquila. He himself went into the synagogue and reasoned with the Jews. ²⁰When they asked him to spend more time with them, he declined. ²¹But as he left, he promised, "I will come back if it is God's will." Then he set sail from Ephesus.

²⁴Meanwhile a Jew named Apollos, a native of Alexandria, came to Ephesus. He was a learned man, with a thorough knowledge of the Scriptures. ²⁵He had been instructed in the way of the Lord, and he spoke with great fervor and taught about Jesus accurately, though he knew only the baptism of John. ²⁶He began to speak boldly in the synagogue. When Priscilla and Aquila heard him, they invited him to their home and explained to him the way of God more adequately.

²⁷When Apollos wanted to go to Achaia, the brothers encouraged him and wrote to the disciples there to welcome him. On arriving, he was a great help to those who by grace had believed. ²⁸For he vigorously refuted the Jews in public debate, proving from the Scriptures that Jesus was the Christ.

UNDERSTANDING THE SCRIPTURE

Acts 18:1-17. In this lesson, we see Paul working as a missionary with forming congregations and overhear his hopes for future work. He is on his second missionary trip and has come to Corinth, which is a likely site for evangelization. Corinth, a provincial capital and a major commercial center in Greece, was built on an isthmus over which cargo was transported between the Aegean and Adriatic Seas. The city's diverse population included a large colony of about forty thousand Jews. The text also provides a general date: The expulsion of certain Jews from Rome by Claudius began in A.D. 49. The expulsion was prompted by the "constant disturbances at the instigation of Chrestus" (Christ), the probable group being Roman Christians who caused disputes within the Jewish community. Furthermore, since Nero rescinded Claudius's order when he came to power in A.D. 54, we can date Paul's missionary work in Corinth to the early A.D. 50s. Upon his arrival, Paul began missionary efforts with the synagogue, established a tentmaking practice with the deportees from Rome, Aquila and Priscilla, and was soon embroiled in arguments with a significant opposition within the synagogue.

Once Silas and Timothy arrived with the collected funds from Macedonia, the ministry expanded; for a while Paul devoted himself to full-time evangelical work. However, resistance among the Jews led to a division of the synagogue. Some members left with Paul, Silas, Timothy, Priscilla, and Aquila to establish a house church next door to the synagogue in the home of Titius Justus, a Gentile God-fearer; even the leader of the synagogue joined the Christians next door. Paul was aware of the difficulties that were ahead; by a vision, he was strengthened to face those difficulties. However, when the synagogue leaders attempted to expose Paul as the leader of a "new religion"—rather than a "reform movement" within Judaism—the proconsul dismissed the charges as frivolous. By this brief incident, Luke indicated that the Roman government would not become involved in an internal religious dispute about which it had neither authority nor interest.

Acts 18:18-23. Paul's approach to missionary work had two phases. First came the actual preaching and teaching of the gospel, always beginning with the synagogue and usually continuing with Jews and Gentile God-fearers. Paul also developed leaders for the congregation; when he departed the mission continued as a self-directing congregation. The second phase of missionary work was the follow-up visit. Paul returned to these young congregations to encourage the leaders, to assist with difficult moral issues, and to offer further instruction. Luke's brief description of Paul's return visit to these congregations stressed the importance of the Spirit's direction of Paul's work. For example, as Paul left Corinth, he paused in Ephesus and promised to return. The Spirit once again held open a door and Paul once again hoped he would enter as an evangelist. Although Paul's relationship with the synagogue in Corinth had ended badly, he continued his practice of sharing the gospel in a synagogue before preaching to a wider audience. Although self-described as a "missionary to the Gentiles," Paul apparently took a Nazarite vow (see Numbers 6:1-21) to purify himself before worshiping God at the temple in Jerusalem. Paul remained a Jew throughout his life: he participated in temple worship, worshiped on the Sabbath in a synagogue, and taught as a rabbi of Israel. At the center of his faith, however, was Jesus, the one sent by God to usher in the season of divine favor.

Acts 18:24-28. Luke's next sketch suggests the rich diversity of ministries conducted during the missionary phase. First we meet an impressive orator, Apollos. He was an Alexandrian Jew, influenced by the sophisticated Alexandrian Jewish scholars renowned for a type of allegorical interpretation relating Torah to Hellenistic cultural values. Apollos spoke with beauty, authority, and, according to the text, with enthusiasm (a burning spirit); however, Priscilla and Aquila sensed a deficiency. Although Apollos understood the Scriptures and accurately testified to Jesus as God's Messiah, he knew only John's baptism of repentance. He had not moved from repentance to new life. This couple, a husband and wife with a shared ministry, privately took the spirited preacher aside and gave him a fuller understanding of Christian faith and practice. Their training was, evidently, effective; Apollos was encouraged by the Ephesian congregation to begin a mission in Achaia. There his efforts proved to be both faithful and successful.

By way of another small detail, Luke displayed an important aspect of congregational life: the leadership of women. With the exception of the first reference, whenever the missionary couple from Rome was mentioned, Priscilla's name came first. This probably signified her leadership and authority was greater in the community than that of her husband, Aquila. The witness of women in the early church has long been disputed; there are as many voices disclaiming the significance of women as there are affirming their ministries. Women leaders were as counter-cultural as community property and Jews sharing table fellowship with Gentiles. Every counter-cultural activity was criticized, defended, maligned, and changed as the church grew into a more organized institution; not surprisingly, the witness of women changed from the first to the second century. Still, Luke's testimony stands: Priscilla was a leader and a teacher.

Acts 19:1-10. As missionaries' paths crossed, various teachers visited the new congregations. When Paul returned to Ephesus, he followed the path of Apollos only to discover that the error that Priscilla and Aquila had corrected was still rooted among some believers. As Paul interviewed these believers, he discovered that they had more in common with disciples of John the Baptist than with Jesus' disciples. Those who had accepted "John's baptism" understood their need for repentance; they had turned to God and reformed their ethics. Moreover, they understood that Jesus was the Messiah; however, they did not understand that his lordship both required and offered a unique spiritual dimension. The requirement was, of course, baptism in the name of Jesus and the offering was, of course, the Holy Spirit. As Paul taught the twelve disciples, they recognized the truth he presented. They were baptized and as Paul laid his hands upon them, the Holy Spirit graced them with the spiritual manifestation of speaking in tongues and edifying speech (prophecy). Paul continued his missionary work in Ephesus for about two years; he taught in the synagogue, debated in a public forum, the Hall of Tyrannus, and made the gospel of Jesus broadly known throughout the region.

INTERPRETING THE SCRIPTURE

A Focused Ministry

The unfolding story of Acts is a testimony to the Holy Spirit. Although difficulties abound, grace opens unnoticed doors and provides exceptionally gifted leaders. When Paul arrived in the city of Corinth, the Spirit's providence was evident in the gift of two mature Christians, Aquila and Priscilla. This couple was from a Diaspora synagogue in Rome and Aquila was a tentmaker. What better companions for Paul? It is easy to imagine this Christian couple opening their modest home—after all, they were religious refugees—to a brother in the Lord. The morning hours were devoted to tentmaking; surely testimonies were exchanged as they stitched and stretched the leather and fabric. In the afternoon, while the city rested, the trio visited with the members of the synagogue and held informal teaching assemblies in the synagogue or homes of interested Jews. On the Sabbath, Paul would be invited to teach in the synagogue or debate during an open teaching time. As a rabbi, Paul found spiritual grace in working at a skill that engaged his hands; honest labor freed him for honest teaching without another's financial control. The ministerial trio of Paul, Priscilla, and Aquila worked and witnessed together; their everyday conduct of life was their approach to "new church development." Their ministry revealed Jesus through everyday events and encounters. By such an ordinary witness, something extraordinary came into existence: the Corinthian congregation.

An Itinerant Ministry

The focused ministry, however, soon reverted to the itinerant ministry. Paul was not a restless individual incapable of staying in one place; he was a Spirit-led individual who understood that God's mission was greater than any one location. After a period of mutual ministry with Priscilla and Aquila, Paul left to visit some of the congregations he had previously organized. This trip was intended to encourage and support leaders, but also to foster a sense of connection among the congregations. From the very beginning, the church of Jesus Christ faced the temptation of isolation. Congregations always need prophets, preachers, evangelists, and itinerant pastors to strengthen ties that bind the whole church together. In his commentary *Acts: The Gospel of the Spirit*, Justo González discusses the necessity of a connectional relationship among the churches by listing the consequences of failing to be connected. In summary these are:

- Personal belief in Jesus takes precedence over the church's mission and ministry—"I can be a Christian without the church."
- The church becomes a means of satisfying individual needs—"If I don't like what is going on at the church on a particular Sunday, I'll drop out."
- The church becomes a matter of taste; believers become "spiritual tourists" seeking ever-new forms of diversion.
- It is easy to separate from an "optional" church: "If disagreement begins, I'll find another church home."
- Divided churches debate internal issues and cease to witness to Christ; the unity that Christ taught and for which Christ prayed has not a tangible presence in the world.

By Paul's attention to his relationship with his former congregations, the history of the early church outlines our contemporary issues. As we struggle to hold together when disagreements, disappointments, and divisions erupt, so the early Christians were tempted to "go it on their own." But, an itinerant pastor, whose heart was full of love for many congregations, knew their relationship had to be unified and maintained. Therefore, Paul returned to teach, preach, pastor, and counsel the congregations he established. As he did so, he crafted lines of communication, channels of mutual support, and a vision of the unity of all believers in Christ. His itineration was as necessary as his focused ministry for the development of the early church.

An Error in Ministry

Luke frequently creates small windows in his narrative. As we stand gazing through those windows, a much richer, more diverse ministry emerges. He doesn't pretend to tell everything about the church and its development during the first century. In the first volume of his work, the Gospel According to Luke, Luke explained his work as an orderly account to assure Theophilus of the truth in his religious instruction. A similar guideline persists in Acts; however, this book so full of action and drama (and so little known compared with the Gospels) presents such richness that it is difficult to imagine the wealth of untold tales. Nonetheless, there were many more tales that Luke could have recorded. Many missionaries went out from congregations in Judea; Christians fleeing political and religious oppression became witnesses to new communities in foreign cultures. Early congregations were nourished by a remarkable stew spiced with the dynamics of a Spirit-led community, the relatively brief history of Christian witness, and the human tendency toward cultural adaptation, self-preservation, and idolatry. The results were at times remarkable—and at times heretical. The error displayed in Acts 18:24-28 was Luke's open window on the spicy diversity of the early church experience. Through that window we see: (1) the preaching of a message derived from John the Baptist, but lacking a full confession of Jesus Christ; (2) the power of rhetoric in the service of heresy; (3) the wisdom of quiet correction rather than public argument in matters of faith; (4) the willingness of the community to trust its leaders; and (5) the necessity of balancing enthusiasm with correct teaching. Without the formal supports of written guidelines (for example, the four Gospels), a centralized school for leadership training (colleges, seminaries, and lay training institutes), or an official church structure (a council of elders or bishops and overseers) it is amazing the church held onto authentic faith. The diversity glimpsed through the window, especially the errors that led to heresy, however, was guided and corrected by a greater power: the Holy Spirit.

A Spirit-filled Ministry

When did you receive the Holy Spirit? How has that gift from God been manifest in your life? Are you aware of your spiritual gifts? Do you doubt the vibrancy of your faith? Have you ever grieved the Holy Spirit? When we are honest, our understanding of the Holy Spirit is one of the most problematic aspects of Christian faith. We are taught that the gift of the Holy Spirit is for all Christians. We know that the Holy Spirit is sensed, rather than intellectually apprehended. Yet, we slip down opposite sides of the Holy Spirit issue by assuming too much at times and disclaiming too much at other times. We are frequently confused, sometimes arrogant, and often humbled in our awareness of the work of the Holy Spirit among us. Perhaps this is because our view is too narrow and much too personal.

Acts' singular message boldly announces the Spirit is in charge of the growth, witness, and development of the church. The leaders led in response to the Spirit's direction. Congregations grew by the Spirit's confirmation. Ethical and social choices were determined after prayer and the Spirit's consensus. On page after page, visions and dreams, sermons and lessons, prayers and patient waiting demonstrated the close guidance of the Holy Spirit in the early church. Why is the Spirit so evident in Acts and so distant from our lives in the church? Perhaps because we, unlike the earliest Christians, are more interested in our personal spiritual experience than in God's great spiritual deeds through the church. Humbly, Acts helps us confess: The Holy Spirit enlivens the whole church, not just our particular corner.

SHARING THE SCRIPTURE

PREPARING TO TEACH

Preparing Our Hearts

This week's devotional reading, which is found in Luke 10:1-11, tells the familiar story of Jesus sending out the seventy in mission. Note that they worked in teams of two to accomplish the purposes for which Jesus sent them. How have you worked with a team to minister by, with, and for others? Write about at least one positive experience in your spiritual journal.

Pray that you and the adult learners will strive, by the power of the Holy Spirit, to work together in community so as to help spread the good news to the ends of the earth.

Preparing Our Minds

Study the background from Acts 18:1–19:10, and lesson Scripture, Acts 18:1-4, 18-21, 24-28. As you do your preparatory Scripture reading, be alert for models of team ministry that you find in this week's lesson.

Write on newsprint:

❑ six ideas found in "Characteristics of Powerful Ministry Teams" in the "Explore Modern Examples of Team Ministry" section.

❑ information for next week's lesson, found under "Continue the Journey."

LEADING THE CLASS

(1) Gather to Learn

❖ Welcome the class members and introduce any guests.

❖ Pray that each one who has come today will be open to the whispering of the Holy Spirit in their own lives.

❖ Encourage the students to recall a time when they worked with a highly effective team or group. This might have been a sports team, a group at work, a community group, a social organization, or some other kind of group. Ask them to answer this question: **What are the marks of a team that can accomplish its mission effectively?** List their ideas on newsprint, and leave the paper posted.

❖ Read aloud today's focus statement: **People need to work together to do God's work. What models of team ministry do we have? Acts describes how Aquila and Priscilla, mentored by Paul, learned to minister to others as a team.**

(2) Discover How People of Various Trades, Gifts, and Skills Ministered to Others

❖ Study Acts 18:1-4.

■ Choose a volunteer to read these four verses.

■ Locate on a map the cities mentioned.

■ Read or retell the first paragraph in the Understanding the Scripture portion, Acts 18:1-17, to provide information about Corinth and the reason Aquila and Priscilla were there.

■ Note that in this stage of Paul's ministry he had two vocations: tentmaker (leather worker) and evangelist. Ask the class to comment on why they believe Paul would have chosen to work two vocations.

❖ Consider Acts 18:18-21.

■ Distribute paper and pencils. Ask the students to read this passage silently and to write down any questions that occur to them about it.

■ Discuss the students' questions.

■ Use the map again to trace Paul's journey.

❖ Examine Acts 18:24-28.

■ Post three sheets of newsprint headed "Apollos," "Aquila and Priscilla's Influence on Apollos," and "Apollos's Ministry After Working with Aquila and Priscilla." After reading the passage aloud, invite the students to call out ideas to list on each sheet. Or, divide into three groups and ask each group to work with one heading.

■ Look back at the ideas brainstormed earlier in the session. Identify any parallels you see between your ideas and the ways that the people in today's lesson worked together.

■ Wrap up the Bible study by discussing this question: **What lessons in teamwork can you glean from the way the early Christians we have studied today worked together?**

(3) Explore Modern Examples of Team Ministry

❖ Present the following information, summarized from "Characteristics of Powerful Ministry Teams" by Chuck Allen, to the students, either on newsprint or in a brief lecture. According to Allen, six characteristics consistently describe teams that work effectively in ministry:

(1) **A common purpose or task that all the team members are committed to achieving.**

(2) **Well-defined roles that allow the**

team members to effectively divide and do the necessary work.

(3) Christ-centered leadership that is accepted by the team.

(4) Effective processes that are understood and embraced by all the team members.

(5) Solid relationships based on interdependence and mutual accountability.

(6) Clear, fast, accurate communications among the group members.

❖ Invite the students to note committees or other groups within your congregation (or other churches) where these characteristics seem to be operative. Talk about how these characteristics aid a group.

(4) Develop a Plan for Engaging in an Act of Ministry Together

❖ Divide the class into teams of four to six adults. Give each team a sheet of newsprint and a marker. Ask them to take the following steps:

(1) Identify a social justice issue or marginalized group needing some kind of ministry.

(2) Brainstorm ideas that you could use to create a team-based ministry that would address at least one of the needs you have identified.

(3) Develop a plan of action for meeting these needs as a team. The plan should include: what you will do, for whom, with whom, by when, at what cost, and how you will evaluate the merit of the project.

(4) Make whatever plans are necessary to meet outside of class and fulfill your goals.

❖ Allow time for each of the teams to report on their goal and the reasons they made their choices.

❖ Invite the students who are willing to make a commitment to repeat these words after you: **I will work together with my partners in ministry to . . . (add here what the groups said they would do).**

(5) Continue the Journey

❖ Pray that the participants will continue to grow in their ability to work effectively together as team players focused on furthering the reign of God.

❖ Read aloud this preparation for next week's lesson. You may also want to post it on newsprint for the students to copy. **Prepare for next week's session, entitled "Saying Good-bye," by reading Acts 20:17-38. Our session will focus on verses 17-28, 36-38. As you study the lesson, consider these ideas: People who care for one another feel great sadness when they must part permanently. What can help us get through these painful experiences? We have an example in Paul, who prayerfully helped the elders at Ephesus say good-bye to him.**

❖ Read aloud the following three ideas. Challenge the students to commit themselves to use these activities as a springboard to spiritual growth.

(1) **Think about your ministry, as well as that of people you know. Describe how several of you are using "secular work" (paid or volunteer) to minister to others.**

(2) **Recall a time when you were a member of a team. Write in your journal about that experience. What were the positive aspects? What were the negatives? How did you work together to overcome problems?**

(3) **Identify at least one person who you could mentor in the faith. Review the story of Apollos, Priscilla, and Aquila to glean ideas about how to help and encourage others in their faith and ministry.**

❖ Sing or read aloud "O Church of God, United."

❖ Lead this benediction to conclude the session: **May the Holy Spirit empower you to be witnesses for Jesus Christ in your community, in your nation, and to the ends of the earth. Amen.**

UNIT 3: TO THE ENDS OF THE EARTH
SAYING GOOD-BYE

PREVIEWING THE LESSON

Lesson Scripture: Acts 20:17-28, 36-38
Background Scripture: Acts 20:17-38
Key Verse: Acts 20:28

Focus of the Lesson:
People who care for one another feel great sadness when they must part permanently. What can help us get through these painful experiences? We have an example in Paul, who prayerfully helped the elders at Ephesus say good-bye to him.

Goals for the Learners:
(1) to overhear Paul's farewell and his friends' reactions.
(2) to identify some of the "sad good-byes" that they might experience.
(3) to identify and express gratitude for sources of support during such times.

Pronunciation Guide:
Miletus (mi lee' tuhs)

Supplies:
Bibles, newsprint and marker, paper and pencils, map, hymnals, optional art supplies such as clay, pipe cleaners, or crayons/colored pencils

---

READING THE SCRIPTURE

NRSV
Acts 20:17-28, 36-38

[17]From Miletus he sent a message to Ephesus, asking the elders of the church to meet him. [18]When they came to him, he said to them:

"You yourselves know how I lived among you the entire time from the first day that I set foot in Asia, [19]serving the Lord with all humility and with tears, enduring the trials that came to me through the plots of the Jews. [20]I did not shrink from doing anything

NIV
Acts 20:17-28, 36-38

[17]From Miletus, Paul sent to Ephesus for the elders of the church. [18]When they arrived, he said to them: "You know how I lived the whole time I was with you, from the first day I came into the province of Asia. [19]I served the Lord with great humility and with tears, although I was severely tested by the plots of the Jews. [20]You know that I have not hesitated to preach anything that would be helpful to you but have taught you pub-

NOVEMBER 27

helpful, proclaiming the message to you and teaching you publicly and from house to house, [21]as I testified to both Jews and Greeks about repentance toward God and faith toward our Lord Jesus. [22]And now, as a captive to the Spirit, I am on my way to Jerusalem, not knowing what will happen to me there, [23]except that the Holy Spirit testifies to me in every city that imprisonment and persecutions are waiting for me. [24]But I do not count my life of any value to myself, if only I may finish my course and the ministry that I received from the Lord Jesus, to testify to the good news of God's grace.

[25]"And now I know that none of you, among whom I have gone about proclaiming the kingdom, will ever see my face again. [26]Therefore I declare to you this day that I am not responsible for the blood of any of you, [27]for I did not shrink from declaring to you the whole purpose of God. [28]**Keep watch over yourselves and over all the flock, of which the Holy Spirit has made you overseers,** to shepherd the church of God that he obtained with the blood of his own Son.

[36]When he had finished speaking, he knelt down with them all and prayed. [37]There was much weeping among them all; they embraced Paul and kissed him, [38]grieving especially because of what he had said, that they would not see him again. Then they brought him to the ship.

licly and from house to house. [21]I have declared to both Jews and Greeks that they must turn to God in repentance and have faith in our Lord Jesus.

[22]"And now, compelled by the Spirit, I am going to Jerusalem, not knowing what will happen to me there. [23]I only know that in every city the Holy Spirit warns me that prison and hardships are facing me. [24]However, I consider my life worth nothing to me, if only I may finish the race and complete the task the Lord Jesus has given me—the task of testifying to the gospel of God's grace.

[25]"Now I know that none of you among whom I have gone about preaching the kingdom will ever see me again. [26]Therefore, I declare to you today that I am innocent of the blood of all men. [27]For I have not hesitated to proclaim to you the whole will of God. [28]**Keep watch over yourselves and all the flock of which the Holy Spirit has made you overseers.** Be shepherds of the church of God, which he bought with his own blood.

[36]When he had said this, he knelt down with all of them and prayed. [37]They all wept as they embraced him and kissed him. [38]What grieved them most was his statement that they would never see his face again. Then they accompanied him to the ship.

UNDERSTANDING THE SCRIPTURE

Acts 20:17-24. With characteristic style, Luke signals a change in the direction and purpose of Paul's ministry. The opening of chapter 20 deals with Paul's last visit to Greece; again his preaching inspired faith as well as incited resistance. He set sail with the hope of being in Jerusalem for the Jewish celebration of Pentecost, a festival that held a rich significance for his brothers and sisters in the church. His ship did not stop at the port of Ephesus, but because of a message, the Ephesian elders met Paul in Miletus. This message was more of a summons than an invitation. The meeting between Paul and the representatives from the church in Ephesus was not casual; attendance and spiritual preparation was expected. The meeting was the occasion for

Paul's farewell speech. This is Act's only record of Paul's direct teaching and counsel with Christians; all other speeches in Acts were before nonbeliever audiences ranging from keenly interested to greatly offended. Here, Paul speaks formally but intimately with those who studied with him, labored for the gospel beside him, and looked to Paul for spiritual guidance in all matters, but especially in matters relating to the church. There are three parts to the speech:

- Paul's faithfulness to his ministry and his spiritual empowerment.
- Paul's transfer of gospel ministry to the elders.
- Paul's final commendation and blessing for the leaders.

In the speech, Paul stressed the openness and accountability of his ministry. He described his work among the Ephesians as steadfast and helpful; he ascribed his accomplishments to the guidance and power of the Holy Spirit. Especially noting that suffering always accompanied his ministry, he stated that his captivity to the Spirit perfected his only hope: to finish his ministry as a testimony to God's grace in Jesus. Paul's labor for the Lord was difficult, fruitful, and Spirit-held; he spoke as a man without regret.

Acts 20:25-31. As Luke described the transfer of leadership he emphasized the finality of Paul's decision. Paul's statement that the elders would never again see his face set the context for the transition. He was not talking about his death; Paul did not set his face, as Jesus did, toward Jerusalem to encounter persecution and death. Rather, Paul was intensely aware of the next mission. Paul's face was set toward Jerusalem because from there a new mission (to Rome) began. Paul's comments were bold; he declared an end to his responsibility for the spiritual nurture of the elders and he affirmed their knowledge of the whole purpose of God. Just as Jesus appealed to his disciples in the Garden of Gethsemane, so Paul appealed to these elders: Keep watch and be alert. Paul's daily spiritual diet was danger and suffering;

therefore, he commanded the elders to be vigilant. He asserted their responsibility to pastor in imitation of the Good Shepherd Jesus. Paul described the wolves from within the flock; these were probably "the Judaizers," Christians who continued to rely on Jewish spiritual practices to ensure a relationship with God. Paul also warned of wolves attacking from outside the flock; perhaps he was referring to Hellenistic philosophical systems such as Gnosticism. Paul's words were voiced as imperatives. Nothing had more importance for the leaders than the safety of the flock. And nothing was more expensive. God purchased the flock's security with the blood of his own. Notice that this sentence is variously completed. In the NIV, God's "own blood" may have multiple meanings but in any case is unclear as it stands. The NRSV adds the word "Son" specifying the ultimate sacrifice of Jesus on the cross.

Acts 20:32-35. Paul's speech provoked strong emotions. The leaders now understood that this was a final meeting, that they had full responsibility for the congregation, and that gospel ministry required vigilance before dangers within and without the community. With the two words "and now," the tone of the speech shifted. The suffering, the dangers, the trials and the tribulations for the Lord were set to the side as a pastor talked about practical and mundane issues. The final commendation was a simple reminder: Conduct yourself as you have seen me conduct myself. Paul's illustrations came from the ethics of mutuality: Do not covet; work with your hands to earn your living; use your resources to support the weak. By these examples, Luke connected the congregation in Ephesus to the original charter of the Jerusalem congregation: "All who believed were together and had all things in common; they would sell their possessions and goods and distribute the proceeds to all, as any had need" (Acts 2:44-45). Once again, Luke stressed that spiritual maturity had specific economic consequences. With an imaginative flair, Paul's speech concluded with a saying of Jesus not recorded in the Gospels. This beloved quotation evidently was written on the hearts of believers: "It is more blessed to give than to receive."

Acts 20:36-38. After all was said, something must be done. Luke's attention to the details of the parting reminds us of the importance of actions—practical, symbolic, and ritual. These church leaders who had shared so much would not depart from one another without prayer. But, they had to demonstrate to each other (and to themselves) that this prayer was different from all other prayers they shared. They did something physical and practical: They knelt in prayer, a posture that indicated a solemn vow or a deeply felt emotion. Then,

the emotions rose up. The symbolic gestures of embracing and kissing were ordinary blessings when friends separated; these gestures became symbols softened by tears. This was truly the last touch and symbolized the depth of love that bound these men together. One last deed was yet to be accomplished: Paul had to board the ship and take his leave. With the purposefulness of a ritual procession, the elders escorted Paul to the ship. They accompanied him as far as possible; then, they released him. Their journey together was filled with faith and fire, sadness and suffering, joy and jubilation; all that belonged to the past. As Paul sailed south, the church leaders turned north. They would not meet again, but their spiritual unity was sure to endure.

INTERPRETING THE SCRIPTURE

When It Is Time to Part

The closure depicted in this lesson is familiar to all church members: A pastor and a congregation say good-bye. There are literally hundreds of ways such endings occur; however, the story of Paul's final meeting with the church leaders from Ephesus presents an issue contemporary Christians will never face. This was the first generational transition. Although not a disciple of Jesus and, therefore, not an eyewitness to his ministry, Paul was an apostle by order of the whole church. When an apostle left, the whole church was bereft of an intimate connection to Jesus; yet new leaders accepted the situation with courage. They held onto the apostles' teachings. By a gentle, yet firm touch, the process of apostolic succession began. It was neither formal nor ritualized, yet each farewell to an apostle was, literally, a once in a lifetime event. As contemporary Christians trace roots back to the church of the apostles, we acknowledge this apostolic succession despite the many fractures

within the church of Jesus Christ. However, for these elders, Paul was their root connection to Christ. Because they held onto his teaching, their congregation continued to be nourished by the authority of the apostles.

Captive to the Spirit

Was Paul thinking about the prophet Jeremiah as he meditated in preparation for his farewell speech? Jeremiah, the weeping prophet, endured great physical suffering in his prophetic career; in that way he and Paul are similar. Jeremiah faced resistance from his own people, from religious authorities and from political powers; that's another similarity. Jeremiah also experienced a burning spiritual passion he could not resist; this is the most obvious similarity. The fire shut up in Jeremiah's bones became his witness just as the Holy Spirit inspired Paul's final speech. Truly, these men demonstrate the meaning of being "captive to the Spirit." In Paul's speech, the fire of the Spirit produced hope and confidence as well as passionate preaching. The Holy Spirit led Paul to places and people he could not have imagined. Through the Spirit, Paul learned patience as he began each evangelical outreach within the confines of a Jewish synagogue; there he was as frequently rejected as accepted. He learned collegial ministry as he found himself laboring beside men and women who were younger and older, Jewish and Gentile. He learned to listen to his dreams and to persevere with his prayers. He learned the everyday lessons of community life and the exceptional lessons of community turmoil. Wherever he went, whatever he did, his life was filtered through one reality: The Holy Spirit directed his gospel ministry. Finally he declared, "I do not count my life of any value to myself" (20:24)—his only goal was to complete his ministry and offer his unique testimony to Jesus. Paul's captivity to the Spirit brought him a final sense of peaceful purpose; he belonged to his Lord completely.

Watching Over the Flock

When a pastor leaves a flock, there is always a momentary concern: Will there be faithful leadership for the congregation? Whether a new pastor arrives immediately or a lengthy delay separates the time between pastors, congregations are equipped with leaders. Frequently, these leaders have a blessed opportunity to receive their new responsibilities and authority directly. That is what happens in this farewell speech: Paul hands over responsibility and authority to the elders from Ephesus. This transition is graceful, yet firm. Grace abounds as Paul acknowledges the spiritual maturity of the leaders. Have you ever noticed the tendency of contemporary leaders to notice their deficits rather than their attributes? Imagine having a beloved pastor shaking your hand while saying, "I've shared the whole purpose of God with you!" Surely, such knowledge is sufficient for the leadership challenges ahead. A grace we can offer to leaders is the grace of naming spiritual gifts—and further setting those within the whole purpose of God. As you greet your pastor or teacher following the next sermon or lesson, why not shake spiritual awareness as well as hands? Say something such as this: Your humor (or wisdom or compassion or leadership or meekness or courage or vulnerability) is just what God needs to redeem the world. When gifts are conscientiously named, grace abounds. This was part of Paul's formal speech: a graceful affirmation.

But Paul, who could catalogue the sufferings he endured for the Lord, was also firm with the new leaders. Their position was that of pastor; they were not to be preoccupied with status or standing; rather, their only preoccupation was the safety and security of their flock. This firm standard is also a spiritual blessing best known through experience. The pastor or church leader whose eyes are steadily focused on the needs of the congregation rarely feels distant from Jesus. The pastor or church leader whose eyes continually check the mirror, adjusting self-presentation and perfecting image, misses intimacy with the Lord. These self-absorbed leaders are looking in the wrong direction. Jesus promised to be among the community, with the weak and the lowly, and beside those who testify to the truth of God's great purposes. Jesus never promised an exclusive club composed of "Me and Jesus"—Jesus initiated a community able to hold a Holy Spirit. Within that community, some members were set aside as leaders with the singular duty of protecting the flock. These firm words established the responsibility and authority of the elders; it was a necessary part of the leadership transition.

A Faithful Farewell

The last words were spoken. There came a holy pause. Then, the elders and Paul knelt for prayer. They had experienced intense ministry with one another; they were deeply connected as brothers in the Lord; they were also full of poignant human emotions. The time had come for a faithful farewell, and a last walk was all that remained. In a similar fashion, we have come to the end of this study. Together we traced the outline of the early church from Pentecost through persecution, by apostolic leadership and accidental recruitment, with foreign tongues and peals of laughter. Our faithful farewell to the book of the Acts of the Apostles is rich with the stories we studied. But, hopefully, more remains than interesting encounters and difficult verses. These lessons are not only a testimony of the Spirit's guidance of the early church, but they are also the Spirit's guidance of the contemporary church. As you prepare to say farewell, consider: What has challenged your faith? What made you stop and ponder? What comforted you and what confused you? What is the Spirit's message to your congregation through Acts? This is something to pray about. It may be also something to weep about. As the elders escort Paul to the ship they make their faithful farewell. As you close this study of Acts and replace your notes and bookmarks, you also are saying farewell. Dear saints of the church, make your farewell to Acts faithful.

SHARING THE SCRIPTURE

PREPARING TO TEACH

Preparing Our Hearts

This week's devotional reading is found in Acts 20:31-35, which is part of our background Scripture. After warning the elders at Ephesus about the false teachers—"savage wolves"—that Paul expects will come when he is gone, he implores his hearers to "be alert" even as he commends them to God. Recall a mentor in the faith with whom you are no longer in contact. Which words and actions of this mentor had a profound impact on your life? Did he or she have any parting words of counsel for you that you still remember?

Pray that you and the adult learners will allow the good influence of the lives of other Christians to help guide you in God's holy path for living.

Preparing Our Minds

Study the background, Acts 20:17-38, and lesson Scripture, verses 17-28, 36-38. As you prepare this session think about how people get through the painful experience of saying good-bye to a loved one.

Write on newsprint:
❏ top ten factors on the Holmes-Rahe Stress Scale, as found in the "Gather to Learn" portion. You can find the complete list on the Internet if you choose to use it.
❏ information for next week's lesson, found under "Continue the Journey."

LEADING THE CLASS

(1) Gather to Learn

❖ Welcome the class members and introduce any guests.

❖ Pray that the participants will be led by the Holy Spirit as we consider examples of "sad good-byes" in the biblical story and in our lives.

❖ Post the newsprint on which you have written the highest ten factors from the Holmes-Rahe Stress Scale:

- Death of a spouse 100
- Divorce 73
- Marital Separation 65
- Jail term 63
- Death of close relative 63
- Personal injury or illness 53
- Marriage 50
- Fired from job 47
- Marital reconciliation 45
- Retirement 45

❖ Discuss which ones of these relate in some way to a good-bye. Try to identify why these good-byes are so stressful for most people. Encourage the students to name strategies for coping with these losses.

❖ Read aloud today's focus statement: **People who care for one another feel great sadness when they must part permanently. What can help us get through these painful experiences? We have an example in Paul, who prayerfully helped the elders at Ephesus say good-bye to him.**

(2) Paul's Farewell and His Friends' Reactions

❖ Use a map to locate Ephesus, where the church elders are, and Miletus, where Paul is staying. Note that both places are on the west coast of Asia Minor, by the Aegean Sea.

❖ Select two volunteers, one to read the narrator's part and the other to read the words of Paul, in Acts 20:17-28, 36-38. Ask the students to imagine themselves as the elders who are listening to Paul bid them farewell. After the reading, invite the students to describe their feelings as they realize that they will not see Paul again.

❖ Ask the students to look in their Bibles at Acts 20:18-24 and discuss these questions.

    (1) What does Paul say about himself?

    (2) What does he say about his ministry?

    (3) What examples can you think from the Scriptures to support Paul's statement? (Suggest that the students look back through Acts or at some of Paul's letters to find such examples.)

❖ Note that in verse 27, Paul asserts that he has proclaimed "the whole purpose of God." Divide the class into teams of three to four and give each team a sheet of newsprint and marker. Set a short time limit. Ask each team to list as many things as they think of to describe "the whole purpose of God." Call time. Either ask each team to report on what they have listed, or have the teams post their newsprint and provide time for the participants to circulate around the room to see what has been written. Wrap up this activity by inviting the students to suggest ways that they, both individually and as members of the church, can go about proclaiming "the whole purpose of God."

❖ Read again today's key verse, Acts 20:28. Discuss what "overseeing the flock" might have meant to the elders of Ephesus. Also talk about what it might mean in the contemporary church.

❖ Conclude this portion of the session with a time of silence. Ask the students to envision themselves accompanying Paul, or a beloved one they know, to the boat, knowing that they will never see this person again. Suggest that they think about what they would like to say as they part company.

(3) Identify Some of the "Sad Good-byes" the Learners Might Experience

❖ Refer to the Holmes-Rahe Stress Scale list. Invite the participants to add other difficult good-byes that people might experience. Write these ideas on the newsprint. Encourage the group to include in their list some good-byes specifically associated with the church, such as a pastor leaving, an active family moving away, or the death of a beloved member.

❖ **Option:** Recognize that many people have difficulty expressing in words the profound sorrow that they feel about a loss. Distribute malleable art supplies, such as clay or pipe cleaners, or crayons/colored pencils and paper. Invite the students to try to release their grief by using color (they need not draw any recognizable object) or molding a shape. Let the artworks themselves be a silent testimony to the sad good-byes that class members have experienced.

(4) Identify and Express Gratitude for Sources of Support During Such Times

❖ Distribute paper (or index cards) and ask the students to write one source of support that they felt as they had to say good-bye to a dear one. Ask them to use generic terms, such as "my daughter," rather than give a name.

❖ Collect these papers, shuffle them, and read them aloud as a litany to remind the class members that even under very painful circumstances they do have support. You can create the litany by telling the participants that their response is **"we give you thanks, O God."** Then begin by reading the first sheet and add, **"For this source of support..."** and cueing the class to respond.

(5) Continue the Journey

❖ Pray that the adults will recognize that God and others are present to offer love and support even during the most difficult good-byes.

❖ Read aloud this preparation for next week's lesson. You may also want to post it on newsprint for the students to copy. **Prepare for next week's session, entitled "Serving Others," by reading background Scripture from Isaiah 41–42 and focusing on Isaiah 42:1-8. As you study, keep these main ideas in mind: Injustices run throughout human relationships on both a** personal and a societal level. **What can help us continue to hope and work for justice despite the overwhelming reality of our experience? Isaiah promises that God will bring justice to the world.**

❖ Read aloud the following three ideas. Challenge the students to commit themselves to use these activities as a springboard to spiritual growth.

(1) **Call or visit a friend who may be terminally ill. Without being maudlin, let the person know how deeply you love and appreciate him or her. Offer words of encouragement.**

(2) **Remember a "sad good-bye" in your life. What were the circumstances? How did you cope? How did your faith and your church community help you to get through this difficult experience?**

(3) **Be a source of strength for someone who is facing a loss due to death, divorce, or separation. Do whatever you can to assist this person.**

❖ Sing or read aloud "God Be with You Till We Meet Again."

❖ Lead this benediction to conclude the session: **May the Holy Spirit empower you to be witnesses for Jesus Christ in your community, in your nation, and to the ends of the earth. Amen.**

SECOND QUARTER
God's Commitment—Our Response

DECEMBER 4, 2005–FEBRUARY 26, 2006

This winter we will explore God's redeeming acts of love and some appropriate responses that we can make to move toward spiritual wholeness. The lessons for the first unit of this quarter are based on passages from Isaiah and Luke. The remainder of the quarter focuses on three books collectively known as the Pastoral Letters: 1 Timothy, 2 Timothy, and Titus.

Unit 1, "God's Redeeming Love," looks at familiar prophecies from Isaiah, and Mary's *Magnificat* and Jesus' birth story in Luke, as we move through Advent to Christmas. We begin on December 4, the second Sunday in Advent, with a session entitled "Serving Others," based on Isaiah 41–42. Here we will see how God intends to bring about justice for all. On December 11 we move to Isaiah 49–50 to examine how those who are weary can gain "Strength from God." "Hope for Those Who Suffer," the session for December 18, looks at both Isaiah 53 and Luke 1 to discern how God offers hope. The unit concludes on Christmas Day with readings from Isaiah 61:1-3 and Luke 2:8-20. In this lesson entitled "Be Joyful" we hear again the good news of great joy that the shepherds heard as angels announced the Messiah's birth.

In Unit 2, "God's Gifts of Leadership," we will spend five weeks investigating 1 Timothy to understand how the development of gifts that God has given for leadership is part of our faithful response to God's love. "Finding Strength to Serve," the session for January 1, delves into 1 Timothy 1 to reassure us that we do not serve in our own strength but rather by the strength that God has given us for our appointed ministries. On January 8 we turn to 1 Timothy 2 to learn about several types of prayers, for "Everyone Needs Prayer." We explore 1 Timothy 3 on January 15 in a session entitled "Leading God's People" to discern the behaviors, attitudes, and traits of faithful leaders of God's people. "Set an Example," the lesson for January 22, looks at 1 Timothy 4 to discern the guidance that Timothy—and we—are given for teaching. The unit concludes on January 29 with directions on "Practicing Justice and Mercy," based on 1 Timothy 5.

During Unit 3, "Faithful Followers, Faithful Leaders," we will spend four weeks examining passages from 2 Timothy and Titus. The unit opens on February 5 with "A Heritage of Faith," based on 2 Timothy 1. This lesson calls us to look at those who have taught us the faith and urges us to be true to that heritage. "Pursue Righteousness," the lesson for February 12, explores 2 Timothy 2 to discern how we can develop Christian character. On February 19 we consider "The Marks of a Helpful Mentor," as outlined in 2 Timothy 3–4. The quarter closes on February 26 as we turn to "Teach Sound Doctrine by Example," rooted in Titus 2, to see how we are to live and teach the truth.

MEET OUR WRITER

THE REVEREND JOHN INDERMARK

John Indermark is an ordained minister in the United Church of Christ and a freelance writer. His writings focus on resources for Christian education curricula and spiritual formation books. John lives in southwest Washington state in the town of Naselle with his wife, Judy, a 911 dispatcher for Pacific County. John and Judy enjoy traveling in British Columbia, fly fishing, beachcombing, and singing in their community's Finnish American Choir.

John received a bachelor of arts degree in history from St. Louis University in 1972. In 1976, he received a masters of divinity degree from Eden Seminary in Webster Groves, Missouri, and was ordained in his home church of Salvator United Church of Christ in St. Louis.

From 1976 until 1992, John served full-time pastorates in the Pacific Northwest Conference of the United Church of Christ (Metaline Falls, Carnation, and Naselle). From 1992 until 2002, he served a variety of interim and supply pastorates in Presbyterian, Methodist, and Lutheran congregations in southwest Washington and northwest Oregon. He also served as an associate chaplain at a state juvenile detention facility in Naselle.

John began work as a freelance writer in 1990, which he now does full-time along with occasional preaching. His published books include *Genesis of Grace, Neglected Voices, Setting the Christmas Stage, Traveling the Prayer Paths of Jesus,* and *Turn Toward Promise,* all published by Upper Room Books. He co-authored with his son Jeff Indermark *Seekers, Saints, and Other Hypocrites,* a young adult study book published by the Presbyterian Church U.S.A. in its "Real Life Real Faith" series. The curriculum projects he has worked on include *The New International Lesson Annual, Seasons of the Spirit, Present Word, Adult Bible Studies, Bible Quest,* and *The Inviting Word.*

GOD'S COMMITMENT— OUR RESPONSE

Welcome to this winter quarter of studies. If you have already looked ahead at the contents, you will note the material has been divided into three units. The first, "God's Redeeming Love," uses passages from Isaiah and Luke to explore promises of hope and renewal that set the stage for love's incarnation. The second, "God's Gifts of Leadership," addresses instructions and guidance for leadership in the church given in the epistle of 1 Timothy. The third, "Faithful Followers, Faithful Leaders," reviews texts from 2 Timothy and Titus to understand and encourage faithful discipleship of Jesus Christ.

You may already have been struck by the seeming disjunction between the first unit and the second two. There are large differences between the times and cultural contexts addressed by Isaiah and those by the Pastoral Letters (a title often applied to Titus and 1 and 2 Timothy). The transition between those two also parallels the shift in the seasons when you study these materials, beginning in Advent/Christmas and then moving into Epiphany.

For these reasons, this introduction will begin by addressing separately these two sets of materials. We will first look at the issues and settings that generated the work of Isaiah, and briefly at Luke. We will then explore the context from which the Pastoral Epistles arose. At the end, we will look at how these texts, and the seasons in which they are studied, find common ground under the covenantal theme of "God's Commitment—Our Response."

Setting the Context: Isaiah

Perhaps in no other biblical book is context so critical to discerning and applying the message. The writings collected in Isaiah address three critical moments in the history of the southern kingdom (Judah).

The first involves a period of crises running from the invasion and destruction of the northern kingdom by Assyria in 722 B.C. to the unsuccessful siege against Jerusalem by Assyria at the close of that century. With some exceptions, much of the material in the first thirty-nine chapters of Isaiah arises from that situation. The second major period of crisis involves Judah's conquering by Babylon, Jerusalem's destruction in 587 B.C., and the reality of exile and dispersion over the next generation. The third crisis comes in the wake of return from exile in 537 B.C., and the subsequent difficulties of rebuilding the temple and walls and finding connection between the lofty promises made during exile and the harsh realities experienced upon return.

Three of our readings from Isaiah this quarter come from that exilic period, when despair gnawed away at hope. How could God possibly undo what was done? How could justice ever be established, given the loss of land and the failings of the final dynasty? The fourth reading from Isaiah, on Christmas Day, comes from that last period, when the reality of return seemed so far removed from the earlier promises of restoration.

None of our passages come from that earlier period, when the prophetic word in greatest need of speaking was not hope but judgment and challenge. When we fail to take seriously the context, we tend to fall back on what we like to hear most. We want to be comforted by Isaiah 40, for example—even though the times may be more in need of challenging present practices, as in Isaiah 1 or 5.

Listening to what these texts say is advanced and sharpened by understanding *when* and *to what circumstances* they say it. Such concerns relate directly to your teaching. One of the most important functions you will have is enabling the learners to hear these passages in their time, so as to understand where (and to whom) these passages speak most powerfully in our time. The fervent hope for justice, for example, in the first session's text (Isaiah 42) addresses those who have suffered most from the oppressive injustice of exile—and who wonder where God is in all of this. Who are such persons today? Where do your learners experience or perceive such despair as underlies these words of hope? Helping learners make such connections—and so listening to the text in context in your own experience—will bring fresh life to these words in your sessions.

Another interpretive task has to do in general with the place of Isaiah in Christian theology, and in particular with the identity of Isaiah's "Servant." Every one of this quarter's texts from Isaiah relates directly or indirectly to a figure known only as the "Servant" (or "Suffering Servant"). The church has long read these texts through the lens of Jesus' life and ministry. Jesus himself uses the fourth of our texts (from Isaiah 61) to open his sermon in Nazareth, identifying its "fulfillment" in him (Luke 4:16-21).

Does Isaiah write of the Servant with Jesus only and exclusively in mind? Sometimes the church makes it seem that way. But Jewish and some Christian scholars also identify the Servant with Israel. To appropriate Isaiah as if it was only written to predict Jesus ignores a crucial element of the prophetic tradition: addressing the people of God in the prophet's time with God's word of judgment or hope. That does not mean Isaiah cannot be read through the lens of Jesus' coming and ministry. It simply means the historical and Jewish contexts of Isaiah's words and images need to be taken seriously at the same time.

Setting the Context: Luke

Two passages from Luke's Gospel are used as lesson Scriptures: Mary's Song or *Magnificat* (1:47-55) and the Christmas narrative (2:8-20).

The song of Mary closely resembles that of Hannah in 1 Samuel 2:1-10. The miraculous birth of her child (Samuel) results in a celebration of God's overturning of the powerful and exalting of the vulnerable. So when Mary offers this song to God, the parallel is not simply God's ability to provide for miraculous conceptions. The parallel between Luke and 1 Samuel, and Luke and Isaiah, is God's recreating the world in ways that reverse injustice and fashion a new order. Mary's song will ring consistent with Luke's narrative of Jesus' ministry. There, too, reversals abound. A prodigal goes welcomed. A despised Samaritan becomes the object lesson of faith and good works. Women serve as Easter's first witnesses.

That theme even takes shape in the Christmas narrative. Shepherds are the ones who receive the birth announcement. Shepherds at this time were not revered, but held in low esteem. They were not to be trusted. Yet, God entrusted the news of a Savior to them. Isaiah had earlier called on Judah in exile not to fear because of the approach of God (40:9-10). So in Luke does God's coming bring a new word of "do not be afraid" (Luke 2:10) to these "exiles" in the hills outside Bethlehem.

Setting the Context: The Pastoral Epistles

The Pastoral Epistles of Titus and 1 and 2 Timothy bring peculiar concerns of their own. First and foremost are those that surround issues of authorship. Traditional scholarship accepts the affirmation made in the salutation (opening) verses of all three epistles as coming from the hand of Paul. Bolstering that position is not only the same attribution by the early church fathers, but also some of the personal details regarding Paul's relationship to Timothy and Titus, along with some touching words evoked by his imprisonment and the approach of winter.

On the other hand, recent scholarship has mounted strong challenges to Pauline authorship. Primary in their objections are issues of language, theology, and church order. The Pastorals use a large number of words that occur nowhere else in the Pauline epistles. The theological objection comes in the way in which faith has shifted from a dynamic exercised by persons in trust to a settled body of accepted doctrine. The formal orders of ministry (elder, deacon, bishop) apparent in these works move beyond church structure noted elsewhere in Pauline epistles. For these reasons, variously weighted in their importance by individual commentators, the Pastorals are held to come from another hand than Paul's.

If you wish to pursue the details of such different approaches, two resources provide good summaries. *The New Interpreter's Bible* (volume 11) gives a fair account of the reasons that scholars question Pauline authorship. *The Interpretation Series Commentary on First and Second Timothy and Titus* (by Thomas Oden) provides a reasonable statement of the traditional position. The commentary and interpretation provided in these sessions lean toward Pauline authorship for the bulk of the material, with the understanding that final compilation may have been at a later date. As a result, for matters of shorthand, Paul will be used in references to the author so that we do not have to rehash every possibility of authorship at every reference.

The dating of the epistles relies somewhat on how one views the authorship question. To be completely written by Paul would involve a date no later than the mid A.D. 60s. Non-Pauline authorship would allow a later date, with an end-period being the first decade of the second century. This end date has been established because the Pastorals were quoted by Ignatius in works written in the 110's. Even those who opt for a source other than Paul place these sometime in the last two decades of the first century.

Timothy lived in Ephesus, while Titus lived in Crete, according to the epistles. Ephesus is a seaport on the western coast of modern-day Turkey, while Crete is an island situated south of Asia Minor and Greece.

One of the intriguing mysteries involved in both of these epistles is the identity of the "false teachers." Identity there has less to do with their personal names, and more to do with what they taught that brought such scorn and energy to the epistles' words to these colleagues and their churches.

A variety of opinions have been expressed about the false teachers over the centuries. Only in a few places do we get an isolated reference to what some opponents took issue with: dietary concerns and marriage (1 Timothy 4:3) and the nature of the resurrection (2 Timothy 2:8). On occasion, Paul does give us names: Hymenaeus, Alexander, Philetus. Names, however, without histories that summarize teachings, do not shed light.

Some have conjectured that the opponents represent an early form of Gnosticism in the church, a heresy that gained prominence in the second century A.D. "Gnosticism" comes from *gnosis*, meaning "wisdom" or "knowledge" (see 1 Timothy 6:20). The occupation with "endless genealogies" comment in 1 Timothy 1:4 suggests a connection with a similar interest in Jewish apocryphal works about the patriarchs or angels. The identification in Titus 1:14 of "Jewish myths" (1 Timothy 1:4 mentioned only "myths") makes such a connection more likely. The problem, however, is that the Pastorals never do identify what the specific "myths" or "genealogies" are.

Perhaps that vagueness serves the church today better. If the danger can be specified to one narrow instance, then as long as that teaching or movement is not apparent among us— we would seem to be fine. But leaving the false teaching in vague terms encourages a sense of vigilance to see that what passes for faithful discourse in our time does not in fact take us down unfruitful paths. Remember also: The emphasis in the Pastorals is not only upon "the faith"—it is upon good works. How one lives in response to the gospel proves revealing in and of itself of that gospel.

One final note about the setting of the Pastoral Epistles merits attention. There is a strong underlying concern for conduct that does not cause affront to the wider community. This word comes explicitly in 1 Timothy 3:7 in describing qualifications for bishop: "Moreover, he must be well thought of by outsiders." This word, along with other such inferences (1 Timothy 5:14; Titus 2:5, 8), reveals a genuine concern about how the faith community is perceived by society at large. If this were a period of active persecution, such conformity or at least "not rocking the boat" would provide a measure of safety to the community. Or perhaps the motive moves in the direction of living model lives so that others would be attracted to it (see Acts 2:47).

Covenant in Word and in Season

"God's Commitment—Our Response" invokes covenant. God acts, we respond. God graces, we trust. God invites, we follow. The church lives in the balancing of the commitments God has kept with our response exercised in faithful discipleship.

Isaiah holds that covenant at the core of its theology. God remains active in creation. God's works are not only the mighty deeds of old, but what is yet coming and on the way. "See, the former things have come to pass, and new things I now declare" (Isaiah 42:9a). Isaiah invites Judah, and through her faithful persons in every time, to respond to the "new things" God declares and enacts in a covenant that moves forward toward God's promised and sovereign realm.

The Pastoral Epistles also affirm such a covenantal understanding. The God who has fashioned and ordered the whole of creation is now about the fashioning and ordering of the church. God's commitment has been kept in the gift of the Spirit, who in turn gifts persons to upbuild the community of faith (1 Timothy 4:14). The word of grace with which Paul opens these letters originates in the grace revealed in Jesus Christ and experienced in the call and ministry (Titus 2:11). Such grace is indeed what strengthens and enables our faithful response in this covenant (2 Timothy 2:1). Faithful response in the Pastorals comes both in holding to the faith entrusted and evidencing good works. Covenant permeates our spiritual foundation and transforms our daily living.

That is the covenantal message commitment and response in these texts you will explore. That is also the message of these seasons in which you will encounter them.

Advent and Christmas celebrate the awesome commitment God brings through incarnation. A Word present with God and active in creation's fashioning now becomes the Word Incarnate. God invests the very gift of Self in a new and unique way in Jesus Christ. That commitment involves entering into the heart and depth of this life we know: its joys and sorrows, its pains and aspirations. The old promise of Emmanuel, "God with us," finds keeping. Our response, in the example of Mary, invites wonder and trust. Like her, we are invited to "treasure" this gift of God's commitment—and to do so in thought and word and deed. Our response, in the example of shepherds, beckons us to "go and see"—and having done so, to live without fear.

Epiphany celebrates the revealing of Jesus Christ to the world. That revealing underlies the injunctions of the epistle: to reveal the truth of God's coming in our belief and in our good works. The church responds to God's commitments by an embodiment of that faith we have received. In our ministries, in our relationships with one another, we find opportunity to respond to the grace given with lives lived graciously toward one another.

UNIT 1: GOD'S REDEEMING LOVE
SERVING OTHERS

PREVIEWING THE LESSON

Lesson Scripture: Isaiah 42:1-8
Background Scripture: Isaiah 41–42
Key Verse: Isaiah 42:6

Focus of the Lesson:
Injustices run throughout human relationships on both a personal and a societal level. What can help us continue to hope and work for justice despite the overwhelming reality of our experience? Isaiah promises that God will bring justice to the world.

Goals for the Learners:
(1) to review Isaiah's prophecy concerning God's promise to send justice through God's servant.
(2) to discern how Isaiah's prophecy relates to Jesus Christ, and consider what challenge this brings for the learners today.
(3) to commit to ways to work for God's justice.

Pronunciation Guide:
Levitical (li vit' i kuhl)
mishpat (mis pawt')
Yahweh (yah' weh)

Supplies:
Bibles, newsprint and marker, paper and pencils, hymnals

READING THE SCRIPTURE

NRSV
Isaiah 42:1-8
¹Here is my servant, whom I uphold,
  my chosen, in whom my soul delights;
I have put my spirit upon him;
  he will bring forth justice to the nations.
²He will not cry or lift up his voice,
  or make it heard in the street;
³a bruised reed he will not break,

NIV
Isaiah 42:1-8
¹"Here is my servant, whom I uphold,
  my chosen one in whom I delight;
I will put my Spirit on him
  and he will bring justice to the nations.
²He will not shout or cry out,
  or raise his voice in the streets.
³A bruised reed he will not break,

and a dimly burning wick he will not
quench;
he will faithfully bring forth justice.
⁴He will not grow faint or be crushed
until he has established justice in the
earth;
and the coastlands wait for his teaching.
⁵Thus says God, the LORD,
who created the heavens and stretched
them out,
who spread out the earth and what comes
from it,
who gives breath to the people upon it
and spirit to those who walk in it:
⁶I am the LORD, I have called you in
righteousness,
I have taken you by the hand and kept
you;
I have given you as a covenant to the
people,
a light to the nations,
⁷   to open the eyes that are blind,
to bring out the prisoners from the
dungeon,
from the prison those who sit in darkness.
⁸I am the LORD, that is my name;
my glory I give to no other,
nor my praise to idols.

and a smoldering wick he will not snuff
out.
In faithfulness he will bring forth justice;
⁴he will not falter or be discouraged
till he establishes justice on earth.
In his law the islands will put their hope."
⁵This is what God the LORD says—
he who created the heavens and stretched
them out,
who spread out the earth and all that
comes out of it,
who gives breath to its people,
and life to those who walk on it:
⁶"I, the LORD, have called you in righteousness;
I will take hold of your hand.
I will keep you and will make you
to be a covenant for the people
and a light for the Gentiles,
⁷to open eyes that are blind,
to free captives from prison
and to release from the dungeon those
who sit in darkness.
⁸"I am the LORD; that is my name!
I will not give my glory to another
or my praise to idols.

UNDERSTANDING THE SCRIPTURE

Isaiah 41:1-7. Isaiah opens this passage by "staging" a courtroom trial with God bringing an opening argument against rivals, political and religious. The first half of God's argument (41:2-4) raises questions about who has initiated a new power moving from the east. This likely refers to the rise of the Persian Empire under Cyrus II, who will soon overrun Babylon and set the Israelite exiles free. The second half of the argument (41:5-7) mocks the fearful, and ultimately impotent, response of those whose gods stand helpless before the God who is "first, and will be with the last"—that is, the One who precedes and outlasts all other powers.

Isaiah 41:8-13. Whereas Israel had been "offstage" during the previous scene, now the exiles come to the forefront. God's stance shifts from prosecutor to comforter and advocate. The reference to Jacob and Abraham underscores how God's saving and calling activity in the past will now be repeated. The theme of Israel as "servant" (41:8, 9) will loom large in Isaiah, even as the words written here and later about the "servant" will figure in the church's understanding of Jesus' identity and mission. Israel's fear in exile is directly addressed by God's repeated assertions of "do not fear" and "I am with you." Exile had brought the terrifying possibility of God's abandonment. God declares, that is not so. God is here. God will help.

Isaiah 41:14-16. The language of "worm" and "insect" for Israel shocks. The terms seem more fitting to the abusive words of captors. Yet, these verses use them to heighten the reversal about to take place. The "worm" and "insect" will take an active role in dismantling those who stand as their captors. This imagery may trace to plagues of locusts sweeping over the land and devouring all vegetation. Such a plague had been part of the narrative of God's bringing freedom from Egypt (Exodus 10:13-15), an act of deliverance to be paralleled in release from exile.

Isaiah 41:17-20. The identification of the "poor and needy" brings this session's theme of justice to the forefront. God's advocacy for the vulnerable traces back in law to the Levitical codes, and in story to the plight of Israel in Egypt. As in Egypt, God now answers in saving ways. In Isaiah, God's acts of redemption on behalf of those in need spills out into the whole of creation. The theme of re-creation, particularly the transformation of wilderness, is key in Isaiah's vision (see also chapters 35 and 65). The end result is not simply the restoring of life, but the revealing of God. Isaiah 41:20 parallels stories, for example, in John's Gospel, where a need for healing (John 9:3) and raising (John 11:4) serve larger purposes of revealing the works and glory of God.

Isaiah 41:21-29. The courtroom scene returns. God as prosecutor cross-examines the nations concerning the divinity of their idols. The questioning echoes that of Job 38-41, except the tone is hostile. In middle (41:24) and end (41:29), judgment is rendered: These idols amount to nothing. They have no substance. In spite of the appearance of power, they can do nothing. It is important to remember these words address Israel. Encouragement is intended in the revelation, for there is nothing to fear in Babylon.

Isaiah 42:1-4. We have already noted how "servant" brings dual associations with Israel and, through the church's interpreting of these words, Jesus Christ. In these four verses, "justice" (Hebrew: *mishpat*) occurs three times, revealing it to be a central concern. The Spirit's empowerment does not bring the type of power whose wielding bowls people over. The imagery of verses 2-3 reveals gentleness to the Servant's work, not unlike the image of God's might being revealed in the gathering of lambs and leading of those with child in Isaiah 40:11. The reference to "coastlands" along with "nations" (Hebrew: *goi*, also translated as "Gentiles") suggests this Servant will somehow minister beyond the boundaries, physical and theological, of Israel in ways the text leaves unidentified.

Isaiah 42:5-9. Introduced by a return to creation imagery, the Servant's calling now finds explicit description. Covenant and light form "identity" factors, even as "nations" make the Servant's mission parallel to the Abrahamic covenant's intent to bring blessing to all the families of the earth (Genesis 12:3). Twice in these verses, the name of God given to Moses at the burning bush (*YHWH* or *Yahweh*) is introduced by "I am." The name *YHWH* itself is believed to be some form of the verb "to be" (such as, "I am who I am"). So as Moses, and through him Israel, received this name in pledge of promised deliverance, so now that name comes in pledge of God's new deliverance of Israel.

Isaiah 42:10-17. Isaiah begins this passage with a song of praise, whose opening line echoes that of Psalm 96. As the Servant's mission connected to the "nations," so does this song invoke not just Israel but a variety of peoples and even elements of creation. The militancy of the song's closing verse (42:13) makes for an interesting transition into the passage's next image: childbirth. Victory shouts become birthing shouts. Isaiah depicts God in childbirth, to declare the gift of new life in exile's end. The leading of the blind (42:16) returns God's concern for the vulnerable to the forefront of God's actions in a promise not to forsake those least able to make the trip home.

Isaiah 42:18-25. Isaiah here shifts the tone of address to Israel from pastoral to prodding and even warning. The language of seeing without recognition and hearing without understanding (42:20) recalls the pre-exilic judgment on those with eyes who cannot see and with ears who cannot hear (Jeremiah 5:21). Exile has placed Israel in a precarious situation (42:22) not limited to captivity. It is the precariousness of not being able to hear the word of hope, not being able to see the One who brings promise. Verse 25 warns that same lack of hearing and seeing resulted in exile.

INTERPRETING THE SCRIPTURE

Inspired for Justice

The gift of God's Spirit evokes several associations from the church. The gift of God's Spirit on Pentecost established the Christian community. The gift of God's Spirit led the biblical writers in fashioning what we have come to designate as Scripture. Here in Isaiah, though, the gift of God's Spirit connects to the bringing and establishing of justice.

And what is justice? Contemporary nuances of meaning abound among us. "Bringing to justice" suggests apprehension of a criminal. "Justice system" may call to mind part or all of the institutions of law, ranging from legislators to police to courts. Justice has taken on a definite punitive edge in its understanding of late. Biblical justice, however, moves in a different direction. Justice (*mishpat*) has less to do with specific individual ordinances than with a general ordering of life and relationship in ways that ensure right treatment of others. Of particular concern, especially in the prophetic tradition, is justice as a safeguarding of those most vulnerable in society. Widows and orphans, the poor and those physically at risk: For these persons, Isaiah and Amos and others declare God bears special concern. Justice involves their care and keeping, rather than their abuse and discarding and devaluing.

"I have put my spirit upon him; he will bring forth justice to the nations" (Isaiah 42:1). The "servant" receives this commissioning to seek and to do justice. This is a critical text for the Christian community, for the church has long associated Isaiah's "servant" with the identity and mission of Jesus. As such, the church sees in Christ (and in itself, given its calling to be the "body of Christ") the same commissioning to justice. Luke 4:18 recalls Jesus' quoting another passage in Isaiah (61:1-2), whose opening lines link the servant's anointing by God's Spirit with preaching the gospel to the poor. Other inspired actions there are taken on behalf of the brokenhearted, the captives, the blind, and the oppressed.

Justice concerns the individual and community of faith. That is not because justice is politically correct (or not), nor because it is socially polite (or not). Rather, justice issues from God's bestowing of Spirit for the sake of the vulnerable among us: bruised reeds who might otherwise be broken, dimly burning wicks who might otherwise be quenched. So Isaiah prophesied, so Jesus ministered, so the church keeps faith.

Called to Servanthood

For Isaiah, the gift of God's Spirit and the resulting call to servanthood is not impersonal. Listen to the parallel declarations of verse 6 where God addresses the Servant: "I have called you...I have taken you...I have given you. . . ."

Servanthood is bestowed through personal encounter with and address by God.

What does such servanthood consist of? Isaiah offers two general instructions: "covenant to the people" and "light to the nations" (42:6). Covenant speaks of a history of gracious and saving relationship. Covenant with Noah came on the heels of the flood, and bore the promise of "never again." Covenant with Abraham came in God's leading to a land unseen and an heir unborn. Covenant with Moses came in the aftermath of God's deliverance from Egypt. God's promising presence marks the gift of covenant, and here the Servant finds commissioning to serve as (sign of) covenant with the people. "Light to the nations" marks servanthood with a broader perspective and audience. Some disagreement exists among scholars about whether the intent of Isaiah is to speak words of mission to all the nations, or to the Jewish exiles who had been scattered therein. What is clear, however, is the church's interpretation and use of such texts to understand the scope of Christian mission to be universal.

The challenge of servanthood comes in making its acts specific. *Servant* means nothing as a noun unless it finds expression as a verb. Isaiah's commissioning to servanthood is not simply "to be" a covenant or a light. As the writer continues, the Servant engages in actions that "open" and "bring out" (a familiar word in Exodus for God's deliverance). For the church, this passage strongly suggests that talking about service, or even Jesus as servant, is not enough. Servanthood requires demonstration. And again, as emphasized in the previous section, servanthood is to benefit those in greatest need (here identified in verse 7 as the blind and the prisoners).

Consider the community in which you not only worship, but also work and live and shop. Who are the ones at the margins, vulnerable to shifts in economy and health?

There you will find the ones for whom this passage commissions God's servants to be of service.

But commissioning is not: "Here's a job to do, so go at it the best you can." The means, the energy, the power, by which such service can be rendered by the likes of us returns us to the One who not only commissions, but also empowers.

The God "I Am"

Isaiah 42:1-8 does not merely clarify who or what the servant is or does. At its core, this passage reveals God.

The revelation at the heart of this passage is of God the Creator, of God the breath and Spirit giver. Remember these words originally addressed exiles, living in captivity. For them, the power of Babylon to wreak chaos and destruction loomed large. What Isaiah does is return Israel to her roots, and to its foundation story of the God who fashioned life out of chaos. What God has done before, the author seems to say, God can—and will—do again.

There is another foundational story to which Isaiah returns the exiles who may well have been wondering about what sign they could have to believe the remarkable promise of homecoming. In Exodus 3, Moses protested his calling from God to lead Israel from Egypt. Even when promised God's presence, Moses replied that the people would want to know the name of this God that would defeat Pharaoh. The answer? *YHWH*, or "I am who I am." Twice in our passage in Isaiah, the prophet relates the answer of God to such concerns: "I am the LORD" (42:6, 8). The name given at the burning bush as guarantor for deliverance from Egypt now comes as a sign of this present-day deliverance. "I am 'I am who I am'" would be one way of literally translating the message.

So what do such names mean today? When we hear the biblical promises of justice and mercy, of compassion and homecoming, we too may well wonder how in the world such things can be trusted. We too may seek for some guarantee we are not chasing after dreams. As with Israel, our hope roots in a name, the name, of the One who can be trusted. "At the name of Jesus," Paul wrote in Philippians 2:10—we work and serve and trust in the name of the One

who revealed God in the fullness not only of time but also of grace.

"I am the LORD, I have called you. . . . I have taken you by the hand" (42:6). Our source of Spirit, our hope of justice, our example of servanthood—all are rooted in the God whose promises Isaiah anticipated and whose grace Jesus made incarnate.

SHARING THE SCRIPTURE

Preparing Our Hearts

This week's devotional reading is found in Isaiah 41:8-13, which is part of our background Scripture. As you read this passage in which God promises to be with Israel no matter what, ponder what it means to be God's servant. How are you acting as a servant now? What else could you be doing?

Pray that you and the adult learners will claim your role as servants, recognizing that you have nothing to fear, for God will uphold you in all circumstances.

Preparing Our Minds

Study the background from Isaiah 41–42 and the lesson Scripture, Isaiah 42:1-8, which is the first of the four Servant Songs found in Isaiah. As you prepare the lesson consider how the promise that God will bring justice to the world motivates Christians to continue to work for justice, despite current realities.

Be sure to read the introduction to the winter quarter, which gives you an overview of the lessons we will study. Also read the background article, which will help you set the lessons within the context of their respective biblical books. Both articles are located at the beginning of this quarter's lessons.

Optional: You may wish to read all four of the Servant Songs, found in Isaiah 42:1-4; 49:1-6; 50:4-9; and 52:13–53:12. Consider reasons why the church may have associ-

ated these songs with Jesus. Note that we will be studying more Servant passages in the coming weeks.

Write on newsprint:
❏ information for next week's lesson, found under "Continue the Journey."

LEADING THE CLASS

(1) Gather to Learn

❖ Welcome the class members and introduce any guests.

❖ Pray that the participants will be open to the Spirit's leading as you study together.

❖ Encourage the students to name injustices that they have experienced or have witnessed. List these ideas on newsprint. Try to identify and categorize reasons for these injustices. For example, if a female class member said she was denied a managerial job in the 1960s, could her rejection have been based on her gender or marital status? Review the list. Which injustices have been remedied, at least to some extent? Which still exist? What steps need to be taken to eliminate them?

❖ Read aloud today's focus statement: **Injustices run throughout human relationships on both a personal and a societal level. What can help us continue to hope and work for justice despite the overwhelming reality of our experience? Isaiah promises that God will bring justice to the world.**

(2) Review Isaiah's Prophecy Concerning God's Promise to Send Justice Through God's Servant

❖ Read aloud Isaiah 42:1-4.

■ Draw a vertical line to divide a sheet of newsprint into two columns. Label the left side "God's Relationship with the Servant" and the right side "Traits of the Servant." Invite the students to list as many ideas as possible. Encourage the use of multiple translations to create a richer description of the Servant.

■ Note that the word "justice" is used three times: in verses 1, 3, and 4. Ask the students to define "justice" as the word seems to be used here.

■ Point out that according to verse 4, the Servant is to establish justice throughout the earth. The justice he brings is not only for Israel but rather for all people. The Servant acts to bring justice not in a punitive, power-wielding sense, but rather by means of gently leading.

❖ Choose a volunteer to read Isaiah 42:5-8.

■ Read aloud the Understanding the Scripture explanation under Isaiah 42:5-9 to unpack this passage.

■ Discuss these questions.

(1) What does this passage say to you about God?

(2) What does this passage say to you about God's relationship with humanity?

(3) If you were an Israelite in exile in Babylon, would this passage comfort or afflict you? Why?

(3) Discern How Isaiah's Prophecy Relates to Jesus Christ, and Consider What Challenge This Brings for the Learners Today

❖ Refer to the list of ideas the class recorded on newsprint for Isaiah 42:1-4. Ask the class to make connections between this prophecy regarding the Servant and their understanding of Jesus' role and mission. What comparisons and contrasts can they draw between Jesus and the Servant?

❖ Point out that the Servant's identity has long been debated. Israel itself is referred to as God's chosen servant (Isaiah 41:8-9; 44:1-2, 21; 45:4; 48:20). The church, however, has seen in the first four verses of Isaiah 42 a description of Jesus and have claimed that he is indeed God's Servant.

❖ Suggest that the learners look again at Isaiah 42:6-8 and compare that to Luke 4:18 and 7:18-23. Discuss with the group how Jesus fulfilled the role of the Servant.

❖ Divide the class into small groups to discuss these questions:

(1) How does Jesus' role as God's Servant challenge you to be a more faithful servant?

(2) Who are the vulnerable people at the margins of society that need liberation and healing?

(3) What barriers prevent you from working to bring justice to these people?

(4) How might these barriers be overcome?

❖ Bring the groups together to report on their ideas. Create a list on newsprint of those whom the students have identified as vulnerable and in need of justice.

(4) Commit to Ways to Work for God's Justice

❖ Look again at the list of marginalized, vulnerable people the students have just created. Work together to identify the ones that the class can reasonably be expected to be able to reach. Likely, these groups will live right in your community. Brainstorm ideas for helping these people. Here are some ideas to get the discussion started:

• collect toys, clothing, and food for a homeless shelter or facility for battered women and their children.

• visit nursing home patients to provide companionship (perhaps with a pet), a listening ear, and prayer, Bible study, or worship.

- tutor immigrants who are trying to learn English.

❖ Ask the group to select one idea that they as a class would commit to acting upon. If time permits, make decisions about how you will undertake this project: who will be involved, what will be accomplished, when, where, and how it will be done. If time is short, appoint a task force to shape the project and report back to the entire group at a mutually agreed upon date.

(5) Continue the Journey

❖ Pray that the participants will go forth to serve God by serving others and working for justice.

❖ Read aloud this preparation for next week's lesson. You may also want to post it on newsprint for the students to copy. **Prepare for next week's session, "Strength from God," by reading Isaiah 49–50. Our lesson will focus on Isaiah 49:5-6 and 50:4-9. As you read, direct your attention to these ideas: Everyone experiences physical, emotional, or mental weariness at some point. Where can we draw strength during our own times of weariness? The Isaiah passage indicates that our strength comes both from God and from people like Isaiah who carry God's comfort to us.**

❖ Read aloud the following three ideas. Challenge the students to commit themselves to use these activities as a springboard to spiritual growth.

(1) **List at least two steps you will take to "be a light" to a person or group who needs to experience God's loving justice/righteousness. Take action.**

(2) **Keep an eye on the media for stories of injustice. Write to elected officials and your local newspaper to voice your concern. Do whatever else you can to assist those who have been unjustly treated. Pray for victims of this injustice.**

(3) **Pray daily for citizens of nations affected by systemic oppression and injustice.**

❖ Sing or read aloud "Go Forth for God."

❖ Lead this benediction to conclude the session: **May you go forth as servants in whom the Lord delights to bring justice to the nations by the power of God's Spirit. Amen.**

UNIT 1: GOD'S REDEEMING LOVE

STRENGTH FROM GOD

PREVIEWING THE LESSON

Lesson Scripture: Isaiah 49:5-6; 50:4-9
Background Scripture: Isaiah 49–50
Key Verse: Isaiah 50:7

Focus of the Lesson:
Everyone experiences physical, emotional, or mental weariness at some point. Where can we draw strength during our own times of weariness? Our strength comes both from God and from people like Isaiah who carry God's comfort to us.

Goals for the Learners:
(1) to explore the assurance of God's comfort, as brought to humankind by the prophet Isaiah.
(2) to consider Isaiah's words in light of their own views on how God brings strength to the weary.
(3) to discern and commit to helping those who are weary.

Pronunciation Guide:
adamah (ad aw maw')
goy (go'ee)

Supplies:
Bibles, newsprint and marker, paper and pencils, concordances, tape or tacks, hymnals

---

READING THE SCRIPTURE

NRSV
Isaiah 49:5-6
⁵And now the LORD says,
   who formed me in the womb to be his
      servant,
to bring Jacob back to him,
   and that Israel might be gathered to him,
for I am honored in the sight of the LORD,
   and my God has become my strength—
⁶he says,

NIV
Isaiah 49:5-6
⁵And now the LORD says—
   he who formed me in the womb to be his
      servant
to bring Jacob back to him
   and gather Israel to himself,
for I am honored in the eyes of the LORD
   and my God has been my strength—
⁶he says:

"It is too light a thing that you should be my
servant
    to raise up the tribes of Jacob
    and to restore the survivors of Israel;
I will give you as a light to the nations,
    that my salvation may reach to the end of
    the earth."

Isaiah 50:4-9
[4]The Lord GOD has given me
    the tongue of a teacher,
that I may know how to sustain
    the weary with a word.
Morning by morning he wakens—
    wakens my ear
    to listen as those who are taught.
[5]The Lord GOD has opened my ear,
    and I was not rebellious,
    I did not turn backward.
[6]I gave my back to those who struck me,
    and my cheeks to those who pulled out
    the beard;
I did not hide my face
    from insult and spitting.
[7]The Lord GOD helps me;
    therefore I have not been disgraced;
therefore I have set my face like flint,
    and I know that I shall not be put to
    shame;
[8]he who vindicates me is near.
Who will contend with me?
    Let us stand up together.
Who are my adversaries?
    Let them confront me.
[9]It is the Lord GOD who helps me;
    who will declare me guilty?
All of them will wear out like a garment;
    the moth will eat them up.

"It is too small a thing for you to be my
servant
    to restore the tribes of Jacob
    and bring back those of Israel I have kept.
I will also make you a light for the Gentiles,
    that you may bring my salvation to the
    ends of the earth."

Isaiah 50:4-9
[4]The Sovereign LORD has given me an
    instructed tongue,
    to know the word that sustains the weary.
He wakens me morning by morning,
    wakens my ear to listen like one being
    taught.
[5]The Sovereign Lord has opened my ears,
    and I have not been rebellious;
    I have not drawn back.
[6]I offered my back to those who beat me,
    my cheeks to those who pulled out my
    beard;
I did not hide my face
    from mocking and spitting.
[7]Because the Sovereign LORD helps me,
    I will not be disgraced.
Therefore have I set my face like flint,
    and I know I will not be put to shame.
[8]He who vindicates me is near.
    Who then will bring charges against me?
    Let us face each other!
Who is my accuser?
    Let him confront me!
[9]It is the Sovereign LORD who helps me.
    Who is he that will condemn me?
They will all wear out like a garment;
    the moths will eat them up.

UNDERSTANDING THE SCRIPTURE

Overview. The "Servant Songs" in Isaiah, of which Isaiah 49:1-6 and 50:4-9 are the second and third, raise the question of the identity of the Servant. Judaism has traditionally associated the Servant with the nation Israel. Christian theology has at times sought to read the songs through the person or work of Christ, or to identify the Servant with some other individual in history. While the argument that Isaiah intended to "predict" Jesus' life presumes more than the book reveals, the Servant passages certainly do echo themes consistent with critical elements of Jesus' ministry and self-understanding.

Isaiah 49:1-4. The Servant begins by addressing the coastlands and peoples "far away," a reference suggestive of the extent of Israel's dispersion in exile. An assertion follows a divine call upon the Servant's life prior to birth, echoing Jeremiah's understanding of that same call (Jeremiah 1:5). Such a calling does not come without conflict. The litany of "vain," "nothing," and "vanity" hints that faithfulness to the call does not always reap immediate rewards or success. Still, that "lament" moves into an articulation of trust in God.

Isaiah 49:5-7. The speech of God picks up the message consistent since the opening of the fortieth chapter: the returning of Jacob and Israel from exile. The land of promise will once again be restored. While that hope might at the moment seem inconceivable, God's saving purposes move in even more astounding directions. An end of exile is "too light"—perhaps an interesting contrast with "glory," whose literal meaning in Hebrew is "weight." As if the end to exile were not enough, God enlarges the Servant's task to bringing light to the nations (Hebrew *goy*, which can also be translated as "Gentiles"). How that will happen does not depend upon the Servant's status in the world, identified here in the negative terms of "despised" and "abhorred" and "slave." This will happen because of the Sovereign God who is faithful.

Isaiah 49:8-12. God next addresses the Servant with the calling, first stated in Isaiah 42:6, that the Servant has been given as a "covenant to the people." To the "prisoners" (exiles), God calls the Servant to declare an imperative verb: "Come out." A new exodus is about to take place. As with the first, reluctance abounds. Some scholars suggest life in Babylon for many exiles proved comfortable, if not desirable. The summons here to "come out" aims not at obtaining release from captors, but at breaking loose those who may have been quite content to stay where they were (as, apparently, many did). God's care for those who risk the journey finds expression in the imagery of a guiding and sheltering shepherd (compare 49:10*b* with Psalm 23:1-2).

Isaiah 49:13-18. The narrator summons all creation to share in a liturgy of celebration. The causes identified for such joy are God's comforting (as in 40:1) and compassion (as in 40:11, 49:10). A counter theme follows, stirred by the experience of exile that suggests God has forsaken and forgotten, two verbs common to laments (see Psalm 13:1; 22:1). God's response does not condemn the exiles for such questioning, but makes two powerful affirmations of God's bond. The first compares God's attachment to Israel in the image of God as mother to her birth child Israel. The second depicts Israel "marking" the palms of God's hands as a tattoo not to be removed.

Isaiah 49:19-26. An almost playful statement of irony declares to exiles that a land now devastated and emptied will fill to overflowing with "your children." As with Abram and Sarai, or Hannah, God transforms the barren into the blessed. The landscape is further reversed and turned upside down. Kings and queens, those who formerly carried Israel into exile, will now be the ones who will bear them back home. The served become the servants. How can this be? God is in the business of turning the world upside down—or perhaps the better expression would be, right side up. God will be advocate and redeemer.

Isaiah 50:1-3. Can God's promises be trusted, given what happened to Israel in exile? The narrative takes up challenging words to Israel from God. Those who say God has irretrievably "divorced" Israel have it wrong. The guilt for exile belongs to those who broke covenant with God, not the other way around. God's ability to save and redeem went untested (for example, in the pleadings earlier in Isaiah to trust God, such as 30:1-17). As a result, judgment (not abandonment) came.

Isaiah 50:4-9. This Third Servant Song asserts that God has made possible the work of the Servant ("The Lord GOD has given me . . . the Lord GOD has opened . . . The Lord God helps me" [twice]). The emphasis on "word," whether listening or speaking, echoes the Genesis 1 narrative of a word-begotten creation. There, God speaks to summon life into being. Here, word connects to the Servant's task in the promise of "new creation," an important theme in the latter half of Isaiah (40:12-31; 65:17-25). The end to exile will be not only a new "exodus," but also a new creation. To be sure, that newness will not come without opposition and contention to God's Servant,

as verses 5-6 make clear. What matters, however, is the core affirmation of why the Servant (and we) can trust in and work toward such promise: the advocacy of God. Those who serve can stand resolute, knowing who it is who stands with them (see also Romans 8:31-39).

Isaiah 50:10-11. Verses 10-11 begin with an "interrogation" of the exiles, and conclude with a rather negative challenge to the Israelites in exile. The words here follow in spirit the opening three verses of this chapter. Taken together, they serve as a call to choose where loyalties will be when exile does come to an end. In that sense, they parallel Joshua's words spoken to the tribes in the covenant ceremony at Shechem, particularly Joshua 24:19-28. Choices do matter.

INTERPRETING THE SCRIPTURE

The God Who Forms and Strengthens

Isaiah asserts God "formed" the Servant "while I was in my mother's womb" (49:1, 5). The verb translated as "formed" is the same Hebrew verb used in Genesis 2:7, where God "forms" *Adam* out of the dust of the ground (in Hebrew, *adamah*).

Formed in the womb may stir remembrances, or quarrels, with theologies of predestination. It is critical to keep in mind here the context in which Isaiah makes this assertion. What looms before the exiles in Babylon is the issue of who is in control of history. The Babylonian Empire has staked its claim by subjugating Israel and holding its exiles in captivity. Isaiah claims Yahweh to be the One whose purposes will be sovereign. The Servant's *in utero* call demonstrates that claim in a declaration that God has begun working in saving ways even before those involved could claim any conscious recognition.

Isaiah's interest resides in forming hope among exiles who might, at the moment, have seen no evidence of the "birthing" of

God's saving intent. The Servant's call before birth asserts God's purposes need not always be seen in order to be viable or trustworthy. God's redemptive purposes unfold beyond our sight or determination. One does not need to affirm every minuscule act of human life to be predetermined in order to say, with Isaiah, that God forms us in ways, and even in times, beyond our knowledge for the sake of good.

Beyond that, Isaiah affirms that the consequence of the Servant's being formed of God is to be strengthened by God. In the lesson Scriptures of this session, the importance of strength can readily be seen. A major task awaits the Servant, as does significant opposition. "Going it alone" is not an option, at least if the call is to be kept. Strength will be needed. Strength still is needed to live faithfully in the face of opposition or apathy, to endure when the way seems long for us.

Not Settling

From the opening of chapter 40, Isaiah has plainly stated God's intention to return the exiles from Babylon to the land of promise. One might have thought this would have been enough of a surprising turn of events. Hundreds of miles of high desert steppe land still separated the exiles from Israel. The power of Babylon continued to hold them in captivity. Surely, the home-gathering of Jacob and Israel provided sufficient challenge to the faith of the exiles in general, and the task of the Servant in particular. Yet God declares, "It is too light a thing" (49:6). The promises for Jacob and Israel do not go far enough. Words now come of the Servant's work to extend to the nations, to the very ends of the earth.

Scholars debate whether this actually means a "Gentile" mission for the Servant, or if perhaps the words intend a reaching and gathering of those exiles who have been dispersed to the far corners of the world. But these words, at the very least, push the boundaries of hope's expectations.

Consider, for example, the season in which you read these words from Isaiah: "It is too light a thing." The expectations of Advent involve God once again promising, and acting, in a way that exceeded expectation. God would not settle for a word merely written on a scroll: Advent awaits, in the language and hope of John's Gospel, the Word made flesh.

This passage from Isaiah has likewise deeply influenced the church's understanding of call. "It is too light a thing" to just be the church for ourselves. As with Isaiah's Servant, we understand our calling to include the nations, and the ends of the earth. The church exists for others, for the sake of light.

Speaking and Listening That Sustain

Isaiah identifies God's gifting both the tongue and the ears of the Servant. Listening and speaking are critical to the task at hand—for the Servant in Isaiah, and in our service.

Speaking we can readily see and appreciate. "To sustain the weary with a word" (50:4) may trigger remembrances of someone whose words lifted you with precisely the gift or nudge or comfort you needed at some critical moment. The liturgy of the synagogue and later the church centered around a ministry of the spoken word, where the Spirit somehow fashions through our words an encounter with God.

Speaking, however, is only part of the equation. Note that while Isaiah mentions the tongue but once, he affirms the ears twice: "[God] wakens my ear . . . the Lord God has opened my ear" (50:4b, 5a). The emphasis is understandable, both practically and theologically. Practically, one learns to speak only by listening. Theologically, in Hebrew the word for "hear" (shama) also is translated as "obey." Obedience to God, faithfully carrying out God's purposes, begins with ears that listen.

From such faithful listening comes faithful speaking—and living. One learns how to sustain with a word by listening to the words God speaks to sustain: words of hope, words of promise. The "wakening" of the ear carries that sense of having one's life opened by attending to the words God brings to us. The tongue of a teacher emerges from the ears of a listening student. So Isaiah wrote of the Servant then, and so it remains true for Servants today. May those who have ears, listen.

The God Who Helps

Is God removed from history and personal experience, a deity who set creation into motion and now sits back to watch impassively as life unfolds? Some have proposed that idea of God. Isaiah did not. God is neither removed nor uninvolved. The Third Servant Song confesses God as the One who helps.

The sort of help Isaiah asserts takes shape in decisive moments, when standing firm does not come easily. Because of such help: disgrace is turned aside, shame is eliminated, vindication comes near, and God stands as advocate for the Servant in the face of adversaries and accusers.

The structure of 50:7-9 moves back and forth from questions of who will stand against the Servant to answers rooted in the affirming presence God will bring. That structure closely parallels that of Romans 8:31-39. There, Paul asserts God as advocate in the face of powers that threaten separation from God in a similar series of questions and answers. For Paul, God allows nothing to separate us from God's help. In Isaiah, the Servant asserts the help of God to render all the aid required to stand and live faithfully.

"It is the Lord GOD who helps me." Those words, and their promise, continue to enliven persons and communities of faith. For we know in their light we do not live alone, or left only to our own resources. We live in the grace and hope of God's help. Notice that God's help does not mean adversaries or difficult times will never be faced. It means that, in the midst of them, we may trust in and rely upon God's help: to walk with us, to stand by us, to see us through to whatever end may come. And to know, come what may, God will not forsake us.

SHARING THE SCRIPTURE

Preparing Our Hearts

This week's devotional reading is found in Isaiah 49:7-13. These verses follow the Second Servant Song, part of which is included in our lesson. God, the "Redeemer of Israel," will provide strength and compassionate care for the "prisoners," that is, those who are exiles in Babylon and scattered elsewhere, as God brings them home. What situations in your life are causing you to be physically, emotionally, mentally, or spiritually exhausted? What words of comfort and strength do you need to hear from God today? Meditate with a "listening ear" so that God may speak to you.

Pray that you and the adult learners will experience God's strength and redeeming love.

Preparing Our Minds

Study the background in chapters 49 and 50 of Isaiah and the lesson Scripture, Isaiah 49:5-6 and 50:4-9. Note that Isaiah 49:1-6, which we are reading in part, is generally known as the Second Servant Song. Isaiah 50:4-9 is the third of the Servant Songs. As you prepare this lesson, consider how God acts as a source of strength in times of weariness.

Write on newsprint:
❑ information for next week's lesson, found under "Continue the Journey."

LEADING THE CLASS

(1) Gather to Learn

❖ Welcome the class members and introduce any guests.

❖ Pray that those who are weary will find God's strength revealed in today's session.

❖ Note that people around the world have experienced hurricanes, tornadoes, flooding, fires, extreme temperatures, and other natural disasters that have caused great stress and weariness. Invite students who have had such experiences to describe briefly:

    (1) the problems they faced;

    (2) how these problems affected them physically, emotionally, mentally, and/or spiritually;

(3) how and where they found the strength to continue on.

If your community has had such experiences, you may want to divide into groups so that more students will have an opportunity to speak.

❖ Read aloud today's focus statement: **Everyone experiences physical, emotional, or mental weariness at some point. Where can we draw strength during our own times of weariness? The Isaiah passage indicates that our strength comes both from God and from people like Isaiah who carry God's comfort to us.**

(2) Explore the Assurance of God's Comfort, as Brought to Humankind by the Prophet Isaiah

❖ Set the stage for today's lesson by pointing out that Isaiah 49:5-6 is part of the Second Servant Song (Isaiah 49:1-6), and Isaiah 50:4-9 is the Third Servant Song.

❖ Choose a volunteer to read Isaiah 49:5-6.

■ Discuss these questions, or answer them yourself in a brief lecture.
 (1) **What does this passage tell you about the relationship between God and the Servant?**
 (2) **What is God's purpose for the Servant?**
 (3) **Had you been the one called even before birth to be the Servant, what kinds of resources and support could you imagine needing from God?**

■ Provide quiet time for the adults to think about the kinds of resources and support they need from God to fulfill their own mission. How have they experienced this support in the past? What help do they need most right now?

❖ Select someone to read Isaiah 50:4-9.
 ■ Give background for these verses, known as the Third Servant Song, by creating a brief lecture from the Understanding the Scripture por-

tion. Note that the intended audience is the exiled Israelites who have turned away from God.

■ Study the Bible passage in depth by discussing these questions or answering them in a lecture.
 (1) **What does this passage say about God and the Servant?** (You may want to address this issue by distributing paper and pencils and asking the students to work individually or with a group to write these verses in their own words.)
 (2) **What meaning do you think Isaiah was trying to convey to his original listeners, the Israelites who were living in exile in Babylon?**
 (3) **What meaning does this passage have today for your congregation or the wider church?**
 (4) **What personal message can you glean from this passage?** (One way to discern a personal message is to ask the participants to read verses 4-9 silently and focus on a word or phrase that "pops out." What does that word or phrase say to them?)

(3) Consider Isaiah's Words in Light of the Learners' Views on How God Brings Strength to the Weary

❖ Divide the class into groups, and give each group a sheet of newsprint and a marker. Ask the students to list on their sheets any Bible passages that they like to turn to when they are feeling weary and overwhelmed. Provide at least one concordance so that the students may locate a favorite passage. Post the newsprint around the room and invite the students to walk around the room and note verses that appear on more than one list. Encourage the class members to talk about why the passages they have chosen are meaningful for them.

❖ Brainstorm other ways that the participants find God's strength in times of weariness. List these ideas on newsprint. Suggest that the students each select one or two new ideas that they will try.

(4) Discern and Commit to Helping Those Who Are Weary

❖ Distribute paper and pencils to each participant. Ask them to identify at least two people they know who are physically, emotionally, or mentally weary. State that their lists are to be kept confidential. Suggest that the students think of people who are carrying heavy burdens, such as trying to find employment, caring for elderly family members, or tending a chronically ill child.

❖ Invite the adults to list several concrete actions they could take on behalf of each person on their lists.

❖ Suggest that the students write these words on their papers and complete the sentence as a sign of their commitment to take action: **With God's help, I will uphold . . . , who is weary because. . . . I will assist by taking this action: . . . .**

(5) Continue the Journey

❖ Pray that the participants will go forth knowing that God will refresh, uphold, and strengthen them, even as they offer strength to others.

❖ Read aloud this preparation for next week's lesson. You may also want to post it on newsprint for the students to copy. **Prepare for next week's session, "Hope for Those Who Suffer," by reading Isaiah 53 and Luke 1. Our lesson will focus on Isaiah 53:1-3 and Luke 1:47-55. As you study, keep these ideas in mind: Suffering is an inescapable aspect of human life, and some suffer far more than others. What hope can we have in the midst of our suffering, whatever it may be? Isaiah's words affirm that Jesus suffered as we do and, indeed, freed us by his willingness to suffer even more on our behalf. Mary's song in Luke celebrates the release from suffering that will be brought about by her yet-unborn child.**

❖ Read aloud the following three ideas. Challenge the students to commit themselves to use these activities as a springboard to spiritual growth.

(1) **Make a list of several Scripture passages that you turn to, or could turn to, to find comfort and strength in times of weariness and discouragement. Keep this list handy.**

(2) **Offer an encouraging word to someone who is weary from ongoing challenges, such as illness, caring for a loved one, or searching for a job. See if there is some way you can assist this person.**

(3) **Meditate and pray about a situation that causes you to be weary. Seek God's guidance and strength.**

❖ Sing or read aloud "God Will Take Care of You."

❖ Lead this benediction to conclude the session: **May you go forth as Servants in whom the Lord delights to bring justice to the nations by the power of God's Spirit. Amen.**

UNIT 1: GOD'S REDEEMING LOVE
HOPE FOR THOSE WHO SUFFER

PREVIEWING THE LESSON

Lesson Scripture: Isaiah 53:1-3; Luke 1:47-55
Background Scripture: Isaiah 53; Luke 1
Key Verse: Luke 1:50

Focus of the Lesson:
Suffering is an inescapable aspect of human life, and some suffer far more than others. What hope can we have in the midst of our suffering, whatever it may be? Isaiah's words affirm that Jesus suffered as we do and, indeed, freed us by his willingness to suffer even more on our behalf. Mary's song in Luke celebrates the release from suffering that will be brought about by her yet-unborn child.

Goals for the Learners:
(1) to compare the Isaiah passage to Mary's *Magnificat*.
(2) to reflect on the Scripture passages in light of the learners' own views of suffering and the kind of release that Jesus brought into the world.
(3) to praise God for the hope that Jesus brings to those who suffer.

Pronunciation Guide:
Magnificat (mag nif' uh kat) (Latin word meaning "magnify")
Theophilus (thee of' uh luhs)
vicarious (vi ker'e us) (here used with "suffering" to mean "suffering for others")
Zechariah (zek uh ri' uh)

Supplies:
Bibles, newsprint and marker, paper and pencils, newspapers and/or current news magazines, hymnals

---

READING THE SCRIPTURE

NRSV
Isaiah 53:1-3
[1]Who has believed what we have heard?

NIV
Isaiah 53:1-3
[1]Who has believed our message

And to whom has the arm of the LORD
  been revealed?
²For he grew up before him like a young
  plant,
  and like a root out of dry ground;
he had no form or majesty that we should
  look at him,
  nothing in his appearance that we should
  desire him.
³He was despised and rejected by others;
  a man of suffering and acquainted with
  infirmity;
and as one from whom others hide their faces
  he was despised, and we held him of no
  account.

Luke 1:47-55
  ⁴⁷And my spirit rejoices in God my Savior,
⁴⁸for he has looked with favor on the lowliness of his servant.
  Surely, from now on all generations will
  call me blessed;
⁴⁹for the Mighty One has done great things
  for me,
  and holy is his name.
⁵⁰His mercy is for those who fear him
  from generation to generation.
⁵¹He has shown strength with his arm;
  he has scattered the proud in the thoughts
  of their hearts.
⁵²He has brought down the powerful from
  their thrones,
  and lifted up the lowly;
⁵³he has filled the hungry with good things,
  and sent the rich away empty.
⁵⁴He has helped his servant Israel,
  in remembrance of his mercy,
⁵⁵according to the promise he made to our
  ancestors,
  to Abraham and to his descendants forever."

and to whom has the arm of the LORD
  been revealed?
²He grew up before him like a tender shoot,
  and like a root out of dry ground.
He had no beauty or majesty to attract us to
  him,
  nothing in his appearance that we should
  desire him.
³He was despised and rejected by men,
  a man of sorrows, and familiar with
  suffering.
Like one from whom men hide their faces
  he was despised, and we esteemed him
  not.

Luke 1:47-55
  ⁴⁷And my spirit rejoices in God my Savior,
⁴⁸for he has been mindful
  of the humble state of his servant.
From now on all generations will call me
  blessed,
  ⁴⁹for the Mighty One has done great
  things for me—
  holy is his name.
⁵⁰His mercy extends to those who fear him,
  from generation to generation.
⁵¹He has performed mighty deeds with his
  arm;
  he has scattered those who are proud in
  their inmost thoughts.
⁵²He has brought down rulers from their
  thrones
  but has lifted up the humble.
⁵³He has filled the hungry with good things
  but has sent the rich away empty.
⁵⁴He has helped his servant Israel,
  remembering to be merciful
⁵⁵to Abraham and his descendants forever,
  even as he said to our fathers."

UNDERSTANDING THE SCRIPTURE

Isaiah 53:1-3. The questions of verse 1 hearken back to the opening of the Fourth Servant Song in 52:13-15. There, the nations go startled and muted from what they see revealed in the appalling sight of the Servant. The "arm of the LORD" is a phrase suggestive of God's power (see also Luke 1:51). The powerful irony of this expression in Isaiah comes in the one who will reveal that very strength through suffering. The language of the second verse depicts the Servant in a series of negatives ("no" and "nothing"), matching the barren image of a root parched in dry ground. The Servant's apparent state of "nothingness" finds ultimate expression in the third verse. Despised, rejected, suffering, infirm, of no account: Who could believe this?

Isaiah 53:4-6. The theme of vicarious suffering dominates. The verbs and their modifiers become quite graphic in the experience of such suffering: *stricken, struck down, afflicted, wounded, crushed.* The one upon whom this falls is the Servant. As noted in earlier sessions, the identity of the Servant remains a mystery, as does the process of how exactly suffering in the place of another "works." Is this Israel, suffering in exile for the nations? Is this Jesus, hanging on the cross for sinners? Isaiah leaves that open. What Isaiah does disclose is the identity of those for whom the Servant suffers: "our infirmities," "we like sheep," "the iniquity of us all." These verses lead to confession that our hope is inseparable from the Servant's suffering.

Isaiah 53:7-9. Justice looms large in Judeo-Christian ethics. It is part of God's purposes for humanity (Micah 6:8). It is part of the Servant's calling (Isaiah 42:4). Yet justice goes denied to the Servant (53:8). The very one through whom God works finds the covenant's protections absent. In the face of that denial, the Servant does not cry out. He remains silent. Vulnerability goes

enacted in no words raised in defense or protest, even when suffering leads to death and further indignity (53:9). It is a nonverbal turning of the other cheek. Violence and injustice go absorbed in that silence, as does our culpability in the suffering of verses 4-6. How? Isaiah does not reveal. Isaiah simply invites belief.

Isaiah 53:10-12. The Fourth and last Servant Song culminates in reversal and restoration. The mystery inherent in previous sections regarding the process of vicarious suffering and the identity of the Servant now finds an even greater enigma. Isaiah declares that the Servant's suffering and pain trace to "the will of the LORD" (53:10). That will, however, does not end for the Servant in defeat. The one once "nothing" will be made great. Suffering will neither be in vain nor without vindication. One does not read the whole of this Servant Song in the season of Advent without catching glimpses of the purposes of the awaited birth. For Christians, the vicarious suffering undergone by Isaiah's Servant only deepens the redemptive meaning of Isaiah 9:6: "For a child has been born for us." For us.

Luke 1:1-4. A single complex sentence forms this prologue to Luke. "Since" introduces the opening clause—a recognition of the existing accounts of the life of Jesus handed on by eyewitnesses (from which Luke, therefore, seems to exclude himself). The main body of the sentence ("I, too, decided . . .") declares Luke's intent to author his own "orderly account." The identity of Theophilus remains an intriguing mystery. Was he the "patron" who sponsored Luke's writing? Was he a well-known figure in the community? Or was Theophilus, which literally means "lover of God," simply a symbol for Luke to include every Christian as the addressee?

Luke 1:5-25. As Luke will do to preface the birth of Jesus, so now he introduces the story of John by placing these events in historical context (the reign of Herod). Likewise, the archangel Gabriel announces the promised birth to Zechariah, as will be the case with Mary. The promise of a child to a barren couple is more than simply a familiar theme from the Hebrew Scriptures. The "song" Mary later offers in joy to Elizabeth (1:46-55) closely resembles in structure and style the prayer of Hannah (1 Samuel 2:1-10), whose own barrenness ended with the birth of Samuel. Zechariah's service as priest required occasional travels to Jerusalem for tours of duty there (see also 10:29-31).

Luke 1:26-38. Tradition names this narrative the "annunciation," for its announcement of the birth. Betrothal, while not marriage, represented a definite and formalized relationship. Very often, the woman could be quite young (early to mid-teens) while the man was much older. In contrast to Matthew, Luke has virtually no role in the prebirth narrative for Joseph, save his lineage from the house of David. Gabriel's concluding response of "nothing will be impossible with God" (1:37) forms a close parallel to words spoken to an equally incredulous Sarah: "Is anything too wonderful for the LORD?" (Genesis 18:14).

Luke 1:39-56. This narrative of the visitation begins with Elizabeth's blessing of Mary and the child her cousin carries with her. John's *in utero* leap when his mother hears Mary's greeting serves to accentuate the role John will have in his ministry of pointing to Jesus as the one for whom he prepares. Mary's lengthy "song" in reply is often called the *Magnificat* from its opening word in Latin. Its connection to the prayer of Hannah has already been mentioned. Mary's remaining with Elizabeth for three months before leaving allows Luke to clear the stage for John's birth. The next time we meet Mary will be in Bethlehem for the birth of Jesus.

Luke 1:57-80. The birth of John comes accompanied eight days later by the miraculous loosing of Zechariah's tongue (1:20, 64). Thus, the father is able to fulfill the traditional role of naming the son at the time of circumcision. Zechariah offers a priestly benediction for John and the one whose way he will prepare (1:67-79). The passage closes with words of John's growth (1:80), similar to a later word concerning Jesus (2:52).

INTERPRETING THE SCRIPTURE

Incredible!

What stretches your capacity to believe? How does faith test your limits of credibility? Isaiah 53:1 moves into such territory, and draws us there as well. Its opening question of "Who has believed . . . ?" strongly implies that such an act of trust is not universal among those addressed, and perhaps not even frequent. What stretches the possibility of belief here is what has been heard along with what has been seen ("revealed").

We rely on the senses of sight and sound to assess the world. In matters of faith, those two senses are heightened. Paul asserts, "faith comes from what is heard" (Romans 10:17). Sight can hold even more sway in what we believe or not, and that is not just Thomas insisting on seeing the wounds of Jesus before he will believe. At the end of the book of Job, Job speaks about his own maturing in faith: "I had heard of you by the hearing of the ear, but now my eye sees you" (Job 42:5).

But what happens when what we hear and see conflicts with faith, or our understandings of God's purposes? In the time of Isaiah 53, the sight and sound (silence, actually) of the figure of the Suffering Servant seemed incredible. In the time of Jesus, Peter could not abide by what he heard of a suffering Messiah. Several of the Gospels record that none of the disciples could bear the sight of a Crucified One either. In our time, plenty of evidence abounds in sight and sound that this world spins out of the control—and out of the love—of God. In all such times, hope seems incredible. In all such times, faith requires more than what is seen or heard to verify it. Faith summons trust and action that reflects God's incredible grace.

A Man of Suffering

Image dominates our postmodern world. Advertisements may carry few or no words to hawk products, relying instead on images of beautiful people doing attractive things while wearing the jeans or guzzling the drink only subtly identified. Media consultants advise candidates or incumbents for office concerning which image looks best and appeals most widely. A senator wearing a bow tie, no matter how bad or good his ideas may be, could not ever hope to win the presidency—at least, not until styles change.

If Isaiah relied upon image, all hope would be lost. The Servant to whom he points comes up short on all counts. He looks bad: no form, no desirability. He repels: rejected by others, one from whom others hide their faces. He embodies the kind of life none of us would want or choose: suffering, infirmity. Just to make sure we do not miss the point, twice in verse 3 Isaiah states the Servant was "despised," a Hebrew word whose meaning involves contempt and utter disregard.

Nothing in the Servant would attract attention to self—which is why "incredible" headlines the previous section. God has chosen to reveal God's power through the one least likely to be seen, least likely to be associated with power, to work in saving ways intended to bring hope. You can't just accept what God does in such a one on face value. Faith is required—a suspension of belief in this world's conventional wisdoms

concerning where help and hope normally are found—in order to trust Isaiah's word. You cannot avoid the need to trust beyond appearances to believe that hope emerges from the Servant's suffering. Then again, you need to trust beyond appearances in order to celebrate a Savior who is, for the moment, curled in Mary's womb before wriggling in a manger's hay.

The Joy of God's Favor

Magnificat. Rejoice. Every now and then, Scripture bursts into song. We are used to that in the Psalms, which are themselves a collection of songs. But in other scriptural works, where narrative and story dominate, we also find such occasional eruptions of praise. When Egypt's chariots disappear under the waters, the prophetess Miriam takes tambourine in hand and sings a song of victory (Exodus 15:20-21). Paul searches for words to express a theology of Christ's humiliation and exaltation, and ends up using what many believe is a hymn of the early church in Philippians 2:5-11. And here, Luke's narration of the birth "preludes" of both John and Jesus breaks with the interlude of Mary's song of praise.

Those of us from the Protestant tradition sometimes do not know what to do with Mary. In our over-reactions to perceived indulgences in Marian devotion, we ignore her at best—to our detriment. Listen to the opening verses of the hymn (1:47-49). Mary's joy resides in the joy of God's grace and blessing extended to her. God's grace sometimes does scandalize us by its particularity. God chooses Israel, a choice not made by Israel's numbers but rather completely out of God's grace (Deuteronomy 7:7-8). The lowliness ("humility") of Mary reflects a similar grace at work here. The blessedness understood by Mary traces not to her, but to what God has done for her and through her.

God's "regarding" of Mary offers hope to all the rest of us, particularly to those who are otherwise routinely overlooked or ignored. God's grace does not rely upon celebrity, or upon self-promotion. God's blessings fall upon the faithful, who open themselves to the gracious word and ways of God in their lives (Luke 1:38). Mary's rejoicing in God's favor anticipates our own.

The Gospel as Topsy-Turvy

The core of Mary's song (1:51-54), in one sense, extends the news and celebration of God's favor to Mary to all who are lowly. To do so, Mary sings a song whose theme will loom large in all the Gospel accounts, but especially Luke: the great reversal that grace and justice bring to the normal order of things. Mary's tune rises and falls on notes of lifting up (the lowly) and bringing down (the powerful), of filling (the hungry) and emptying (the rich).

God's reversals bring extraordinary hope to those whom the world has given no cause to hope: the poor, the suffering, the lowly. Likewise, those who have all of the world (figuratively if not literally) find hope resides not in what you have but rather in whom you trust. And the only one trustworthy in Mary's song, and this Gospel, is the One who shows mercy and remembers promises, the God who "helps" Israel. Luke uses an unusual word for "help," which occurs only two other times in all of the New Testament. In one of those, Paul enjoins the elders at Ephesus in his farewell to them to "support the weak" (Acts 20:35). God's help shows a particular concern for those who are vulnerable: the suffering, the poor, the weak, and the humble.

Mary's song underscores that theme deeply rooted in the Hebrew Scriptures, and clearly announced in the Song of Hannah that so closely parallels the *Magnificat* (see especially 1 Samuel 2:2-8). Mary's song sets the stage for Luke's Gospel, where outcast Samaritans go honored (10:29-37) and destitute prodigals find welcome (15:11-24); where Beatitudes bless the poor and the hungry and the suffering (6:20-22). Mary sings hope of God's turning the world topsy-turvy by grace that regards the lowly. She herself and the child she carries are signs of this coming reversal.

SHARING THE SCRIPTURE

Preparing Our Hearts

This week's devotional reading is found in Romans 12:9-16, where Paul outlines the traits of a Christian. Note in verse 12 that we are told to "be patient in suffering," an admonition that relates to today's lesson in which those who suffer are assured of hope. As you read verses 9-16, examine your own life. How many of these traits can you claim? Which ones are you earnestly striving toward? Which ones do you need to begin to focus on? Write your thoughts in a spiritual journal.

Pray that you and the adult learners will live as true believers whose actions and attitudes bear witness to their faithfulness.

Preparing Our Minds

Study the background from Isaiah 53 and Luke 1, and the lesson Scripture, Isaiah 53:1-3 and Luke 1:47-55, often called Mary's *Magnificat*. As you study, consider how the messages of Isaiah and Mary offer hope to those in the midst of suffering.

Write on newsprint:

❑ quotations concerning suffering for the "Reflect on the Scripture Passages in Light of the Students' Views of Suffering and the Kind of Release That Jesus Brought into the World" portion of the lesson.

❑ information for next week's lesson, found under "Continue the Journey."

LEADING THE CLASS

(1) Gather to Learn

❖ Welcome the class members and introduce any guests.

❖ Pray that participants who are currently experiencing some form of suffering will be especially aware of God's presence and comfort today.

❖ Distribute whatever news magazines and newspapers you have available. Ask the students to scan these resources for examples of human suffering. List these examples on newsprint. Provide a few moments for silent prayers for all who suffer.

❖ Read aloud today's focus statement: **Suffering is an inescapable aspect of human life, and some suffer far more than others. What hope can we have in the midst of our suffering, whatever it may be? Isaiah's words affirm that Jesus suffered as we do and, indeed, freed us by his willingness to suffer even more on our behalf. Mary's song in Luke celebrates the release from suffering that will be brought about by her yet-unborn child.**

(2) Compare the Isaiah Passage to Mary's Magnificat

❖ Choose a volunteer to read aloud Isaiah 53:1-3, which is part of the Fourth Servant Song.

❖ Brainstorm answers to this question: **What does this passage tell you about the person and work of the Servant?** List ideas on newsprint. Post this paper where everyone can see it.

❖ Select someone to read Mary's *Magnificat*, found in Luke 1:46-55.

■ Brainstorm answers to this question: **What does this passage tell you about God and divine intentions** **for humanity?** List ideas on newsprint. Post this paper next to the one your created for Isaiah 53.

❖ Compare the two lists the students have made by asking the following questions.

(1) What relationship, if any, do you see between the Servant and Jesus the Messiah?

(2) How do you see promises that Isaiah made to Israel in exile fulfilled?

(3) How do you see the promises of "great things" that Mary sings about fulfilled?

(4) What hope does this prophecy and song of praise offer to you?

(3) Reflect on the Scripture Passages in Light of the Students' Views of Suffering and the Kind of Release That Jesus Brought into the World

❖ Point out that the suffering of the Servant was "for us."

❖ Post newsprint on which you have written the following quotations concerning suffering.

(a.) The first thing Jesus promises is suffering: "I tell you . . . you will be weeping and wailing . . . and you will be sorrowful." But he calls these pains birth pains. And so, what seems a hindrance becomes a way; what seems an obstacle becomes a door; and what seems a misfit becomes a cornerstone. Jesus changes our history from a random series of sad incidents and accidents into a constant opportunity for a change of heart (Henri J. M. Nouwen, 1932–1996).

(b.) Remember this: all suffering comes to an end. And whatever you suffer authentically, God has suffered from it first (Meister Eckhart, about 1260–about 1327).

(c.) Unearned suffering is redemptive (Martin Luther King Jr., 1929–1968).

(d.) We look on the woes of the world. We hear the whole creation, to use Paul's language, groaning and laboring in pain. We see a few good men vainly striving to help the world into life and light; and in our sense of the awful magnitude of the problem and of our inability to do much, we cry out: "Where's God? How can he bear this? Why doesn't he do something?" And there is but one answer that satisfies: and this is the Incarnation and the Cross. God could not bear it. He has done something. He has done the utmost compatible with moral wisdom. He has entered into the fellowship of our suffering and misery and at infinite cost has taken the world upon his heart (Borden P. Bowne, 1847–1910).

❖ Provide time for the students to read these quotations silently and choose one that best describes their attitude toward or beliefs about suffering.

❖ Divide into groups and invite the adults to talk about how the quotations they have chosen reflect their attitudes or beliefs about suffering. How do Jesus and his suffering fit into their views?

(4) Praise God for Providing Hope to Those Who Suffer

Invite the class members to read aloud Psalm 34. If you have a hymnal that includes a Psalter (the Psalms), you may want to have the psalm read responsively.

Encourage the students to read silently the words of praise in verses 1-3 and offer praise in their hearts to God for deliverance from suffering, especially as that deliverance comes through Jesus.

(5) Continue the Journey

❖ Pray that each participant will experience the hope that God offers through Jesus to those who suffer and share that hope with others.

❖ Read aloud this preparation for next week's lesson. You may also want to post it on newsprint for the students to copy. **Prepare for next week's session, "Be Joyful," by reading Isaiah 6:1-3 and Luke 2:8-20. The lesson will focus on Isaiah 6:1-2 and Luke 2:8-20. Keep this focus in mind as you study: People enjoy hearing and sharing good news. What good news can we share with others? The good news of the Isaiah passage is that God will one day establish wholeness, freedom, and joy. In Luke's passage, the angels announce that this new day has begun with Jesus' birth.**

❖ Read aloud the following three ideas. Challenge the students to commit themselves to use these activities as a springboard to spiritual growth.

(1) **List all the ways that you are suffering right now. Pray about each of these situations. Meditate on these questions: How do you experience God's love in the midst of this suffering? What gives you hope to carry on?**

(2) **Recall that the Servant suffered for a redemptive purpose, on behalf of others. Who are you serving? What are you willing to give up, perhaps even suffer for, to help others? Take action, based on your answers, to help someone.**

(3) **Visit someone who is having a difficult time right now. Perhaps you could perform a small kindness, such as bringing dinner or babysitting a child or just listening to one who needs to know that God's love is present even in the midst of painful situations.**

❖ Sing or read aloud "My Soul Gives Glory to God."

❖ Lead this benediction to conclude the session: **May you go forth as Servants in whom the Lord delights to bring justice to the nations by the power of God's Spirit. Amen.**

UNIT 1: GOD'S REDEEMING LOVE
BE JOYFUL

PREVIEWING THE LESSON

Lesson Scripture: Isaiah 61:1-2; Luke 2:8-20
Background Scripture: Isaiah 61:1-3; Luke 2:8-20
Key Verse: Luke 2:11

Focus of the Lesson:

People enjoy hearing and sharing good news. What good news can we share with others? The good news of the Isaiah passage is that God will one day establish wholeness, freedom, and joy. In Luke's passage, the angels announce that this new day has begun with Jesus' birth.

Goals for the Learners:

(1) to explore Isaiah's prophecy of the One to come in light of Luke's account of Jesus' birth.
(2) to relate the meaning of Jesus' birth to their own lives.
(3) to celebrate Christmas Day!

Pronunciation Guide:

cinquain (sin' kan) (a poem that is five lines long)
euaggelizo (yoo ang ghel id zo)
mashach (maw shakh')

Supplies:

Bibles, newsprint and marker, paper and pencils, hymnals, optional light refreshments

---

READING THE SCRIPTURE

NRSV
Isaiah 61:1-2
¹The spirit of the LORD GOD is upon me,
  because the LORD has anointed me;
he has sent me to bring good news to the
    oppressed,
  to bind up the brokenhearted,
to proclaim liberty to the captives,
  and release to the prisoners;

NIV
Isaiah 61:1-2
¹The Spirit of the Sovereign LORD is on me,
  because the LORD has anointed me
  to preach good news to the poor.
He has sent me to bind up the broken-
    hearted,
  to proclaim freedom for the captives

²to proclaim the year of the LORD's favor,
and the day of vengeance of our God;
to comfort all who mourn;

Luke 2:8-20

⁸In that region there were shepherds living in the fields, keeping watch over their flock by night. ⁹Then an angel of the Lord stood before them, and the glory of the Lord shone around them, and they were terrified. ¹⁰But the angel said to them, "Do not be afraid; for see—I am bringing you good news of great joy for all the people: **¹¹to you is born this day in the city of David a Savior, who is the Messiah, the Lord.** ¹²This will be a sign for you: you will find a child wrapped in bands of cloth and lying in a manger." ¹³And suddenly there was with the angel a multitude of the heavenly host, praising God and saying,

¹⁴"Glory to God in the highest heaven,
and on earth peace among those whom he favors!"

¹⁵When the angels had left them and gone into heaven, the shepherds said to one another, "Let us go now to Bethlehem and see this thing that has taken place, which the Lord has made known to us." ¹⁶So they went with haste and found Mary and Joseph, and the child lying in the manger. ¹⁷When they saw this, they made known what had been told them about this child; ¹⁸and all who heard it were amazed at what the shepherds told them. ¹⁹But Mary treasured all these words and pondered them in her heart. ²⁰The shepherds returned, glorifying and praising God for all they had heard and seen, as it had been told them.

and release from darkness for the prisoners,
²to proclaim the year of the LORD's favor
and the day of vengeance of our God,
to comfort all who mourn,

Luke 2:8-20

⁸And there were shepherds living out in the fields nearby, keeping watch over their flocks at night. ⁹An angel of the Lord appeared to them, and the glory of the Lord shone around them, and they were terrified. ¹⁰But the angel said to them, "Do not be afraid. I bring you good news of great joy that will be for all the people. **¹¹Today in the town of David a Savior has been born to you; he is Christ the Lord.** ¹²This will be a sign to you: You will find a baby wrapped in cloths and lying in a manger."

¹³Suddenly a great company of the heavenly host appeared with the angel, praising God and saying,

¹⁴"Glory to God in the highest,
and on earth peace to men on whom his favor rests."

¹⁵When the angels had left them and gone into heaven, the shepherds said to one another, "Let's go to Bethlehem and see this thing that has happened, which the Lord has told us about."

¹⁶So they hurried off and found Mary and Joseph, and the baby, who was lying in the manger. ¹⁷When they had seen him, they spread the word concerning what had been told them about this child, ¹⁸and all who heard it were amazed at what the shepherds said to them. ¹⁹But Mary treasured up all these things and pondered them in her heart. ²⁰The shepherds returned, glorifying and praising God for all the things they had heard and seen, which were just as they had been told.

UNDERSTANDING THE SCRIPTURE

Isaiah 61:1-2. A connection between Isaiah and Luke emerges in these verses.

Jesus opens his inaugural sermon in Nazareth by quoting from these words.

After reading them, he adds: "Today this scripture has been fulfilled in your hearing" (Luke 4:21). These words originally addressed the people of Israel, either in exile or the difficult post-exilic period of rebuilding. As the books of Ezra and Nehemiah make clear, the rebuilding did not move smoothly. Opposition arose. Hopes fell. Even a rebuilt Jerusalem did not match memories of what had once been. The unidentified speaker of these words has been sent to serve as one who not only brings good news, but also acts in ways to bring freedom and comfort. The phrases "liberty to the captives" and "the year of the LORD's favor" bring the promise of Jubilee back into the spirit and imagination of Israel (see Leviticus 25). Jubilee was a tradition that called for the forgiveness of debt and the restoration of land and personal freedom. It was to occur every fiftieth year: after the seventh of seven cycles of seven years, a Sabbath for the land and its people. Who would be the one upon whom the Spirit of God would rest and accomplish these things? Intriguingly, Isaiah identifies him with the Lord's "anointed." In Hebrew, that word is *mashach*, the root for "Messiah."

Isaiah 61:3. "Zion" was the mount upon which Jerusalem had been built. The actions of reversal begun in the opening two verses find evidence in a triad of "insteads" in verse 3. A garland replaces ashes, the latter being a traditional symbol of mourning (as the ashes imposed on Ash Wednesday reflect mourning and repentance for sin). Oil, instead of mourning, draws on the symbol of oil as a sign of hospitality and joy (see Psalm 133:2). Likewise the wrapping of a mantle (of praise) provides protection and shelter. The verse closes by describing those who find themselves encouraged by good news and ministered to by these comforting and freeing actions as "oaks. . . the planting of the LORD." The image hearkens back to Psalm 1:3, where those who tend to God's purposes are like "trees planted by streams of water."

Luke 2:8-9. The Old Testament prophets referred to Israel's kings as "shepherds," often in unflattering comparisons to God's shepherding of the people (see Ezekiel 34). Shepherds in the day of Jesus carried and provided an equally mixed metaphor. David as the shepherd king continued to exercise appeal. Yet, Jewish society of that day held shepherds in contempt. In a vocation that separated them from community, shepherds found little welcome in that community when they were not out keeping watch over flocks. So in a Gospel that will elevate the role of outcasts (Samaritans, prodigals), it is perhaps not surprising to see shepherds there at the beginning. The "glory" of the Lord, portrayed as a shining (see also 9:29-31), evokes an understandable response of fear. "They were terrified" translates an unusual Greek phrase that literally means, "to fear with a great fear."

Luke 2:10-12. The angelic pronouncement of "do not be afraid" has occurred twice already in this Gospel, first to Zechariah (1:13) and then to Mary (1:30). The reason given not to fear echoes Isaiah 61:1: the bringing of good news. The Greek verb Luke uses for that action echoes another word you may find familiar: *euaggelizo*, "evangelize." The recipients of this news are not shepherds alone, but all people. The city of David is not Jerusalem but Bethlehem, the birthplace of the shepherd king. Luke identifies the One born there as Messiah (*Christos* in Greek), the meaning of which is "anointed" (Isaiah 61:1). The other titles ascribed here to Jesus are "Savior" and "Lord," with Luke alone among the Synoptic Gospels (Matthew, Mark, Luke) using "Savior" in reference to Jesus. The wrapping of an infant in bands of cloth represented a Palestinian custom for care of newborns.

Luke 2:13-14. In the Old Testament, the "host(s)" of heaven derived from a military term for men of war or an army. The heavenly hosts came to be associated with God's angelic army, symbolic of God's might (see

Genesis 32:1). In the night sky over Bethlehem, the symbols and messengers of God's power become those entrusted with a song of praise that promises peace. Textual differences between manuscripts of the last phrase in the fourteenth verse account for the difference in translations from "on earth peace, goodwill toward men" (King James Version); to "on earth peace among those whom he [God] favors" (New Revised Standard Version). The angels' song finds ironic parallel in Luke's account of the entry into Jerusalem (19:38).

Luke 2:15-17. The visit and report of the shepherds takes center stage. These outcasts, whose testimony in a legal procedure would have been held suspect, will become the first witnesses to God's workings. Their unlikely role in the Gospel's opening anticipates that of the women who will witness at the climax of this Gospel to an empty tomb in the face of initially unbelieving disciples (24:11). The sight of mother and father and child trigger their witness (2:16-17).

Luke 2:18-20. "All who heard it were amazed." "All" suggests a larger audience than a set of parents and a cooing infant. "All" makes room in the scene for "all" who overhear, and overlook, the manger's scene and the shepherds' report through Luke. Amazement summarizes the response of all. Luke singles out Mary for "treasuring" and "pondering" these words. When Gabriel had greeted her months before, Mary then had "pondered" his greeting (1:29). Later, Luke will depict Mary as one who "treasured all these things in her heart" (2:51b). The mother of Jesus is more to the story than a mere vehicle of birth. She is a person of deep faith. The shepherds' return at the close of the story mirrors its angelic beginnings. They go their way "glorifying and praising God," the very same actions as the heavenly host. Heaven and earth unite to sing the Messiah's birth song.

INTERPRETING THE SCRIPTURE

Spirited Works

In this season of Advent now birthed into Christmas, Isaiah gives voice to actions for which Messiah had been awaited. We have noted before how Jesus used this text in affirming his ministry led by God's Spirit. Consider now the verbs Isaiah uses in the first verse of that passage as descriptive of Christ's ministry that, for the moment, comes in cradled form.

To bring good news to the oppressed. You would think the bearer of good news would be always welcomed everywhere. That depends on whether you hear it as good or not. To outcasts (shepherds), to folks on the margin (Samaritans), to those not routinely included among the powers that be (women), Jesus brought words of invitation and inclusion and commendation.

To bind up the brokenhearted. Restoring what had been lost and grieved forms a core of Jesus' healings. Lepers found in their healings not only restoration of body but also to community. In the raising of a little girl and then Lazarus, hearts broken by grief found the new possibilities of grace at work in Jesus' touch and word.

To proclaim liberty to the captives and release to the prisoners. Exorcisms, the casting out of unclean spirits, pose problems for the modern mind. The exorcisms of Jesus, however one understands them, represent acts of liberation. People under the dominion of that which brought only self-abuse now find freedom. Jesus looses the human spirit for its God-intended freedom.

The one who now rests in a manger will be the same one upon whom God's Spirit will descend at baptism. And in every case, the actions of Isaiah's Anointed One find incarnation in the ministry of Jesus the Christ.

Do Not Live Afraid

Faith intends to move persons out of fear. "Do not be afraid" speaks a message consistent with the biblical witness as a whole. So God spoke to Abram (15:1) and then to Israel (Deuteronomy 7:18) to move them from fear to promise. So an angel spoke to Mary and Joseph at the beginning of Jesus' story (Luke 1:30, Matthew 1:20) to change their fear into trust. So an angel would speak to women come to the tomb (Matthew 28:5) to transform fear into hope. And so now, in this session's text, does an angel speak to shepherds to replace their fear with joy.

Notice that none of these texts say, "don't be afraid *because there's nothing to be afraid of.*" Sometimes we make the mistake of thinking the only way to get rid of fear is to deny any cause for it. There are times when denial is the way to go. When we tell a child at night there is not a monster under the bed so you don't have to be afraid, that is true. But when a person is genuinely frightened by something all too real, it does little good—and sometimes very great harm—to say there's nothing to be afraid of. When a widow or widower looks at life for the first time without a beloved companion, there is cause for fear. When a patient faces risky surgery or the prospect of a lengthy and difficult therapy for cancer, there is reason to fear. When people live in dangerous places, where attempts to bring peace come at high risk, there is justification for fear.

The gospel speaks to such people and situations, not out of fear's denial, but from the possibility of fear's transformation. Perhaps what the angel speaking to shepherds and would-be parents and mourners of death soon to be witnesses of life is really saying is: Do not *live* afraid. By the grace of Jesus Christ, by the gift of community with those who proclaim that grace: Fears may

still arise, but we need not live our lives under their control. We live by faith.

The Jubilee of God's Favor

Scholars concur that the year of Jubilee, as described in Leviticus 25 and alluded to in Isaiah 61:1, most likely was never observed in Israel in any extensive way (see also Isaiah 61:1-2 in "Understanding the Scripture"). Certain specific practices such as the redemption of land or kinsmen seem to have worked their way into society on individual cases (see Ruth 4:1-7).

Why then bring up Jubilee, especially on the day set aside to celebrate Jesus' birth? Isaiah's reference to "the year of the LORD's favor" is generally understood to be a reference to Jubilee. The time of God's favor looms large in the birth narrative of Jesus, particularly in the angels' song: "Glory to God in the highest heaven, and on earth peace among those whom he favors" (Luke 2:14). The awaited time of God's favor comes in the birth at Bethlehem.

The meaning of that favor in Luke traces back to this child's identity as "Savior." The Jubilee practices of Leviticus relied on the actions of persons who "redeemed" family from slavery or debt and land from another's possession. Consider how those actions parallel themes encountered in our understandings of the purpose of Jesus' coming. Redemption and liberation figure largely in those purposes: from sin and oppression and death, for grace and freedom and life. The Jubilee of God's favor can justifiably describe this day's celebration.

Treasuring and Pondering

The works of Luke, both his Gospel and Acts, offer Mary as an example of faith. Her earlier "let it be with me according to your word" (Luke 1:38) offers a remarkable statement of trust and openness to God's purposes. Acts 1:12-14 lists Mary among those who returned to Jerusalem after the ascension. That is, Mary was part of the earliest Christian community, who devoted themselves to prayer in expectation of the promised Spirit (Acts 1:8).

Luke's Christmas narrative (2:8-20) offers further insight into the faith and spirituality of this woman. Here (as noted in "Understanding the Scripture"), Mary is described as one who "treasured" and "pondered." "Treasured" translates a verb whose meaning suggests "preserving." Other occurrences of this verb in Scripture relate to instances where the preserving was of something not quite fully understood, but held on to anyway. Faith invites the treasuring or preserving of some things that we, too, do not fully grasp. Who among us understands perfectly the mystery of Incarnation, or the presence of Christ in sacrament? If we only held on to those things that we understood, our faith would be one-dimensional and without a sense of holy mystery.

Likewise, Luke commends Mary for her "pondering." To ponder something is to reflect on its meaning. For some folks, faith has no subtleties. *God said it, I believe it, that's all there is to it.* Mary trusts the angel's word, and now comes to hear the shepherds' refrain. Nothing suggests she does not believe it. Mary also continues to mull it over in her mind and heart; she "ponders" it. Mary's pondering offers us a wise model for ways to approach Scripture and even our prayer life. Move within it, look from different angles, ponder its meaning, rather than simply go on previous assumptions. Ponder the gift of Christmas: What is fresh and new in its meaning or experience this day? Where have you grown in your experience of the Word made flesh in the past year? Let Mary lead you in faithful pondering. Let her joy be your joy.

SHARING THE SCRIPTURE

Preparing Our Hearts

This week's devotional reading is found in Isaiah 52:7-12. George Frideric Handel (1685–1759) used an excerpt from verse 7 in the *Messiah* to create a beloved aria, "How beautiful are the feet of them that preach the Gospel of peace." Who has brought you good news? With whom have you shared good news? As you "break forth together into singing" (52:9) the joyous music of this Christmas season, capture the excitement once again of the news that the shepherds heard announced by the heavenly choir so long ago.

Pray that you and the adult learners will proclaim the glad tidings of Jesus' birth, for he came bringing salvation and peace for all people.

Preparing Our Minds

Study the background, Isaiah 61:1-3 and Luke 2:8-20, and lesson Scripture, Isaiah 61:1-2 and Luke 2:8-20. As you read these passages, give thanks for Isaiah's good news that God will one day establish wholeness, freedom, and joy. Recognize that with the birth of Jesus this new day has begun.

Write on newsprint:
❏ list of tasks for section entitled "Explore Isaiah's Prophecy of the One to Come in Light of Luke's Account of Jesus' Birth."
❏ chart for section entitled "Explore Isaiah's Prophecy of the One to Come in Light of Luke's Account of Jesus' Birth."
❏ information for next week's lesson, found under "Continue the Journey."

Option for "Explore Isaiah's Prophecy of the One to Come in Light of Luke's Account of Jesus' Birth": Plan a brief lecture in which you give examples of specific events or stories from the Gospels that illustrate how Jesus fulfilled the prophecy of Isaiah 61:1-2.

Option: Plan to provide some light refreshments, such as cookies, for today's session.

LEADING THE CLASS

(1) Gather to Learn

❖ Welcome the class members and introduce any guests. Be sure to offer a special welcome to those who may be visiting on this Christmas Day.

❖ Pray that all who have come will hear and receive the good news that Jesus Christ has come to earth as Savior, Messiah, Lord—God with us.

❖ Invite the participants to tell brief stories of good news they have heard recently. Suggest that they think about notes or letters they have received with Christmas cards. If the class is large, divide into groups so that more adults will have an opportunity to participate.

❖ Read aloud today's focus statement: **People enjoy hearing and sharing good news. What good news can we share with others? The good news of the Isaiah passage is that God will one day establish wholeness, freedom, and joy. In Luke's passage, the angels announce that this new day has begun with Jesus' birth.**

(2) Explore Isaiah's Prophecy of the One to Come in Light of Luke's Account of Jesus' Birth

❖ Choose a volunteer to read Isaiah 61:1-2.
  ■ List on newsprint the tasks that the one to whom this passage refers is expected to do.
  ■ Ask the class to turn to Luke 4:16-21. Note that verses 18-19 are quotations from Isaiah 58:6 and 61:1-2. Point out that in Luke 4:21 Jesus claims that the Scripture from Isaiah has been fulfilled through him.

■ Invite the class members to cite examples of ways in which they believe Jesus fulfills Isaiah's prophecies. You may want to list these ideas on newsprint. Or, you may prefer to create a brief lecture in which you give examples of specific events or stories from the Gospels.

❖ Select a narrator, angel, and two or three shepherds to read Luke 2:8-20 as a drama. Enlist the entire class to read verse 14 in unison as the heavenly host.
  ■ Post this chart on newsprint. Reread the passage from Luke and work as a class or in groups to complete it.

Who?	What happened?	Where?	When?

■ Read or retell the information on Luke 2:8-9 in Understanding the Scripture. Discuss these questions.
  (1) Why do you think God chose shepherds to be the first to hear and tell the good news?
  (2) What responses did the shepherds make? (Be sure to note their initial terror, their immediate decision to go to Bethlehem, their conversation with Mary and Joseph, their sharing of the good news with others, and their praise to God.)
  (3) Suppose Jesus had just been born this morning. Who are the "shepherds" in our contemporary world to whom God would first announce the good news?
  (4) Why do you think those whom you identified would be the first to hear?

(3) Relate the Story of Jesus' Birth to the Learners' Lives

❖ Invite the students to relate stories of past Christmases, discussing times when they really felt "plugged into" the true meaning of Christmas. Consider what made these particular Christmases so meaningful.

❖ Go around the room, or work in groups, asking each person to complete this sentence: **For me, Jesus' birth means. . . .**

(4) Celebrate Christmas Day

❖ Distribute paper and pencils. Encourage the students to write a short, nonrhyming poem, known as a *cinquain*, in which they express joy for the good news of Jesus' birth. The pattern for a cinquain, which is twenty-two syllables, looks like this example, but self-expression is more important than getting the exact number of syllables.

     ■ **Line 1:** Jesus *(two syllables)*
     ■ **Line 2:** God's Messiah *(four syllables)*
     ■ **Line 3:** Born to heal, cleanse, and free. *(six syllables)*
     ■ **Line 4:** We sing for joy because of you. *(eight syllables)*
     ■ **Line 5:** Savior. *(two syllables)*

❖ Invite the class members to read aloud their poems.

❖ **Option:** Enjoy a fellowship time with refreshments.

❖ **Option:** Sing some carols that are class favorites.

(5) Continue the Journey

❖ Pray that the students will experience the deep joy that the good news of God's redeeming love, enfleshed in Jesus, brings to all the world.

❖ Read aloud this preparation for next week's lesson. You may also want to post it on newsprint for the students to copy.

Prepare for next week's session, "Finding Strength to Serve," by reading 1 Timothy 1. Our lesson will focus on verses 12-20. Keep these ideas in mind as you study: People need strength to execute their assigned tasks. How can we become empowered with the strength needed to do ministry? In his first letter to the young minister Timothy, Paul says this strength comes from Christ Jesus and he gives thanks for it.

❖ Read aloud the following three ideas. Challenge the students to commit themselves to use these activities as a springboard to spiritual growth.

     (1) Recognize that the holidays are not a joyous time for everyone. Some people are lonely, grieving, sick, or feeling hopeless. Identify someone who needs to hear and experience God's good news. Do whatever you can to proclaim these glad tidings in word and deed.

     (2) Read the Christmas story from Luke 2 to family and/or friends. If you have a crèche in your home, gather with your loved ones around it as you read.

     (3) Page through a hymnal or Christmas carol book. Read the words. What messages of hope, comfort, and healing do you find there?

❖ Sing or read aloud "Once in Royal David's City."

❖ Lead this benediction to conclude the session: **May you go forth as servants in whom the Lord delights to bring justice to the nations by the power of God's Spirit. Amen.**

UNIT 2: GOD'S GIFTS OF LEADERSHIP
FINDING STRENGTH TO SERVE

PREVIEWING THE LESSON

Lesson Scripture: 1 Timothy 1:12-20
Background Scripture: 1 Timothy 1
Key Verse: 1 Timothy 1:12

Focus of the Lesson:
People need strength to execute their assigned tasks. How can we become empowered with the strength needed to do ministry? In his first letter to the young minister Timothy, Paul says this strength comes from Christ Jesus and he gives thanks for it.

Goals for the Learners:
(1) to explore Paul's assertions and appreciation that God provides strength for ministry and that powerful results come from this strength.
(2) to identify areas where God has given them strength for ministry.
(3) to commit to serve in whatever way God has called and given gifts to do so.

Pronunciation Guide:
diakonia (dee ak on ee' ah)
Gnosticism (nos' tuh siz uhm)
hubris (hew' bres)
Hymenaeus (hi muh nee' uhs)
oikonomia (oy kon om ee' ah)
pistos (pis tos')

Supplies:
Bibles, newsprint and marker, paper and pencils, hymnals

READING THE SCRIPTURE

NRSV
1 Timothy 1:12-20

¹²I am grateful to Christ Jesus our Lord, who has strengthened me, because he judged me faithful and appointed me to his service, ¹³even though I was formerly a

NIV
1 Timothy 1:12-20

¹²I thank Christ Jesus our Lord, who has given me strength, that he considered me faithful, appointing me to his service. ¹³Even though I was once a blasphemer and

blasphemer, a persecutor, and a man of violence. But I received mercy because I had acted ignorantly in unbelief, [14]and the grace of our Lord overflowed for me with the faith and love that are in Christ Jesus. [15]The saying is sure and worthy of full acceptance, that Christ Jesus came into the world to save sinners—of whom I am the foremost. [16]But for that very reason I received mercy, so that in me, as the foremost, Jesus Christ might display the utmost patience, making me an example to those who would come to believe in him for eternal life. [17]To the King of the ages, immortal, invisible, the only God, be honor and glory forever and ever. Amen.

[18]I am giving you these instructions, Timothy, my child, in accordance with the prophecies made earlier about you, so that by following them you may fight the good fight, [19]having faith and a good conscience. By rejecting conscience, certain persons have suffered shipwreck in the faith; [20]among them are Hymenaeus and Alexander, whom I have turned over to Satan, so that they may learn not to blaspheme.

a persecutor and a violent man, I was shown mercy because I acted in ignorance and unbelief. [14]The grace of our Lord was poured out on me abundantly, along with the faith and love that are in Christ Jesus.

[15]Here is a trustworthy saying that deserves full acceptance: Christ Jesus came into the world to save sinners—of whom I am the worst. [16]But for that very reason I was shown mercy so that in me, the worst of sinners, Christ Jesus might display his unlimited patience as an example for those who would believe on him and receive eternal life. [17]Now to the King eternal, immortal, invisible, the only God, be honor and glory for ever and ever. Amen.

[18]Timothy, my son, I give you this instruction in keeping with the prophecies once made about you, so that by following them you may fight the good fight, [19]holding on to faith and a good conscience. Some have rejected these and so have shipwrecked their faith. [20]Among them are Hymenaeus and Alexander, whom I have handed over to Satan to be taught not to blaspheme.

UNDERSTANDING THE SCRIPTURE

1 Timothy 1:1-2. The letter opens with an address typical of Pauline epistles. It declares the identity and authority of the author, indicates the recipient, and offers a greeting. Paul asserts himself to be an "apostle," a term originally used for the Twelve who had been eyewitnesses to Jesus' ministry. Earlier letters suggest an initial resistance among some to Paul's appeal to this title (see Galatians 1:1; 1 Corinthians 9:1-2, 15:8-10). "Apostle," however, is not Paul's personal claim: It results from God's command (1:1). "Savior" will be used repeatedly in the correspondence to Timothy and Titus, in contrast to only two occurrences in any other letters of Paul. The author identifies Timothy as the recipient of

this epistle. "Child" refers to the role Paul has played as "parent" to Timothy's faith (Acts 16:1-3). Timothy had shared in Paul's ministry previously, and Paul now commends Timothy's loyalty in that relationship. "Faith" appears for the first of many times in this epistle. "Grace, mercy, and peace" (1:2) combines the Jewish greeting of shalom ("peace") with a wordplay, as Paul replaces the popular Hellenistic *charein* ("greetings") with *charis* ("grace").

1 Timothy 1:3-7. In all but one of the earlier letters of Paul (Galatians), greetings were followed by a thanksgiving for the community addressed (or the individual, as in 2 Timothy 1:1-7). Like Galatians, 1 Timothy moves directly from greeting to confronting problems that have triggered the epistle. Paul urges Timothy to give instructions to certain people within the community. The clues of "myths" and "endless genealogies" do not reveal precisely in our day the nature of what these false teachings were. A movement called Gnosticism, which held salvation came through special knowledge (*gnosis*), had begun to develop. Some form of it may be indicated by Paul's contrast of the opponents' speculation to what is "known" by faith (1:4). The "divine training" (*oikonomia*, "household law"), which refers to Timothy's work of instructing, aims at love. The problem Paul identifies involves those who would be teachers, who have no grasp of their subject: in this case, the law. Some deduce from this accusation a Judaizing tendency among at least some of the opponents.

1 Timothy 1:8-11. The opening verse here asserts the positive role of the law, as long as it is employed legitimately (the Greek word literally means "lawfully"). Paul's following statement of the law's purpose "not for the innocent but for the lawless . . ." implies the opponents may have used the law to impugn innocent persons rather than confront those engaged in what the law identifies as sin. To give illustration, Paul follows with a list of behavior outside the bounds of the law. Some of the transgressions are portrayed in general if not vague ways. What, for instance, falls under the category of disobedient, or profane? The charges then become specific, including one ("sodomite") whose interpretation vexes the church today. A closing word ("whatever else is contrary to the sound teaching. . .") wraps in anything else that may not have been named as unlawful above.

1 Timothy 1:12. The epistle's thanksgiving appears now. Instead of offering thanks for the community or individual addressed, however, the author renders gratitude to Jesus Christ for three actions done in Paul's life. Christ has strengthened Paul (see also Philippians 4:13). Christ has judged Paul

faithful, that faithfulness setting the stage for what will be a major theme in this letter. Christ has appointed Paul to ministry (*diakonia*), even as ministry will form another important theme in the correspondence to Timothy and Titus.

1 Timothy 1:13-16. Why Paul feels such gratitude becomes readily apparent in his confession that follows. "Blasphemer" likely refers to Paul's vigorous denial of God's presence in Jesus, as evidenced in his earlier persecution of the church. "Man of violence" translates *hubris*, a word whose original meaning connoted arrogance and pride. Twice in this passage, Paul declares his actions in these regards made him foremost among sinners. He was, if you will, the living example of what not to be and do. These extremities of vices make the declaration of God's grace and mercy in Jesus Christ stand out all the more. "The saying is sure and worthy of full acceptance . . ." introduces a formula the author will return to in this correspondence (4:9; see also 2 Timothy 2:11 and Titus 3:8) to emphasize teachings or insights of peculiar significance. Here, the words point to the role of Jesus as bringing salvation for sinners, clarifying how exactly Paul "received mercy." Such grace transforms Paul from foremost sinner to "example" of faith.

1 Timothy 1:17. The epistle makes a transition in this verse from confession back to instruction. The transition takes the form of an act of praise, a natural response to the recitation of Paul's deliverance. God as "King" offers a traditional Jewish understanding of God's rule and reign in life. It may also subtly assert how the dominion exercised in this era by Rome stands under the dominion of God. "The only God" gives affirmation to the monotheism Christianity inherited from Judaism (Deuteronomy 6:4). "Honor and glory forever" anticipates part of the acclamation of praise sung by the elders and angels in honor of the Lamb (Revelation 5:12, 13).

1 Timothy 1:18-20. Paul closes this

chapter by returning to the instructions given Timothy in 1:3. What "prophecies" made about Timothy are not specified, nor is it clear if this connects to the experience pointed to in 4:4. What is clear, however, is that what looms ahead for Timothy is a struggle. "Fight the good fight" has both military and athletic meanings. Its use here encourages such efforts through faith and a good conscience (see 1:5). Failure of conscience has led some of Paul's opponents to shipwreck, a vivid term for a genuine peril of travelers in that day. Two of them are singled out (see also 2 Timothy 2:17). Paul's action indicates some form of excommunication or disfellowship, though it is done in hopes they will learn—as he did.

INTERPRETING THE SCRIPTURE

The Weave of Faith

Some form of the Greek root for faith (*pistos*) occurs six times in this passage, whether as a noun (faith), verb (believe), or adjective (faithful, sure). The importance of faith in these verses serves as prelude to the way faith will be a central concern in the correspondence to Timothy and Titus.

This focus on faith is not new to Pauline epistles. Commentators do note, however, a shift in emphasis between faith in the Pastoral Epistles and those of earlier writings of Paul. In those earlier writings, faith primarily described the act of radical trust in God. In the Pastorals, faith is more and more used in reference to an accepted body of belief, as in "the" faith (see 1:19).

Those two dimensions of faith form an important balance in the church's life and teaching. Faith is, and must always be, a personal act of deep trust. Christian faith invites such encounter and experience in the God made known to us in Jesus Christ and present with us in the Holy Spirit. But who is God? And who is Jesus Christ? And who or what is the Holy Spirit? Christian faith is not deep trust in just anything we please. Faith to be Christian requires some basic mooring in what it is that justifies the adjective of "Christian" to such trust. So correspondence like the Pastorals, and later efforts of the church such as creeds and catechisms, simply seek to establish those moorings. Abuses of such efforts lead to the danger of confusing agreement with this or that statement of doctrine or social ethics with the radical act of trust in God. Authentic Christian faith resists such substitutes. Teaching informs the trust. Trust enlivens the teaching. Faith needs both for embodiment.

A Case Study in Grace

Although many scholars question whether Paul actually wrote the letters to Timothy and Titus, one of the persuasive arguments for Pauline authorship of the Pastorals in general and 1 Timothy in particular are verses strongly autobiographical in tone. In this session's passage, such verses relate Paul's confession of his life before receiving mercy, and that mercy's purposes.

If you have read Paul much, you will know he does not have a "retiring" personality. Who he is, what he has done for good or ill, usually remain close to the surface in his writings. Paul's intent here is to provide concrete illustration to the meaning of Christ's grace and mercy. He looks no further than himself to do so. Paul cuts himself no slack in describing his life before Christ. He was, if you will, everything you would not want your son or daughter—or self—to be. In other epistles, Paul uses the language of boasting in ways both positive and negative (compare Romans 15:17 with Galatians 6:14). Here in 1 Timothy 1:15, Paul boasts about his being the "foremost" (in Greek, *protos* as in "prototype") of sinners.

Sometimes, persons use their shortcomings or fallibilities to excuse their inabilities, or to protest they are "not worth it." Paul inflicts his own self-indictment for the purpose of elevating the work of Christ in his life. The argument implied runs something like this: *if you think you're irredeemable, I was way worse, yet Christ transformed me.*

So in a sense, the point of Paul's recitation of sinfulness is not who Paul is or was, but who Jesus Christ is. The core affirmation of this section is simple: "Christ Jesus came into the world to save sinners" (1:15). The Greek word for "save" also carries with it the meaning of *making whole* and *healing.* Like Paul, our lives can find wholeness and healing in Christ.

Doxology

Paul pauses in the midst of opening this epistle to write a brief verse of praise (1:17). At first sight, this might seem an interruption in the flow of the passage. Once we read it, we can get back to the "important" things.

Think of this verse as a parable about the whole of our lives: as individuals, as members of congregations. Busyness abounds among us. Significant work needs to be done. Critical decisions need to be made. Places and persons need to be visited. It can become quite easy to move acts of devotion to the periphery, to "when we can find the time."

Paul interrupts the text with praise, and in doing so invites us to do the same. Look at what he has just written about himself, about the work of Jesus Christ in his life. Praise is simply a spontaneous and natural response. To be sure, there remain in this epistle important fights to be fought, instructions to be given. But for the moment, praise flows.

Doxology can interrupt our lives as well. In the midst of all that terribly important business we have to do, do you remember you are loved of God? Do you ever pause to reflect on what an extraordinary gift creation truly is? In the midst of some encounter that brings joy or reflection that reminds us of God's grace writ on our lives, it would be a natural and faithful thing to pause for grateful remembrance. That is, on a larger scale, the gift brought to us by Sabbath: the necessary interruption of our important busyness with the grace of rest and worship and renewal.

Let the people take time to say, Amen!

Fight the Good Fight

A growing and healthy movement in the church today aims at the use of consensus in decision-making. We can each likely tell stories of churches and communities battered by divisive sidetaking, where those left standing at the end of the battle wonder whether it was worth it.

That being said, consensus may not always be possible. The attempt to reach consensus would not have desegregated lunch counters in the 1950's. The attempt to reach consensus would not protect a battered spouse from an abuser.

The epistle here urges Timothy to "fight the good fight" (1:18). Fighting the "good" fight recognizes that not all conflicts are good. A professor of mine once remarked that too many conflicts in the church trace to our lack of trust in God. Unable to trust God for what we have, or who we are, or what makes us one, we think it is up to us to seize and define those things for ourselves. In such conflicts, persons become easier targets than ideas. The epistle is not advocating violence to other persons, physically or emotionally or theologically. Rather, the encouragement is to stand firm with the faith and instructions entrusted in the face of those who may well oppose them.

What also helps define the fight or struggle as "good" or worth engaging in comes in what is sought from those with whom we disagree. In 1 Timothy, Paul has some hard sayings in verse 20 about two such persons. Yet, the declared intent is that they "learn." The Greek word, *paideuo*, typically refers to instruction given children in order for them to grow into maturity. Growth, not expulsion or elimination, is the desired outcome.

Faith also tempers the meaning of the "good" fight. The One who fought against moneychangers in the temple also forgave executioners. To follow Jesus Christ invites following his way, which nowhere makes victims of those with whom he comes into conflict.

SHARING THE SCRIPTURE

Preparing Our Hearts

This week's devotional reading is found in Romans 16:17-27. In these closing verses of his letter to the church in Rome, Paul particularly warns his readers against teachers who have corrupted the gospel. In his greetings in verse 21, Paul mentions Timothy, calling him "my coworker." Spend some time meditating on the moving benediction, found in verses 25-27. What do you learn from these few words about salvation and the church's commission? You may wish to memorize these benedictory verses.

Pray that you and the adult learners will find the strength needed to serve God, following in the footsteps of two early servants, Paul and Timothy.

Preparing Our Minds

Study the background from 1 Timothy 1 and the lesson Scripture, verses 12-20. As you study, mull over ways in which you can become empowered with the strength necessary to serve God.

Write on newsprint:
❑ litany for "Commit to Serve in Whatever Way God Has Called and Given Gifts to the Learners to Do So."
❑ information for next week's lesson, found under "Continue the Journey."

LEADING THE CLASS

(1) Gather to Learn

❖ Welcome the class members and introduce any guests.

❖ Provide time for the students to exchange brief stories about their Christmas celebrations.

❖ Pray that all who have come will be ready to make a fresh start.

❖ Read this quote from Joni Eareckson Tada, a well-known author, speaker, and advocate for persons with disabilities: **The weaker we feel, the harder we lean on God. And the harder we lean, the stronger we grow.**

❖ Invite the students to tell the class or a small group about a situation that led them to the same conclusion as Mrs. Tada. Talk about how that situation brought them into a closer, stronger relationship with God.

❖ Read aloud today's focus statement: **People need strength to execute their assigned tasks. How can we become empowered with the strength needed to do ministry? In his first letter to the young minister Timothy, Paul says this strength comes from Christ Jesus and he gives thanks for it.**

(2) Explore Paul's Assertions and Appreciation That God Provides Strength for Ministry and That Powerful Results Come from This Strength

❖ Select a volunteer to read 1 Timothy 1:12-20, as if Paul were reading this letter aloud to Timothy.

❖ Discuss these questions. Or, use these questions, along with ideas in the

Interpreting the Scripture section, to create a brief lecture about Paul and his aims in writing to Timothy, as revealed in verses 12-20.

(1) **What do you learn about Paul from this passage?** (List ideas on newsprint.)

(2) **Why do you think Paul writes so much about himself if his purpose is to encourage Timothy as a leader in God's service?**

(3) **Paul writes a doxology in verse 17. Why do you suppose he inserts these words of praise here?** (See "Doxology" in the Interpreting the Scripture portion.)

(4) **In verse 18, Paul writes that he is giving Timothy "instructions." How does Paul's handling of Hymenaeus and Alexander relate to the idea of instruction?**

❖ Read or retell "Fight the Good Fight" in Interpreting the Scripture. Add information from 1 Timothy 1:18-20 in Understanding the Scripture. Talk with the class about these ideas.

(1) **Describe what you think Paul meant by "the good fight."**

(2) **Identify situations in which ministry or service for God has been a real struggle for you. How have you continued to "fight the good fight" even though it was difficult?**

(3) **Name situations that the church is struggling with today. Do you think all of these issues are truly "good fights"? Why or why not?**

(3) Identify Areas Where God Has Given Each Learner Strength for Ministry

❖ Read aloud today's key verse, 1 Timothy 1:12. Note that Paul expresses gratitude to Christ for the strength he has been given for service and ministry.

❖ Brainstorm with the class a list of arenas in which the students might serve. This list should include ideas for service in the church, home, community, and school/workplace, related to national/global issues, especially concerning peace and justice. Here are some ideas if the group needs help getting started: serve on a church committee or board; volunteer for a Habitat for Humanity build; participate in a short-term mission project, such as Volunteers in Mission; become an advocate for the homeless, hungry, or poor; make regular visits to a homebound neighbor or a nursing home.

❖ Distribute paper and pencils. Invite the students to choose two items from the list. Ask them to divide their paper in half and head each column with one of the items. Under each heading they are to list God-given talents or strengths that they believe will enable them to offer service in their selected areas.

❖ Suggest that the students talk with a team of three or four about their lists. The learners may be able to add to the lists strengths that they see in one another.

❖ Close this portion of the session by asking the students to read in unison the key verse, 1 Timothy 1:12.

❖ Provide a few moments of meditation so that the adults may give thanks for the strength they have received from Christ to undertake the service to which he has called them.

(4) Commit to Serve in Whatever Way God Has Called and Given Gifts to the Learners to Do So

❖ Post the following litany, which you will have written on newsprint prior to class, where everyone can see it. Note that the response is adapted from 1 Timothy 1:17.

■ LEADER: For the gifts that you have given us for service,

■ GROUP: We give to you, the King of the ages, immortal, invisible, the only God, honor and glory forever and ever.

■ LEADER: For the strength to undertake this service,

■ GROUP: We give to you, the King of the ages, immortal, invisible, the only God, honor and glory forever and ever.

■ LEADER: For instruction to know how we are to conduct ourselves and lead your people,

■ GROUP: We give to you, the King of the ages, immortal, invisible, the only God, honor and glory forever and ever.

■ ALL: And all the people of God said, "amen and amen."

(5) Continue the Journey

❖ Pray that the participants will give thanks for the strength and gifts God has given them to serve.

❖ Read aloud this preparation for next week's lesson. You may also want to post it on newsprint for the students to copy. **Prepare for next week's session, "Everyone Needs Prayer," by reading 1 Timothy 2. Our time together will focus on 1 Timothy 2:1-8. Keep these thoughts in mind as you study the lesson: Everyone stands in need of prayer. Why should we pray for the needs of others? In his letter, Paul says this kind of intercessory prayer is right and acceptable to God.**

❖ Read aloud the following three ideas. Challenge the students to commit themselves to use these activities as a springboard to spiritual growth.

(1) Create a list of new intentions you have for mission, ministry, and service to God in 2006. Perhaps you will be assuming leadership of a committee or volunteering time for a certain task. Prayerfully consider this list and make adjustments as God leads. Commit yourself to follow through.

(2) Encourage someone who is stepping into a new role of leadership and/or service. If you have filled leadership roles in the church, offer to mentor this new leader.

(3) Identify those areas of service where you feel inadequate. Write about them in your spiritual journal. Ask God to give you the strength to fulfill your tasks, and wisdom to know which tasks you need to jettison because they do not fit with your current sense of calling.

❖ Sing or read aloud "God of Grace and God of Glory."

❖ Lead this benediction to conclude the session: **May you go forth as servants in whom the Lord delights to bring justice to the nations by the power of God's Spirit. Amen.**

UNIT 2: GOD'S GIFTS OF LEADERSHIP
EVERYONE NEEDS PRAYER

PREVIEWING THE LESSON

Lesson Scripture: 1 Timothy 2:1-8
Background Scripture: 1 Timothy 2
Key Verse: 1 Timothy 2:1

Focus of the Lesson:
Everyone stands in need of prayer. Why should we pray for the needs of others? In his letter, Paul says this kind of intercessory prayer is right and acceptable to God.

Goals for the Learners:
(1) to review Paul's admonition that prayers and thanksgiving be given for everyone.
(2) to discern the role of prayer in their own lives.
(3) to offer a prayer.

Pronunciation Guide:
eusebia (yoo seb' i ah)
thelo (thel' o)

Supplies:
Bibles, newsprint and marker, paper and pencils, hymnals, optional: meditative CD or tape and appropriate player

---

READING THE SCRIPTURE

NRSV
1 Timothy 2:1-8

¹First of all, then, I urge that supplications, prayers, intercessions, and thanksgivings be made for everyone, ²for kings and all who are in high positions, so that we may lead a quiet and peaceable life in all godliness and dignity. ³This is right and is acceptable in the sight of God our Savior, ⁴who desires everyone to be saved and to come to the knowledge of the truth. ⁵For there is one God;

NIV
1 Timothy 2:1-8

¹I urge, then, first of all, that requests, prayers, intercession and thanksgiving be made for everyone—²for kings and all those in authority, that we may live peaceful and quiet lives in all godliness and holiness. ³This is good, and pleases God our Savior, ⁴who wants all men to be saved and to come to a knowledge of the truth. ⁵For there is one God and one mediator between God and men, the man Christ Jesus, ⁶who gave

there is also one mediator between God and humankind,

Christ Jesus, himself human,

[6]who gave himself a ransom for all

—this was attested at the right time. [7]For this I was appointed a herald and an apostle (I am telling the truth, I am not lying), a teacher of the Gentiles in faith and truth.

[8]I desire, then, that in every place the men should pray, lifting up holy hands without anger or argument. . . .

himself as a ransom for all men—the testimony given in its proper time. [7]And for this purpose I was appointed a herald and an apostle—I am telling the truth, I am not lying—and a teacher of the true faith to the Gentiles.

[8]I want men everywhere to lift up holy hands in prayer, without anger or disputing.

UNDERSTANDING THE SCRIPTURE

1 Timothy 2:1-2. The list of four "prayer" words in verse 1 touches on different aspects of prayer as conversation with God. Supplication likely refers to prayer for one's own needs, while intercession lifts the needs of another to God. This "interceding" anticipates an affirmation Paul makes in verse 5 for Jesus as "mediator." The scope of those to be prayed for is without limit: "everyone." Paul tightens that focus as he goes on to urge prayer specifically for those in positions of public leadership. The church addressed in this epistle sought to maintain good relations with local and imperial authorities in an era when hostility toward and distrust of the church was the norm. Paul identifies that aim through prayer for life that is "quiet and peaceable," two terms that depict serenity in one's inner life and outer relationships. "Godliness" translates *eusebia*, a critical word in the Pastoral Epistles, which connotes devotion, reverence, or piety.

1 Timothy 2:3-4. Paul here clarifies why such prayer "is right and is acceptable in the sight of God." The confession of God as Savior has already been made (1:1). These verses link God's saving activities with the previously urged prayers. "Everyone" is to be prayed for because God "desires everyone to be saved" (2:4). "Desire" is a weak translation of the Greek *thelo*, which can also

mean "to will." Thus, Paul affirms salvation to be God's will for all.

1 Timothy 2:5-6. An apparent fragment of an early creedal statement of the early church appears in verses 5-6a. "One God" asserts the monotheism of Judaism, whose most clear statement comes in the *Shema* ("Hear, O Israel") of Deuteronomy 6:4. "One mediator" communicates the unique role played by Jesus as the one who stands between the "one God" and humanity. Such mediation does not suggest the contemporary understandings of mediator as a neutral figure between two hostile parties. Rather, Jesus serves as the instrument who mediates the grace of God to us. Paul further describes Christ's mediation by the metaphor "ransom" (see also Mark 10:45). In that era, ransom referred to money paid to bring about the release of a slave or hostage. As Paul expressed God's saving purpose for "all," so now does he affirm Christ's ransom is for "all."

1 Timothy 2:7. This verse carries the undertone of conflict, a situation where Paul's authority and even honesty have been called into question. As he had done earlier in 1:12, Paul asserts he does not do this work on his own but as one "appointed." "Herald" literally means "one who cries out," and this is the only place Paul so refers to himself. His declaration of his ministry among the Gentiles repeats a theme central to his sense of call (Romans 11:13).

1 Timothy 2:8-15: An Overview. In this section of the epistle, Paul gives instructions for men and women about worship and "order" that resist quick summaries much less easy resolutions. The instructions cannot be heard apart from the culture in which Paul lived, and in particular the dominant authority of the husband in its households. Secular literature contemporary to this time abounded with household "codes" that described the ordering of household relationships in ways that can only be termed patriarchal at best. The fact that most churches still gathered in the households of members would have encouraged using existing traditions, particularly if the church did not seek to give offense to the wider community. Does this mean every ordering designated in this passage and others remains in effect, unchanged by huge differences between the culture of that day and our own? Remember that such household codes, including several in the New Testament, also described the proper relationship between slaves and masters (see Ephesians 6:5-9). Do those hold equal force for the church today as these gender-identified roles?

1 Timothy 2:8-10. Prayer provides the link between the preceding words and the instructions for ordering worship and the household of faith that begin here. "Without anger or argument" recognizes we do not always come with pure motives before God, even in acts of devotion. Vigilance is always and everywhere required: beginning not with others, but with ourselves. "Men" and "women" in this passage may also be translated as "husbands" and "wives." Verse 9 describes the appropriate "dress" for wives

or women in this household. The richness of several of those details suggests the existence of significant wealth in this community, believed to be in Ephesus (1:3). In that light, the advice for dress may encourage against shows of wealth that could highlight divisions rather than unity in the faith. Good works provide the attire most appropriate for "reverence."

1 Timothy 2:11-14. Here the instructions become even more complicated. Some commentators alleviate difficulties by saying Paul's permitting women to learn (2:11) at least exceeds the norm of its day in Judaism and Greek culture. Even so, the words seem far removed from Paul's earlier affirmation that in Christ "there is no longer male and female" (Galatians 3:28). Paul complements his instructions to Timothy in verses 13-14 with a line of argument that does not simply blame Eve for the fall, but absolves Adam of being deceived. Read Romans 5:12-19 alongside of these verses, and you will find Scripture (and Paul himself) in conversation with itself on this issue.

1 Timothy 2:15. Salvation through childbearing has been variously understood. Some mitigate the reading by relating that, in Greek, "childbearing" is preceded by "the." Their argument goes something like this: "The childbearing" makes reference to women's salvation (as for all) as coming in the birth of Jesus Christ. Others offer the interpretation that "saving" through childbirth, connected with "faith and love and holiness," suggests these qualities will help women through the hazards of childbirth. Neither argument seems persuasive. The primary role of wife as child-bearer was strong in that culture, and this may simply be yet another example of a text strongly conditioned by the culture of its day.

INTERPRETING THE SCRIPTURE

The Prayers of the People

The opening and closing verses of the lesson Scripture give instructions for the nature and conduct of Christian prayer. At the outset, this text nowhere singles out Timothy or any other leader as the one who always and everywhere offers prayer on behalf of the people. The early church did not know of a professional class of "prayers" whose function was to vocalize prayers so that others did not have to. Lending order to corporate worship, another desire of Paul's (see 1 Corinthians 14:40), probably did encourage the development of one or two praying on behalf of all in public liturgy. But "on behalf of" does not mean "in place of." The instructions Paul gives here are offered to any and all for our prayers, to which we are all urged (1 Thessalonians 5:17).

Prayer is not "monotone." That is, prayer takes different forms and shapes, as reflected in the language Paul uses here to describe prayer according to some of its different purposes. Paul invites prayer that "supplies" (supplication) our needs. Prayer for one's own life and circumstances does not imply selfishness. It recognizes providence and grace to be part of the daily rhythm of our lives. It also humbles us, at times, with the reminder that what we think we need and what we truly need may not always be the same. "Thanksgivings" celebrate and name the gifts of providence that come to us, and all creation, by the grace of God. Thanksgiving arises from the joy and humility of knowing we live in not a self-made, but a God-graced, world. "Intercession" balances supplication by including in our prayers the needs and situations of others. Intercession also reminds us that praying on another's behalf invites speaking and acting on their behalf. At best, prayer weaves its way into our lives—we bring our lives and world into prayer.

Community Context

This passage, like Romans 13:1-7, sometimes gains for Paul and the church a reputation of "cozying up" to institutional and governmental power. Clearly, there are times when the desire for leading a "quiet and peaceable life" must be superceded by the need to speak truth and cry for justice in the face of falsehood and injustice.

But context is important. When the church is in a position to wield influence, but refuses to speak for the sake of not rocking the boat, we err. That was by no means the context of the community addressed in 1 Timothy. That community formed a minority in its society, and a small one at that. The church did not yet own the protections given to it in later centuries. Persecution loomed in the near future, if Paul was the author of this letter to Timothy. If, as many argue, the letter came closer to the end of the first century, the church had already borne the brunt of imperial abuse.

The author's seeking of prayers for authorities so as to bring about a "quiet and peaceable life" represented not compromise, but prudence. In our own day, individuals and communities of faith labor in similar contexts of hostility. It may be easy to suggest "counter-cultural" witness in situations from which we are far removed, simply because we happen to disagree with the political regime or religious majority in those places.

It is not that 1 Timothy does not take community context seriously. It takes it so seriously it will lift up leaders in prayer who may have given the community no reason to trust them or hope for behavior other than hostility from them. And it lifts prayers for these leaders, not against them. A community transformed in Jesus Christ prays the same for others.

The Importance of "Everyone"

Usually it is the "big" words that catch our attention and deepen our understanding of God's majesty: grace, love, and justice. In our text, a less flashy pair of words provide revealing insight into God's purposes: "everyone" and "all." More than linguistic style connects their repetition through these verses.

As noted earlier in the commentary section, prayers for "everyone" flow naturally from God's saving will for "everyone."

Why? Remember one of the petitions of the Lord's Prayer: "your will be done." Doing God's will represents one of the fundamental petitions of Christian prayer. So if God's will finds expression in the salvation of everyone, it follows that our prayers for doing God's will lift up those for whom God exercises that saving will: everyone.

The church finds itself challenged by the scope of these two words: "all" and "everyone." For in them, we recognize that in Jesus Christ we cannot settle for parochial visions of faith that simply take into account my corner of the town, much less the world. "Everyone" and "all" are missional words that stretch the reach of our faith's practice. First Timothy does not voice this vision in isolation. Isaiah 49:6 announces that God intends for the Servant to raise up not just Israel, which would be a challenging undertaking in itself. Rather, God gives the Servant to be "a light to the nations"—to everyone. Even before that, Genesis 9:16 records the very first covenant of the Bible to be between God and not just Noah, not just human creation, but "every living creature of all flesh that is on the earth."

God's saving purposes, like Christ's "ransom," are for the sake of everyone. All find inclusion in the gracious will of God!

Prayer and the Mediation of Christ

In the biblical era, "mediator" represented one who intervened between two parties, typically in striking a contract or settling a dispute. Does Jesus intervene with God, as if God could not be satisfied? And if Jesus forms the second person of the Trinity, does God mediate with God? Metaphors have their limits. Clearly, though, Christ as mediator in this passage affirms the interceding of Jesus on our behalf.

Consider what it means to intercede for another. You place yourself between that person and some need or crisis he or she faces. Jesus interceded for a woman caught in adultery and facing judgment (John 8:1-11). Jesus interceded for children whom his own disciples tried to abruptly dismiss (Mark 10:13-16). Interceding intends to change a situation by your placing yourself within it. As such, interceding carries the potential of risk and even sacrifice. This text closely allies Jesus Christ as "mediator" and "ransom." Both terms involve interceding, and ransom in particular is linked with Jesus' sacrifice on the cross (see Mark 10:45).

Intercessory prayer on our part involves us in Christ's ministry of mediation. Prayer does not end our participation in that ministry. The Epistle of James underscores that prayers on behalf of others that go unmatched by action are empty (James 2:14-17). In some situations where we are far removed physically or otherwise, prayers of intercession may be the only intercessory option available to us . . . for the moment. But intercessory prayer beckons us to search out ways in which we can intercede on Christ's behalf for the good of others. It may be risky. There may be sacrifice. But in Jesus Christ, we are called to prayers and lives of intercession by the light of his example.

SHARING THE SCRIPTURE

Preparing Our Hearts

This week's devotional reading is found in 1 Thessalonians 5:16-22. Here we find Paul writing a series of commands to the church members at Thessalonia. Try listing these exhortations in your spiritual journal. Which ones can you check off, saying, "yes, I try to do that"? Pray about the ones that you are not able to say that you are doing right now. Consider especially the one to "pray without ceasing" (5:17), which directly relates to today's lesson. Spend time in prayer right now for others in need and for guidance in your own life.

Also pray that you and the adult learners will practice all facets of prayer in your lives.

Preparing Our Minds

Study the background, which includes all of 1 Timothy 2, and the lesson Scripture, verses 1-8. As you study, consider what Paul teaches about why you should pray for others.

Write on newsprint:
❑ questions for "Discern the Role of Prayer in the Learners' Lives."
❑ information for next week's lesson, found under "Continue the Journey."

Plan brief lectures, as suggested under "Review Paul's Admonition That Prayers and Thanksgiving Be Given for Everyone."

If you choose to use meditative background music as the learners work in the "Offer a Prayer" segment, select the music and secure the appropriate player and extension cord, if needed.

LEADING THE CLASS

(1) Gather to Learn

❖ Welcome the class members and introduce any guests.

❖ Pray that each participant will find new meaning and purpose in prayer so as to deepen his or her personal prayer life.

❖ Distribute slips of paper. Ask each participant to write a person's first name, the name of a place, or a brief description of a situation for which prayer is needed. Collect the papers, shuffle them, and give each person a paper. If possible, go around the room and ask each person to lift up a sentence prayer for the person, place, or event noted. If the class is large, divide into groups to offer this prayer. As each prayer is read, ask the students to respond with the words, **"Lord, in your mercy, hear our prayer."**

❖ Read aloud today's focus statement: **Everyone stands in need of prayer. Why should we pray for the needs of others? In his letter, Paul says this kind of intercessory prayer is right and acceptable to God.**

(2) Review Paul's Admonition That Prayers and Thanksgiving Be Given for Everyone

❖ Note that in today's passage, Paul gives instructions concerning prayer. In verses 1-7, he urges believers to pray, and gives theological reasons as to why people should pray. Then, in verse 8 (through verse 15, though we will only study verse 8), Paul writes about how men and women in his day are to worship.

❖ Select a volunteer to read 1 Timothy 2:1-8.

❖ Write the words "supplications," "intercessions," and "thanksgivings" on newsprint. Invite the students to offer definitions or descriptions of these three types of prayer. You will find a brief statement about each type in the 1 Timothy 2:1-2 portion of Understanding the Scripture.

❖ Look especially at verses 2-4. In a brief lecture or as a class discussion, draw a link between prayers for everyone and God's desire for salvation. Information may be found in Understanding the Scripture and "The Importance of 'Everyone'" in Interpreting the Scripture.

❖ Look now at verses 5-7. Discuss these questions or present possible answers in a lecture.

(1) **What does this passage tell you about God?**

(2) **What does this passage tell you about Jesus?** (Check Understanding the Scripture for these verses and "Prayer and the Mediation of Christ" in the Interpreting the Scripture portion for help in explaining "ransom" and "mediator.")

(3) **What does this passage tell you about Paul?** (See information on verse 7 in Understanding the Scripture.)

❖ Read again verse 8. Encourage the class members to think of examples of people praying together who are experiencing "anger or argument." Do not let this become a personal discussion spotlighting individual divisions. Rather, focus on ideas that may separate Christians, such as disagreements on church policy, national politics, moral issues, or issues of social justice. Consider how Paul's admonition can help church members to learn how to handle their differences so as to live and worship peaceably.

(3) Discern the Role of Prayer in the Learners' Lives

❖ Divide the class into groups and assign one or two questions to each group. Write the questions on newsprint prior to the session. Give each group paper or newsprint and a pencil or marker to record their answers. Provide time for the groups to report back to the entire class.

(1) **How do you define "prayer"?**

(2) **How did you learn to pray?**

(3) **Why do you pray?**

(4) **What difference does prayer make in your life?**

(5) **Some people claim that they are so busy that they have no time to pray. Perhaps you are one of them. How would you respond to Saint Francis of Sales' (1567–1622) comment: "Every Christian needs a half hour of prayer each day, except when he is busy, then he needs an hour"?**

(6) **People sometimes question God when their supplications or intercessions are not answered in the way that they would like. What does your experience suggest about how to respond to such people?**

❖ Ask the learners to open their Bibles to passages on prayer. If you have a group of seasoned Bible students, they will likely have favorite verses that they can name. Otherwise, you may wish to look at any of the following passages and ask the question: **What does this passage teach you about prayer?**

■ 1 Samuel 2:1-10.

■ Psalm 28.

■ Matthew 6:9-13.

■ Luke 18:1-8.

■ John 15:7.

(4) Offer a Prayer

❖ Distribute paper and pencils. Challenge the learners to write a prayer, which will not be read aloud. Suggest that they include:

(1) *supplications* that God will fulfill their needs;

(2) *intercessions* for others who have special needs, such as those facing illness, death, or family crisis; and

(3) *thanksgivings* for God's grace, mercy, and answers to prayers.

❖ Provide time for the learners to work in a prayerful environment. If possible in your setting, play some quiet, meditative background music.

(5) Continue the Journey

❖ Break the quiet time with a prayer that each participant will make the spiritual discipline of prayer for all people an integral part of their own life with Christ.

❖ Read aloud this preparation for next week's lesson. You may also want to post it on newsprint for the students to copy. **Prepare for next week's session, "Leading God's People," by reading 1 Timothy 3, paying particular attention to verses 2-15. As you study this lesson, keep these ideas in mind: People seek leaders who have a good reputation. What behavior and qualifications should we look for in church leaders? Paul indicates that good church leaders have strong Christian faith and character and that they are well respected by all in the community.**

❖ Read aloud the following three ideas. Challenge the students to commit themselves to use these activities as a springboard to spiritual growth.

(1) Spend extra time in prayer this week for both people in high places and victims of violence, that they might "lead a quiet and peaceable life in all godliness and dignity" (2:2).

(2) Read a book about prayer this week, such as Richard Foster's *Prayer*. Foster is a contemporary Quaker writer whose books on spiritual disciplines have already become classics.

(3) Offer daily prayers for individuals, groups, or countries that you consider enemies. How does prayer change your attitude about that person or group? If you are praying for a country and its leaders, how do you hope your prayers will change this "enemy"?

❖ Sing or read aloud "Sweet Hour of Prayer."

❖ Lead this benediction to conclude the session: **May you go forth as servants in whom the Lord delights to bring justice to the nations by the power of God's Spirit. Amen.**

UNIT 2: GOD'S GIFTS OF LEADERSHIP
LEADING GOD'S PEOPLE

PREVIEWING THE LESSON

Lesson Scripture: 1 Timothy 3:2-15
Background Scripture: 1 Timothy 3
Key Verse: 1 Timothy 3:9

Focus of the Lesson:

People seek leaders who have a good reputation. What behavior and qualifications should we look for in church leaders? Paul indicates that good church leaders have strong Christian faith and character and that they are well respected by all in the community.

Goals for the Learners:

(1) to examine Paul's description to Timothy of the characteristics of good church leaders.
(2) to compare Paul's view with their views about characteristics that make good church leaders.
(3) to name and give thanks for the good leaders in their congregation and denomination.

Pronunciation Guide

anegkletos (an eng' klay tos)
Cenchreae (sen' kree uh)
diakonos (dee ak' on os)
ekklesia (ek klay see' ah)
episkope (ep is kop ay')
martureo (mar too reh' o)
paterfamilias (pa ter fe mi' le es)

Supplies:

Bibles, newsprint and marker, paper and pencils, hymnals

JANUARY 15

READING THE SCRIPTURE

NRSV

1 Timothy 3:2-15

²Now a bishop must be above reproach, married only once, temperate, sensible,

NIV

1 Timothy 3:2-15

²Now the overseer must be above reproach, the husband of but one wife, temperate,

respectable, hospitable, an apt teacher, [3]not a drunkard, not violent but gentle, not quarrelsome, and not a lover of money. [4]He must manage his own household well, keeping his children submissive and respectful in every way—[5]for if someone does not know how to manage his own household, how can he take care of God's church? [6]He must not be a recent convert, or he may be puffed up with conceit and fall into the condemnation of the devil. [7]Moreover, he must be well thought of by outsiders, so that he may not fall into disgrace and the snare of the devil.

[8]Deacons likewise must be serious, not double-tongued, not indulging in much wine, not greedy for money; [9]they must hold fast to the mystery of the faith with a clear conscience. [10]And let them first be tested; then, if they prove themselves blameless, let them serve as deacons. [11]Women likewise must be serious, not slanderers, but temperate, faithful in all things. [12]Let deacons be married only once, and let them manage their children and their households well; [13]for those who serve well as deacons gain a good standing for themselves and great boldness in the faith that is in Christ Jesus.

[14]I hope to come to you soon, but I am writing these instructions to you so that, [15]if I am delayed, you may know how one ought to behave in the household of God, which is the church of the living God, the pillar and bulwark of the truth.

self-controlled, respectable, hospitable, able to teach, [3]not given to drunkenness, not violent but gentle, not quarrelsome, not a lover of money. [4]He must manage his own family well and see that his children obey him with proper respect. [5](If anyone does not know how to manage his own family, how can he take care of God's church?) [6]He must not be a recent convert, or he may become conceited and fall under the same judgment as the devil. [7]He must also have a good reputation with outsiders, so that he will not fall into disgrace and into the devil's trap.

[8]Deacons, likewise, are to be men worthy of respect, sincere, not indulging in much wine, and not pursuing dishonest gain. [9]They must keep hold of the deep truths of the faith with a clear conscience. [10]They must first be tested; and then if there is nothing against them, let them serve as deacons.

[11]In the same way, their wives are to be women worthy of respect, not malicious talkers but temperate and trustworthy in everything.

[12]A deacon must be the husband of but one wife and must manage his children and his household well. [13]Those who have served well gain an excellent standing and great assurance in their faith in Christ Jesus.

[14]Although I hope to come to you soon, I am writing you these instructions so that, [15]if I am delayed, you will know how people ought to conduct themselves in God's household, which is the church of the living God, the pillar and foundation of the truth.

UNDERSTANDING THE SCRIPTURE

1 Timothy 3:1-7. By the time of 1 Timothy's writing, the development of separate church offices of bishop, deacon, and elder had begun to take place (for elder, see 5:19). The term "bishop" translates the Greek word *episkope,* a term meaning "overseer." The letter of 1 Timothy is less interested in

the functions of a bishop than the qualities required. As a result, it sheds little light on what distinguishes a bishop from an elder or deacon at this point and time in history. Later writings of the early church fathers, such as the letter of Ignatius, bishop of Antioch in the first decade of the second century, provide details of office that had developed by then. "Married only once" (in Greek, "the husband of one wife") raises interesting questions. Polygamy does not seem to have been a practice acceptable in this era. The text is unclear whether then this refers to remarriage after divorce or the death of a spouse, or to acts of adultery. Beyond the "individual" traits detailed in the first three verses, there are three categories of "communal" characteristics the passage identifies for those who would be bishops. The first set of characteristics relates to the bishop's ability to manage relationships within his (and at this time, that would be the correct pronoun) own household. The second "community" quality requires that the bishop not be a newcomer to the faith. The third quality has already been touched on in previous sessions: The bishop must be one who has the respect of the community outside the church. In an interesting play on words in verse 7, the bishop must be well "thought of" by outsiders. The verb there is *martureo*, "witness." The bishop, who was to be a witness to the community, here relies upon the "witness" of the community.

1 Timothy 3:8-10. "Deacon" comes directly from the Greek word *diakonos*, whose original meaning referenced a servant who waited tables. As with "bishop," 1 Timothy ignores the duties of this office in favor of identifying its qualifications. The office of deacon had already been identified, lifted up in two of Paul's letters (Romans 16:1, Philippians 1:1), as well as traditional ascriptions of the office to Stephen and the seven set apart in Acts 6:1-6. "Conscience" in verse 9 repeats a theme raised earlier in 1:5 (positively) and 1:19 (negatively). The word for "conscience" in Greek derives from a root meaning "to know in common with." In the wider culture surrounding 1 Timothy's church, "conscience" referred to a self-knowledge that exercised moral insight or restraint. This passage links a "clear" conscience to the holding of faith.

The words may suggest a deep integrity of faith, where what is professed truly reflects what individuals believe in heart and mind.

1 Timothy 3:11. This verse presents an interesting task for interpreters. In the middle of a passage (8-13) concerned with deacons, it inserts instructions for "women" (or "wives" as the term can also be translated). Who exactly does the author have in mind? It could be the wives of deacons, but it is odd they would be singled out, while the wives of bishops are not given similar instruction in the previous passage. It could be women in the church in general, but why interrupt the flow of this passage that has to do with qualifications for church office? The third option for the identity of this group is deacons who are women. Lest we think such an interpretation lays modern thinking upon an ancient text, refer to Romans 16:1. There, the first person Paul singles out in the greetings to those in the church at Rome is "Phoebe, a deacon of the church at Cenchreae."

1 Timothy 3:12-13. The section on deacons concludes with these two verses. The thirteenth verse in particular raises an interesting perspective: namely, the issue of "advancement." It would be a gross misreading of this text to equate it with approval of ministry that climbs the career ladder. The "good standing for themselves" attained by such service in this verse links directly with "boldness in the faith." The personal value of rendering faithful service as a deacon thus relates to the growth and confidence of one's faith, a deepening relationship in Jesus Christ. This may also indirectly relate to the importance of being viewed by the wider community (not just the church) with respect.

1 Timothy 3:14-15. In Romans 8:28, Paul wrote of God's ability to have "all things work together for good." Had Paul been immediately able to make this visit represented by his expressed hopes here, this epistle would not have been written. Verse 15 represents the overarching theme of this epistle: how to conduct life within the "household" of God, which is the church. Here, the epistle uses the New Testament's chief word for Christian community: *ekklesia*, "called out." In the context of this letter in particular, that to which the church has been called is to serve as the "pillar and bulwark of the truth." Those two terms are architectural in origin, allowing the author to speak of the church as a building (see 1 Corinthians 3:9*b*-15 for another "structural" image).

1 Timothy 3:16. Verse 9 made reference to the "mystery of the faith." In this chapter's closing verse, 1 Timothy provides a glimpse of what that mystery entails. It is worth noting that in verse 16, the word translated as "religion" is *eusebeia*. The commentary on 1 Timothy 2:2 in the session for January 8 noted this same word is crucial in both of the Timothy epistles as well as Titus. Its meaning (and translations in the NRSV) range from "reverence" to "godliness" to "religion." The structure of these verses strongly resembles a hymn, either of the author's composition or more likely a fragment of some liturgical creation of the early church. Six parallel lines assert a faith that is at once deeply incarnational and broadly missional. Without mentioning once the name of Jesus, the references leave no doubt as to whom this faith is anchored in and to whom it bears witness.

INTERPRETING THE SCRIPTURE

Leadership Qualities

The measure of leadership has typically sought a blending of "doing" and "being." That is, we want our leaders to be able to *do* certain things, and we also want them to *be* certain things. We do that in the church. In denominations that use call systems for placement rather than appointments, profiles of churches and ministers will usually have a page devoted to "skills" or "competencies" for ministry. Pastoral leadership does come in the "doing."

First Timothy 3 approaches the measure of leadership from the side of "being." That is, it identifies the qualities or characteristics needed for ministry. To be sure, every one of these qualities identified for both bishops and deacons takes shape in action. You are not "hospitable" by just talking about the welcome extended to others. You are "not violent but gentle" not by merely thinking good thoughts, but by not exploding when push really does come to shove. But it is not so easy to place such characteristics on a checklist, and develop consensus statements on what constitutes a "skill" of hospitality or gentleness.

At the time of 1 Timothy's writing, the assignment of specific responsibilities to these offices still seemed to be in a state of flux and development. So it is natural that the epistle weighs in most strongly on these criteria of "being." Does that mean that 1 Timothy teaches that clergy need not be competent or skilled? Absolutely not. But neither does it mean, in our day that stresses the professionalism of ministry, that matters of character in religious leadership are merely secondary to the skills one can show. Some of the crises that most vex the church today, particularly in areas of ministerial ethics, trace not to competency levels but to issues of personal integrity. As 1 Timothy rightly underscores, who we are figures just as largely as what we can do in the identification and authorization of Christian leadership.

Church and Home

The last session's Understanding the Scripture touched briefly on the role of "household" in the wider society in general, and in the church in particular. We need now to look more deeply at that issue, as issues of household loom large in the qualifications of bishops (3:4-5) and deacons (3:12). As mentioned in that previous section, "household codes" existed in the wider culture that defined the roles and obligations of every member of the household, even slaves. The intent of those codes was to give order to those relationships. And the order in those codes was very much top-down—with the so-called *paterfamilias* (father of the family) in charge of all.

The influence of this structure upon the developing church and its leaders was multiplied by the fact that churches at this date primarily met in homes. Another factor deepening this influence had to do with the church's desire to be at peace with the wider community. Those already suspicious about the nature of Christian community did not need further ammunition by having the Christian community organize itself in ways radically distinct from its neighbors.

So when we hear 1 Timothy speaking of church office being directly related to the ability to "manage his own household" (3:4, 12), we ought not be surprised. This passage closes by referring to the purpose of this letter as instruction as to "how one ought to behave in the household of God" (3:15). That simply underscores what was, for this community, its strategy for co-existence.

Does co-existence with culture mean compromise of faith? Before we cast too many stones for this community's adoption of the household model of authority, we may want to examine how many of our own traditions in the church, including those related to leadership, trace far more to culture than to Christ.

Experience

It is the inevitable challenge for recent graduates of high school or college: help wanted, five years of experience required. How do you get experience in your field if you have not been able to work in your field? Experience is valued, and valuable.

First Timothy recognized this truth, and applies it to bishops and deacons in slightly differing ways.

To bishops, the need for experience comes in this clause: "he must not be a recent convert" (3:6). The fact it is made hints that the experiment has been tried of elevating folks new to the faith to this office and responsibility. The epistle identifies the problem with not doing so to be that of pride. It is not simply an ancient problem, nor is it limited to church office. Rises to power that have come too quickly do tend to have an inflationary effect on one's sense of self. "Too big for your britches" was my mother's phrase for Timothy's theology. It is the problem confronted when Jesus lectures the disciples on the differences between power in the church and in the world (Mark 10:35-45). "It is not so among you" still warrants our heeding, whether for bishops or any other church position.

For deacons, the need for experience comes in an indication in verse 10 of some probationary or testing period. What is intriguing there is that the time of testing is not identified with discovering whether they can do the work. Rather, the test will be whether "they prove themselves blameless" or not. It would be misleading to understand "blameless" as not making any mistakes. The word translated as "prove blameless" is *anegkletos*. Its meaning in the wider culture referred to one against whom no accusation could be made. That meaning would apply here to one who, in the probationary conduct of this office, had not committed any offense or abuse that would warrant some accusation or charge. And experience in the office, or at least in some limited exercise of its power and responsibility, provided the best determination for its full authorization.

Hold Fast to Mystery

The key verse in this session, while spoken in regard to deacons, truly invites everyone in the Christian community: "hold fast to the mystery of the faith" (3:9).

Holding fast to a mystery might seem something of an oxymoron. Mysteries are, by nature, things that escape our total grasp. There is much of faith that has that quality. We do not totally grasp the mystery of God. Like Job standing before the whirlwind, we marvel in awe—not control—at the wonders of God's workings in the far universe and in the very building blocks that compose our bodies. Mystery surrounds us. Yet God does not say: *Too bad you don't get it.*

God bids us with grace to hold on to that which sheds light on minds and hearts—and to trust good and gracious purposes for that which escapes us.

The historical context of 1 Timothy adds yet another meaning to holding on. Those times were lived at the edge of persecution, where discipleship sometimes came at great cost. Holding on to faith was not keeping culturally acceptable and even expected values as it is for some of us today. Holding on meant just that: holding on to hope, when despair pressed hard. Holding on to love, when suffering what was unloving. And to know, and trust, in our holding that we are held on to by the One revealed to us in Jesus Christ.

SHARING THE SCRIPTURE

Preparing Our Hearts

This week's devotional reading is found in Mark 9:33-37. Here we read about Jesus' response to the disciples' argument about greatness. Reflect on the following questions. How does Jesus define "greatness"? How do you define it? How does society or your social group define it? What does Jesus' definition suggest about how leaders in the church should function?

Pray that you and the adult learners will seek to experience the kind of true greatness that Jesus urges his followers to embrace.

Preparing Our Minds

Study the background, 1 Timothy 3, and the lesson Scripture, verses 2-15. As you focus on this session, consider the kinds of behaviors and qualifications that you seek in a good church leader. How do your expectations square with Paul's?

Write on newsprint:

❏ information for next week's lesson, found under "Continue the Journey."

LEADING THE CLASS

(1) Gather to Learn

❖ Welcome the class members and introduce any guests.

❖ Pray that the participants will not only learn about what it means to live as a good leader in the church but also live out that teaching.

❖ Head a sheet of newsprint *Leadership*. Divide it into three columns labeled "Community," "Workplace," "Church." Invite the students to brainstorm ideas about the characteristics that people need to be effective leaders in the community, workplace, and church, respectively. Encourage the adults to point out differences in expectations for leaders among the three groups. Discuss why such differences might exist. Consider issues of integrity, morality, and ethics each group might encounter.

❖ Read aloud today's focus statement: **People seek leaders who have a good reputation. What behavior and qualifications should we look for in church leaders? Paul**

indicates that good church leaders have strong Christian faith and character and that they are well respected by all in the community.

(2) Examine Paul's Description to Timothy of the Characteristics of Good Church Leaders

❖ Ask the students to open their Bibles to 1 Timothy 3:2-7. Invite them to call out the characteristics of bishops. Write these ideas on newsprint. Encourage as many responses as possible because different translations of the Bible will give a variety of nuances to these traits. The more responses you have, the more thorough the students' understandings will be.

❖ Repeat this activity for 1 Timothy 3:8-13, which deals with the qualifications of deacons. Be sure to note that the word "women" in verse 11 may refer to "the deacons' wives," or it may also be a reference to "women who are deacons." Both interpretations are possible in the Greek. This variation may open the door for discussion about the role of women in leadership positions.

❖ Leave both lists posted where everyone can see them. Discuss the standards of accountability for the bishops and deacons. Talk with the class about whether or not they think church leaders, especially clergy, are held to a higher standard than other members. If the adults believe that leaders are held to a higher standard, talk about whether or not this should be the case. Shouldn't all who bear the name of Christ live upright, model lives that serve as an example to others? If not, why not?

(3) Compare Paul's View with the Learners' Views About Characteristics That Make Good Church Leaders

❖ Use the brainstorming technique again to encourage the adults to list traits of church leaders. Use two or three sheets of newsprint:

■ one for clergy. Focus on spiritual behaviors and attitudes and personal traits that enable clergy to be good leaders for God's people.

■ one for lay volunteers. When you discuss lay volunteers try to think of all the different unpaid jobs that are done in your church. These might include: singing in the choir, ushering, teaching Sunday school, maintaining the building and grounds, working in the church office, serving on or leading committees. You do not need to list specific talents, such as being able to sing, but focus on spiritual behaviors and attitudes and personal traits that enable laity to be good leaders for God's people.

■ one (if this applies to your church) for paid leaders who are not clergy. These people might include church musicians, director of Christian education/spiritual formation, youth leader, secretary/administrative assistant, or other such positions. Again, focus on spiritual behaviors and attitudes and personal traits that enable these workers to be good leaders for God's people.

❖ Look now at the two or three lists of characteristics you have created and compare them to the ones that Paul says are essential for church leaders. Discuss similarities between the two lists.

❖ Add to your class lists or note any characteristics that are essential for leaders in the contemporary church that Paul does not mention. Why are these traits important today? Are there any on Paul's list that you believe are not important today? Why?

(4) Name and Give Thanks for the Good Leaders in the Learners' Congregation and Denomination

❖ Distribute paper and pencils. Ask the students to write the name of leaders, both ordained and lay, who they believe are (or have been) especially effective in moving the church closer to the reign of God.

❖ Ask the students to call out, at random, the name(s) they have written. More than one student may have chosen a particular individual. (Consider posting these papers on a bulletin board where the students may be reminded of these leaders as we continue the unit, "God's Gifts of Leadership.")

❖ **Option:** If time permits, invite the students to tell brief stories of how particular leaders have influenced their own journey of faith.

❖ Use this prayer and invitation to support leaders, adapted from "An Order for Installation or Recognition of Leaders in the Church" found in *The United Methodist Book of Worship.*

■ *Prayer:* **Almighty God, we give you thanks for these persons who have answered the call to lead us. Continue to pour out your blessings upon these your servants. Grant them grace to give themselves wholeheartedly in your service. Keep before them the example of our Lord, who did not think first of himself, but gave himself for us all. Guide them in their work. Reward their faithfulness with the knowledge that through them your purposes are accomplished; through Jesus Christ our Lord. Amen.**

■ *Invitation:* **Dear friends, rejoice that God provides laborers for the vineyards. Will you do all you can to assist and encourage them in the responsibilities to which they have been called, giving them your cooperation, your counsel, and your prayers?**

■ *Response:* **If so, please answer, we will.**

(5) Continue the Journey

❖ Pray that the students will continue to support and uphold the faithful leaders in

their church and denomination so that they may point the church in the direction of God's coming reign.

❖ Read aloud this preparation for next week's lesson. You may also want to post it on newsprint for the students to copy. **Prepare for next week's session, "Set an Example," by reading 1 Timothy 4. During our class meeting we will look at that entire chapter. As you study, think about the lesson with these ideas in mind: People need to be taught the truth. What rules can guide us in what and how we teach? Paul admonishes Timothy to teach godliness and the good news of Jesus Christ.**

❖ Read aloud the following three ideas. Challenge the students to commit themselves to use these activities as a springboard to spiritual growth.

(1) **Consider the leadership you give to the church through any positions you may hold. What qualifications do you feel are essential for these tasks? Which of these qualifications do you believe you possess? What kind of example do you set for the people you lead?**

(2) **Offer to mentor someone else as a teacher and/or leader. Just as Timothy needed Paul to set an example and give him guidance, so too inexperienced leaders need the example and guidance you have to share.**

(3) **Make it a point to call or write to at least two church leaders whose example and/or work have positively influenced you. Thank them and let them know how they have touched your life.**

❖ Sing or read aloud "A Charge to Keep I Have."

❖ Lead this benediction to conclude the session: **May you go forth as servants in whom the Lord delights to bring justice to the nations by the power of God's Spirit. Amen.**

UNIT 2: GOD'S GIFTS OF LEADERSHIP
SET AN EXAMPLE

PREVIEWING THE LESSON

Lesson Scripture: 1 Timothy 4
Background Scripture: 1 Timothy 4
Key Verse: 1 Timothy 4:16

Focus of the Lesson:
People need to be taught the truth. What rules can guide us in what and how we teach? Paul admonishes Timothy to teach godliness and the good news of Jesus Christ.

Goals for the Learners:
(1) to investigate Paul's admonition to Timothy to teach consistently God's instructions for living and Jesus' good news.
(2) to explore how they discern truth.
(3) to commit to teaching the truth through example.

Supplies:
Bibles, newsprint and marker, paper and pencils, hymnals

READING THE SCRIPTURE

NRSV
1 Timothy 4

[1]Now the Spirit expressly says that in later times some will renounce the faith by paying attention to deceitful spirits and teachings of demons, [2]through the hypocrisy of liars whose consciences are seared with a hot iron. [3]They forbid marriage and demand abstinence from foods, which God created to be received with thanksgiving by those who believe and know the truth. [4]For everything created by God is good, and nothing is to be rejected, provided it is received with thanksgiving; [5]for it is sanctified by God's word and by prayer.

[6]If you put these instructions before the

NIV
1 Timothy 4

[1]The Spirit clearly says that in later times some will abandon the faith and follow deceiving spirits and things taught by demons. [2]Such teachings come through hypocritical liars, whose consciences have been seared as with a hot iron. [3]They forbid people to marry and order them to abstain from certain foods, which God created to be received with thanksgiving by those who believe and who know the truth. [4]For everything God created is good, and nothing is to be rejected if it is received with thanksgiving, [5]because it is consecrated by the word of God and prayer.

brothers and sisters, you will be a good servant of Christ Jesus, nourished on the words of the faith and of the sound teaching that you have followed. [7]Have nothing to do with profane myths and old wives' tales. Train yourself in godliness, [8]for, while physical training is of some value, godliness is valuable in every way, holding promise for both the present life and the life to come. [9]The saying is sure and worthy of full acceptance. [10]For to this end we toil and struggle, because we have our hope set on the living God, who is the Savior of all people, especially of those who believe.

[11]These are the things you must insist on and teach. [12]Let no one despise your youth, but set the believers an example in speech and conduct, in love, in faith, in purity. [13]Until I arrive, give attention to the public reading of scripture, to exhorting, to teaching. [14]Do not neglect the gift that is in you, which was given to you through prophecy with the laying on of hands by the council of elders. [15]Put these things into practice, devote yourself to them, so that all may see your progress. [16]**Pay close attention to yourself and to your teaching; continue in these things, for in doing this you will save both yourself and your hearers.**

[6]If you point these things out to the brothers, you will be a good minister of Christ Jesus, brought up in the truths of the faith and of the good teaching that you have followed. [7]Have nothing to do with godless myths and old wives' tales; rather, train yourself to be godly. [8]For physical training is of some value, but godliness has value for all things, holding promise for both the present life and the life to come.

[9]This is a trustworthy saying that deserves full acceptance [10](and for this we labor and strive), that we have put our hope in the living God, who is the Savior of all men, and especially of those who believe.

[11]Command and teach these things. [12]Don't let anyone look down on you because you are young, but set an example for the believers in speech, in life, in love, in faith and in purity. [13]Until I come, devote yourself to the public reading of Scripture, to preaching and to teaching. [14]Do not neglect your gift, which was given you through a prophetic message when the body of elders laid their hands on you.

[15]Be diligent in these matters; give yourself wholly to them, so that everyone may see your progress. [16]**Watch your life and doctrine closely. Persevere in them, because if you do, you will save both yourself and your hearers.**

UNDERSTANDING THE SCRIPTURE

1 Timothy 4:1-3a. Already in the teachings of Jesus, faithfulness was expected to encounter opposition and betrayal (see Matthew 10:16-23). Such expectations formed a familiar component of writings addressing the "last times," both Jewish and Christian. The opposition depicted in these verses, however, is not limited to some distant future moment. Renunciation of the faith is a present threat to and dilemma of the church. The nature of the dilemma is not merely misguided individuals. The mention

of "spirits" and "demons" communicates that the struggle goes much deeper (see Ephesians 6:11-12). "Hypocrisy" and "liars" identify the presence of false teachers within the community. The two issues identified with false teaching both involve abstinence: one from marriage, the other from certain foods. These issues had already been addressed in 1 Corinthians 7 and 8. Their presence in this later correspondence suggests a movement (an early form of Gnosticism?) that has persisted in the church.

1 Timothy 4:3b-5. The author argues against the opponents on the basis of creation theology. Genesis 1 is here the primary text in mind, with its repeated refrain of "and God saw that it was good" following the days of creation. These ascetics will argue, as do some later Gnostics, that the material world is evil and thus something to be escaped. The ban on marriage would thus move persons out of the realm of the flesh and into the realm of the spirit. Holiness becomes defined as an increasing separation from the things of this world, whether food or authentic sexuality. For the author of 1 Timothy, nothing could be further from the truth. The very things denied by the opponents have been fashioned by God and deemed "good" in their creation. What sets persons and things apart—that is to say, what brings holiness—is "God's word and prayer." The practical measure employed by the author about what is good or appropriate becomes whether it can be received with thanksgiving and prayer. A more extended presentation of this argument may be found in 1 Corinthians 10:23-31.

1 Timothy 4:6. There is some question as to whether these verses offer a summary to teach the preceding verses (1-5) or those following (7-11). In either case, they assert Timothy's call to a ministry of teaching. "Servant" in this verse translates *diakonos*, a term elsewhere rendered as "minister" or "deacon." The context here suggests the author does not mean a specific office in the church (as in deacon, elder, bishop), but rather the word is used as a general term for ministry. "Nourished" may be an ironic play on the opponents' abstinence from foods. What "feeds" Timothy, and likewise any "good" servant of Christ Jesus, are the teachings followed. In the Timothy correspondence, "teaching" and "the faith" are essentially synonyms, along with truth and belief/believe. Even as these epistles sought to provide a basic framework for ordering offices of ministry, so too do they seek to assert a basic framework of teaching that is "the faith." Opposition and conflict make both movements necessary.

1 Timothy 4:7-10. A pair of imperative verbs introduces this section: "have nothing to do" and "train yourself." The first brings the reminder that not all things are good for faith. While the opponents are given some identification in verse 3, verse 7 gives us little to understand what specifics are involved with such "myths" and "tales." Some suggest a preoccupation with genealogies, particularly since that association occurs in 1:4. To go any further, however, would be speculation—which is itself what the author weighs in against here. Unhelpful speculation that does nothing to equip the person or community of faith has no value. In contrast, the next imperative moves toward that which does have value: training in "godliness." As we have noted earlier, "godliness" (*eusebia*) is a key word throughout the Pastoral Letters. Literally meaning "good devotion," it has in mind the way in which faith works itself out in the course of life. "Piety" would be a synonym, in the sense not merely of a religious attitude toward life but of that attitude being "enacted." The title of God as "Savior" occurs with frequency in the Pastorals (see 1 Timothy 1:1, 2:3).

1 Timothy 4:11. This is another summary verse that could work equally well with the preceding verses (7-10) or the following (12-16). Since the following verses speak more of the author's concern for Timothy's own actions, however, this verse's emphasis on what must be insisted upon and taught seems to fit more in expression with the preceding.

1 Timothy 4:12-16. In a community where one ministerial office takes its name from an age designation ("elder"), "youth" could be a definite hindrance for the exercise of authority. Jeremiah 1:6-7 reflects a similar concern. But where the authority of years is lacking, the author encourages Timothy to seek that authority which arises out of example. In one sense, verse 11's insistence upon Timothy's teaching does relate to these verses: Only here, Timothy is to teach not only by word but by conduct, love, faith, and purity. He is himself to be the text. The author mentions a possible visit in verse 13: Whether or not it came to pass, if this is Paul writing, is unclear. The verse in one way lends the author's (Paul's?) authority to Timothy in the meantime, as it entrusts this ministry and teaching to Timothy. The particular gift of ministry, while unidentified in verse 14, requires Timothy's cultivation. "Do

not neglect" makes clear that it can be neglected. The specific episode of commissioning by the laying on of hands also is referred to in 2 Timothy 1:6. Again, the ordering of ministry that has been a theme in this and other of the Pastoral Letters finds early practical evidence in this rite, by which the community had set apart Timothy for ministry. The closing verse underscores the significance of these instructions to Timothy. While God is Savior, the actions of Timothy and others in ministry have a share in that "saving" activity.

INTERPRETING THE SCRIPTURE

Bad Examples

The letter's urging of Timothy's example of the faith becomes all the more critical by the presence and influence of "bad examples." Not all who undermine faith stand outside of it or in opposition to it. Some speak its name, and make its claims, but only in ways that serve their purposes.

The opponents in the case outlined in 1 Timothy make a show of abstinence. It is not always so. Hypocrisy can also sugarcoat the gospel so that it becomes a means or even vehicle to personal enrichment in the most material of ways. Abstinence makes a claim to spiritual superiority by pointing to what is denied oneself as the secret of faithfulness. In our own day, affluence makes a claim to spiritual superiority by pointing to what is accumulated to oneself as the proof of faithfulness. Either can be harmful.

The author uses the word "hypocrisy" here to describe the posturing of such persons. The word "hypocrite" originated in ancient Greek theater, where it was used of actors. For in the plays of that day, a single actor might play several roles, each signified by a different mask put on. Hypocrisy

in life in general, and in the church in particular, functions in a similar way. What is real and true to one's identity is covered by a superficial visage. It might be the appearance of self-denial, as in this text. It may be the trappings of affluence, as is displayed in some corners of the church today. It may be the guise of humility, which barely covers greed or pride.

As in the day of 1 Timothy, the church still wrestles with bad examples of faithfulness. Witness still is needed to confront hypocrisy for what it is, no matter how deeply it wraps itself in the name of God or nation or congregation.

Spiritual Training

The imagery of training resonates in our culture, even as it did among the ancient Greeks. They, too, devoted considerable time to honing physical skills and appearances for the sake of athletic competition.

The text borrows that imagery of athletic training to emphasize the importance of spiritual training. The use of such imagery would lend itself to those who believe Paul to be author of this epistle. For elsewhere (1 Corinthians 9:24-25, Philippians 3:12-14),

Paul makes vivid use of training and competition to speak of faith and endurance.

How do you go about "spiritual training?" The last decade and more has seen a rise in interest for spiritual exercises and disciplines. Biblical study that moves beyond information into issues of personal formation and faith experience reflects this interest. Many church growth advocates categorize the current and upcoming generation as "seekers." The name grows from a perceived thirst on their part for religious experience not always available to them in the formalism of worship or narrow doctrine. What the church will have to offer to those folks will, in part, grow out of how we come to terms with what the author seeks here of Timothy: training in "godliness."

The image may seem a bit pietistic to some. But consider this: How do we cultivate in ourselves an awareness of and responsiveness to the presence of God in our midst? Corporate worship and text-oriented study are by no means the only ways to grow in Christ. The text invites you and those with whom you share this class to engage in conversation about how you go about such "training"—what you find valuable, what you might like to see. Imagine if your congregation were a spiritual fitness center. What would it offer that would be of help to you? To those who rarely darken a church's door but who are still very much on a spiritual quest? Such training, the author affirms, will be "valuable in every way."

The Good News of Hope and Salvation

Interpreting the Scripture in the session for January 8 touched on the theme of Christ's ransom being for all persons (1 Timothy 2:6). Now, in 4:10, yet another affirmation is made about the scope of God's saving activity: "the living God, who is the Savior of all people, especially of those who believe."

Does this mean God saves all persons, and that those who believe are just especially blessed because they know their status in grace? Does this mean God *offers* to save all persons, and that those who believe are the only ones who have benefit of the offer? It is important to keep this text in conversation with others on this topic, both those that imply the necessity of belief for salvation (Galatians 3:21-22) and those that imply universalism (Ephesians 1:9-10), a doctrine that states that all will be saved by God's grace regardless of what they believe.

The primary audience of 1 Timothy 4:10 is folk within the church. And the primary function of these words is to engender hope among them—which is to say, among us. The toil and struggle alludes back to the effort made in training. Those words may also have in the background the labor involved in living faithfully in the midst of a society at best suspicious of the community and persecuting at worst. The text does not imply that hope cuts us free from earthly worries, not to mention faith's disciplines. Hope does not set its roots in the outward circumstances of life, good or bad. Hope sets its roots in the living God (not the make-believe God promoted by the opponents in verse 3). The God of hope is the God of creation, and creation is still where the church fashions our witness to the God who is Savior of all.

Getting Personal

The God who came incarnate in Jesus still seeks "incarnation" in the lives of faithful persons. This portion of the letter closes with the author's encouraging of Timothy's "incarnation" of the faith. The calling is to be an example of the faith in his life for the sake of others.

The words in verse 15 sound like a return to the imagery of training: "put into practice," "devote yourself," "progress." There are no shortcuts to faithfulness. Nor are there options that allow us to have others live our faith for us. The author is not instructing Timothy to be an example of faith so that others do not have to. No, the example is given so that others can follow.

Sometimes we seek our leaders, church or secular, to be surrogates for us. Let them take the risks; let them do the work. Such effort not only puts leaders on unfair pedestals, it creates a spirit of passivity among the followers. Timothy is a leader in this congregation. This epistle calls upon him to offer his life as an example in every way possible. But nowhere does it suggest that Timothy is to do this in place of the equivalent of religious spectators. Timothy's example is for the sake of providing others with a role model that they can follow. Timothy's peculiar call rests in the ritual of commissioning described in these verses. But Timothy's call shared with every one in that congregation, and in our own, is his baptism. In our baptism, God calls each one of us to ministry. God calls each one of us to be, with Timothy, an example of faith.

SHARING THE SCRIPTURE

Preparing Our Hearts

This week's devotional reading is found in 1 Corinthians 3:6-11. Here we find Paul writing about the distinctive work that different servants in the church perform. These workers are to be seen not as competitors but as those who, collectively, contribute to the building up of the body of Christ. They do not work on their own but are assigned their tasks by God. How do you think about the leaders in your congregation? How do you see yourself as a congregational leader? Are these leaders seeking personal status, or truly working as God's servants? What difference does the example of the leaders make?

Pray that you and the adult learners will set an example of faithful living in Christ Jesus.

Preparing Our Minds

Study the background and lesson Scripture, both of which are chapter 4 of 1 Timothy. As you read, consider the rules that guide what and how we teach, remembering that Timothy was told to teach godliness and the good news of Jesus Christ.

Write on newsprint:

❑ Questions under "Gather to Learn."
❑ information for next week's lesson, found under "Continue the Journey."

Plan a lecture on 1 Timothy 4:1-6 for the "Investigate Paul's Admonition to Timothy to Teach Consistently God's Instructions for Living and Jesus' Good News" portion.

LEADING THE CLASS

(1) Gather to Learn

❖ Welcome the class members and introduce any guests.

❖ Pray that the students will be open to the Spirit's leading as they study together today.

❖ Invite the learners to recall a favorite teacher of any subject in elementary or secondary school, college, or Sunday school. Discuss these questions either with the class or in small groups. If you want to work in groups, post the questions on newsprint.

(1) **Why did this teacher make such an impression on you?**

(2) **How did this person gain your confidence so that when he or she spoke you could trust the truth of his or her teachings?**

(3) **How did this teacher's character help to shape you? In other words,**

how did this teacher set an example that you chose to follow?

❖ Read aloud today's focus statement: **People need to be taught the truth. What rules can guide us in what and how we teach? Paul admonishes Timothy to teach godliness and the good news of Jesus Christ.**

(2) Investigate Paul's Admonition to Timothy to Teach Consistently God's Instructions for Living and Jesus' Good News

❖ Choose a volunteer to read 1 Timothy 4:1-6.

■ Use the information from Understanding the Scripture for these verses and "Bad Examples" in Interpreting the Scripture to create a lecture in which you:
  • discuss the concerns related to renunciation of the faith.
  • look at Paul's arguments against the ascetics' positions on marriage and abstinence from certain foods.
  • explore the meaning of verse 6, especially as it relates to Timothy and his ministry.

❖ Choose a volunteer to read 1 Timothy 4:7-16.

■ Divide a sheet of newsprint into two columns, one headed "Do" and the other, "Don't Do." Encourage the adults to look in their Bibles at the verses that have just been read and call out things that Timothy (and by extension, anyone who ministers in the name of Jesus) is to do and those things that one is to refrain from doing.

■ Talk with the class about the ways in which they do what Timothy was commanded to do.

■ Consider with the class how the metaphor of athletic training is appropriate for training in godliness. Perhaps some members of the class work out regularly at a gym, exercise at home, or prepare for athletic competitions. Encourage them, in particular, to talk about similarities between athletic and spiritual training.

■ Read today's key verse, 4:16. Help the class members see that what they do affects not only themselves but also those they teach, through lessons and/or the example of their lives.

■ Provide quiet time for the adults to reflect on the lessons they've taught this week by the way they have acted and treated other people.

(3) Explore How the Learners Discern Truth

❖ Point out that we can be influenced by "the hypocrisy of liars" (4:2) and may then turn away from "the words of the faith" and "sound teaching" (4:6), possibly to follow "myths" and "tales" (4:7).

❖ Ask the class to give some examples of current false teaching or lies in the realm of faith. (Avoid discussions of politics, economics, or other areas where students believe leaders are lying so as not to get sidetracked from faith issues.) Challenge the adults to talk about why they are so certain that the teaching they have labeled as "false" or "a lie" really is untrue. This discussion will lead into the next activity.

❖ Make a list on newsprint of the criteria the participants use to determine whether or not a religious teaching is true. Recognize that different people will use different criteria for determining truth. Some will rely solely on Scripture; others may look to reason, church tradition, and/or their own experience.

❖ Place a check mark next to any of the criteria listed on newsprint that the entire class can agree on. Where differences exist, encourage the adults to say why a certain standard is important to them.

❖ Talk about how whatever we believe to be true influences our behavior and attitudes.

(4) Commit to Teaching the Truth Through Example

❖ Distribute paper and pencils. Invite the students to consider how they can teach the truth of godliness and the good news of Jesus to others. Ask them to jot down at least one action they will take this week to be an example of this truth for others.

❖ Read to the class, as a commission, 1 Timothy 4:15-16.

(5) Continue the Journey

❖ Pray that the students will go forth as servants of the word who by their example teach others the good news of Jesus Christ.

❖ Read aloud this preparation for next week's lesson. You may also want to post it on newsprint for the students to copy. **Prepare for next week's session, "Practicing Justice and Mercy," by reading the background passage from 1 Timothy 5, focusing on the lesson Scripture from verses 1-8, 17-24. Keep these ideas in mind as you read: People want not only to be treated fairly but also to receive mercy. How can we show both justice and mercy? Paul advises Timothy on how to be just and merciful, particularly in regard to the older and younger members of the church and to widows.**

❖ Read aloud the following three ideas. Challenge the students to commit themselves to use these activities as a springboard to spiritual growth.

    (1) Be alert for opportunities to teach others about Jesus this week. Look especially for ways to teach by example.

    (2) Spend extra time preparing for next week's session. Imagine how you would lead it if you were the teacher. Why would you plan to teach it in the way you have chosen?

    (3) Ponder the ways in which you discern truth. How do you know what you know? Why do you believe it to be true? Think about a specific belief you hold. What might be able to change your mind? Write your thoughts in your spiritual journal.

❖ Sing or read aloud "This Little Light of Mine."

❖ Lead this benediction to conclude the session: **May you go forth as servants in whom the Lord delights to bring justice to the nations by the power of God's Spirit. Amen.**

UNIT 2: GOD'S GIFTS OF LEADERSHIP
PRACTICING JUSTICE AND MERCY

PREVIEWING THE LESSON

Lesson Scripture: 1 Timothy 5:1-8, 17-24
Background Scripture: 1 Timothy 5
Key Verses: 1 Timothy 5:1-2

Focus of the Lesson:
People want not only to be treated fairly but also to receive mercy. How can we show both justice and mercy? Paul advises Timothy on how to be just and merciful, particularly in regard to the older and younger members of the church and to widows.

Goals for the Learners:
(1) to explore how Paul's instructions amount to a call to enact justice and mercy.
(2) to express their understanding of how Paul's words apply to particular situations in their lives.
(3) to identify an issue where they can advocate for justice and mercy and commit themselves to action.

Pronunciation Guide:
presbuteros (pres boo' ter os)

Supplies:
Bibles, newsprint and marker, paper and pencils, hymnals

READING THE SCRIPTURE

NRSV
1 Timothy 5:1-8, 17-24

¹Do not speak harshly to an older man, but speak to him as to a father, to younger men as brothers, ²to older women as mothers, to younger women as sisters—with absolute purity.

³Honor widows who are really widows. ⁴If a widow has children or grandchildren,

NIV
1 Timothy 5:1-8, 17-24

¹Do not rebuke an older man harshly, but exhort him as if he were your father. Treat younger men as brothers, ²older women as mothers, and younger women as sisters, with absolute purity.

³Give proper recognition to those widows who are really in need. ⁴But if a widow has

they should first learn their religious duty to their own family and make some repayment to their parents; for this is pleasing in God's sight. ⁵The real widow, left alone, has set her hope on God and continues in supplications and prayers night and day; ⁶but the widow who lives for pleasure is dead even while she lives. ⁷Give these commands as well, so that they may be above reproach. ⁸And whoever does not provide for relatives, and especially for family members, has denied the faith and is worse than an unbeliever.

¹⁷Let the elders who rule well be considered worthy of double honor, especially those who labor in preaching and teaching; ¹⁸for the scripture says, "You shall not muzzle an ox while it is treading out the grain," and, "The laborer deserves to be paid." ¹⁹Never accept any accusation against an elder except on the evidence of two or three witnesses. ²⁰As for those who persist in sin, rebuke them in the presence of all, so that the rest also may stand in fear. ²¹In the presence of God and of Christ Jesus and of the elect angels, I warn you to keep these instructions without prejudice, doing nothing on the basis of partiality. ²²Do not ordain anyone hastily, and do not participate in the sins of others; keep yourself pure.

²³No longer drink only water, but take a little wine for the sake of your stomach and your frequent ailments.

²⁴The sins of some people are conspicuous and precede them to judgment, while the sins of others follow them there.

children or grandchildren, these should learn first of all to put their religion into practice by caring for their own family and so repaying their parents and grandparents, for this is pleasing to God. ⁵The widow who is really in need and left all alone puts her hope in God and continues night and day to pray and to ask God for help. ⁶But the widow who lives for pleasure is dead even while she lives. ⁷Give the people these instructions, too, so that no one may be open to blame. ⁸If anyone does not provide for his relatives, and especially for his immediate family, he has denied the faith and is worse than an unbeliever.

¹⁷The elders who direct the affairs of the church well are worthy of double honor, especially those whose work is preaching and teaching. ¹⁸For the Scripture says, "Do not muzzle the ox while it is treading out the grain," and "The worker deserves his wages." ¹⁹Do not entertain an accusation against an elder unless it is brought by two or three witnesses. ²⁰Those who sin are to be rebuked publicly, so that the others may take warning.

²¹I charge you, in the sight of God and Christ Jesus and the elect angels, to keep these instructions without partiality, and to do nothing out of favoritism.

²²Do not be hasty in the laying on of hands, and do not share in the sins of others. Keep yourself pure.

²³Stop drinking only water, and use a little wine because of your stomach and your frequent illnesses.

²⁴The sins of some men are obvious, reaching the place of judgment ahead of them; the sins of others trail behind them.

UNDERSTANDING THE SCRIPTURE

1 Timothy 5:1-2. Earlier texts in 1 Timothy on the characteristics for church leaders leaned heavily upon qualities exhibited in the household. Now, in instructions to Timothy about relating to diverse folks within the community, the author once more employs imagery from family relationships. The primary issue here is communication (speaking), but actually it goes deeper. *Presbuteros* is the Greek word translated here as "older man." The passage later renders this same word as "elder," in recognition of those ensuing verses dealing with the office of elder in the church. First Timothy 4:12 already identified Timothy's relative "youth." As a result, the first verse provides practical advice for bridging the generation gap in Timothy's exercise of authority. The text counsels communication and relationship as if with parents. Similarly, with peers and those younger, the counsel to Timothy is to maintain relationships as within family. The text adds further explanation and protection to Timothy's relating to younger women by qualifying it with the word meaning "absolute purity." That word in the Greek shares the same root as "holy."

1 Timothy 5:3-8. These verses focus on the place of widows in the Christian community. They also underscore the support owed by families to widowed parents and relatives. The imperative that begins the passage, "honor," echoes the Decalogue's commandment to "honor your father and your mother" (Exodus 20:12). Distinctions are made in this text between widows with children or other means of support and those who are "left alone" and therefore in need of the community's support. As in Judaism, the early Christian community would provide support from a common fund administered by the church and used for monetary support or needed goods (see Acts 6:1). The responsibilities of family, to be examined in more detail in the Interpreting the Scripture section, find powerful statement. "Honoring" widows involves not just attitudes, but "repayment" that supports them in their time of need. To fail in such obligations is not simply bad manners—it is denial of the faith (5:8).

1 Timothy 5:9-16. The "list" spoken of in verse 9 refers to an enrollment of widows. The list does not merely have to do with who receives charity. Those enrolled seem

to have taken vows (5:12). Some understand the pledge to be related to not remarrying, and thus making clear they rely on the support of the community. Others see connected in those vows various acts of ministry (5:10) and prayer (5:5). The presence of younger widows, a major concern in this passage, may be attributed to the marriage of girls at a young age to older men as well as a shortened life expectancy of men in the military. The fact that the epistle devotes so much focus in these verses to the issue of younger widows suggests the situation was a familiar one. There seems to be a contradiction in the attitude against remarriage in verse 11 with the encouragement to do so in verse 14. While various explanations related to the vows of those enrolled are possible, the text does not speak with enough clarity to settle all questions. Once again in verse 16, the responsibility of family to assist widows is restated.

1 Timothy 5:17-18. These verses address the development of paid leadership in the early church, at least of those in the office of "elders who rule." Taken by itself, verse 17 might be heard as simply an encouragement to offer due respect ("honor") to those persons, particularly those whose "ruling" involves the ministry of the word ("preaching" here translates *logos*, which simply means "word"). Verse 18 clearly moves the conversation and context into financial support. This is the only time where 1 Timothy quotes Scripture—and what is quoted is intriguing. The first quotation about not muzzling an ox comes from Deuteronomy 25:4. The second quotation, however, is from Jesus (Luke 10:7). Does this mean that at the time 1 Timothy was written the collections of Jesus' teachings or Gospels had already attained the status of Scripture in the church (remember: verse 18 declares "for the scripture says")?

1 Timothy 5:19-20. The author earlier advised that bishops and deacons should be "above reproach" or "blameless" (3:2, 10). In case reproach or blame was forthcoming, these verses now deal with how to handle such charges. In line with the traditions associated with Judaism (Deuteronomy 19:15) and the teachings of Jesus (Matthew 18:16), a minimum of two witnesses would be required before accepting (which does not necessarily presume agreeing with) any accusation. Verse 20 addresses the uncomfortable situation where such sin persists. The bringing to light of the matter is to be public, in order that the example may be brought to bear upon the whole community.

1 Timothy 5:21-22. These words of warning to Timothy have the sound of instructions given to a judge or jury. As such, they reflect on how the assessment of matters in verses 19-20 is to be handled. The rejection of prejudice and partiality reflects a theme encountered elsewhere in the reception of Gentiles into the community (Acts 10:34) as well as how to maintain community in the face of inequities (James 2:1, 9). The injunction against hasty "ordinations" (the Greek there is literally "lay hands on") resonates with earlier instructions about requiring experience and even probation for those entrusted with leadership (3:6, 10).

1 Timothy 5:23. This remarkable personal touch to the epistle reminds the readers that wholeness is a matter of not only the spirit but the body as well. Previous admonitions about sobriety in this epistle ensure this is not meant to be an advertisement for inordinate drinking. Rather, it is the recognition that, for Timothy, an ailment he has may call for a reasonable use of wine.

1 Timothy 5:24-25. These closing words suggest the sins (and good works) of some are obvious, while others are not so apparent. Those who rush to judgment in either case based on mere appearances may not know the truth. But all is known to God, and will be revealed in good time.

INTERPRETING THE SCRIPTURE

Speaking to Community

Language shapes life. We can use words to abuse and batter a spouse or a child as surely as with a fist. We can use words to raise another's spirit or bring hope. Language also shapes community. Before a holocaust can be enacted, words of hatred must sear consciences. Before transformation can come, words of hope must open minds and spirits to new possibilities.

The author of 1 Timothy well understands the power of language to shape relationship and community. And why not? Christian faith comes revealed through and in "word." God speaks, and creation comes into being. The Word becomes flesh, and we encounter God in our midst in Jesus. Scripture bears witness to God's purposes and serves as authority for shaping our life together.

Beyond those overarching themes, our text homes in on practical ways in which language plays a formative role in community. First Timothy 5 counsels the language of family for the church's "conversations."

To elders, words spoken aim at the goal of respect extended to parents. Such deference does not equate with giving in on every matter. Timothy still must exercise the authority the author of this epistle entrusts to him. Yet, it is to be done in a way that honors the wisdom and experience of age.

The author's instructions to Timothy about peers invoke the language and relationship of brothers and sisters. Our own family experiences will shape how we hear those words (as well as the "parental" language above). The intent, it seems, aims at a goal of honesty and camaraderie in such relationships. The qualification of the relationship toward younger women "with absolute purity" identifies an issue still very much alive and troublesome in the church. Just as there is language that abuses, so can there be relationships that abuse. To use the office of leadership in the church for one's sexual needs or advantage represents just such an abuse. Given the language of familial relationship invoked by the author, such abuse is incestuous in nature.

Responsibilities in Church and Family

"Charity begins at home" is sometimes invoked as an excuse for not engaging in ministry and mission beyond the comfortable confines of that which is local—whether that is defined as one's own church, community, or nation. In the case of 1 Timothy 5, however, it underscores a sometimes grossly overlooked responsibility in that time and in our own: responsibility for one's own family.

If the (extended) family could not support a widow, or there was no family left to do so, the Christian congregation, like the Jewish synagogue, took up such slack. The author apparently knows of cases where family support was not forthcoming. Otherwise, why would this reminder be necessary? Verse 8 speaks to the responsibility of "providing for," a role understood at this time to belong to the *paterfamilias*, or elder male of an extended family. Verse 16 extends that care-giving to women of means. The context of the passage points in the direction of the church having limited means at its disposal to care for every widow, which made the responsibility of extended families more pressing.

Clearly, the era in which 1 Timothy was set did not have the social service safety nets that ours does—at least, for some of us. Some of the responsibilities for caring for elders and others made vulnerable have been assumed by the wider community—but not all. For a family to presume state or church will take over all needs for care-giving of one of its members, simply to save

money or time, is no less offensive to the faith now than it was then. We are connected to one another: in family as well as in congregation. First Timothy simply connects the exercise of covenant faithfulness to family relationships as well as church community.

Leadership: Support and Accountability

In verses 17-20, the author of 1 Timothy links leadership in Christian community with two key issues: support and accountability.

To be supported, leaders in the Christian community need the means to live and find their work honored. The quotations used by the author make clear that, while other means of support and honor are to be considered, financial support is the topic at hand. First Timothy does not say what the level of support should be. We find no advice as to whether to base the local elder's salary on the equivalency of the local blacksmith, the local schoolteacher, or the local centurion. This much we do know: The ministry of the word is a labor, and it deserves financial recognition. Over the last quarter of a century, the emphasis on ministry as profession has pressed the awareness of such recognition in local churches and denominations, and rightly so. Nothing in this text suggests ministry should be compensated at a level only slightly different from indentured servanthood. On the other hand, nothing in this text suggests ministry should be vying for Wall Street wages either.

The issue of accountability finds initial statement in words that insist on another form of support: fairness. Even though the author brings significant expectations for leadership qualifications in the church (3:1-13), fairness is to be the rule of the day when it comes to assessing accusations. An elder has the same right of two or three witnesses before an accusation is considered as any other person according to the law of Moses and the teaching of Jesus (see

Understanding the Scripture on verses 19-20). But when the accusation proves itself true, accountability requires that the elder not be cut any special favors or allowed to "persist in sin" (5:20). Not so long ago, accusations of sexual indiscretion were not met with censure, but with a move to another parish or conference or diocese. "Out of sight, out of mind" may be convenient, but it solves nothing for the offender—and certainly not for victims, past or future.

Forewarned Is Forearmed

The author cautions Timothy in this passage's concluding section against the sort of things that would get him, and the church and leaders who follow him, in hot water. Avoid prejudice. Avoid partiality. Don't put anyone into ordained leadership too quickly. Commentators believe that much of what is said here relates directly to the issues in verses 19-20.

Such advice also merits wider hearing and application. Prejudice and partiality have never served the church or Jesus Christ. Because of the former, we still wrestle with such things as 11 A.M. Sunday morning being the most segregated hour in the United States. Because of the latter, we have inherited the ability to be turned by appearances and won over by style versus substance.

The ordination issue is an intriguing one. Perhaps in some free-church traditions, and certainly thanks to mail-in divinity degree factories, ordinations may still be done too quickly. On the other hand, this writer would suppose that most of the traditions using this material have lengthy tracks for ordination. Some folks, and communities, in special circumstances may find it easier to find the blessing of God's Spirit than the blessing of God's church for needed ministry. How do you hear these words of 1 Timothy on ordination speaking to the church today?

SHARING THE SCRIPTURE

Preparing Our Hearts

This week's devotional reading is found in Matthew 23:23-28. Here Jesus issues a scathing attack on "scribes and Pharisees" whose actions, while appearing pious, are motivated by "hypocrisy and lawlessness" (23:28). These people who like to consider themselves faithful are "full of greed and self-indulgence" (23:25). Jesus denounces these leaders for following minute aspects of the law, while ignoring the larger issues of "justice and mercy and faith" (23:23). How are you practicing the kind of justice and mercy that God expects? Does the image you project to the world mirror who you are in your heart? If not, what disparities exist? What changes do you need to ask God to help you make?

Pray that you and the adult learners will recognize how important it is for believers to practice justice and mercy.

Preparing Our Minds

Study the background from 1 Timothy 5 and the lesson Scripture, verses 1-8, 17-24. Consider Paul's advice to Timothy concerning how we are to show justice and mercy, especially to those who are most vulnerable.

Write on newsprint:
❏ questions for the "Explore How Paul's Instructions Amount to a Call to Enact Justice and Mercy" portion.
❏ information for next week's lesson, found under "Continue the Journey."

LEADING THE CLASS

(1) Gather to Learn

❖ Welcome the class members and introduce any guests.

❖ Pray that the participants will be open to the gracious ways in which God offers justice and mercy and expects Jesus' followers to do likewise.

❖ List on newsprint the ways that your congregation provides for vulnerable members, such as widows. Do you have an organized "caring committee" that offers services such as transportation, meals, and/or household chores? What can this class do to expand or initiate such services for those who are most in need of help?

❖ Read aloud today's focus statement: **People want not only to be treated fairly but also to receive mercy. How can we show both justice and mercy? Paul advises Timothy on how to be just and merciful, particularly in regard to the older and younger members of the church and to widows.**

(2) Explore How Paul's Instructions Amount to a Call to Enact Justice and Mercy

❖ Choose two volunteers, one to read aloud 1 Timothy 5:1-8 and the other, verses 17-24.

❖ Divide the class in half. Assign half the group (or groups, if the class is large) to 1 Timothy 5:1-8, and the other to verses 17-24. Distribute paper and pencils or newsprint and markers to each group. Ask each group to discuss these questions and jot down answers. Post these questions on newsprint where all the groups can see them.

(1) **Why do you think Paul speaks in terms of family relationships? (5:1-8)**

(2) **Do you agree with Paul's way of handling vulnerable widows? Why or why not? (5:1-8)**

(3) **What does Paul say is the duty of**

believers toward their spiritual leaders? (5:17-24)

(4) **Why is the conduct of the leader so apparently important for Paul? (5:17-24)**

(5) **How do Paul's points reflect the kind of justice and mercy to which God calls us? (5:1-8, 17-24)**

(6) **What does this passage suggest to you about how contemporary church members are to treat their families and church leaders? (5:1-8, 17-24) Do we act in accordance with Paul's teachings? If not, why not?**

❖ Provide time for the groups to report to the entire class.

(3) Express Understanding of How Paul's Words Apply to Particular Situations in the Learners' Lives

❖ Read one or both of the following case studies and ask the class, either as a whole or in smaller groups, to respond.

■ Case 1: Blanche Jackson's husband of 55 years died last year after a lengthy illness. Blanche had cared lovingly for him but now is clearly failing herself. Although she lives at home, a mild stroke has left her unable to drive and do many of the chores she used to do by herself. Her son and daughter, both of whom are married with families of their own, live out of state and are not very attentive to their mother. What role can the church play in helping these grown children to reconnect with her? How can the church assist her while she is apparently without support?

■ Case 2: Pastor Jonathan Dowe found a way to embezzle funds from the church. His theft had gone unnoticed for months, but when it was discovered, the church was in an uproar and immediately taking sides. How would you handle such a situation in your own church? What guidelines would you use to ensure that Pastor Dowe was treated with justice and mercy?

❖ Provide quiet time for the class members to reflect on situations that require attention in their own lives, particularly with aging and/or dependent family members. Encourage them to think about how their handling of the situation reflects—or needs to reflect—God's justice and mercy.

❖ Break the silence by reading today's key verses, 1 Timothy 5:1-2.

(4) Identify an Issue Where the Learners Can Advocate for Justice and Mercy and Commit Themselves to Action

❖ Invite the students to discuss local issues where justice and mercy seem to be lacking. Here are some examples: Is the tax structure unfair to the poor? Do unsatisfactory schools keep children from achieving their full potential? Are families who need public assistance treated with prejudice or partiality?

❖ Encourage each participant to choose one issue that he or she feels passionate about and serve as an advocate for those who need justice and mercy. Distribute paper and pencils. Ask each learner to write a sentence or two stating the selected issue and possible action to be taken.

(5) Continue the Journey

❖ Pray that the participants will practice justice and mercy to all, especially those who are the most vulnerable members of society. Or, if you have hymnals that include "The Prayer of Saint Francis," ask the class to pray this prayer in unison.

❖ Read aloud this preparation for next week's lesson. You may also want to post it on newsprint for the students to copy. **Prepare for next week's session, "A Heritage of Faith," by reading 2 Timothy 1.**

Our lesson will highlight verses 3-14. As you read, keep these ideas in mind: People are often shaped significantly by their heritage and seek to stay true to it. What constitutes being true to one's Christian heritage? Paul reminds Timothy to follow the correct teachings that he received from his mother and grandmother and from the apostle, and to let the faith and love of Christ be his model in life.

❖ Read aloud the following three ideas. Challenge the students to commit themselves to use these activities as a springboard to spiritual growth.

(1) **Locate information on Medicare and/or Social Security or other public programs. From what you know—and possibly experience firsthand—do you believe these programs reflect the kind of justice and mercy for the vulnerable that God would want? If not, what changes need to be made in these programs to make them more just? What action will you take to let your voice be heard by decision-makers?**

(2) **Select someone in your congregation who is facing a major challenge. See what you can do to show God's mercy to this individual and help him or her get through the current crisis.**

(3) **Look within your family. Is there someone—a widow or widower; a child; a loved one with a physical, mental, or emotional handicapping condition—who needs special care? Lend support to this person in whatever way is needed and possible.**

❖ Sing or read aloud "What Does the Lord Require?"

❖ Lead this benediction to conclude the session: **May you go forth as servants in whom the Lord delights to bring justice to the nations by the power of God's Spirit. Amen.**

UNIT 3: FAITHFUL FOLLOWERS, FAITHFUL LEADERS
A HERITAGE OF FAITH

PREVIEWING THE LESSON

Lesson Scripture: 2 Timothy 1:3-14
Background Scripture: 2 Timothy 1
Key Verse: 2 Timothy 1:5

Focus of the Lesson:

People are often shaped significantly by their heritage and seek to stay true to it. What constitutes being true to one's Christian heritage? Paul reminds Timothy to follow the correct teachings that he received from his mother and grandmother and from the apostle, and to let the faith and love of Christ be his model in life.

Goals for the Learners:

(1) to explore how Paul encouraged Timothy to be true to his Christian heritage by boldly proclaiming the sound teaching he received from Lois, Eunice, and Paul.
(2) to identify how their own spiritual formation has occurred.
(3) to share their faith with a member of a younger generation.

Pronunciation Guide:

anapsucho (an aps oo' kho)
ekklesia (ek lay see' ah)
euaggelion (yoo an ghel' ee on)
marturion (mar too' ree on)
Onesiphorus (on uh sif' hu ruhs)

anuhpokritos (an oo pok' ree tos)
enoikeo (en oy keh' o)
Johannine (joh han' in)
oikos (oy' kos)
paratheke (par ath ay' kay)

Supplies:

Bibles, newsprint and marker, paper and pencils, hymnals

READING THE SCRIPTURE

NRSV

2 Timothy 1:3-14

³I am grateful to God—whom I worship with a clear conscience, as my ancestors did—when I remember you constantly in my prayers night and day. ⁴Recalling your tears, I long to see you so that I may be filled

NIV

2 Timothy 1:3-14

³I thank God, whom I serve, as my forefathers did, with a clear conscience, as night and day I constantly remember you in my prayers. ⁴Recalling your tears, I long to see you, so that I may be filled with joy.

with joy. **⁵I am reminded of your sincere faith, a faith that lived first in your grandmother Lois and your mother Eunice and now, I am sure, lives in you.** ⁶For this reason I remind you to rekindle the gift of God that is within you through the laying on of my hands; ⁷for God did not give us a spirit of cowardice, but rather a spirit of power and of love and of self-discipline.

⁸Do not be ashamed, then, of the testimony about our Lord or of me his prisoner, but join with me in suffering for the gospel, relying on the power of God, ⁹who saved us and called us with a holy calling, not according to our works but according to his own purpose and grace. This grace was given to us in Christ Jesus before the ages began, ¹⁰but it has now been revealed through the appearing of our Savior Christ Jesus, who abolished death and brought life and immortality to light through the gospel. ¹¹For this gospel I was appointed a herald and an apostle and a teacher, ¹²and for this reason I suffer as I do. But I am not ashamed, for I know the one in whom I have put my trust, and I am sure that he is able to guard until that day what I have entrusted to him. ¹³Hold to the standard of sound teaching that you have heard from me, in the faith and love that are in Christ Jesus. ¹⁴Guard the good treasure entrusted to you, with the help of the Holy Spirit living in us.

⁵I have been reminded of your sincere faith, which first lived in your grandmother Lois and in your mother Eunice and, I am persuaded, now lives in you also. ⁶For this reason I remind you to fan into flame the gift of God, which is in you through the laying on of my hands. ⁷For God did not give us a spirit of timidity, but a spirit of power, of love and of self-discipline.

⁸So do not be ashamed to testify about our Lord, or ashamed of me his prisoner. But join with me in suffering for the gospel, by the power of God, ⁹who has saved us and called us to a holy life—not because of anything we have done but because of his own purpose and grace. This grace was given us in Christ Jesus before the beginning of time, ¹⁰but it has now been revealed through the appearing of our Savior, Christ Jesus, who has destroyed death and has brought life and immortality to light through the gospel. ¹¹And of this gospel I was appointed a herald and an apostle and a teacher. ¹²That is why I am suffering as I am. Yet I am not ashamed, because I know whom I have believed, and am convinced that he is able to guard what I have entrusted to him for that day.

¹³What you heard from me, keep as the pattern of sound teaching, with faith and love in Christ Jesus. ¹⁴Guard the good deposit that was entrusted to you—guard it with the help of the Holy Spirit who lives in us.

UNDERSTANDING THE SCRIPTURE

2 Timothy 1:1-2. The opening two verses of this letter closely mirror 1 Timothy 1:1-2. (For review, see the Understanding the Scripture portion on those verses in the session for January 1.) Two slight differences with the first epistle's opening merit further comment. First, Paul in verse 1 identifies the "promise of life" in Christ. Some commentators see this as anticipating the controversy related in 2:18, where Paul's

opponents claim that the resurrection has already occurred. If so, the opening verse underscores the promissory nature of hope against those who say it has already been realized. Second, Paul identifies Timothy as his *"beloved* child" (1 Timothy 1:2 has *"loyal* child"). A more endearing or relational tone is set in this epistle, a tone that flows quite naturally into the affirmation of verse 4.

2 Timothy 1:3-5. Paul makes an intriguing statement when he links his service rendered in clear conscience with "as my ancestors did." Sometimes, the Christian tradition seeks to make the break between Judaism and Christianity too abrupt—implying Paul must have repudiated his entire tradition. Passages such as this and Romans 11 refute such attempts. The constancy of Paul's prayer life (1:3) suggests a spirituality where conversation with God is ongoing, responsive to passing events and thoughts. The "longing" to see Timothy echoes other texts where Paul yearned to see those from whom he was at the moment separated (Romans 1:11; Philippians 1:8). The tears of Timothy likely refer to some specific experience of parting, perhaps the last time these two saw each other. The tears give embodiment to Paul's earlier "beloved" comment. Timothy's "sincere faith" reflects the goal Paul identified in 1 Timothy 1:5. "Sincere" translates the Greek word *anupokritos* ("not hypocritical"). That faith, Paul relates, first "lived in" Timothy's mother Eunice and grandmother Lois. The words "live in" translate in Greek to *enoikeo*. *Oikos* was the word for house or dwelling. Therefore, one might say Timothy's household "housed" his faith's origins.

2 Timothy 1:6-7. The first of this epistle's charges to Timothy is that of "rekindling" the gift (*charisma*) received in the rite of laying on hands. That ritual likely has in mind the same community event referenced in 1 Timothy 4:14. This ordination as a bestowing of the Spirit finds witness in Paul's assertion that the Spirit given Timothy involved power, love, and self-discipline. The Spirit as power resonates with the empowerment associated with Pentecost. The Spirit as love echoes particularly the Johannine texts, where Jesus promises the Spirit in the imminence of his departure and the command to love one another (John 14 and 15, especially 14:15-17). The Spirit as self-discipline reflects an earlier Pauline linkage of the Spirit with self-control (Galatians 5:23).

2 Timothy 1:8-10. Verse 8 contains the first of three references to "not ashamed" in this chapter. Here, it comes in the form of a charge to Timothy about testimony (*marturion*) to Christ. Paul's self-reference as a prisoner is the only such reference in all of the Pastoral Letters. Suffering and gospel and community with Paul all come linked in this invitation to Timothy in the second half of verse 8. The power (same word as in verse 7) to do so arises within not self but God. God as Savior, an affirmation that opened 1 Timothy, now finds assertion in a more narrative form in the opening of 2 Timothy 1:9-10. "Calling" (*klesis*) points back to Israel's understanding of itself as called of God, and forward to the church's identity as the *ekklesia* ("called out"). God's grace, not our works, forms the genesis of that saving and calling activity in both cases. Paul affirms such grace to be in place from the very foundation of the world. Its revelation in Christ is associated first and foremost with the abolition of death (Revelation 21:4; Isaiah 25:8) and the revealing of life and immortality (1 Corinthians 15:53-54).

2 Timothy 1:11-12a. Paul returns to the theme of his having been designated an apostle, though now joined also with "herald" and "teacher" of the gospel (*euaggelion*). "This gospel" references the summary of God's action in Christ made in verses 9-10. "This gospel," however, is not merely a statement of Paul's authority to speak and act as he does. It is this gospel that brings Paul to suffer (1:12), a suffering to which he invites Timothy to join him in ministry. Paul's present imprisonment (1:8) may be the immediate experience of suffering in mind behind these words. Yet before this imprisonment, Paul asserts that suffering and gospel are frequent traveling companions (see especially 2 Corinthians 4:7-18).

2 Timothy 1:12b-14. Paul's second "not ashamed" becomes a testimony of his own willingness to trust wholly in God. In verses 12 and 14, "entrusted" (*paratheke*) is used:

first of what Paul entrusts to God, secondly of what has been entrusted to Timothy. The Greek word originally referred to a deposit, or of property left in the hands of another. Verses 13-14 represent a concluding charge in this passage to Timothy to "hold" and "guard" the teaching entrusted to him in ministry. That grace is still operative becomes clear in Paul's asserting Timothy's task is to be done with the help of the Spirit "living" (*enoikeo*, as in verse 5) in us.

2 Timothy 1:15-18. Paul does not point to himself as the only example for Timothy's faith and ministry. Verse 15 recounts the negative witness of some who rejected Paul. "All in Asia" sounds very much like hyper-bole on Paul's part. No specific details beyond the two names given illuminate what generated such a sweeping statement of opposition or betrayal. Faith's positive witness comes in the example of Onesiphorus and his household (1:16-18). Apparently during Paul's imprisonment in Rome, Onesiphorus sought out the apostle and ministered to him with frequency. "Refreshed me" translates *anapsucho*, whose literal meaning runs closer to "renew the soul." The reference to Ephesus underscores the continuity of this individual's service from before. Onesiphorus, like Paul, like Eunice and Lois, forms the example of faith in which Timothy now lives.

INTERPRETING THE SCRIPTURE

Faith "In House"

Previous sessions and their passages have highlighted the importance of the household in the ordering of the early church. At least one of those passages presumed roles for women that sound demeaning at best to modern ears and eyes (1 Timothy 2:11-15). The issue before Paul in 2 Timothy 1 is no longer "order" per se: It is faith's origins. Household once again comes to the fore, but Paul makes an amazing testimony here to faith's "dwelling."

For Timothy, the decisive sources for faith (besides Paul) resided in his grandmother Lois and his mother Eunice. In a society where family lines and inheritance were determined by male ancestry, this is a powerful word about the way God works through those whom the world tends to overlook. Absent from this passage are any words about Timothy's grandfather and father. All we know of his father (Acts 16:1) is that he was Greek (presumably a Gentile, as that verse specifies Timothy's mother was Jewish). Second Timothy 1:5 does not disparage the importance of fathers in religious upbringing, or having two parents actively involved in religious training. It simply yet profoundly asserts Timothy's faith drew first nurture from the household provided by mother and grandmother.

Recall from the commentary that verb translated as "lived in" in this verse: *enoikeo*. Faith is given a dwelling in the lives of these two women, which in turn enables faith's development in Timothy. In contrast to the dramatic experience of conversion of Paul, Timothy represents one nurtured within the faith—a third-generation Christian! Persons come into the faith, then and now, in different ways and paths. Second Timothy 1 witnesses to the importance of systems of family and church that provide places of birth and growth for new generations of faith. The witness of Timothy is also of God's providence in using persons outside the usual mainstream to bring such faith into being.

Continuity and Community: Gifts and Suffering

The lesson Scripture witnesses to the theme of continuity and community in faith—for Timothy, and for us.

Think of the ways in which these verses underscore the heritage of faith that sustains persons. Paul relates that his worship or service rendered to God was in company with his ancestors. The faith of Timothy is connected to that of his grandmother and mother. The gift that Paul wants Timothy to rekindle is related to a rite in which the hands of Paul (and those of elders in his community, 1 Timothy 4:14) were placed upon him in some act of ordination. Paul speaks of his own imprisonment, and then invites Timothy to "join with me in suffering" (2 Timothy 1:8). Finally, Paul affirms the trustworthiness of God in his life and in the Spirit's help of Timothy. No one stands alone in the Christian life. Paul urges Timothy—and us—to stand in continuity with these persons, and this God, who gift and grace our lives with such a heritage.

"Gift" and "grace" speak of our enrichment, and rightly so. Yet Paul also, as noted, invites Timothy to share "in suffering for the gospel" (1:8). These are not easy words to hear, much less follow. Yet they ring consistent with Paul's earlier words about the cruciform life (1 Corinthians 1:18-25). They resonate with Jesus' own invitation in the Gospels to discipleship that takes up one's cross and follows (Mark 8:34-38). These are not words that sit easily with contemporary theologies that entice persons to faith as the means to prosperity, or to prayer as naming and claiming our desires. Our reliance is upon the power of God, not the power of materialism or privilege or "might makes right." To stand in continuity and community with Paul and Timothy we must embrace a gospel that bears gifts and suffering in its keeping.

The Gospel: Saved and Called by Grace

Paul's letter to the Romans, perhaps his closest effort at a systematic theology, begins with a statement that closely echoes how 2 Timothy 1:8-10 speaks of the gospel: "For I am not ashamed of the gospel; it is the power of God for salvation to everyone who has faith" (Romans 1:16).

"Save" or "salvation" describes what God does for us in grace. The word in Greek also carries with it the meaning of "safety" and "wholeness," and frequently is used in the Gospels in connection with Jesus' healings. Paul's invitation to Timothy to "join with me in suffering" (1:8) makes clear that "saving" does not magically deliver us from situations and circumstances that may be difficult or trying. Rather, God's saving assures us that nothing can finally separate us from God (Romans 8:38-39).

It is perhaps not coincidental that 2 Timothy 1:9 follows immediately the affirmation of God "who saved us" with the words that God "called us with a holy calling." Salvation is for a purpose: changed lives. Paul would have been at ease with the understanding of being called of God from his Jewish background. Israel had been called of God: out of Egypt, through the Torah. God's calling was to be a peculiar people devoted to God. The church now shares in that calling. The initiative for that call, as well as its fulfilling, reside in the purpose and grace of God. As important as human effort is, and this epistle will later place great stress on our works as did 1 Timothy, Paul recognizes discipleship gains its moorings in God's grace. We still live, and serve, and hope, by that same grace.

Entrusted

Have you ever been entrusted with something of value from another person, or done the same to another? Letting go is not easy, unless there is substantial trust in that other person to do what is right with what has been given.

Paul knows the One in whom he has placed his trust. Written in imprisonment, perhaps near the time of his death, such words carry weight. The one who once wrote of nothing separating him from the love of God in Christ faces powers able to inflict suffering and death with ease. Yet Paul trusts in the God who is able (the same root word as that used in "power" in verse 8) to guard what has been entrusted to God.

Timothy also has been entrusted with the heritage of faith given him by Eunice and Lois and Paul, the "good treasure" of verse 14. By the Spirit's help, Paul writes, Timothy is to guard that gift.

And what of us? Much has been entrusted to our hands. The church in which you worship, the mission in which you engage with your community, the faith that is yours: We have a heritage entrusted to our care and keeping. And we have that heritage entrusted for the sake of others, those who follow us and depend upon our witness. And we also find ourselves, like Paul, able to entrust God with our lives. We will not be disappointed by the grace of God. We will not be cut loose by the love of God. So the close of this passage returns us to Paul's opening: "I am grateful" (1:3). For what God has given to us, for what we may entrust into God's sure keeping—let us be grateful, and faithful!

SHARING THE SCRIPTURE

Preparing Our Hearts

This week's devotional reading is found in 2 Thessalonians 2:13-17. "Stand firm and hold fast to the traditions that you were taught by us," Paul writes in verse 15. As you think about your own spiritual formation, what traditions have been writ large on your heart and mind? Who passed these traditions on to you? How are you passing them on to others? How do you feel about new ideas that can become traditions for future generations? Write your answers in a spiritual journal.

Pray that you and the adult learners will appreciate and give thanks for your spiritual heritage.

Preparing Our Minds

Study the background from 2 Timothy 1 and the lesson Scripture, verses 3-14. As you read, consider what constitutes being true to one's spiritual heritage.

Write on newsprint:

❑ the chart shown under "Explore How Paul Encouraged Timothy to Be True to His Christian Heritage by Boldly Proclaiming the Sound Teaching He Received from Lois, Eunice, and Paul."

❑ questions for "Identify How the Learners' Spiritual Formation Has Occurred."

❑ information for next week's lesson, found under "Continue the Journey."

LEADING THE CLASS

(1) Gather to Learn

❖ Welcome the class members and introduce any guests.

❖ Pray that the students will recall and give thanks for the spiritual foundation upon which they have built their life in Christ.

❖ Encourage the students to think about sayings they heard at home that helped to shape their character and view of the world. These might be "mom's sayings" or Ben Franklin quotations, such as "Never leave that till tomorrow which you can do today," or "A spoonful of honey will catch more flies than a gallon of vinegar."

❖ Read aloud today's focus statement: **People are often shaped significantly by their heritage and seek to stay true to it. What constitutes being true to one's Christian heritage? Paul reminds Timothy to follow the correct teachings that he** received from his mother and grand-mother and from the apostle, and to let the faith and love of Christ be his model in life.

(2) Explore How Paul Encouraged Timothy to Be True to His Christian Heritage by Boldly Proclaiming the Sound Teaching He Received from Lois, Eunice, and Paul

❖ Choose a volunteer to read today's lesson from 2 Timothy 1:3-14.

❖ Copy this chart onto newsprint and fill it in with the class. Determine what the text discloses and/or implies about each of these people. If the class is large, divide into groups and ask each group to work on one name. Provide time for the groups to report back.

Lois	Eunice	Timothy	Paul	Jesus

❖ Read the third paragraph in the section in Interpreting the Scripture entitled "Continuity and Community: Gifts and Suffering." Recall that the epistle makes reference in verse 8 to Paul as a prisoner. Talk with the class about what they are willing to suffer or sacrifice to keep the gospel alive in their own lives and pass it on to others. Consider how a life lived in the shadow of the cross contrasts with some current theologies that make the Christian way sound like a free coupon for anything people want.

❖ Read the first, second, and third paragraphs of "Entrusted" in Interpreting the Scripture. Discuss these questions.

(1) What faith traditions have been entrusted to you by the ancestors of your congregation and/or your denomination?

(2) How are you as a body living out this faith?

(3) How are you intentionally pass-

ing on these faith traditions to younger generations?

(4) What additional steps, if any, do you need to take to ensure that the faith is passed on? Remember the adage that Christianity is always just one generation away from extinction.

(3) Identify How the Learners' Spiritual Formation Has Occurred

❖ Distribute paper and pencils. Ask the students to draw a line down the center of the page. At the top, ask them to write the year of their birth, and at the bottom, 2006. Set a time limit and invite them to fill in specific dates that were especially meaningful to them in their faith journey. These may be events, such as baptism or confirmation, but they may also be a meaningful time spent with someone from whom the students learned about the faith.

❖ Invite volunteers to tell about a particular event in their own life. Suggest that as they speak they address these questions, which you will post on newsprint.

(1) Who was involved?

(2) How did this event help to shape your life of faith?

(3) What faith traditions, if any, were handed on to you as a result of this event?

(4) If you had to name three people most influential on your spiritual development, who would they be? Why?

(5) What kind of church "family" most nurtured you in your faith development?

❖ Suggest that the students try to detect any patterns regarding how faith is shared and formed. Talk about these patterns. Perhaps you will note some generational differences if your class includes a variety of age groups.

(4) Share the Faith with a Member of a
Younger Generation

❖ Encourage the participants to talk about how they share the faith with children, grandchildren, or other children in their lives. Do they tell the faith, show the faith, or a bit of both? Invite them to be open about the difficulties they have encountered in trying to share the faith.

❖ Distribute paper and pencils. Suggest that the students write a letter to a spiritual son or daughter in which they tell about how their own faith was formed, traditions that are important to them, and their dreams for spiritual growth and direction for the son or daughter they have addressed.

❖ **Option:** Invite several class members to read or retell what they have written.

❖ Close this portion of the session by suggesting that the adults hand carry or mail this letter to the addressee.

(5) Continue the Journey

❖ Pray that the students not only have identified their Christian heritage but also will remain true to it and pass it on to others.

❖ Read aloud this preparation for next week's lesson. You may also want to post it on newsprint for the students to copy. **Prepare for next week's session, "Pursue Righteousness," by reading 2 Timothy 2, which is the background, and focusing on verses 14-26. As you study, keep these main ideas in mind: People need to** develop Christian character so they may live as people of God. How can church leaders help members develop Christian character? Paul advises Timothy to exercise self-discipline, especially in his speech and attitudes, and to deal gently with those who would start quarrels.

❖ Read aloud the following three ideas. Challenge the students to commit themselves to use these activities as a springboard to spiritual growth.

(1) **Give a monetary donation or gift of time in honor or memory of someone who has been very influential in your faith journey.**

(2) **Plan an intergenerational activity with family that includes persons from three or four generations. Be alert for opportunities to bear witness to your faith as you interact with your loved ones.**

(3) **Draw a family tree showing as many ancestors as possible. Write a sentence or two about each one who has influenced your faith journey. Remember that that influence may not be direct, but handed down through several generations. If you do genealogical research, see what you can find out about the beliefs of your ancestors.**

❖ Sing or read aloud "Happy the Home When God Is There."

❖ Lead this benediction to conclude the session: **May you go forth as servants in whom the Lord delights to bring justice to the nations by the power of God's Spirit. Amen.**

UNIT 3: FAITHFUL FOLLOWERS, FAITHFUL LEADERS
PURSUE RIGHTEOUSNESS

PREVIEWING THE LESSON

Lesson Scripture: 2 Timothy 2:14-26
Background Scripture: 2 Timothy 2
Key Verse: 2 Timothy 2:22

Focus of the Lesson:
People need to develop Christian character so they may live as people of God. How can church leaders help members develop Christian character? Paul advises Timothy to exercise self-discipline, especially in his speech and attitudes, and to deal gently with those who would start quarrels.

Goals for the Learners:
(1) to study Paul's instructions regarding the development of Timothy's Christian character.
(2) to develop a profile of Christian character based on this passage and identify their own strengths and weaknesses in light of this profile.
(3) to repent of any behavior that does not fit with this Christian profile, and to commit to the self-discipline Paul describes.

Pronunciation Guide:
antiphon (an' te fan)   *asebeia* (as eb' i ah)
hagiazo (hag ee ad' zo)   Hymenaeus (hi muh nee' uhs)
logomacheo (log om akh eh' o)   *metanoia* (met an' oy ah)
paideuo (pahee dyoo' o)   Philetus (fi lee' tuhs)

Supplies:
Bibles, newsprint and markers, paper and pencils, tacks or tape, hymnals

READING THE SCRIPTURE

NRSV
2 Timothy 2:14-26

14Remind them of this, and warn them before God that they are to avoid wrangling over words, which does no good but only ruins those who are listening. 15Do your best

NIV
2 Timothy 2:14-26

14Keep reminding them of these things. Warn them before God against quarreling about words; it is of no value, and only ruins those who listen. 15Do your best to present to present yourself to God as one approved by him, a worker who has no need to be ashamed, rightly explaining the word of truth. [16]Avoid profane chatter, for it will lead people into more and more impiety, [17]and their talk will spread like gangrene. Among them are Hymenaeus and Philetus, [18]who have swerved from the truth by claiming that the resurrection has already taken place. They are upsetting the faith of some. [19]But God's firm foundation stands, bearing this inscription: "The Lord knows those who are his," and, "Let everyone who calls on the name of the Lord turn away from wickedness."

[20]In a large house there are utensils not only of gold and silver but also of wood and clay, some for special use, some for ordinary. [21]All who cleanse themselves of the things I have mentioned will become special utensils, dedicated and useful to the owner of the house, ready for every good work. **[22]Shun youthful passions and pursue righteousness, faith, love, and peace, along with those who call on the Lord from a pure heart.** [23]Have nothing to do with stupid and senseless controversies; you know that they breed quarrels. [24]And the Lord's servant must not be quarrelsome but kindly to everyone, an apt teacher, patient, [25]correcting opponents with gentleness. God may perhaps grant that they will repent and come to know the truth, [26]and that they may escape from the snare of the devil, having been held captive by him to do his will.

yourself to God as one approved, a workman who does not need to be ashamed and who correctly handles the word of truth. [16]Avoid godless chatter, because those who indulge in it will become more and more ungodly. [17]Their teaching will spread like gangrene. Among them are Hymenaeus and Philetus, [18]who have wandered away from the truth. They say that the resurrection has already taken place, and they destroy the faith of some. [19]Nevertheless, God's solid foundation stands firm, sealed with this inscription: "The Lord knows those who are his," and, "Everyone who confesses the name of the Lord must turn away from wickedness."

[20]In a large house there are articles not only of gold and silver, but also of wood and clay; some are for noble purposes and some for ignoble. [21]If a man cleanses himself from the latter, he will be an instrument for noble purposes, made holy, useful to the Master and prepared to do any good work. **[22]Flee the evil desires of youth, and pursue righteousness, faith, love and peace, along with those who call on the Lord out of a pure heart.** [23]Don't have anything to do with foolish and stupid arguments, because you know they produce quarrels. [24]And the Lord's servant must not quarrel; instead, he must be kind to everyone, able to teach, not resentful. [25]Those who oppose him he must gently instruct, in the hope that God will grant them repentance leading them to a knowledge of the truth, [26]and that they will come to their senses and escape from the trap of the devil, who has taken them captive to do his will.

UNDERSTANDING THE SCRIPTURE

2 Timothy 2:1-2. As in 1:2, Paul refers to Timothy as his "child." The term sets a tone of both authority and tenderness for what follows. As has been the case in his own life, Paul begins by encouraging Timothy to draw strength from the grace of Christ. Grace is fundamental to Paul's understanding of God as revealed in Christ. Faith itself relies upon grace for its own efficacy (Ephesians 2:8). In verse 2, Paul reminds

Timothy not only of keeping the faith passed on through him (and others), but also of Timothy serving as such a conduit for coming generations. "Entrust" repeats the same word and message sounded in 1:12, 14.

2 Timothy 2:3-7. The invitation of Paul to Timothy in 1:8 to join in his suffering now prefaces verses that make clear that call to "be strong" in verse 1. Paul follows with three parable-like images to depict what such suffering involves. Soldiering underscores the "chain of command" of obedience, where following the word of a higher authority and not just going it alone takes precedence. The athlete conveys, in this passage, the importance of following rules not necessarily of one's own choosing much less creation. The image of the farmer points here to the rewards of one's work, a theme that will play a large role in the lesson Scripture.

2 Timothy 2:8-13. Once again, Paul directly connects gospel and suffering in his own life—and implicitly, in preparing Timothy for his own gospel ministry. The paradox of gospel and suffering finds match in the affirmation of Jesus' Davidic descent and his resurrection (which presumes crucifixion). "The saying is sure" in verse 11*a* repeats a phrase used earlier in 1 Timothy (1:15, 3:1, 4:9). As in those cases, here it is used to communicate some element of the tradition Paul saw to be normative and critical. The verses following it here serve as an "antiphon" formed of four "if" clauses followed by their consequences. Our living and dying in Christ reiterates a Pauline theme developed earlier in Romans 6:1-11. More difficult to understand is the relationship between the final two affirmations, where denial that seems irrevocable yet faithlessness on our part is met by faithfulness by God. Such a paradox is reflected later in this chapter by Paul's thoughts about his opponents.

2 Timothy 2:14-18. Where 2 Timothy opened with Paul "reminding" Timothy, so now he calls upon Timothy to do such

reminding of others that is linked with a warning. "Wrangling over words" translates an unusual compound word: *logomacheo*, whose literal meaning would be "word battle." The grave risk of such uses of words to spar rather than up-build or save comes when Paul declares its effect of "ruin" (*katastrophe*) for its listeners (2:14). In contrast, Timothy's urging to be one "approved" by God comes precisely in the intended use of words ("rightly explaining the word of truth"). After this brief positive exhortation, Paul returns to critique those whose talk only leads folks into "impiety" (*asebeia*), the very opposite of the attitude of piety and godliness (*sebeia*) affirmed in the epistles to Timothy and Titus. Of the pair whom Paul censures here, Hymenaeus had already been identified in 1 Timothy 1:20.

2 Timothy 2:19. Paul earlier drew on the image of foundations in writing of the church (1 Corinthians 3:10-15). Here, he adds to that the image of an inscription placed upon a building. The "inscription" on this foundation consists of one clear quotation (Numbers 16:5) and another that brings together various sources of calling on God and turning from evil. The context of the first quotation (Numbers 16) tells the story of a revolt against the authority of Moses that led to disaster for those who made that challenge. If Paul's opponents were familiar with the text, it would have been a confrontational gauntlet thrown down before them in their challenge of Paul's authority.

2 Timothy 2:20-21. Paul turns next from the imagery of foundations to that of household utensils. Given the previous emphasis in 1 Timothy on the connections between the church and the household, Paul's words here take on greater meaning. He speaks of utensils made of various materials and their uses. His point in this passage is not the same as in 1 Corinthians 12:22-24, where the seeming "inferior" members are honored as well as those more "respectable." Rather, Paul urges here such "cleansing" as will enable persons to take on the special or honored uses. "Dedicated" translates *hagiazo*, the root word for "holy." "Usefulness" to the owner of the house comes in being "ready for every good work." The same chapter that stresses reliance upon the grace of God (2:1) now asserts that grace intends to result in lives actively doing good works.

2 Timothy 2:22-25a. Given the conflict in the previous verses, "shun youthful passions" probably has to do not only with sexual issues but with argumentative spirits. Paul follows this negative charge with a positive one. Closely paralleling the instructions given to Timothy to close the first epistle (6:11), Paul identifies four qualities to be pursued. The one quality not identified in that previous listing is "peace." In a conflicted church community, "peace" would

not be a given—and perhaps not without some suffering for its sake. Such conflict returns to Paul's concern in verse 23. "Quarrels" translates *mache*, echoing the second half of the compound verb in verse 14. Contrasting with the harshness generated by such conflicts, Paul urges leadership marked by "correcting opponents with gentleness." Fire is not met with fire.

2 Timothy 2:25b-26. "Repent" translates *metanoia*, "change of mind." In the Pastorals, "truth" (2:25) serves as a synonym for "the faith" (see 2:18 for the opponents' risk in losing sight of the truth). The use of "captive" in verse 26 hearkens to Paul's own captivity and imprisonment. Yet the contrast is clear: Paul (as he calls Timothy in 2:24) is God's servant. The opponents fall captive to an entirely different power whose will they end up doing.

INTERPRETING THE SCRIPTURE

"Wrangling Over Words"

For someone whose ministry largely consisted of the communication and explication of words, it might seem that Paul sounds too restrictive. Where does the line get drawn to separate healthy debate from "stupid and senseless controversies" (2:23)? In the context of 2 Timothy, the measure comes in the results. Those consequences that Paul urges against come stated in various ways in this passage: "does no good," "ruins those who are listening" (both in 2:14), "quarrels" (2:23).

Now Paul is not saying conversations about different views or disputations over theological concepts are to be absolutely avoided. Read Galatians, where Paul takes opponents to task in a spirited confrontation over the meaning of such words as "grace" and "liberty." Debate is not squelched in 2 Timothy. But it is tempered by consideration of its results. The freedom to yell "fire" in a crowded theater does not make it right, precisely because of what it may lead

to. The freedom to engage in theological wrangling in the church does not make it right, if it results in undermining the very community it should up-build. Hold Paul's words of consequences in tandem with contemporary "wranglings" in the church. Sometimes the "talk" is small in nature but large in effect. Petty disputes about church furnishings or committee turf more often than not fail to serve any good. Sometimes, the talk is large in nature and immense in effect. Standards for ordination, issues surrounding sexual orientation, the interface between gospel and political action, decisions about moving between traditional and "seeker" styles of worship: These are important debates. They are words that cannot be avoided. Even so, 2 Timothy's caution over what results from such conversations needs to be heard and heeded. For if such words do no good and bring catastrophe to those caught in their wake, no amount of piety or relevance will cloak their assessment by 2 Timothy as "stupid and senseless . . . profane chatter" (2:23, 16).

"Ready for Every Good Work"

How does a person prepare to render faithful service to God? That theme underlies Paul's addressing Timothy—and through him, us.

The preparation begins in relationship with God: "present yourself to God as one approved by him [God]" (2:15). The verb "present" carries connotations in Greek of an offering or even sacrifice brought forward. Our preparation for Christian service thus originates in the recognition that what we do in response to faith's call is an "offering" we extend to God.

Timothy's particular work to which Paul urged him was a ministry of teaching ("rightly explaining the word of truth," 2:15). Whether we preach sermons or knit layettes, ladle soup for homeless folk or participate on a committee, we render an offering of our selves to God in that act. We do so not to merit being "approved" by God. That approval has already come as a gift of God's grace in Jesus Christ (2:1). Rather, our service flows out of thanksgiving for God's grace and out of the example of Christ's own serving of others.

Toward that service and good work, Paul urges Timothy (and us) to "do your best" (2:15). Paul elsewhere uses the noun form of that verb as a gift of God to be developed (as in Ephesians 4:3, regarding unity). There is discipline involved in that word and urging. God has graced us. That is fundamental. But we are to act upon that grace by developing its gifts in our lives and giving expression to them in our works. We are saved by grace through faith, yet that grace and faith seek embodiment in our actions. As in the imagery of the utensils in verses 20-21, we are to ready our lives to do the good works of God as faithful servants.

Character Worth Seeking

Building character, Christian or otherwise, requires two distinct types of discipline. The first discipline involves avoiding involvements and attitudes that would harm character. The second discipline involves seeking after such qualities and practices as would build character.

Paul's advice in 2 Timothy travels both paths. On one hand, the counsel is to avoid "wrangling over words" (2:14) and "profane chatter" (2:16) and to "shun youthful passions" (2:22). On the other hand, Paul in verse 22 urges the pursuit of such qualities ("righteousness, faith, love, and peace") and relationships ("those who call on the Lord from a pure heart") as would build Christian character. In light of his opponents' fondness for quarrels, Paul summons kindness and patience. Even "correction" (*paideuo*, a word originally used in reference to the instruction of children) of opponents is needed, but it is to be done with gentleness.

The discipline of character formation in individuals (and communities) remains a calling of the church. At times, that formation comes in the discipline of avoiding and rejecting that which undermines us as persons and congregations. Some things are not needed in faith: gossip, intolerance, deceit. You may add to that list those attitudes or forces that detract from the gospel of grace and its service to Jesus Christ.

As with Paul advising Timothy here, Christian formation also requires an active pursuit of those qualities and purposes that lend themselves to good. Some things are always needed in faith: love that seeks the good of others, humility, courage. Again, you may add to that list anything that communicates and embodies the gospel of grace and its service to Jesus Christ.

Character worth seeking says no to what does not honor or do justice to our calling as servants of Jesus Christ. Character worth seeking says yes to what does. Neither discipline comes without struggle or cost. But both disciplines result in individuals and communities formed more closely in the image of Christ.

Grace Possibilities

When you compare the effect of some persons' words and actions to the spread of gangrene (2:17) and when you refer to some ongoing conversations as "stupid and senseless" (2:23), you cannot be accused of mincing your words. These comments, and the identification by name of two such troublemakers, make it clear that Paul verges on the edge of his own counsel to correct opponents with gentleness (see also 1 Timothy 1:19-20).

As impassioned as Paul may be toward those folks, however, he leaves room for grace (2:25b-26). As bad as they are, they have not left the orbit of God's reach. Perhaps Paul remembers his own history. A willing and approving accomplice to the killing of Stephen (Acts 7:58–8:1), a violent persecutor of the church himself (Acts 9:1-2): Paul then Saul might have seemed outside the pale of God's grace. But the Damascus Road proved otherwise.

Sometimes, we become convinced—and often for good reason—some individual or group is evil incarnate. They have no hope. They deserve no love. They merit no grace. Yet that is the problem, and the scandal, of grace. Deserving is not the issue. God's unconditional love is.

Second Timothy 2:25b-26, even in its tentative way, reminds us of that truth. The worst of scoundrels may yet undergo change. Grace never was for the spiritually fit among us. How did Jesus put it? "I have come to call not the righteous but sinners" (Mark 2:17). Such grace comes with the territory of faith.

SHARING THE SCRIPTURE

Preparing Our Hearts

This week's devotional reading is found in 1 Peter 2:1-10. In verse 5 we are called to let ourselves "be built into a spiritual house, to be a holy priesthood, to offer spiritual sacrifices acceptable to God through Jesus Christ." Peter goes on to write that God has chosen us to proclaim God's mighty acts. By our words, our deeds, our very character, we show others who God is. What is your life saying to others about God and the precious cornerstone, Jesus, who is the foundation on which we stand?

Pray that you and the adult learners will recognize that their behaviors and attitudes reflect their relationship with God through Jesus Christ. Consequently, we all need to be careful about what we say and do.

Preparing Our Minds

Study the background from 2 Timothy 2 and the lesson Scripture, verses 14-26. As you prepare, ponder how you and other church leaders can help members develop Christian character. Paul offers advice to Timothy on this matter, which you will find in these Scripture readings.

Write on newsprint:
❏ information for next week's lesson, found under "Continue the Journey."

LEADING THE CLASS

(1) Gather to Learn

❖ Welcome the class members and introduce any guests.

❖ Pray that the participants will see the Scriptures with "fresh eyes" today as they study and fellowship together.

❖ Read aloud this German proverb on character:

When wealth is lost, nothing is lost;
When health is lost, something is lost;
When character is lost, all is lost!

❖ Discuss these questions.

(1) Do you agree with this proverb? Why or why not?

(2) How do you define "character"? (Note ideas on newsprint and leave posted.)

(3) What are some basic qualities found in a person with good character? (Note ideas on newsprint and leave posted.)

❖ Read aloud today's focus statement: **People need to develop Christian character so they may live as people of God. How can church leaders help members develop Christian character? Paul advises Timothy to exercise self-discipline, especially in his speech and attitudes, and to deal gently with those who would start quarrels.**

(2) Study Paul's Instructions Regarding the Development of Timothy's Christian Character

❖ Select a volunteer to read 2 Timothy 2:14-26.

❖ Divide the class in half. Ask one half (either together or in smaller groups) to identify a list of "Do's" appropriate for one striving to live righteously. These are traits believers are to cultivate. Ask the other half of the class to develop a list of "Don'ts" that Paul warns Timothy against. Give each group a sheet of newsprint, markers, and tacks or tape to post the list they have created.

❖ Invite both groups to report back. Or, ask the participants to circulate around the room to see what has been written.

❖ Discuss these questions.

(1) In your church and/or denomination, how do you see the positive aspects of righteous character being lived out? What examples can you give?

(2) How can you tell the difference in the church between healthy debate and "stupid and senseless controversies" (2:23)? What's important enough to discuss seriously? (See "Wrangling Over Words" in Interpreting the Scripture.)

❖ Encourage the participants to imagine that Paul has come to their church as a consultant. As he explores your congregation's programs and opportunities for mission and ministry, he discerns ways that you are helping people to build Christian character so as to pursue righteousness. And he has also seen some activities that are counterproductive to the goal of Christian character building. Ask the following questions.

(1) What would Paul say are the ways for building Christian character that our congregation has developed? How can we expand these opportunities?

(2) Are there activities or behaviors that are counterproductive? If so, what are they? How can these kinds of behaviors be held in check?

(3) What advice might Paul have for our congregation?

3) Develop a Profile of Christian Character Based on This Passage and Identify the Learners' Own Strengths and Weaknesses

❖ Invite the class to look again at the definitions of "character" and qualities of persons with good character that you brainstormed during the "Gather to Learn" portion. Discuss with the group what should be added or deleted from these lists, based on Paul's instructions to Timothy.

❖ Distribute paper and pencils. Encourage the students to choose from the list traits that they believe are personal strengths and others that they feel are weaknesses and write these on their papers.

❖ Provide quiet time for the adults to reflect on how their character reflects and/or denies the character of Jesus Christ.

(4) Repent of Any Behavior That Does Not Fit with This Christian Profile, and Commit to the Self-Discipline Paul Describes

❖ Distribute paper and pencils if you have not already done so. Invite each participant to write a prayer, which will not be shared with the group, in which they confess behaviors identified as weaknesses that do not reflect Christian character.

❖ Invite the students to recommit themselves to Christ by reading "A Covenant Prayer in the Wesleyan Tradition" (page 607, *The United Methodist Hymnal*). If you do not have this hymnal, read these words line-by-line and ask the students to echo you.

I am no longer my own, but thine.
Put me to what thou wilt, rank me with
  whom thou wilt.
Put me to doing, put me to suffering.
Let me be employed by thee or laid
  aside for thee,
exalted for thee or brought low by thee.
Let me be full, let me be empty.
Let me have all things, let me have
  nothing.
I freely and heartily yield all things
to thy pleasure and disposal.
And now, O glorious and blessed God,
Father, Son, and Holy Spirit,
thou art mine, and I am thine. So be it.
And the covenant which I have made
  on earth,
let it be ratified in heaven. Amen.

(5) Continue the Journey

❖ Read aloud this preparation for next week's lesson. You may also want to post it on newsprint for the students to copy. **Prepare for next week's session, "The Marks of a Helpful Mentor," by reading chapters 3 and 4 of 2 Timothy. Our lesson will highlight 3:10–4:8. Carefully consider** these ideas as you read: **People choose mentors or role models with whom they identify. What makes a good mentor or role model? As a mentor for Timothy, Paul set an example by trying to follow the teachings of Scripture in all that he did. Paul celebrates God's word as the ultimate guide for all that we do.**

❖ Read aloud the following three ideas. Challenge the students to commit themselves to use these activities as a springboard to spiritual growth.

(1) **Name one or two people who in your opinion are examples of high Christian character. Jot down any traits that contribute to their character. Which of these traits can you adopt? What steps can you take now to try to develop these traits in your life?**

(2) **Consider areas of your life where you need to be more self-disciplined. Perhaps you eat too much, fail to exercise enough, or talk too much. Pray for guidance about your problem areas. Find some visual cues, such as a note on the refrigerator door, to remind you of your resolve to be better disciplined.**

(3) **Be alert to situations in which you are likely to engage in a dispute. Why are you arguing? How might you be more open to other points of view without necessarily compromising your own position?**

❖ Sing or read aloud "Take Time to Be Holy."

❖ Lead this benediction to conclude the session: **May you go forth as servants in whom the Lord delights to bring justice to the nations by the power of God's Spirit. Amen.**

UNIT 3: FAITHFUL FOLLOWERS, FAITHFUL LEADERS

THE MARKS OF A HELPFUL MENTOR

PREVIEWING THE LESSON

Lesson Scripture: 2 Timothy 3:10–4:8
Background Scripture: 2 Timothy 3–4
Key Verse: 2 Timothy 3:14

Focus of the Lesson:

People choose mentors or role models with whom they identify. What makes a good mentor or role model? As a mentor for Timothy, Paul set an example by trying to follow the teachings of Scripture in all that he did. Paul celebrates God's word as the ultimate guide for all that we do.

Goals for the Learners:

(1) to describe how Paul mentored Timothy through the way he followed and taught the Scriptures.
(2) to identify people who have been significant mentors in their own faith journey.
(3) to discern ways they can become good mentors to others in the faith and then take action to do so.

Pronunciation Guide:

Antioch (an' tee ok)
Iconium (i koh' nee uhm)
Jannes (jan' iz)
Lystra (lis' truh)
paideia (pahee di' ah)
Telemachus (tuh-lem'-a-kuhs)
theopneustos (theh op' nuoo stos)

eschatological (es kat uh loj' i kuhl)
Jambres (jam' briz)
kairos (kahee ros')
meno (men'o)
sophizo (sof id' zo)
teleo (tel eh' o)

Supplies:

Bibles, newsprint and marker, paper and pencils, hymnals

READING THE SCRIPTURE

NRSV

2 Timothy 3:10-17

[10]Now you have observed my teaching,

NIV

2 Timothy 3:10-17

[10]You, however, know all about my

my conduct, my aim in life, my faith, my patience, my love, my steadfastness, [11]my persecutions and suffering the things that happened to me in Antioch, Iconium, and Lystra. What persecutions I endured! Yet the Lord rescued me from all of them. [12]Indeed, all who want to live a godly life in Christ Jesus will be persecuted. [13]But wicked people and impostors will go from bad to worse, deceiving others and being deceived. **[14]But as for you, continue in what you have learned and firmly believed, knowing from whom you learned it,** [15]and how from childhood you have known the sacred writings that are able to instruct you for salvation through faith in Christ Jesus. [16]All scripture is inspired by God and is useful for teaching, for reproof, for correction, and for training in righteousness, [17]so that everyone who belongs to God may be proficient, equipped for every good work.

2 Timothy 4:1-8

[1]In the presence of God and of Christ Jesus, who is to judge the living and the dead, and in view of his appearing and his kingdom, I solemnly urge you: [2]proclaim the message; be persistent whether the time is favorable or unfavorable; convince, rebuke, and encourage, with the utmost patience in teaching. [3]For the time is coming when people will not put up with sound doctrine, but having itching ears, they will accumulate for themselves teachers to suit their own desires, [4]and will turn away from listening to the truth and wander away to myths. [5]As for you, always be sober, endure suffering, do the work of an evangelist, carry out your ministry fully.

[6]As for me, I am already being poured out as a libation, and the time of my departure has come. [7]I have fought the good fight, I have finished the race, I have kept the faith. [8]From now on there is reserved for me the crown of righteousness, which the Lord, the righteous judge, will give me on that day, and not only to me but also to all who have longed for his appearing.

teaching, my way of life, my purpose, faith, patience, love, endurance, [11]persecutions, sufferings—what kinds of things happened to me in Antioch, Iconium and Lystra, the persecutions I endured. Yet the Lord rescued me from all of them. [12]In fact, everyone who wants to live a godly life in Christ Jesus will be persecuted, [13]while evil men and impostors will go from bad to worse, deceiving and being deceived. **[14]But as for you, continue in what you have learned and have become convinced of, because you know those from whom you learned it,** [15]and how from infancy you have known the holy Scriptures, which are able to make you wise for salvation through faith in Christ Jesus. [16]All Scripture is God-breathed and is useful for teaching, rebuking, correcting and training in righteousness, [17]so that the man of God may be thoroughly equipped for every good work.

2 Timothy 4:1-8

[1]In the presence of God and of Christ Jesus, who will judge the living and the dead, and in view of his appearing and his kingdom, I give you this charge: [2]Preach the Word; be prepared in season and out of season; correct, rebuke and encourage—with great patience and careful instruction. [3]For the time will come when men will not put up with sound doctrine. Instead, to suit their own desires, they will gather around them a great number of teachers to say what their itching ears want to hear. [4]They will turn their ears away from the truth and turn aside to myths. [5]But you, keep your head in all situations, endure hardship, do the work of an evangelist, discharge all the duties of your ministry.

[6]For I am already being poured out like a drink offering, and the time has come for my departure. [7]I have fought the good fight, I have finished the race, I have kept the faith. [8]Now there is in store for me the crown of righteousness, which the Lord, the righteous Judge, will award to me on that day—and not only to me, but also to all who have longed for his appearing.

UNDERSTANDING THE SCRIPTURE

2 Timothy 3:1-9. "Last days" refers to the closing times of this age that will precede God's coming sovereign realm. The association of those days with evil finds testimony in both Jewish and Christian writings. The list of vices in verses 2-5 compares with other such lists in Pauline writings (Galatians 5:19-21). Love is occasionally offered in the church (and elsewhere) as a remedy for all ills, without specifying what such love involves. This list clarifies that there are "loves" to be avoided (self, money, pleasure). Verses 6-7 pose problems in the portrayal of "silly women." The underlying critique, by no means limited in practice to one gender, is of persons who flit from one truth to another without ever setting down roots or firming up commitments. Those who mislead such naiveté are compared to the figures of Jannes and Jambres. Jewish tradition outside Scripture identifies these individuals as the magicians of Pharaoh who attempted to duplicate Moses' miracles (Exodus 7:11-12, 22).

2 Timothy 3:10-13. "Observe" in verse 10 translates a Greek word that connotes following or paying close attention to. Paul invites not a cursory look, but rather a deep examination borne of experience on Timothy's part to scrutinize his example of faith. The epistle's previous emphasis upon the difficulty of witness emerges in the language of these verses: *patience* (the word literally means "long suffering"), *persecutions, suffering, persecutions, persecuted*. At the core of this recounting comes Paul's affirmation (and experience) of trust: "the Lord rescued me from all of them." The presence of opponents, like those in mind with the previous reference to Jannes and Jambres, surfaces once more in verse 13. The problem is not only their deception of others, but also the fact that they themselves are deceived. Change becomes even more difficult when, as a result of that self-deception, no need for change is seen.

2 Timothy 3:14-17. "Continue" translates the Greek word *meno*, meaning "to dwell." The invitation to Timothy to "dwell" in the tradition received perhaps subtly echoes the "household" theme in 1 Timothy. Two other words with special meanings occur in this text. "Instruct" translates *sophizo*, "to make wise" (as philo-*sophy* means "love of wisdom"). In the Hebrew tradition, wisdom was less a measure of abstract intelligence and more an indication of the practical ability to live one's life in the light of such knowledge. "Inspired by God" translates *theopneustos*, literally "God breathed." Paul defines Scripture here in a dynamic way, primarily in terms of the functions which it may serve and the purposes for which it is given. As with wisdom, those purposes in verse 17 find expression in a recurring theme in the Timothy correspondence: the equipping for "every good work."

2 Timothy 4:1-5. "I solemnly urge you" recalls the tone and emphasis Paul used earlier with Timothy in 2:14 and 1 Timothy 5:21. The three-part linking of Jesus with "judge," "appearing," and "kingdom" places a decided eschatological (end-times) slant on these words (as "last days" had at the beginning of chapter 3). The initial "urging" comes in the form of five imperative verbs invoking Timothy's action. "Persistent" translates a verb that carries the sense of "standing ready" or "being on call," no matter whether the time for action is convenient and expected or not. The coming "time" (*kairos*, "opportune season," the same root of the words rendered "favorable" and "unfavorable" in the previous verse) once again hints at the close of history. The actions of others in such times recall the vices singled out at the start of chapter 3. "As for you" returns the focus upon Timothy, through yet another set of imperative verbs that Paul uses to summon his exercise of ministry.

2 Timothy 4:6-8. "As for me" connects what Paul had to say to Timothy in the preceding verse to what is to follow now. "Poured out as a libation" uses the imagery of sacrifice to describe Paul's imminent status and fate. The image of athletic competition in verses 7-8 is one Paul used earlier in 1 Timothy 6:12. Only now, the words do not come as charge to Timothy but as summary of Paul's own strivings toward faithfulness. "Finish" translates *teleo*, "to complete." Victory is not Paul's to achieve or "win," but God's to give ("the crown of righteousness"). Once again, Christ as judge and "his appearing" come as conclusion to words that strongly suggest Paul knows he has come to the end of his life.

2 Timothy 4:9-18. There is poignancy about the details Paul asks Timothy to handle in these verses. They resemble the way one might settle affairs or wrap up loose ends when some ending draws close to hand. The fondness of relationship with Timothy courses through the appeal, "do your best to come to me soon." It is as if not many opportunities, or times, remain to do so. The detail of Luke's presence with Paul supports the tradition that Luke used Paul directly as a source for much of the second half of the book of Acts. The notes about the cloak and books and parchment perhaps suggest Paul wishes to have more to read (or write!), and more clothing for warmth in his confinement. Once more, Paul offers witness to God's rescue, even though he now faces a situation when death may finally come for him.

2 Timothy 4:19-22. The request to offer personal greetings is a shorthand version of Romans 16:3-16. The naming of Prisca and Aquila, also mentioned in several other works, affirms a special affinity with this couple (Acts 18:2-3, 1 Corinthians 16:19, and the Romans text). "Do your best to come before winter," reiterates Paul's already stated desire to see Timothy once more. Winters could be difficult times in prison, where a damp cell made cooler might itself become the executioner. Paul speaks of a community (4:21*b*) from whom he sends greetings to Timothy. With that, Paul closes the epistle, as he opened it and 1 Timothy, with the invocation of God's grace upon his younger colleague.

INTERPRETING THE SCRIPTURE

Paul as Mentor

In Greek mythology, Mentor was the trusted counselor of Odysseus, who also lent guidance to his son Telemachus. From those stories, "mentor" enters our language as one with experience and/or wisdom who guides a younger protégé.

Paul does not use the word "mentor" in this epistle. But clearly, Paul served as mentor to Timothy. The best of mentors do offer instruction or advice based not on theoretical constructs, but on time-tested experience. Paul's mentoring of Timothy here is a far cry from "do as I say, not as I do." Instead, Paul points to his experiences as the textbook for Timothy's ministry.

Taken out of context, the recurrence of "my" and "me" in 3:10-11 might sound like the ramblings of someone overly taken with himself. There is risk involved in assuming or accepting the role of mentor, for the focus is on self as example. But Paul does not place himself in the limelight to promote his own self-righteousness. Paul earlier critiqued opponents who hold "the outward form of godliness" (3:5). Appearances can deceive. That is why Paul as mentor invites Timothy to take a hard and deep look at his modeling of the faith. This is not about appearances or making a good show. Conduct, aim, faith, patience, love, steadfastness—all point to the way in which the whole of one's life needs to be shaped by this gospel.

Contemporary mentoring sometimes settles on issues of style, or shortcuts for doing things. No shortcuts exist for the mentoring of faith. A helpful mentor is one who lives the message being communicated. Who are the persons you would name as mentors of your faith?

Scripture's Mentoring Purposes

Persons serve as our mentors in faith. It would not be wrong to add that Scripture serves that same purpose: to guide and shape our lives by example.

The previous commentary on 3:14-17 closed by saying Paul focuses here on a dynamic view of Scripture. That is, 2 Timothy defines the Scriptures primarily by their function. Even its origin as "God breathed" portrays movement and purpose in its genesis. Paul confirms to Timothy they intend to "instruct you for salvation" (3:15). Notice Paul does not say, they intend to serve as your textbook for mathematics or science. That is not their focus. That is not their intent. Instruction, or more literally "wising," for salvation is.

Their usefulness aims to equip the individual and community of faith for good works. Sometimes that occurs in teaching, the communication of faith's substance recounted in the stories told. Sometimes that occurs in reproof and correction, the critical word aimed at separating what is gospel from opinion, what it faith from superstition. Sometimes that occurs in "training" (the Greek word *paideia* is the typical word used for the nurture of children) in righteousness. But always, Scripture's concern is salvation and good works—not in producing "profane chatter" and "senseless controversies" and "quarrels" as critiqued earlier in chapter 2 by Paul.

For Scripture to serve as such a mentor, persons and communities of faith need to hold that focus in mind. Sometimes our arguments over Scripture, whether in matters of interpretation or application, go far afield of salvation and good works. If Scripture is God-breathed in origin, as Paul testifies, those who wield its words would benefit from a greater seeking of God's breathing in their interpretations and applications of it. For inspired writing needs inspired persons to discern God's word afresh to each generation.

A Charge to Faithfulness

In traditions that use services of installation for pastors, Paul's words to Timothy may strike a familiar chord. Perhaps you have even heard them invoked in such situations. But make no mistake: While Paul's address is a personal one to Timothy's ministry, the charge does not fall exclusively upon the circle of the ordained. The ministry of the baptized, the ministry we all share, is addressed.

Faith is not a seasonable pursuit, to be set aside when ill winds blow, or when the illusion of "self-made success" breeds apathy. The gospel of Christ intends to shape and guide us in every path we travel. All of the imperatives Paul employs underscore discipleship as *discipline*. To be saved by grace, to be set at liberty by the gospel, does not mean we have no obligations placed upon us. At the close of John's Gospel, Jesus informed a newly restored Peter he would be taken "where you do not wish to go" (John 21:18). We may not want to be taken to that place where the gospel challenges our prejudices. We may not want to be taken to that place where crosses are carried, or where encounter with Christ involves coming face-to-face with the least of these my brothers and sisters. In the most extraordinary of understatements, Paul elsewhere says, in Romans 13:8, we are under no obligation—except to love one another!

Alternatives to faith demands abound. Paul speaks of them here in the guise of "itching ears"(4:3) and piling up teachers who say what we like to hear. Unlike much conventional wisdom, the gospel ordinarily does not tell us what we want to hear, but what we *need* to hear. So Paul charged Timothy . . . and us.

Life as Benediction

Imagine that you know your life nears its end. What would you want to say about your life, about your trust, about your hope for community?

Paul ends the lesson Scripture on such a note. He sees his approaching death not as a tragedy to be cursed, but in the form of a sacrifice. Romans 12:1 had spoken of offering our lives as a living sacrifice to God. For Paul, a life lived sacrificially is viewed now in its conclusion in that same perspective. The words carry echoes of Stephen and Jesus entrusting themselves into God's hands at the time of their deaths.

Before that departure comes, Paul the evangelist bears witness to his life's witness: the good fight, the completed race, the kept faith. Paul sometimes strikes persons as having a large ego in his self-referencing affirmations. As Walt Whitman and later Dizzy Dean are reported to have said, though: "If you done it, it ain't bragging." What Paul says of his life in verse 7 rings congruent with his living. Words once used to encourage Timothy's (and our) ministry in 1 Timothy 6:12 now serve as a fitting epitaph to a life faithfully lived. Those same words move us to examine our own discipleship. Are the fights we fight the good ones, or the ones that demean others and cheapen ourselves? Are the races we run worth completing, or simply the ones that keep us busy in motion with little accomplishment? Do we keep the faith, or simply try and let faith keep us safe and happy and isolated from a world God so loved?

Paul concludes with hope firmly planted in God's grace. As one who labored so long in the life of the church, he sees that hope as not simply his own, but "also to all who have longed for his appearing" (4:8). Even in the face of death, Paul lives and hopes community and continues to mentor others in the faith.

And let the people say, Amen!

SHARING THE SCRIPTURE

Preparing Our Hearts

This week's devotional reading is found in Psalm 119:9-16. This wisdom psalm praises the teachings (torah) of God. In verse 9 the psalmist asks how young people can "keep their way pure." The response that follows encourages young people to obey God's commandments. As you read, think about how this passage applies to you, regardless of your age. Think also about how it might apply to the young church leader Timothy as Paul is trying to guide him.

Pray that you and the adult learners will seek after God and delight to learn God's ways.

Preparing Our Minds

Study the background, chapters 3 and 4 of 2 Timothy, and the lesson Scripture, 2 Timothy 3:10–4:8. As you delve into Paul's message to Timothy consider what you believe makes a good mentor or role model.

Note that in three weeks we will be moving into our spring quarter, "Living In and as God's Creation." You may want to look ahead at this material, which explores Wisdom literature in Psalms, Job, Ecclesiastes, and Proverbs.

Write on newsprint:

❑ information for next week's lesson, found under "Continue the Journey."

Plan a lecture for the "Describe How Paul Mentored Timothy Through the Way He Followed and Taught the Scriptures" portion.

LEADING THE CLASS

(1) Gather to Learn

❖ Welcome the class members and introduce any guests.

❖ Pray that the adults will be motivated to search God's word and act on what they find there.

❖ Read aloud this story about a student who needed and found a mentor. **After earning his bachelor's degree, "George" went to graduate school because he had no idea what he wanted to do. Since his parents thought that he was going to school to avoid getting a real job, George worked in a professor's science lab to earn money. The professor liked George, and George became interested in the research. The professor spent hours talking with George about his hopes for the future and where and how he might be able to fulfill them. The professor also shared his own dreams, mistakes, and experiences. When George finished his degree, he felt well prepared to work as a university professor. When he retired decades later, he looked back with gratitude to the professor whose mentoring helped him to enter a rewarding career.**

❖ Discuss these questions.

(1) **How did this professor serve as a role model or mentor to George?**

(2) **What are the characteristics of a good mentor?** (You may want to list these ideas on newsprint.)

(3) **Do people need mentors in the faith, as well as career mentors? Why or why not?**

❖ Read aloud today's focus statement: **People choose mentors or role models with whom they identify. What makes a good mentor or role model? As a mentor for Timothy, Paul set an example by trying to follow the teachings of Scripture in all that he did. Paul celebrates God's word as the ultimate guide for all that we do.**

(2) Describe How Paul Mentored Timothy Through the Way He Followed and Taught the Scriptures

❖ Select a volunteer to read the charge that Paul gives to Timothy in 2 Timothy 3:10–4:8.

❖ Describe how Paul mentored Timothy by discussing these categories. Some ideas will overlap categories.

(1) **Ways Paul demonstrated the behaviors he hoped Timothy would observe and imitate.**

(2) **Explanations by Paul as to how he was doing what he did, and/or how Timothy should follow suit.**

(3) **Explanations by Paul as to why he was doing what he did.**

(4) **The role Scripture played in Paul's teaching of Timothy.**

(5) **Paul's comments on his own life and the challenges he faced.**

❖ Use information from Understanding the Scripture for 2 Timothy 3:10-13, 3:14-17, 4:1-5, and 4:6-8 for a brief lecture in which you highlight points that may be unfamiliar to the class.

(3) Identify People Who Have Been Significant Mentors in the Learners' Faith Journey

❖ Distribute paper and pencils. Invite the participants to list persons who have been significant in their faith journey.

❖ Ask the students to buddy with a partner or small group and share one example (more if time permits) of how one of these mentors made an impact on their lives.

(4) Discern Ways the Learners Can Become Good Mentors to Others in the Faith and Then Take Action to Do So

❖ Recall that when we discussed Paul as a mentor we considered:

■ Ways Paul demonstrated the kind of behavior Timothy was to imitate.

■ Paul's explanations of how Timothy should take certain actions.

■ Paul's explanations of why Timothy should take certain actions.

❖ Head three sheets of newsprint: "Demonstrate," "Explain How," "Explain Why." Invite the participants to list ideas of actions they could take in each of these categories to mentor someone in the faith. Also talk about ways that the adults could monitor the performance of their protégés.

❖ Ask the adults to think silently about someone they could mentor.

❖ Conclude this portion of the lesson by asking the class members to repeat after you this Congregational Pledge from a Baptismal Covenant of The United Methodist Church. Every time this pledge is made, members of the congregation are promising to be mentors to a new child in the faith. As they make this pledge today, class members are to insert the name of the person they identified when you reach that point in the pledge. **With God's help we will so order our lives after the example of Christ, that [NAME], surrounded by steadfast love, may be established in the faith, and confirmed and strengthened in the way that leads to life eternal.**

(5) Continue the Journey

❖ Pray that the students will give thanks for those who have mentored them even as they pledge themselves to mentor others in the faith.

❖ Read aloud this preparation for next week's lesson. You may also want to post it on newsprint for the students to copy. **Prepare for next week's session, "Teach Sound Doctrine by Example," by reading Titus 2, which is both the background and lesson Scripture. Consider these ideas as you study: People often learn through the life experiences of others. How can we be trained to live as the people of God? Paul instructed Titus to teach only sound Christian doctrine so that others could learn the attitudes and actions appropriate for Christians.**

❖ Read aloud the following three ideas. Challenge the students to commit themselves to use these activities as a springboard to spiritual growth.

(1) **Think of an individual who has been an important mentor in some area of your life. What effect do you think this person had on your life? How do you think you would be different if this person had not influenced you? What does his or her impact say to you about the value of a good mentor?**

(2) **Consider volunteering for an agency such as Big Brothers or Big Sisters where you can serve as a mentor for a child or teen. If your church pairs mentors with confirmands, work with a young person as he or she prepares to make a public confession of faith.**

(3) **Take a young church leader under your wing, if you are an experienced leader yourself. Help this person to understand the biblical and theological basis for why your church does things the way it does. Also teach this person about your church's history, identity, and culture.**

❖ Sing or read aloud "Rejoice in God's Saints."

❖ Lead this benediction to conclude the session: **May you go forth as servants in whom the Lord delights to bring justice to the nations by the power of God's Spirit. Amen.**

UNIT 3: FAITHFUL FOLLOWERS, FAITHFUL LEADERS
TEACH SOUND DOCTRINE BY EXAMPLE

PREVIEWING THE LESSON

Lesson Scripture: Titus 2
Background Scripture: Titus 2
Key Verses: Titus 2:7-8*a*

Focus of the Lesson:
People often learn through the life experiences of others. How can we be trained to live as the people of God? Paul instructed Titus to teach only sound Christian doctrine so that others could learn the attitudes and actions appropriate for Christians.

Goals for the Learners:
(1) to delve into Paul's instructions to Titus regarding the appropriate attitudes and actions for Christians.
(2) to evaluate Paul's instructions as they apply to the learners' lives.
(3) to affirm their own commitment to teaching and living out God's word.

Pronunciation Guide:
ecumenism (e kyu' me ni zem)   *epiphaino* (ep ee fah' ee no)
epiphaneia (ep if an' i ah)   *hieroprepes* (hee er op rep ace')
oikouros (oy koo ros')   *zelotes* (dzay lo tace')

Supplies:
Bibles, newsprint and marker, paper and pencils, hymnals

READING THE SCRIPTURE

NRSV
Titus 2

¹But as for you, teach what is consistent with sound doctrine. ²Tell the older men to be temperate, serious, prudent, and sound in faith, in love, and in endurance.

³Likewise, tell the older women to be

NIV
Titus 2

¹You must teach what is in accord with sound doctrine. ²Teach the older men to be temperate, worthy of respect, self-controlled, and sound in faith, in love and in endurance.

reverent in behavior, not to be slanderers or slaves to drink; they are to teach what is good, ⁴so that they may encourage the young women to love their husbands, to love their children, ⁵to be self-controlled, chaste, good managers of the household, kind, being submissive to their husbands, so that the word of God may not be discredited.

⁶Likewise, urge the younger men to be self-controlled. **⁷Show yourself in all respects a model of good works, and in your teaching show integrity, gravity, ⁸and sound speech that cannot be censured;** then any opponent will be put to shame, having nothing evil to say of us.

⁹Tell slaves to be submissive to their masters and to give satisfaction in every respect; they are not to talk back, ¹⁰not to pilfer, but to show complete and perfect fidelity, so that in everything they may be an ornament to the doctrine of God our Savior.

¹¹For the grace of God has appeared, bringing salvation to all, ¹²training us to renounce impiety and worldly passions, and in the present age to live lives that are self-controlled, upright, and godly, ¹³while we wait for the blessed hope and the manifestation of the glory of our great God and Savior, Jesus Christ. ¹⁴He it is who gave himself for us that he might redeem us from all iniquity and purify for himself a people of his own who are zealous for good deeds.

¹⁵Declare these things; exhort and reprove with all authority. Let no one look down on you.

³Likewise, teach the older women to be reverent in the way they live, not to be slanderers or addicted to much wine, but to teach what is good. ⁴Then they can train the younger women to love their husbands and children, ⁵to be self-controlled and pure, to be busy at home, to be kind, and to be subject to their husbands, so that no one will malign the word of God.

⁶Similarly, encourage the young men to be self-controlled. **⁷In everything set them an example by doing what is good. In your teaching show integrity, seriousness ⁸and soundness of speech that cannot be condemned,** so that those who oppose you may be ashamed because they have nothing bad to say about us.

⁹Teach slaves to be subject to their masters in everything, to try to please them, not to talk back to them, ¹⁰and not to steal from them, but to show that they can be fully trusted, so that in every way they will make the teaching about God our Savior attractive.

¹¹For the grace of God that brings salvation has appeared to all men. ¹²It teaches us to say "No" to ungodliness and worldly passions, and to live self-controlled, upright and godly lives in this present age, ¹³while we wait for the blessed hope—the glorious appearing of our great God and Savior, Jesus Christ, ¹⁴who gave himself for us to redeem us from all wickedness and to purify for himself a people that are his very own, eager to do what is good.

¹⁵These, then, are the things you should teach. Encourage and rebuke with all authority. Do not let anyone despise you.

UNDERSTANDING THE SCRIPTURE

Titus 2:1. As the previous session had dealt with opponents who misled the community with false teaching, "as for you" shifts the address back upon Titus (the identical words mark a similar transition in 2 Timothy 4:5). The emphasis in the whole epistle of Titus, as with Timothy, rests upon sound teaching of the faith. "Doctrine" translates a word whose literal meaning would be closer to "that which is taught."

The opening imperative verb, "teach," is actually a more general term for what one says or speaks. Perhaps using this generic term at the outset, rather than one specific to formal teaching situations, suggests that any and all opportunities for bringing the word of faith to voice must be done with care. In a context where much teaching, true and false, abounds, Paul urges Titus to that which is "sound." That word is a key modifier of faith or teaching throughout Titus (used five times) and Timothy (also used five times).

Titus 2:2-6. Paul here assesses the pastoral care needs for this community in four categories based on age and gender: older men, older women, young women, and younger men. The instruction for older men mirrors closely the qualities invoked for bishops and deacons in 1 Timothy 3:2, 8, 11. "Soundness" once more depicts faith, and along with it love and endurance (see also 1 Timothy 6:11). Instructions for the older women include an unusual word (*hiero-prepes*). It is translated here as "reverent," though its root suggests something akin to "priestly." Paul indicates they do have a teaching role in the community of mentoring younger women. "Good managers of the household" translates *oikouros*, "home- or house-workers." Echoing a theme encountered earlier in 1 Timothy 3:7 (also indirectly in 2:2), this behavior aims at preventing the church from being viewed with suspicion or scandal by the wider community.

Titus 2:7-8. Once more, Paul directly addresses Titus with a call to teach by example. "Good works" forms another key element of the correspondence to Titus (1:16, 3:8, 3:14) as well as 1 Timothy (2:10, 5:10, 5:25). Faith seeks enacting in daily living. The framing of the previous instructions to the composition of the typical "household" makes the same point by insisting how life in the most ordinary settings is to seek faith's transformation. "Sound" now modifies "speech," so that the whole of one's communication is addressed by the importance of not bringing shame upon the community or faith.

Titus 2:9-10. A final set of members of the household of Paul's day is now addressed: slaves. "Submissive" repeats the same word used in verse 5 to indicate the nature of relationship of wife to husband in this culture. "Give satisfaction" translates a word used in Romans 12:1-2 and other Pauline texts to describe service or sacrifice acceptable to God. More practical and specific advice for behavior follows in the injunction to not "talk back" or "pilfer." It may be safely assumed that such advice indicated such things did occur. "Fidelity" translates the New Testament's most common word for faith. Such imagery that casts the slave's position in the language of faith finds ultimate expression in the purpose for such behavior: to adorn "the doctrine of God." Paul's perspective is that even those trapped in such a dehumanizing situation can participate in the witness of faith and a life of good works. (Please refer to "Texts in Context" in Interpreting the Scripture for further comments.)

Titus 2:11-12. Paul provides the theological framework for the previous instructions in this and the next set of verses. The "appearance" (*epiphaino*) of God's grace forms the first half of Paul's argument. The incarnation brings God's salvation "to all" (1 Timothy 2:4-6). Such salvation, however, influences not merely what we believe—but what we do and how we live. The verb translated as "training" is *paideuo*, the word in Greek culture used to describe the education and nurture of children into responsible adulthood. Such Christian "maturity" invites disciplines that not only renounce irresponsibility ("impiety and worldly passions"). In a positive vein, they demonstrate qualities of life that would have been honored in that wider culture. The word for "upright" means "just," a virtue of both Judaism and Hellenism. "Godly" translates *eusebos*, a word we have underscored in previous sessions as key in the Pastoral Epistles for an attitude of reverence and piety.

Titus 2:13-14. The second half of Paul's theological framework seeks motive for our faith and living in the hope we have. The "manifestation" (*epiphaneia*, see 2:11) is now of the God who will come at the end of history. Theologians recognize in these words to Titus a "high" Christology. That is, Jesus Christ is identified here as both Savior and "great God." "Redeem" makes reference to the payment made for the release of hostages or slaves. The aim of that redemption and ensuing purification is the creation of community: "a people of his own" (see 1 Peter 2:9-10). Paul next uses a highly charged word: *zelotes*. "Zealots" in Judea referred to a group of revolutionaries, many with deep ties in Judaism. Depending upon the time of this letter's writing, they were either drawing close to an armed revolt against Rome that would lead to the temple's destruction in A.D. 70—or that revolt had run its course, and the community of Israel had been largely dispersed because of it. Paul urges zealousness of good deeds for the Christian community, not those who would bring down persecution and destruction upon its practitioners.

Titus 2:15. The passage closes where it began: with a command to "declare" (it is the same verb used to open verse 1) these things. "Exhort and reprove" reflect the dual function of the gospel's proclamation: declaration of the gospel's truth that is good news, and confrontation of falsehood that detracts from its purpose for faith and good works. Paul closes by advising Titus, as he had Timothy (1 Timothy 4:12), to not let others look down on him—that is, to not honor the authority he bears.

INTERPRETING THE SCRIPTURE

A Model of Words and Works

With some biblical texts, the structure conveys the message, or at least the unifying theme. We see that more often in poetical writings—but we encounter it here in Titus. The beginning (2:1), the ending (2:15), and the center (2:7-8) all assert the call of Titus to teach with consistency and to act as a model of those words with integrity.

Teaching (speaking) with consistency is not always an easy task. Grace may flow smoothly when its current runs in our direction. But when grace embraces those with whom we disagree, do we speak it so quickly? Likewise, it is one thing to critique an opponent for a perceived action contrary to our understanding of the gospel. But when we, or our friends, engage in the same action, are we as quick to reprove? Consistent teaching challenges us to allow the gospel's light to shine on our strengths and our weaknesses.

Likewise, the closing charge to Titus provides another challenge: "exhort and rebuke." A mentor of mine once spoke at the installation of a younger colleague. As he recited the traditional words of "comfort the afflicted"—he paused and added, "and afflict the comfortable." Exhort and rebuke. To exhort is to comfort, to encourage, to rally the troops with support. To rebuke is to challenge, to get in the face of another— or one's self—with the word that cuts to the core. Some of us prefer dwelling wholly in exhortation. A few of us scrape by never seeming to get beyond rebuking. Paul understood the gospel needs both.

At the core, Paul reveals an even greater challenge: The messenger is the message. Good words rely on good works. "Practice what you preach" is another way of framing this critical truth for the church and Christian in every age.

Community Formation   *Texts in Context*

The sessions for January 8 and January 15 addressed how "households" formed a key concept in the understanding and organizing of church responsibilities in Timothy's day. Now in Titus 2:2-10, the structuring of households in that era forms the pattern for Paul's instructing of Titus regarding ministry to and by the constituents in the household of the church.

One overriding theme emerges. Everyone is addressed. By age and by gender, no one is left out of this epistle's concern. Even those who are slaves, whom that day's society considered without rights and whose primary value came measured in economics—even such persons are worked into the framework of those to be ministered to . . . and those who ministered.

Secular household codes of this era resemble some of the affirmations made in this text. The kinds of qualities sought here (prudence, piety, justice, self-control) would have been familiar to persons who had no connection at all with the church. The witness of the church, then and now, finds evidence in conduct and attitudes that contribute to the public good. The secular world ought not define that good for the church. But neither should the church assume that living faithfully means living at odds with neighbors and breaking down the wider community.

The difficult task comes in understanding when the church's witness meshes with that of the wider community, and when we are called to a "counter-cultural" witness. The Pastorals certainly lean in the direction of living so that "the word of God may not be discredited" (2:5). The book of Revelation certainly affirms an outlook where the faithful cannot help but come into conflict with powers that deny justice and mock love and deal only in control. The church in the twenty-first century listens to both sets of texts to navigate our way to living the gospel faithfully in sanctuary and in community.

If the previous commentary on verses 4-5 and 9-10 seemed to be an unquestioning acceptance of the role of women and acceptance of slavery—it was not. Commenting on what the text says is one thing. Interpreting how that text is to be heard and applied in our day can be quite another.

In the context of the times and culture in which these words came to be written, these verses represented a moderating if not cautiously liberating view. Women taught women. Slaves were apparently seen as participants in the church.

Do we then "baptize" these positions as stated here true everywhere and in every time and in every context? Some traditions have. No doubt, more than one white preacher prior to the American Civil War would have taken this as a proof text that slavery was acceptable in the sight of God. More than a few still view the position of a young woman's primary calling in life to be *oikouros* ("house worker"), where exceptions are neither the norm nor encouraged.

Such texts can be very vexing for the church. Some pose the only options to be "God said it, I believe it, so get used to it" theology—or a total rejection of all scriptural authority. Both of those two extremes are far too rigid for the dynamics of Scripture. Did not Jesus say, "you have heard it said. . . . but I say to you" (see Matthew 5:21-22, 27-28, 31-32, 33-34, 38-39). Did not Paul write that in Christ "there is no longer Jew or Greek, there is no longer slave or free, there is no longer male and female; for all of you are one in Christ Jesus" (Galatians 3:28)?

That unity took form when Scripture traditions about no Gentiles in the community of God fell to the movement of God's Spirit. That unity took form when slavery was revealed as an affront to human dignity and divine creation. God continues to invite the church to be open to the movement of the

Spirit in breaking open the word of Scripture in faithful ways.

Theology Matters

In the early days of ecumenism, the saying went: "Theology divides, but service unites." Some say the current mood in church cooperation, given the huge gulf over some societal issues such as abortion and gay rights, reverses that: "Service divides, but theology unites."

The writer of the Pastorals, and in particular verses 11-14 and this whole chapter, would probably take issue with both statements. For Paul, theology and service ("good works") form a common cloth. In these four verses in particular, the author lays out the theological argument for why the church's life and witness has any significance at all.

God has entered human history in the life and person of Jesus Christ. This life, this history, has sacred possibilities. It carries the memory, and hope, of God's appearing. And as a result, it evokes "in the present age" lives of discipline and witness. The redemption of God and the fashioning of a "people of his own" aim at the creation of a community "zealous for good deeds." Notice Paul did not write zealous to be rid of this world or zealous to be extricated out of it ASAP. No, redemption and purification are intended as acts that bear and do good in this world—in the example of Jesus' own life and ministry. What we say about God (theology) *does* matter because it reveals not only God's grace but also God's intentions for our faithful living now.

SHARING THE SCRIPTURE

Preparing Our Hearts

This week's devotional reading is found in Ephesians 4:11-16. In this passage we read about the gifts that God has given, not for the glorification of the individual, but rather for the upbuilding of the church. These gifts are needed until the whole church grows to spiritual maturity and "unity of the faith" (4:13). Think back to people whose example has made such an impression on you that you felt your faith increased. What did these persons do or say to help you? How are you leading others by example?

Pray that you and the adult learners will be open to learning from the life experiences of others, and living in such a way that people will learn from you how to live as a Christian.

Preparing Our Minds

Study the background and lesson Scripture, both of which are found in the second chapter of Titus. As you study, consider what this passage says about how we can be trained to live as the people of God.

Write on newsprint:

❑ information for next week's lesson, found under "Continue the Journey."

Plan a brief lecture for the "Delve into Paul's Instructions to Titus Regarding the Appropriate Attitudes and Actions for Christians" portion.

LEADING THE CLASS

(1) Gather to Learn

❖ Welcome the class members and introduce any guests.

❖ Pray that the participants will examine their lives in light of the Scriptures to see how they can live as faithful followers and faithful leaders.

❖ Ask the class members to think back to an incident in their childhood or teen years in which an admired adult disappointed them by his or her conduct or expression of an attitude. Invite several volunteers to tell their stories briefly, being careful not to disclose names. In addition to telling what happened, the storytellers should also say how this incident affected them and possibly their faith if this person was someone they looked up to as a Christian role model.

❖ Read aloud today's focus statement: **People often learn through the life experiences of others. How can we be trained to live as the people of God? Paul instructed Titus to teach only sound Christian doctrine so that others could learn the attitudes and actions appropriate for Christians.**

(2) Delve into Paul's Instructions to Titus Regarding the Appropriate Attitudes and Actions for Christians

❖ Choose a volunteer to read Titus 2:1-15.

❖ Invite the students to list on newsprint words that describe how Christians are to behave.

❖ Entertain questions and discussion concerning how these words to Titus apply to the modern church.

❖ Give a brief lecture based on "Texts in Context" in Interpreting the Scripture. Include ideas on Titus 2:2-6 and 9-10, as found in the Understanding the Scripture portion. Your purpose is to set the words written to Titus in a modern context. The students may want to add other ideas or comments.

❖ Read paragraphs three and four of "Community Formation" in Interpreting the Scripture.

❖ Talk with the class about areas in which the church needs to be "a counter-cultural witness." These areas may include social, economic, political, or other issues. Brainstorm ideas as to how the church can live as an example to the culture but not be co-opted by it. You may want to use this quotation from David Jackson (1944–) to get the discussion started: **Somehow the pressures of modern society were making it increasingly difficult for us to live by the values we had been taught. We thought our church should constitute a community of believers capable of withstanding these pressures, yet it seemed to go along with things as they were instead of encouraging an alternative. The "pillars" of the church seemed as severely trapped by material concerns and alienation as most non-Christians we knew.**

❖ Wrap up this section of the lesson by discussing how the members of this class could make a difference in their cultural setting by living as good examples of Christ's followers.

(3) Evaluate Paul's Instructions as They Apply to the Learners' Lives

❖ Ask the students to reread silently Titus 2:11-13.

❖ Recall that Titus 2:12 states that we are "to renounce impiety and world passions" and "to live lives that are self-controlled, upright, and godly."

❖ Distribute paper and pencils. Invite the students to make two confidential lists concerning their own lives: one that includes attitudes and behaviors that could be seen as impious or worldly, and the other that indicates how they are living "self-controlled, upright, and godly" lives.

❖ Provide quiet time for the class members to reflect on how their actions are or are not teaching others what it means to live faithfully as a disciple of Jesus Christ.

❖ Break the silence with these words adapted from verse 1: **May you by your words and deeds teach what is consistent with sound doctrine.**

(4) Affirm Commitment to Teaching and Living Out God's Word

❖ Make the point that the words of Titus 2 teach us that all of us can be good role models, whatever our social status. We can, indeed, all choose to live righteous lives.

❖ Help the students commit to such living by creating a prayer in which they promise to be good examples for others. You may want to divide into groups of four to six and give each group newsprint and a marker or paper and pencil. Each prayer should end **"and all the people of God said, amen."** At a specified time, ask a representative from each group to read aloud their prayer as a sign of their commitment to live as examples who are faithful to the sound doctrine of the gospel.

(5) Continue the Journey

❖ Pray that the students will show by their example what it means to live according to sound Christian beliefs.

❖ Read aloud this preparation for next week's lesson. You may also want to post it on newsprint for the students to copy. **Prepare for next week's session, "God Made Us Special," by reading Psalm 8, which is both our background and lesson Scripture. This is the first lesson in our spring unit on Wisdom literature, "Living in and as God's Creation," which will explore Psalms, Job, Ecclesiastes, and Proverbs. As you read, keep these ideas in focus: People wonder about their place in a vast universe. What does our faith say about our inherent worth within the context of all creation? The psalmist affirms** that we hold a place of honor in God's creation: We are special to God and cared for by God, to whom we owe our highest praise.**

❖ Read aloud the following three ideas. Challenge the students to commit themselves to use these activities as a springboard to spiritual growth.

(1) **Spend some extra time in Bible study this week so as to become more familiar with the "sound doctrine" that you are called to teach by example.**

(2) **Write down one area of your life that needs improvement. Carry this slip of paper with you and note each day what you have done to move in the direction that God would have you to go.**

(3) **Listen to others with whom you interact on a regular basis. Do you hear or see yourself in their words or deeds? Whether we intend to or not, we do teach others all the time. What would Jesus say about how you are teaching others, based on how your ideas and behaviors are played back to you?**

❖ Sing or read aloud "Take My Life, and Let It Be."

❖ Lead this benediction to conclude the session: **May you go forth as servants in whom the Lord delights to bring justice to the nations by the power of God's Spirit. Amen.**

THIRD QUARTER
Living in and as God's Creation

MARCH 5, 2006–MAY 28, 2006

During our spring course of study, "Living in and as God's Creation," we will consider portions of Wisdom literature from Psalms, Job, Ecclesiastes, and Proverbs that emphasize our life as created beings within God's world. Be sure to read the background article, "Learning Wisdom with the People of God," to gain a clearer understanding of the focus and intent of the wisdom tradition. As you work with this unit, keep in mind that wisdom was important not only for the Israelites but also for many neighboring cultures.

Unit 1, "The Glory of God's Creation," delves into the Psalms. This four-week unit begins on March 5 with a look at Psalm 8 in a lesson entitled "God Made Us Special," which considers the place of humanity amid the universe. On March 12 we read in Psalm 104, which praises God for creation, that "God Created Wonderful Things." "Searched and Known by God," the session for March 19, explores selected verses from Psalm 139 to remind us that God the Creator intimately knows our amazingly intricate bodies. The unit ends on March 26 with a session entitled "Worthy of Praise," based on a glorious hymn of praise to God, Psalm 145.

We will spend five weeks on Unit 2, "Living with Creation's Uncertainty," which explores selections from Job and Ecclesiastes. Job 1–3, the Scripture for April 2, helps us cope in "Living with Tragedy" as we hear the many losses that Job sustained. "When All Seems Hopeless," the lesson for April 9, looks at Job's predicament as recorded in Job 14; 32:1-8; 34:10-15; 37:14-24 and affirms his reliance on God. The Easter session for April 16, "From Death to Life," continues to explore Job 38:1-4, 16-17; 42:1-6, and looks closely at Mark 16, which is this Gospel's account of Jesus' resurrection. On April 23 Ecclesiastes 1:1-11 and John 20:19-23 raise the question, "Where Is Peace Found?" The unit concludes on April 30 with the very familiar passage from Ecclesiastes 3 that reminds us that "Everything Has a Season."

Unit 3, "Lessons in Living," takes us on a four-week journey through Proverbs. The first week, May 7, we will study Proverbs 2–3 to discern how wisdom is "A Treasure Worth Seeking." On May 14 we will read Proverbs 8–9 to discern "Wisdom's Invitation" to seek the wisdom that God makes available to all who desire it. Proverbs 11, the focus of the session for May 21, emphasizes "Choosing the Path of Integrity," which will help us to overcome the negative traits of pride and dishonesty. The quarter concludes on May 28 with a session on Proverbs 31 entitled "Living Out Wisdom." Here we see the teachings of King Lemuel's mother on criteria for living that are wise and prudent, as exemplified by the wise woman described in this chapter.

MEET OUR WRITER

DR. PATRICK J. WILLSON

Patrick J. Willson is a minister of the Presbyterian Church (USA) and pastor/head of staff at Williamsburg Presbyterian Church in Williamsburg, Virginia.

This is Willson's fourth contribution to *The New International Lesson Annual*. His sermons have appeared regularly in *Pulpit Digest, Biblical Preaching Journal, Lectionary Homiletics, Preaching Great Texts,* and *Preaching: Word and Witness.* He has written articles for *Interpretation, The Christian Century,* and *The Register of the Company of Pastors;* and he has reviewed books for *The Christian Century, Theology Today, The Princeton Seminary Bulletin,* and *Homiletic.*

Willson has previously served parishes in Texas, Alabama, Mississippi, and Tennessee. He has taught preaching as adjunct professor of Homiletics at Brite Divinity School of Texas Christian University in Fort Worth, Texas, and as instructor in preaching and worship for the Doctor of Ministry program at Columbia Theological Seminary in Decatur, Georgia. Working with Dr. Beverly Roberts Gaventa of Princeton Theological Seminary, he has taught preaching workshops at Princeton Theological Seminary, Claremont School of Theology, Emmanuel School of Religion, and assorted Presbyterian continuing education events.

He is married to Nancy W. Willson, who is vice president for advancement at Union Theological Seminary/Presbyterian School of Christian Education in Richmond, Virginia. They have two daughters, Robyn and Polly, and a charming new grandson, Willson James Hattaway.

LEARNING WISDOM WITH THE PEOPLE OF GOD

To study faithfully the Wisdom literature of Israel requires different skills and strategies than we customarily employ in reading other portions of the Scriptures. Wisdom literature includes the books of Proverbs, Job, and Ecclesiastes, and in the broader canon of Roman Catholicism also the documents named Sirach (or Ecclesiasticus) and the Wisdom of Solomon.

Among the religious authorities of ancient Israel were three groups: (1) the priests who presided over the worship of the people and edited much of the Hebrew Scriptures; (2) the prophets whose words are recorded in their books; and (3) the sages or teachers of wisdom whose instructions, thoughts, and ruminations are found in Wisdom literature.

The priests mediate the traditions of the people: God said to Moses, say to Aaron and the priests (Numbers 6:22-23). The prophets have heard a word from the Lord not otherwise available to the community of faith; the word burns within them and they announce: "thus says the Lord." In the New Testament the Gospel writers report God doing something unprecedented and utterly unique, and to hear them rightly we must attune our reading to these extraordinary events. In the Revelation to John, the seer has seen astonishing things no one else has ever seen before, and he bursts to tell us about them.

Wisdom literature, by contrast, invites us to examine the ordinary, unexceptional stuff of human life in order to discern the lessons we need to live as God's faithful people. Wisdom literature does not say: "Let me tell you what I have heard and seen"; but rather says: "Listen to your life, and let me help you discern what you are hearing. Look around you, and let me help you see things as they truly are." The Wisdom literature invites us to explore our lives each day as a classroom in which God gladly would teach us how to live humanly and faithfully.

Other portions of the Scriptures may find their energy and center in God's mighty works, in miracles, astonishing disruptions of history, and the drama of human salvation, but Wisdom literature grounds its teaching in the orderliness of creation. Although the Psalms are not properly located within the Wisdom literature of Israel, many psalms (for example, Psalm 37) share wisdom's confidence in an elegantly ordered creation where human beings may discern God's truth through the predictable structures of earthly existence. God has fashioned everything with wisdom (Psalm 104:24) and those who are wise will learn to discern wisdom woven in the fabric of the creation. So perfectly available is this wisdom and so widely strewn that Proverbs counsels, "Go to the ant" and "consider its ways and be wise" (Proverbs 6:6). Even the tiny, humble ant can teach us wisdom if we will only be receptive students. The ordinary rhythms of human life and the ordinary events of every day offer lessons so that we may live a life of blessing for ourselves and for others. The emphasis is on common sense and congruity.

That Wisdom literature interprets a theology of creation is not to suggest by any means that we should expect to find nuggets of gold lying on the surface of reality. The book of

Proverbs recognizes that many things masquerade as wisdom and much would seduce us from the path wisdom teaches. Not everything that looks appealing is wise; many things that appear to work in the short run will finally betray us. Wisdom consistently strives to distinguish itself from foolishness. The very soul of foolishness assumes that we can do as we please, that reality will bend itself to our desires, and we can live without concern for God or neighbor. The arrogant willfulness of fools brings disaster not only upon themselves but also upon their households and nation. The reality of creation cannot be contoured to suit our personal taste. From within the Wisdom literature the books of Job and Ecclesiastes provide a critique of the wisdom tradition. Yes, contemplating the creation may teach us wisdom, the book of Job allows, but considering the whole of creation may also utterly overwhelm us (Job 38–42) so much that a daunted Job surrenders saying, it is all "too wonderful for me" (Job 42:3). Qohelet, the writer of Ecclesiastes, does not doubt that wisdom is woven all through the fabric of the creation, but he is deeply skeptical of our human ability finally to discern the threads of wisdom and foolishness. Studying the rhythms of creation he is able to recognize that there is "a time to be born, and a time to die," but he also acknowledges that we never quite know when those times are (Ecclesiastes 3:2, 11).

Although wisdom is to be found within God's creation, that creation is by no means an open book. We need, therefore, an able teacher to instruct us in the ways of wisdom. The teacher has reflected on life and experience and has gathered up the reflections of others to make them available to new generations. Such teaching is precisely what the Wisdom literature offers, most directly in the book of Proverbs, which is something of a textbook to provide a young Jewish man the practical education he needs to make his way in the world, achieve material success, and receive God's favor. We find similar books of wisdom, such as *Life's Little Instruction Manual* in the self-help section of our bookstores. That the book intends to educate young men should not be understood, however, as utterly limiting the scope of its influence. In the Hebrew Scriptures we meet "wise women" (2 Samuel 14:2; 20:16; Proverbs 14:1) who have certainly inculcated the lessons Proverbs provides. In contrast to the hotheaded and rebellious Sheba, the "wise woman" of Abel (2 Samuel 20) does not provoke the anger of the king (Proverbs 16:14; 20:2) but rather speaks respectfully and persuasively (Proverbs 15:1, 18) to the general of King David's armies, thus becoming an example of how a single wise person may withstand the force of a horde of warriors (Proverbs 21:22). The lessons of life compiled for young men probably during the Persian reign over Israel provide wisdom for all who would read, give attention, and learn.

Little is known about the arrangements for formal education existing in ancient Israel, but the lessons taught in the Wisdom literature suggest three sources: the household, the royal court, and probably, the school. Wisdom was passed from parents (Proverbs 1:8) and other familial leaders to nurture the young into the values and ways of the family. A stable family life could sustain people amidst the turbulent changes of an uncertain economy, so the student was admonished to give attention to his parents (Proverbs 1:8); to live in loyalty with "the wife of your youth" (5:18); and warned against the temptations of other men's wives (6:24, 26, 29). This wisdom centered in family life stresses the importance of finding a suitable mate (12:4; 18:22); highlights the miseries of living with a quarrelsome spouse (21:9, 19; 25:24); and recognizes that a happy marriage is finally a gift of God's grace (19:14). Of such overwhelming importance is the life of the family that the book of Proverbs concludes with a marvelous description of a superlative woman who is praised not only by her husband and children (31:28) but also by the entire community (31:31).

The royal courts were traditionally associated with wisdom, and some lessons directly instruct young rulers in the ways of statecraft (Proverbs 25:1; 31:1-9). Just as David is the poetic inspiration for the Psalter in addition to being composer of many psalms, so is his son Solomon the royal sponsor for Wisdom literature. In the traditions of the Davidic dynasty, Solomon was remembered as a composer of proverbs (1 Kings 4:32) and the book of Proverbs is introduced with the title "The proverbs of Solomon son of David, king of Israel" (Proverbs 1:1), though the book clearly points out other sources of proverbs (22:17, 30:1, 31:1-9). Many proverbs may have had their origin in the rustic village life of common people and, indeed, some proverbs give hints of social positions that are anything but royal (20:2, 22:11; 23:1-3; 25:6-7), but it seems likely they were collected and edited by the royal court, as is indicated in Proverbs 25:1. The wisdom tradition intended to provide stability by respect for the royal household (24:21) while recognizing that not only should kings rule with wisdom but wisdom should also rule the king (25:5; 29:4; 30:21-22, 27). Wisdom literature provides instruction for kings but also for those ruled by the king, with the implied royal recommendation that if kings rule by wisdom, so should we rule ourselves with wisdom.

People may be surprised to discover that no direct evidence for schools in ancient Israel has been found. Biblical scholars are therefore left to infer educational strategies from what is known of Egyptian and Mesopotamian pedagogy. Most societies do provide means beyond the household for nurturing and socializing their children, and the existence of some institutions beyond the family seems more than likely. Cities like Abel (2 Samuel 20:18-19) and Tekoa (2 Samuel 14:2) seem to have had reputations for wisdom paralleling the university towns of our age. In the ancient Near East education was carried on by laborious repetition and memorization. Students copied our their letters carefully and archaeologists in Israel have found clay pieces on which students practiced their alphabet. These particular potshards are called "abecedaries." Learning was largely memory work. The teacher would speak a proverb and ask students to repeat it. When the father enjoins the son to keep his commandments on his heart (Proverbs 3:1-3) he almost certainly means for the boy to memorize the lessons. Though out of fashion among educational strategies these days, memorizing proverbs remains a formidable way of learning wisdom. Discipline in the classrooms of the ancient Near East, though so strict as to allow for corporal punishment, served as an incentive to serious concentration on study and was a pedagogical strategy enthusiastically applauded in the book of Proverbs (10:13; 13:24; 22:15, 23:13-16).

That the wisdom tradition of Israel was taught to young men who then became teachers of wisdom is strikingly evidenced in the New Testament. The epistle traditionally ascribed to James the brother of Jesus contrasts a wisdom that is "earthly, unspiritual" with a wisdom that is heavenly (James 3:15-17). This wisdom from above, implying God as the giver of wisdom, is characterized as being filled with peace, submission, mercy, good works, and impartiality, all qualities lauded in the wisdom tradition. James has learned from observing the creation, and in making the point that our mouths cannot bless God and then curse our neighbor, he observes that the same spring cannot produce both fresh water and salty (3:11). In this concern for the quality of conversation among the people of God (3:1-12), James mirrors a persistent theme of the Wisdom literature (Proverbs 10:18-21, 31-32; 11:12-13).

Even more striking perhaps are the ways the Gospels depict Jesus as a teacher of wisdom. In the "Sermon on the Plain" recorded in Luke's Gospel we find strings of proverbs (Luke 6:43-45). The "Sermon on the Mount" in Matthew's Gospel concludes with a wisdom parable contrasting the wise person who builds on rock with the foolish person who builds on sand (Matthew 7:24-27). In Matthew, Jesus takes on the mantle of wisdom to invite disciples to take his yoke (11:28-30), a yoke being a traditional metaphor expressing a relationship with wisdom (Sirach 6:30). The opening verses of the Gospel of John use the wisdom category of "the Word" to declare Jesus as the very wisdom of God (John 1:1-5, 14-18), and the apostle Paul agrees, writing to the church in Corinth that Christ is "the wisdom of God" (1 Corinthians 1:24). By no means are the wisdom traditions of Israel confined to a few seldom studied documents in the Old Testament; they inform our central proclamations of the gospel because Jesus, James, Matthew, and Paul, obviously diligent students who paid attention, learned wisdom through their families and in their education.

If we would learn the ways of the wisdom tradition we might borrow their educational strategies. We might reasonably decline to share their fondness for the rod, but memorization has much to recommend it. As you engage in this study of the Wisdom literature you might commit to memory each week one wisdom saying, or if memorization does not work well with you, write down the saying on an index card and keep that saying with you throughout the day. Speak the proverb aloud; this literature means to be heard. Writing is secondary. Listen to the rhythm; hear the contrasts and comparisons. Use the saying as a lens to examine the texture of your living. Where does the saying or proverb wisely inform you? Where is the saying not so helpful? The Wisdom literature understands that proverbs may not be perfectly appropriate to every circumstance: The wise person learns to discern the usefulness of the lesson. Fools can readily misuse or misspeak the wisest of proverbs (Proverbs 26:7, 9), but the wise understand that discernment is required in each circumstance. Sometimes it is appropriate to correct someone; sometimes it is prudent to keep silence (26:3-4). We can learn from following the path that proverbs guide, but we can learn something also from those places where we resist their teaching.

Such resistance is by no means alien to the wisdom tradition of Israel. In their own way the books of Job and Ecclesiastes protest: "It's not that simple!" To enter into the wisdom tradition is to join a conversation that has been going on for centuries. We rightly appropriate and honor these Scriptures not by keeping silence and submitting to a monologue, but by joining in their conversation and allowing their questions to draw us deeper into faith. The questions proposed in the wisdom tradition are dark and difficult:

"Why am I alive at all?" (Job 3:11).

"Who is this human creature who lives before the face of God?" (Psalm 8:4).

"What difference does all my work make?" (Ecclesiastes 1:3; 3:9).

"Where is authentic wisdom to shape human life?" (Job 28:20).

"Why be honest when cheating works so well?" (Proverbs 11:3).

"How do we live with the heavy knowledge of our own mortality?" (Ecclesiastes 3:19-22).

"What help dare we expect in living our lives?" (Psalm 145).

The sayings of the wisdom tradition address these questions, and although they appear to provide ready-made answers in the form of proverbs, these are not conclusions so much as contributions to an ongoing conversation. To read the Wisdom literature we enter into the conversation, placing our own lives on the line. Only within the conversation will we discover true wisdom and come to know the utterly trustworthy God to whom the wisdom tradition bears witness.

UNIT 1: THE GLORY OF GOD'S CREATION
GOD MADE US SPECIAL

PREVIEWING THE LESSON

Lesson Scripture: Psalm 8
Background Scripture: Psalm 8
Key Verses: Psalm 8:4-5

Focus of the Lesson:
People wonder about their place in a vast universe. What does our faith say about our inherent worth within the context of all creation? The psalmist affirms that we hold a place of honor in God's creation: We are special to God and cared for by God, to whom we owe our highest praise.

Goals for the Learners:
(1) to hear how the psalmist describes the place of humankind in God's creation.
(2) to consider what this description implies about human worth and responsibility.
(3) to acknowledge and affirm their own worth in God's eyes.

Supplies:
Bibles, newsprint and marker, paper and pencils, hymnals; optional: magazines, scissors, glue, large paper

---

READING THE SCRIPTURE

NRSV
Psalm 8
[1]O LORD, our Sovereign,
  how majestic is your name in all the earth!
You have set your glory above the heavens.
[2] Out of the mouths of babes and infants
you have founded a bulwark
    because of your foes,
  to silence the enemy and the avenger.
[3]When I look at your heavens,
    the work of your fingers,
  the moon and the stars that
    you have established;

NIV
Psalm 8
[1]O LORD, our Lord,
  how majestic is your name in all the earth!
  You have set your glory
    above the heavens.
[2]From the lips of children and infants
  you have ordained praise
because of your enemies,
  to silence the foe and the avenger.
[3]When I consider your heavens,
  the work of your fingers,

---

⁴ **what are human beings that you
　are mindful of them,
　mortals that you care for them?
⁵Yet you have made them a little lower
　than God,
　and crowned them with glory and honor.**
⁶ You have given them dominion over
　the works of your hands;
　you have put all things under their feet,
⁷ all sheep and oxen,
　and also the beasts of the field,
⁸ the birds of the air, and the fish of the sea,
　whatever passes along the paths of
　the seas.
⁹ O LORD, our Sovereign,
　how majestic is your name in all
　the earth!

the moon and the stars,
　which you have set in place,
⁴**what is man that you are mindful of him,
　the son of man that you care for him?
⁵You made him a little lower than the
　heavenly beings
　and crowned him with glory and honor.**
⁶You made him ruler over the works of
　your hands;
　you put everything under his feet:
⁷all flocks and herds,
　and the beasts of the field,
⁸the birds of the air,
　and the fish of the sea,
　all that swim the paths of the seas.
⁹O LORD, our Lord,
　how majestic is your name in all the earth!

UNDERSTANDING THE SCRIPTURE

Psalm 8:1, 9. Although the hymn of praise we hear announced in 8:1 may appear commonplace, such a call to praise has not sounded thus far in the book of Psalms. This is the first hymn of praise in the Psalms. The psalms preceding it sing in more desperate keys: "O LORD, how many are my foes!" (Psalm 3:1); "Answer me when I call, O God of my right!" (Psalm 4:1); "Give ear to my words, O LORD; give heed to my sighing" (5:1); "O LORD, do not rebuke me in your anger" (Psalm 6:1). Psalm 8, in contrast, asks God for nothing, but praises God for everything.

Among the psalms this would be categorized as a hymn of praise, but it is a hymn of praise with particular elements of the wisdom tradition of Israel: It sings of a world well-ordered, mysterious to human beings in many ways but comprehensible and under the control of a "sovereign" or governor who has also ordered and provided a place for humankind.

The hymn is held in an utterly awestruck parenthesis of praise (8:1, 9). Such enthrallment is perfectly appropriate, however, for the Wisdom literature of Israel that declares, "The fear of the LORD is the beginning of wisdom (knowledge)" (Psalm 111:10, Proverbs 1:7), and it is perfectly appropriate in light of the God we are given to contemplate. What can one do but wonder and praise?

Psalm 8:2-8. Praise is at the heart of the matter for Psalm 8, and praise is powerful stuff. Praise builds a fortress capable of withstanding the threats mentioned and implied in Psalms 2–7. So potent is praise that even the innocent, poorly articulated praise of babbling infants provides adequate shelter from all that would assail us. Even as the psalm invites us to reflect on the naïve, trustful praise of children, it also invites us to imagine how much more powerful are the praises of those who have brought the concentrated command of their creative powers to bear to the task of praising God.

Like a child the psalmist wanders under the stars of night with face upturned to mysteries of the universe. The contemplation only hinted at in the second portion of verse 1 now begins in earnest. The sky full of far-flung stars is immense, and the more that we know about the stars and sky, the larger they become. When the psalmist declares of the heavens that they are the work of God's fingers, that estimation by no means diminishes the size of the universe but only establishes the even greater sovereignty of God. Although the psalmist may be naïve about relativity theory and quantum hypotheses, the naïveté of the psalm's central metaphor is exaggerated to make a point about the utter immensity of God and God's design and God's creativity: God places the stars in the heavens like a master jeweler handling diamonds, "the work of your fingers" (8:3).

The dazzling heavens can dizzy us with thoughts of our own diminutive stature, and the psalmist turns from the heavens to contemplate the humans: Who are they? Who are we? Notice, however, the psalmist does not frame the question without reference to God. We do not know, indeed, we cannot know who human beings authentically are without reference to God. However vast the spread of stars in the night sky, however glorious the passage of the sun through the heavens, the human creatures are the ones of whom God is "mindful"; they are the ones for whom God "cares," in the sense of a gardener caring for a garden, a shepherd caring for the sheep. The emphasis falls on the grace of God demonstrated in remembering and caring, not on what fascinating creatures we are to contemplate or what valuable creatures we are to look after. God's "mindful" care provides only one more reason for praise. Remembrance and concern, however, are merely a prelude when it comes to contemplating the place of the human creature in God's universe.

Having begun the psalm by contemplating God's sovereign rule, the psalmist, who has turned attention to the human creature, now recognizes that God has entrusted to the human creature a dominion also. As the stars in the heaven, the work of God's fingers, crown God with "glory and honor" (8:5), so also are the human ones crowned by the works of their hands. In the beginning God gave human creatures responsibility for and stewardship of the creation and other creatures (Genesis 1:26-31). This psalm sings of God's goodness in doing so, and praises God for the height of human accomplishment: the domestication of animals. The ancient psalm was sung when the ox collar was the pinnacle of technology and the epitome of human achievement. That the psalmist should take such pride may strike us as quaint. No matter: This psalmist could praise God just as confidently for this computer that whisks my words on a screen in front of me. How do such things happen? Well, I certainly can't explain my computer (I mean, I do know how to turn it on and load paper, sure), but the psalmist can: God has given it all into our hands as a gift of God's goodness. Our place in the creation is not established by some natural order or hierarchy of creatures, but is entrusted to us by God. Moreover, God has demonstrated the manner in which a wise ruler exercises dominion: God is "mindful," God is caring. So are we to be mindful and caring. The psalmist borrows the language of monarchy ("dominion") to describe the place God has given the human creature in creation. In another psalm, King David's final words describe how all of nature flourishes when the king rules wisely and fairly: "One who rules over people justly, ruling in fear of God, is like the light of morning, like the sun rising on a cloudless morning, gleaming from the rain on the grassy land" (2 Samuel 23:3-4). That vision indeed stirs us to praise: "how majestic is your name in all the earth" (8:1, 9).

INTERPRETING THE SCRIPTURE

Wondering About Our Place in the Cosmos

The experience recounted in Psalm 8 is timeless and universal: A human being wanders in the night and looking up is dazzled and dizzied by the utter vastness of the stars in the sky. With a sky so immeasurable and stars so innumerable, what does human life matter? Are we lost in the immensity of the stars? All the preoccupations that daily accompany us seem tiny compared with the endless sky. We ourselves may feel tiny and insignificant.

As if that experience were not daunting enough, physics and astronomy magnify our smallness. Modern scientific achievements have made human life longer and more comfortable, but so also they may have increased our sense of anxiety and inconsequence. Yes, look into the night sky, say physics and astronomers, but know that what you see is only the barest fraction of all that exists. Radio telescopes and spacecraft traveling far from Earth discover vast galaxies hidden from our sight. If it were not enough to heighten our sense of smallness, they tell us that what can be seen is only a fraction of what actually is, and that most of the matter of the universe is not visible at all, but "dark matter" floating in the emptiness of space or hidden in what they call "black holes."

Renaissance astronomers regarded the heavens as stable, with the planets spinning majestically around the sun and the stars standing sentinel in the heavens, but more recent scientific assessments born of radio telescopes and relativity physics tell of unspeakable violence and chaos in the stars. A star a thousand times larger than our sun grows larger still, bloating with super-heated gases until it supernovas and explodes in fiery fury to engulf a thousand solar systems the size of our own. Another star in its maturity does not explode but instead collapses upon itself to create a "black hole" of such density that even its own light cannot escape its unrelenting gravity. Such chaos takes place light years away but still we shudder in vulnerability: Is this universe any place to live? How can we ever find a home here?

Wandering Home

The psalmist finds home in the cosmos by knowing the name of the Lord: "How majestic is your name in all the earth!" (8:1, 9). The psalmist knows "the name" of the One with whom we have to do, the One who made heaven and earth, the One who is our help in all things (Psalm 124:8). The cosmos is not regarded as an alien place, full of threat, because the psalmist knows and reflects poetically upon the creation story of Genesis 2. Because the psalmist knows God's "name," the psalmist knows also that this cosmos is nothing other than the creation of God's hands, and God's gracious design has been to fashion a home for human beings.

This season of Lent is a time of homecoming. Often in Lenten worship we tell the story of the prodigal son who, in the midst of his alienation and distance from his father, could still remember his father's address, a place where even the servants had food to eat and plenty of it. Just as the prodigal son remembers his father's address, the psalmist remembers the name of the Lord and knows One who remembers and cares for the children of earth and welcomes them home.

To remember the name of the Lord is to recognize the character and works of the one named. This God created at the beginning and gave the earth as a home to the human ones, placing them in dominion over the creation (Genesis 1:26-31). This vision is sung elsewhere in the psalms: "The heavens are the LORD's heavens, but the earth he has given to human beings" (Psalm 115:16). We are God's stewards on earth to manage the creation responsibly. Jesus pointed to this relationship as he told parables where servants are left in charge while the householder is away (Matthew 24:45-51; 25:14-28).

The psalmist does not come to this recognition by observing nature. The creation in this psalm does not reveal God, but is recognized as God's good gift by those who know God's "name." The cosmos is intelligible only in relationship to God. Only those who can call on the name of the Lord see beyond the randomness and chaos of the world to discern a habitation made for humans. The question addressed here is not "who is man" or "what does it mean to be human," but rather "who is this human creature who is given such dignity that God would not overlook or forget but remember and care?" Our finitude and smallness, far from diminishing us, become our dignity because they are the occasion of God's remembering and care. God "remembers we are dust" (Psalm 103:14), and thus knowing our vulnerability and regarding us with tenderness, God provides for our care.

Wondering and Worshiping

The psalmist fulfills the human vocation by praising God. As God has shown delight in the human creatures by preparing for them a home and caring for them, so now the psalmist expresses our human delight in being the recipients of God's creation and care. Beginning and ending the psalm with the same exclamation of praise (8:1, 9), the poet wraps the whole cosmos in God's majesty. Whatever is hidden in the darkness of the skies belongs to God and is part of

God's grand design for the creation. This universe is not a random collection of stars and stones, but nothing less than the work of God's hands. We learn this truth by singing it.

By praise, we name the earth as the Lord's; by praise, we claim the earth as our inheritance as God's children. Only those who can worship and wonder can penetrate the mysteries of stone and stars to recognize their earthly home. The rock we cling to in the darkness of space becomes hospitable only when we know and praise "the name"—that is the character and will—of the one who gives it. Even the simplest praise and thanksgiving of children (8:2) is formidable enough to stake our claim in the universe against all that would intimidate human life. Though the foes of meaninglessness and insignificance and chaos threaten human life, even the unsuspecting praise of children is bulwark enough to hold back the dark. The house we are given on the earth is the house of praise, the home we have is thanksgiving, the only appropriate responses to such a gift. We sing the secrets of the stars hidden to those who do not participate in the mystery of worship.

Naming and claiming a house of faith within God's creation we build our home. Though unpredictability pounds against the door, it is God's unpredictability, a driving force of creativity. Though chaos blows at the house, we trust in God's creative power to triumph finally over chaos. Even though meaninglessness surrounds the house, in praise and thanksgiving we remember who we are and whose we are. Worship leads us again to our truest meaning: God means for us to be here, and we are given the human tasks of glorifying God and delighting in God forever.

SHARING THE SCRIPTURE

Preparing Our Hearts

This week's devotional reading is found in Genesis 1:26-31. In this beloved account of God's creation of humanity we learn that we have been given "dominion" over that which God has created here on earth. This "dominion" is not meant to be exploitative, but rather we are to rule as God would rule. If you think about "dominion" in that sense, what could you and other Christians do to be better stewards of God's creation? Brainstorm some ideas and list them in your spiritual journal.

Pray that you and your class participants will be aware of your special place in God's creation and the responsibility attached to that place.

Preparing Our Minds

Study the background and lesson Scripture, both of which are Psalm 8. As you ponder this psalm, think about what our faith says about our inherent worth within the context of all creation.

To help orient yourself to this quarter's material, please read the overview of each week's lessons and the background article that introduces you to Wisdom literature. Both of these articles are found just prior to this lesson.

Write on newsprint:
❑ information for next week's lesson, found under "Continue the Journey."

Decide which of the options you will use for the "Gather to Learn" portion. Collect necessary supplies.

LEADING THE CLASS

(1) Gather to Learn

❖ Welcome the class members and introduce any guests.

❖ Pray that those who have come today will experience the wonder of humanity's place within God's creation.

❖ Choose one of these options to introduce the lesson.

■ **Option 1:** Provide magazines that can be cut, scissors, glue, and some large paper. As a class or in smaller groups, ask the students to make a collage of pictures of humans. Try for as much diversity as possible. Talk about why the students believe God created humanity. What is our purpose?

■ **Option 2:** Take a short nature walk with the class, weather permitting. Ask the adults to point out facets of God's creation that they find particularly fascinating.

❖ Read aloud today's focus statement: **People wonder about their place in a vast universe. What does our faith say about our inherent worth within the context of all creation? The psalmist affirms that we hold a place of honor in God's creation: We are special to God and cared for by God, to whom we owe our highest praise.**

❖ **Option:** This would be an appropriate time to introduce the quarter's theme: Wisdom literature. You may wish to highlight some points made in the article entitled "Learning Wisdom with the People of God."

(2) Hear How the Psalmist Describes the Place of Humankind in God's Creation

❖ Invite the class to read Psalm 8. If you have a hymnal that includes a Psalter, distribute the hymnal and read responsively. If not, select one person to read the entire psalm.

❖ Discuss these questions.

(1) What does this psalm say to you about God?

(2) What does this psalm say to you about God's creation and the place of humanity within that creation? (Be sure to note that we cannot know who we are and what our place is unless we recognize who God is.)

(3) What does this psalm suggest about the response of humanity to creation?

❖ Distribute paper and pencils. Ask the students, individually or in groups, to write their own psalm or poem about God's creation.

❖ Encourage volunteers to read their psalm or poem.

(3) Consider What This Description Implies About Human Worth and Responsibility

❖ Look again at verses 5-8. Point out that humans are made "a little lower than God," or as some other ancient manuscripts read, "than the divine beings" or "angels." Furthermore, we have been given "dominion" over the creation here on earth. Talk with the class about their understanding of "dominion" and how that understanding may have changed. (See the first paragraph under "Preparing Our Hearts" for a comment on "dominion.")

❖ Discuss whether or not humanity has been true to its high calling as God's stewards by caring for creation as God would. Identify situations that indicate humanity has been faithful and list these ideas in one column on a sheet of newsprint. In a second column, list examples of unfaithful care.

❖ Brainstorm with the students ways that they can be true to their high calling by being responsible stewards of God's good creation. In this list, include ideas for taking care of creation at home (recycling, creating a backyard habitat) and as a citizen of their community, nation, and world (writing letters to encourage public policy that supports care of the earth, belonging to a stewardship-focused organization, such as the Nature Conservancy). As you do the brainstorming, some participants may briefly tell how they have implemented a particular idea.

❖ Invite the learners to select at least one idea and commit themselves to implementing it.

(4) Acknowledge and Affirm the Learners' Worth in God's Eyes

❖ Read aloud this quotation by A. W. Tozer (1897–1963) and ask the students to comment on it in light of their understanding of Psalm 8: **If a poll should be taken to name the six greatest men [people] in the world and our names would not be included, we would still have the same privileges in God's world that they have! We can breathe God's beautiful air, look at his blue sky, gaze into a never-ending array of stars in the night sky. We can stand upon the hard earth and stamp our little feet—and our big feet, too—and know that it will sustain us. We are as much a part of this human race as the greatest men and women.**

❖ Provide quiet time for the class members to meditate on this quotation as it relates to their own self-worth.

❖ Conclude this portion of the lesson by reading this quotation from Minnie Smith: **I am as my Creator made me, and since he is satisfied, so am I.**

(5) Continue the Journey

❖ Pray that the participants will recognize their special place in God's vast universe and give thanks for all that God has entrusted to their care.

❖ Read aloud this preparation for next week's lesson. You may also want to post it on newsprint for the students to copy. **Prepare for next week's session, "God Created Wonderful Things," by reading Psalm 104. Our session will focus on verses 1-13. Contemplate these ideas as** you study: People often experience awe and wonder in response to the natural world. Who created the creatures and landscapes that cause such feelings in us? The psalmist praises God for being the Creator of all living and nonliving things, seen and unseen on earth.

❖ Read aloud the following three ideas. Challenge the students to commit themselves to use these activities as a springboard to spiritual growth.

(1) **Offer praise to God by writing your own psalm, reading a psalm with enthusiasm, or singing a hymn that focuses on praise to God.**

(2) **Participate in a roadside clean-up** or other activity that will give you an opportunity to be a good steward of the earth.

(3) **Observe nature, either at night or during the day. Perhaps you are in a place where the season is changing and the earth is being renewed. Give thanks to God for each facet of creation that you observe.**

❖ Sing or read aloud "For the Beauty of the Earth."

❖ Lead this benediction to end today's session: **With all of your creatures, most majestic God, we sing your praises and pray that you would empower us to be wise people and faithful stewards of your creation. In Jesus' name. Amen.**

UNIT 1: THE GLORY OF GOD'S CREATION

GOD CREATED WONDERFUL THINGS

PREVIEWING THE LESSON

Lesson Scripture: Psalm 104:1-13
Background Scripture: Psalm 104
Key Verse: Psalm 104:1

Focus of the Lesson:

People often experience awe and wonder in response to the natural world. Who created the creatures and landscapes that cause such feelings in us? The psalmist praises God for being the Creator of all living and nonliving things, seen and unseen on earth.

Goals for the Learners:

(1) to discover how the psalmist expresses praise to God for being the Creator of all things.
(2) to recognize and affirm that all nature is created by God.
(3) to develop a plan for contributing to the care of God's creation.

Pronunciation Guide:

Leviathan (li vi' uh thihn)

Supplies:

Bibles, newsprint and marker, paper and pencils (colored pencils, if possible), hymnals, pictures of the created world

---

READING THE SCRIPTURE

NRSV

Psalm 104:1-13

¹ **Bless the LORD, O my soul.**

O LORD my God, you are very great.

You are clothed with honor and majesty,

² wrapped in light as with a garment.

You stretch out the heavens like a tent,

NIV

Psalm 104:1-13

¹ **Praise the LORD, O my soul.**

O LORD my God, you are very great;

you are clothed with splendor and majesty.

²He wraps himself in light as with a garment;

3   you set the beams of your chambers on
        the waters,
    you make the clouds your chariot,
        you ride on the wings of the wind,
4   you make the winds your messengers,
        fire and flame your ministers.
5   You set the earth on its foundations,
        so that it shall never be shaken.
6   You cover it with the deep as with a
        garment;
        the waters stood above the mountains.
7   At your rebuke they flee;
        at the sound of your thunder they take
        to flight.
8   They rose up to the mountains,
        ran down to the valleys
    to the place that you appointed for them.
9   You set a boundary that they may not
        pass,
    so that they might not again cover the
        earth.
10 You make springs gush forth in the
        valleys;
    they flow between the hills,
11 giving drink to every wild animal;
    the wild asses quench their thirst.
12 By the streams the birds of the air have
        their habitation;
    they sing among the branches.
13 From your lofty abode you water the
        mountains;
    the earth is satisfied with the fruit of your
        work.

he stretches out the heavens like a tent
3and lays the beams of his upper chambers
    on their waters.
He makes the clouds his chariot
    and rides on the wings of the wind.
4He makes winds his messengers,
    flames of fire his servants.
5He set the earth on its foundations;
    it can never be moved.
6You covered it with the deep as with a
    garment;
    the waters stood above the mountains.
7But at your rebuke the waters fled,
    at the sound of your thunder they took to
    flight;
8they flowed over the mountains,
    they went down into the valleys,
    to the place you assigned for them.
9You set a boundary they cannot cross;
    never again will they cover the earth.
10He makes springs pour water into the
    ravines;
    it flows between the mountains.
11They give water to all the beasts of the
    field;
    the wild donkeys quench their thirst.
12The birds of the air nest by the waters;
    they sing among the branches.
13He waters the mountains from his upper
    chambers;
    the earth is satisfied by the fruit of his
    work.

UNDERSTANDING THE SCRIPTURE

Introduction. Psalm 104 is a hymn of praise from the wisdom tradition of Israel. It sings praises of the One who created the world and arranged all its parts in an intricate but reliable order. The Wisdom literature of Israel assumes a well-ordered creation even if at times it may also protest the order, as in Job, or question the meaning of the way things are ordered, as in Ecclesiastes.

Psalm 104:1a. The writer of this psalm has neither complaint nor question, however, only sheer, ebullient rejoicing: "Bless the LORD, O my soul!" That familiar exhortation to praise is found only in four places: the opening and closing verses of Psalm 103 and Psalm 104. Thus, "Bless the LORD, O my soul!" becomes a bracket holding both psalms in the Scripture and in our memory. These two psalms are intended to be read together, with Psalm 103 praising God's "steadfast love" (103:11) and Psalm 104 rejoicing in all God has made.

Psalm 104:1b-4. Psalm 104 catalogs the creation for reasons to praise God. God should be praised for creating the heavens. As in Psalm 8 the heavens provide no threat (as they did for many people of the ancient Near East), but belong to God alone. The clouds are God's chariot riding majestically on the roads made by the wind. The sky itself is like a tent, a place provided for shelter and designed for human habitation.

Psalm 104:5-13. The earth offers no fewer reasons for praise. It is founded solidly and immovably. The waters that often seem a threat in the Scriptures (Genesis 8 and 9; Psalm 32:6; 46:3; 144:7) bear no menace here. God has established their bounds, and life may safely endure on the land while the water blesses the land with growth and abundance. Trees grow to provide home for singing birds. Wild donkeys drink their fill from gushing springs. On this earth each creature finds what it needs.

Psalm 104:14-26. The human creature also finds satisfaction, for the psalmist sings that God has not only provided the necessary "food from the earth" (104:14) but also the "extras" of "wine to gladden the human heart, oil to make the face shine" (104:15). The picture of abundance is exuberant. God has placed human beings in a home on the earth, just as God provides homes also for birds in the trees and rocks for the coneys. The Eighth Psalm's vision of human dominion over the creation and other creatures is absent here: Human beings are a part of the creation, living in something of a "peaceable kingdom," no less and no more the object of God's affection than other creatures. This kingdom is not entirely peaceable, however, for we hear the roaring of "the young lions . . . for their prey" (104:21). In the glorious vision of this psalm, however, those roars are more like a prayer of thanksgiving to their Maker, a leonine version of "Bless, O Lord, this food to our use, and us to thy

service." Every creature has a place and a service in this creation, and the psalmist praises God that "In wisdom you have made them all" (104:24).

Even the Leviathan—the mythic chaos monster that in much Near Eastern folklore stood in opposition to God's ordering of creation as the force of disorder and misrule—is recognized as tame and no longer fierce and frightening. The dreaded chaos monster is finally revealed as God's own creation, and the psalmist dares to declare that God created Leviathan as a happy plaything. The psalmist states that God made the Leviathan "to sport in it" (104:26 NRSV) or "to frolic" (104:26 NIV) in the sea, which is to say that God made this awesome creature for the sheer delight of it.

Psalm 104:27-30. All the creatures depend upon God for food, for the warmth of God's face shining upon them, and finally, for breath. The psalmist confronts the facts of creaturely contingency poetically but also realistically. Death also is given a place within the great mystery of God's creation. The creatures of Disney's *The Lion King* could sing of "The Circle of Life," but the psalmist of Psalm 104 hymns the mystery of all creatures living and dying beneath the generous and caring face of God. No less than life, death is part of the order of the creation God has in wisdom made. Death is not a threat to the design of creation but is an inevitable part of that order.

Psalm 104:31-35. The whole creation finds its source in the joy of God. Just as nothing threatens God's creation so also nothing compels God to create. Creation is the act of God's joy, and the psalmist begins the conclusion with the prayer in verse 31 that God may find joy always in the creation: "May the LORD rejoice in his works." The psalmist resolves to rejoice in the Lord: "I will sing to the LORD as long as I live" (104:33). The psalmist knows that the day comes when breath will slip away and the harp will fall to the ground and the song will end; the psalmist knows that human life is not forever; but still the psalmist prays, "May the glory of the LORD endure forever" (104:31).

Because not everyone enjoys existence as a creature of a generous Creator and because not everyone desires to live in harmony with God's creation, the psalmist adds the surprising and discordant note of verse 35: "Let sinners be consumed."

The psalms ends as it begins, "Bless the LORD, O my soul." This is fitting. Our lives end as they begin—in the grace and generosity of God, who has ordered all things well. While we have eyes to behold the ordered creation and ears to hearken to the psalmist's invitation to "Bless the LORD," it is fitting to muster our breath to sing God's praise.

INTERPRETING THE SCRIPTURE

Naming the Creation: A Human Vocation

With our words we not only describe the creation we are given, we construct an order and meaning to the creation. The singer of Psalm 104 engages in a creative enterprise of naming the creation. This should not surprise us. From the very beginning, the task of faithfully naming the creation has been part of the human vocation: God parades all the creatures before the human one so that they may receive their names (Genesis 2:19-20). We organize the world that passes before us not simply by what we notice but by the way we name it.

Peter Berger, a sociologist of religion and lay theologian, describes how this happens with a commonplace example. A child cries out in the night, awakened by a bad dream. Mother comes into the room, gathers the child into her arms, turns on a small light; she speaks to the child reassuringly or sings, and the message of her speech and song are predictable and very much an echo of Psalm 104: everything is okay, all is in order, there's no need to be afraid. It's a familiar scene, almost all of us have been in such a room, but in *A Rumor of Angels: Modern Society and the Rediscovery of the Supernatural* Peter Berger asks the question: "Is the mother lying to the child?"

It is a troubling question, troubling precisely because it is so basic, so formidable.

As I prepare this lesson I contemplate the morning news: Our government warns of terrorist missile strikes against commercial airliners, a strange disease ravages Asia, businesses lay off more employees, and three mummified infant bodies have been found in an abandoned storage facility. Everything is certainly not okay or in order, and fear seems a perfectly reasonable response.

To declare that things are in order, that everything is okay, and that there's nothing to fear is not simply a response to observable events; it is an articulation of a faith that does not ignore what it sees but is grounded deeper in trust and faith (Romans 8:24). Psalm 104 sings its song of praise from those depths. It announces the creation as the theater of God's glory. There are other ways of looking at it. The psalm sees evidence of God's providential care as lions feast on their prey. We might expect that creatures lower on the food chain do not find this so praiseworthy!

Naming the Creation as God's

Naming the creation as a creation is a creative act in itself. Many people look around at the world encircling them and see only a random collection of events and artifacts that mean nothing, intend nothing, came from nowhere, and are going nowhere; a universe as deaf to the psalms we sing as it is unsympathetic to our hopes and fears and loves and lives. To construe this ramshackle, thrown-together collection as a creation requires an act of creative imagination. The deepest truths of our lives can only be spoken in hints and metaphors and similes, the stuff of imagination.

If we are regular churchgoers we may take faith so much for granted that we forget what a creative and imaginative enterprise our faith is. With daring imagination Psalm 104 surveys literally everything and names it all as God's creation. Though the heavens may be dark and shake the earth with thunder and lightning, the heavens are God's and the storm belongs to God (see also Psalm 29). Though the waters churn with uncertainty they also are God's good gift to provide life to all that dwell upon the land. In the psalmist's vision even the dreaded Leviathan, the dragon-like chaos monster usually understood as utterly inimical to God's creative purposes, has been tamed to an enjoyable house pet. Far from being a haphazard assortment, the world has been ordered by a creative hand, the work of a Creator who looks with generous care upon all the creatures. Wild donkeys in the fields and birds in the air, fierce lions and timid coneys, all are the objects of God's care and providence. And if God so cares for storks and sea monsters, how much more does God care for his human creations (Matthew 6:25-33), giving them "food from the earth and wine to gladden the human heart" (104:14-15); not to mention the gracious and delicious superfluity of "oil to make the face shine" (104:15).

Claiming the Creation as Home

With such daring and dazzling poetry, the psalmist reassembles the world into a theater where God's great providence is daily enacted. Moreover, the song invites us to recognize this world as a place for human habitation; it invites us to find our home in God's care. Like a mother reassuring a restless child, "everything is in order, there is nothing to fear," so the psalmist invites us to discover our place in God's ordered creation. The world exists in God's care; the creation is utterly dependent upon the Creator. Although the psalmist extravagantly celebrates the wonder of the world, the psalmist also recognizes that the world has no life apart from God's life, God's breath, God's creative ordering of all. The psalmist points out the solemn order God has provided: There is a time for the moon and a time for the sun, a time for darkness and a time for dawn (104:19-22). God arranges dry land and water (104:9). Food appears "in due season" (104:27), there is a time to go to work (104:23), and, as in Ecclesiastes 3, there is a time to be born and a time to die (104:29-30). It is characteristic of the Wisdom literature of the Bible to see the world as ordered, reliable, and predictable. The book of Proverbs provides instruction appropriate to living in this well-arranged world, but for Psalm 104 we find our way in the world most truly by worship. The appropriate response to the psalmist's creative vision of reality is a life lived in praise: "I will sing to the LORD as long as I live" (104:33).

With the sound of thunder (104:7), the young lions roaring (104:21), and the trembling of the earth (104:32), we are called to "sing praise to God." Our worship brings us to the task of creatively imagining the world as God's creation. God's creation is unfinished; God is preparing a new heaven and a new earth (Revelation 21:1), and we participate already in that new creation (2 Corinthians 5:17) in our praise of God. Knowing the architecture of justice that will adorn the city of God, we join the psalmist now in naming the world theologically. We refuse the familiar economic naming of reality that speaks of the world only in terms of what can be bought and sold and used. That man laid off is not named "expendable," but is a child of God, baptized into Christ; that child with Down syndrome is not "an unprofitable burden" but a citizen of God's kingdom and heir of a fabulous inheritance (Ephesians 1:3-14). We can see this gospel truth because Psalm 104 teaches us how to name our world as God's creation; and when we can name our world as God's creation, we name God's creation as our home.

SHARING THE SCRIPTURE

Preparing Our Hearts

This week's devotional reading is found in Psalm 104:31-35, which is part of our background reading for today. Verse 33 proclaims: "I will sing to the LORD as long as I live." Spend time singing praise to God for the majesty revealed in the created universe. You may want to write your own hymn of praise, or sing a praise song that is especially meaningful to you.

Pray that you and your class participants will recognize that God has created wonderful things and praise God for the glories of creation.

Preparing Our Minds

Study the background Scripture, Psalm 104, and lesson Scripture, verses 1-13. As you read, consider the awe and wonder that many people experience in response to the natural world and contemplate God as the Creator of these things.

Write on newsprint:
❏ sentence in "Develop a Plan for Contributing to the Care of God's Creation."
❏ information for next week's lesson, found under "Continue the Journey."

Locate several pictures of the created world that highlight its beauty and majesty. Your local library will likely have books of photographs by Ansel Adams, pictures of Georgia O'Keeffe's paintings of flowers, landscape scenes, or pictures of God's creatures in their natural habitats.

Plan a brief lecture as suggested in "Discover How the Psalmist Expresses Praise to God for Being the Creator of All Things."

LEADING THE CLASS

(1) Gather to Learn

❖ Welcome the class members and introduce any guests.

❖ Pray that the students will enter into a spirit of awe, wonder, and praise as they contemplate creation and the God who made it.

❖ Show pictures of nature that you have collected. If the class is large, you may want to pass around the book(s) or pictures. Encourage the class members to discuss these ideas:
  ■ how they experience God within creation and even through art that captures creation's beauty and power.
  ■ ways in which the wonders of nature prompt them to praise God.
  ■ how they feel about nature: Is it stable or unpredictable?

❖ Read aloud today's focus statement: **People often experience awe and wonder in response to the natural world. Who created the creatures and landscapes that cause such feelings in us? The psalmist praises God for being the Creator of all living and nonliving things, seen and unseen on earth.**

(2) Discover How the Psalmist Expresses Praise to God for Being the Creator of All Things

❖ Introduce today's reading from Psalm 104 by pointing out that this psalm and

Psalm 103 are related to one another. Psalm 104 begins with the same words that began and ended 103, "Bless the LORD, O my soul." In Psalm 103 the psalmist gives thanks for God's goodness, forgiveness, and love. In Psalm 104, the focus is on God's creation of each aspect of creation for its own purpose, apart from any purpose we humans may derive from it. The psalmist praises God, who creates and provides for all of creation.

❖ Choose a volunteer to read Psalm 104:1-13. Better still, if you have a hymnal that includes the psalms, ask the students to read this passage responsively.

❖ Read aloud or lecture briefly on the information found in Understanding the Scripture for verses 1a, 1b-4, and 5-13.

❖ Ask the adults to work together to identify sensory images in this passage. In other words, what can they see, hear, taste, touch, or smell as they read the psalmist's description of creation?

❖ Distribute paper and pencils—if possible, colored pencils. Ask the students to look again at verses 1-13 and select an image that particularly appeals to them. Invite them to sketch that image, but assure them that artistic ability is not important. What is important is that the learners use their imaginations to envision God's creation.

❖ Conclude this portion of the lesson by inviting volunteers to show their pictures and/or tell about the image that most captivated them and why this image resonated with them.

(3) Recognize and Affirm That All Nature Is Created by God

❖ Read these quotations from leading scientists concerning their views of creation. Invite the students to respond to these views. Some may express surprise that scientists would voice these perspectives.

■ *Alan Sandage (winner of the Crawford prize in astronomy):* "I find it quite improbable that such order came out of chaos. There has to be some organizing principle. God to me is a mystery but is the explanation for the miracle of existence, why there is something instead of nothing."

■ *John O'Keefe (astronomer at NASA):* "We are, by astronomical standards, a pampered, cosseted, cherished group of creatures. . . . If the Universe had not been made with the most exacting precision we could never have come into existence. It is my view that these circumstances indicate the universe was created for man to live in."

■ *Frank Tipler (professor of mathematical physics):* "When I began my career as a cosmologist some twenty years ago, I was a convinced atheist. I never in my wildest dreams imagined that one day I would be writing a book purporting to show that the central claims of Judeo-Christian theology are in fact true, that these claims are straightforward deductions of the laws of physics as we now understand them. I have been forced into these conclusions by the inexorable logic of my own special branch of physics."

■ *Arthur L. Schawlow (professor of physics at Stanford University, 1981 Nobel Prize in physics):* "It seems to me that when confronted with the marvels of life and the universe, one must ask why and not just how. The only possible answers are religious. . . . I find a need for God in the universe and in my own life."

❖ Discuss these questions.

(1) What do you believe about God's role in the creation of the universe? (Note that one can believe that God is the Creator without accepting the stories in Genesis 1 and 2 as the "scientific explanation" for the creation.)

(2) What can you affirm about God if you believe that God did create and is still creating the universe?

(4) Develop a Plan for Contributing to the Care of God's Creation

❖ Distribute paper and pencils. Ask the adults to look again at the pictures they drew earlier in the session. Suggest that they discern some way to care for the facet of creation that most captured their attention. For example, if they were intrigued by water images, encourage them to think about what they can do to keep water in their community pure. If they liked the image of the wind as messengers, consider how can they keep the air unpolluted.

❖ Invite the class members to copy the verse(s) from Psalm 104 that contain the images that attracted them. Then they are to complete this sentence on their paper: **To be a good steward of the** _____ (for example, water or air) **of God's creation, I will** _____.

(5) Continue the Journey

❖ Pray that the learners will give thanks for, and do their utmost to care for, all that God has created and entrusted to humanity to tend.

❖ Read aloud this preparation for next week's lesson. You may also want to post it on newsprint for the students to copy.

Prepare for next week's session, "Searched and Known by God," by reading Psalm 139. Note especially verses 1-3, 7-14, and 23-24. As you study, keep these ideas before you: People often forget how unique and amazing our bodies are. What is the source of these amazing bodies of ours? The psalmist celebrates God as the One who creates us in this wonderful, intricate form and who therefore knows us intimately.

❖ Read aloud the following three ideas. Challenge the students to commit themselves to use these activities as a springboard to spiritual growth.

   (1) Sing a praise song as part of your devotions each day this week.

   (2) Sketch, paint, or make a collage showing the beauty of God's world.

   (3) Plant a tree, shrub, or flowers, if possible in your climate. If you cannot plant something outdoors, consider adding an indoor plant to your home. Give thanks to God for this plant as you tend it.

❖ Sing or read aloud "O Worship the King."

❖ Lead this benediction to end today's session: **With all of your creatures, most majestic God, we sing your praises and pray that you would empower us to be wise people and faithful stewards of your creation, in Jesus' name. Amen.**

UNIT 1: THE GLORY OF GOD'S CREATION
Searched and Known by God

PREVIEWING THE LESSON

Lesson Scripture: Psalm 139:1-3, 7-14, 23-24
Background Scripture: Psalm 139
Key Verse: Psalm 139:14

Focus of the Lesson:
People often forget how unique and amazing our bodies are. What is the source of these amazing bodies of ours? The psalmist celebrates God as the One who creates us in this wonderful, intricate form and who therefore knows us intimately.

Goals for the Learners:
(1) to delve into this psalm, which celebrates God as the creator of our wonderfully designed human forms.
(2) to consider how they respond to the idea that God knows them intimately.
(3) to identify ways that they need to be better stewards of their own bodies and to make a commitment to act.

Pronunciation Guide:
imprecatory (im' pri ke tor e)
omnificence (am ni' fe sence)
omnipotence (am ni' pe tents)
omnipresence (am ni pre' zents)
omniscience (am ni' shents)
Sheol (shee' ohl)

Supplies:
Bibles, newsprint and marker, paper and pencils, hymnals

READING THE SCRIPTURE

NRSV
Psalm 139:1-3, 7-14, 23-24
¹O Lord, you have searched me and
   known me.

NIV
Psalm 139:1-3, 7-14, 23-24
¹O Lord, you have searched me
   and you know me.

2 You know when I sit down and when I
    rise up;
  you discern my thoughts from far away.
3 You search out my path and my lying
    down,
  and are acquainted with all my ways.
7 Where can I go from your spirit?
  Or where can I flee from your presence?
8 If I ascend to heaven, you are there;
  if I make my bed in Sheol, you are there.
9 If I take the wings of the morning
  and settle at the farthest limits of the
    sea,
10 even there your hand shall lead me,
  and your right hand shall hold me fast.
11 If I say, "Surely the darkness shall cover
    me,
  and the light around me become night,"
12 even the darkness is not dark to you;
  the night is as bright as the day,
  for darkness is as light to you.
13 For it was you who formed my inward
    parts;
  you knit me together in my mother's
    womb.
**14 I praise you, for I am fearfully and
    wonderfully made.
  Wonderful are your works;
that I know very well.**
23 Search me, O God, and know my heart;
  test me and know my thoughts.
24 See if there is any wicked way in me,
  and lead me in the way everlasting.

2You know when I sit and when I rise;
  you perceive my thoughts from afar.
3You discern my going out and my lying
    down;
  you are familiar with all my ways.
7Where can I go from your Spirit?
  Where can I flee from your presence?
8If I go up to the heavens, you are there;
  if I make my bed in the depths, you are
    there.
9If I rise on the wings of the dawn,
  if I settle on the far side of the sea,
10even there your hand will guide me,
  your right hand will hold me fast.
11If I say, "Surely the darkness will hide me
  and the light become night around me,"
12even the darkness will not be dark to you;
  the night will shine like the day,
  for darkness is as light to you.
13For you created my inmost being;
  you knit me together in my mother's
    womb.
**14I praise you because I am fearfully and
    wonderfully made;
  your works are wonderful,
I know that full well.**
23Search me, O God, and know my heart;
  test me and know my anxious thoughts.
24See if there is any offensive way in me,
  and lead me in the way everlasting.

UNDERSTANDING THE SCRIPTURE

Psalm 139:1-6. Psalm 139 ends as it begins, but as we compare beginning and ending, we may wonder if they are not in the wrong order. The psalmist begins by wondering at what God has already accomplished—"you have searched me and known me"—but ends by requesting that God do precisely that in the future: "search me . . . and know my thoughts." This curious order makes the psalm a powerful prayer to be prayed again and again, and probably derives from the original function of the psalm.

Although biblical scholars can only speculate about such things, those who try to locate socially the texts of Scripture within the life of the Israelite people suggest that this psalm may have played a role in a testing ritual (Numbers 5:16-22). Like Psalms 7, 17, and 26, this psalm may have provided a liturgy for a person pleading innocent to a charge of idolatry (the word translated "wicked" in verse 24 has more specific connotations of worshiping other gods). Similar psalms may engage in lengthy protestations of innocence (Psalm 26), but this psalm finds its sole confidence in the God who shall act as judge. The psalm invites the supplicating worshiper to take the measure of the God who will judge the matter (139:1-18) and allows the worshiper to stand on God's side against those who oppose God (139:19-22) and finally to make the plea, "Search me, O God."

So astonishing is the poetry in which that plea is voiced, however, that Psalm 139 soars above its original context to find new locations wherever people ponder their lives in the light of God. These new locations are by no means alien to the intent of the psalm: Scholars recognize in Psalm 139 many wisdom elements teaching people about the God who is utterly and relentlessly intertwined in their lives.

As the psalmist begins to contemplate what it means to say that God has "searched and known me," all the everyday events of the day come to mind: "I sit down. . . . I rise up" (139:2). The commonplace words we speak are known beforehand by God. God's searching might seem uncanny, might feel uncomfortable; we might sense an assault on our privacy or even ourselves, but fear does not intrude on the psalmist's reverie. Instead, we experience a calm but poignant companionship. God's help is everywhere available. The psalmist introduces an image of God's care: You "lay your hand upon me" (139:5). God's hand may have been the instrument of execution for Israelites fleeing slavery in Egypt (Exodus 9:3; 16:3), and God's hand may have been a threat to Job (Job 12:9), but for this psalmist God's hand reassures, encourages, sustains, vindicates, and guides. Contemplating God's hand, the psalmist bursts out with the exclamation, "Such knowledge is too wonderful!" (139:6).

Psalm 139:7-12. God's hand rests upon the psalmist wherever he goes. Even if the psalmist flees to Sheol, the land of the dead where by definition God is not (see Psalms 6:5; 30:3, 9; 88:3-6), definitions and logic crack before the steadfastness of God's guiding hand. The dazzling imagery of verse 9 invites worshipers to imagine catching the sun at the dawn—when it appears to be touching the earth—and cruising with the sun as it wakens dawn over the earth (in something of the same way that Greek mythology might have imagined riding in Apollo's bright chariot of the sun) and landing finally in the far countries to the west at "the farthest limits of the sea" (139:9). Imagine that span and distance from east to west, the psalmist sings, and "even there your hand shall lead me" (139:10). The brightness of the morning and the darkness of night show only the faithfulness of God.

Psalm 139:13-18. From the darkness of night the psalmist turns attention to the darkness of the womb. There, in the most secret and mysterious place, God's hand also may be found weaving together bone and muscle, weaving weft and warp of veins and arteries and nerves to fashion a physical human body. The English translation "knit" attempts to speak of this, and just as women do most of the knitting in our time, so also women did most of the weaving in ancient Israel. That people could be spoken of as "woven in the depths of the earth" (139:15) echoes Genesis 2. No sooner has the psalmist invited us to imagine God as a woman weaving than another image appears: God as a scribe. God's hand holds a stylus and records in wet clay tablets the chronicle of the psalmist's days. No matter that these days have not yet dawned, God writes of them, because each day will be lived within God's knowledge and each day God's hand will hold, keep, and guide.

Psalm 139:19-24. That such utterly sublime praise should be interrupted by harrowing hostility may shock us, but it is typical of the Psalms. Verses 19-24 are the sort of lament that we might anticipate preceding verses 1-18, but this psalmist is determined to sing a song of praise. These verses seem less directed toward actual persecutors (compare to Psalm 140) and more of an acknowledgment that not everyone wishes to praise God, that God has enemies also, and that this worshiper takes a stand with God. In Luke 10:1-12, Jesus sends out his disciples as emissaries with power to bless—"say 'Peace to this house!'"—and the message of the gospel—"the kingdom of God has come near"—with the clear understanding that not everyone will wish to receive their blessing or the good news of the kingdom. Israel's Wisdom literature consistently differentiates between wisdom and foolishness. These imprecatory verses, which would usually invoke evil on an enemy, are less like a curse than a confession of faith: The psalmist takes a stand with God and the wisdom of God and against all that opposes God for evil.

In these final verses we finally reach the one petition of Psalm 139, "Search me, O God . . . test me" (139:23), which now pleads that God reveal and purge anything within the supplicant that does not belong to God. The psalmist cannot do this alone. Only God possesses the knowledge and power and love and justice required to accomplish such soul searching.

INTERPRETING THE SCRIPTURE

Bone Deep Theology

Classical Christian theology has spoken of God's omniscience, omnipresence, omnipotence, and omnificence. God is *omniscient* in that God *knows* all things. God is *omnipresent* in that God is not located in a single place but in all places and everywhere. Likewise, God's *omnipotence* declares that God is acting and powerful in all places and things. These assertions can be made because God is *omnificent*, the creator and fashioner of all things. These Latinate words with several syllables each provide a useful and accurate vocabulary for understanding God and speaking of God. The singer of Psalm 139 would doubtless agree with the claims for God made by these words. Yet, this singer speaks of God not in abstract theological terms but rather in the concrete, lived experience of human life. The psalmist explicates faith not from the top of his head, but from bone and muscle and organs knowing God who knows them intimately. The psalm begins not with airy philosophical musings about omniscience, but with the experience of being completely and utterly *known*.

To be known so intimately and so entirely can be an unsettling experience. Children coming to terms with God's omniscience and omnipresence often ask, "Can God see me naked?" They thought they had some privacy in the shower, just as adults sometimes naively assume there is some place in their lives that God does not know and where God is not seeking to work. God knows us in our nakedness: the innocence of our nakedness as well as the vulnerability of our nakedness in the physician's examining room, our naked need, and our naked aloneness. We cloak ourselves in so many different outfits that we may lose ourselves and forget who we are in the many roles we must play in a complicated society, but although we forget God remembers and God knows. So unsettling may this experience be that we can resonate with the psalmist's cry "Where can I flee from your presence?" (139:7). The answer, of course, is nowhere. Wherever we turn God is there. The news is at once terrifying and reassuring: God does not surrender us up to our self-deceptions, and we are freed to pray, "Search me, O God, and know my heart" (139:23). Although we may not know our own hearts, God knows and may be trusted.

Bodily Theology

No less than our hearts, God knows our physical form, our human anatomy. The psalmist exults that God has "knit" the human form together so that we are "fearfully and wonderfully made" (139:14). Fear and wonder are appropriate to contemplating our physical human existence before the Lord who made us. We fear because we know nothing in this creation requires our being here. Our human life is a gift we never asked for. One day we will no longer be alive, but for the time being here we are and what a marvel it is that our bodies work the way they do! We may take these intricate operations of our body for granted until something goes wrong, but illness and aging finally cause us to marvel that bodies work at all.

Although Psalm 139 is attributed to David, many biblical scholars would recognize that simply as an attribution and declare the psalm anonymous. If we cannot know for certain who wrote this psalm celebrating our "fearfully and wonderfully made" bodies we may be quite certain the author was neither a model for Ralph Lauren men's wear nor one of the lovelies out of the *Sports Illustrated* swimsuit issue. The body that is "fearfully and wonderfully made" is the ordinary body that is also aging, balding, sagging, graying, sometimes limping, sometimes aching, sometimes broken, sometimes desperately ill, and almost always in need of healing of one sort of another. That ordinary body provides the occasion of praise: "I will praise you because I am fearfully and wonderfully made" (139:14).

Hospitalized and enduring a horrendous series of surgeries a parishioner shyly asked, "Would it be okay for me to pray for a bowel movement?" This person was unsure. Is it permissible to approach the High and Holy One with a matter as ordinary and even profane as defecation? The answer, of course, is that the Omnificent One who knitted together human bodies with consummate skill is also the Omniscient One who knows our need even before we ask and is also the Omni-compassionate One who deigns to hear every prayer. On better days we may not think at all about the exquisite operations of our bodies. Signs placed miles before tunnels may warn drivers to turn aside and take another route if they are carrying HAZ-MATS (hazardous materials), but every day the tunnels in our bodies carry hazardous materials through us without our ever thinking about it. More marvelous and vastly more complicated than the computers that throw letters and words upon a screen is the one whose mind signals the touching of the keys. The mechanics of the machine are simple compared with the dazzling complexities to be found in the mind of one who contemplates them.

"Search Me, O God"

We are complicated creatures, and if we are capable of dazzling achievements of human thought and insight, we know we are also capable of astonishing self-deception. The wisdom tradition of Israel understood how enslavement to self could lead to foolishness. "There is a way that seems right to a person," says Proverbs 14:12, "but its end is the way to death" (NRSV; NIV: "in the end it leads to death"). We think we know what is wise, what is good, what is healthy, what is true, but our clamoring self obscures our vision. Encased in our bodies, we are creatures of a single location. Our social location in a complex society causes us to see things in a particular way. The experiences we have had or not had have taught us how to regard other persons. The politics of gender that press upon us remind us that women and men really do see things differently. As North American Christians engage in conversations with African Christians we discover how different our perceptions are regarding poverty, medicine, mission, and the life of the church of Jesus Christ. Because our knowing is inevitably limited by our time, our age, our social location, our experiences, our physical well-being, the psalmist cries out: "Search me, O God, and know my heart" (139:23). The psalmist's knowledge, even of himself, is limited, but he trusts God, who is able to know intimately, completely, and perfectly.

Psalm 139 refuses to be content with self-righteousness. The one who prays it has endured serious self-examination but does not rest content with self-examination. Knowing the human capacity for self-deception and self-righteousness, the psalmist pleads for God's superior knowledge, for God's truth, and for God's righteousness. The posture is that of the wise person who can accept correction (Proverbs 3:11, 5:12; 13:18). The wise person is the one who is so filled with knowledge as to know the limits of knowledge and to know also the unlimited knowledge of God and to seek it. This psalm's knowledge of God leads us to wonder and a place where God can teach us. We do not have to know everything because we know One who does know everything and everyone in utter intimacy and in complete compassion.

SHARING THE SCRIPTURE

Preparing Our Hearts

This week's devotional reading is found in Psalm 100. This beloved song calls "all the earth" to praise God. Verse 3 reminds us that we belong to God, for God is our Maker. How does the knowledge that God has made you influence how you care for your body—or does it? What changes might you need to make in how you care for your body?

Pray that you and your class participants will give thanks to God, who created and sustains you.

Preparing Our Minds

Study the background Scripture, which includes all of Psalm 139, and lesson Scripture, which focuses on verses 1-3, 7-14, 23-24. As you contemplate this psalm, consider the unique creation that is your body, and the Creator God who knows you intimately.

Write on newsprint:

❑ information for next week's lesson, found under "Continue the Journey."

LEADING THE CLASS

(1) Gather to Learn

❖ Welcome the class members and introduce any guests.

❖ Pray that the learners will be open to knowing God more intimately, even as God the Creator knows each one of them so completely.

❖ Read aloud these fun facts about the human body to help the students get a sense of how amazing our bodies are. Invite the class to comment on any they choose.

(1) **An average human scalp has 100,000 hairs. We lose an average of 40 to 100 strands of hair each day.**

(2) **Humans shed about 600,000 particles of skin every hour—about 1.5 pounds a year. By age 70 an average person will have lost 105 pounds of skin.**

(3) **It takes 17 muscles to smile and 43 to frown.**

(4) **There is enough phosphorous inside the human body to make about 250 match heads.**

(5) **Humans are born with 300 bones. Adults have 206 bones. There are 29 different bones in your head.**

(6) **Human thighbones are stronger than concrete.**

(7) **During a 24-hour period, the average human will breathe 23,040 times.**

(8) **Every time you lick a stamp you are consuming one tenth of a calorie.**

(9) **By the time you turn 70, your heart will have beat some two and a half billion times (based on an average of 70 beats per minute).**

(10) **Human blood travels 60,000 miles (96,540 kilometers) per day on its journey through the body.**

❖ Read aloud today's focus statement: **People often forget how unique and amazing our bodies are. What is the source of these amazing bodies of ours? The psalmist celebrates God as the One who creates us in this wonderful, intricate form and who therefore knows us intimately.**

(2) Delve into This Psalm, Which Celebrates God as the Creator of Our Wonderfully Designed Human Forms

❖ Choose a volunteer to read Psalm 139: 1-3, 7-14, 23-24. Or, if you have access to a Psalter in your hymnal, divide the class in half and read the entire psalm responsively.

❖ Note that the text can be divided this way:

■ 139:1-6　　　God intimately knows each of us.

■ 139:7-12　　　God's presence is inescapable.

■ 139:13-18　　God as the Creator of each person.

■ 139:19-24　　implications of God's knowledge of us and constant presence with us.

❖ Explore what each of the verses in today's Scripture lesson indicates about God and God's relationship with humanity.

❖ Invite the students to agree with, modify, or disagree with the psalmist's views of God and God's relationship to humanity. Probe the reasons for their statements.

❖ **Option:** Look particularly at verses 13-14 (or extend to verse 18). This text certainly affirms the sanctity of life, even in the womb. Since each person is such a unique creation, all of life deserves to be sanctified. Talk with the class about "sanctity of life" issues, which include: abortion, stem cell research, euthanasia, death penalty, murder, war, poverty that deprives people of life's basic necessities, and other ideas the class may raise. If the students take seriously the psalmist's beliefs about God's intimate relationship with and plan for each person, what does that suggest about the positions they are likely to take on these issues? How do we deal with the psalmist's views three thousand years later in the midst of a vastly different culture?

(3) Consider the Learners' Response to the Idea That God Knows Them Intimately

❖ Ask the students to look in their own Bibles and count the number of times some form of the word *know* is used. Results may vary, depending on the translation, but the idea is to make the adults aware of this important theme.

❖ Discuss these questions.

(1) **Most Christians are seeking a close personal relationship with God through Jesus Christ. Why, then, would people want to flee from God (139:7)?**

(2) Does the knowledge that God is always intimately present with you frighten you? If so, why?

(3) How does this knowledge of God's constant presence comfort you?

(4) Identify Ways That the Learners Need to Be Better Stewards of Their Own Bodies and Make a Commitment to Act

❖ Read or retell portions of "Bodily Theology" in "Interpreting the Scripture," as time permits.

❖ Provide a brief opportunity for volunteers to tell stories of how an illness or accident assaulted their body and how their body was able to heal.

❖ Distribute paper and pencils. Ask the students to list in one column ways that they care for their bodies properly, and in another column ways in which they do not care for their bodies as good stewards. For example, do they overeat or eat the wrong foods? Are they couch potatoes? (Note that even elderly nursing home residents benefit from exercise.) Do they smoke or abuse drugs, even ones that have been prescribed? Assure the students that their lists are to be kept confidential, for their eyes only.

❖ Challenge the students to review their lists and select one problem that they will try to overcome. Ask them to write on their papers what they will try to do, when they will do it, who they will tell about this decision, and what kind of support they will need.

(5) Continue the Journey

❖ Pray that the adults will be better stewards of the bodies that God has so "fearfully and wonderfully made" for them.

Also pray that the participants will open their hearts and minds to ask God to search and know them.

❖ Read aloud this preparation for next week's lesson. You may also want to post it on newsprint for the students to copy. **Prepare for next week's session, "Worthy of Praise," by reading Psalm 145. Our time together will focus on verses 1-13. Ponder these ideas as you study: People like to praise that which is worthy of praise. Why should we praise God? The psalmist says that God is great, abundantly good, gracious, merciful, abounding in love, almighty, and everlasting in power.**

❖ Read aloud the following three ideas. Challenge the students to commit themselves to use these activities as a springboard to spiritual growth.

(1) Attend a health fair or visit your physician if you have not had a routine check-up recently. Follow through on advice regarding tests or treatments that you need to keep your body operating effectively.

(2) Give thanks each day for your body and its amazing ability to function and heal.

(3) Spend time asking God to search you, know you, and reveal to you anything you need to know in order to live more faithfully.

❖ Sing or read aloud "All People That on Earth Do Dwell."

❖ Lead this benediction to end today's session: **With all of your creatures, most majestic God, we sing your praises and pray that you would empower us to be wise people and faithful stewards of your creation, in Jesus' name. Amen.**

UNIT 1: THE GLORY OF GOD'S CREATION
WORTHY OF PRAISE

PREVIEWING THE LESSON

Lesson Scripture: Psalm 145:1-13
Background Scripture: Psalm 145
Key Verse: Psalm 145:8

Focus of the Lesson:
People like to praise that which is worthy of praise. Why should we praise God? The psalmist says that God is great, abundantly good, gracious, merciful, abounding in love, almighty, and everlasting in power.

Goals for the Learners:
(1) to examine the reasons the psalmist gives for praising God.
(2) to identify their own reasons for praising God.
(3) to offer personal praise to God.

Pronunciation Guide:
aleph (ah lehf)
beth (beht)
gimel (ghee mehl)

Supplies:
Bibles, newsprint and marker, paper and pencils, hymnals; optional: praise music on CD or tape and appropriate player

---

READING THE SCRIPTURE

NRSV

Psalm 145:1-13

1 I will extol you, my God and King,
    and bless your name forever and ever.
2 Every day I will bless you,
    and praise your name forever and ever.
3 Great is the LORD, and greatly to be
        praised;
    his greatness is unsearchable.

NIV

Psalm 145:1-13

1I will exalt you, my God the King;
    I will praise your name for ever and ever.
2Every day I will praise you
    and extol your name for ever and ever.
3Great is the LORD and most worthy of
        praise;
    his greatness no one can fathom.

4 One generation shall laud your works to
      another,
   and shall declare your mighty acts.
5 On the glorious splendor of your majesty,
      and on your wondrous works, I will
      meditate.
6 The might of your awesome deeds shall
      be proclaimed,
   and I will declare your greatness.
7 They shall celebrate the fame of your
      abundant goodness,
   and shall sing aloud of your
      righteousness.
8 The LORD is gracious and merciful,
   slow to anger and abounding in
      steadfast love.
9 The LORD is good to all,
   and his compassion is over all that he
      has made.
10 All your works shall give thanks to you,
      O LORD,
   and all your faithful shall bless you.
11 They shall speak of the glory of your
      kingdom,
   and tell of your power,
12 to make known to all people your mighty
      deeds,
   and the glorious splendor of your
      kingdom.
13 Your kingdom is an everlasting kingdom,
      and your dominion endures throughout
      all generations.
   The LORD is faithful in all his words,
      and gracious in all his deeds.

4One generation will commend your works
      to another;
   they will tell of your mighty acts.
5They will speak of the glorious splendor of
      your majesty,
   and I will meditate on your wonderful
      works.
6They will tell of the power of your awesome
      works,
   and I will proclaim your great deeds.
7They will celebrate your abundant
      goodness
   and joyfully sing of your righteousness.
8The LORD is gracious and compassionate,
   slow to anger and rich in love.
9The LORD is good to all;
   he has compassion on all he has made.
10All you have made will praise you,
      O LORD;
   your saints will extol you.
11They will tell of the glory of your kingdom
   and speak of your might,
12so that all men may know of your mighty
      acts
   and the glorious splendor of your
      kingdom.
13Your kingdom is an everlasting kingdom,
   and your dominion endures through all
      generations.
   The LORD is faithful to all his promises
   and loving toward all he has made.

UNDERSTANDING THE SCRIPTURE

Introduction. The English translation conceals the most obvious feature of Psalm 145: This song is an alphabet of praise. Like Psalms 9 and 10 (together), 25, 34, 37, 111, 112, and 119, each verse begins with a letter of the Hebrew alphabet and each succeeding verse begins with the next letter of the alphabet. (The verse corresponding to the Hebrew letter *nun*—beginning in verse 13, "The Lord is faithful"—was lost in the best Hebrew manuscripts, and this reading reflects translations from Greek and Syriac translations of the Psalms.) Translators have had to choose between a faithful translation of the structure of the psalm and a faithful translation of the words of the psalm, and they have chosen the latter. Attempting a rough translation of the form, one might come up with something like:

Aleph: Alleluia! I will extol you, my God and King . . .

Beth: Blessing your name every day . . .

Gimel: Great is the Lord and greatly to be praised . . .

That the psalmist should choose such a simple and elementary form to communicate praise already articulates theological convictions about the reliable order of the world our God has fashioned for us. God is trustworthy, and the world is arranged in a way that the appropriate ways of living in it and responding to God are part of that order and can be taught in the psalmist's song.

Psalm 145:1-13a. In the first three verses the psalmist begins by praising and addressing God as a ruling monarch beyond all comparison and comprehension. Given such a vision of God, what can one do but "bless" and "praise" not only today but "forever and ever," never falling silent but joining in the procession of generations (145:4) that rises up to glorify and enjoy God's goodness to them. Although this is a hymn of praise from an individual ("I will extol/exalt"), this individual's praise is accompanied by an astonishing chorus sung by all the things God has made as well as a choir of human creatures who know fittingly how to respond to God (145:10). They offer praise for God's gracious and orderly rule that is again imagined in monarchial terms as a "kingdom." Note the repetitions of "king" and "kingdom" in verses 11, 12, and 13a. In verse 13, readers of Psalm 145 can scarcely keep from remembering God's promise to David of an everlasting kingdom (2 Samuel 7:12-16) and anticipating the New Testament's vision of Christ ruling for all time (Revelation 11:15-17).

The reason for the psalm's extravagant praise is revealed in verse 8, a verse echoing from the voice of Mount Sinai. As God renews the covenant with Israel, Moses fashions new tablets of stone to replace those he shattered previously, God reveals the divine name, "the LORD," and God announces this ineffable truth to Moses, and through Moses to the people (Exodus 34:4-7). This message of God's grace, mercy, and steadfast love is the oldest and most central theological affirmation of Hebrew Scriptures. Only after the character of God has been revealed does God give the replacement tablets of the commandments to the people. Without the grace, mercy, and compassion of God, the law is bad news and unbearable. Some people, like the prophet Jonah (Jonah 4:2), chafe under such an extravagance of grace, mercy, and compassion, but Psalm 145 sings rapturously of the character of God.

Psalm 145:13b-20. As the first section of the psalm largely occupies itself with rich description of all the creation praising God (145:1-7, 10-13a), the second portion of Psalm 145 focuses attention on describing the enactment of God's grace, mercy, and steadfast love (145:13b-20). As in Psalm 104:27-28, God's hands open to sustain the life of all the creation, "every living thing" (145:16). As the rule of an earthly king provides prosperity to the citizens, so God's wise rule over the creation grants plenty to all creatures.

God's particular attention to those who fall and those who "are bowed down" begins a series of descriptions of God's care that continues on into Psalm 146, where God is particularly the Lord of those who have no earthly help: the hungry, the prisoners, the blind, the strangers, the orphan and the widow, precisely those who cry out in 145:19 for God's help. These need God's assistance because there are others who do not praise God, who do not fear and respect God's design, and therefore verse 20 recognizes that the wicked will be destroyed by the enactment of God's grace, mercy, and steadfast love. Although the destruction of verse 20 may startle us, we have heard of this before: Mary singing of God toppling thrones and lifting up the lowly, filling the hungry with good things and sending the sated away hungry. When Jesus begins his ministry in the Gospel of Mark, he begins by preaching and teaching about the kingdom—about the reign of God's grace, mercy, and steadfast love—and demons immediately recognize the threat to their power: "have you come to destroy us?" (Mark 1:21-28).

Psalm 145:21. Envisioning God's performance of grace, mercy, and steadfast love that will at once rescue the needy and destroy their oppressors, the psalmist takes a stand and sings a confession of faith:

However others may decide, I will praise the Lord, indeed all flesh and all creatures, all the voices God has made will praise God's name not only now but everlastingly.

In English we may miss the fun of the Hebrew acrostic, but that doesn't mean we can't hum along with the tune. We can at least start. In Psalm 145, A is for *all*. *All* is the big word for Psalm 145. In twenty-one verses, the psalmist uses the word *all* nineteen times. All the creation praises God and so may we. Our praise, like all else in this creation, is the gift of a generous and gracious God.

INTERPRETING THE SCRIPTURE

Worship Is as Natural as Breathing

Week after week we worship. Is worship something we learn? Is worship something we are taught?

Listening to Psalm 145, it would seem that nothing is more natural than praise. If worship does not rise up within us spontaneously, as naturally as breath, as fundamental as a heartbeat, then worship is something we easily catch from others, so contagious is worship. Psalm 145 is a hymn of praise for an individual to sing, but this individual is by no means alone. It is a bit like walking into worship and being swept up into it. The worshiper begins in verse 1, "I will extol you, my God and King," and soon recognizes that the song has been sung from generation to generation, a song received from parents and a song to be passed to children. Encountering this God and King, the worshiper soon recognizes that the whole creation is singing a hymn of praise: "All your works shall give thanks to you, O LORD, and all your faithful shall bless you" (145:10). When we hear the chorus the whole creation sings, when we recognize that everything God has made sings in

praise, we cannot help being caught up in song and worship.

Is anything more natural than worship? Is anything more natural than praise?

And Idolatry Is as Natural as Worship

If worship is natural, so is idolatry. We take that which is made by God and serve it instead of God. We take God's creation and treat it as if it were our creation. We take the good gifts of God and misuse them, misplace them, misappropriate them. If the song of praise has been going on from the very beginning, so also has idolatry. You remember that episode with the golden calf? Aaron explained it: "They gave [their gold] to me, and I threw it into the fire, and out came this calf" (Exodus 32:24). What could be more natural?

Gold is God's good gift; but we can turn it into an idol and worship it. We don't make idols out of bad things; we're not that kind of people. The essence of idolatry is taking what is good and making it God. We take what is good and misuse it and misplace it. God gives us the good gift of food—"you give them their food in due season," sings Psalm 145:15, but we overeat, eat the wrong things, and we become ill. Psalm 104:15 sings that God gives us "wine to gladden the human heart." What is wine for? To gladden our hearts—but few have not known the sadness and heartbreak of a family member who misused the good gift of wine and strong drink. God gives us the gift of sexuality to cement loving relationships, and misplacing this good gift, we betray loving relationships. God gives us the good gift of worship, and we make worship a venue for our entertainment. We measure worship not by our giving of ourselves to God, but by asking, "what did I get out of it?"

We Learn How to Worship God

Nothing is more natural than worship. Nothing is more natural than idolatry. Therefore Psalm 145 methodically teaches us how to worship God, how to focus praise and worship and attention and love on the One with whom we have to do.

The psalm is an A-B-C of praise. This is the way we learn to worship. This is the way we learned language in the beginning with the little alphabet books of our childhood: A is for apple, B is for ball, C is for cat. One letter follows another, one step proceeds to the next. The psalm orients us to a way of life lived in the presence of God. In the early 1980s a lot of people were moving to Texas and some enterprising writer produced a book to orient foreigners to their new home: A is for armadillo; B is for barbecue; C is for cowboy. Step by step, we learn to make our way in an unfamiliar world.

Just so, Psalm 145 orients us to a life of worship. It calls our attention directly to God, who is like no other: "Great is the LORD, and greatly to be praised; his greatness is unsearchable" (145:3). That is the One we praise: great beyond comparison, beyond our estimation, beyond our searching.

Worship has to do with God. That's a startling thing to say when so much of what passes for worship is about us. Worship is not about our amusement, our entertainment. Worship has to do with God. Worship is the encounter of the created with the Creator. Psalm 145 makes clear the distinction between God and what God has made in order to avoid that mistaking of the "creature" for the "Creator" that gives birth to idolatry (see Romans 1:25). "All your works shall give thanks to you, O LORD" (145:10).

Praising God at "All" Times

All is the key word for Psalm 145 because we can be distracted from our praise not only by the temptations of idolatry, but also by hardships we endure. This psalm understands frankly that *all* includes the hard things of life. *All* contains our disappointment and heartbreak, our disillusionment and despair; *all* encloses sickness and loss, disorientation and death.

Worship is not a natural inclination at times like those. We wonder how to praise in the darkness. There are days when we cannot draw spit to pray, times when we don't know what we believe or if we believe anything at all. The psalm teaches us, step-by-step, letter-by-letter to worship nonetheless. When you cannot pray, come to surround yourself with people praying with you and for you. When you cannot say the creed, come to worship and let us say the creed for you. When you aren't sure who you are and what you believe, the worshiping community remembers: You are a child of God, baptized into Christ.

All of the darkness of our lives we bring to God in our worship because the psalm reminds us, "The LORD is near to all who call" in their need (145:18); "The LORD upholds all who are falling" (145:14) and "hears their cry, and saves them" (145:19). Psalm 145 is bold to say that because the psalmist knows and teaches the real God, not a god of our own making, not a god fashioned in the image of our wants or even our needs.

"The LORD is gracious and merciful, slow to anger and abounding in steadfast love" (145:8, today's key verse). That is the God our idolatries cannot imagine; that is the God we cannot fashion for ourselves. That is the God our Scriptures proclaim, and that is the God we gather to worship. That is the God whom Psalm 145 teaches us about as we worship, for we are always learning the ways of this God who is "gracious and merciful, slow to anger and abounding in steadfast love." As we worship we learn to worship, and we pray continually that we might also be fashioned into a people who are "gracious and merciful, slow to anger and abounding in steadfast love."

SHARING THE SCRIPTURE

Preparing Our Hearts

This week's devotional reading is found in Psalm 150, a hymn calling "everything that breathes" (150:6) to praise God. The psalmist explains how to praise, summoning an entire orchestra to resound because of God's "mighty deeds" and "surpassing greatness" (150:2). Notice that the psalmist does not ask for anything, but simply gives praise to God. Spend time right now praising, not for what God has done, but rather, for who God is. Write a psalm, sing a hymn of praise, or move to music, perhaps with arms stretched upward.

Pray that you and your class participants will give glory to God, the Creator who is worthy of our praise.

Preparing Our Minds

Study the background Scriptures from Psalm 145 and the lesson Scripture, verses 1-13. As you delve into this text think of reasons why you want to praise God.

Write on newsprint:

❑ information for next week's lesson, found under "Continue the Journey."

Plan a brief lecture as suggested under "Examine the Reasons the Psalmist Gives for Praising God." Note that in this same section there is an optional lecture for you to consider.

LEADING THE CLASS

(1) Gather to Learn

❖ Welcome the class members and introduce any guests.

❖ Pray that all who have come today will experience the presence of the God who is to be praised.

❖ Go around the room asking each person to state one praiseworthy event that occurred this past week. These may be "secular" events, such as a favorite team winning a game, a child earning good grades, an inspiring performance by the local symphony, or the community banding together to help neighbors in need. If the class is large, divide into groups so that everyone may participate. Some students may wish to say "pass" if they have no ideas to add.

❖ Read aloud today's focus statement: **People like to praise that which is worthy of praise. Why should we praise God? The psalmist says that God is great, abundantly good, gracious, merciful, abounding in love, almighty, and everlasting in power.**

(2) Examine the Reasons the Psalmist Gives for Praising God

❖ Introduce Psalm 145 by creating a brief lecture from the Introduction in Understanding the Scripture to explain the acrostic structure of this psalm. If you have access to the *New Jerusalem Bible*, you will be able to see all the Hebrew letters shown at the beginning of each verse.

❖ Ask students to each read one verse of Psalm 145:1-13. Be sure to choose volunteers, because some adults are uncomfortable about reading even one verse aloud. Some students may need to read more than one verse.

❖ Look with the class line by line at these thirteen verses. List all of the action words (verbs) on newsprint. These verbs will vary with the translations used by the students, and some words are used more than once, but here are verbs from the NRSV: *extol, bless, praise, laud, declare, meditate, proclaimed, celebrate, sing, give thanks, speak, tell, make known, endures.* Invite the students to comment on the mood the psalmist creates by using these verbs. Ask the students to consider whether they would want to join the psalmist in praise, based on these words.

❖ Point out that Psalm 145 is a psalm of worship and praise. Read aloud the last two paragraphs of "We Learn How to Worship God" in the Interpreting the Scripture portion. Ask these questions:

(1) **How do you define authentic worship?**

(2) **Compare your view of authentic worship with these statements from "And Idolatry Is as Natural as Worship": "God gives us the good gift of worship, and we make worship a venue for our entertainment. We measure worship not by our giving of our selves to God, but by asking, 'what did I get out of it?'" How is your view similar to or different from this one?**

❖ Look at Psalm 145:8, today's key verse. Divide into groups and assign to each group one or more of the following passages, all of which are similar to verse 8. Ask the students to determine the context in which this description was used and what this passage suggests about the nature of God. Provide time for each group to report to the class. If you prefer, present this information as a lecture.

■ Exodus 34:6
■ Numbers 14:18
■ Nehemiah 9:17
■ Psalm 86:15
■ Psalm 103:8
■ Joel 2:13
■ Jonah 4:2

❖ Conclude this portion of the lesson by inviting the students to comment on why the nature of God prompts people to (or discourages them from) praising God.

(3) Identify the Learners' Reasons for Praising God

❖ Distribute paper and pencils. Ask the students to list every reason they can think of for praising God. Limit their work time to two minutes. If you brought a CD or tape of praise music, play it softly as background music while the learners work.

❖ Challenge the students to make another list, this time including only reasons related to God's own Self, rather than related to actions that God may have taken on behalf of the adults. Again, play praise music in the background.

❖ Invite volunteers to state any items from either list.

❖ Solicit ideas from the class concerning these points:

■ why we sometimes feel reluctant to praise God in public, even in a church setting;

■ how praise can become contagious, such that when one person starts to praise others join in; and

■ why praise is a natural part of worship. (See "Worship Is as Natural as Breathing" in Interpreting the Scripture for ideas.)

(4) Offer Personal Praise to God

❖ Ask each student to choose a partner and have each one lift a word of praise to God for an item from the list they made in the previous section.

❖ Invite them to repeat this activity with another partner, choosing another word of praise. If your group is small enough, participants may want to mill around so that most of them have an opportunity to offer a word of praise to all the other students in the class.

❖ End this activity with a clap offering to God. Omit this activity if the sound of applause would disturb other groups.

(5) Continue the Journey

❖ Pray that the learners will continually lift praise to God.

❖ Read aloud this preparation for next week's lesson. You may also want to post it on newsprint for the students to copy. **Prepare for next week's session, "Living with Tragedy," by reading chapters 1, 2, and 3 of Job. Our session will focus on Job 1:14-15, 18-19, 22, and 3:1-3, 11. As you explore these passages, keep these thoughts in mind: When tragedy occurs, some people conclude that it would be better to die than to live. What can help us survive tragedy when it comes to us? These passages from Job imply that the** desire to end pain is a basic human reaction, yet death is not really the answer. Set in the larger context of the book as a whole, we see that God can overcome our pain and grief, eventually leading us to rejoice again in life.

❖ Read aloud the following three ideas. Challenge the students to commit themselves to use these activities as a springboard to spiritual growth.

(1) **Offer daily praise to God this week. Praise may be spoken, sung, danced, drawn, written, or offered through another medium of your choice.**

(2) **Attend a prayer and praise service if one is available at your church or a nearby congregation.**

(3) **Meditate on God's nature as described in Psalm 145:8-9. While humans can in no way mirror the perfection of God, try this week to be gracious, merciful, slow to anger, loving, and compassionate to all.**

❖ Sing or read aloud "All Creatures of Our God and King."

❖ Lead this benediction to end today's session: **With all of your creatures, most majestic God, we sing your praises and pray that you would empower us to be wise people and faithful stewards of your creation, in Jesus' name. Amen.**

UNIT 2: LIVING WITH CREATION'S UNCERTAINTY
LIVING WITH TRAGEDY

PREVIEWING THE LESSON

Lesson Scripture: Job 1:14-15, 18-19, 22; 2:10; 3:1-3, 11
Background Scripture: Job 1–3
Key Verse: Job 2:10

Focus of the Lesson:
When tragedy occurs, some people conclude that it would be better to die than to live. What can help us survive tragedy when it comes to us? These passages from Job imply that the desire to end pain is a basic human reaction, yet death is not really the answer. Set in the larger context of the book as a whole, we see that God can overcome our pain and grief, eventually leading us to rejoice again in life.

Goals for the Learners:
(1) to encounter the story of how Job remained blameless and upright as he suffered tragedy, pain, and grief.
(2) to confront the problem of suffering in their own lives.
(3) to affirm that God's goodness endures, despite tragedies.

Pronunciation Guide:
Chaldean (kal dee' uhn)
Chebar (kee' bahr)
Edomite (ee' duh mite)
Sabean (suh bee' uhn)
satan (saw tawn')

Supplies:
Bibles, newsprint and marker, paper and pencils, hymnals

READING THE SCRIPTURE

NRSV
Job 1:14-15, 18-19, 22

¹⁴[A] messenger came to Job and said, "The oxen were plowing and the donkeys were feeding beside them, ¹⁵and the Sabeans fell on them and carried them off, and killed

NIV
Job 1:14-15, 18-19, 22

¹⁴[A] messenger came to Job and said, "The oxen were plowing and the donkeys were grazing nearby, ¹⁵and the Sabeans attacked and carried them off. They put the

the servants with the edge of the sword; I alone have escaped to tell you.". . . [18]While he was still speaking, another came and said, "Your sons and daughters were eating and drinking wine in their eldest brother's house, [19]and suddenly a great wind came across the desert, struck the four corners of the house, and it fell on the young people, and they are dead; I alone have escaped to tell you."

[22]In all this Job did not sin or charge God with wrongdoing.

Job 2:10

[10]**But he said to her [his wife], "You speak as any foolish woman would speak. Shall we receive the good at the hand of God, and not receive the bad?" In all this Job did not sin with his lips.**

Job 3:1-3, 11

[1]After this Job opened his mouth and cursed the day of his birth. [2]Job said:
[3] "Let the day perish in which I was born, and the night that said,
'A man-child is conceived.'
[11] "Why did I not die at birth, come forth from the womb and expire?"

servants to the sword, and I am the only one who has escaped to tell you!"

[18]While he was still speaking, yet another messenger came and said, "Your sons and daughters were feasting and drinking wine at the oldest brother's house, [19]when suddenly a mighty wind swept in from the desert and struck the four corners of the house. It collapsed on them and they are dead, and I am the only one who has escaped to tell you!"

[22]In all this, Job did not sin by charging God with wrongdoing.

Job 2:10

[10]**He replied [to his wife], "You are talking like a foolish woman. Shall we accept good from God, and not trouble?"**

In all this, Job did not sin in what he said.

Job 3:1-3, 11

[1]After this, Job opened his mouth and cursed the day of his birth. [2]He said:
[3]"May the day of my birth perish, and the night it was said, 'A boy is born!'
[11]"Why did I not perish at birth, and die as I came from the womb?"

UNDERSTANDING THE SCRIPTURE

Introduction. "Understanding" is too confident a word to apply to our reading of the book of Job. Biblical scholars approach Job respectfully, knowing they will never master this book. "Understanding" lacks the humility and sense of wonder that Job finally demonstrates at the conclusion of his story. Let us speak instead of "encountering" Job to discover what will become of us in this encounter.

Job 1:1-5. Job is introduced immediately as a man "blameless and upright, one who feared God and turned away from evil" (1:1). To encounter Job and his story we must trust the narrator's characterization.

Not only is Job "blameless and upright," he is fortunate in his family of "seven sons and three daughters" and he is fabulously wealthy (1:3). The storyteller does not suggest any causal connection between Job's piety and his wealth, but rather that connection is frequently made in the Scriptures (see, for example, Deuteronomy 6:3) and assumed particularly in Wisdom literature: God curses the wicked and blesses the righteous (Proverbs 3:33). The only cloud in Job's sky is a fretful worry that his children may "have sinned and cursed God in their hearts" (1:5).

The conventional translation "cursed"

obscures an artful ambiguity in the Hebrew. The Hebrew reads "blessed," not "cursed," but the meaning clearly is "cursed," as in our usage: "Tom blessed out the parking attendant for scratching his new car." The Hebrew reader must decide with each use of "blessed" in Job if it means "blessed" or "cursed." Indeed, the entire story of Job asks readers to contemplate meanings of blessing and curse far more complicated than the proverbial wisdom of Proverbs 3:33.

Job 1:6-7. The book of Job begins in the land of Uz, probably referring to Edomite territory but offering a narrative equivalent to "in a land far away" (1:1). The scene shifts quickly in verse 6 to the heavenly courts where heavenly creatures present themselves before the Lord. Translating the Hebrew literally they would be "sons of God," but in the sense that Israelites are "sons of Israel," not in the sense that the New Testament employs that title for Jesus. Among these heavenly creatures is the "ha-satan," the accuser, God's prosecuting attorney. The translation as "satan" is probably unfortunate: This is not a proper name, but simply a common noun meaning "adversary" or "accuser," and that is what "the satan" does. In this respect the creature is more like the accuser who detects weak faith among Jesus' disciples and helpfully offers to "sift" them for impurities (Luke 22:31) than the opponent of God's anointed and kingdom (Luke 22:3; Acts 5:3).

Job 1:8-12. Although God looks on Job with pride, this accuser has reservations: Of course Job is "blameless and upright." Why wouldn't he be "blameless and upright" when it works so well for him? What is at stake in these opening chapters of the book of Job is a question of disinterested piety: Does Job serve God for nothing? (1:9), or does Job serve God because serving God works to Job's advantage? The Lord and the accuser work a bargain in the heavenly council: The accuser may wreak havoc with all that Job "has" (1:12), but the narrator

numbers among Job's possessions his children.

Job 1:13-22. When the scene returns to the earthly land of Uz, we discover that among the things Job "has" that are now given over to the adversary are not only his property and livestock, but also his children. A "great wind" collapses the house where Job's children gather and seven sons and three daughters are killed. In the face of this horrific tragedy, Job grieves and laments (1:20-21), but he does "not sin" or accuse God (1:22). Job passes the adversary's test.

Job 2:1-10. The accuser is by no means satisfied, and as the scene shifts again to the council chamber in heaven, the accuser taunts the Lord with what may echo an ancient proverb: "Skin for skin" (2:4). Though Job can tolerate the pain of loss, can he tolerate physical agony without cursing God? Another bargain is struck, and the accuser is freed to torment Job himself with ghastly sores all over his body. Again, the storyteller assures us, Job remained "blameless and upright," refusing to curse God even when his wife recommends such a merciful surrender: "Curse God and die" (2:9).

Job 2:11-13. Three friends appear to console Job. Each is identified by a geographical location though those locations are obscure. Their intentions testify to their wisdom and nobility. Suffering alone magnifies desolation (Psalm 69:20). Approaching Job, they can scarcely recognize him, so transformed is Job by the weight of loss and the appalling skin condition, but to their manifest horror they do recognize him. They join Job in grief, tearing their robes and heaving dust into the air, perhaps a symbol of human frailty and the ephemeral quality of life. For "seven days and seven nights" (2:13) the three sit in silence, stunned by the suffering that has come upon their friend. The seven days and nights of silence may be a traditional period of grief: Ezekiel sits in silence for seven days among the exiles at the river Chebar before the word of the Lord comes to him (Ezekiel 3:15-16). After the seven days and nights the friends will begin to talk and not stop talking for many chapters, but their silence here at the beginning of Job's story may be their best wisdom and greatest consolation.

Job 3:1-26. Slipping into chapter 3 you will immediately notice a change: Suddenly we are reading poetic verse with only the slightest narrative to hold it together. Everything has been lost, there is nothing

more to lose, and the next thirty-nine chapters will reflect on the mystery of loss and tragedy and the ways of God in the world. The storyteller of chapters 1 and 2 has set the stage for the Job poet to ponder the mysteries of living. The first item on the poet's agenda is the question of why we live at all. Job himself raises the question, howling that he wishes he had never been born. Chapter 3 puts the question in utterly dazzling poetry, but no answer appears, only the question.

INTERPRETING THE SCRIPTURE

The Narrative Context

The book of Job raises an anguished cry of protest against every simple and smug explanation of suffering and tragedy. For people of faith tragedy and suffering are at the heart of the matter. Tragedy and suffering visit the homes of those who trust in God and those who are utterly indifferent. Our religious faith may sustain us with the most remarkable resources to deal with tragedy and suffering—or our religious faith may mock us and add to our ache because we expected something else from God. The book of Job restrains itself in dealing with these matters. Instead of providing answers it tells a story and proposes poetic visions.

At the heart of the book of Job rests the theological axiom that God's blessing follows righteous human behavior. This idea is sometimes unequivocally spoken in the Scriptures (Deuteronomy 28; Proverbs 3:33). So often when we use the word *bless* it sounds so small, so frail, so "spiritual." But when the Hebrew Scriptures speak of blessing they mean for us to smell the spring rain on the rich soil, to taste the sweetness of wine and ripe fruit, to feel sensation of skin touching skin, to hear the sound of a newborn crying, to see the goodness of the Lord

in the land of the living. To "bless" invokes everything God intends for human creatures: life, joy, land, fertility, health, children, long life, and wealth. All of these blessings Job had received. The storyteller introduces Job as a man "blameless and upright" (1:1), but shies away from directly connecting Job's abundant blessings to his righteousness.

The satan, who tests humans, does not shy away from making the connection between Job's blessedness and his righteousness. The challenge the satan makes to God is that Job is righteous because righteousness works, righteousness pays off well. Job fears God (1:1, 8) because that strategy succeeds so well. Remove the blessings, dares the satan, and Job will curse God (1:9-11).

God accepts the wager and the trials of Job begin. The premise of the first two chapters of the book of Job has the unfortunate tang of a bet laid down in a sports bar: "Yeah, well, Ruth wouldn't have hit sixty home runs if he had stayed at Fenway Park!" The storyteller imaginatively describes a scene hidden in the heavenly council chamber where human beings are not permitted entrance. In order to probe mysteries finally beyond human comprehension the narrator construes an agreement to permit tragedy and suffering in order to determine the true motivation of religious faith. Does Job fear God because fearing God has been endlessly profitable for Job, or does Job fear God because Job seeks communion with God above every other thing? Does Job want to be blessed, or does Job want the One who blesses?

Losing Everything

Tragedy falls upon Job in what the storyteller obviously intends as an escalating series, but most of us would have lost heart long before our skin erupted with pustules. Three sets of messengers come to Job describing the loss of his wealth in livestock, donkeys, sheep and camels; then another messenger announces the death of Job's children. This loss kills our soul. What the satan may be allowed now to do to us is nothing compared with this. In modern society with modern medicine we do not expect to attend the funerals of our children. Certainly this was different in the ancient Near East, and certainly it is different in much of our world today, but we ache with those who have endured the death of a child and shudder to consider the situation. Job has lost all his children, seven sons and three daughters, all in an instant. The contemplation of such an unbearable loss drives the plot of the Stephen Spielberg film *Saving Private Ryan*, in which a squad of soldiers seeks one last infantryman of a family whose older brothers had all been lost in the initial carnage of D-Day. With the collapse of a house killing his children everything is lost for Job. Although the satan is given a second permission to torture Job, the gruesome skin ailments might seem a welcome distraction from inventorying all that has been lost in the fall of the house of Job.

On Not Losing God

The satan expects Job to lose faith in God and we might expect it as well. When every-

thing is lost, we may feel abandoned by God. Indeed, Job may well have felt abandoned by God, but he does not examine his feelings or act on them but rather confesses a faith in God that is deeper than even his grief and loss (Job 2:10, today's key verse; 1:22). Nothing that he can see speaks of God's goodness; the grief that sweeps over him tells only of utter desolation, yet Job neither curses God nor gives up on God but only later asks for an audience with God (Job 23:1-7). Though God may give him evil where in the past he has received good things, Job seeks God. His "faith" is not a faith "about" God, that God will do certain things, but a longing for God. Job wants to take up his loss with God.

Silence and Speech

Our first reaction to loss is silence. There is nothing to say. Job breaks silence to correct his wife (Job 2:10), but falls into silence again. When three friends appear who have heard of Job's loss they do not bring with them bouquets of comforting words or self-help volumes on living with grief. Instead, they bear a holy and respectful silence. They are wise enough at the beginning to know there are no words, and for seven days and seven nights no one speaks a word to Job. The afternoon and evening of September 11, 2001, news commentators again and again declared that there were no words. That did not stop them talking because talking was their job, but their wisdom understood there are times when there are no words. Christian faith has much to say about grief and loss. We have wonderful words full of hope, faith, endurance, and healing, but on the day of terrible loss the words are too soon, too easily spoken and a betrayal of faith: better to sit in silence with God and suffering.

When the words come to Job they come in dazzling poetry. Sometimes poetry, with its careful measuring of words around silences, speaks our heart's hurt and hope better than prose. In the days after the September 11 terrorist attacks, literary critics and booksellers alike noticed an unaccustomed surge in the poetry market.

Poetry says the unsayable, and in his loss Job declares he wishes he had been lost as well, that he had never been born. Our first experiments of speaking of terrible loss may exaggerate in just such ways: "I wish I were dead instead!" "I will never get through this!" "I wish I could just lie down and sleep and not wake up!" At this point the worst thing about living with loss is that we go on living and the loss is for keeps. We do not know how we will endure and we cannot know. Job moves forward by addressing his poetic lament to the heavens, to anyone who will hear, finally to God. With God we can go forward for the next few minutes, the next hour, the day, and finally, forever.

SHARING THE SCRIPTURE

Preparing Our Hearts

This week's devotional reading is found in Psalm 22:1-11. This psalm opens with familiar words that Jesus cried from the cross: "My God, my God, why have you forsaken me?" The psalmist continues pleading with God to be delivered from the suffering he is experiencing and the hostility other people are heaping upon him. When have you experienced such anguish? How has God brought you through that difficult time?

Pray that you and your class participants will go to God when pain and tragedy strike, knowing that God is willing and able to help you.

Preparing Our Minds

Allow extra time to study the lengthy background from chapters 1, 2, and 3 of Job. The lesson will focus on Job 1:14-15, 18-19, 22, and 3:1-3, 11. Job 2:10 is our key verse. As you read, consider how we can respond to and survive tragedy.

Write on newsprint:

❏ information for next week's lesson, found under "Continue the Journey."

Plan a brief lecture as suggested in "Encounter the Story of How Job Remained Blameless and Upright as He Suffered Tragedy, Pain, and Grief."

LEADING THE CLASS

(1) Gather to Learn

❖ Welcome the class members and introduce any guests.

❖ Pray that the adults will recognize that loss is part of life, but that God offers us positive ways to deal with the tragedies we face.

❖ Read this information to the class: **Christopher Reeve, an accomplished actor perhaps best known as Superman, faced an unthinkable tragedy when the six-foot-four athletic star was thrown from a horse during a competition in 1995. He sustained a spinal cord injury that left him paralyzed. Although Reeve had briefly considered suicide after his accident, he stated: "I refuse to allow a disability to determine how I live my life." He worked tirelessly at therapy to improve his own health. He advocated for spinal cord research, including stem cell research. Reeve lobbied Congress to provide better insurance for catastrophic injury. He challenged Hollywood to make more films dealing with social issues. Despite his paralysis, he played a leading role in the 1998 remake of Hitchcock's *Rear Window*, for which he won a Screen Actors Guild award for best actor. He died at age 52 in 2004, but the** power of his personal struggle continues to touch us.

❖ Discuss these questions with the class.

(1) **How would you describe Christopher Reeve's response to tragedy?**

(2) **How might Mr. Reeve be a role model for you in dealing with tragedy?**

❖ Read aloud today's focus statement: **When tragedy occurs, some people conclude that it would be better to die than to live. What can help us survive tragedy when it comes to us? These passages from Job imply that the desire to end pain is a basic human reaction, yet death is not really the answer. Set in the larger context of the book as a whole, we see that God can overcome our pain and grief, eventually leading us to rejoice again in life.**

(2) Encounter the Story of How Job Remained Blameless and Upright as He Suffered Tragedy, Pain, and Grief

❖ Present a brief lecture from verses 1-5, 6-7, 8-12 of the "Understanding the Scripture" portion to set the stage for today's lesson.

❖ Read or retell "The Narrative Context" in Interpreting the Scripture to further set the stage. Be sure to make three important points:

(1) Suffering and tragedy are part of the human condition, whether one believes in God or not.

(2) A major tenet of Wisdom literature is that God blesses those who are good and brings destruction upon the wicked.

(3) Job's story challenges the wisdom understanding because he suffers greatly and yet is "blameless and upright" (1:1).

❖ Choose a volunteer to read Job 1:14-15, 18-19, 22. Or, if you have time to present the full story, read verses 13-22.

(1) **What has Job lost?**

(2) **How do you think most people would respond to such a loss?**

(3) **How does Job respond?**

(4) **What do you believe motivates his response?**

❖ Look at today's key verse, Job 2:10. Note that Job is covered with sores and is physically suffering. Job's wife is urging him to "Curse God and die," but Job refuses.

❖ Select someone to read aloud Job 3:1-3, 11. Note that in chapter 3 the text shifts from prose to poetry, which can say the unsayable.

❖ Compare Job's response in 2:10 to his words in 3:1-3, 11. Discuss why Job's attitude seems to have changed. Consider this change in light of Napoleon Bonaparte's statement: "It requires more courage to suffer than to die."

(3) Confront the Problem of Suffering in the Learners' Lives

❖ Distribute paper and pencils. Ask the students to write about a painful or tragic episode in their own lives. Suggest that they focus on these ideas:

■ questions that came to mind when they first heard the news.

■ their response to this loss.

■ resources, such as faith and family, that helped them to survive this loss.

■ how this event affected their relationship with God.

■ how this event changed them.

❖ Invite volunteers to read or retell what they have written.

❖ Encourage the class to draw conclusions, if possible, about:

■ how we cope with tragedy and loss.

■ whether our means of coping are generally positive or negative.

■ how our faith affects our ability to sustain loss.

(4) Affirm That God's Goodness Endures,
Despite Tragedies

❖ Affirm God's goodness by reading responsively Psalm 107:1-9, 33-43. Use the Psalter in your hymnal, if possible.

❖ **Option:** Help the participants write a short litany in which they affirm God's enduring goodness and love, no matter what the circumstances.

(5) Continue the Journey

❖ Pray that the participants will seek from God positive ways for coping with loss and tragedy.

❖ Read aloud this preparation for next week's lesson. You may also want to post it on newsprint for the students to copy. **Prepare for next week's Palm Sunday session, "When All Seems Hopeless," by reading Job 14; 32: 1-8; 34: 10-15; and 37: 14-24. Our class session will focus on Job 14: 1-2, 11-17; 32:6, 8; 34:12; and 37:14, 22. Be alert for ways that these ideas may inform your study: When bad things happen, it can seem that things will never get better. How can our hope be renewed? These texts from Job affirm that, even when we feel hopeless, we can count on God to be good, just, and all-powerful.**

❖ Read aloud the following three ideas. Challenge the students to commit themselves to use these activities as a springboard to spiritual growth.

(1) **Recall loss and tragedy that you have faced in your own life. How were you able to move through the loss? What role did God play in your healing?**

(2) **Compose an answer to someone who said to you that God sends tragedy to teach a lesson.**

(3) **Read the entire book of Job. Try to look at Job's situation from his point of view; from the point of view of his friends, who believe that God rewards the just and punishes only those who are wicked; and from God's point of view.**

❖ Sing or read aloud "Come, Ye Disconsolate."

❖ Lead this benediction to end today's session: **With all of your creatures, most majestic God, we sing your praises and pray that you would empower us to be wise people and faithful stewards of your creation, in Jesus' name. Amen.**

UNIT 2: LIVING WITH CREATION'S UNCERTAINTY
WHEN ALL SEEMS HOPELESS

PREVIEWING THE LESSON

Lesson Scripture: Job 14:1-2, 11-17; 32:6, 8; 34:12; 37:14, 22
Background Scripture: Job 14; 32:1-8; 34:10-15; 37:14-24
Key Verse: Job 14:14

Focus of the Lesson:
When bad things happen, it can seem that things will never get better. How can our hope be renewed? These texts from Job affirm that, even when we feel hopeless, we can count on God to be good, just, and all-powerful.

Goals for the Learners:
(1) to hear Job's words of despair and hopelessness and analyze Elihu's argument that God is greater than human beings and controls all of life.
(2) to examine their own beliefs about God's presence in difficult circumstances.
(3) to trust God to help them solve a problem and to give God the glory when that problem has been resolved.

Pronunciation Guide:
Barachel (bair' uh kuhl)
Buzite (byoo' zit)
Elihu (i li' hyoo)
Sheol (shee' ohl)

Supplies:
Bibles, newsprint and marker, paper and pencils, hymnals

READING THE SCRIPTURE

NRSV
Job 14:1-2, 11-17

¹ "A mortal, born of woman, few of days
    and full of trouble,
² comes up like a flower and withers,
    flees like a shadow and does not last.
¹¹ As waters fail from a lake,

NIV
Job 14:1-2, 11-17

¹"Man born of woman
    is of few days and full of trouble.
²He springs up like a flower and withers
    away;
    like a fleeting shadow, he does not endure.

and a river wastes away and dries up,

12 so mortals lie down and do not rise again;
    until the heavens are no more, they will
        not awake
    or be roused out of their sleep.

13 O that you would hide me in Sheol,
    that you would conceal me until your
        wrath is past,
    that you would appoint me a set time, and
        remember me!

14 If mortals die, will they live again?
    All the days of my service I would wait
    until my release should come.

15 You would call, and I would answer you;
    you would long for the work of your
        hands.

16 For then you would not number my steps,
    you would not keep watch over my sin;

17 my transgression would be sealed up in a
        bag,
    and you would cover over my iniquity.

Job 32:6, 8

6 Elihu son of Barachel the Buzite answered:
    "I am young in years,
        and you are aged;
    therefore I was timid and afraid
    to declare my opinion to you.

8 But truly it is the spirit in a mortal,
    the breath of the Almighty, that makes for
        understanding.

Job 34:12

12 Of a truth, God will not do wickedly,
    and the Almighty will not pervert justice.

Job 37:14, 22

14 "Hear this, O Job;
    stop and consider the wondrous works
        of God.

22 Out of the north comes golden splendor;
    around God is awesome majesty.

---

11 As water disappears from the sea
    or a riverbed becomes parched and dry,

12 so man lies down and does not rise;
    till the heavens are no more, men will not
        awake
    or be roused from their sleep.

13 "If only you would hide me in the grave
    and conceal me till your anger has passed!
If only you would set me a time
    and then remember me!

14 If a man dies, will he live again?
    All the days of my hard service
    I will wait for my renewal to come.

15 You will call and I will answer you;
    you will long for the creature your hands
        have made.

16 Surely then you will count my steps
    but not keep track of my sin.

17 My offenses will be sealed up in a bag;
    you will cover over my sin.

Job 32:6, 8

6 So Elihu son of Barakel the Buzite said:
    "I am young in years,
        and you are old;
    that is why I was fearful,
        not daring to tell you what I know.

8 But it is the spirit in a man,
    the breath of the Almighty, that gives him
        understanding.

Job 34:12

12 It is unthinkable that God would do
        wrong,
    that the Almighty would pervert justice.

Job 37:14, 22

14 "Listen to this, Job;
    stop and consider God's wonders.

22 Out of the north he comes in golden
        splendor;
    God comes in awesome majesty.

UNDERSTANDING THE SCRIPTURE

Job 14:1-22. Scholars familiar with the book of Job recognize the different voices in the poetry; the rest of us must pay careful attention to who is speaking. Here, in chapter 14, Job speaks, meditating on the frailty of human life and longing for a hearing with God. He speaks of the shortness and insignificance of human life and wonders why God would pay any attention at all (14:1-3). Why would God bother to judge? Job flaunts the logic with clean/unclean or pure/impure polarities that can never come into contact: Just so, God and the human creature would not be fitting adversaries in a court of law. God has only to glance away and this vulnerable creature wilts like a flower in the heat of the sun.

Trees are a different matter, Job asserts, demonstrating that he is a lively observer of nature and a sage of the wisdom tradition. An apparently dead tree, cut down or dormant, may spring again to life with rainfall, sprouts erupting from the old stump and buds appearing on wood given up for dead. Human beings, however, are not like trees (14:10). Evidencing Wisdom literature's typical lack of confidence in resurrection or afterlife, Job declares they do not rise from death (14:12).

If Job does not have hope in an afterlife he at least proposes a scheme: If God would only hide him away in Sheol, the place of the dead, until God's anger fades, then things could be as they once were between God and Job, with God calling and Job responding (14:15; also 13:22), a lively and imaginative description of a relationship to God. This proposal for judgment after death anticipates later developments in the faith of the people of God as they began to hope for God's final justice for martyrs given no earthly justice.

Sheol offers no justice, only pain and sadness (14:22). This land of the dead is not a place where people "live" after death, so much as they "dead" after death, living in a shadowy imitation of life, unaware of the fate of others (14:21) and preoccupied with their own loss.

Job 32:1-8. Elihu appears as a surprising interruption in the book of Job, and many scholars believe his speeches to be a later addition: Elihu's name appears neither in the prose narrative that begins the book (2:11) nor in God's rebuke to Job's friends at the end (42:9). Others see him as integral to the design and written in congruent style. In this case Elihu may be something of a comic figure of the wisdom tradition: the youth who assumes he is wiser than his elders and who speaks rashly. Elihu explains he has kept silence in respect for his elders, but when he declares that it is "the spirit . . . the breath of the Almighty" (32:8) that gives "understanding," he is utterly confident that he possesses that spirit (and the others are somehow deficient).

Elihu finds fault not only in Job's self-justifying defenses but also in the three friends' failure to convince him of his grievous errors. Elihu is absolutely confident that he can do better, and he speaks through chapter 37 without permitting any interruption. The preceding chapters poetically described a dialogue between Job and his friends; Elihu provides a long monologue, occasionally quoting Job.

Job 34:10-15. Elihu's long speech continues as he responds to chapters 29–31, in which Job asserts his innocence. Elihu speaks the conventional theology of the wisdom tradition that God responds to human goodness with goodness and blessing and that God responds to human wickedness with retribution and suffering. Job's situation of suffering, Elihu hints here, is obviously evidence of his wickedness. The only alternative to such a conclusion, Elihu explains, would be to accuse God of wickedness and injustice (34:12), a wholly unacceptable premise. Elihu buttresses his argument by appealing to the sovereignty of God: God is creator of all things and in charge of all things. No one elected God as God or has surrendered this sovereignty to God, indeed everything that lives relies on the breath of God to animate it (compare Psalm 104, lesson for March 12). Our lives utterly depend upon God, declares Elihu, with the implication that we are poorly postured to complain about the way God exercises sovereignty over the creation.

Job 37:14-24. Elihu invites Job to "stop and consider" the wonders God accomplishes, because Elihu believes that if Job does "stop and consider" he will recognize immediately the folly, impudence, and inappropriateness of his protests of innocence before God. As he considers the wonders of God's creation, Elihu assaults Job's human limitations, asking twice, "Do you know?" (37:15, 16), a phrasing that might be rudely translated, "Well, if you know so much, Mr. Smarty-pants." Elihu taunts Job not only with the limits of his knowledge,

but also with his limited power: "Can you" (37:18)? Finally Elihu—whose speech is now in its sixth chapter—faults Job for speaking too much, and sarcastically taunts Job, asking him to help the others know what to say before God because they cannot prepare their legal briefs for court in the darkness of their human limitations (37:19). Elihu explains that the glorious light of God overwhelms humans in their darkness as if they were looking straight into the sun. Our reverence before God depends not solely upon God's incomparable majesty and glory, however, but also on God's inviolable sense of justice. God is not only glorious but also good. Elihu concludes his oration appealing to the glorious God's justice before which wise mortals bow down in reverence. Job has argued that matters are not so simple; thus Elihu's conclusion is something of an unspoken condemnation of Job. He does not appropriately reverence God's glory and justice; Job is foolish in his refusal to recant.

INTERPRETING THE SCRIPTURE

Talking About God and Talking with God

Shortly after his troubles began three friends came to visit Job (chapter 2). Now they are joined by a fourth, Elihu, who has a great deal to say about say about God's faithful and just dealings with humankind. Elihu speaks with dazzling eloquence and his grasp of his theological heritage is evident. Most preachers would envy the style as well as the substance of Elihu's sermon to Job. He has a lot to say and his manner of speaking is quite persuasive. Elihu is confident that he has the answers to Job's dilemma.

Job does not have answers, but he does have trust in God. Job has questions, and he asks his questions of God.

Throughout his long sermon Elihu has

much to say about God and God's way of dispensing justice in the universe God has made. Job enters into dialogue with his three friends, but most of all he wants to address his case to God. He doesn't seek answers, even good answers and theologically correct answers; Job wants to speak to God.

Earlier Job had expressed his longing "to speak to the Almighty" (Job 13:3), and that is precisely what he does here in chapter 14. Like us, Job cannot tell whether God is listening or not. God has been silent since chapter 2 and will not speak again until chapter 38, but Job will speak with God nonetheless.

Job characterizes his relationship with God in terms of call and response: God calls and Job responds (14:15). Often we contemplate our prayer life in exactly the opposite terms: We call and God responds. Certainly much of the Scriptures invite us to call to the Lord in our need, but Job does not pray that his fortunes be reversed, his wealth restored, and his suffering ended. What matters to Job is the conversation of call and response; what matters is the relationship.

The four friends have answers about God, perhaps even answers from God, but Job has God, even if his "having" God is experienced mostly in the absence and silence of God, only in the longing for God and finally only hoping in God. Job waits for the Lord (see also Psalm 27:14), trusting that with God "release" (14:14 NRSV) and "renewal" (14:14 NIV) will accompany a refreshed conversation with the Almighty.

Trusting God in Life and in Death

Job meditates on the frailty and brevity of human life as he turns his prayers to God. That human beings are "born of woman" (14:1) is by no means meant to be disparaging to women, but rather a reminder of our utter mortality. We enter this world in a process that involves the tearing of flesh, the shedding of blood, and terrible pain and risk. That is just the beginning. And before our days are counted out, what will the world do to us? Our life is as beautiful and as graceful as a flower bloom, but it also withers just as quickly (14:2). Whatever grand pretensions we may aspire to in human life, they are as insubstantial and as passing as shadows (14:2).

Contemplating this does not cause Job to despair but rather turns his thoughts to the One who gave human life and whose goodness and justice are the guarantors of human existence. Job speaks the conventional wisdom of the Hebrew Scriptures that when human beings die they enter a sleep from which there is no waking (14:12); yet Job also looks beyond conventional wisdom, looks beyond death even, looks toward the mystery of God's creating life,

and raises the question from the grave: Might we live again? Job asks the question to God, in whom the mysteries of life and death find their conclusion. Job doesn't know the size of his question and he doesn't know the answer, but he does know that the question ultimately must be addressed to the Author of Life. Some questions can only be asked of God.

God in Our God-forsakenness

One reason Job so trusts in God is that he remembers happier days when God managed to maintain the other side of a conversation of call and response (14:14). Job looks forward to the time when the conversation may resume. In the meantime, however, Job prays in the dark without answers or assurances.

We remember another who prayed in the dark. Reading Job's prayer in this season of Lent and particularly on this Palm/Passion Sunday when so many churches read the Gospel of Mark, and we hear Jesus' cry, "My God, my God, why have you forsaken me" (Mark 15:34, quoting Psalm 22:1), we are reminded that Job's story is not the only story of a righteous man enduring undeserved suffering and crying out to God of his God-forsakenness.

If we take Job and Jesus at their word we discover the curious paradox that in experiences of utter God-forsakenness God is somehow present in absence, whispering in the silence, hidden from the light but nearby in the darkness. Job's and Jesus' experiences of God-forsakenness should not be brushed off by pious talk, but neither should we overlook the resilient faith that caused them to address their God-forsakenness to no one other than God. Good Friday assures us that God may be trusted with our God-forsakenness.

The Spirit of God Draws Us to God

To cry out to God even of our God-forsakenness evidences God's work within us even in the most extreme circumstances. That we can draw breath to cry out is no accident but the very gift of God. That we should cry out to God is the work of God's spirit. Elihu bears witness to this in his attempt to remind Job (32:8), and Christian faith affirms that it is God's own spirit working within us that causes us to turn to God in prayer (Romans 8:15-16).

When we are at the end of our human resources it is not, as we might suspect, our utter lack of other help that causes us to seek God; rather, it is God's own spirit drawing us near in spite of all other evidence of God's presence. When we seek a justice the world refuses to give, we know that there is one who can be trusted to do the right thing, one who would never allow injustice to reign (34:12). Although we cannot see God's approach, the God to whom

Elihu bears witness will come in "golden splendor" and "awesome majesty" (37:22) finally to set things right.

When Elihu invites Job and us to "stop and consider" (37:14) the marvelous works of God, he is not simply asking us to look around to examine the physical evidence of God's presence and protection; rather, he is summoning us to go deeper into our faith and "consider" the One who is utterly and ultimately trustworthy. Our eyes and ears may not be able to see or hear the slightest confirmation of our faith, and we may wonder what God is doing. In that case our wondering itself testifies to God. Our wondering about God, our longing for God, our praying to God: What are these but the ways God's spirit plies our spirits as we seek after "understanding" (32:8)?

SHARING THE SCRIPTURE

Preparing Our Hearts

This week's devotional reading is found in Job 36:24-33. Here Elihu, a young man who feels certain that he understands the reasons for Job's problems, proclaims God's majesty by pointing out God's creative powers as seen so clearly in nature. God gives food to nourish us but also thunderstorms that can terrify us. Meditate on the power and splendor of God. Do you find God to be comforting, terrifying, or both?

Pray that you and your class participants will recognize and affirm God's creative power and majesty.

Preparing Our Minds

Study the background Scripture in Job 14; 32:1-8; 34:10-15; 37:14-24. The session will focus on Job 14:1-2, 11-17; 32:6, 8; 34:12; 37:14, 22. As you read this lesson, think about how hope can be renewed when bad

things happen.
 Write on newsprint:
 ❏ information for next week's lesson, found under "Continue the Journey."

LEADING THE CLASS

(1) Gather to Learn

❖ Welcome the class members and introduce any guests.
 ❖ Pray that the participants will experience God's presence, even in the midst of seemingly hopeless situations.
 ❖ Suggest that the adults recall a time when they felt mired in a difficult situation and hopeless, perhaps even abandoned by God. Let them meditate on this situation for a few moments.
 ❖ Read aloud these brief excerpts from chapter 10 of the spiritual classic *Dark Night of the Soul* by the Spanish mystic Saint John of the Cross (1542–1591). **(1) During**

the time, then, of the aridities of this night of sense . . . spiritual persons suffer great trials, by reason not so much of the aridities which they suffer, as of the fear which they have of being lost on the road, thinking that all spiritual blessing is over for them and that God has abandoned them since they find no help or pleasure in good things. (2) It is well for those who find themselves in this condition to take comfort, to persevere in patience and to be in no wise afflicted. Let them trust in God, Who abandons not those that seek Him with a simple and right heart, and will not fail to give them what is needful for the road, until He bring them into the clear and pure light of love.

❖ Invite the class members to respond to Saint John's words, which reassure us that those who trust in God will never be abandoned, no matter how hopeless they feel.

❖ Read aloud today's focus statement: **When bad things happen, it can seem that things will never get better. How can our hope be renewed? These texts from Job affirm that, even when we feel hopeless, we can count on God to be good, just, and all-powerful.**

(2) Hear Job's Words of Despair and Hopelessness and Analyze Elihu's Argument That God Is Greater Than Human Beings and Controls All of Life

❖ Choose a volunteer to read Job 14:1-2, 11-17.

■ Identify the images of life and death that appear in this passage. You may want to list the images on newsprint.

■ Discuss the following ideas with the class. Add, as appropriate, ideas from "Trusting God in Life and in Death" from Interpreting the Scripture.

(1) how Job's thoughts on life and death are similar to and different from their own.

(2) situations that have prompted

them to sink into the hopelessness that Job experienced.

(3) connections they can make between Job's story and the events of Holy Week and Palm/Passion Sunday.

❖ Select another volunteer to read Job 32:6, 8; 34:12; and 37:14, 22. Write these passages where the reader can see them, or let the reader borrow your copy of *The New International Lesson Annual* if class members do not have their own copies.

■ Discuss these questions.

(1) What do you know about Elihu? (Add to the discussion points from Job 32:1-8; 34:10-15; 37:14-24 in the Understanding the Scripture portion.)

(2) What does Elihu believe, or think he knows, about God?

(3) Do you agree with the points Elihu makes? Why or why not?

(4) Recall that in the wisdom tradition justice was understood to mean that the good were rewarded and the evil punished. Elihu states in Job 34:12 that it would be unthinkable for God to do wrong or pervert justice. What is he implying about Job's situation?

(5) How do you think God defines justice?

(3) Examine the Learners' Beliefs About God's Presence in Difficult Circumstances

❖ Read aloud the last paragraph in "The Spirit of God Draws Us to God" in the Interpreting the Scripture portion.

❖ Encourage the students to think silently about difficult situations in their own lives when they wondered where God was and what God was doing.

❖ Discuss these questions with the class.

(1) Why do you—or don't you— believe that God is present in all circumstances?

(2) **What evidence do you need to be assured that God is present in difficult circumstances?**

(3) **If someone lamented that he or she had been abandoned by God, what response or witness could you give concerning God's abiding presence?**

❖ Distribute paper and pencils. Ask each student to write a prayer or psalm of thanksgiving about God's presence. If some students cannot affirm God's abiding presence, encourage them to write a psalm of lament, asking where God is in their time of trouble.

❖ Invite volunteers to read their psalms or prayers. The expressions of one's heart, not the format, are most important.

(4) Trust God to Help Solve a Problem and Give God the Glory When That Problem Has Been Resolved

❖ Ask the students to brainstorm answers to this question: **Where in the world are situations that seem hopeless?** Record their ideas on newsprint, adding a few words about why the situation is so dire.

❖ Invite volunteers to pray on behalf of those who are involved in the situations and give thanks for God's presence in each one of these situations. Try to make sure that each of the identified situations has been lifted up in prayer.

(5) Continue the Journey

❖ Conclude the prayer time of the previous section by praying that the participants will know that they can place their full trust and confidence in the Creator God, even when all seems hopeless.

❖ Read aloud this preparation for next week's lesson. You may also want to post it on newsprint for the students to copy. **Prepare for next week's Easter session, "From Death to Life," by reading Job 38:1-4, 16-17; 42:1-6; Mark 16. Our session will explore Job 38:1, 4, 16-17; 42:1-2, 5; Mark 16:1-7, 9-14, 20. As you study focus on these ideas: People want to believe that they will live again after physical death. What hope of new life can we find through the resurrection of Jesus Christ? The Job texts point to God as the One powerful enough to overcome death itself, and Mark's account of the first Easter gives us confidence that believers can look forward to resurrection.**

❖ Read aloud the following three ideas. Challenge the students to commit themselves to use these activities as a springboard to spiritual growth.

(1) **Read *J.B.* by Archibald MacLeish. This play in verse is a modern version of the Job story. What new insights on Job's story do you get from this play?**

(2) **Recall "dark night of the soul" experiences when you felt that God had truly forsaken you. What kinds of situations prompted these experiences? What resources did you have for holding on to you faith until the conversation with God again resumed?**

(3) **Support someone who is grieving or in the midst of a crisis by offering whatever assistance you can.**

❖ Sing or read aloud "Stand by Me."

❖ Lead this benediction to end today's session: **With all of your creatures, most majestic God, we sing your praises and pray that you would empower us to be wise people and faithful stewards of your creation, in Jesus' name. Amen.**

UNIT 2: LIVING WITH CREATION'S UNCERTAINTY
FROM DEATH TO LIFE

PREVIEWING THE LESSON

Lesson Scripture: Job 38:1, 4, 16-17; 42:1-2, 5; Mark 16:1-7, 9-14, 20
Background Scripture: Job 38:1-4, 16-17; 42:1-6; Mark 16
Key Verse: Mark 16:6

Focus of the Lesson:
People want to believe that they will live again after physical death. What hope of new life can we find through the resurrection of Jesus Christ? The Job texts point to God as the One powerful enough to overcome death itself, and Mark's account of the first Easter gives us confidence that believers can look forward to resurrection.

Goals for the Learners:
(1) to learn how the Job texts affirm God's power, even over death, and to see how this power brings hope for new life found in the resurrection of Jesus Christ.
(2) to explore their beliefs about God's power, which is great enough to bring life out of death.
(3) to celebrate Easter!

Pronunciation Guide:
Salome (suh loh' mee)

Supplies:
Bibles, newsprint and marker, paper and pencils, hymnals; optional: Easter foods, napkins, plates, cups, beverage

---

READING THE SCRIPTURE

NRSV
Job 38:1, 4, 16-17
1 Then the LORD answered Job out of the
   whirlwind:
4 "Where were you when I laid the
   foundation of the earth?
   Tell me, if you have understanding.
16 "Have you entered into the springs of the
   sea,

NIV
Job 38:1, 4, 16-17
1 Then the LORD answered Job out of the
storm. He said:
4 "Where were you when I laid the earth's
   foundation?
   Tell me, if you understand.
16 "Have you journeyed to the springs of the
   sea

or walked in the recesses of the deep?

¹⁷ Have the gates of death been revealed to
you,

or have you seen the gates of deep
darkness?

Job 42:1-2, 5

¹ Then Job answered the LORD:

² "I know that you can do all things,
and that no purpose of yours can be
thwarted.

⁵ I had heard of you by the hearing of
the ear,

but now my eye sees you.

Mark 16:1-7, 9-14, 20

¹When the sabbath was over, Mary
Magdalene, and Mary the mother of James,
and Salome bought spices, so that they
might go and anoint him. ²And very early
on the first day of the week, when the sun
had risen, they went to the tomb. ³They had
been saying to one another, "Who will roll
away the stone for us from the entrance to
the tomb?" ⁴When they looked up, they saw
that the stone, which was very large, had
already been rolled back. ⁵As they entered
the tomb, they saw a young man, dressed in
a white robe, sitting on the right side; and
they were alarmed. ⁶**But he said to them,
"Do not be alarmed; you are looking for
Jesus of Nazareth, who was crucified. He
has been raised; he is not here. Look, there
is the place they laid him.** ⁷But go, tell his
disciples and Peter that he is going ahead of
you to Galilee; there you will see him, just as
he told you."

⁹[[Now after he rose early on the first
day of the week, he appeared first to
Mary Magdalene, from whom he had cast
out seven demons. ¹⁰She went out and
told those who had been with him, while
they were mourning and weeping. ¹¹But
when they heard that he was alive and
had been seen by her, they would not
believe it.

¹²After this he appeared in another form
to two of them, as they were walking into

or walked in the recesses of the deep?

¹⁷Have the gates of death been shown to
you?

Job 42:1-2, 5

¹Then Job replied to the LORD:

²"I know that you can do all things;
no plan of yours can be thwarted.

⁵My ears had heard of you
but now my eyes have seen you.

Mark 16:1-7, 9-14, 20

¹When the Sabbath was over, Mary
Magdalene, Mary the mother of James, and
Salome bought spices so that they might go
to anoint Jesus' body. ²Very early on the first
day of the week, just after sunrise, they were
on their way to the tomb ³and they asked
each other, "Who will roll the stone away
from the entrance of the tomb?"

⁴But when they looked up, they saw that
the stone, which was very large, had been
rolled away. ⁵As they entered the tomb, they
saw a young man dressed in a white robe sitting on the right side, and they were
alarmed.

⁶**"Don't be alarmed," he said. "You are
looking for Jesus the Nazarene, who was
crucified. He has risen! He is not here. See
the place where they laid him.** ⁷But go, tell
his disciples and Peter, 'He is going ahead of
you into Galilee. There you will see him, just
as he told you.' "

⁹When Jesus rose early on the first day of
the week, he appeared first to Mary
Magdalene, out of whom he had driven
seven demons. ¹⁰She went and told those
who had been with him and who were
mourning and weeping. ¹¹When they heard
that Jesus was alive and that she had seen
him, they did not believe it.

¹²Afterward Jesus appeared in a different
form to two of them while they were walking in the country. ¹³These returned and
reported it to the rest; but they did not
believe them either.

¹⁴Later Jesus appeared to the Eleven as
they were eating; he rebuked them for their

the country. [13]And they went back and told the rest, but they did not believe them.

[14]Later he appeared to the eleven themselves as they were sitting at the table; and he upbraided them for their lack of faith and stubbornness, because they had not believed those who saw him after he had risen.

[20]And they went out and proclaimed the good news everywhere, while the Lord worked with them and confirmed the message by the signs that accompanied it.]]

lack of faith and their stubborn refusal to believe those who had seen him after he had risen.

[20]Then the disciples went out and preached everywhere, and the Lord worked with them and confirmed his word by the signs that accompanied it.

UNDERSTANDING THE SCRIPTURE

Job 38:1-4, 16-17. Job asked for an audience with God. He has a complaint, actually a sort of lawsuit: "I would speak to the Almighty, and I desire to argue my case with God" (13:3; also 31:35-37). Finally God appears in chapter 38, challenging Job with words echoing Job's original appeal (38:3b; 13:22). God responds to Job's plea and God's response goes on through chapter 41 with some of the most dazzling poetry the world has heard.

Job's world has fallen apart, sundered by God's permission, which the reader knows from the opening chapters. Job only knows that something has gone terribly wrong that he cannot understand; his friends assure him everything is perfectly understandable and everything remains in good working order; it is only that Job has somehow, perhaps inadvertently, violated the order of the creation. When God speaks from the whirlwind God speaks of the creation in such a way as to challenge our human capacity fully to understand it: You have complaints about the order of the creation, but where were you when all things began? God's speech dazzles as it recounts the bustling variety of wild creatures—lions, ravens, mountain goats—precisely the sorts of creatures not domesticated to human purposes in Psalm 8. God tours Job through those places of the creation that human beings cannot go and live: the depths of the sea where springs give life to the ocean and the

gates of death and deep darkness. Those who have seen these gates do not return to report their travels. Such knowledge belongs to God alone.

Job 42:1-6. God's response to Job does not merely give more information about the creation for Job to learn and manage. Nor does God give Job new understanding, but Job does receive insight: "now my eye sees you" (42:5). A transformation, not merely learning, has taken place, and Job finds a new place in the creation. Job seems strangely comforted, consoled and at home.

If you find verse 6 difficult to understand, please know that you are in the very best company. The finest biblical scholars have disagreed and continue to disagree about what the writer means to say. Sometimes "dust and ashes" signifies profound humiliation: I have been proud, I have insisted on my own way, now I have learned better. (That seems to be the tack favored by both the NIV and NRSV.) "Dust and ashes" are also signs of mourning. In the Scriptures, however, "dust and ashes" represent the human condition and even the human dignity whereby a human can stand before God in protest (as Abraham, Genesis 18:27). In recognizing that we are dust (Genesis 2:7), we may also recognize we are dust deeply cared for and remembered by God (see Psalm 103:14).

Mark 16:1-8. Mark's story of Easter

Sunday begins Saturday evening at sundown as the Sabbath ends and shopkeepers open their shops. The three women Mark noticed at the cross (15:40), Mary Magdalene, Mary the mother of James and Joses, and Salome, buy spices, fragrant oils, and ointments to mask the smell of a corpse. The customary care for the deceased had been postponed late Friday afternoon because of the Sabbath's arrival. Tending to a body now will be a ghastly ordeal evidencing deep devotion and no small risk: Primitive taboos about touching corpses reveal a hygienic truth. The women are by no means sure, however, how they will access the body of Jesus securely encased in a tomb. Although verse 3 has been pressed into heavy service for sermons on the futility of worrying about things beforehand, the narrative thrust prepares us for the surprise of the stone rolled back in verse 4, and insists on the women's innocence to charges of tampering with a tomb. At the tomb they find not only the stone moved but also a young man in a white robe. Mark probably understands this as an angel—Matthew certainly does (Matthew 28:5)—and undoubtedly the young man's function in the story is angelic: He has a message to deliver. He identifies Jesus as the one "who was crucified," perhaps echoing language from early Christian worship or creeds. The verb form of "raise" is passive, so the NRSV translation is to be preferred: "He has been raised" with the clear implication that God has done this unexpected thing. What the women are to do now is to "go" and "tell" the disciples that Jesus goes before them (just as Jesus had gone before them on the roads leading to Jerusalem) and they will see him precisely as Jesus himself had told

them in 14:28. Verse 8 reports that instead of speaking as the angel had commanded them, the women fled in terror and kept silent. The "resurrection appearances" in the Gospel of Mark come by promise and anticipation. Jesus has kept other promises; therefore, we can trust that we will encounter him as we follow in his way.

Mark 16:9-20. Many Christians have found that conclusion to the Gospel of Mark profoundly unsatisfying, but most biblical scholars concede that the writer ends the story in 16:8 as the women rush away from the tomb in fear. Matthew and Luke, writing a decade or more later, and using Mark as a source and outline for their Gospels, ended their Gospels with more astonishing stories of the risen Christ's appearing to his disciples. This section appended to the Gospel of Mark, which begins with verse 9, is conventionally known as "the longer ending." A pious Christian scribe apparently added it to Mark sometime in the late second or early third century. The finest ancient manuscripts of the New Testament do not include it. Mark certainly did not write it, but it is part of our Bible and heritage.

The scribe has combined brief references to stories from the other Gospels to round out and smooth down the roughness of Mark 16:1-8. Verses 9-11 in which Jesus appears to Mary Magdalene recall Luke 24:10-11 and John 20:14-28. Luke's wonderful story on the road to Emmaus (Luke 24:13-35) is echoed in verses 12-13. Mark 16:15 reminds us of the Great Commission, Matthew 28:19-20. The ending continues by recounting the signs that will accompany believers. Following Jesus' ascension, the disciples proclaim the good news, which is confirmed by accompanying signs.

INTERPRETING THE SCRIPTURE

The God of the Depths

The modern proverb "Be careful what you ask for, you might just get it" applies in this circumstance. Job has asked—that is, pleaded and demanded—for an audience with God. Given the righteousness of his cause and the ample evidence of injustice done to him we quite naturally sympathize with Job: His case should be heard. What we overlook in our sympathy, however, are the necessary dimensions and location of the courtroom. The chambers of justice are cosmic in proportion. With a sweep of hand God gestures to the pillars that hold up the earth and interrogates Job as to his whereabouts when they were erected. A man with such wealth as Job must be well traveled: "Have you toured the bottom of the seas, Job, where the springs surge up from the depths of rock? Have you visited the densely populated but dimly lit land of the dead?" Job's silence concedes his inexperience in such matters. It is difficult to know how to read God's response to Job. Is this a blast from a threatened deity or a playful parody by a smiling, benevolent parent or a lecture to a slow-learning student? However we read God's lines, this much seems clear: God is God and Job is not up to the task. The immensity of God's creation insists that we approach ultimate questions with humility. Certainly the Scriptures teach us enough about justice so that we should know injustice when we see it and be able to name it for what it is. Just as certainly, however, we should measure our words by recognizing we haven't seen everything and we haven't seen any particular issue from every angle. Job's misunderstanding is not asking for God's judgment but rather presuming he would be able to understand the language. In another courtroom scene in the movie *A Few Good Men* Jack Nicholson as Colonel Nathan Jessep shouts, "You can't handle the truth!" So it is with Job. He cannot manage or grasp the truth about God and God's ultimate justice. This failure is not the result of any moral failure on the part of Job; both God and the storyteller have already told us that he is "blameless" (Job 2:3, 1:1). Job is simply human with human limitations.

Meeting the God We Thought We Knew

Job concedes his human limits in his response to God's questions. Once the court

proceedings begin God dazzles Job not only by pointing out the dimensions of the venue in which the hearing takes place but also by the astonishing diversity of witnesses God provides: lions, mountain goats, wild donkeys, wild oxen, ostriches, hawks, and eagles. If that were not enough, enter the primal creatures of myth and wonder, Leviathan and Behemoth, who are nothing other than God's pets. When all the testimony has been heard, Job does not respond by confessing some hidden sin, as his friends had insisted he must do, and he does not apologize for having asked for an audience with God. Job simply confesses his faith—which has been shaken and tested and agonized throughout his story—and says (perhaps he sings): "I know that you can do all things" (42:2). Job does not have an answer for his suffering, but he has what he has asked for, he has *Who* he has asked for, he has God. In his suffering and questioning his relationship to God has been so renewed that he can modestly say that he had *heard of* God, but now he *sees* in the sense of an inward illumination. He thought he knew before, but now he really knows God.

The Promised Easter Story

Just as Job has discovered God in his own experiencing of suffering, loss, and questioning, so an angelic visitor on Sunday morning promises the women gathered at the tomb and Jesus' disciples and us that we will discover the risen Christ in our own experience: "you will see him" (Mark 16:7). The original ending of the Gospel of Mark apparently did not include any of the familiar and treasured stories of the appearances of the risen Lord. The Gospel of Mark ended at 16:8 with the women rushing from the tomb in fear and bewilderment. Does that mean that the Gospel of Mark's confidence in the resurrection of Jesus is somehow diminished? Far from it! Mark is so utterly confident regarding the power and presence of the risen Lord Jesus Christ that he is certain that you will discover his presence alive in your life. "You will see him," Mark says, and he is confident that you will. Throughout the Gospel he has charted an unmistakable path to recognize the presence of the risen One. Look for suffering, rejection, betrayal, and death and you will find resurrection also (Mark 8:31; 9:31; 10:34). This has always been difficult for Jesus' disciples to grasp (Mark 9:32; 10:35), but the risen One appears again and again. "Appearing in theaters in your neighborhood," movie advertisements used to boast; "appearing in lives just like yours," the Gospel of Mark promises. The Easter story is not simply what we hear when we come to church on Easter Sunday morning; the Easter story tries continually to tell itself in the story of our lives.

Story After Story

The Easter Story is not just the one story of women coming to the tomb on Sunday morning but many stories as men and women come to know the presence of the risen Jesus Christ. It happened to Mary Magdalene, say the writers of the added ending to Marks' Gospel, and it happened to two disciples in the country. The resurrection happened, but when these people tried to tell others, they would not believe them. When the resurrection happens to you, what will you believe? Listen to those who have seen him. Their testimony is reliable. Their stories are true. More stories want to be told of the risen Lord among his disciples. We will discover him as before, wrapped with suffering, rejection, betrayal, and death. He shares our suffering and God-forsakenness, and as he shares it teaches us to speak to God of it all. The risen One does not shrink from the shelter for the homeless, the AIDS treatment center, or the hospice room prepared on your street. As one filled with resurrection life he invades the territory of death. Out of the whirlwind God asks Job if he has seen "the gates of death" (38:17). The question is meant for Job, but Jesus the Christ of God, another human being well acquainted with suffering, answers, saying that he has indeed seen "the gates of death," invaded them, kicked them down, and rescued those contained behind them. The ancient Christian story of "the harrowing of hell" is alluded to in 1 Peter (3:19; 4:6), and is one more story evoked by the triumphant story of Easter Sunday. The story told in worship this morning is told again and again in the lives of Christian people every day.

SHARING THE SCRIPTURE

Preparing Our Hearts

This week's devotional reading is found in Luke 24:1-9, which is Luke's account of the resurrection. Try to read this account as if it were the first time you had encountered it. Think about what you can see, hear, taste, touch, and smell. What questions does this amazing incident raise for you? How might it challenge your faith? How does it strengthen your faith? Had you been one of the women, what might you have said to the others after the "two men in dazzling clothes" (24:4) left you? Ponder these ideas and/or write about them in your spiritual journal.

Pray that you and your class participants will recognize that God has the power even to raise Jesus from the dead.

Preparing Our Minds

Study the background Scripture from Job 38:1-4, 16-17; 42:1-6; Mark 16. Our lesson will highlight Job 38:1, 4, 16-17; 42:1-2, 5;

Mark 16:1-7, 9-14, 20. As you read, think about how we find hope of new life through the power of God, who resurrected Jesus.

Write on newsprint:

❏ resolution for the debate in "Explore the Learners' Beliefs About God's Power, Which Is Great Enough to Bring Life Out of Death."

❏ information for next week's lesson, found under "Continue the Journey."

Plan a brief lecture on the longer ending of Mark as suggested in "Learn How the Job Texts Affirm God's Power, Even over Death, and See How This Power Brings Hope for New Life Found in the Resurrection of Jesus Christ."

Plan for appropriate Easter foods, such as hot cross buns or Easter eggs, if you will use them in the "Celebrate Easter!" portion. Contact class members early in the week to enlist donations.

Locate information about Easter symbols, as suggested in "Celebrate Easter!"

LEADING THE CLASS

(1) Gather to Learn

❖ Welcome the class members and introduce any guests.

❖ Pray that the participants will be open to the scriptural message that the Creator God responds to death with new life.

❖ Invite volunteers who grew up in the church to recall Easter services and family celebrations from their childhood. What seemed so special about Easter? What traditions did their family observe? At what age did they recall beginning to understand that Easter was a celebration of God raising Jesus from the dead to new life? If the class is large, divide into groups so that more people can participate.

❖ Read aloud today's focus statement: **People want to believe that they will live again after physical death. What hope of new life can we find through the resurrection of Jesus Christ? The Job texts point to** God as the One powerful enough to overcome death itself, and Mark's account of the first Easter gives us confidence that believers can look forward to resurrection.

(2) Learn How the Job Texts Affirm God's Power, Even over Death, and See How This Power Brings Hope for New Life Found in the Resurrection of Jesus Christ

❖ Choose a volunteer to read Job 38:1, 4, 16-17. If time permits, read all of chapter 38 to get a sense of the majestic poetry with which God speaks to Job concerning creation. Ask another person to read Job 42:1-2, 5.

◼ Discuss these questions.

(1) How would you describe God's attitude in answering Job? (See "The God of the Depths" in Interpreting the Scripture for ideas.)

(2) What words would you use to describe the picture of creation that God paints for Job?

(3) When Job actually meets God, what new insights does he gain? (See "Meeting the God We Thought We Knew" in "Interpreting the Scripture" for ideas. Add ideas from verse 6. See the second paragraph of Job 42:1-6 in Understanding the Scripture for help.)

◼ Invite the students to contemplate silently this idea: **What is the difference between knowing God and knowing about God? Which label best describes your own relationship? What changes would you like to make?**

❖ Select someone to read an account of Jesus' resurrection from Mark 16:1-7, 9-14, 20.

◼ Use information from Mark 16:9-20 in Understanding the Scripture to point out that Mark has a longer ending, which begins with verse 9, and a shorter ending (verse unnumbered in NRSV) that was added sometime after the third century.

Most scholars believe that Mark's actual work ended with verse 8. Comment, or ask the class to comment, on what would be lost if the Gospel ended with verse 8.

■ Look at verses 11 and 13, which both speak of unbelief. Encourage the students to envision themselves with the disciples. How would they have reacted to the news? Would they believe? Why or why not?

(3) Explore the Learners' Beliefs About God's Power, Which Is Great Enough to Bring Life Out of Death

❖ Set up an informal debate on this resolution: **Resolved, that since an angelic young man appeared to the women and assured them of Jesus' resurrection, an integral part of Christian belief is that Jesus was bodily resurrected.**

❖ Choose two teams to give opposite views on this resolution. Or, if the class is small, include everyone. This debate will give students an opportunity to express their beliefs and doubts about the resurrection and hear how other people view this amazing event.

(4) Celebrate Easter!

❖ Celebrate Easter with the class by studying some of the symbols commonly associated with Easter, such as: *Paschal Lamb, the cross, Easter eggs, Easter bunny, Easter clothes and bonnets, Easter lilies, hot cross buns, butterfly,* and *sunrise.* You can find information in books and on the Internet under "Easter symbols." You may wish to contact class members during the week and ask each one to research a different symbol.

❖ **Option:** Enjoy some hot cross buns and Easter eggs if you and/or members of the group choose to bring them. Be sure to have napkins, plates, and cups for a beverage.

❖ Talk with the class about why Easter is important to them.

(5) Continue the Journey

❖ Pray that the Spirit of the living Christ will abide in the hearts of all who call upon the name of the Lord.

❖ Read aloud this preparation for next week's lesson. You may also want to post it on newsprint for the students to copy. **Prepare for next week's session, "Where Is Peace Found?" by reading Ecclesiastes 1:1-11 and John 20:19-23. We will look especially at Ecclesiastes 1:1-9 and John 20:19-23. Focus on these ideas as you study: People are searching for a purpose in life that brings them peace. How can we find the meaning and peace in life for which we search? The writer of Ecclesiastes, who tradition says was Solomon, implies that it is our nature to seek meaning and peace, but that we might not find this in our lifetime. John, on the other hand, affirms that we find meaning and peace in life when we receive the Spirit of Christ Jesus.**

❖ Read aloud the following three ideas. Challenge the students to commit themselves to use these activities as a springboard to spiritual growth.

(1) **Read accounts of the resurrection from the other Gospels: Matthew 28:1-10; Luke 24:1-12; John 20:1-18. Compare these accounts with Mark 16. What new insights do you gain from each of the Gospel writers?**

(2) **Read God's response to Job in its entirety in Job 38–39.**

(3) **Tell at least one other person about God raising Jesus from the dead, and what that news means for all creation. Invite that individual to make a response to this good news.**

❖ Sing or read aloud "Up from the Grave He Arose."

❖ Lead this benediction to end today's session: **With all of your creatures, most majestic God, we sing your praises and pray that you would empower us to be wise people and faithful stewards of your creation, in Jesus' name. Amen.**

UNIT 2: LIVING WITH CREATION'S UNCERTAINTY
WHERE IS PEACE FOUND?

PREVIEWING THE LESSON

Lesson Scripture: Ecclesiastes 1:1-9; John 20:19-23
Background Scripture: Ecclesiastes 1:1-11; John 20:19-23
Key Verse: John 20:19

Focus of the Lesson:

People are searching for a purpose in life that brings them peace. How can we find the meaning and peace in life for which we search? The writer of Ecclesiastes, who tradition says was Solomon, implies that it is our nature to seek meaning and peace, but that we might not find this in our lifetime. John, on the other hand, affirms that we find meaning and peace in life when we receive the Spirit of Christ Jesus.

Goals for the Learners:

(1) to connect teachings in Ecclesiastes about the meaning, purpose, and peace for which we search with John's account of Jesus' post-resurrection appearance.
(2) to identify places in their own lives where they need God's peace.
(3) to recognize and affirm how Jesus provides purpose and peace in their lives.

Pronunciation Guide:

hebel (heh' bel)
Qoheleth (koh hel' ith)
shalom (sha lom')

Supplies:

Bibles, newsprint and marker, paper and pencils, hymnals

READING THE SCRIPTURE

NRSV
Ecclesiastes 1:1-9
1 The words of the Teacher, the son of
    David, king in Jerusalem.
2 Vanity of vanities, says the Teacher,
    vanity of vanities! All is vanity.
3 What do people gain from all the toil
    at which they toil under the sun?

NIV
Ecclesiastes 1:1-9
1The words of the Teacher, son of David,
    king in Jerusalem:
2"Meaningless! Meaningless!"
    says the Teacher.
"Utterly meaningless!
    Everything is meaningless."

4 A generation goes, and a generation
    comes,
  but the earth remains forever.
5 The sun rises and the sun goes down,
    and hurries to the place where it rises.
6 The wind blows to the south,
    and goes around to the north;
  round and round goes the wind,
    and on its circuits the wind returns.
7 All streams run to the sea,
    but the sea is not full;
  to the place where the streams flow,
    there they continue to flow.
8 All things are wearisome;
    more than one can express;
  the eye is not satisfied with seeing,
    or the ear filled with hearing.
9 What has been is what will be,
    and what has been done is what will
      be done;
  there is nothing new under the sun.

3What does man gain from all his labor
    at which he toils under the sun?
4Generations come and generations go,
    but the earth remains forever.
5The sun rises and the sun sets,
    and hurries back to where it rises.
6The wind blows to the south
    and turns to the north;
  round and round it goes,
    ever returning on its course.
7All streams flow into the sea,
    yet the sea is never full.
To the place the streams come from,
    there they return again.
8All things are wearisome,
    more than one can say.
The eye never has enough of seeing,
    nor the ear its fill of hearing.
9What has been will be again,
    what has been done will be done again;
  there is nothing new under the sun.

John 20:19-23

19**When it was evening on that day, the
first day of the week, and the doors of the
house where the disciples had met were
locked for fear of the Jews, Jesus came and
stood among them and said, "Peace be with
you."** 20After he said this, he showed them
his hands and his side. Then the disciples
rejoiced when they saw the Lord. 21Jesus
said to them again, "Peace be with you. As
the Father has sent me, so I send you."
22When he had said this, he breathed on
them and said to them, "Receive the Holy
Spirit. 23If you forgive the sins of any, they
are forgiven them; if you retain the sins of
any, they are retained."

John 20:19-23

19**On the evening of that first day of the
week, when the disciples were together,
with the doors locked for fear of the Jews,
Jesus came and stood among them and
said, "Peace be with you!"** 20After he said
this, he showed them his hands and side.
The disciples were overjoyed when they saw
the Lord.

21Again Jesus said, "Peace be with you! As
the Father has sent me, I am sending you."
22And with that he breathed on them and
said, "Receive the Holy Spirit. 23If you forgive anyone his sins, they are forgiven; if
you do not forgive them, they are not forgiven."

UNDERSTANDING THE SCRIPTURE

Ecclesiastes 1:1-11. Reading Ecclesiastes
(especially the first Sunday after Easter) can
startle people who expect the Scriptures to
speak in a single tone of voice. The writer
Qoheleth, usually translated "the teacher"
or "the preacher"—the Hebrew word

derives from the word for the assembly or
congregation—takes getting used to. It is
too easy to dismiss him as depressed or
despondent, a cynic or nihilist or curmudg-
eon. He has written a dense, complicated,
and sometimes contradictory document

that does not shrink from the density, complications, and contradictions of living in our world. The apostle Paul reflected on his world in the light of what he witnessed God doing in the cross and resurrection of Jesus Christ and announced, "everything has become new!" (2 Corinthians 5:17); Qoheleth, no less a man of faith than Paul, looked upon his world and declared "there is nothing new under the sun" (Ecclesiastes 1:9).

"All things are *hebel*," announces Qoheleth: The NRSV translates with the traditional "vanity"; the NIV translates "meaningless"; others translate "absurdity," "emptiness," "futility," "useless." All of these translations pick up pieces of Qoheleth's truth, but no one translation fully captures all of the nuances. The Hebrew root meaning would be "vapor" or "breath," that which is evanescent and ephemeral, but also that which we cannot grasp, hold, and master. All that seems so permanent, enduring, and significant in time blows away like smoke. *Hebel* is an important word for Qoheleth, occurring thirty-eight times in these twelve chapters.

Another characteristic usage is "under the sun," repeated twenty-nine times. "Under the sun" refers to life among the living. The only life beyond death Qoheleth imagines is the life of succeeding generations and their remembrance, but finally even that fades like mist as one generation comes and goes and finally is forgotten. God may be praised from generation to generation (Psalm 79:13), but human endeavor slips into the forgetfulness of history.

What does anything matter, Qoheleth asks, and what is the significance of human "toil under the sun" (1:3)? The wisdom tradition of Israel honors the respectability of hard work: "In all toil there is profit, but mere talk leads only to poverty" (Proverbs 14:23). One thing consistently frustrating Qoheleth in his attempts to find consistency in the world is the way that neither wisdom nor folly provides guarantees of success

(2:12-16; 7:15). Although Qoheleth would not dispute the possible short-term benefits, this too is finally *hebel*, and who can finally know whether hard work finally leads to profit or poverty?

Human beings do not have a place of privilege from which they may make that sort of judgment; that belongs to God alone. From where we must live our lives in "toil under the sun," the sun is predictably rising and setting to no purpose, and the rivers are flowing to the sea without ever filling the sea.

The unfilled sea mirrors the human condition of dissatisfied emptiness. Verse 8 states "all things are wearisome," also translated, "all words are wearisome," which would fit better with the next thought: Things are more tedious than Qoheleth can possibly say. One might almost translate colloquially, "but why am I telling you this?" Why bother with more unsatisfactory words? Why bother with anything at all? But Qoheleth does bother, and beyond the words incessantly announcing that nothing matters very much, we sense that everything is at stake in this writer's words. The words may not fill us up and they may not satisfy us, but Qoheleth's astringent honesty compels a hearing, even a grudging hearing.

John 20:19-23. The church calendar reckons time according to Luke's calculation: Jesus is raised from death on Easter, then fifty days later at Pentecost the Spirit is given (Acts 2:1-13). The Gospel of John places both events on the same day. In the morning Mary Magdalene, Peter, and "the other disciple" (20:4) go to the tomb and find it empty. The two disciples return home, but Mary, remaining at the tomb with her tears, sees the risen Lord. The day passes and at evening Jesus comes to his disciples. The disciples huddle behind locked doors "for fear of the Jews" (20:19), one of the Gospel of John's curious ways of speaking about Jesus' opponents, as if Jesus and all the disciples were not Jews. That manner of speaking reflects the situation when the Gospel of John was written, probably sixty years or so after that first Easter, when Jews who followed the way of Jesus were no longer welcome in synagogues. The risen Christ's words to the disciples are utterly Jewish, drawing on the deep hopes of the Scriptures: "Peace be with you," he says, echoing the blessing given by God to Moses to give to the children of Aaron (Numbers 6:24-26). God's promise of peace, *shalom,* is the heartbeat of Isaiah's words of comfort and hope (Isaiah 52:7; 54:10). *Shalom* is not simply the absence of war or an interval between conflicts, but the healing of the creation into the harmony God has always intended. Christ's blessing, "Peace be with you," draws from the deep wells of God's promise of peace, but who could believe such a promise could be coming true after everything that had happened that weekend? It is precisely the signs of Jesus suffering—"he showed them his hands and his side" (20:20)—that validate the blessing of peace. When the disciples see the wounds they rejoice as Isaiah expected people to rejoice in response to peace (Isaiah 55:12), and Jesus blesses them a second time and sends them out as emissaries of God's peace. Those who have been disciples (followers of a master) become apostles (those who are sent). Jesus breathes the Spirit upon them (or in them), a daringly intimate picture of the giving of the Spirit. The Spirit in the Gospel of John is the Spirit of the crucified One: Until Jesus is simultaneously crucified and glorified there is no Spirit to give (John 7:39). The gift of forgiveness bears witness to God's *shalom:* it is not merely a juridical transaction ("you are forgiven this deed or that neglect"), but a part of God's healing of all that has been broken by sin.

INTERPRETING THE SCRIPTURE

Raising the Tough Questions

It is good to have the book of Ecclesiastes in our Bible. It is good also that the contemplations and questions and critique of Ecclesiastes are bound up together along with the high praise of the Psalms, the confidence of the prophets, and the hope of the Gospels. Read by itself the book of Ecclesiastes is so astringent that we might shudder to hear our existence described in such terms, but reading Ecclesiastes as one more witness to our life lived in the presence of God can provide a strange comfort and an unexpected hope.

The voice we hear in Ecclesiastes is that of Qoheleth, a preacher or teacher, one who gathers a congregation for a time of learning. Qoheleth has seen a thing or two, he has engaged in experiments in living (Ecclesiastes 2:1), and he wants to raise questions with us. It is good to have someone in class who is not afraid to ask the hard questions and to raise the most unsettling concerns. Sometimes we are timid with our questions. We fear what others might think. We fear our own doubts. We fear the questions themselves. Some classes do not permit questions. They think religious faith is a matter only of answers. It is good to have Qoheleth to ask the questions, because his questions are our questions, and the voice we hear in Ecclesiastes is a voice we also hear in our own minds.

That our Scriptures include the book of Ecclesiastes confidently signals that questions are welcomed in our faith. Jesus included among his disciples Thomas, who on at least one occasion risked asking the question that all the disciples must have been thinking. "You know the way," Jesus tells them (John 14:4), but Thomas blurts that they don't know "the way" at all, and asks "how can we know the way?" (John

14:5). On this second Sunday of Easter many congregations read each year the story of Thomas questioning the resurrection. He was not present when Jesus appeared to the disciples; he has questions. Jesus does not rebuke his questions but welcomes his skepticism and invites him to experience his risen body firsthand (John 20:27).

Our Life Is a Breath

Qoheleth observes what we all see: the sun rising and setting, the wind blowing this way and that, the generations rising and falling. Nothing seems permanent except the unending repetition, and from what can be directly observed, there seems no point to it all. Everything is transient, insubstantial, and as evanescent as breath.

The meanings we would like to find in life slip away like fog. The success we thought would thrill us was wonderful, but did not entirely satisfy us, and so we look for something else even though we may not quite be certain what it is we seek. The tragedy we thought would destroy us didn't, and so we live with loss and sadness even as other events appear to give us moments of joy and happiness we never expected. We meet the goals we set, but to what avail? Or we fall short of our best dreams for ourselves, and what does it matter? The world turns on and our triumphs and disappointments weigh no more than a breath on its turning. The phrase "toil under the sun" refers not only to the work human beings do to survive but also the very burden of our own living. How do we live out our brief interlude—our moments of breath—in the never-ceasing procession of the generations that come and go?

The wisdom tradition of Israel occupied itself with providing reliable instruction for life, but Qoheleth observes that those who are wise will die just as fools die (2:15-16). What is the point of wisdom? Still, Qoheleth speaks wisdom. He laments the vanity of more contemplations and more words (1:8), but still he gathers his congregation to teach what wisdom frail, limited human creatures may know.

Seeking Wisdom

Again and again the wisdom tradition entreats learners to seek wisdom as they would search for "hidden treasure" (Proverbs 2:4), promising that those who find wisdom will be happy (Proverbs 3:13), enticing students with the incomparable value of wisdom (Proverbs 3:15), and declaring of Woman Wisdom that "all her paths are peace" (Proverbs 3:17). The wisdom tradition warns of distractions on this search (Proverbs 2:12-19), especially the temptation to believe that one is already wise or has sufficient wisdom (Proverbs 3:5). (In one sense Qoheleth's acknowledgment of the limits of wisdom is nothing less than the epitome of wisdom. We can only know so much.) The end of our human searching is not simply that one finds wisdom (Proverbs 3:13) but one discovers that it is the gracious will of God to give wisdom to those who seek (Proverbs 2:3-6).

Nothing less than this grace is enacted in the resurrection story found in the Gospel of John. The first verses of John's Gospel identify Jesus as the personified Wisdom of God. "The Word" had become a way of speaking of wisdom by the first century. At the beginning of John's Gospel two disciples of John the Baptist begin following Jesus and he asks them, "What are you looking for?" (John 1:38 NRSV); or "What do you want?" (John 1:38 NIV). They respond, calling Jesus "Rabbi," and John highlights the title translating it as "teacher." They place themselves as learners before a teacher. In this case, their teacher is no one other than the very Wisdom of God. The two disciples do not answer Jesus' question about what they are searching for; it may be as difficult to articulate a statement of what we are looking for as it is to find it. Perhaps they are looking for a way through life. "Ways" were a customary manner of speaking in the wisdom tradition. Perhaps they were seeking a depth of life and the truth about life. As we read John's Gospel, Jesus—who we know to be the Wisdom of God—reveals himself saying, "I am the way and the truth and the life" (John 14:6) and "I am the resurrection" (11:25). The disciples are learning wisdom.

Receiving Wisdom and Peace

At the conclusion of the Gospel of John, Jesus teaches his disciples no longer. They have learned what they need to know about who he is. They do not need lessons about him, they need life like his, and this Jesus gives them as he breathes upon them. The breath that for Qoheleth epitomizes the fearful futility of human existence conveys in this story the very gift of life. When Jesus gives his disciples his own breath he means

for them to have a life filled with the breath/spirit that animated his own living. The Way of Jesus Christ—the Way that *is* Jesus Christ—is characterized by peace. With the gift of his peace and his Spirit, Jesus also gives the disciples a commission to share that peace and that Spirit by offering forgiveness. His is a gift—if we may dare say it—that keeps on giving, even from generation to generation.

The contrasts between Ecclesiastes and the Gospel of John are so many and so enormous that it may not be fair to compare them, but perhaps one ironic point is worth noting. Qoheleth's acidic ruminations about human existence begin by asking the question about what do humans *gain* from their toil under the sun. Jesus sends his disciples out inviting them to imagine what they might *give* to a world badly in need of a word of peace.

SHARING THE SCRIPTURE

Preparing Our Hearts

This week's devotional reading is found in Luke 24:36-48, which records a post-resurrection appearance of Jesus to his disciples. Jesus greets his startled followers with the words "Peace be with you." For Jesus, peace, or in Hebrew *shalom*, is not simply the absence of conflict, but health and wholeness; in fact, it denotes the healing of all God's creation. Where do you need peace in your own life? What steps can you take to move toward peace?

Pray that you and your class participants will do your utmost to bring about the peaceable kingdom that God intends for all creation.

Preparing Our Minds

Study the background from Ecclesiastes 1:1-11 and John 20:19-23. Our lesson will focus

on Ecclesiastes 1:1-9 and John 20:19-23. As you prepare to teach, ponder what the Scriptures say about how we can find the meaning and peace in life for which we search.

Write on newsprint:

❑ information for next week's lesson, found under "Continue the Journey."

Plan a lecture if you choose to use one for "Connect Teachings in Ecclesiastes About the Meaning, Purpose, and Peace for which We Search with John's Account of Jesus' Post-resurrection Appearance."

LEADING THE CLASS

(1) Gather to Learn

❖ Welcome the class members and introduce any guests.

❖ Pray that the participants will recognize the relationship between meaning and peace in their lives.

❖ Read this anecdote quoted by Rick Warren in *The Purpose-Driven Life:* **Andrei Bitov, a Russian novelist, grew up under an atheistic Communist regime. But God got his attention one dreary day. He recalls, "In my twenty-seventh year, while riding the metro in Leningrad (now St. Petersburg) I was overcome with a despair so great that life seemed to stop at once, preempting the future entirely, let alone any meaning. Suddenly, all by itself, a phrase appeared:** *Without God life makes no sense.* **Repeating it in astonishment, I rode the phrase up like a moving staircase, got out of the metro and walked into God's light.**

❖ Challenge the class members to discuss experiences in their own lives when they no longer felt in the dark about their purpose in life but realized that purpose in the light of God's love.

❖ Read aloud today's focus statement: **People are searching for a purpose in life that brings them peace. How can we find the meaning and peace in life for which we search? The writer of Ecclesiastes, who tradition says was Solomon, implies that it is our nature to seek meaning and peace, but that we might not find this in our lifetime. John, on the other hand, affirms that we find meaning and peace in life when we receive the Spirit of Christ Jesus.**

(2) Connect Teachings in Ecclesiastes About the Meaning, Purpose, and Peace for Which We Search with John's Account of Jesus' Post-resurrection Appearance

❖ Choose a volunteer to read Ecclesiastes 1:1-9.
■ Point out the variety of meanings for *hebel,* translated as "vanity" in the NRSV, as found in the second paragraph of Ecclesiastes 1:1-11 in "Understanding the Scripture."
■ Talk about how the examples the Teacher gives in these verses seem to support his belief that all is *hebel.*

■ Read "Our Life Is a Breath" from Interpreting the Scripture and ask these questions.
(1) **Why do you agree or disagree with the Teacher?**
(2) **In what ways does a relationship with Christ change the Teacher's perspective on life— or does it?**

❖ Select one student to read the part of the narrator and one to read the words of Jesus in John 20:19-23. Note that this encounter takes place on the evening of Easter.
■ Identify in a lecture or a class discussion any changes that occur in this brief story.
(1) In verse 19, fear (based on the unwillingness of the disciples to believe Mary Magdalene's report of her meeting with the risen Lord) is banished by Jesus' words of peace.
(2) In verse 20, the sorrowing disciples now rejoice because they see proof that the one before them is the risen Lord.
(3) In verse 21, the disciples will no longer be barricaded behind closed doors but are being sent out to do Jesus' work.
(4) In verse 22, the disciples will be transformed by the gift of the Holy Spirit, which Jesus had promised to them in John 14:26; 15:26-27; 16:7-11; and 16:12-15.
(5) In verse 23 the disciples receive the power to forgive sins. As *The New Interpreter's Study Bible* explains, in John's Gospel, "forgiveness of sins is the community's Spirit-empowered mission to continue Jesus' work of making God known in the world and through that work to bring the world to judgment and decision through its response to Jesus."
■ Conclude this section of the lesson by reading the final paragraph of

"Receiving Wisdom and Peace" in Interpreting the Scripture. Encourage the class to talk about the contrast between gaining and giving.

(3) Identify Places in the Learners' Lives Where They Need God's Peace

❖ Distribute paper and pencils. Invite the students to write confidentially or meditate on a situation that has disrupted their sense of God's peace. Note that these situations may be normal transitions that many people look forward to, such as the last child leaving home or retirement. Suggest they consider these questions: What happened? Who was involved? What do I think needs to happen in order for this situation to be resolved and my peace to be restored?

❖ Close this time by asking the students to read today's key verse, John 20:19, in unison. Then encourage the students to say to one another, **"The peace of our Lord Jesus Christ be with you."**

(4) Recognize and Affirm How Jesus Provides Purpose and Peace

❖ Encourage the class members to tell stories of how Jesus has provided purpose and peace in their own lives. If the class is large, consider dividing into groups so that more people can relate their stories.

❖ Invite the students to make a commitment to share with others what they have learned about God's purpose and peace from their own lives and from today's Scripture study.

(5) Continue the Journey

❖ Pray that the participants will experience God's peace in their lives and share that peace with others.

❖ Read aloud this preparation for next week's lesson. You may also want to post it on newsprint for the students to copy. **Prepare for next week's session, "Everything Has a Season," by reading Ecclesiastes 3. We will pay particular attention to verses 1-8, 14-15 during our session. As you read, think about these ideas: People want to believe there is a time for everything that occurs in life. How does God's time schedule relate to our lives? This text reveals that God does everything at the right time in our lives.**

❖ Read aloud the following three ideas. Challenge the students to commit themselves to use these activities as a springboard to spiritual growth.

   (1) Read Rick Warren's book *The Purpose-Driven Life*. How does this book affirm or challenge understandings of your own life's purpose?

   (2) Write in your spiritual journal about experiences in life that have given you a sense of peace and meaning. Do these experiences still touch your life? If not, how can you regain this sense of peace and meaning?

   (3) Identify experiences that disrupt your sense of peace. What steps can you take when such disruptions occur to regain your sense of shalom?

❖ Sing or read aloud "It Is Well with My Soul."

❖ Lead this benediction to end today's session: **With all of your creatures, most majestic God, we sing your praises and pray that you would empower us to be wise people and faithful stewards of your creation, in Jesus' name. Amen.**

UNIT 2: LIVING WITH CREATION'S UNCERTAINTY
EVERYTHING HAS A SEASON

PREVIEWING THE LESSON

Lesson Scripture: Ecclesiastes 3:1-8, 14-15
Background Scripture: Ecclesiastes 3
Key Verse: Ecclesiastes 3:1

Focus of the Lesson:
People want to believe there is a time for everything that occurs in life. How does God's time schedule relate to our lives? This text reveals that God does everything at the right time in our lives.

Goals for the Learners:
(1) to examine the philosopher's thoughts on how there is a time for everything.
(2) to draw a connection between the text's teachings about God's timetable and events in their lives.
(3) to be mindful about balancing how time is spent.

Pronunciation Guide:
Qoheleth (koh hel' ith)

Supplies:
Bibles, newsprint and marker, paper and pencils, copy of the words of Peter Seeger's "Turn, Turn, Turn" and/or recording of it with appropriate player

---

READING THE SCRIPTURE

NRSV
Ecclesiastes 3:1-8, 14-15

¹For everything there is a season, and a time for every matter under heaven:
2 a time to be born, and a time to die;
   a time to plant, and a time to pluck up
      what is planted;
3 a time to kill, and a time to heal;
   a time to break down, and a time to build
      up;

NIV
Ecclesiastes 3:1-8, 14-15

**¹There is a time for everything,
and a season for every activity under
   heaven:**
2 a time to be born and a time to die,
   a time to plant and a time to uproot,
3 a time to kill and a time to heal,
   a time to tear down and a time to build,
4 a time to weep and a time to laugh,

⁴ a time to weep, and a time to laugh;
   a time to mourn, and a time to dance;
⁵ a time to throw away stones, and a time to
   gather stones together;
   a time to embrace, and a time to refrain
   from embracing;
⁶ a time to seek, and a time to lose;
   a time to keep, and a time to throw away;
⁷ a time to tear, and a time to sew;
   a time to keep silence, and a time to speak;
⁸ a time to love, and a time to hate;
   a time for war, and a time for peace.
¹⁴I know that whatever God does endures
forever; nothing can be added to it, nor anything taken from it; God has done this, so
that all should stand in awe before him.
¹⁵That which is, already has been; that which
is to be, already is; and God seeks out what
has gone by.

a time to mourn and a time to dance,
⁵ a time to scatter stones and a time to
   gather them,
   a time to embrace and a time to refrain,
⁶ a time to search and a time to give up,
   a time to keep and a time to throw away,
⁷ a time to tear and a time to mend,
   a time to be silent and a time to speak,
⁸ a time to love and a time to hate,
   a time for war and a time for peace.
¹⁴I know that everything God does will
endure forever; nothing can be added to it
and nothing taken from it. God does it so
that men will revere him.
¹⁵ Whatever is has already been,
   and what will be has been before;
   and God will call the past to account.

UNDERSTANDING THE SCRIPTURE

Ecclesiastes 3:1-8. This best-known passage of Ecclesiastes is this poem of fourteen
antitheses opposing twenty-eight different
human activities. Such an arrangement of
opposites is often used in the Old Testament
to signify completeness. The parallel structure of the introductory verse 1, in which
the general statement of the first words ("a
time for everything," NIV; "For everything
there is a season," NRSV) is focused and
intensified by the second half of the statement, leads us expectantly into the list of
activities. The word translated "season"
indicates a time predetermined and
ordained, not one arranged by human initiative. The list begins with birth and death,
though biblical scholars disagree whether
this should be translated "a time to be born"
or "a time to give birth." Beginning with
birth and death, and ending with war and
peace, this list means to circumscribe the
human enterprise. Birth and death, war and
peace stand at the limits of human existence: These are beyond our control as indi-

viduals. Although human beings have
somewhat more control over the other activities cataloged in between these limit experiences we must still concede the "seasons"
are not ours to decide. Even our own tears
and laughter are not ours to determine. The
activities are the stuff of ordinary human
existence: planting a field or clearing it;
building or destroying; embracing or not
embracing. The stones that are scattered or
gathered raise many questions. Some suggest this recalls a wartime strategy of scattering stones in a field to prevent an
enemy's planting it; others see a
euphemistic reference to lovemaking as
scattering and abstinence as gathering; still
others to the employment of stones as a
bookkeeping method in an agricultural
economy. The two oppositions of verse 6
enjoin generosity by placing a limit on our
acquisitiveness: There is a time for surren-
dering our possessions. Tearing and sewing
(3:7) most likely refer to the experience of
grief: One tears one's garments as a sign of

grief (Genesis 37:29; 2 Samuel 1:11) and makes repairs after a suitable time of mourning. The opposition of silence and speaking in verse 7 is characteristic of the wisdom tradition of Israel that knows the power and refreshment of the right word at the right time (Proverbs 15:23; 25:11). Beginning with birth and death and progressing to love and hate, we might expect the next opposition to be peace and war, but the poet somewhat unexpectedly ends, "war and peace."

Ecclesiastes 3:9-15. Qoheleth, the wisdom teacher of Ecclesiastes, shifts into prose to reflect on the meaning of these many and varied activities. He asks a rhetorical question in verse 9 wondering about the point of all this busyness—implying that there is no "gain" or profit to be found—and then in verse 10 shifts attention from contemplating human activity to God's activity. God has given all these activities just as God has given the seasons in which they are to be done. What God has given the human creature is not a gift to be regarded lightly. The NIV's translation of "burden" (3:10) is to be preferred over the NRSV's "business"—the Hebrew word in question carries a ponderous weight in Ecclesiastes. We bear the weight of our work even as we try to discern the seasons in which to take the appropriate action, but our vision and understanding are limited. We know that there is an appropriate season for every activity, but we cannot know when that is and we cannot know when prudently to act. Only God knows such things. We cannot fully know the meaning of time; nor can we fully understand "eternity" (3:11 NIV; the word invokes a sense of timelessness, and "eternity" is probably a closer match than "a sense of past and future" as found in the NRSV). From God we have received intimations of eternity, but we must live out our lives in the ambiguities of times beyond our control. Though we might easily despair, Qoheleth has been conducting experiments in experience (Ecclesiastes 2:1, 12) and has come to

some conclusions. In 3:12 and 14 he announces the results of his tests: "I know." The words "I know" are uncharacteristic of the reflective, pondering posture of Ecclesiastes, so when we hear something announced with such certitude, we do well to listen. Although we may have no "gain" from our burdensome work, Ecclesiastes invites us to discover the enjoyment of the work itself. Every day is the appropriate season for discovering the goodness God gives. Our labors can neither add nor diminish what God has prepared, but we can live as reverent and grateful recipients of the time given us. God keeps us "from this time on and forevermore" (Psalm 121:8).

Ecclesiastes 3:16-22. Qoheleth trusts God even with his disillusionment and skepticism. Much he does not understand and much he does not know, but he commends it all to God who gave it. He surveys the world seeking for God's promised justice, but his eyes fall upon injustice ruling in the place of justice. Nevertheless, he trusts that God will finally judge both "the righteous and the wicked"(3:17), and that justice will finally rule. His trust anticipates our confidence in praying "thy kingdom come" and our hope that God's justice and mercy will finally rule. In the meantime, he examines the facts: Animals die and human beings die: "as one dies, so dies the other" (3:19). As we have come from the dust of the earth so we return to dust, human and animal alike. A man of the world, Qoheleth has heard rumors, most likely from Greek thought, that the human spirit rises upward. Perhaps this is so, he concedes, but "who knows" (3:21). He will consider the matter thoughtfully, but he will not be consumed by vain speculation about what he cannot know will be. His concern is for wisdom by which we may live in the present where the human task is to find enjoyment in work. Qoheleth has learned (3:22) that the real reward of work is found in the joy of work itself, not in anticipated profits that may or may not be returned.

INTERPRETING THE SCRIPTURE

Knowing Time and Not Knowing

Some people, especially baby boomers, cannot read this poem from Ecclesiastes 3 without hearing as background music the tune of the Byrds' rendition of the Pete Seeger song "Turn, Turn, Turn." We heard that music when we were much younger, and we recognized the deep wisdom of the words. Nowadays this generation is more likely to hear these words read at funerals and memorial services. The seasons have "turn, turn, turned," and looking back and looking forward, we wonder where the time has gone and we wonder what time it is. Song and Scripture promised "a time to every purpose under the heaven" (Ecclesiastes 3:1, KJV), but as the years go by we may find ourselves wondering if we really can discern the right times for things. We know that there was a right time to buy Dell stock and a right time to get out of Enron. We know there is a time to be born and a time to die, but our death is, for most of us, hidden from our eyes, and as for birth we wonder if we should have had children sooner or maybe later, or more of them or not so many, or we wish that single people adopting had become an acceptable alternative sooner, or maybe there's still time. But we do not know the time to give birth any more than we know precisely the hour of our death.

Qoheleth's poem tantalizes us because we cheerfully acknowledge the truthfulness and wisdom of his observations. We know that there is a time for everything, and we exercise our best judgment to discern the times. We do not plant in the fall that which cannot endure the winter. We carefully consider when an embrace might be a comfort and when it might be an affront. We try to postpone our time to die by cutting back on the cholesterol and exercising, and then we hear that the cute thirty-ish fellow in the next pew has a chest full of cancer even though he never smoked, had no family history or particular risk. We know there is a time but we know we don't know the time.

Trusting Time to God

Far from being a counsel of despair or an enthronement of discouragement, Qoheleth's observations propose to lead us directly to God, who is the Author of Time. That there are seasons we know and that there are human actions to be taken we know, but we know also the One who has made both the seasons and work humans are given to do, and Qoheleth tells us that God has provided a right time for everything. The "rightness" of the time is expressed in an elegant Hebrew word. The NRSV's translation of "suitable" (3:11) is perfectly adequate, but in the Hebrew there are also connotations of a harmonious fit, and the NIV's translation of "beautiful" stresses that theme.

In the passing seasons things happen that we did not plan and would not have asked for, but we also discover sometimes an elegant "fit" in which we are given not so much what we would want but perhaps what we need. Where we cannot discern that "fit" Qoheleth invites us to trust in God and finally recognize our own place in the drama of creation by standing in awe and reverence of God. No, we do not understand the plan, and no, we do not understand the seasons, but we can trust ourselves to God's plans in every season.

Living in Wonder

Contemplating the changing times and seasons of human life upon the earth, Qoheleth turns his eyes heavenward to the One who does not change and before Whom we live out our days. We build and tear down, we plant and pluck up what has been planted, we sew and tear away, and the impermanence of our accomplishments characterizes human life. Each day there are dishes to be washed, each week new loads of laundry, each month bills to be paid, each quarter quotas to be met, each year annual reports and evaluations. Within the rhythms of human activity there are satisfactions and frustrations, joys and regrets, but what is not there is permanence, and sometimes we cannot help wondering at the meaning of it all. Time has a way of eroding the work of our hands: The lawn does not stay mowed, the last quarter's growth is not matched by this quarter's flat charts. Qoheleth looks up from the world of our work and activity to wonder at God's work. "I know," he says with great assurance, that what "God does endures forever" (3:14). What Qoheleth points to is a construction that transcends the erosions of time and is so vast that "nothing can be added to it, nor anything taken from it" (3:14).

The appropriate response to this is "awe" (3:14 NRSV) or reverence ("revere," NIV). The book of Proverbs invites us to recognize that "The fear of the LORD is the beginning of knowledge" (Proverbs 1:7; also Psalm 111:10), and Psalm 19:9 declares that "the fear of the LORD is pure, enduring forever": just as whatever God does endures forever, so also the fear of the Lord endures forever. Awe, wonder, and reverence may be present as we begin our seeking of wisdom, but we will never conclude our contemplation of what God has done without awe, wonder, and reverence.

Earlier Qoheleth had observed the persistence of the past into the present and the future's repetition of what has been, and observed "there is nothing new under the sun" (1:9). Here he explains that this is so because God is not through with the past but summons it to return again, perhaps for judgment, perhaps to reclaim and heal the time. (Readers will recognize the difficulty as they compare the two different translations of 3:15 in the NRSV and NIV.) If the past encroaches upon the present and future this is for Qoheleth no mere assertion of the repetitiveness of time. God causes this to happen because God who lives out of time is working in our time.

God's Triumph

Although some would dismiss Qoheleth as a cynic, he is by no means a man without hope. Observing the inequities of this world, some would shrug and say that is the way it always has been and always will be, but for Qoheleth the inequities bear witness to and anticipate the time of God's judgment (3:17). That time has not arrived; thus we see wickedness in the place of judgment, but Qoheleth anticipates another time. In this respect he is like the prophets of Israel in looking to the horizon for God's victory. He anticipates Jesus of Nazareth by preaching a time when God will establish justice in an everlasting kingdom (Matthew 25:31-46). Qoheleth entrusts time, its goodness and wickedness, to the hands of God who made time.

As Christians, we are inevitably tempted to over-interpret the book of Ecclesiastes, but I am haunted by that startling and unexpected juxtaposition of "war and peace" that concludes his catalog of human enterprises. How remarkable that he should end with peace, just as the Gospel of John begins its conclusion with Jesus blessing the disciples with peace (John 20:26) and the Revelation to John concludes with a vision of a city blessed with the peace of God (Revelation 22:1-5). When the time comes, when the time is right, the final word will be God's word of peace.

SHARING THE SCRIPTURE

Preparing Our Hearts

This week's devotional reading is found in Psalm 34:1-8, which is a wisdom psalm. In these verses the psalmist offers praise and thanks for God's goodness and salvation. Praise God now as you prepare to teach this lesson. What reasons do you have to give thanks to God? How have you tasted and seen God's goodness?

Pray that you and your class participants will be open to the Spirit's leading as we continue our study of Wisdom literature.

Preparing Our Minds

Study the background Scripture from Ecclesiastes 3 and the lesson Scripture, verses 1-8, 14-15. As you prepare, think about how God's time schedule relates to your life.

Write on newsprint:
❏ information for next week's lesson, found under "Continue the Journey."

Plan a brief lecture as suggested under "Examine the Philosopher's Thoughts on How There Is a Time for Everything."

Locate a recording of Pete Seeger's adaptation of Ecclesiastes 3:1-8, known as "Turn, Turn, Turn" and sung by the Byrds. Most baby boomers in the class will know this music that was popular in the 1960s. You can also find the words on the Internet.

LEADING THE CLASS

(1) Gather to Learn

❖ Welcome the class members and introduce any guests.

❖ Pray that those who have come will recognize that everything does work out in God's time.

❖ Encourage the class members to relate stories of how events in their lives worked out in God's time. Often these events hap-

pen unexpectedly. For example, a student enrolls in a college course because a preferred one was filled and in that class meets a future spouse. Or a family tries unsuccessfully to sell a house to move locally and then a few months later is transferred out of state.

❖ Read aloud today's focus statement: **People want to believe there is a time for everything that occurs in life. How does God's time schedule relate to our lives? This text reveals that God does everything at the right time in our lives.**

(2) Examine the Philosopher's Thoughts on How There Is a Time for Everything

❖ Read Ecclesiastes 3:1-8 responsively. To do this, have half of the class read the first set of each of the fourteen pairs of activities (for example: "a time to be born"), and the other half read the second set (for example: "and a time to die"). This echo effect will draw attention to the stark contrasts.
- ■ Talk about the rhythmic order that these verses convey. Discuss with the students whether this notion that everything has a proper time squares with their understanding of how the world works.
- ■ See if there are other contrasting pairs that the adults would add to this list.

❖ Choose a volunteer to read Ecclesiastes 3:14-15.
- ■ Discern what these verses say about God.
- ■ Read the information for Ecclesiastes 3:9-15 from Understanding the Scripture or make these points in a brief lecture. You may also want to include information from "Living in Wonder" in Interpreting the Scripture.

(1) Although God has made everything suitable in its own time, humans cannot grasp the entire course of history from beginning to end and therefore cannot know what is truly happening because they cannot put events in a larger context.

(2) Even though we cannot comprehend history's "big picture," we can all be happy because what God has given us is good.

(3) God's activities endure forever.

(4) The appropriate human response to what God has done is awe and reverence.

(3) Draw a Connection Between the Text's Teachings About God's Timetable and Events in the Learners' Lives

❖ Distribute paper and pencils. Ask the students to hold the paper horizontally and draw a line near the top of the page. Label the far left side with the date of their birth and the far right side with today's date. Suggest that they divide the line into roughly five-year periods. Directly below the line, they are to record personal events that were meaningful in their own lives. Make sure they save space to write underneath their personal events.

❖ Ask the students to review the timeline and beneath their personal events record newsworthy events that had an impact on society in general or their community or family in particular.

❖ Suggest that the students once again add information, this time near the bottom of the page. As they review their personal events and newsworthy events, they may be able to discern evidence of God working. Write those ideas in the appropriate time frame.

❖ Offer the students an opportunity to share any insights they have gleaned from this activity.

❖ Talk with the participants about how life does (or does not) seem to have a rhythm, and clues that they discern for seeing God at work in the history of their lifetime.

(4) Be Mindful About Balancing How Time Is Spent

❖ Ask the students to look again at Ecclesiastes 3:1-8. Note that, depending upon the specific context, some of these "times" are positive while others are negative. Yet, in our society we always want to be on top and have things going well for us. Failure and other negatives are not options. Our culture prizes youth and encourages us to do whatever possible to remain forever young. In doing so, our society rails against the challenges of aging and the experiences it brings. Ecclesiastes reminds us that there is a balance between positive and negative.

❖ Invite the participants to think about how they spent their time this past week. As they recall the week, were most things positive or negative or was there some kind of balance? Which of the activities would the students like to have engaged in more often? Which would they prefer not to do at all?

❖ Close this section of the lesson by challenging the students to be mindful of how they spend their time in the coming week. Perhaps they will become aware of how their time and God's time touch or overlap.

(5) Continue the Journey

❖ Pray that the participants will learn to live in God's time, trusting that there is a season and time for all things.

❖ Read aloud this preparation for next week's lesson. You may also want to post it on newsprint for the students to copy. **Prepare for next week's session, "A Treasure Worth Seeking," by reading chapters 2 and 3 of Proverbs. Study especially**

Proverbs 2:1-5; 3:1-6, 13-18. Contemplate these ideas as you read: Many people seek guidance that will help them successfully navigate life. Where can we find the guidance we need? According to Proverbs, wisdom comes as we acknowledge and trust in God with all our heart.

❖ Read aloud the following three ideas. Challenge the students to commit themselves to use these activities as a springboard to spiritual growth.

(1) Keep a log of how you spend your time this week. Prior to doing so, estimate how much of your time you devote to family, church, recreation, spiritual development, volunteer activities, or other things you normally do. At the end of the week, compare the time you actually spent with your "guesstimate." Do you need to make any changes? If so, how will you do that?

(2) Memorize Ecclesiastes 3:1-8 as it appears in your favorite Bible translation. How do the Preacher's words apply to your own life?

(3) Ponder how human time and God's time are different. What assurances do you receive from knowing that whatever God does endures eternally? How does that knowledge affect the way you live?

❖ Sing or read aloud "Turn, Turn, Turn" by Pete Seeger.

❖ Lead this benediction to end today's session: With all of your creatures, most majestic God, we sing your praises and pray that you would empower us to be wise people and faithful stewards of your creation, in Jesus' name. Amen.

UNIT 3: LESSONS IN LIVING

A Treasure Worth Seeking

PREVIEWING THE LESSON

Lesson Scripture: Proverbs 2:1-5; 3:1-6, 13-18
Background Scripture: Proverbs 2–3
Key Verse: Proverbs 3:13

Focus of the Lesson:
Many people seek guidance that will help them successfully navigate life. Where can we find the guidance we need? According to Proverbs, wisdom comes as we acknowledge and trust in God with all our heart.

Goals for the Learners:
(1) to examine what Proverbs says regarding wisdom as a treasure that can help us be happy and blessed.
(2) to articulate a biblical understanding of wisdom.
(3) to pray for God's wisdom and open themselves to God's guidance.

Pronunciation Guide:
aleph (ah lehf)
lamed (lah mehd)

Supplies:
Bibles, newsprint and marker, paper and pencils, hymnals

READING THE SCRIPTURE

NRSV
Proverbs 2:1-5
1 My child, if you accept my words
    and treasure up my commandments
        within you,
2 making your ear attentive to wisdom
    and inclining your heart to
        understanding;
3 if you indeed cry out for insight,
    and raise your voice for understanding;

NIV
Proverbs 2:1-5
1My son, if you accept my words
    and store up my commands within you,
2turning your ear to wisdom
    and applying your heart to
        understanding,
3and if you call out for insight
    and cry aloud for understanding,
4and if you look for it as for silver

4   if you seek it like silver,
    and search for it as for hidden
        treasures—
5   then you will understand the fear of the
        LORD
    and find the knowledge of God.

Proverbs 3:1-6, 13-18
1   My child, do not forget my teaching,
    but let your heart keep my
        commandments;
2   for length of days and years of life
    and abundant welfare they will give
        you.
3   Do not let loyalty and faithfulness forsake
        you;
    bind them around your neck,
    write them on the tablet of your heart.
4   So you will find favor and good repute
    in the sight of God and of people.
5   Trust in the LORD with all your heart,
    and do not rely on your own insight.
6   In all your ways acknowledge him,
    and he will make straight your paths.
13 **Happy are those who find wisdom,**
    and those who get understanding,
14   for her income is better than silver,
    and her revenue better than gold.
15   She is more precious than jewels,
    and nothing you desire can compare
        with her.
16   Long life is in her right hand;
    in her left hand are riches and honor.
17   Her ways are ways of pleasantness,
    and all her paths are peace.
18   She is a tree of life to those who lay hold of
        her;
    those who hold her fast are called
        happy.

and search for it as for hidden treasure,
5then you will understand the fear of the
    LORD
and find the knowledge of God.

Proverbs 3:1-6, 13-18
1My son, do not forget my teaching,
    but keep my commands in your heart,
2for they will prolong your life many years
    and bring you prosperity.
3Let love and faithfulness never leave you;
    bind them around your neck,
    write them on the tablet of your heart.
4Then you will win favor and a good name
    in the sight of God and man.
5Trust in the LORD with all your heart
    and lean not on your own understanding;
6in all your ways acknowledge him,
    and he will make your paths straight.
13**Blessed is the man who finds wisdom,**
    the man who gains understanding,
14for she is more profitable than silver
    and yields better returns than gold.
15She is more precious than rubies;
    nothing you desire can compare with her.
16Long life is in her right hand;
    in her left hand are riches and honor.
17Her ways are pleasant ways,
    and all her paths are peace.
18She is a tree of life to those who embrace
        her;
    those who lay hold of her will be blessed.

UNDERSTANDING THE SCRIPTURE

Overview of Proverbs 2. Proverbs begins with several poetic lessons and hymns orienting those who would seek wisdom. The second chapter of Proverbs is a single poem (actually one long sentence) declaring the value of wisdom. By its own carefully ordered structure it tells how wisdom may be found in the ordered structure of the world. The poem consists of twenty-two lines, the number of Hebrew consonants. The word translated "if" begins with *aleph;* that translated "saved" begins with *lamed.* The structure itself assures that "if" students will seek wisdom "then" they will be saved from pitfalls on their way. Each of the verse halves of the poem is further divided into strophes of four (1-4, 12-15), four (5-8, 16-19), and three (9-11, 20-22) lines. Penciling in lines in your Bible to indicate this structure will show you how elegantly this teacher invites the student to learning the way of wisdom. The poem's graceful structure suggests how wisdom would shape our lives to grace and beauty.

Proverbs 2:1-11. The first section (1-4) invites the student to listen to wise instruction. The student is "my child" (NRSV) or "my son" (NIV), evidencing not only the instruction parents were to give their children but the familial affection appropriately shown by a teacher toward students. The education envisioned in Proverbs was directed at young Jewish men, but the universal wisdom of Proverbs is available to people of both genders and many religious traditions. Those who seek wisdom may find it, for such is the nature of the God who gives wisdom. The search for wisdom culminates not in our seizing and grasping but in receiving it as a gift from God's hand. The second section (5-8) describes God's gracious response to those who seek wisdom. True wisdom is hidden with God (as in the book of Job) and those who seek happiness and success without "the fear of the LORD" doom themselves. Those who find "the knowledge of God" receive ample reward and protection (9-11).

Proverbs 2:12-22. The second half of the poem focuses on "the way" to which the first half invited the student. The first section (2:12-15) assures the student that wisdom will thwart the ways of evil, even the temptations of the "loose" woman (2:16-19). It is typical of the Wisdom literature to characterize both wisdom and foolishness as women: The wise woman who invites students to a glorious banquet and the deceitful woman who invites students to fleeting pleasures and final doom. (More about these two in the next lesson.) The poem concludes (2:20-22) promising protection and prosperity for those who "walk in the way of the good." "The land" in this case not only refers to real estate but also symbolizes abundance for people who had lost land in exile and whose ownership of home and fields was sometimes precarious.

Proverbs 3:1-12. Chapter 3 is made up of two related pieces of poetic instruction (3:1-12, 21-35) interrupted by an anthem praising the worth of wisdom (13-20). These poems parallel Jesus' teaching of the great commandment (Matthew 22:36-40): Proverbs 3:1-12 instructs the student in love of God and verses 21-35 teach love of neighbor. The command to love God and love neighbor are found in Deuteronomy 6:4-5 and Leviticus 19:18, respectively.

The teacher asks the student to attend to the words of instruction and to memorize them so they may always be available in conscience. This ancient method of learning is unfortunately out of fashion today. More than mere rote memorization the teacher asks for "loyalty and faithfulness," and invites the student "to bind them around your neck," echoing the covenant injunctions of Deuteronomy 6:7-8. The teacher contrasts trust in God with trust in self (3:5, 7). One honors God by making the offering (3:9-10). Note the logic: The worshiper does not make an offering because barns burst with plenty and vats overflow with wine; rather, barns burst with plenty and vats overflow because a worshiper knows Whom to honor with the first fruits. By no means is this to say that all will be easy and pleasant for those who seek God's wisdom, but they will learn to recognize even hard times as occasion also for God's instruction and discipline (3:11-12).

Proverbs 3:13-20. The teacher's instruction is interrupted as the chorus comes on to sing an anthem about the incomparable value of wisdom (3:13-20). Show us silver, gold, or rubies, they sing; they are nothing measured against wisdom. "A tree of life" echoes Psalm 1:3, a wisdom psalm, as well as Genesis 2:9. In the primeval garden God plants two trees: "the tree of life" and "the tree of the knowledge of good and evil." The human creatures were forbidden only to eat of this second "tree of the knowledge of good and evil" (2:16-17). Disobeying, they were exiled from the garden, and an angel placed as guard at "the tree of life" (3:24). This hymn announces wisdom as "the tree of life" and reasserts our original human privilege to eat the fruit of its branches. Wisdom has authority to dismiss the angel from guard duty because the final verses (3:19-20) reveal wisdom as the source of the creation, the blueprint of the world's order and structure.

Proverbs 3:21-35. The order and structure of the creation continues in community relationships. Trusting in the gracious God who made all things (3:26) one may greet one's fellows with grace. Prohibitions fence the good life. We can certainly understand not plotting or doing evil (3:29), but we are enjoined not to withhold doing good (3:27-28). The violent will receive their own reward from God, as will the just (3:32). Those who scorn wisdom and God are particularly hopeless in Wisdom literature (Psalm 1:1) because they denigrate the very things that would make them whole. The teacher shows the student how to live by entrusting them all—the scorners and the humble, the wise and the foolish—to God.

INTERPRETING THE SCRIPTURE

A Truth to Teach

The people whose wisdom inhabits the book of Proverbs believed they had something to teach their children. They were not shy about asserting their faith, their view of the world, and their values. We see the advertisements on television and in magazines imploring parents: Talk to your children—about drugs; about sexual behavior; and (God help us) about sexually transmitted diseases. Here among the people of God we might add: Talk to your children about what God means to you. (No, not the conversation about "Why we have to go to church this morning"; rather the one about "Why you are a disciple of Jesus Christ." That conversation can be a learning experience for both of you.)

One of the expressions young people often use these days is the one word "Whatever," spoken with a verbal shrug of the shoulders. "Whatever"—it doesn't matter. "Whatever"—the choice is up to you. "Whatever"—it doesn't make any difference. The book of Proverbs insists that human life matters deeply and the choices we make—or don't make—make all the difference.

Parents who ask their children to determine the course of their religious education would seldom assume the same laissez–faire attitude toward dental hygiene: "We want our children to make their own decisions about taking care of their teeth. Dental floss can be so irritating, and standing in front of a mirror brushing, brushing, brushing is such a boring, tedious business. They're just kids: They should have fun now and make their own decisions about their teeth when they're more mature."

The book of Proverbs recognizes that all our decisions are made among competing claims for our loyalty spoken with perverse words (2:12) and seductive speech (2:16). To make our way in this moral fray we must be centered on one thing.

Seek Wisdom First

Proverbial wisdom of our day, inscribed on plaques and posters in offices, advises, "Keep first things first." The book of Proverbs persuades students that wisdom comes first before all else. If you wish happiness, seek wisdom first. If you want wealth and the good things of life, seek wisdom first. If you would be honored, seek wisdom first. If you would have a long life, seek wisdom first. Some readers may feel embarrassed that wisdom is so blatantly advertised as the means to worldly success and material gain, but we should not attempt to be more spiritual than the Scriptures themselves. Although we may not have ambitions to be wealthy, very few of us aspire to lives of poverty, misery, ill repute, and failing health. Wisdom holds the blessings God would give us: "Long life is in her right hand; in her left hand are riches and honor" (3:16). Those who seek wisdom will receive the blessings that wisdom alone can give, but wisdom comes first.

If this still seems woefully unspiritual, you might wish to recall that Jesus also took up matters concerning our need for material goods (food, drink, clothing, shelter, and long life) and invited his disciples to seek first God's kingdom and God's righteousness, "and all these things will be given to you as well" (Matthew 6:33). For Jesus' disciples it is important to keep first things first.

Those who hurry after wealth alone doom themselves to failure and punishment (Proverbs 28:20, 22), but those who seek wisdom find treasures greater than silver, gold, and jewels (3:14-15); indeed, they find happiness (3:13).

A Teachable Spirit

The wisdom poem of Proverbs 3 recognizes that the opponents of wisdom are not only those voices outside calling with their perverse words and seductive speech, but there are voices inside us assuring us that we know what is wise and good and that we have learned enough already. Among the temptations that would lure us from the way of wisdom are self-assertion, self-absorption, self-confidence, self-sufficiency, self-satisfaction, self-centeredness, in short, "self." We laud the importance of self-esteem in our schools and society—and certainly there is nothing praiseworthy about what we call "poor self-esteem"—but we should remember also that many a dictionary defines "self-esteem" as "belief in one's self," which is exactly the wisdom teacher's point. The great enemy of wisdom is that of believing in one's own wisdom (hence the downfall of Job's friends, Job 42:8). "Do not be wise in your own eyes" (Proverbs 3:7), the sage warns. Being wise "in your own eyes" discards the humility required to learn wisdom from others and from God. Proverbs warns repeatedly of the danger of the misplaced self-confidence of being wise in one's "own eyes" (26:5, 12).

Again and again the sage of Proverbs enjoins the student, "listen," "accept my words," "pay attention," "do not forget my teaching": Instruction in wisdom requires attention and openness to learn. The teachers of the Protestant Reformation spoke of "a teachable spirit" being a precondition for receiving the truth of God. "A teachable spirit" inclines people to learn and provides a posture for life-long learning. People who already know everything have nothing left to learn. People already full have nowhere to receive the blessings wisdom would gladly offer.

The Fear of the Lord:
The Beginning and End of Wisdom

The antithesis to "Do not be wise in your own eyes" is not, as some might expect, "regard yourself as stupid and wallow in low self-esteem," nor is it "assume everyone knows better and posture yourself victim to their pretended wisdom," but rather, simply, "fear the LORD." The posture of human humility fits exactly the contours of divine goodness. The motto of the book of Proverbs is found in 1:7: "The fear of the LORD is the beginning of knowledge." The word *fear* is appropriately used. When we recognize our utter dependence upon the One with whom we have to do, what can we do but fear? Knowing more of God, fear modulates into awe and reverence. The book of Proverbs would cringe to hear cheery comments about God being our cosmic buddy.

The motto "The fear of the LORD is the beginning of knowledge" also connotes that the fear of the Lord is the epitome of knowledge. The fear of the Lord begins our journey into wisdom, but it is also the destination of our wisdom. Here, at the beginning of the book of Proverbs the sage counsels, "Trust in the LORD with all your heart" (3:5), and the end of all your search for wisdom will be to "Trust in the LORD with all your heart" (3:5). The way of wisdom is a journey in God, through God, with God, toward God (Romans 11:36).

The book of Proverbs knows we live in a vast, complicated world and it speaks of many things in many ways. In order to speak wisdom regarding the many, however, the book of Proverbs teaches "Trust in the LORD with all your heart," which is to say, know this and know this first and best because without knowing this you cannot know anything else truly and well. Knowing God is the first principle for knowing anything else. Without God everything else you know will be misplaced and misshapen because you do not know the center. When you know "the fear of the LORD"—that is, when you respect and wonder and regard with awe the One with whom we have to do—all of your knowledge will become a blessing not only for you but also for your community.

SHARING THE SCRIPTURE

Preparing Our Hearts

This week's devotional reading is found in Proverbs 2:6-15, which is part of our background Scripture. The writer tells us that wisdom is a gift from God that bestows many blessings upon us. Make a list of these blessings. How have you seen them enacted in your own life? What evidence can you cite to show that you are actively seeking God's wisdom?

Pray that you and your class participants will be open to receiving God's gift of wisdom.

Preparing Our Minds

Study the background Scripture from chapters 2 and 3 of Proverbs and our lesson Scripture, Proverbs 2:1-5; 3:1-6, 13-18. As you encounter these passages, consider where you go to find the guidance you need to navigate through life.

Write on newsprint:
❑ information for next week's lesson, found under "Continue the Journey."

Prepare a brief lecture if you plan to use one for the Gather to Learn portion of the session.

LEADING THE CLASS

(1) Gather to Learn

❖ Welcome the class members and introduce any guests.

❖ Pray that the participants will come to this session with a teachable spirit, ready to receive what God has to offer them.

❖ Discuss with the class, or present in a

brief lecture, sources of wisdom that society offers to them. List these sources on newsprint. The list may include: schools and other educational institutions, media, stories passed from generation to generation, and corporate cultures.

❖ Review the list and talk about how these sources provide guidance for daily living. Evaluate the quality of guidance these sources provide.

❖ Read aloud today's focus statement: **Many people seek guidance that will help them successfully navigate life. Where can we find the guidance we need? According to Proverbs, wisdom comes as we acknowledge and trust in God with all our heart.**

(2) Examine What Proverbs Says Regarding Wisdom as a Treasure That Can Help Us Be Happy and Blessed

❖ Read "Overview of Proverbs 2" in Understanding the Scripture to set the stage for today's lesson.

❖ Ask a volunteer to read Proverbs 2:1-5.
  ■ Note that in English these verses are one "if-then" statement. The class may find it helpful to more clearly identify all the "ifs" and "thens" and list them on newsprint. You might write them as follows, or you may prefer to write out each statement.
    ○ If you accept. . . .
    ○ If you treasure. . . .
    ○ If you make your ear attentive. . . .
    ○ If you incline your heart. . . .
    ○ If you cry out. . . .
    ○ If you raise your voice. . . .
    ○ If you seek. . . .
    ○ If you search. . . .
    ○ Then you will understand. . . .
    ○ Then you will find. . .
  ■ Use information from "The Fear of the Lord: The Beginning and End of Wisdom" in Interpreting the Scripture to clarify what it means to "fear the Lord." Indicate that a

knowledge of God comes not from a single encounter, but rather, from a relationship that develops over time.
  ■ Provide time for participants to review the list and ponder silently how they are pursuing wisdom (the "ifs") and reaping its rewards (the "thens").

❖ Select someone to read Proverbs 3:1-6.
  ■ Ask the students to call out the positive (+) and negative (-) admonitions found in verses 1-6. Write these on newsprint. Your list might look like this.
    – do not forget my teaching
    + let your heart keep my commandments (*Note that this instruction includes the notions of "learning by heart" and "taking to heart."*)
    - do not let loyalty and faithfulness forsake you
    + bind them around your neck and write them on the tablet of your heart
    + trust in the Lord with all your heart
    - do not rely on your own insight
  ■ Identify the rewards, found in verses 2 and 4, for those who follow the instructions.

❖ Choose a reader for Proverbs 3:13-18.
  ■ Note the blessings that come to those who seek wisdom, here personified as a woman ("her" and "she").
  ■ Read or retell the section in Interpreting the Scripture entitled "Seek Wisdom First."
  ■ Explain the image of wisdom as "a tree of life" (3:18) by reading or retelling Proverbs 3:13-20 in Understanding the Scripture.

❖ Wrap up this portion of the lesson by inviting the students to summarize what they have learned about wisdom and why it is so valuable.

*(3) Articulate a Biblical
Understanding of Wisdom*

❖ Begin a time of meditation by reading aloud this quotation from Charles Swindoll (1934–): **Don't expect wisdom to come into your life like great chunks of rock on a conveyor belt. It isn't like that. It's not splashy and bold . . . nor is it dispensed like a prescription across a counter. Wisdom comes privately from God as a by-product of right decisions, godly reactions, and the application of spiritual principles to daily circumstances. Wisdom comes . . . not from trying to do great things for God . . . but more from being faithful to the small, obscure tasks few people ever see.**

❖ Talk with the class about how they think Swindoll's understanding of wisdom affirms, modifies, or challenges the vision of wisdom we have seen in Proverbs 2 and 3.

❖ Invite the learners to define or describe "wisdom" as they now understand it. Write these definitions on newsprint.

❖ Review the definitions. Consider how the writer of Proverbs might respond to these ideas.

❖ Conclude this portion of the lesson by discussing how a biblical understanding of wisdom, as opposed to the secular understanding we considered in Gather to Learn, can provide us with unfailing guidance.

*(4) Pray for God's Wisdom and Be Open to
God's Guidance*

❖ Distribute paper and pencils. Encourage each student to write a prayer seeking God's wisdom.

❖ Invite volunteers to read these prayers as the class sits quietly or gathers in a prayer circle.

(5) Continue the Journey

❖ Pray that those who have come will seek God's gift of wisdom and treasure it.

❖ Read aloud this preparation for next week's lesson. You may also want to post it on newsprint for the students to copy. **Prepare for next week's session, "Wisdom's Invitation," by reading chapters 8 and 9 of Proverbs. Our session will delve into Proverbs 8:1-5, 22-31. Keep these ideas in mind as you read: People need wisdom in order to make wise choices. How can we acquire wisdom? Proverbs affirms that God's wisdom, which has existed since before creation, is available to whoever seeks it.**

❖ Read aloud the following three ideas. Challenge the students to commit themselves to use these activities as a springboard to spiritual growth.

(1) **Be aware of the values you are consciously or unconsciously passing on to younger generations. Are you instilling the importance of God's gift of wisdom, or are you encouraging others to seek wisdom elsewhere? What steps can you take to be more intentional about teaching your values?**

(2) **Write in your spiritual journal about how your life is blessed and happy because you have sought God's wisdom.**

(3) **Recall a time when you sought wisdom from sources other than God. How did the decisions you made or actions you took based on these sources turn out? What lessons did you learn?**

❖ Sing or read aloud "Immortal, Invisible, God Only Wise."

❖ Lead this benediction to end today's session: **With all of your creatures, most majestic God, we sing your praises and pray that you would empower us to be wise people and faithful stewards of your creation, in Jesus' name. Amen.**

UNIT 3: LESSONS IN LIVING
WISDOM'S INVITATION

PREVIEWING THE LESSON

Lesson Scripture: Proverbs 8:1-5, 22-31
Background Scripture: Proverbs 8–9
Key Verse: Proverbs 8:1

Focus of the Lesson:
People need wisdom in order to make wise choices. How can we acquire wisdom? Proverbs affirms that God's wisdom, which has existed since before creation, is available to whoever seeks it.

Goals for the Learners:
(1) to explore the imagery Proverbs uses to describe the availability of God's wisdom to us.
(2) to relate the theological implications of the passage that describes wisdom's origins and role in creation to their own lives.
(3) to commit to answering wisdom's call.

Pronunciation Guide:
`āmôn (aw mone')

Supplies:
Bibles, newsprint and marker, paper and pencils, hymnals

READING THE SCRIPTURE

NRSV
Proverbs 8:1-5, 22-31

¹ **Does not wisdom call,**
   and does not understanding raise her
   voice?
² On the heights, beside the way,
   at the crossroads she takes her stand;
³ beside the gates in front of the town,
   at the entrance of the portals she cries out:
⁴ "To you, O people, I call,

NIV
Proverbs 8:1-5, 22-31

¹**Does not wisdom call out?**
   Does not understanding raise her voice?
²On the heights along the way,
   where the paths meet, she takes her stand;
³beside the gates leading into the city,
   at the entrances, she cries aloud:
⁴"To you, O men, I call out;
   I raise my voice to all mankind.

MAY 14

and my cry is to all that live.
5 O simple ones, learn prudence;
   acquire intelligence, you who lack it.
22 The LORD created me at the beginning of
      his work,
   the first of his acts of long ago.
23 Ages ago I was set up,
   at the first, before the beginning of the
      earth.
24 When there were no depths I was brought
      forth,
   when there were no springs abounding
      with water.
25 Before the mountains had been shaped,
   before the hills, I was brought forth—
26 when he had not yet made earth and
      fields,
   or the world's first bits of soil.
27 When he established the heavens, I was
      there,
   when he drew a circle on the face of the
      deep,
28 when he made firm the skies above,
   when he established the fountains of
      the deep,
29 when he assigned to the sea its limit,
   so that the waters might not transgress
      his command,
   when he marked out the foundations of
      the earth,
30 then I was beside him, like a master
      worker;
   and I was daily his delight,
      rejoicing before him always,
31 rejoicing in his inhabited world
   and delighting in the human race.

5You who are simple, gain prudence;
   you who are foolish, gain understanding.
22"The LORD brought me forth as the first of
      his works,
   before his deeds of old;
23I was appointed from eternity,
   from the beginning, before the world
      began.
24When there were no oceans, I was given
      birth,
   when there were no springs abounding
      with water;
25before the mountains were settled in place,
   before the hills, I was given birth,
26before he made the earth or its fields
   or any of the dust of the world.
27I was there when he set the heavens in
      place,
   when he marked out the horizon on the
      face of the deep,
28when he established the clouds above
   and fixed securely the fountains of the
      deep,
29when he gave the sea its boundary
   so the waters would not overstep his
      command,
   and when he marked out the foundations
      of the earth.
30Then I was the craftsman at his side.
I was filled with delight day after day,
   rejoicing always in his presence,
31rejoicing in his whole world
   and delighting in mankind.

UNDERSTANDING THE SCRIPTURE

Proverbs 8:1-3. Wisdom personified as a woman invites disciples to learn from her and follow her way at the beginning of Proverbs (1:20-33), and now she reprises her invitation and elaborates upon it in a long, dazzlingly beautiful poem. The teacher's introduction begins with a rhetorical question, "Does not wisdom call?" (8:1), in order to summon learners to attention: Can't you hear her? Wisdom calls all through the city to those who can hear, give attention, and learn. She calls "on the heights"; on street corners in the midst of the city's traffic; and at the gates, where the significant matters of business, law, and social policy were discussed and determined. Wisdom personified thrusts her invitation into the competitive fray of conversations and distractions that characterize every city of every age.

Proverbs 8:4-9. Wisdom's invitation is addressed to everyone, but she speaks particularly to those characterized as "simple": the inexperienced, the naïve, and not so much the uninformed as those as yet unformed in character. Surely she hopes to attract the attention of the young man who from the beginning has been the implied audience for Proverbs (1:8, 10), but she will gladly act as host to all who would receive her abundance.

Proverbs 8:10-21. The marketplace in which Wisdom calls out her invitation clamors with advice about how wealth may be made, but what she would offer is better than gold or silver or jewels (8:10-11, 19). By no means, however, are her blessings only spiritual. Far more convincing than the marketplace's cheap claims for quick profits and easy rewards, Wisdom promises that "riches and honor" accompany her (8:18). Kings know her, Wisdom tells the student, and by wisdom they reign. The association of wisdom and royal rule runs deep in the Scriptures. Much of Wisdom literature is associated with Solomon (Proverbs 1:1; 25:1; Ecclesiastes 1:1; 1 Kings 4:29), as well as with Hezekiah (Proverbs 25:1) and King Lemuel (Proverbs 31:1). If kings rule by wisdom, should not others allow wisdom to rule their lives? Those who love Wisdom will be loved by her (8:17) and receive not only wealth but also treasuries overflowing. Earlier the young man had learned how the wrong kind of woman could strip him of his honor, wealth, and home (5:3-10), but in Wisdom he encounters a powerful, loving and prudent woman who would gladly fill his life with good things.

Proverbs 8:22-34. Woman Wisdom's extravagant promises are guaranteed by her unique relationship to God and her unique place in God's cosmos. Before God created anything else, God "created" (8:22 NRSV) or "brought forth" (NIV) Wisdom. The language employed certainly permits the construal that God is both father and mother to Wisdom: The word translated "created" or "possessed" (KJV) frequently describes fathering, and mothering is expressed in "I was given birth" (8:24, 25 NIV), more dramatically expressing the NRSV's "brought forth." God births Wisdom before all else, and Wisdom highlights this by listing all the magnificent creations she preceded: before the world, oceans, mountains, and hills (8:24-26). Wisdom delights in her place of privilege with God, delights as well in the marvelous creation her parent has fashioned, and this abundance of delight overflows to benefit humankind. Translation problems abound, but whether one translates Wisdom as saying, "I was daily [God's] delight" (8:30 NRSV) or "I was filled with delight day after day" (8:30 NIV), this much is clear: The relationship between God and Wisdom is one of utter delight, a delight that brims over to delight "in mankind" (8:31 NIV) or "in the human race" (8:31 NRSV). The joy God and Wisdom share they intend for humankind. "Craftsman" (8:30 NIV) and "master worker" (NRSV) translate the word `āmôn` in verse 30, which some other commentators persuasively argue should be translated "little child," offering an enchanting image of a child playing in her parents' workroom, enjoying her parents' creative ability and achievements while offering her own play for their enjoyment.

Proverbs 8:35-36. Having shown her true identity, Wisdom personified urges students to listen. Everything is at stake in listening: "whoever finds me finds life" (8:35) and "all who hate me love death" (8:36). Like Moses, Wisdom puts before people "life and death, blessings and curses" (Deuteronomy 30:19) and invites them to choose.

Proverbs 9:1-6. Like a generous householder, Wisdom has prepared a lavish banquet and has invited guests (see also Matthew 22:1-4). The wisdom teacher catalogues her preparations: building a grand house, preparing meat (a luxury item), adding festive spice to her wine, and sending her female servants as messengers throughout the town. She asks only that people come, laying aside "simple ways" (9:6 NIV) and "immaturity" (NRSV). In that respect she asks for what the church has called "repentance": a turning to go in another direction. To enter her house is to leave behind foolishness and childishness.

Proverbs 9:7-12. If verses 7-12 seem an odd interruption of Wisdom's invitation, you recognize an oddness biblical scholars note. Commentators are virtually unanimous in explaining that a scribe (not the most skillful editor) added these proverbs later. Verse 10 reiterates Proverbs 1:7, and proclaims once again the deep relationship between true wisdom and knowledge of God. Self-sufficient "scoffers" (9:8 NRSV) and "mockers" (NIV) turn away from good advice and correction; they are hopeless. The wise person listens seriously to reproof and learns, a familiar theme in Proverbs (13:1, 17:10; 25:12, 27:5).

Proverbs 9:13-18. Wisdom invites guests to her banquet, but not far away Folly has her own party going. She also issues her invitation publicly and invites passersby into her house. With the same words she invites the "simple" to come and be filled. In contrast to Wisdom, who speaks enchanted poetry, Folly is "loud" (9:13) and as lacking in wisdom as those she invites to her way. She has made no preparations, built no house, prepared no meat or wine, sent no messengers, but instead offers the seductions of an unwise proverb: "Stolen water is sweet" (9:17). "Stolen water" may euphemistically refer to an illicit sexual liaison (as in Proverbs 5:15-17), but can more broadly point to all manner of clandestine pleasures made "sweeter" by being forbidden. They appear exciting, enticing, and just wickedly delicious, but "the simple" soon discover that the only guests at Folly's banquet are "the dead" and those on the way to death (9:18).

INTERPRETING THE SCRIPTURE

Wisdom with a Face

That the wisdom poets chose to personify wisdom as a woman generates astonishing theological possibilities. Consider the metaphorical alternatives to personifying wisdom: Wisdom is not a mythical beast like a unicorn remote from our experience, transcendent in its utter purity; wisdom is not a fearsome creature like dragon, hoarding its treasure, threatening to devour humans; wisdom is not a mountain, stony and immovable, indifferent to those who scale it; wisdom is not a machine, mechanically grinding out rewards for those who tend it; wisdom is not a mindless force of nature, like gravity or magnetism, aloof in perfect neutrality. Wisdom is a person and therefore one with whom we may have a

personal relationship. Imagine all that is good and enriching and delightful in human relationships; this and more wisdom promises to those who would enter into this friendship (Proverbs 7:4).

Moreover, the wisdom tradition of Israel imagines wisdom as Wisdom, God's female companion who wishes to be our companion also. How do we imagine God? Probably male, aged, bearded, stern, speaking "thou shalt nots." Imagine beside God a companion: a woman promising us wonderful gifts and speaking poetry. They stand together, a family. Nowhere, however, does the wisdom tradition of Israel so much as hint that Wisdom is God's spouse or consort. Although they lived surrounded by cultures worshiping pairs of fertility gods like Baal and Asherah, the sages of Israel imagined the relationship of Wisdom to God in quite different ways. That there is a romance going on is not to be doubted, but it is a different sort of romance, and one that invites human beings to join in the feast of love. Wisdom is God's creation, and the language of creating and birthing invites us to imagine Wisdom as God's child, the daughter of God's delight. A true daughter of her parent, she invites humans into relationship, she wishes to teach them, she promises to guide them in ways of righteousness, and she offers them the blessings God intends for all of God's children.

Wisdom's Invitation

Wisdom calls to everyone—"to all who live" (8:4)—because Wisdom particularly delights in the human race (8:31). Her call is universal but she particularly addresses the "simple" and the "foolish" (8:5 NIV) or those who lack intelligence (8:5 NSRV). In her general summons these two particular and discrete groups are invited.

The "simple" are those who lack "prudence." They are inexperienced, callow, naïve. In Proverbs 14:15 (NIV) the terms of "simple" and "prudence" are paired again to describe the utter credulity of those who are "simple" in contrast to the practiced caution of the "prudent" (or "clever" in NRSV). The "simple" would typically be the young Jewish male who is the assumed audience for the book of Proverbs. He needs to learn his way around or he will naïvely fall into all manner of traps. He is not wicked; the problem is that he cannot identify wickedness when he sees it and must be warned by Wisdom (for example, Proverbs 2:11-19). Wisdom's invitation to the "simple" evidences a motherly care for a child too easily led astray.

The "foolish" (NIV) or those lacking in intelligence (NRSV) have had experience with the world but have refused to learn from it. They have abandoned paths of wisdom and understanding to pursue their own willful schemes. Unlike the "simple," these people know better but do not do it. In Proverbs 10:23 we discover the fool delighting in wrongdoing while the discerning person delights in wisdom. Wisdom's invitation to these people is to change direction and follow her instructions. Hers is a call to repentance, the New Testament word for repentance meaning literally to turn and go another direction.

Whatever our circumstance, Wisdom invites us to follow. In some respects we lack experience and do silly, thoughtless things that cost us heavily; in other respects we make bad choices when we know better and suffer consequences. Wisdom calls us, those of us who don't know any better and those who do, and promises for us something much better.

A Theology of Delight

Although translation problems abound, this much is clear: Wisdom invites us to a relationship filled with delight. Whether we picture her as a craftswoman shaping God's creation as it is being fashioned in the workshop or a child frolicking in her parent's workroom, the image is unexpected and enchanting. Whether Woman Wisdom was filled with delight (as in 9:30 NIV) or God was filled with delight (NRSV), Wisdom's poetry summons us to delight. We seldom think of delight as a theological category, but that is only because we know so little of Wisdom.

Wisdom recognizes that human beings may find delight in all the wrong things: in cynicism about sacred things and in getting away with wrongdoing. She invites us instead to find a more authentic delight in a relationship that has been going on since the world began. The delight that passes between God and Wisdom is a delight wanting to be shared with women and men. Delight is not merely serendipitous happiness; we learn the ways of delight. We did not delight the first time we picked up a tennis racket or a hand of bridge but as we learned the discipline we discovered delight as well. With much the same logic the book of Proverbs instructs us in behavior that delights God: walking in blameless ways (11:20), speaking and acting truthfully (12:22), and praying sincerely (15:8). These are ways of delight for our journey.

Invitation to Delight

Exuberance and happy energy characterize the poetry of Wisdom's invitation. The words and cadence mean to charm listeners and persuade them to join in the joy of Wisdom's company. Her happy call can be heard everywhere a person can go: in the marketplace (where the roads cross), in houses and households (along the way), in the place of worship (the heights), in the place of state where decisions are deliberated and judgments meted out (at the city gates). Those who would answer her invitation are not summoned to leave these places in favor of a lecture hall or a dreary classroom, but rather are called to make Wisdom their tour guide wherever they may go. She is the ideal traveling companion—she knows the language and customs of every place and will teach those who would learn; she knows the terrain of the entire creation from the oceans to the mountains and will guide those who hearken to her voice; she is welcome everywhere because of her gracious ways, and those who make her their companion will learn those ways.

To refresh us on our journeys Wisdom invites us to a banquet of delight (9:1-5). Banquets (like Greek symposia) were held in the ancient world not only as occasions for dining but also for conversing about philosophy and the world of ideas. Wisdom invites us to such a table where wisdom might be discussed, shared, and celebrated. The book of Proverbs knows feasts lavish with malice as well as meat (Proverbs 15:17), and it knows of treats that trick (Proverbs 23:3), but in Wisdom's house everything on the table is a banquet of pure delight where every cup overflows with joy.

SHARING THE SCRIPTURE

Preparing Our Hearts

This week's devotional reading is found in Proverbs 8:10-21, which is part of our background Scripture. Wisdom speaks here in the first person, "I." What do you learn about Wisdom from this passage? What does Wisdom have to offer to those who follow her ways? How does wisdom relate to righteousness and justice? What role does wisdom play in your life?

Pray that you and your class participants will seek Wisdom and find all that she has to offer.

Preparing Our Minds

Study the background Scripture from chapters 8 and 9 of Proverbs and the lesson Scripture, 8:1-5, 22-31. Since we need wisdom in order to make wise choices, think about how Proverbs indicates that we can acquire wisdom.

Write on newsprint:
❏ information for next week's lesson, found under "Continue the Journey."

LEADING THE CLASS

(1) Gather to Learn

❖ Welcome the class members and introduce any guests.

❖ Pray that the students will seek and find wisdom as they study together this day.

❖ Read aloud this scenario: **Arlo Wilson**

has been offered a new job in another city. If he takes the job, he will receive a promotion and handsome raise. His wife Jennie will be able to find a suitable job in the new city. In short, this would be a good career move for Arlo and would not disrupt Jennie's career. However, Arlo's elderly mother would not be able to receive the special medical care she needs in the new city. Arlo and his wife Jennie have faithfully cared for the elder Mrs. Wilson, and there is no one else able to help her.

❖ Invite the class to make a list on newsprint of "pros" and "cons" of accepting this new job.

❖ Choose two volunteers to role-play a conversation between Arlo and Jennie as to what decision they will make.

❖ Debrief the role-play by discussing how people go about making wise decisions.

❖ Read aloud today's focus statement: **People need wisdom in order to make wise choices. How can we acquire wisdom? Proverbs affirms that God's wisdom, which has existed since before creation, is available to whoever seeks it.**

(2) Explore the Imagery Proverbs Uses to Describe the Availability of God's Wisdom to Us

❖ Choose someone to read Proverbs 8:1-5.

◼ Look at where Wisdom is said to be located. (You may wish to add information from the first paragraph of "Invitation to Delight" in Interpreting the Scripture.)

◼ Look at the kind of people to whom Wisdom calls and what you know about them. (In addition to, or instead of, a discussion you may want to read or retell "Wisdom's Invitation" in Interpreting the Scripture.)

❖ Select a volunteer to read Proverbs 8:22-31.

◼ Invite the students to call out images that caught their attention as the passage was read. Class members may want to comment on why these images are memorable.

◼ Discuss these questions.

(1) **What relationship do you sense between God and Wisdom, personified as a woman?** (Note the variety of meanings of the Hebrew word translated as "master worker" in the NRSV. See Proverbs 8:22-34 in "Understanding the Scripture." The word may also mean "nursing child" or "confidante.")

(2) **What does Wisdom report seeing created?**

(3) **How does Wisdom seem to relate to creation in general and humanity in particular?**

◼ **Option:** If time permits, consider how this passage in Proverbs compares or contrasts with Job 38–39 in which God questions Job concerning his whereabouts during creation.

(3) Relate the Theological Implications of the Passage That Describes Wisdom's Origins and Role in Creation to the Learners' Lives

❖ Invite the students to raise questions, concerns, or insights they have gained so far in today's discussion. (Be aware that some adults will express discomfort with the personification of Wisdom as a woman. Several class members may raise questions concerning the relationship between Wisdom and God the Creator, or between Wisdom and Christ. Others may voice questions about whether Wisdom is God's consort, which she is not. See the second paragraph of "Wisdom with a Face" in Interpreting the Scripture for help with this question.)

❖ Work with the class to define "wisdom" in a way that is faithful to the Bible and also relates to the learners' lives. You may want to use these questions as prompts. List ideas on newsprint.

(1) **Is wisdom an accumulation of information, such as one might need to play** *Trivial Pursuit* **or** *Jeopardy,* **or does it have other dimensions? If so, what are those other dimensions?**

(2) **Where can we find wisdom?**

(3) **What are some of the ways that wisdom can be used in our daily lives?**

❖ Encourage the students to talk with the class or a small group about ways that wisdom makes a difference in their daily lives.

(4) Commit to Answering Wisdom's Call

❖ Distribute paper and pencils. Read aloud Proverbs 8:1, today's key verse. Ask the students to write confidentially about how they needed wisdom at a previous time in their lives. Did they seek or ignore wisdom? What difference did wisdom make in a decision they had to make or in the way they acted in that situation?

❖ Provide a few moments for the students to process what they have written so they can recognize how wisdom previously touched them.

❖ Invite the students to write confidentially about a situation that requires wisdom now. Suggest that they consider how their previous experience in seeking and finding wisdom can help them in their current circumstances.

❖ Suggest that the students make a silent commitment to answer wisdom's call so that they may benefit from the guidance wisdom can bring to bear on this current situation.

(5) Continue the Journey

❖ Pray that the participants will accept Wisdom's invitation to seek and find her.

❖ Read aloud this preparation for next week's lesson. You may also want to post it on newsprint for the students to copy. **Prepare for next week's session, "Choosing the Path of Integrity," by reading Proverbs 11, noting especially verses 1-14. As you study, think about these ideas: Personal integrity is destroyed by pride and dishonesty. How can we overcome these negative traits? Proverbs teaches that pride and dishonesty must be replaced by wisdom and right behavior.**

❖ Read aloud the following three ideas. Challenge the students to commit themselves to use these activities as a springboard to spiritual growth.

(1) **Consider the value of wisdom in your own life. What role does it play in your decision-making? Do you try to act with prudence, or are you more apt to make a snap decision? What changes do you need or want to make in this regard?**

(2) **Listen to someone who needs to make a decision. Without telling this individual what to do or giving your own advice, try to help him or her recognize how God's wisdom can provide guidance.**

(3) **Pray for wisdom for yourself, for the church, and for political leaders. Meditate on whatever need you have to connect more closely with God.**

❖ Sing or read aloud "God, Who Stretched the Spangled Heavens."

❖ Lead this benediction to end today's session: **With all of your creatures, most majestic God, we sing your praises and pray that you would empower us to be wise people and faithful stewards of your creation, in Jesus' name. Amen.**

UNIT 3: LESSONS IN LIVING

Choosing the Path of Integrity

PREVIEWING THE LESSON

Lesson Scripture: Proverbs 11:1-14
Background Scripture: Proverbs 11
Key Verse: Proverbs 11:3

Focus of the Lesson:

Personal integrity is destroyed by pride and dishonesty. How can we overcome these negative traits? Proverbs teaches that pride and dishonesty must be replaced by wisdom and right behavior.

Goals for the Learners:

(1) to summarize Proverbs' teachings on the ways one can overcome pride and dishonesty, which destroy one's personal integrity.
(2) to consider the marks of integrity in themselves and people they know.
(3) to commit themselves to living with integrity in all aspects of their lives.

Supplies:

Bibles, newsprint and marker, paper and pencils, hymnals

READING THE SCRIPTURE

NRSV
Proverbs 11:1-14
1 A false balance is an abomination to the
    LORD,
      but an accurate weight is his delight.
2 When pride comes, then comes disgrace;
      but wisdom is with the humble.
3 **The integrity of the upright guides them,**
    but the crookedness of the treacherous
    destroys them.
4 Riches do not profit in the day of wrath,
      but righteousness delivers from death.
5 The righteousness of the blameless keeps

NIV
Proverbs 11:1-14
1The LORD abhors dishonest scales,
      but accurate weights are his delight.
2When pride comes, then comes disgrace,
      but with humility comes wisdom.
3**The integrity of the upright guides them,**
    but the unfaithful are destroyed by their
    duplicity.
4Wealth is worthless in the day of wrath,
      but righteousness delivers from death.
5The righteousness of the blameless makes a

their ways straight,
but the wicked fall by their own
wickedness.
6 The righteousness of the upright saves
them,
but the treacherous are taken captive by
their schemes.
7 When the wicked die, their hope perishes,
and the expectation of the godless
comes to nothing.
8 The righteous are delivered from trouble,
and the wicked get into it instead.
9 With their mouths the godless would
destroy their neighbors,
but by knowledge the righteous are
delivered.
10 When it goes well with the righteous,
the city rejoices;
and when the wicked perish, there is
jubilation.
11 By the blessing of the upright a city is
exalted,
but it is overthrown by the mouth of the
wicked.
12 Whoever belittles another lacks sense,
but an intelligent person remains silent.
13 A gossip goes about telling secrets,
but one who is trustworthy in spirit
keeps a confidence.
14 Where there is no guidance, a nation falls,
but in an abundance of counselors there
is safety.

straight way for them,
but the wicked are brought down by their
own wickedness.
6The righteousness of the upright delivers
them,
but the unfaithful are trapped by evil
desires.
7When a wicked man dies, his hope
perishes;
all he expected from his power comes to
nothing.
8The righteous man is rescued from trouble,
and it comes on the wicked instead.
9With his mouth the godless destroys his
neighbor,
but through knowledge the righteous
escape.
10When the righteous prosper, the city
rejoices;
when the wicked perish, there are shouts
of joy.
11Through the blessing of the upright a city is
exalted,
but by the mouth of the wicked it is
destroyed.
12A man who lacks judgment derides his
neighbor,
but a man of understanding holds his
tongue.
13A gossip betrays a confidence,
but a trustworthy man keeps a secret.
14For lack of guidance a nation falls,
but many advisers make victory sure.

UNDERSTANDING THE SCRIPTURE

Introduction. Chapter 11 of Proverbs is part of the larger collection, "the proverbs of Solomon" (10:1–22:16), which contains 375 proverbs (375 being the numerical value of the name "Solomon"). Solomon asked God for an understanding mind in order to govern the people, and his prayer so pleased God that Solomon was given wisdom and discernment beyond all others (1 Kings 3:3-14). Solomon's spirit endures in Proverbs:

Here are lessons for governing our families and ourselves wisely.

Proverbs 11:1-2. The sage who composed the proverb in verse 1 borrows the language of ritual sacrifice to condemn unjust business practices: Just as golden idols are "abhorrent to the LORD your God" (Deuteronomy 7:25), so is a shaved balance on the scales. And just as God delights in right offerings (Psalm 51:19), so God delights in an accurate balance. Verse 2 warns against the wrong companions. Choose pride and disgrace follows, but wisdom accompanies humility.

Proverbs 11:3-8. Although the proverbs seem oddly sorted, the theme of integrity and righteousness winds through Proverbs 11. The overarching question is "Do integrity and righteousness really reward a person?" If I cheat my neighbor with my substandard weights and she never notices, does it matter? The chapter concludes with the assurance that integrity and righteousness matter deeply: "The fruit of the righteous is a tree of life" (11:30) giving nourishment, shelter, and healing to all (compare Revelation 22:2). The sage describes how this happens with a series of antithetical (opposite) pairs: The second half of the proverb restates the premise of the first half but in reverse. We see this rhythm in verses 3-6: Here is how it is with the righteous, but with the wicked it is the opposite. The righteous are guided, delivered, kept, and saved by their righteousness, but the wicked, betrayed by their wickedness, are destroyed, fallen, and trapped without hope.

Proverbs 11:9-14. Nothing so betrays wisdom as foolish talk, and Wisdom literature consistently concerns itself with the way we talk to each other. The sage counsels a language capable of building up neighbors (11:9), cities (11:10-11), and the nation (11:14). A language builds relationships and a language tears down relationships (compare Ephesians 4:29). Those who diminish and demean others speak without thinking—a sign of careless folly in Wisdom literature—whereas wise people know how to remain discreetly quiet. Gossips are a special case of not knowing when to be silent. They betray confidence along with relationships and diminish the trust on which families, communities, and nations must rely. Solomon casts his shadow over verse 14 as he sees nations falling for lack of guidance and recommends gathering a cabinet of wise guides.

Proverbs 11:15-16. The three proverbs in verses 15-16 appear utterly conventional, and perhaps it is their utter obviousness that recommends them alongside the arguments for integrity and righteousness: Since you know that this is so, you may trust what the sage says about righteousness as well. The sage counsels against securing a loan for another person, but in Proverbs 6:1-5 we are provided advice for extricating ourselves from such a dubious business arrangement. The differences between NRSV and NIV translations attest to the difficulty of translating the two proverbs in verse 16.

Proverbs 11:17-23. Proverbs regarding the outcome of our actions bear witness to the endurance and rewards of righteousness. We may advocate kindness because of its benefits to others, but the sage promises that kindness does us good. By the same logic cruelty injures not only those treated cruelly but also those who are cruel. This backfire invites us to contemplate what we should like to receive and how we should like to be. Verse 18 acknowledges the apparent contradiction that the wicked seem to be doing very well indeed, but assures the student that such visible results are "deceptive wages" (NIV) and "no real gain" (NRSV). Authentic and enduring rewards come to the righteous in spite of what we might momentarily observe. Both the righteous and the wicked are following inexorable paths, the righteous to life, the wicked to death, and the final outcome is certain. The wicked may lead tempting, attractive lives, but we should not be misled by surface appearances (11:22). Although the wicked may thrive before our eyes, and in our perplexity we may wonder about this, the sage invites students to find comfort in the assurance that "the wicked will not go unpunished" (11:21) while "the desire of the righteous ends only in good" (11:23).

Proverbs 11:24-29. Although Proverbs can be sharp in business matters, generosity is always in order in social relationships.

Just as kindness, shown to others, rewards the kind, so also those who give generously receive generosity. This notion is first expressed in the antithetical parallelism of verse 24, then reiterated in verse 25. Blessings and curses attend the seller of grain, depending upon business practices. Conventional market wisdom might recommend hoarding grain until prices rise, but merchants employing such tactics are cursed (even as their strategy is a curse to the community). Those who sell their grain—they are not enjoined to donate it; this is a business after all—are blessed. Verse 27 provides a terse summary that those who seek good find good, and those who seek evil find evil. Once again the righteous appear in verse 28, their righteousness recognized in contrast to those who trust in their own riches. The concern for wise governance of a household appears in the sad proverb of verse 29 depicting the honor and wealth of a family "gone with the wind" and the foolish family reduced to a life of servitude to a wiser householder.

Proverbs 11:30-31. The sage reiterates the theme of the rewarding of the righteous and the punishment of the wicked with a familiar Hebrew construction of arguing in verse 31 from the lesser to the greater: "if. . .then how much more" (Proverbs 19:7; Job 25:5-6; 1 Peter 4:18). The construction implies that the repayment of the righteous is an irrefutable truth that can be depended upon, and the repayment of the wicked is even more certain. The translation of verse 30 is difficult, as seen by comparing the translations in the NRSV, which refers to violence taking away life, and the NIV, which refers to winning souls.

INTERPRETING THE SCRIPTURE

Righteousness and Its Rewards

The righteousness of the righteous person will receive a reward, but the wicked will finally be frustrated in their efforts, declares a common theme in the Wisdom literature of Israel (11:5-8). Wisdom literature promises to show learners the authentic way of life. The introduction of the book of Proverbs announces that it means to instruct its pupils in the discipline of righteousness (1:3) so that students who give attention to wisdom will understand what is right (2:9).

"Righteousness" may be minimally defined as conforming to the law and ordinances of our "righteous" God, but in the Wisdom literature "righteousness" also discerns what is "right" in a particular situation and acts accordingly. Righteousness has to do with enormous matters like worshiping the Lord and it has to do with mundane affairs like having honest, consistent business practices. A righteous person in the wisdom tradition is one who knows how to live in fellowship with God and community, trusting and worshiping God and offering generous care to neighbors and particularly to the needy. The presence and actions of the righteous person strengthen the community (11:11); the presence and actions of the wicked undermine our common life (11:12-13).

The Opponents of Righteousness: Pride and Greed

Chief among the threats to righteousness are pride (11:2) and greed (11:4) because both of these "deadly sins" inevitably destroy relationships with God and neighbor.

"Pride" does not simply mean taking an appropriate satisfaction in one's abilities and accomplishments. In Proverbs "pride" is the very opposite of "the fear of the LORD" and therefore, a seductive substitute for God (8:13). At the beginning of the book the parent counseled the pupil to "Trust in the LORD with all your heart" (3:5) and not to be willfully self-reliant. Certainly there is a place for self-confidence in the book of Proverbs (which is, after all, a most self-confident book), but self-confidence is no substitute for trusting God.

Greed is the opposite of righteousness in the book of Proverbs because greed can never be satisfied and ultimately subverts just relationships within the community. The trust the unrighteous wicked place in their financial resources and possessions cannot finally endure; their fate is that of the rich fool in Jesus' parable (Luke 12:16-21), while the righteous are promised they will finally be delivered from death (11:4). Proverbs speaks of wisdom's reward in terms of treasure and wealth and it gladly offers business advice, but Proverbs understands clearly that righteous living with modest means is to be preferred to wealth and wickedness (15:16; 16:8).

Integrity in the Marketplace

We may think of "righteousness" as being right with God, and for the Israelite that was customarily accomplished through worship and sacrifice. The book of Proverbs appreciates that insight, but it also borrows the language of worship to describe a life of faithfulness in the workplace. False scales betray our worship as an "abomination," but accurate weights "delight" God (11:1). For the book of Proverbs balances and weights were not merely practical matters or secular concerns, but rather it is God who has provided the world of commerce with honest scales and weights (16:11). Our business standards are as much of God's creation as the mountains and oceans and the people who do business together. The manner in which we do our weekly business is no less an act of worship than what we do in the sanctuary on Sunday morning. With this remarkable use of language the sages invite us to see our desk as an altar, our workplace as a temple, our business transactions as offerings to God.

Living in a consumer economy we inevitably enjoy finding a bargain, a good deal at a good price. Our economy is founded on such transactions and businesses prosper that can provide the better "deals." We enjoy the inexpensive hamburger at the fast food chain, but when we hear of illness caused by contaminated meat and read about the small salaries and nonexistent benefits for workers in the fast food industry, we may very well wonder if this is such a "good deal" after all. We know buying a quart of milk at the convenience store down the street will be more expensive than at the superstore on the edge of town, but when we hear that same quart of milk costs even more in the poorer parts of town, we hear echoes of Proverbs' warning against using false balances and different weights for different people.

Integrity Will Guide You

Sometimes the book of Proverbs exhorts the seeker of wisdom by prescribing a proper course of behavior: "Do not wear yourself out to get rich" (Proverbs 23:4). More often, however, Proverbs simply describes the way things are in this world God has created, and that is precisely what 11:3 does: "The integrity of the upright guides them." The proverb does not exhort the student to seek integrity or insist the student follow the way of integrity; rather the proverb quietly insists that integrity has its own force and energy. The proverb suggests a minidrama in which integrity is by no means a passive quality to be sought but one of the leading actors on the stage.

You are embarking on a journey through unknown territory. You have heard the terrain can be stunningly beautiful but you have also been warned of many dangers. You decide to take on a guide for the trip.

Two applicants appear. One is jittery, looking this way and that, a little evasive answering your questions, but assuring you the trip will be grand fun, you can pack as light as you like, choose the paths that appeal to you, and the journey will require little effort on your part. The other applicant looks you straight in the eye and speaks clearly and confidently: "Yes, the trip can be very dangerous, and yes, there are marvelous vistas ahead, but you will have to pack the proper equipment, pay careful attention, and stay on the marked trail." Which guide will you choose for the way ahead?

Those who give the car keys to duplicity or allow treachery behind the wheel should not be surprised to discover themselves in a ditch, their lives wrecked by the choices they have made. Integrity is the reliable mentor. For the wisdom teacher who proposed this proverb integrity was not merely a virtue to be sought, but a pilot who will steer us through difficult channels.

When we are faced with complicated decisions the wisdom teacher is utterly confident that integrity will assert its own energy to provide us guidance. We are not cast alone in the moral fray. Integrity is our companion who would gladly guide us through the intricate passageways. That we should doubt the moral force of integrity may evidence how broken and divided our lives really are. "Integrity" speaks of a singleness of purpose, just as duplicity and treachery speak of divided and false loyalties. "One thing I asked of the LORD" (Psalm 27:4), sings the psalmist; "This one thing I do" (Philippians 3:13), says Paul. What "one thing" inhabits our hearts and souls? As we become more clear about that "one thing," this proverb is confident we will hear integrity whispering discernments and guiding our paths in ways of righteousness.

SHARING THE SCRIPTURE

Preparing Our Hearts

This week's devotional reading is found in Proverbs 10:27-32. These verses immediately precede our lesson. Note the structure of these proverbs: The first half makes a statement and the second half states a contrast, beginning with the word *but*. What do you learn about the righteous person in these verses? What do you learn about the wicked ones? Try writing some proverbs of your own stating something positive about the righteous and contrasting that with a comment about the wicked.

Pray that you and your class participants will choose to live with the integrity of those who are righteous.

Preparing Our Minds

Study the background Scripture from chapter 11 of Proverbs and the lesson Scripture, verses 1-14. Ponder how pride and dishonesty, which destroy personal integrity, can be overcome.

Write on newsprint:
❏ meditation questions under "Consider the Marks of Integrity in the Learners Themselves and People They Know."
❏ information for next week's lesson, found under "Continue the Journey."

LEADING THE CLASS

(1) Gather to Learn

❖ Welcome the class members and introduce any guests.

❖ Pray that those who have gathered will glean lessons for living from today's session.

❖ Read this information, some of which is taken from a June 30, 2003, article by Rolf

Rosenkranz in *The Business Journal* of Minneapolis–Saint Paul: **Integrity is an important issue in our current business climate. Many people, from high profile chief executive officers of major corporations to lesser-known employees, compromise their integrity by committing white collar crimes. Their crimes hurt not only themselves but others, sometimes many others. In an event in Minneapolis focused on such crimes, George Kline, who was serving a fifty-four month sentence for insider trading and other financial crimes, stated that he neither saw himself above the law nor needed the money. In fact, he had no explanation for what he did. Brian Herron, convicted on federal bribery charges, "urged the audience to abide by the law and develop moral standards and conduct for everyday life." He claimed that his crime "wasn't about power and greed," but "a lack of self worth." Tom Mengler, dean of the University of Saint Thomas School of Law, stated, "we have to take personal responsibility for our actions."**

❖ Invite the students to comment on the role of personal integrity in the workplace and life in general. What kinds of actions and attitudes destroy our integrity?

❖ Read aloud today's focus statement: **Personal integrity is destroyed by pride and dishonesty. How can we overcome these negative traits? Proverbs teaches that pride and dishonesty must be replaced by wisdom and right behavior.**

(2) Summarize Proverbs' Teachings on the Ways One Can Overcome Pride and Dishonesty, Which Destroy One's Personal Integrity

❖ Choose different persons, fourteen of them if possible, to each read a verse from Proverbs 11:1-14. Ask the students to listen as each verse is read to see if they hear any patterns.

❖ Talk about the patterns the adults heard. Likely they will have recognized that each verse (except 7) has a statement about the righteous and another contrasting statement about the wicked. On a sheet of newsprint that has been divided in half vertically, list on the left side the comment about the righteous, and on the right side, the comment about the wicked.

❖ Look at the list and identify any themes. Add information in "The Opponents of Righteousness: Pride and Greed" and "Integrity in the Marketplace" from Interpreting the Scripture as appropriate.

❖ Talk with the class about how these themes are—or are not—applicable to life in the twenty-first century.

(3) Consider the Marks of Integrity in the Learners Themselves and People They Know

❖ Divide the class into groups and give the students paper and pencils. Challenge the groups to write a description of a person who lives with integrity. You may want to ask one group to look specifically at the marks of a person who acts with integrity in the workplace, another group to consider how ones lives with integrity at home, a third group to consider how integrity shows itself in the church, and another to discern how one lives with integrity as a neighbor and citizen. Note that God's people act with integrity in all areas of their lives; this activity is simply highlighting several different lenses through which integrity can be viewed.

❖ Ask the groups to report back. List ideas on newsprint.

❖ Provide quiet time for the learners to ponder these questions posted on newsprint. They may choose to write their thoughts on the paper that has already been distributed.

(1) How does my life reflect the marks of integrity that we and the writer of Proverbs have identified?

(2) When I think of people who live with integrity, who immediately comes to mind? Why?

(3) When I think of people whose integrity has been compromised, who comes to mind? What actions or attitudes compromised their integrity?

(4) Commit to Living with Integrity in All Aspects of Life

❖ Invite the class to read in unison today's key verse from Proverbs 11:3.

❖ Ask the students to comment on how they interpret this verse. Be prepared for discussion on how and where treachery destroys those who are crooked. Some students may point to "high profile" cases in which someone was punished for failing to act with integrity, but other class members may suggest situations in which blatant "crookedness" went unpunished, or worse, was lauded.

❖ **Option:** If you have access to *The United Methodist Hymnal*, invite the students to read in unison "For Holiness of Heart" (page 401) by Howard Thurman. Let this prayer express their desire to commit themselves to living with integrity.

❖ **Option:** Ask the students to take the hand of a neighbor and together repeat these words after you: **God, I seek your wisdom so that I might live with the integrity and righteousness of those who are upright in your sight. I commit myself to walking in the path of integrity that you have set before me, and humbly pray in Jesus' name that you will guide me on this narrow way. Amen.**

(5) Continue the Journey

❖ Pray that the participants will be faithful to their commitment to follow the path of integrity.

❖ Read aloud this preparation for next week's lesson. You may also want to post it on newsprint for the students to copy. **Prepare for next week's session, "Living Out Wisdom," by reading Proverbs 31. We will look particularly at verses 8-14, 25-30. As you study this familiar description, consider these thoughts: People choose the criteria for living to which they commit and by which they are thus guided to make decisions. Which wise criteria for living should one be committed to and guided by in order to achieve prudent behavior? King Lemuel's mother praises the women who respect God and follow God's guidance in loving and caring for their families.**

❖ Read aloud the following three ideas. Challenge the students to commit themselves to use these activities as a springboard to spiritual growth.

(1) **Look for news articles concerning people who have compromised their integrity by engaging in dishonest or unethical activities. What caused these individuals to fall? How could they have avoided such a fall? How could you avoid a similar fall?**

(2) **Be alert to situations in which you could be tempted to act dishonestly or with conceit. What triggers such temptations? How can you deal with them?**

(3) **Pray for persons whose integrity has been compromised. Do whatever is in your power to help them restore their integrity.**

❖ Sing or read aloud "I Want a Principle Within."

❖ Lead this benediction to end today's session: **With all of your creatures, most majestic God, we sing your praises and pray that you would empower us to be wise people and faithful stewards of your creation, in Jesus' name. Amen.**

UNIT 3: LESSONS IN LIVING
LIVING OUT WISDOM

PREVIEWING THE LESSON

Lesson Scripture: Proverbs 31:8-14, 25-30
Background Scripture: Proverbs 31
Key Verse: Proverbs 31:30

Focus of the Lesson:
People choose the criteria for living to which they commit and by which they are thus guided to make decisions. Which wise criteria for living should one be committed to and guided by in order to achieve prudent behavior? King Lemuel's mother praises the women who respect God and follow God's guidance in loving and caring for their families.

Goals for the Learners:
(1) to summarize the description of the wise woman that King Lemuel learned from his mother.
(2) to explore how they and others they know live with wisdom.
(3) to make a commitment to try to live with God's wisdom.

Pronunciation Guide:
hayil (khah' yil)
Lemuel (lem' yoo uhl)

Supplies:
Bibles, newsprint and marker, paper and pencils, hymnals

READING THE SCRIPTURE

NRSV
Proverbs 31:8-14, 25-30
8 Speak out for those who cannot speak,
     for the rights of all the destitute.
9 Speak out, judge righteously,
     defend the rights of the poor and needy.
10 A capable wife who can find?
     She is far more precious than jewels.

NIV
Proverbs 31:8-14, 25-30
8"Speak up for those who cannot speak for
     themselves,
     for the rights of all who are destitute.
9Speak up and judge fairly;
     defend the rights of the poor and needy."
10A wife of noble character who can find?

¹¹ The heart of her husband trusts in her,
　　and he will have no lack of gain.
¹² She does him good, and not harm,
　　all the days of her life.
¹³ She seeks wool and flax,
　　and works with willing hands.
¹⁴ She is like the ships of the merchant,
　　she brings her food from far away.
²⁵ Strength and dignity are her clothing,
　　and she laughs at the time to come.
²⁶ She opens her mouth with wisdom,
　　and the teaching of kindness is on her
　　tongue.
²⁷ She looks well to the ways of her
　　household,
and does not eat the bread of idleness.
²⁸ Her children rise up and call her happy;
　　her husband too, and he praises her:
²⁹ "Many women have done excellently,
　　but you surpass them all."
**³⁰ Charm is deceitful, and beauty is vain,
　　but a woman who fears the LORD is to
　　be praised.**

She is worth far more than rubies.
¹¹Her husband has full confidence in her
　　and lacks nothing of value.
¹²She brings him good, not harm,
　　all the days of her life.
¹³She selects wool and flax
　　and works with eager hands.
¹⁴She is like the merchant ships,
　　bringing her food from afar.
²⁵She is clothed with strength and dignity;
　　she can laugh at the days to come.
²⁶She speaks with wisdom,
　　and faithful instruction is on her tongue.
²⁷She watches over the affairs of her
　　household
　　and does not eat the bread of idleness.
²⁸Her children arise and call her blessed;
　　her husband also, and he praises her:
²⁹"Many women do noble things,
　　but you surpass them all."
**³⁰Charm is deceptive, and beauty is
　　fleeting;
but a woman who fears the LORD is to be
　　praised.**

UNDERSTANDING THE SCRIPTURE

Proverbs 31:1. The book of Proverbs began with the invitation, "Hear, my child, your father's instruction, and do not reject your mother's teaching" (1:8), but much in the initial chapters suggested that the pedagogical relationship was confined to a father addressing a son. Here, at the conclusion of the book of Proverbs, the women take over the instruction: A queen, the mother of King Lemuel, instructs her son in lessons of statecraft; and a dazzlingly effective woman appears clothed in poetry to complete the book's vision of the habits and benefits of wisdom.

The queen teaches her son about the temptations and obligations of being a king. The presumed situation may be that the

young man's father has died and he is about to become King Lemuel. Some translators prefer "King Lemuel of Massa" (31:1 NIV margin) rather than speaking of the queen's instruction as "an oracle," in which case King Lemuel might have been regent of an Arabian tribe, because Massa is located in Arabia. The wisdom offered in Proverbs is international and ecumenical, and the queen's instruction applicable not only to kings but to presidents, prime ministers, CEO's, pastors, and all who would live wisely.

Proverbs 31:2-7. In verse 31:2 the repeated "No—No" (NRSV) or "O—O" (NIV) could be even more literally translated "What?—What?" That emphatically negative "What?" causes many to remember their parent's admonition: "You're going to do WHAT?" (The clear message being: You're not going to do that!) What young Prince Lemuel is not going to do when he becomes King Lemuel is to exhaust himself among the royal harem. This advice parallels earlier warnings in Proverbs 7:10-27 about the temptations of the wrong kind of woman (the right kind of woman will soon be described). Women are not the only temptation in the palace, however, and the Queen Mother warns against the dissolutions of wine and beer (31:6 NIV; "strong drink" in NRSV). Filled with wisdom and experience, this royal mother counsels against the use of alcohol by those in power because of its effect on memory and judgment. Let the suffering drink to ease their pain and the poor to ease their misery, but the king cannot afford to risk misusing alcohol.

Proverbs 31:8-9. It is a mercy for the poor and suffering to forget their misery, but King Lemuel cannot forget who he is: a voice for the voiceless and a righteous judge for "the rights of the poor and needy." This instruction echoes the vision of the righteous king's rule in Psalm 72 where the king's attention to the weak and needy mirrors God's cosmic compassion upon all the creation.

Proverbs 31:10. The woman described as *hayil* in Proverbs 31:10 could be thought of as "a woman of strength" or "a woman of worth" or "a woman of substance" or "valiant woman." She is more than "a capable wife" or "a wife of noble character." When the Hebrew Bible employs the word *hayil* it describes strong officers and valiant warriors. Only a few verses before, *hayil* is translated "strength" in reference to King Lemuel (31:3). When Boaz is described as *hayil* the NRSV translates "prominent rich man" and NIV offers "a man of standing" (Ruth 2:1). The woman we meet in Proverbs 31:10-31 is *hayil*, and therefore, not easily translated into our terms, but "capable wife" is a bland rendering. Like Woman Wisdom herself, this woman is "more precious than jewels" (3:10 "rubies," NIV; compare Proverbs 3:15; 8:11). She exceeds our valuations and vocabulary to name her.

Proverbs 31:11-31. The wisdom poet of Proverbs 31:10-31 is less interested in naming this outstanding woman than describing her activities in a lavish poem or hymn. The poem is an acrostic twenty-two lines, each line beginning with the next letter of the Hebrew alphabet. Acrostics provide an easily remembered teaching device, and this structure can be seen in Psalms 9 and 10 (together), 25, 34, 37, 111, 112, 119, and 145 (see lesson for March 26). Like many of the psalms this poem is a hymn of praise, but in this case the one praised is this extraordinary woman. Like hymns addressed to the Lord, it describes strength demonstrated, wisdom shown, and success achieved (compare Exodus 15, Judges 5, and 2 Samuel 22). The hymn of praise begins as a solo, but in verse 28 the woman's children and husband join the acclamation. This husband was mentioned at the beginning of the poem (31:11) but has been largely absent except in verse 23—where as a result of his wife's wise management and productivity he is recognized with honors at the gate. Now the husband and children acclaim her announcing that her achievements bring her honor at the city gates.

The hymn that began within the privacy of a household concludes in the most public place of an Israelite town, the city gates. The gates were not merely portals to the city, but the place of gathering. Though they may have been physically located at the perimeter of the city, the gate was the "center" of the city with respect to the city's social, economic, religious, and legal affairs. Elders gathered at the gates to decide legal matters (Deuteronomy 17:5, 21:19; 25:7; Psalm 69:12). Amos the prophet indicted those who "push aside the needy in the gate" (Amos 5:12) and announced that Israel should "Hate evil and love good, and establish justice in the gate" (Amos 5:15). The gate was a place for settling family affairs, as when the *hayil* man Boaz goes to claim Ruth (Ruth 4:1-2). The scribe Ezra read the law of God at the gate (Nehemiah 8:3). Archaeological digs find evidence that the gates were also a place of worship (sometimes of false worship, 2 Kings 23:8). The male elders of Israel ruled at the city gates.

That the book of Proverbs should conclude with this vision of a woman's achievements being so acclaimed at the center of community life is both appropriate and astonishing. The exceptional woman of chapter 31, surely a daughter of Wisdom, has made her way to the very center of her world. What is left to do but sing praise?

INTERPRETING THE SCRIPTURE

A Woman Full of Surprises

The book of Proverbs concludes with a poetic portrait of Wisdom inhabiting the life and manners of a single human being, in this case a woman described as *hayil*, a word variously translated "prominent," "effective," "valiant," "strong," and "capable." Proverbs began with poems inviting human beings to learn wisdom and then provided collections of proverbs to guide learners in the ways of wisdom. Now Proverbs shows us how wisdom looks walking around in a household and community. The acrostic form, moving from the A to Z of the Hebrew alphabet, suggests completeness and perfection, and provides a satisfying but also somewhat surprising conclusion for Proverbs.

The astonishing woman of 31:10-31 is not identified as being a member of her husband's household (or father's or eldest son's), as she might customarily be named in the Scriptures, but she is said to have "her household" (31:15, 21, 27). The designation, far from threatening or diminishing her husband, provides for his well-being (31:11-12), ensures his trust (31:11), and summons his praise (31:28-29). When we read the word *household* in the Scriptures we do well to remember that our experience that divides home and workplace, house and office, is a modern invention. A "household" was also a place of commerce and business, and so

we see this woman supervising other women, also members of the household, in their work (31:15). The distinction our language frequently (and unfortunately) makes between "housewife" and "business woman" simply does not apply to households of the ancient world. The household is a place of production and this woman is productive indeed. The book of Proverbs has consistently warned against laziness (Proverbs 10:26; 12:24, 13:4, 15:19; 20:4, 21:25; and 26:13-16), and this woman has no appetite for "the bread of idleness" (31:27).

Another surprise is that this woman, like Wisdom personified and like the sages who gathered wisdom for the book of Proverbs, is a teacher (31:26). She offers wisdom and instruction in the covenant loyalty—sometimes spoken of as "loving kindness"—the quality that describes God's relationship to human beings as well as the affiliation binding households and communities. In this poem she teaches not only by the words of her mouth but also by her every action and gesture.

Perplexed by Perfection?

The acrostic form of the poem suggests perfection, a perfect form for a perfect woman, or for that matter, a perfect human being. No other human in all the Hebrew Scriptures is so praised as this woman. Whatever she does she does excellently, surpassing all others (31:29).

Because she is so utterly perfect many people discover unpleasant negative emotions surging up within them. She's too good! Some people resent her because she's too perfect: No one person can be that complete. Others may feel she presents an overwhelming demand: Isn't it challenge enough to balance family and work without watching Wonder Woman? She may intimidate us by her completeness: Maybe she can do it all, but I sure can't! Being aware of our visceral reaction to a reading from Scripture is particularly useful in reading Wisdom literature—we can learn not only from what we willingly accept but also from what we resist—but we do well in our reading to push beyond first thoughts, immediate reactions, and emotional responses to a more reflective consideration of what the Scripture is trying to teach us.

This surprising woman does not appear in the last verses of the book of Proverbs to cow us or irritate us, but rather she comes to bless us. She proposes to welcome us into God's presence. The phrase "girds herself with strength" (31:17) is typically used as a preparation for an encounter with God (Job 38:3; 40:7; Nahum 2:1). Her perfection does not mean to alienate us but means to mediate God's goodness to us. The Epistle to the Hebrews assures of the perfection and sinlessness of Jesus Christ so that we might understand that he is perfectly capable of being the mediator of God's grace and salvation (Hebrews 4:15-16, 5:9). Her "perfection" is for our sake and means to teach us how we can live with blessing. Before we dismiss her as "too good to be true," we do well to remember a proverb, "Fools think their own way is right, but the wise listen to advice" (Proverbs 12:15). This woman is formidable, no doubt about that, but she intends "good, not harm" (31:12) not only for her husband but for all.

Living Like a Queen

The song of praise hymning her productivity and profitability does not overlook her concern for those in need. Because Wisdom literature focuses on instructing individuals we may be tempted to think of human life lived autonomously in isolation from a larger society, but wisdom recognizes that there is more to the good life than personal prosperity. The NRSV translation best captures the poetic repetition of "hands" in verse 20: This splendid woman's hands are busy not with work alone but with reaching out to the poor and needy. She embodies the queenly wisdom that the mother of King Lemuel gives her son, and does not forget those who cannot speak out for themselves (31:8-9). Just as the whole creation benefits from the rule of the righteous monarch (2 Samuel 23:3-4), so her entire household, including servants, reaps the benefits she provides (31:21). Although the greed of the kings of Israel and Judah is well documented in the Scriptures, Psalm 72, attributed to Solomon, speaks of the wise ruler who does not overlook the weak and needy. This woman embodies the royal wisdom of Proverbs.

The Fear of the Lord Is the Beginning . . . and Ending

Just as the book of Proverbs began with the inviting motto "The fear of the LORD is the beginning of knowledge" (1:7), so it concludes with this marvelous poem and the declaration that "a woman who fears the LORD is to be praised" (31:30). The woman might have been praised for her business sense or her household management or her acts of mercy or her wise teaching—and all of these "works" do indeed praise her (31:31)—but the poet sums it all up by inviting us to praise her for her "fear of the LORD."

To fear the Lord diminishes every other fear. Though we may fear death, we need not fear death as those "who have no hope" (1 Thessalonians 4:13), because in life and death "we are the Lord's" (Romans 14:8). This woman does not fear the caprices of the weather (Proverbs 31:21) nor the unpredictable turns the future may take (31:25) because fearing God she knows her place in God's creation. Trusting in God with all her heart (3:5) she has a strong place to stand when wool and flax markets collapse or merchant ships founder. Even the wise cannot escape misfortune, the wisdom tradition has taught us, but the wise have a foundation that cannot be shaken by the ever-changing days. Although the woman of Proverbs 31:10-31 sounds very beautiful indeed, she has wisdom to know that beauty is fleeting and insight to know that wisdom endures because it belongs to God. The laughter with which the woman laughs at the future is the laughter of one whose delight is in the Lord (Psalm 37:4). Wisdom invites us to fear God and treat all else with good humor and gentle laughter.

SHARING THE SCRIPTURE

Preparing Our Hearts

This week's devotional reading is found in Proverbs 4:10-15. Here we read the words of a parent urging his child to walk in the way of wisdom, as he has been taught to do. Wisdom leads one in the path of "uprightness," but those who stray find themselves on "the path of the wicked." What kind of advice about following the right way did you hear from significant adults in your life? What kind of advice are you passing on to the next generation? What evidence can others see that you are walking in the way of wisdom?

Pray that you and your adult learners will teach and act as role models for those who want to follow the path of God's wisdom.

Preparing Our Minds

Study the background Scripture from Proverbs 31 and the lesson Scripture, verses 8-14, 25-30. As you study, think about criteria for living that should guide your decision-making and behavior.

Write on newsprint:

❑ information for next week's lesson, found under "Continue the Journey."

Plan a brief lecture as suggested under "Summarize the Description of the Wise Woman That King Lemuel Learned from His Mother."

LEADING THE CLASS

(1) Gather to Learn

❖ Welcome the class members and introduce any guests.

❖ Pray that those who have come will commit themselves to living according to God's wisdom.

❖ Encourage the class to list qualities they would use to describe a "good" person. List these ideas on newsprint. Discuss the differences, if any, between the qualities that a woman would be praised for and those for which a man would be praised. If differences were noted, invite the class to comment on reasons that these differences exist.

❖ Read aloud today's focus statement: **People choose the criteria for living to which they commit and by which they are thus guided to make decisions. Which wise criteria for living should one be committed to and guided by in order to achieve prudent behavior? King Lemuel's mother praises the women who respect God and follow God's guidance in loving and caring for their families.**

(2) Summarize the Description of the Wise Woman That King Lemuel Learned from His Mother

❖ Introduce today's text by creating a brief lecture based on the explanations of

Proverbs 31:1, 2-7, as found in Understanding the Scripture.

❖ Select someone to read Proverbs 31:8-9. Note the following points:

■ These verses are part of King Lemuel's mother's teachings. Most of Proverbs has focused on a father teaching his son, but here we have the mother doing so. (See Proverbs 1:8.)

■ Defending the vulnerable and judging righteously are attributes of the righteous king. (See Psalm 72.)

■ The responsibility of a monarch to care for the vulnerable was not only seen in Israelite society but also in neighboring societies. King Lemuel may have been from Massa in Arabia.

❖ Choose a volunteer to read Proverbs 31:10-14, or if time permits, 10-24.

■ List on newsprint reasons for which the capable wife is to be praised.

■ Compare this list to the one the class created in the "Gather to Learn" portion of the lesson. Identify similarities and differences between the two lists.

■ Invite the students to respond to this woman by discussing these questions.

(1) **Does this woman seem real? Why or why not?** (You may wish to read or retell "Perplexed by Perfection?" in Interpreting the Scripture.)

(2) **How do her abilities make you feel?**

(3) **How might women who are not wives and/or mothers relate to this woman?**

(4) **How might men relate to this woman's strengths?**

❖ Have a student read Proverbs 31:25-30.

■ Read or retell "The Fear of the Lord Is the Beginning . . . and Ending" in Interpreting the Scripture.

■ Ask the learners to recall previous discussions concerning "the fear of the LORD" and consider how this "fear" is related to wisdom.

(3) Explore How the Learners and Others They Know Live with Wisdom

❖ Divide the class into groups. Give each group a sheet of newsprint and a marker. Ask each group to list three to five criteria for living that they feel are most important. Then have them brainstorm names of people—either famous or locally known to many of the participants—who seem to fit these criteria.

❖ Provide time for each group to report to the class. If you have space, post the sheets of newsprint around the room. As an option, encourage the students to walk around the room to get ideas from what the groups have written.

❖ Lead a discussion by asking the students to note which criteria for living seem to be mentioned most often. Invite them to relate any insights they have gathered about the ways of those who live wisely.

(4) Make a Commitment to Try to Live with God's Wisdom

❖ Distribute paper and pencils. Ask the students to list three to five criteria for living that guide their own lives. They are not to share their lists.

❖ Do this guided imagery activity with the students by reading aloud and pausing so that they can meditate.

■ **See yourself alone in a quiet place. Suddenly, the woman of Proverbs 31, who has learned to live wisely, appears to you. Listen to what she has to say to you about the criteria for living you have identified in your own life.** (Pause)

■ **She points out some other criteria for living that you and your classmates identified earlier and sug-**

gests that you would do well to adopt these. Which ones does she suggest? Why does she say you need to consider them? (Pause)

■ **Respond silently to this wise woman. Make whatever commitment you feel is appropriate about living with wisdom.** (Pause)

(5) Continue the Journey

❖ Break the silence by praying that those who have participated today will go forth committed to live as wise and upright people of God.

❖ Read aloud this preparation for next week's lesson. You may also want to post it on newsprint for the students to copy. **Prepare for next week's session, "Living in Unity," by reading 1 Corinthians 1:10-17. This session marks the beginning of our summer quarter, "Called to Be a Christian Community," which explores 1 and 2 Corinthians. Consider these ideas as you study today's lesson: Many people have experienced the divisiveness of misguided loyalties. What demands our loyalty to the point that we are united rather than divided? Paul says that the Christian community finds its unity in Jesus Christ, to whom we owe complete loyalty.**

❖ Read aloud the following three ideas. Challenge the students to commit themselves to use these activities as a springboard to spiritual growth.

(1) **Watch your behaviors this week. Do you tend to live a self-disciplined life, or are you a procrastinator or someone who shirks responsibility? What changes do you need to make, if any?**

(2) **Identify three to five criteria for living that most drive your actions and attitudes. Examine these criteria in light of biblical teaching. Do you believe that these criteria enable you to live according to God's wisdom, or do you need to modify or change your criteria?**

(3) **Do something this week to show your gratitude for someone who has been a role model for you or otherwise helped you.**

❖ Sing or read aloud "Shalom to You."

❖ Lead this benediction to end today's session: **With all of your creatures, most majestic God, we sing your praises and pray that you would empower us to be wise people and faithful stewards of your creation, in Jesus' name. Amen.**

FOURTH QUARTER
Called to Be a Christian Community

JUNE 4, 2006–AUGUST 27, 2006

This summer we will be looking in depth at 1 and 2 Corinthians. In these highly practical letters, Paul addresses problems that church members in Corinth struggled with as they tried to live faithfully amid a culture inhospitable to Christianity. Even though our world is admittedly quite different, these letters continue to provide us with valuable insights.

Unit 1, "Servants of God," explores 1 Corinthians to discern how the Christian community becomes God's servant people. "Living in Unity," the session for June 4, examines 1 Corinthians 1:10-17 to discover Paul's teaching that the church finds its unity in Jesus, to whom we owe undivided loyalty. First Corinthians 2, the background for "Finding Wisdom" on June 11, proclaims that God is the source of true wisdom, which we receive through the power of the Holy Spirit. The session for June 18, "Building Together," delves into 1 Corinthians 3:1-15 to consider how spiritual formation takes place within the community of faith with the aid of teachers and mentors. The unit ends on June 25 with "Serving Responsibly," a lesson rooted in 1 Corinthians 4:1-13 that encourages us to follow through on appropriate attitudes and actions as disciples.

We continue our study of 1 Corinthians for another five weeks in Unit 2, "Called to Obedience." The unit begins on July 2 with "Living in Relationships," taken from 1 Corinthians 7:1-20, 23-40, which considers vital human relationships, particularly marriage and singleness. Paul urges believers to live so as not to cause others to sin, as detailed in "To Eat or Not to Eat," a session on July 9 from 1 Corinthians 8:1-13. "Called to Win," the lesson for July 16 from 1 Corinthians 9:24–10:13, encourages us to rely on God's strength to follow through on our commitments. On July 23 we move to 1 Corinthians 12:1-13 to consider the spiritual gifts that we have been given for the purpose of building up the body of Christ, as highlighted in the session "All for One." "Love Comes First," our closing lesson for this unit on July 30, taken from the beloved 1 Corinthians 13, describes how love should be the basis for the exercise of our spiritual gifts.

Unit 3, "The Spirit of Giving," includes four lessons from 2 Corinthians concerned with giving as a part of the Christian life. On August 6 in "Forgiving and Reconciling" we will study 2 Corinthians 2:5-11 and 7:2-15 to explore forgiveness as a means of healing broken relationships. "Giving Generously," the lesson for August 13, explores 2 Corinthians 8:1-15, where Paul encourages believers to give. "Reasons for Giving," the session for August 20, investigates 2 Corinthians 9:1-15 to encounter Paul's teaching that we are to give in response to God's generosity. This unit concludes on August 27 with "Leaning on Grace," rooted in 2 Corinthians 12:1-10, which helps us to recognize that no matter what our difficulties are, God is always present and undergirding us with strength.

MEET OUR WRITER

DR. DAVID A. deSILVA

David deSilva lives in Ashland, Ohio, where he serves as professor of New Testament and Greek at Ashland Theological Seminary and as music director and organist at Christ United Methodist Church. He is an ordained elder in the Florida Conference of The United Methodist Church, whose primary ministries are teaching, writing, music, and raising a family.

He is the author of eleven books in the area of biblical studies, including *An Introduction to the New Testament: Context, Methods, and Ministry Formation* (Downers Grove: InterVarsity, 2004); *Introducing the Apocrypha* (Grand Rapids: Baker, 2002); *Honor, Patronage, Kinship, and Purity: Unlocking New Testament Culture* (Downers Grove: InterVarsity, 2000); *Perseverance in Gratitude: A Socio-rhetorical Commentary on the Epistle "to the Hebrews"* (Grand Rapids: Eerdmans, 2000); and *New Testament Themes* (St. Louis: Chalice Press, 2001).

He has written several other books for devotional and small-group use, including *Praying with John Wesley* (Nashville: Discipleship Resources, 2001); *Paul and the Macedonians* (Nashville: Abingdon Press, 2001); and *Afterlife: Finding Hope in the Face of Death* (Nashville: Abingdon Press, 2003). He also has written for *Adult Bible Studies* and *Adult Bible Studies Teacher*. In addition, he has contributed more than sixty articles to journals, collections of essays, Bible dictionaries, and Bible commentaries.

He attended Princeton University, where he earned a bachelor's degree in English, and then matriculated to Princeton Theological Seminary for the degree of master of divinity. In 1995, he was awarded a Ph.D. in religion from Emory University in Atlanta.

He is married to Donna Jean, his wife of fifteen years. They have three sons: James Adrian, John Austin, and Justin Alexander.

THE CHURCHES OF GOD IN CORINTH

The City of Corinth

Although Corinth was an ancient city, it was also a new city in most respects. Whatever "history" it had as a Greek city-state came to an end in 146 B.C., when Roman forces destroyed it. The city remained practically uninhabited for a century until it was re-founded as a Roman colony in 44 B.C. by order of Julius Caesar. Military veterans and freed slaves appear to have made up the bulk of the new colony's settlers, making Corinth a place of fast-paced upward-mobility as these non-elites became the new elites of Corinth.

Corinth was politically important as the center of the province of Achaia, and economically vital as a hub of trade on the route between Italy and the East. The fast-growing city attracted craftspeople of every kind, entrepreneurs in business, and many others who saw a rare opportunity to make a name for themselves in an otherwise static and caste-bound world. People who prospered in business had many opportunities to become public benefactors and to rise in the ranks of the local government, publicizing their generosity and increasing their local reputation through inscriptions testifying to their public improvements.

The blossoming city attracted all manner of philosophers, teachers, orators, and others seeking a new venue for fame and for attracting patrons to support them. The local population would gather around public speakers and form "factions" in support of their favorites, much as people in the United States can become heated and factious about which football team is better. This is the backdrop for the divisions that Paul addresses in 1 Corinthians 1–4, where he finds his converts treating him and the other Christian missionaries as other Corinthians treat rival orators or sophists—local patrons claiming privilege over one another based on being attached to the more accomplished or impressive missionary, factions growing in the church on the basis of connection with one or the other preacher.

Corinth was also a city deeply immersed in athletic events (as the host to the Isthmian games every two years), in the arts, and in religious life. It was truly a city with "many gods" and "many lords" (1 Corinthians 8:5), whose presence and worship surrounded civic life and permeated private and domestic gatherings. The city was filled with impressive temples and shrines to Apollo, Aphrodite, Artemis, the emperors, and exotic cults like the Egyptian cult of Isis and Sarapis. The temples of Demeter and Asclepius had private dining rooms that would have been among the places where Corinthian Christians might have been invited by their neighbors, thus raising the questions about how far Christians could interact with the sacred places and meals of their neighbors (thus enjoying the ongoing business, support, and help of these neighbors as well) without being disloyal to God (see 1 Corinthians 8:1-13; 10:14-33).

Paul's Ministry in Corinth

According to Acts 18, Paul preached in Corinth following his missionary work in Macedonia, where he founded congregations in Philippi and Thessalonica, and Athens. Paul's work in Macedonia exposed him to many hardships, including beatings, imprisonment, and the threat of mob violence. Paul's Letters to the Macedonian churches corroborate the impression we get from Acts on this point (see 1 Thessalonians 1:6; 2:14-16; 2:17–3:4). It is no wonder, then, that he should report coming to Corinth "in weakness and in fear and in much trembling" (1 Corinthians 2:3), faithful to God's call to proclaim Christ crucified, uncertain of what new hardships would await him. The Acts account of Paul's work in Corinth incidentally provides us with one of the very few hard and fast dates we have for constructing a chronology of Paul's career. Paul was in Corinth at the same time that Lucius Annaeus Gallio (Acts 18:12), the brother of the famous philosopher Lucius Annaeus Seneca, was proconsul, namely in 51–52 A.D.

The conversion of a "household" is a common feature in Paul's reports of his own work and in the picture of his ministry in Acts. For example, in Corinth he converts "Crispus, the official of the synagogue, . . . together with all his household" (Acts 18:8; see 1 Corinthians 1:14) and baptizes "the household of Stephanus" (1 Corinthians 1:16). It was vital for Paul to convert householders, since the private home rather than the public religious building was the place where the Christian community would gather for teaching, worship, and celebration of its sacred meals. Prisca and Aquila opened up their home to such a group in Ephesus (1 Corinthians 16:19); Philemon and Nympha were hosts to the churches in the area of Colossae, and so on throughout the Pauline mission. In Corinth, it would appear that the Christians met in "cell groups" in the homes of various householders (like Stephanus), and then came together from time to time as a whole "church" in the house of Gaius (Romans 16:23), notably a person also personally converted and baptized by Paul (1 Corinthians 1:14). The early Christian movement depended on the hospitality of its members of means (see, for example, 1 Peter 4:9); meeting in private homes contributed to the feeling of a new "family" that the early Christian leaders were eager to promote, but it also may have contributed, in part, to factionalism in Corinth.

The Corinthian congregation, which probably numbered no more than fifty believers (if they all were to fit even within one of Corinth's larger houses at one time), was a diverse group. There were people of means supporting the church's meetings, contributing to the collection Paul administered, and supporting itinerant teachers (other than Paul, who worked a trade so as to avoid becoming dependent on a local patron). There were many others who were craftspeople, traders, and slaves. This socio-economic diversity appears to have contributed to divisions in Corinth as well, particularly around the celebration of the Lord's Supper, where the quality and amount of food consumed by different people reinforced differences in social status rather than unity in Christ. Even though Corinth had a strong Jewish presence (Acts 18:8, 17 gives the impression of two synagogues in the city), the church appears to have been predominantly Gentile. Paul speaks of them consistently as former idolaters (1 Corinthians 6:9-11; 8:7; 12:2) rather than as people who had been "slaves to the Torah" or some other such indication of Jewish heritage.

The Ministry of Other Apostles and Missionaries

After Paul left Corinth, the prominent city continued to be visited by Christian preachers. Among these was Apollos, an Alexandrian Jew skilled both in the Old Testament and in public speaking, who was brought into the orbit of the Pauline mission by Prisca and Aquila (Acts 18:24–19:1). His eloquence would certainly appeal to Corinthian sensibilities. Paul himself would come up short by comparison (see 2 Corinthians 10:10; 11:6), but this was in line with his own choice and strategy (1 Corinthians 1:17; 2:1-5). Paul knew the danger of winning people over with impressive displays rather than with words that allowed God to cut to the heart, and this danger was very real for the Corinthians who persistently evaluated their own worth and status, the worth of others, and the legitimacy of their teachers by cultural standards of excellence rather than by the work of God manifest in each. Paul's own relationship with Apollos appears to have been cordial. Paul certainly wants the Corinthians to view them not as rivals, but as partners in the work of God on behalf of the church (1 Corinthians 3:6-9; 16:12).

Paul gives the impression that Cephas, or Peter (see Galatians 2:7-14 on the interchangeability of these names), had also traveled to Corinth, or, at the very least, was represented by other Jewish Christian missionaries in Corinth. First Corinthians 9:5 assumes some acquaintance on the part of the readers with Peter's missionary work (and its details). Finally, 2 Corinthians gives clear evidence of rival Jewish-Christian teachers coming to Corinth and actively trying to claim that ground from Paul. These are not "Judaizers" such as one finds in Galatia, but represent another strain of early Jewish Christianity that was unsupportive of Paul and his gospel.

A Church of "Quarrels"

The Corinthian letters continue to fascinate us because of the insights they give into the tensions between a minister's representation of the gospel and the expectations of a congregation and the guidance they provide for moving beyond a host of other tensions that divide a congregation against itself. These tensions included

- forming factions around their favorite missionary; measuring these preachers against one another and promoting their own as the "best" (and therefore themselves as the students of the "best"); neglecting the fact that all these teachers are God's gifts to them, not grounds for promoting rivalry and boasting.
- looking down upon other believers on the basis of their freedom or lack or freedom from religious scruples, rather than acting out of love and concern to protect one another's consciences.
- flirting with sexual immorality; forgetting that God has sanctified our physical person as well by God's Spirit, and how this body is to be kept for the Lord as the seed of our resurrection body.
- using God's gifts as signs of "spiritual" status, valuing the more obvious and exotic gifts (like speaking in tongues) as visible evidence of being endowed with God's Spirit. This leads to neglect and devaluing of the diversity of gifts God provides the church, as well as a devaluing of those members whose spiritual gifts are not as flamboyant but just as necessary for the whole mission of the church.
- questioning Paul's own legitimacy as an apostle. Judged by cultural standards of skill and charisma, he comes up wanting, and other preachers take advantage of this fact to win over his congregation. Paul must show that relying on external appearances as a measure of one's own or anyone else's worth is a sign of an unconverted mind. The only thing of value is the power of God, transforming us into the image of Jesus and sealing us for our redemption. What value can fleshly strengths have, when the end of all of them is the grave?

The Corinthian Christians continued to evaluate one another, to compete with one another (rather than cooperate), and to evaluate their leaders according to the norms of Greco-Roman society. They needed to hear, as we continue to need to hear, how these strategies run completely counter to the values revealed in the gospel of "Christ crucified," the nature of the church as a family and as a single corporate body, and the lavish generosity of God (which leaves no room for boasting, since all good gifts are gifts received, not achievements attained).

Paul's Long-term, Long-distance Relationship with the Corinthian Christians

What happened after Paul left Corinth at the end of his initial two-year missionary visit? Paul's relationship with the Corinthians is the best represented, the richest, and perhaps the most confusing of his relationships with local Christian communities. Even before writing 1 Corinthians, Paul had written a "previous letter" (referred to briefly in 1 Corinthians 5:9-11), now lost, to provide guidance for the church's life and growth after Paul's departure from Corinth. Sometime after this, the Corinthian church sends a letter to Paul with questions about several matters (sent through the delegation of Stephanus, Fortunatus, and Achaicus; 1 Corinthians 16:17-18). Paul also receives other news about the goings-on in Corinth from "Chloe's people" (1 Corinthians 1:11). Paul responds by sending 1 Corinthians back to Corinth, probably with the returning emissaries.

After some time, and perhaps also after receiving word back from Timothy (1 Corinthians 16:10) about the developments in the congregation, Paul makes a second visit to Corinth on the way to visit his churches in Macedonia (for example, in Philippi and Thessalonica). In so doing, he departs from the plan he stated in 1 Corinthians 16:5, which was to visit them on the way back from Macedonia (see Paul's defense in 2 Corinthians 1:15-17). His unexpected visit, which might have taken the congregation somewhat off guard, ended in a painful confrontation with some unnamed Christian in Corinth (he is referred to simply as "the offender" of 2 Corinthians 2:5-11; 7:11-12). This second visit, then, is the "painful" visit upon which 2 Corinthians looks back. Given the kinds of issues that 2 Corinthians will address, the confrontation probably had to do directly with Paul's legitimacy as an apostle.

Paul leaves Corinth with the relationship between himself and the church in tatters. He proceeds to Macedonia and returns to Ephesus, sending a third letter, the "tearful letter" (referred to in 2 Corinthians 1:23; 2:1-4, 9; 7:8, 12), to Corinth in place of a return visit from Macedonia. Titus carries this letter, and is thus on hand to intervene in the situation personally as well as read Paul's words. The congregation appears, in large part, to have repented of the way they treated Paul, and they respond by excluding the "offender."

Titus leaves Corinth and brings Paul a very encouraging report (see 2 Corinthians 7:6-7, 13-16). Paul is hopeful that reconciliation is on the horizon, but also recognizes that some serious issues remain to be dealt with. In particular, he needs to address the ways in which the believers have responded to intruding missionaries who came to Corinth and sought to undermine Paul's authority and promote their own on the basis of their superior oratorical abilities and other external signs of divine "giftedness." So, Paul composes 2 Corinthians to communicate once again that the legitimate apostle is not the one who has the flashiest presentation and finest appearance, but rather the one who makes the power of God more clearly present, and genuine transformation more accessible. He also seeks to solidify his relationship with the church and to give new impetus to the stalled collection project for the poor in Judea, a very important sign for Paul of the unity of the Gentile and Jewish church (see 2 Corinthians 8–9; see also Romans 15:27-28). This collection project will also be a visible sign that the Corinthians have entered once again into full partnership with Paul, their apostle.

Paul sends Titus and some unnamed "brothers" to take the letter and, if it is successful, oversee the collection. Finally, Paul visits Corinth a third time (see 2 Corinthians 13:1, which envisions such a visit). The Corinthian Christians did in fact contribute to the collection project (Romans 15:25-27), and Paul is able to write Romans from Corinth (Romans 15:25-28; 16:23), looking now to new horizons of ministry. This suggests that the saga with the Corinthian church had a good and God-pleasing ending, even though Paul's troubles would be far from over. When Paul takes the collection to Judea, his visit to Rome is forestalled by the long ordeal narrated in Acts 22–28. The apostle who discovered God's power to deliver in the midst of hardship and the exhaustion of human strengths would enter yet another arena wherein to prove that God's strength, and not human prowess, was the ultimately reliable foundation for his apostleship.

UNIT 1: SERVANTS OF GOD
LIVING IN UNITY

PREVIEWING THE LESSON

Lesson Scripture: 1 Corinthians 1:10-17
Background Scripture: 1 Corinthians 1:10-17
Key Verse: 1 Corinthians 1:10

Focus of the Lesson:
Many people have experienced the divisiveness of misguided loyalties. What demands our loyalty to the point that we are united rather than divided? Paul says that the Christian community finds its unity in Jesus Christ, to whom we owe complete loyalty.

Goals for the Learners:
(1) to explore how Paul addressed the divisions in the church at Corinth by pointing beyond favorite leaders (including himself) to unity in Christ.
(2) to consider how Paul's words reinforce that call to unity for them.
(3) to recognize and affirm that what unites Christians can overcome divisions among them.

Pronunciation Guide:
Achaicus (uh kay' uh kuhs)   Apollos (uh pol' uhs)
Chloe (kloh'ee)   Crispus (kris' puhs)
Fortunatus (for chuh nay' tuhs)   Gaius (gay' yuhs)
Stephanas (stef' uh nuhs)

Supplies:
Bibles, newsprint and marker, paper and pencils, hymnals

READING THE SCRIPTURE

NRSV
1 Corinthians 1:10-17

[10]Now I appeal to you, brothers and sisters, by the name of our Lord Jesus Christ, that all of you be in agreement and that there be no divisions among you, but that you be united in the same mind and the same purpose.

NIV
1 Corinthians 1:10-17

[10]I appeal to you, brothers, in the name of our Lord Jesus Christ, that all of you agree with one another so that there may be no divisions among you and that you may be perfectly united in mind and thought.

¹¹For it has been reported to me by Chloe's people that there are quarrels among you, my brothers and sisters. ¹²What I mean is that each of you says, "I belong to Paul," or "I belong to Apollos," or "I belong to Cephas," or "I belong to Christ." ¹³Has Christ been divided? Was Paul crucified for you? Or were you baptized in the name of Paul? ¹⁴I thank God that I baptized none of you except Crispus and Gaius, ¹⁵so that no one can say that you were baptized in my name. ¹⁶(I did baptize also the household of Stephanas; beyond that, I do not know whether I baptized anyone else.) ¹⁷For Christ did not send me to baptize but to proclaim the gospel, and not with eloquent wisdom, so that the cross of Christ might not be emptied of its power.

¹¹My brothers, some from Chloe's household have informed me that there are quarrels among you. ¹²What I mean is this: One of you says, "I follow Paul"; another, "I follow Apollos"; another, "I follow Cephas"; still another, "I follow Christ."

¹³Is Christ divided? Was Paul crucified for you? Were you baptized into the name of Paul? ¹⁴I am thankful that I did not baptize any of you except Crispus and Gaius, ¹⁵so no one can say that you were baptized into my name. ¹⁶(Yes, I also baptized the household of Stephanas; beyond that, I don't remember if I baptized anyone else.) ¹⁷For Christ did not send me to baptize, but to preach the gospel—not with words of human wisdom, lest the cross of Christ be emptied of its power.

UNDERSTANDING THE SCRIPTURE

1 Corinthians 1:10. 1 Corinthians 1:10–4:21 focuses on the first major issue that Paul plans to correct, namely the use of Christian leaders as rallying points for rivalry and partisanship. Addressing them as "brothers and sisters," Paul reminds them that they are to treat each other as kin rather than as "outsiders." The ethics of kinship called for unity, harmony, solidarity, cooperation, and mutual honoring of one another, especially among siblings. Division and competition among siblings were out of place and shameful, since it ran counter to advancing the good of the whole family. Paul's use of the metaphor of the "body" in chapter 12 will reinforce this ethical lesson. Paul also uses expressions familiar from ethical writings on the virtue of civic unity—being "in agreement" (literally, "say the same thing"), having the "same mind" and "purpose." This is a matter not of parroting the same words, but of putting common ground and common interest ahead of strife and self-interest.

1 Corinthians 1:11-13. Throughout 1 Corinthians, Paul responds to an "official" letter from the church (see 7:1), delivered to Paul by Stephanas, Fortunatus, and Achaicus (see 16:17). Word about the quarrels over leadership, however, came from another source—an oral report brought by "Chloe's people," Christian slaves or freedmen in Chloe's household. Whether Chloe was resident in Corinth (and sending her own "unofficial" delegation to give Paul the "inside scoop") or in the city of Ephesus where Paul was situated (with her people returning from a business trip to Corinth, after observing the situation in the churches) is unknown. If both delegations are from Corinth, this especially signals the disorder there.

Paul speaks of "quarrels" often, and always negatively. Strife and contentiousness between people are marks of unredeemed humanity (see Romans 1:29), of our "fleshly nature" gaining the upper hand (Galatians 5:20; 1 Corinthians 3:3), of unpreparedness for Christ's coming (Romans 13:13). Paul here addresses "quarrels" arising from the way in which the Corinthian Christians have used the teachers that have ministered to the churches there. Promoting one teacher over another—and incidentally promoting oneself over one's neighbors on the basis of following such a superior teacher and receiving his superior wisdom—was quite in keeping with the ethos of the day. Ancient authors like Dio Chrysostom (speaking specifically about Corinth) and Seneca the Elder speak of the followers ("groupies") of different orators and traveling philosophers boasting about their favorite, denigrating others, and forming factions along such lines. These Christians are behaving no differently.

Some promote Cephas (the Aramaic name for Peter), perhaps on the basis of his personal involvement with Jesus and direct authorization by him. Some promote Apollos as the most gifted teacher, which is hardly surprising: His skill as a polished speaker would have appealed to their worldly values. Paul cannot compete with Apollos on this basis, and that by his own choice (1 Corinthians 1:17; 2:1-5). Paul wants people to build their faith and discipleship not on impressive speech, but on a transforming encounter with the power of God. Even those who claim to "belong to Christ" do so not in order to call the whole group to harmony, but as a sort of one-upmanship (which might, incidentally, signify their failure to value human teachers and leaders sufficiently as gifts from God for the church). The impetus for these quarrels comes from the Corinthians, not the leaders. Paul speaks of Apollos not as a rival but as a partner in the work of God on behalf of the whole church (3:6-9; 16:12). We should note that, when certain groups are "puffed up in favor of" Apollos or Cephas or Christ (4:6), they are also calling into question Paul's authority and adequacy as a representative of the gospel. This will remain a major issue through 2 Corinthians. Those who think they are supporting Paul by shouting, "I am Paul's" are not approved either—they, too, play into factionalism rather than understand how all these

Christian leaders work together to fulfill their proper roles in the economy of God on behalf of the church.

In a series of rhetorical questions, all of which expect the answer "no," Paul tries to highlight the absurdity of what the Corinthians are doing. The uniqueness of Christ's redemption of the church, and his lordship over and ownership of the church (see, for example, 1 Corinthians 6:19-20), must be reflected in a unified, harmonious community centered on the Christ who is their single head and Lord.

1 Corinthians 1:14-16. When the head of a household converted to a new religion, his (or her) dependents tended to follow suit (see Acts 16:15, 33-34; 18:8). Crispus and his household were converted and baptized early in Paul's ministry in Corinth (Acts 18:8). Gaius must have been as well, and was sufficiently wealthy to act as host to the whole church in Corinth (Romans 16:23). Stephanas and his companions will be openly praised by Paul as exemplary servants (1 Corinthians 16:15-18), and are all the more likely not to be members of the "Paul party," but neutral believers desiring to see what Paul (indeed, what Christ) would want to see in the church—unity above factionalism. For Paul to have baptized so few people himself during the eighteen months he stayed in Corinth probably means he shared this responsibility not only with his team, but with indigenous Christian leadership early on in the life of the community.

1 Corinthians 1:17. Paul does not seek to minimize the importance of this rite of entrance by which the believers died to sin, rose to newness of life, and clothed themselves with Christ (Romans 6:1-4; Galatians 3:26-29). However, baptism by one, rather than another, of the leaders (which would have led to a sense of special connectedness) probably contributed to the factionalism in the church.

"Eloquent wisdom" is a threat to the cross of Christ having its full effect (especially in Corinth) because snazzy speech focused attention on the visible strengths of the messenger, which were part and parcel of the world that was passing away, rather than the power of God revealed in the cross. Also, dressing up the "outside" of the message would reinforce the worldly values that the cross of Christ sought to turn upside down. Indeed, Paul speaks explicitly about crucifixion and the cross (1:17) here, reminding the hearers of the precise manner of Jesus' death in order to drive home the point that God's wisdom—revealed specifically in the cross—introduces a whole new set of values, ways of valuing, and orientation to others (see Philippians 2:3-11 in this regard). Paul will develop these themes at length in 1 Corinthians 1:18-31 and 2 Corinthians.

INTERPRETING THE SCRIPTURE

United Around the Center

In a situation where Christians are caught up in the diversity of teachers and arguing over their relative merits, Paul calls the congregation's attention back to Jesus, the true center and focal point for the whole church. If we keep coming back to the center, and keep intentionally examining points of conflict and division from the standpoint of God's purposes for us and for God's whole Church, we will be less likely to indulge the cross-purposes we devise against one another and against God's goal of creating a community of love and unity that reflects the unity of the Father and the Son (see John 17).

Being "in agreement" and "united in the same mind" does not imply utter homogeneity of thought. This false premise has, ironically, often been used to create new sects and denominations. "Since you don't agree," or "since you think differently on these points, we will no longer have fellowship with you." Whether or not a people agree on a list of beliefs has come too often to determine who is "in." Paul intended, to the contrary, that all those whom Christ has called to be "in" should "agree," by practicing harmonious and loving relationships with each other, by prioritizing harmony, and by finding common ground and reaching agreement in a spirit of humility and unity rather than nurturing competitive and pig-headed contention. Alas, this last vice is something that our Western culture has encouraged at every turn. One need only think of the myriad of "talk shows" that wallow and revel in contention rather than reconciliation and fostering harmony.

Paul's vision for our own churches can be attained if we prioritize honoring the one Lord through maintaining unity and harmony over proving ourselves "right" or "better" in every debate. There are many occasions thus to "die to ourselves" and to put the best interests of the group ahead of our own in the life of the Christian community (which includes not only our churches, but also our homes).

Leaders and Loyalty

Christian "leaders" are to be found both among the clergy and throughout the laity. Those who have accepted responsibility for facilitating others' involvement in discipleship, whether as choir directors, Christian educators, youth leaders, administrators, missions coordinators, or the like, are all "leaders." And they all have the potential to become focal points for division and partisanship. Some members of the congregation will be attracted more to the style and personality of the associate pastor than to the senior pastor, and begin saying things, like "I wish she got to preach more often; her sermons are so much better than his."

Others will begin talking about the leadership styles of two Sunday school teachers, some putting one down and promoting the other, the others jumping in to defend their favorite. Still others will stop singing in the choir, saying that the new choir director doesn't measure up to the last one. Alas, the leaders are not always free from blame in this regard, either.

This behavior arises, in part, out of quite commendable sentiments. People appreciate the contributions a particular leader has made to the life of the church. But then they begin to use that as a measuring rod for the contributions of others. People may feel a special sense of connectedness or loyalty to a particular leader, as the Corinthian Christians may have felt in regard to who baptized them. But then they begin to feel this attachment as to one leader over against other leaders whose contributions might diminish the status of their favorite.

Paul tries to help us catch the bigger picture, and thus to use God's gifts correctly rather than in a worldly, human, divisive way. He wants us to understand, first, that God's generosity toward the church stands behind what each leader brings to the church universal as each contributes to the building up of particular local congregations or even parts of local congregations. Through the service of Christian leaders, we are all receiving portions of God's one good bounty, and we all belong together to the one God (1 Corinthians 3:21-23). There is thus an essential unity behind all the diversity of gifts manifested by these leaders, behind all the diversity of achievements and contributions made by each. We need to move from playing one leader off another to perceiving and appreciating the complementarity of the gifts and contributions of various leaders to the health of the whole church.

Moreover, God has given the gifts of Christian leaders to build up the church in love and unity, not to become centers for rivalry and quarreling, for breaking the unity and solidarity of the church into little factions favoring one over another. We misuse God's gifts when we make focal points for divisiveness out of Christian leaders. Rather, Paul urges us to honor what God brings for the good of the church through each member (indeed, this is not limited to how we view leaders only), and to receive those gifts in a spirit of humble acceptance and joy rather than competitive boasting and self-assertion. Our ultimate response of loyalty must be to God, and not to one leader over against another; and if we get tangled up in the latter, we have lost sight of the former.

Denominations and the One Church

Can we honestly look at this passage and fail to point out the elephant in the living room here? "Denominationalism" is one of the greatest stumbling blocks on the road to attaining unity and harmony as the body of Christ. Protestantism in particular has fallen prey to division, dissension, and disunity over the centuries. One says, "I follow Luther," another "I follow Calvin," another "I follow Wesley," and, yes, another says "I follow Christ" or "I follow the Spirit."

Can we move toward a theology and a practice of denominationalism that promotes harmony, mutuality, and unity among Christians? One step in this direction would involve doing at the level of denominations what Paul advises we do at the level of local leaders and teachers—discerning the distinctive gifts each brings to the whole of global Christianity, and the ways in which God has strengthened God's church universal through the insights, practice, and service of each denomination. It would also involve looking at the perceived weaknesses in a spirit of love and humility, rather than rejection and judgment. The unity that Jesus desires for his followers—reflected in his prayer on behalf of all who would believe in him through the testimony of his disciples (John 17)—depends upon our willingness to seek out common ground and a sense of partnership in Christ beyond our local congregation and our own denomination.

The Wisdom of God

Verse 17 introduces a key theme, perhaps the key theme, of 1 and 2 Corinthians (see 1 Corinthians 1:18-31). The cross of Jesus proclaims in every generation that God's way of valuing and God's manner of working are completely other than what we expect based on everything our society has taught us. This message is relevant to our discussion here because God calls us away from evaluating people based on external skills or strengths that humans can acquire and exhibit on their own steam (and on the basis of which we can weigh people one against another). God calls us to look instead for the transformation of heart and life that is made possible by the Spirit of God, and to be unified in purpose, nurturing this transformation in ourselves and in one another.

SHARING THE SCRIPTURE

Preparing Our Hearts

This week's devotional reading is found in 1 Corinthians 1:2-9. This salutation to the church at Corinth immediately precedes today's Scripture. Think about Paul's greeting in relation to your own church. What might he give thanks for among the people of your congregation? As you think about your church, what do you give thanks for? Are your church members exercising their gifts so that the congregation is "not lacking in any spiritual gift" (1:7)? If not, what changes need to be made?

Pray that you and the class participants will act as servants of God who use your spiritual gifts to build up the body of Christ.

Preparing Our Minds

Study the background and lesson Scripture, both of which are found in 1 Corinthians 1:10-17. As you study, consider what this passage has to say concerning loyalty, especially that which demands our loyalty to the point that we are united rather than divided.

Write on newsprint:

❑ information for next week's lesson, found under "Continue the Journey."

Plan a brief, optional lecture suggested under "Explore How Paul Addressed the Divisions in the Church at Corinth by Pointing Beyond Favorite Leaders to Unity in Christ."

LEADING THE CLASS

(1) Gather to Learn

❖ Welcome the class members and introduce any guests.

❖ Pray that the adults will work together in a spirit of unity as they study Paul's message to the church at Corinth.

❖ Post a sheet of newsprint on which you have drawn a vertical line down the middle. On the left side write "Unite" and on the right, "Divide." Invite the students to brainstorm ideas in answer to these questions: **As you look at the contemporary church at large (or your denomination in particular), what are the issues or beliefs that unite us? What are the issues or beliefs that divide us?** Leave this sheet posted throughout the session.

❖ Read aloud today's focus statement: **Many people have experienced the divi-**

siveness of misguided loyalties. What demands our loyalty to the point that we are united rather than divided? Paul says that the Christian community finds its unity in Jesus Christ, to whom we owe complete loyalty.

(2) Explore How Paul Addressed the Divisions in the Church at Corinth by Pointing Beyond Favorite Leaders to Unity in Christ

❖ Choose an expressive reader (perhaps yourself) to read 1 Corinthians 1:10-17 as if a church leader were reading Paul's words to the church at Corinth. Ask the students to listen for words or ideas that grab their attention.

❖ Make a list on newsprint of the words and phrases. Talk with the adults about why these words and phrases seem so important.

❖ Discuss or give a brief lecture on the main source of the internal disputes within the Corinthian church, namely, factions. The information in Understanding the Scripture for 1 Corinthians 1:11-13 will be helpful to you.

❖ Look again at the information brainstormed in the Gather to Learn portion of the lesson, focusing especially on the issues and beliefs that divide us in the contemporary church. Consider those reasons for division in light of the ones that Paul discussed in relation to the Corinthian congregation. Discuss similarities and differences between the Corinthian church and the contemporary church.

❖ Distribute paper and pencils. Invite the students, either individually or in groups, to write a letter to the contemporary church (even to your congregation) as Paul might have written if he were ministering today.

❖ Invite volunteers to read what they have written and encourage the class to respond by asking probing questions and/or affirming what has been recorded.

(3) Consider How Paul's Words Reinforce That Call to Unity for the Learners

❖ Read or retell "United Around the Center" and "Denominations and the One Church," both in the Interpreting the Scripture section. Emphasize that diversity can exist within unity. For example, people have different gifts to build up the body of Christ, but each gift is equally important. Point out that we do not need to create divisions just because we don't agree on particular issues, beliefs, or worship styles. Also note that people's social location—where and when they live, their economic status, and other factors—will affect how they read the Bible, understand who they are and whose they are, and practice the Christian faith. Such differences are to be expected and need not create division.

❖ Discuss this scenario: **First Church of the Acts of the Apostles has a proud history of mission and service, dating back more than one hundred years. Recent demographic changes have brought an influx of young families to this formerly rural congregation. To reach these young people, the church has added a contemporary service with keyboard, drums, and guitars, and a very low-key sermon. No emphasis is placed on financial giving or involvement in the work of the church. Established members of the church, while wanting to bring in others, feel that the newcomers are neither sharing leadership responsibilities nor contributing to the church budget. This once strong, unified church is becoming divided. If you were called in as a consultant to First Church, how might you use Paul's concerns to help the church heal its division and move forward together?**

(4) Recognize and Affirm That What Unites Christians Can Overcome Divisions Among Them

❖ Ask the learners to look once more at the list created at the beginning of the session. Focus this time on the "Unite" column. Encourage the students to try to rank at least three to five items listed, with item 1 being the most important and item 5 being least important. If the group has difficulty agreeing on a ranking, see if they can discern what prevents them from reaching consensus.

❖ Write a litany on newsprint affirming the points that the class members have agreed upon. Include a response such as: **We give thanks, O God, for this tie that binds us together.**

❖ Read the litany responsively.

(5) Continue the Journey

❖ Pray that the participants will find unity amid the diversity of the many people who are part of the body of Christ.

❖ Read aloud this preparation for next week's lesson. You may also want to post it on newsprint for the students to copy. **Prepare for next week's session, "Finding Wisdom," by reading 1 Corinthians 2. As you study the lesson, which will focus on verses 1, 6-16, keep these ideas in mind: People are searching for true wisdom. Where can we find an ageless wisdom that transcends time and culture? Paul writes that God is the source of such wisdom,** which Christians receive through the power of the Holy Spirit.

❖ Read aloud the following three ideas. Challenge the students to commit themselves to use these activities as a springboard to spiritual growth.

(1) **Identify at least one source of discord in your own congregation and do whatever is in your power to bring reconciliation and unity.**

(2) **Research the connection between the Corinthian church and Paul, Apollos, Cephas, Chloe, Crispus, and Gaius. A concordance, Bible dictionary, and commentary on 1 Corinthians will help you.**

(3) **Choose either a hymn that speaks about unity or instrumental music that creates a harmonious mood for you. Read, sing, or play this music as a reminder of the unity that is to exist within the church.**

❖ Sing or read aloud "In Christ There Is No East or West."

❖ Close the session with this benediction, which you may want the class members to echo after you: **Go forth committed to serve, obey, and give as people who have been called to live faithfully in Christian community. Amen.**

UNIT 1: SERVANTS OF GOD
Finding Wisdom

PREVIEWING THE LESSON

Lesson Scripture: 1 Corinthians 2:1, 6-16
Background Scripture: 1 Corinthians 2
Key Verse: 1 Corinthians 2:13

Focus of the Lesson:
People are searching for true wisdom. Where can we find an ageless wisdom that transcends time and culture? Paul writes that God is the source of such wisdom, which Christians receive through the power of the Holy Spirit.

Goals for the Learners:
(1) to summarize Paul's text on spiritual wisdom.
(2) to relate ideas on wisdom to their own growth toward Christian maturity.
(3) to make a commitment to live with the mind of Christ.

Supplies:
Bibles, newsprint and marker, paper and pencils, hymnals

READING THE SCRIPTURE

NRSV
1 Corinthians 2:1, 6-16

¹When I came to you, brothers and sisters, I did not come proclaiming the mystery of God to you in lofty words or wisdom.

⁶Yet among the mature we do speak wisdom, though it is not a wisdom of this age or of the rulers of this age, who are doomed to perish. ⁷But we speak God's wisdom, secret and hidden, which God decreed before the ages for our glory. ⁸None of the rulers of this age understood this; for if they had, they would not have crucified the Lord of glory. ⁹But, as it is written,

"What no eye has seen, nor ear heard,
    nor the human heart conceived,

NIV
1 Corinthians 2:1, 6-16

¹When I came to you, brothers, I did not come with eloquence or superior wisdom as I proclaimed to you the testimony about God.

⁶We do, however, speak a message of wisdom among the mature, but not the wisdom of this age or of the rulers of this age, who are coming to nothing. ⁷No, we speak of God's secret wisdom, a wisdom that has been hidden and that God destined for our glory before time began. ⁸None of the rulers of this age understood it, for if they had, they would not have crucified the Lord of glory. ⁹However, as it is written:

what God has prepared for those who
    love him"—

[10]these things God has revealed to us
through the Spirit; for the Spirit searches
everything, even the depths of God. [11]For
what human being knows what is truly
human except the human spirit that is
within? So also no one comprehends what is
truly God's except the Spirit of God. [12]Now
we have received not the spirit of the world,
but the Spirit that is from God, so that we
may understand the gifts bestowed on us by
God. [13]**And we speak of these things in
words not taught by human wisdom but
taught by the Spirit, interpreting spiritual
things to those who are spiritual.**

[14]Those who are unspiritual do not
receive the gifts of God's Spirit, for they are
foolishness to them, and they are unable to
understand them because they are spiritually discerned. [15]Those who are spiritual discern all things, and they are themselves
subject to no one else's scrutiny.

[16]"For who has known the mind of the
    Lord
      so as to instruct him?"
But we have the mind of Christ.

"No eye has seen,
  no ear has heard,
no mind has conceived
    what God has prepared for those who
    love him"—
[10]but God has revealed it to us by his Spirit.

The Spirit searches all things, even the
deep things of God. [11]For who among men
knows the thoughts of a man except the
man's spirit within him? In the same way no
one knows the thoughts of God except the
Spirit of God. [12]We have not received the
spirit of the world but the Spirit who is from
God, that we may understand what God has
freely given us. [13]**This is what we speak, not
in words taught us by human wisdom but
in words taught by the Spirit, expressing
spiritual truths in spiritual words.** [14]The
man without the Spirit does not accept the
things that come from the Spirit of God, for
they are foolishness to him, and he cannot
understand them, because they are spiritually discerned. [15]The spiritual man makes
judgments about all things, but he himself is
not subject to any man's judgment:
[16]"For who has known the mind of the
    Lord
    that he may instruct him?"
But we have the mind of Christ.

UNDERSTANDING THE SCRIPTURE

1 Corinthians 2:1-5. Greeks, and those
who sought to emulate Greek culture,
prized oratorical ability. Rhetoric, or the "art
of persuasion," was part of the core curriculum of Greek education. Those who hoped
to have influence in civic politics, those who
hoped to gather a following for the philosophy or religion they espoused, and those
who simply hoped to make a name for
themselves all devoted themselves to the
mastery of the rhetorical arts. When an itinerant philosopher came into Corinth, the
citizens expected to hear him lay out his
message in ornate, beautiful, rhetorically

powerful speech—much like we might
expect of popular preachers. They expected
to be captivated not only, and not mainly, by
the message that the philosopher brought,
but by the craft and skill of his speech and
the artistry of the delivery.

Paul categorically refuses to play to these
expectations. His co-worker Apollos, who
was known in the early church as an "eloquent man" (Acts 18:24), might appeal more
to the Corinthians' expectations; but Paul
would not. He refuses to base his appeal on
florid and fancy-sounding speech. This is
not to say that he was unskilled in rhetoric,

as he often shows himself quite skilled in pulling together arguments, in appealing not only to the minds but also to the emotions and the allegiance of his hearers, and in utilizing a variety of kinds of proof to make his case. In fact, even the claim not to use "lofty" speech could itself be a rhetorical device. The famous statesman, Dio Chrysostom, says something quite similar in *Orations* (32.39) when he compares himself with other orators as "undistinguished and simple in my speech, though not in my message: for even if the words I use are not all that impressive, my subject matter is of the greatest importance" (my translation). But Paul refused to dress up his speech and try to appear impressive. He knew that his converts needed to encounter God's transforming power, and to be convinced of the truth of the gospel by the work of the Holy Spirit. They did not need to encounter yet another flashy speaker, nor to put their trust in the gospel on the basis of human talent.

Paul expected God to "show up" when he preached the gospel. The activity of the Holy Spirit was of utmost importance to Paul. Just as he knew the Holy Spirit would make himself known to the Galatian converts (Galatians 3:1-5) when he preached Christ crucified, so he knew that the same would happen in Corinth. Another preacher clearly connected in some way with the Pauline mission would also recall how the Holy Spirit confirmed the word preached to him and his church by the apostolic witnesses (Hebrews 2:3-4).

1 Corinthians 2:6-8. Paul uses several contrasting terms to describe different kinds of people in today's lesson and the following lesson. One group is "mature," while another group is composed of "infants" (2:6 and 3:1); the former are "spiritual" (2:15), while the latter are "unspiritual" or "natural" (2:14) or "of the flesh" (3:1, 3). Only those who listen with their spirits attuned to the Spirit of God will receive the wisdom that Paul has to communicate. Those who have been trained in the wisdom taught by

the world will not see this message as anything but folly. As a prime proof of this claim, Paul points to the crucifixion itself, just as he did in 1 Corinthians 1:18-31.

Acting in line with the best wisdom of government and maintaining peace, the authorities in Judea received Jesus as a troublemaker and disposed of him. On the other side of the cross, natural wisdom looks at Jesus as at worst a glorious ruin and at best a fine moral example. But to those who allow God to reveal God's wisdom to them by the Spirit, Jesus shows the way in which God has provided for our deliverance from the human plight of alienation from God, alienation from one another, and, ultimately, alienation from ourselves. This is not something that rational argument can establish; it is a conviction impressed upon the spirit by the Spirit of God.

1 Corinthians 2:9-13. Paul uses a freely modified quotation of Isaiah 64:4 to talk about the "content" of this divine wisdom. The destiny that God has opened up for humankind is beyond our senses and beyond our natural imagination, since it belongs to the realm beyond our natural experience. For this reason, our best thoughts will fail to grasp it. Paul speaks here of a different faculty that we must use if we hope to know the "depths of God," and that faculty is our own spirit listening to the revelation of God's Spirit. This lies beyond anything our academic preparation has tooled us for, beyond anything our experiential knowledge gained from dealing with other people and "the world" has equipped us for. Knowledge of the glorious wholeness that God has prepared for us, an understanding of the path to this wholeness opened up in the crucified and risen Messiah, and an awareness of the gifts God has lavished upon us to nurture us along this journey, come through communion and communication with the living God.

1 Corinthians 2:14-16. Paul continues to underscore the incompatibility of God's wisdom with the human mind operating on its own strength and, more to the point, in accordance with the norms and values it has learned as a result of being shaped in the ways of this world. For those who allow God to open up their spiritual faculties, however, the way of God revealed in Jesus no longer appears as foolishness, but as an astoundingly wise path to fulfill our deepest longings for relationship with God and one another.

Paul quotes Isaiah 40:13, one of many texts in the Hebrew Scriptures teaching the vast difference between God's knowledge and human knowledge (see also Isaiah 55:8-9), to support the point. On our own intellectual strength, we cannot attain to God's knowledge, but God has given "the mind of Christ" to Christ's followers in order to instruct them. Those who have received the "Spirit of Christ" (see Galatians 4:6-7; Romans 8:9-11) are able to see the wisdom of following in Jesus' way. Even though this may look "foolish" to "unspiritual" people, those who follow Christ will not be swayed by the opinions of the unwise.

INTERPRETING THE SCRIPTURE

Upon What Does Your Faith Rest?

In the sequence of my New Testament courses, students inevitably have their faith "challenged" by the ideas and observations offered by critical scholarship. At such times, I put to them the question: "What is your faith ultimately grounded in?" If it is based on rational arguments in favor of the gospel stemming from a certain view of the Scriptures, they will find it very upsetting when I present certain facts that call for an adjustment to that view of the Scriptures. If it is based on their experience of, and their vital relationship with, the living God, I tell them that they have nothing to fear. As they keep building on that foundation, they are building on a deeper level that cannot be shaken by new discoveries—and that does not demand that new discoveries be resisted or refuted in order to keep faith secure.

Building up one's "faith" on the basis of speeches and ideas that appeal to the natural mind as impressive and lofty has another face as well. Many people are caught up in the search for a deeper "spirituality," but are pursuing this search equipped only with their natural faculties. What religious ideas seem wise or helpful? What experiences provide welcome relief from the day-to-day grind? What New Age guru can best appeal to our hopes and aspirations? What ideas are just so novel, mysterious, or different that they command attention? Such people move from fad to fad, left empty at the end of the day. Pursuing "spirituality" without the genuine guidance of God's Holy Spirit, suggested John Chrysostom in *Homilies on 1 Corinthians* 7.9, is like choosing to try to see in a dark house without lighting any lamps.

A seventeenth-century German hymn declares, "Who trusts in God's unchanging love / builds on the rock that naught can move." This is precisely where Paul wants us to build. The hunger for spirituality is God-given, but it can only be satisfied by the feast that God has prepared, and which God communicates by the Spirit.

Winning Arguments Versus Gaining Wisdom

The art of rhetoric was so popular and so important because it was an acknowledged tool for getting what one wanted. Paul refused to base his appeal on the power of clever rhetoric because this power is so often misused to gain our own ends and misses God's ends for us. Rival teachers will emerge on the Corinthian scene, playing to the Corinthians' expectations, and using the power of speech to subvert Paul's authority and his work. Paul will also convict the Corinthian Christians of being decidedly immature and unspiritual (1 Corinthians 3:1-3) because of their own orientation toward using their natural faculties to create rivalries, to compete for precedence and honor within the church.

When Paul sets listening to persuasive rhetoric over against the divine Spirit and power, he cuts to the heart of the human dilemma. We are broken people; we are fragile people; and we will do anything we can to assure ourselves that we are okay and to make sure things come out okay for us when we feel threatened. This often means that when we feel threatened we will turn to rationalization of our actions, self-justifying speech, or putting our argumentative talents in the service of ourselves, our interests, our getting our own way and resisting the feeling of threat.

But there is another voice to which to attend in many such moments, namely the voice of God's Spirit. Perhaps we could learn to rest our sense of self-worth not in our ability to defend our interests or ourselves, but rather in God's boundless love for us. This would free us to quiet our own voice and allow the Spirit to convict us, correct us, and impress upon us what is right and good in God's sight in a particular situation. We would then have an opportunity to hear and yield ourselves to the wisdom that God's own Spirit imparts, and extend that grace to others as well, not forcing them into seeing every encounter as a win-lose situation or a contest of wills and argumentative skills.

Listening to the Spirit with the Spirit

Paul invites us into a wholly "other" dimension of experience (the experience of God's conversation, revealing a dimension that "no eye has seen, nor ear heard," 2:9) and a wholly other dimension of our own humanity (our own spirit). Is that dimension foreign to you, or are you "at home" there? How much time do we spend attending to these "deep things of God" and the "spiritual things" that God's Spirit would communicate to us? How much do we exercise our own "spirit" in the pursuit of maturity in Christ as opposed to exercising our natural faculties in the pursuit of success at work, achieving a certain lifestyle, and gratifying our natural inclinations?

God wants to have intimate access to our being, and to give us intimate access to God's own self. Paul envisions a relationship wherein we allow our own spirit and God's Spirit to search out "the things" in our own heart, and allow the Spirit of God to communicate to us the good things God has given to us and has yet in store for us. This is the path to healing the depths of our brokenness.

Paul's words open up for us the possibility of ceasing and desisting from the rationalizations that help us keep killing the pain of our hearts with addictions to work, food, sex, alcohol, and the like, and that help us to keep avoiding what is "within" us. Rather, as we make room and time for our spirit and the Spirit of God to connect, we yield ourselves to this process of attaining spiritual wisdom for our own healing, for the healing of our relationships, and ultimately for the healing of those who will relate to us in our more mature, whole selves.

The Mind of Christ

Paul speaks here of Christians as having the "mind" of Christ; elsewhere he speaks of having the "Spirit" of Christ (Romans 8:9-11; Galatians 4:6-7). Either word refers to a new reality, a new impetus, within the life of the believer. Paul credits this Spirit with the ability to empower the believer not to be caught in the relationship-destroying snares of envy, rivalry, competition, and malice, or pain-killing addictions like gluttony, excessive drinking, and sexual promiscuity

(Galatians 5:19-21). The Spirit acts as a moral guide, working within us to produce the fruit of a life lived close to the heart of God (Galatians 5:22-25).

God has given us the "mind of Christ" for our instruction, to enable us to progress toward the goal of our calling, the goal of our faith—"to be conformed to the image of his Son" (Romans 8:29; see also Philippians 2:5-11; 3:8-11). The "mind of Christ," however, leads us to act in ways that our natural mind—and those around us who are led by their natural mind—regards as folly. It leads us to "look not to your own interests, but to the interests of others," and "in humility" to "regard others as better than yourselves" (Philippians 2:3-4). It leads us to seek greater avenues for serving others rather than self-promotion and self-advancement (Mark 10:41-45), just as Jesus modeled. It is a cross-shaped life. But just as God raised Jesus from the dead, so also God's Spirit bears us witness that, as we follow the "mind of Christ," we discover a new richness to life and relationships now, and, in the world to come, life everlasting.

SHARING THE SCRIPTURE

Preparing Our Hearts

This week's devotional reading is found in Ephesians 1:15-21. In verses 17-18 Paul prays for "a spirit of wisdom and revelation" for the people of the church at Ephesus, so that their hearts may be "enlightened." Consider how you tap into God's wisdom. How does the Holy Spirit work in your life?

Pray that you and your class participants will seek God's wisdom, which is imparted through the Holy Spirit.

Preparing Our Minds

Study the background Scripture from 1 Corinthians 2 and the lesson Scripture, verses 1, 6-16. As you study think about how we can find ageless wisdom through the power of the Holy Spirit.

Write on newsprint:
❏ chart for "Summarize Paul's Text on Spiritual Wisdom."
❏ questions for "Relate Ideas on Wisdom to the Learners' Own Growth Toward Christian Maturity."
❏ responsive reading for "Make a Commitment to Live with the Mind of Christ."
❏ information for next week's lesson, found under "Continue the Journey."

Plan a brief lecture on Paul's understanding of God's wisdom for "Summarize Paul's Text on Spiritual Wisdom." The entire Interpreting the Scripture portion will be useful to you.

LEADING THE CLASS

(1) Gather to Learn

❖ Welcome the class members and introduce any guests.

❖ Pray that those who have come will open their hearts and minds to the leading of the Holy Spirit as you fellowship and study together this day.

❖ Invite the students to call out the names of contemporary or historical persons they believe are wise. Make a list on newsprint of the characteristics of a wise person. Probe to find out what the adults believe is (are) the source(s) of that wisdom.

❖ Read aloud today's focus statement: **People are searching for true wisdom. Where can we find an ageless wisdom that transcends time and culture? Paul writes that God is the source of such wisdom, which Christians receive through the power of the Holy Spirit.**

(2) Summarize Paul's Text on Spiritual Wisdom

❖ Choose a volunteer to read aloud 1 Corinthians 2:1, 6-16, where Paul writes about the true wisdom of God.

❖ Create a chart in which you illustrate visually the contrasts Paul makes in his writing. Either post the blank chart and let the students fill it in or complete the chart yourself.

Wisdom	Spirit	Representatives
Wisdom of this age	Human spirit	Unspiritual people
God's wisdom decreed before the ages	Spirit of God	Spiritual people

❖ Discuss, or give a brief lecture on, Paul's understanding of God's wisdom. Consider the following questions.

(1) **Why does Paul argue that the "rulers of this age" (2:6) know nothing about the wisdom of God?** (They crucified the Christ.)

(2) **Why is it so important to recognize the Spirit of God within us?** (See "Listening to the Spirit with the Spirit" in Interpreting the Scripture.)

(3) **Why have we been given the "mind of Christ"?** (See "The Mind of Christ" in Interpreting the Scripture.)

❖ Wrap up this portion of the session by asking the students to read in unison today's key verse, 1 Corinthians 2:13.

(3) Relate Ideas on Wisdom to the Learners' Own Growth Toward Christian Maturity

❖ Read or retell "Upon What Does Your Faith Rest?" in Interpreting the Scripture.

❖ Encourage the students to talk with the class or a small group about the basis for their own faith. Is their faith based in facts and rational arguments, or is it based in a vital relationship with the living God? What difference does the basis of one's faith make in how one pursues a deeper spirituality?

❖ Brainstorm with the adults a list of traits that characterize a person who embodies God's wisdom to the point that he or she can be described as spiritually mature. Write these ideas on newsprint.

❖ Provide quiet time for the learners to consider how their own lives reflect these traits.

❖ Divide into groups and ask each group to consider these questions, which you will post on newsprint for all to see.

(1) **How does this congregation provide opportunities and resources for people of all ages to grow spiritually?** (Think in terms of opportunities for worship, witness, mission, hands-on experiences, learning, and fellowship.)

(2) **Which of these opportunities do we avail ourselves of and/or encourage our children to attend?**

(3) **What other opportunities and resources could we provide?**

(4) **What could we do to lead and/or promote any current or new opportunities?**

❖ Give each group time to report their ideas to the class. Focus especially on insights for new programs.

(4) Make a Commitment to Live with the Mind of Christ

❖ Invite the students to make a commitment to live with the mind of Christ by reading responsively this hymn from Philippians 2:5-11.

ALL: [5]Let the same mind be in you that was in Christ Jesus,
GROUP 1: [6]who, though he was in the form of God,
did not regard equality with God
as something to be exploited,
GROUP 2: [7]but emptied himself,

taking the form of a slave,
being born in human likeness.
GROUP 1: And being found in human form,
   8he humbled himself
and became obedient to the point of death—
even death on a cross.
GROUP 2: 9Therefore God also highly exalted
   him
and gave him the name
that is above every name,
GROUP 1: 10so that at the name of Jesus
every knee should bend,
in heaven and on earth and under the earth,
GROUP 2: 11and every tongue should confess
that Jesus Christ is Lord,
to the glory of God the Father.

(5) Continue the Journey

❖ Pray that the participants will continue to be open to God's wisdom as it is imparted by the Spirit so that they too might have the mind of Christ.

❖ Read aloud this preparation for next week's lesson. You may also want to post it on newsprint for the students to copy. **Prepare for next week's session, "Building Together," by reading 1 Corinthians 3:1-15, which is our background and lesson Scripture. Keep these ideas in mind as you study: Many people recognize that spiritual growth depends on the foundation laid by teachers and mentors. How does spiritual formation take place within the community of faith? Paul describes a process by which he first introduced people to the gospel, laying a foundation in Jesus Christ, and then others nurtured the new Christians toward maturity.**

❖ Read aloud the following three ideas. Challenge the students to commit themselves to use these activities as a springboard to spiritual growth.

   (1) Write in your spiritual journal an entry concerning how you have experienced God's wisdom this week. How did the Spirit lead you? Had you been praying for this guidance, or did God provide it for you in an instant when you needed it most?

   (2) Visit your local library or browse the Internet to learn more about New Age philosophy. What wisdom do you believe can be gained from this? How would you compare and contrast that wisdom to the wisdom you gain through a relationship with the living God through Jesus?

   (3) Talk with others about where they find wisdom. Listen respectfully, but be ready to share your thoughts on the wisdom that comes only from God through the Spirit.

❖ Sing or read aloud "Be Thou My Vision."

❖ Close the session with this benediction, which you may want the class members to echo after you: **Go forth committed to serve, obey, and give as people who have been called to live faithfully in Christian community. Amen.**

UNIT 1: SERVANTS OF GOD
Building Together

PREVIEWING THE LESSON

Lesson Scripture: 1 Corinthians 3:1-15
Background Scripture: 1 Corinthians 3:1-15
Key Verse: 1 Corinthians 3:9

Focus of the Lesson:

Many people recognize that spiritual growth depends on the foundation laid by teachers and mentors. How does spiritual formation take place within the community of faith? Paul describes a process by which he first introduced people to the gospel, laying a foundation in Jesus Christ, and then others nurtured the new Christians toward maturity.

Goals for the Learners:

(1) to discover what Paul says about building the church by teamwork based on undivided loyalty to Jesus Christ.
(2) to consider the implications for their spiritual formation that lie in the team process Paul describes.
(3) to identify ways they can become more active in their church's ministry.

Supplies:

Bibles, newsprint and marker, paper and pencils, hymnals

READING THE SCRIPTURE

NRSV
1 Corinthians 3:1-15

¹And so, brothers and sisters, I could not speak to you as spiritual people, but rather as people of the flesh, as infants in Christ. ²I fed you with milk, not solid food, for you were not ready for solid food. Even now you are still not ready, ³for you are still of the flesh. For as long as there is jealousy and quarreling among you, are you not of the flesh, and behaving according to human inclinations? ⁴For when one says, "I belong

NIV
1 Corinthians 3:1-15

¹Brothers, I could not address you as spiritual but as worldly—mere infants in Christ. ²I gave you milk, not solid food, for you were not yet ready for it. Indeed, you are still not ready. ³You are still worldly. For since there is jealousy and quarreling among you, are you not worldly? Are you not acting like mere men? ⁴For when one says, "I follow Paul," and another, "I follow Apollos," are you not mere men?

to Paul," and another, "I belong to Apollos," are you not merely human? ⁵What then is Apollos? What is Paul? Servants through whom you came to believe, as the Lord assigned to each. ⁶I planted, Apollos watered, but God gave the growth. ⁷So neither the one who plants nor the one who waters is anything, but only God who gives the growth. ⁸The one who plants and the one who waters have a common purpose, and each will receive wages according to the labor of each. **⁹For we are God's servants, working together; you are God's field, God's building.**

¹⁰According to the grace of God given to me, like a skilled master builder I laid a foundation, and someone else is building on it. Each builder must choose with care how to build on it. ¹¹For no one can lay any foundation other than the one that has been laid; that foundation is Jesus Christ. ¹²Now if anyone builds on the foundation with gold, silver, precious stones, wood, hay, straw—¹³the work of each builder will become visible, for the Day will disclose it, because it will be revealed with fire, and the fire will test what sort of work each has done. ¹⁴If what has been built on the foundation survives, the builder will receive a reward. ¹⁵If the work is burned up, the builder will suffer loss; the builder will be saved, but only as through fire.

⁵What, after all, is Apollos? And what is Paul? Only servants, through whom you came to believe—as the Lord has assigned to each his task. ⁶I planted the seed, Apollos watered it, but God made it grow. ⁷So neither he who plants nor he who waters is anything, but only God, who makes things grow. ⁸The man who plants and the man who waters have one purpose, and each will be rewarded according to his own labor. **⁹For we are God's fellow workers; you are God's field, God's building.**

¹⁰By the grace God has given me, I laid a foundation as an expert builder, and someone else is building on it. But each one should be careful how he builds. ¹¹For no one can lay any foundation other than the one already laid, which is Jesus Christ. ¹²If any man builds on this foundation using gold, silver, costly stones, wood, hay or straw, ¹³his work will be shown for what it is, because the Day will bring it to light. It will be revealed with fire, and the fire will test the quality of each man's work. ¹⁴If what he has built survives, he will receive his reward. ¹⁵If it is burned up, he will suffer loss; he himself will be saved, but only as one escaping through the flames.

UNDERSTANDING THE SCRIPTURE

1 Corinthians 3:1-4. The contrasts Paul began to introduce in the previous chapter—the "spiritual" person as opposed to the "natural" person, the "mature" person as opposed to the "infant" or "child"—continue in this paragraph. As is quite appropriate for a discussion about different levels of teaching, Paul talks about "milk" as opposed to "solid food," which, together with the contrast between infants and adults, are commonly used metaphors for

one's level of education or mastery of a discipline. The late first-century Stoic philosopher Epictetus frequently uses such images, as when he asks in *Dissertations* (2.16.39): "Do you not yet desire, like children coming of age, to be weaned off milk and to grasp more solid food, rather than cry out for your wet-nurses?" Similarly, the author of Hebrews chides his audience: "You need milk, not solid food; for everyone who lives on milk, being still an infant, is unskilled in the word of righteousness. But solid food is for the mature, for those whose faculties have been trained by practice to distinguish good from evil" (Hebrews 5:12-14).

Paul, like Epictetus and the author of Hebrews, also uses these contrasts to shame his audience out of one mode of behavior, driving them to a different mode of behavior that he deems more appropriate for their place in Christ. On the one hand, the Corinthian Christians enjoy the manifestations of the Spirit in their midst, to the point that individual believers speak in strange languages, receive the ability to interpret those languages, receive words of prophecy, and the like. They have access to deep, spiritual knowledge through the gospel of which their neighbors are still in ignorance. Yet, on the other hand, they have made far less progress than they presume—and pride themselves on. They need to adjust their thinking if they hope truly to be "mature" and "spiritual."

While they have God's Spirit, they are not acting like "spiritual" people. Having the capacity to walk in line with the Spirit rather than with their human drives and culturally-taught responses (being "merely human," 1 Corinthians 3:4), their behavior remains, Paul says, fleshly and carnal. Whatever "knowledge" they might profess, or spiritual gifts they might exercise, the presence of rivalry and strife ("jealousy and quarreling," 3:3) in their congregation betrays their immaturity. Ancient ethicists did not view *zelos* ("emulation, jealousy, rivalry") as uniformly negative. Aristotle regarded it as a character trait of noble people who, seeing someone else achieve fame or other good things by some noble means, fitted themselves to achieve the same. It drove progress and investment in noble ventures then as it still does today. The one place where competition of this kind was "out of place" was among family, especially siblings, who were instead supposed to cooperate, avoid entering into competition, and even find ways in which to help their family members share in any honor or wealth each acquired.

Eris ("strife," "discord"), however, is uniformly negative. Factions disrupted the harmony and unity of a city, and were censured as a political and civic vice. It was an ugly word in the Greco-Roman world, as well as in Pauline ethics, where it was a "work of the flesh" (Galatians 5:19-21) that ran counter to what God seeks to do in the bringing together of people into the one body of Christ, the church (see 1 Corinthians 12). Unity, cooperation, and valuing and honoring one another compose God's vision for the church, attainable as we follow the Spirit rather than our fallen inclinations. This is all the more urgent since Christians are, in fact, "family."

1 Corinthians 3:5-9. Paul tries to provide a proper perspective on Christian leaders and their work using an agricultural metaphor. The ancients frequently affirm that God (or, in pagan authors, the gods) provides the life-giving power to the work of the planters and farmers, without which their work would be for nothing. Similarly, God is the real force and fruit-bearing energy behind the work of any Christian leader. If some came to Christ through Paul, but others through Apollos, this should not become yet another potential source of rivalry and factionalism. It was God who gave to each the fruits of their labors, and neither Apollos nor Paul would claim any convert as "his own" achievement.

God is everything, and Christian missionaries and teachers are united in the common task of tending God's field. It is therefore inappropriate to make Christian leaders into something they are not (that is, rallying points for competition or factions), or to nudge them into a spirit of rivalry with one another, when they are in fact all partners in a joint venture.

1 Corinthians 3:10-15. The metaphor shifts from agriculture to architecture at the end of 1 Corinthians 3:9, from the church as God's field to God's building. Paul again calls attention to the fact that he achieves nothing; any success in his work is a gift from God ("according to the grace of God given to me," 3:10; see 3:5; 4:7). Once again the image emphasizes the way in which Christian teachers work together to complete *God's work,* rather than compete so as to boast of their own achievements.

This "building" is actually "God's temple" (3:16-17). God's dwelling place is no longer conceived of in terms of sacred places (most notably, the temple in Jerusalem). Rather, the Spirit dwells in communities of Christians who have been brought together like stones into a beautiful edifice. The nature of the project calls for caution on the part of builders, who must take great care not to tear down or deface the building. This would be not merely vandalism, but an act of sacrilege against a holy place.

Paul calls the Corinthians to build with a view to lasting rewards, rather than busying themselves with pursuits that have meaning only within the confines of this present world, like self-promotion, prominence, recognition, and one-upmanship. The wise builder looks ahead to the "Day" of judgment, when God will test our works and achievements. Those who worked only to enjoy recognition or prestige will find their works consumed; those who have given the building up of their sisters and brothers first priority in all interactions will find their works survive, to their eternal glory.

INTERPRETING THE SCRIPTURE

We Just Can't Compete

The clearest message of this passage is that competing against fellow Christians and nurturing divisiveness of any kind stand in stark contrast with maturity in Christ and authentic spirituality. As long as believers quarrel with each other, gather support against each other, and regard each other as rivals rather than partners, they are allowing their "flesh" to have the upper hand and neglecting their God-given faculties and charge.

One deep-rooted psychological flaw in many persons is to think, when another is praised or achieves success, oneself to be diminished or one's own achievements to be in jeopardy. We often act as if we lived in a "limited goods" economy, where there is only so much "success" or "affirmation" or "appreciation" to go around. How can we, then, "rejoice with those who rejoice," when we regard their "triumphs" as our "losses," or when we are more concerned with asserting our own importance over their own?

This basic flaw orients us toward others primarily in a competitive mode.

Let's face it. Churches can be hotbeds of quarreling and rivalry. Sarah, who used to be much more prominent in the church before the Administrative Board decided to create a position for a Director of Christian Education, feels displaced by its first incumbent, Karen. She is critical of her, and begins to find ways to impede her work. When Karen wants to introduce home "small group" Bible Studies, Sarah persuades several of her friends to throw a wet blanket on the idea in the Education Committee. Sarah then promotes a new venue for after-school children's ministry, and gets it passed by the Committee, feeling like she's finally gotten the upper hand. Karen, however, senses the personal rivalry and responds in kind. She gets the senior pastor to agree that all educational materials used in the church need to be passed by, and approved by, her as a sort of "quality control" measure. Thus newly empowered, she is able to veto Sarah's first choice for after-school curriculum and substitute it with her own.

Or perhaps you can envision Reverend Smith and Reverend Jones engaged in an ego contest as they boast about what they have been able to do in their churches, or how important and prominent their congregations are in the district. Reverend Jones might finally play his trump card—the fact that he was appointed to a larger, more centrally-involved church than Reverend Smith—to prove that his own ministry has been the more vital for the denomination.

Perhaps there have been incidents when you have yourself allowed personal rivalry or desire for recognition to distract you from the real work of God and embroil you in similar power plays. The point, of course, is that the model for "ministry" behind these rivalries is completely wrong, and the power that drives it is our own fleshly, unredeemed impulses.

In God's economy, there is praise and affirmation and appreciation enough for everyone. There is a never-ending supply, so that there is no need to compete. There is no need to diminish or impede another, so that I might gain my objectives or protect my "stature." Indeed, the more I become concerned about "stature" the more my own true spiritual stature (that of a mere infant in Christ, rather than a mature disciple) becomes evident. Moreover, the new reality of community in Christ is that we are a single field (3:6-9), a unified building (3:10-15), one living organism (1 Corinthians 12), rather than individuals vying against one another. Mature believers will always keep their focus on how they can work together to energize or improve the mission, nurture, and worship of the whole, and will always be looking together to God for direction. "Carnal" believers will focus on how they can improve or maintain their own power or status, and look to themselves for direction.

All This Is from God

Paul sings as a refrain throughout this and the following chapter that Christian leaders are God's gifts to the church, that converts are God's gifts to the missionaries, that spiritual insight and effective work for the kingdom are God's gifts to the believers (3:5, 10, 21-22; 4:7). There is therefore no place for one group of Christians to build themselves up by putting down another group of Christians in a variation of "my daddy is bigger than yours," for we all have the same Daddy. Paul is right to call the Corinthians out for acting like children when they play this game based on the merits or demerits of Paul and Apollos (Paul's main complaint in 1 Corinthians 3:1-4).

The cure Paul presents is the realization that God is the One at work wherever anything good or praiseworthy is occurring in the church. No human being can take credit for it, nor preen himself or herself upon it, nor vie for recognition and stature on the basis of it. We are invited, instead, to look for signs of what God is doing—the gifts God is giving God's church—wherever these are manifest, to appreciate and applaud them, and above all to cooperate with what God is doing through whomever God chooses to do it.

When Sarah mobilized her faction and shot down the small group ministry, she prevented a great gift from being given to her congregation. When Karen chose to reassert herself over Sarah, she failed to recognize or support what God was giving to the church through Sarah. When Reverend Jones and Reverend Smith used their pastoral appointments and ministries as the means by which to feel superior one to another, they lost sight of the fact that they were both tending the same field and working shoulder to shoulder for God. Ultimately, it is God's generosity and God's gifts that are despised or abused when believers engage in competition or partisan wrangling.

A Constant Building Project

As I reflect on my own spiritual journey, I can remember how the foundation of Jesus was laid in my youth through the worship and liturgy of the Episcopal church in which I was raised, and through older friends who nurtured in me a hunger for learning the Scriptures. In the intervening decades, I can remember many men and women of God who invested themselves in me, showed me Christian love and acceptance, taught me more about discipleship, and helped confirm me in my calling. These people built well and selflessly, and I pray God will reward them greatly for the way God built me up through them.

The question in the church is not whether or not we build, but how we build. Every encounter with a sister or brother, every gathering, every avoidance of interaction has an effect on the progress of the "building up" of those around us. Are we building up those around us in such a way that God will honor us on the day of judgment? Are we investing ourselves in the spiritual nurture of our sisters and brothers, or in their physical preservation, or in the care for the little ones at every opportunity? Are we doing it as humble servants looking for God's increase, or as prima donnas looking for our own applause? Paul calls us to examine ourselves now, before that day, so that we will have no reason to regret lost opportunities or misspent energy on that day.

SHARING THE SCRIPTURE

Preparing Our Hearts

This week's devotional reading is found in Matthew 13:3-9, which is the familiar parable of the sower. Try to read this passage as if you had never read it before. Which words "jump out" at you? What does this parable say to you about the Christian life in general and your own discipleship in particular? Write your thoughts in your spiritual journal and/or talk with another believer about your interpretation of this parable.

Pray that you and the class participants will be fertile soil that brings forth an abundant harvest for Christ.

Preparing Our Minds

Study the background and lesson Scripture, both of which are found in 1 Corinthians 3:1-15. As you read, think about how spiritual formation takes place within the community of faith.

Write on newsprint:

❏ the list of questions in Gather to Learn.
❏ information for next week's lesson, found under "Continue the Journey."

Talk with your pastor and prepare a list of ministry opportunities currently available in your church and community. Such a list might already exist.

LEADING THE CLASS

(1) Gather to Learn

❖ Welcome the class members and introduce any guests.

❖ Pray that today's participants will work together to encourage each other in the faith.

❖ Read aloud the first paragraph of "A Constant Building Project" in Interpreting the Scripture.

❖ Ask the students to work in small groups to recall some high points of their own spiritual journeys. They may want to consider these questions, which you will post on newsprint.

(1) **Who helped you to grow in your faith?**

(2) **How did these mentors model what the Christian life is supposed to be?**

(3) **In what ways did their ministry build up your faith and involve you in the life of the church?**

❖ Read aloud today's focus statement: **Many people recognize that spiritual growth depends on the foundation laid by teachers and mentors. How does spiritual formation take place within the community of faith? Paul describes a process by which he first introduced people to the gospel, laying a foundation in Jesus Christ, and then others nurtured the new Christians toward maturity.**

(2) Discover What Paul Says About Building the Church by Teamwork Based on Undivided Loyalty to Jesus Christ

❖ Choose three readers and assign each to a segment of verses: 1 Corinthians 3:1-4, 5-9, 10-15.

❖ Invite the students to state in their own words the concerns that Paul is lifting up to the Corinthians.

❖ Talk with the group about whether or not Paul's words have meaning for today's church. You might consider questions such as these.

(1) **In the Corinthian church there were quarrels concerning leadership. What creates "jealousy and quarreling" among today's church members? How could such divisions be healed?**

(2) **Paul urged his readers to work together for the common good of the church. Where do you currently see examples of Christians working together for a common purpose?**

(3) **Think about the history of your congregation. Who are some of the people who planted or watered the church through the years? How would you describe their legacy?**

(3) Consider the Implications for the Learners' Spiritual Formation That Lie in the Team Process Paul Describes

❖ Point out that Paul writes about a team process where each person does something. No one individual can do it all. Nor can the work of the collective group be worthwhile unless God is in the midst of it.

❖ Read aloud "We Just Can't Compete" in Interpreting the Scripture. Provide a few moments of quiet time for the adults to reflect on (1) the problems created when people undermine or try to outdo each other's work and (2) the idea that there is no need to compete because there is ample praise and affirmation for everyone.

❖ Note that some churches are moving to team-based ministry in order to involve more people in ministry by encouraging them to use their gifts to build up the church.

(1) **Many churches expect the pastor and possibly a few key leaders among the laity to do the work of the church. How might a church that operates this way be different if it did its ministry in teams?**

(2) **What are the advantages of working together as a team?** (List ideas on newsprint.)

(3) **How might teams encourage those persons who have been willing to sit on the sidelines to become involved in ministry?**

❖ Distribute paper and pencils. Give the participants time to meditate on this question and, if they choose, to write a response: **How might you grow spiritually if you participated in a team process for ministry?**

❖ Conclude this portion of the session by inviting the adults to comment on ways they believe the team model that Paul affirms could help individuals and the church as a body grow toward greater spiritual maturity.

(4) Identify Ways to Become More Active in the Church's Ministry

❖ Distribute the list of current opportunities for ministry that you and your pastor discussed. As an alternative, ask the students to brainstorm a list of opportunities for ministry. This list should include work within your local church, as well as ecumenical opportunities in your community (for example, a community soup kitchen or Habitat for Humanity build), and denominational opportunities (for example, a Volunteers in Mission trip sponsored by a district or cluster or churches).

❖ Invite the class members to think about their own gifts and consider ways that they could be used to build up the church's ministry. Encourage them to think of new ministries that they could undertake.

❖ Go around the room (or in smaller groups if the class is large) and ask each person to state one way that he or she will contribute to the harmonious working of the church "team" by using his or her God-given gifts for ministry.

(5) Continue the Journey

❖ Pray that all who have come today will identify themselves as servants of God who will work together harmoniously to build up Christ's church.

❖ Read aloud this preparation for next week's lesson. You may also want to post it on newsprint for the students to copy. **Prepare for next week's session, "Serving Responsibly," by reading 1 Corinthians** **4:1-13, which serves as both the background and lesson Scripture. Ponder these ideas as you study: Following through on responsibility is a major part of life. For what are we responsible? The fact that Paul saw his apostleship as a stewardship from God indicates that we are responsible to God for our attitudes and actions as disciples.**

❖ Read aloud the following three ideas. Challenge the students to commit themselves to use these activities as a springboard to spiritual growth.

    (1) Review your current commitments to your congregation. What other responsibilities might you be able to take on, given your talents, time, and other obligations?

    (2) Encourage a new member or someone who is new to congregational leadership to identify talents and find a ministry where those talents can be used to build up the church.

    (3) Recall that Paul viewed factionalism, jealousy, and quarreling as signs of spiritual immaturity. Be alert for opportunities to bring peace and harmony by emphasizing the complementary nature of work in the church.

❖ Sing or read aloud "O Church of God United."

❖ Close the session with this benediction, which you may want the class members to echo after you: **Go forth committed to serve, obey, and give as people who have been called to live faithfully in Christian community. Amen.**

UNIT 1: SERVANTS OF GOD
SERVING RESPONSIBLY

PREVIEWING THE LESSON

Lesson Scripture: 1 Corinthians 4:1-13
Background Scripture: 1 Corinthians 4:1-13
Key Verse: 1 Corinthians 4:1

Focus of the Lesson:
Following through on responsibility is a major part of life. For what are we responsible? The fact that Paul saw his apostleship as a stewardship from God indicates that we are responsible to God for our attitudes and actions as disciples.

Goals for the Learners:
(1) to explore Paul's view of Christian leadership as servanthood and as stewardship of responsibility.
(2) to compare and contrast Paul's description of the apostles' situation with their own circumstances.
(3) to accept responsibility for their own ministry as servants and stewards of God and act appropriately.

Supplies:
Bibles, newsprint and marker, paper and pencils, hymnals

READING THE SCRIPTURE

NRSV
1 Corinthians 4:1-13

¹Think of us in this way, as servants of Christ and stewards of God's mysteries. ²Moreover, it is required of stewards that they be found trustworthy. ³But with me it is a very small thing that I should be judged by you or by any human court. I do not even judge myself. ⁴I am not aware of anything against myself, but I am not thereby acquitted. It is the Lord who judges me. ⁵Therefore do not pronounce judgment before the time, before the Lord comes, who will bring to

NIV
1 Corinthians 4:1-13

¹So then, men ought to regard us as servants of Christ and as those entrusted with the secret things of God. ²Now it is required that those who have been given a trust must prove faithful. ³I care very little if I am judged by you or by any human court; indeed, I do not even judge myself. ⁴My conscience is clear, but that does not make me innocent. It is the Lord who judges me. ⁵Therefore judge nothing before the appointed time; wait till the Lord comes. He

light the things now hidden in darkness and will disclose the purposes of the heart. Then each one will receive commendation from God.

[6]I have applied all this to Apollos and myself for your benefit, brothers and sisters, so that you may learn through us the meaning of the saying, "Nothing beyond what is written," so that none of you will be puffed up in favor of one against another. [7]For who sees anything different in you? What do you have that you did not receive? And if you received it, why do you boast as if it were not a gift?

[8]Already you have all you want! Already you have become rich! Quite apart from us you have become kings! Indeed, I wish that you had become kings, so that we might be kings with you! [9]For I think that God has exhibited us apostles as last of all, as though sentenced to death, because we have become a spectacle to the world, to angels and to mortals. [10]We are fools for the sake of Christ, but you are wise in Christ. We are weak, but you are strong. You are held in honor, but we in disrepute. [11]To the present hour we are hungry and thirsty, we are poorly clothed and beaten and homeless, [12]and we grow weary from the work of our own hands. When reviled, we bless; when persecuted, we endure; [13]when slandered, we speak kindly. We have become like the rubbish of the world, the dregs of all things, to this very day.

will bring to light what is hidden in darkness and will expose the motives of men's hearts. At that time each will receive his praise from God.

[6]Now, brothers, I have applied these things to myself and Apollos for your benefit, so that you may learn from us the meaning of the saying, "Do not go beyond what is written." Then you will not take pride in one man over against another. [7]For who makes you different from anyone else? What do you have that you did not receive? And if you did receive it, why do you boast as though you did not?

[8]Already you have all you want! Already you have become rich! You have become kings—and that without us! How I wish that you really had become kings so that we might be kings with you! [9]For it seems to me that God has put us apostles on display at the end of the procession, like men condemned to die in the arena. We have been made a spectacle to the whole universe, to angels as well as to men. [10]We are fools for Christ, but you are so wise in Christ! We are weak, but you are strong! You are honored, we are dishonored! [11]To this very hour we go hungry and thirsty, we are in rags, we are brutally treated, we are homeless. [12]We work hard with our own hands. When we are cursed, we bless; when we are persecuted, we endure it; [13]when we are slandered, we answer kindly. Up to this moment we have become the scum of the earth, the refuse of the world.

UNDERSTANDING THE SCRIPTURE

1 Corinthians 4:1-5. Paul turns to a third image to help the Corinthian Christians return to a saner frame of mind regarding their leaders. Farming metaphors (3:5-9) and construction images (3:10-15) helped take the focus off individual teachers and elevate the God who brings gifts to the church through the means God selects. The image of "steward" now draws on the arena of household management. Stewards were usually domestic slaves entrusted with the day-to-day management of the household. It was their responsibility to carry out the instructions and wishes of the master of the house and to manage the business of the household in the best interests of the master.

The steward would act as a kind of business manager in the household with farmlands (as in Luke 16:1-8), as well as care for the needs of the other slaves of the household, according to the master's instructions (as in Matthew 24:45-51).

The "steward" held an important position, but one that existed only for the sake of serving the master's wishes. The Corinthians were evaluating the apostles according to their cultural criteria of the "effective speaker" and the "charismatically gifted teacher." As a steward, however, Paul says he cares nothing about their expectations of him. What counts for a steward, after all, is that the Master finds him faithful and reliable in carrying out his duty. The words translated "human court" in 4:3 are actually "human day" in the Greek. This "day"—any "day" the Corinthians might care to form some judgment about Paul— stands in stark contrast to *the day* when God will judge (see 3:13; 5:5). No person, not even Paul himself, has such clarity of insight as to formulate a completely accurate evaluation of the apostle; only God does, and so he seeks only to be praised by God on that day.

This reinforces what Paul said earlier about deciding not to preach in flashy, polished, and ornamented speech (2:1-5), appealing to the Corinthians' tastes. Rather, he sought, and continues to seek, only to be faithful to the commission his Master gave him, which was to present the Corinthians with Jesus. He presented this in speech, but he also presents it in his life circumstances and in his attitudes. He is no stranger to hardship and persecution; he identifies with the hard-working craftsperson rather than the indolent philosopher; he is poured out rather than puffed up—just like the One he preaches.

1 Corinthians 4:6-8. The enigmatic phrase "nothing beyond what is written" may or may not have been a quotation of a saying current in Paul's time (as the NRSV presents it). Its meaning has been variously explained as (1) an admonition to disciples to "stay within the lines" drawn by the teacher as they learn their alphabet; (2) a reference to Old Testament leadership values, which also emphasize fidelity rather than showmanship; (3) a reference to the things Paul has just written in 1 Corinthians 3:1–4:5, as a corrective against the believers misusing the apostles as rallying points for competition (4:6). Context, I believe, favors the last of these options, which is also the simplest explanation. Having laid out the "way things are," Paul asks the Corinthians, in effect, "who is setting you apart" from walking in line with these realities, accepting not only their apostles, but also their spiritual knowledge and spiritual gifts all as favors they have received from God and not as any basis for claiming superiority over one another in a mad drive for precedence in the church.

When Paul goes on to speak sarcastically about the wealth, the fullness, and the kingly authority the Corinthians have already received, he is making fun of their pretensions for having become models of the sage or wise person, when they are still "unspiritual" (see 1 Corinthians 3:1-4). Both Greco-Roman and Jewish philosophers habitually speak of the "wise person" as king. The author of 4 Maccabees, for example, says that the person who has educated his or her mind in God's law and follows reason rather than the passions of the flesh "will rule a kingdom that is temperate, just, good, and courageous" (4 Maccabees 2:23). In "On the Migration of Abraham" (197) Philo, the Alexandrian Jewish philosopher, writes that wisdom is kingship, for the wise person is a king. In *Moral Epistles* (17.10) Seneca reasons with his reader: Why waste your life waiting for dividends to come due, or for income on your merchandise, or for somebody to leave you money in a will, when you can be rich right now? Wisdom enriches those for whom material wealth has become superfluous.

1 Corinthians 4:9-13. Paul contrasts the

Corinthians' "battles" for the faith—their concern to come out on top in power struggles and other contests—with the apostle's battle for the faith, in which hardships, shame, and sufferings keep pushing him to the limits of human tolerance, where at last they discover the power of God (see 2 Corinthians 4:7-12; 6:3-10; 12:6-10). Hardship, however, is also the arena in which philosophers prove the value of the way of life they stand for and proclaim. Paul embodies conformity with the character and life of Jesus. He blesses when reviled (see Luke 6:28; 1 Peter 2:23); he accepts loss of status and shameful treatment for the sake of doing God's will, even as Jesus did.

The stark juxtapositions Paul constructs between his circumstances and those of his converts cannot help but recall Jesus' statement that "a disciple is not above the teacher, nor a slave above the master" (Matthew 10:24) and the similar struggles Jesus had teaching his disciples about what it meant to follow this master (see especially Mark 10:35-45, where jockeying for precedence is again a major issue). The Corinthians are faced here with the fact that they have been trying to live "above" their teacher, indulging themselves in contests over who is the spiritually superior, who is connected with the better teacher, and the like. They are still trying to remain "upwardly mobile" while following the preacher of a crucified Redeemer. Even though Paul claims not to be trying to shame them (4:14), they should feel ashamed as well as admonished anew to imitate Paul as he imitates Christ (4:16; 11:1).

INTERPRETING THE SCRIPTURE

Christian Leadership

Pride is such an insidious enemy of our souls. It is in many ways more dangerous than other, more obvious "deadly sins" like gluttony, lust, or anger. Those are easy to notice. They lead us to acts or lifestyles in which the sin is obvious, and about which it becomes very difficult to deceive ourselves. But it is easy to deceive ourselves when we give place to pride. When we are occupied in "Christian work," when we can list our arenas of service and our works on behalf of God's mission in the world, when there is no behavior to which people can point and say "this is a sin," self-serving attitudes and self-promoting agendas can creep in alongside the good that we do. Such attitudes were rampant in the Corinthian congregation, and they continue to infect Christian leadership.

The model that Paul embodies is quite different. Paul continually selects images of leadership that help him, as well as his converts, credit God as the prime mover of all his work. He is merely a planter, but God causes the work to flourish; a foreman, but God provides the plan and the design that he labors to execute; the steward, but God is the householder with the only real power. It is enough for this Christian leader to be faithful to his commission by God, whether he is held in honor or dishonor, whether he is recognized for his labors or considered inadequate by those he serves. He distinguishes himself among the churches not by being the most powerful, most applauded, best connected, but by being as fully like Christ as God will permit, pouring himself out for the mission of God, and trusting in God for approval and praise on the last day. All who would be leaders in the church are particularly challenged by his admonition to "be imitators of him," for his is a style of leadership quite different from the style that more naturally appeals to us.

Who, Then, Is the Faithful Steward?

We often act as if our time is our own—something that others can "take up" or "take away." We often think as if we have made our own way in the world, such that the funds in the bank are "my money, which I earned," nay, "which I made." The essence of Christian stewardship is the realization that all we have, and all we are, is a gift from God. Do we truly believe, as Paul expects us to believe, that we have nothing that we did not receive as gifts from God (4:7)?

If so, for what purpose did God give us these gifts? In our imitation of Paul, we are invited to answer this in terms of stewardship—not here primarily thinking in terms of our time, talents, treasures, but rather, and most of all, of the "treasure in the clay jars" (2 Corinthians 4:7) of our own person. God has granted each of us to know something of divine "mysteries," that is, of the love, wholeness, healing, and hope that God has made available through the Holy Spirit to all who have placed their trust in Jesus. Our understanding of God's provisions in Jesus, and our experience of God's power and movement in our lives, is given to us not only for our own good but also for the encouragement, instruction, and strengthening of our sisters and brothers in the faith (see, for example, 1 Corinthians 12:7; 14:12; Hebrews 10:24-25; 1 Peter 4:10-11).

The United Methodist Church and the Episcopal Church, among others, subscribe to a very healthful model of ministry: All baptized Christians are called by God into the work of ministry (Ephesians 4:7-11). All believers are commissioned by God to be "stewards of God's mysteries" (1 Corinthians 4:1). How are you fulfilling God's instructions concerning the use of all that God has given to you for the nurturing and strengthening of God's people?

Who's to Judge?

Some people find themselves consumed in efforts to live up to the expectations of others or the expectations they have of themselves. These expectations can come from different places: the demands of parents, inscribed very early on our consciousness; the vows we make to ourselves as we are growing up; the standards we set for ourselves, learned from our society, our upbringing, or our religion, to measure whether or not our lives are "successful." Very rarely can we live up to them, with the result that we can be caught in a cycle of trying to play to these expectations, measuring ourselves or being measured, being found wanting, feeling defeated, and going back to the beginning of the cycle again. In the process, we can fail to appreciate so much of what we do, who we have become, and what gifts God has set before us. Even more to the point, very often none of these expectations comes from God.

Paul's own attitude commends itself to us for our consideration and imitation, all the more as it promises to deliver us from an abundance of psychological and relational distress. Paul sets aside the expectations his congregations might have of him, and, most astonishingly, does "not even judge" himself (4:3). Rather, his whole concern is to listen in prayer and meditation for what God is calling him to do, and then to do it faithfully. In considering himself answerable to One master, Paul discovers freedom from the tyranny of many masters—including himself.

Lifestyles of God's "Rich and Famous"

Paul's life was not that of a glittering evangelist, traveling in style, moving from stadium to stadium, being cheered on as he went. Taking the gospel to Syria, Asia Minor, and Greece meant journeying by foot for hundreds of miles, being driven out of cities by zealous Jews who opposed what they considered to be a danger to the covenant, being beaten or imprisoned or hauled before magistrates by Gentiles whose religion, livelihood, or family life were disrupted by the anti-idolatrous message Paul brought. It meant being scoffed at, looked down upon, and often treated like garbage. And then Paul will write a few verses later, "be imitators of me" (4:16).

Imitate Paul? His life circumstances are largely the sort of thing we work hard all our lives to avoid, the sort of thing we most fear befalling us. Yet Paul was seeking to imitate Christ, allowing Jesus' cruciform life to take shape in his own life, a spiritual goal that permeates his whole career (see 2 Corinthians 4:7-12; Galatians 2:19-20; Philippians 3:8-11). This would be the life of one who seeks "not to be served, but to serve" (Mark 10:45), to advance not his or her own interests, but the interests of the God who called him or her and the nurture of those God would connect with through him or her (Philippians 2:3-4; 2 Corinthians 5:14-15, 18-20).

Paul did not seek out hardship for its own sake. But he was sufficiently free from most of the concerns that so engulf us that he could endure it for the sake of advancing God's interests in the world. Reputation among people meant far less to Paul than pleasing God. Enjoying creature comforts meant far less than the surpassing value of knowing Jesus and his fellowship in suffering. At the end of the day, what mattered was responding faithfully to God in all things, however this might make him fall short of the expectations of worldly-minded people.

SHARING THE SCRIPTURE

Preparing Our Hearts

This week's devotional reading is found in Matthew 23:8-12. In verse 11 Jesus teaches, "The greatest among you will be your servant." Although servanthood is a familiar theme of Jesus' ministry, it clangs a dissonant note in our ears, for our society teaches that the greatest is the one who is served. Think about your own actions. Are you willing to serve others? What does your service reveal about your relationship with Christ? What commitments will you make this week to serve?

Pray that you and the class participants will be eager and ready to serve others, for in serving others we serve God.

Preparing Our Minds

Study the background and lesson Scripture, both of which are found in 1 Corinthians 4:1-13. As you read, consider how we are responsible to God for our attitudes and actions.

Write on newsprint:
- ❏ ideas for thought in the "Accept Responsibility for Ministry as Servants and Stewards of God and Act Appropriately" portion.
- ❏ information for next week's lesson, found under "Continue the Journey."

Plan a lecture for "Explore Paul's View of Christian Leadership as Servanthood and as Stewardship of Responsibility."

LEADING THE CLASS

(1) Gather to Learn

❖ Welcome the class members and introduce any guests.

❖ Pray that all who have come will be open to the leading of the Spirit as we consider ways in which we can serve God responsibly.

❖ Write "A servant of God is someone who . . ." on a sheet of newsprint. Invite the students to complete the sentence and record their answers. When you have finished, you will likely have a description of ideal leaders and followers in the church. Leave this sheet of newsprint posted.

❖ Read aloud today's focus statement: **Following through on responsibility is a major part of life. For what are we responsible? The fact that Paul saw his apostleship as a stewardship from God indicates that we are responsible to God for our attitudes and actions as disciples.**

(2) Explore Paul's View of Christian Leadership as Servanthood and as Stewardship of Responsibility

❖ Choose a volunteer to read 1 Corinthians 4:1-13. Ask the class to listen as if they were members of the Corinthian church hearing Paul's letter for the first time.

❖ Use information from Understanding the Scripture to create a lecture in which you highlight:

■ the work of the steward in the first-century household.

■ how Paul uses the image of the steward to make his point.

■ possible meanings of the saying in verse 6, "Nothing beyond what is written."

■ how Paul views his own circumstances in contrast to the Corinthian church members' circumstances.

❖ Ask the class to describe Paul's model of leadership. Write these descriptive words and phrases on newsprint. (See "Christian Leadership" in Interpreting the Scripture for additional ideas.)

❖ Point out that an important aspect of Paul's leadership style is that he sets aside the expectations of his congregations—and himself—and listens in prayer and meditation to what God is calling him to do. Then he acts. Discuss with the class:

(1) how such a leadership style would be accepted in many contemporary Protestant churches,

(2) how contemporary churches could benefit from such a leadership style.

(3) any dangers inherent in such a leadership style.

(3) Compare and Contrast Paul's Description of the Apostles' Situation with the Learners' Circumstances

❖ Post side-by-side the descriptions of the ideal leader generated in Gather to Learn and Paul's model of leadership that the class brainstormed as you explored Paul's view of Christian leadership. Divide the class into small groups and ask them to look for similarities and differences between the two lists. Invite the groups to report back to the class.

❖ Encourage the class to imagine this scenario and discuss the following questions: **Paul plans to visit our church next Sunday. He will be speaking with us about the ministry of the apostles and how we can join them as servants in ministry.**

(1) **What do you think Paul will say to us as a congregation about our service as Christ's disciples?**

(2) **How is our contemporary situation different from the one at the church in Corinth? What effect do those differences have on the way we serve?**

(3) **What words of encouragement would you hope to hear from Paul?**

(4) **Are you looking forward to Paul's visit next week? Why or why not?**

❖ Invite the adults to think silently about this question: **How are you fulfilling God's instructions concerning the use of all that God has given to you for the nurture and strengthening of God's people?**

(4) Accept Responsibility for Ministry as Servants and Stewards of God and Act Appropriately

❖ Distribute paper and pencils. Ask the participants to write a few words describing whatever ministries God may be calling them to undertake. Suggest that they consider the following points, which you will need to read aloud or post on newsprint:

■ why this ministry is important.

■ where, when, and how they might become involved in this ministry.

■ gifts God has entrusted to them for this ministry.

■ marks or characteristics of faithful service.

❖ Ask the adults to sign what they have written as the seal of a covenant they have made with God to serve responsibly.

❖ Close this portion of the session by asking the students to read together today's key verse, 1 Corinthians 4:1. If the students do not use the same translation, read a phrase at a time and ask them to repeat it.

(5) Continue the Journey

❖ Pray that the students will recognize their responsibility to serve God and act faithfully in response to the work they have been called to do.

❖ Read aloud this preparation for next week's lesson. You may also want to post it on newsprint for the students to copy. **Prepare for next week's session, "Living in Relationships," by reading 1 Corinthians 7:1-20, 23-40, which is our background Scripture. The lesson will focus on 7:2-15. Keep these ideas in mind as you study:**

Relationships with others are a vital part of life. What kind of relationship is best for us? Focusing on human relationships, Paul gives advice to help Christians discern whether they should marry or stay single.

❖ Read aloud the following three ideas. Challenge the students to commit themselves to use these activities as a springboard to spiritual growth.

(1) Examine the ministries in which you are currently serving. Why are you engaged in these ministries? Are there any that you need to set aside? Why? Are there any other ministries that God may now be calling you to undertake? What response will you make?

(2) Review Paul's comments in today's passage. Clearly, he has suffered to serve Christ faithfully. What have you given up or suffered to serve Christ? What does your list disclose about the depth and breadth of your ministry?

(3) Note that some people think that being a Christian means that life will be trouble-free. How would Paul respond to such an idea? What would you say to Christians who expressed disappointment that life was not easy?

❖ Sing or read aloud "Here, O Lord, Your Servants Gather."

❖ Close the session with this benediction, which you may want the class members to echo after you: **Go forth committed to serve, obey, and give as people who have been called to live faithfully in Christian community. Amen.**

UNIT 2: CALLED TO OBEDIENCE
LIVING IN RELATIONSHIPS

PREVIEWING THE LESSON

Lesson Scripture: 1 Corinthians 7:2-15
Background Scripture: 1 Corinthians 7:1-20, 23-40
Key Verse: 1 Corinthians 7:7

Focus of the Lesson:
Relationships with others are a vital part of life. What kind of relationship is best for us? Focusing on human relationships, Paul gives advice to help Christians discern whether they should marry or stay single.

Goals for the Learners:
(1) to examine Paul's teachings on marriage and singleness.
(2) to identify characteristics of a life-affirming relationship.
(3) to evaluate their own relationships in light of what they have learned.

Pronunciation Guide:
eschatology (es kuh tol' uh jee)

Supplies:
Bibles, newsprint and marker, paper and pencils, hymnals

READING THE SCRIPTURE

NRSV
1 Corinthians 7:2-15

²But because of cases of sexual immorality, each man should have his own wife and each woman her own husband. ³The husband should give to his wife her conjugal rights, and likewise the wife to her husband. ⁴For the wife does not have authority over her own body, but the husband does; likewise the husband does not have authority over his own body, but the wife does. ⁵Do not deprive one another except perhaps by

NIV
1 Corinthians 7:2-15

²But since there is so much immorality, each man should have his own wife, and each woman her own husband. ³The husband should fulfill his marital duty to his wife, and likewise the wife to her husband. ⁴The wife's body does not belong to her alone but also to her husband. In the same way, the husband's body does not belong to him alone but also to his wife. ⁵Do not deprive each other except by mutual consent

agreement for a set time, to devote yourselves to prayer, and then come together again, so that Satan may not tempt you because of your lack of self-control. ⁶This I say by way of concession, not of command. ⁷I wish that all were as I myself am. But each has a particular gift from God, one having one kind and another a different kind.

⁸To the unmarried and the widows I say that it is well for them to remain unmarried as I am. ⁹But if they are not practicing self-control, they should marry. For it is better to marry than to be aflame with passion.

¹⁰To the married I give this command—not I but the Lord—that the wife should not separate from her husband ¹¹(but if she does separate, let her remain unmarried or else be reconciled to her husband), and that the husband should not divorce his wife.

¹²To the rest I say—I and not the Lord—that if any believer has a wife who is an unbeliever, and she consents to live with him, he should not divorce her. ¹³And if any woman has a husband who is an unbeliever, and he consents to live with her, she should not divorce him. ¹⁴For the unbelieving husband is made holy through his wife, and the unbelieving wife is made holy through her husband. Otherwise, your children would be unclean, but as it is, they are holy. ¹⁵But if the unbelieving partner separates, let it be so; in such a case the brother or sister is not bound. It is to peace that God has called you.

and for a time, so that you may devote yourselves to prayer. Then come together again so that Satan will not tempt you because of your lack of self-control. ⁶I say this as a concession, not as a command. ⁷I wish that all men were as I am. But each man has his own gift from God; one has this gift, another has that.

⁸Now to the unmarried and the widows I say: It is good for them to stay unmarried, as I am. ⁹But if they cannot control themselves, they should marry, for it is better to marry than to burn with passion.

¹⁰To the married I give this command (not I, but the Lord): A wife must not separate from her husband. ¹¹But if she does, she must remain unmarried or else be reconciled to her husband. And a husband must not divorce his wife.

¹²To the rest I say this (I, not the Lord): If any brother has a wife who is not a believer and she is willing to live with him, he must not divorce her. ¹³And if a woman has a husband who is not a believer and he is willing to live with her, she must not divorce him. ¹⁴For the unbelieving husband has been sanctified through his wife, and the unbelieving wife has been sanctified through her believing husband. Otherwise your children would be unclean, but as it is, they are holy.

¹⁵But if the unbeliever leaves, let him do so. A believing man or woman is not bound in such circumstances; God has called us to live in peace.

UNDERSTANDING THE SCRIPTURE

1 Corinthians 7:1-9, 32-40. Paul begins here to address questions or concerns about which some Corinthian Christians had actually written to Paul first, seeking his counsel (or perhaps, seeking his backing, since these issues were being debated in the congregation). Among other concerns, these Christians had asked for Paul's advice about sexual relations within marriage,

about divorce (especially in the case of marriage to unbelievers), and about whether or not new marriages (for example, of the engaged, or of widows) should be performed.

Marriage in the ancient world was unlike the practice and ideal of modern marriage in several important respects. Many marriages often involved a substantial difference in age between the older husband and the younger bride. The main purposes for marriage were provision of heirs and disposition of property. When a marriage was arranged, considerations of whether or not two people were "in love" hardly entered into the discussion as a criterion. The process of dating multiple prospects, falling in love, and marrying out of romantic passions was not the norm. Rather, a family (or the adult bridegroom) looked for a union with a compatible family, preferably one which would bring some advantage or social benefit to the whole family. For this reason, philosophers speak of "harmony" and "concord" as the ideal of marriage rather than "love" or "passion" (see, for example, Plutarch's "Advice on Marriage," a treasure trove of popular Roman sentiments on the "good marriage"). Moreover, marriage was not meant to give carte blanche to sexual passion. In *Sentences* 193–194, Pseudo-Phocylides advised husbands not to engage in unbridled passion with their wives because passion is not a god, but a destructive impulse. In *Advice on Marriage* (16) Plutarch advised a wife to consider it a compliment to her if her husband spent his lusts elsewhere, thus honoring her. Nevertheless, people often found satisfying partnerships in marriage, and not a few men still chose their partners for more than practical considerations.

As chapter 7 opens, then, we find Paul dealing with a popular sentiment: It is better not to have sexual relations with a woman/one's wife. Some of the Corinthians may indeed have taken this well beyond Plutarch's advice, regarding sexuality as somehow a distraction or hindrance to attaining the spiritual ecstasy they so prized (see chapters 12 and 14). Paul, however, affirms the importance of marriage as a legitimate channel for sexual energy. Against any one-sided notion of the wife as the husband's sexual object, Paul stresses that each partner has a right to the other's body, and urges mutual considera-

tion and submission in sexual matters. The concession he gives is not that married couples engage in sexual activity, but that they be allowed to suspend sexual activity for periods of special devotion to God—and that only by mutual consent and for limited periods.

Paul indicates a strong preference for the single life, a value choice that runs quite against the grain of Greek and Roman society just as it still does today. The emperor Augustus created fiscal and other incentives to Romans to marry (or, in the case of widows, to remarry) and procreate; Paul urged remaining single if possible. His rationale was not, however, that marriage or sexuality was any less "holy" than singleness, far less that marriage or sexuality was "sin." On the contrary, both singleness and marriage are considered to be special gifts and callings from God. Paul knew, however, that the married would be distracted from the service of God by considerations of what would please the spouse, whereas a single person could serve One Master with undivided heart. A practical man, Paul also knew that passion between man and woman could be strong: If self-control was not effective, marriage would be far better than to be even further distracted by unfulfilled longing.

1 Corinthians 7:10-16. Paul affirms the command of Jesus concerning divorce, following more the content of Mark 10:11-12 and Luke 16:18 than Matthew's version of these sayings (5:32; 19:9). Paul appears to apply this saying as the rule for Christian marriages. With regard to marriages between a believer and a non-Christian, Paul has his own advice to give, however. Believers might be tempted to divorce unbelieving spouses, thinking it improper to continue to have a sanctified person and an unsanctified person "unequally yoked" (though 2 Corinthians 6:14, KJV, where this phrase originates, is not about marriages or dating, as it is most often applied). Paul argues, however, that no change of status is required of the new Christian: The marriage she had before conversion is the locus of her calling. The marriage should not be dissolved, for God's holiness flows through her to the benefit of the whole family, perhaps ultimately to her leading her husband to the faith. If the unbelieving partner wants to leave the marriage, however, Paul absolves the Christian from responsibility. "Peace," or harmony and concord in the home, is God's main objective.

1 Corinthians 7:17-20, 23-31. The heart of the chapter is found here, as Paul shows that the Christian is called to live out the new life within the station in which God called him or her. The single do not have to marry; the married do not have to become celibate or single again; the Gentile need not be circumcised; the Jew need not reverse his circumcision; the slave does not have to worry about his servile status—as soon as they are born of the Spirit, they are all sisters and brothers, with the new status of members of the family of God. Any status ascribed to them by their natural birth or earthly circumstances are relativized, taking on a secondary importance.

Underlying all of Paul's statements in this chapter is his eschatology, his awareness that "the present form of this world is passing away" (7:31). This world, with all its structures of marriage and slavery, and with all its business enterprises and personal pretensions, was already on the way out. The Christian, privy to the knowledge that Christ's resurrection signaled the invasion of the ultimate and eternal into this world, is challenged to live each day with an eye to pleasing God and looking for what has eternal significance, which means not getting too caught up in the temporal affairs that so easily consume the minds and hearts of unbelievers.

INTERPRETING THE SCRIPTURE

The Qualities of Christian Marriage

Paul envisions marriage being guided by great sensitivity and mutual consideration. Speaking to believers thinking about suspending sexual relations within their marriages, imagining this to be the path to greater spirituality, devotion to God, and, perhaps, superior charismatic gifting, Paul warns against making one's spouse feel deprived or shut out. He makes a bold statement about each spouse not having the final authority over his or her own body, but rather that authority being given away to the spouse at marriage. Paul imagines a husband shunning the sexual advances of his wife out of what would now amount to a selfish desire for spiritual advancement, making her feel both ashamed for her "carnal" drives as well as rejected. So he bluntly says that abstinence is not the husband's decision to force on his wife, or vice versa.

It is easy to imagine this verse being abused, as are Paul's other statements about marriage. I remember, as a child, listening to an adult couple with whom my family was quite close (I called them "aunt" and "uncle") arguing, and the husband trying to break down the wife's opposition by quoting Paul: "Wives, submit to your husbands" (Ephesians 5:22, NIV). Of course, he never cited the preceding verse: "Submit to one another out of reverence for Christ" (NIV); nor the following paragraph: "Husbands, love your wives as Christ loved the church and gave himself up for her" (Ephesians 5:25, NIV). That marriage eventually dissolved. In a similar way, one spouse might be tempted to cajole the other with 1 Corinthians 7:4, claiming scriptural authority for his or her "rights" to physical attention from the other.

This is not at all what Paul has in mind. He does not provide ammunition for coercion, but speaks to each partner and calls for mutual consideration in all things. And if one partner really feels the need for abstinence for a special period of spiritual devotion, this also calls for consideration from the other partner. All things are to be done "by agreement." If God has indeed called us to "peace" (7:15), then we fulfill our vocation as married believers when we seek to nurture harmony, concord, and peace in our marriages, which never happens when one spouse "wins" and the other "loses" an argument.

Paul teaches us another lesson about Christian marriage somewhat indirectly by pointing to a potential drawback in 1 Corinthians 7:32-35. Marriage, which often involves the rearing of children, brings a plethora of concerns into a person's life. One is constantly struggling to give enough attention to one's children, to give one's spouse the attention and support he or she needs, and, if any time is left over, to care for oneself and perhaps steal fifteen minutes for quiet time with God. Their "interests are divided" indeed (1 Corinthians 7:34). The challenge laid out for us, then, is to find ways in which to unite our interest in knowing and serving the Lord with the time we spend together as couples or as families. Rather than each spouse thinking about how to please God and the family, the challenge extended is how a couple can think together about meeting and serving God as a family.

The Calling of Singleness

I have heard the "gift of celibacy" sometimes called "the gift nobody wants," the ultimate "white elephant" in the Spirit's warehouse of provisions. Family and friends, then as now, surround an individual with expectations that he or she will marry. The Jewish wisdom tradition reflected in Ben Sira, for example, testifies to a father's anxiety that his daughter might remain unmarried (Sirach 42:9). Roman legislation, moreover, favored the married and those with multiple children (much like our tax schedules and incentives in the United States). People are uniformly made to feel that they should find a mate and that, if they do not, they are somehow "less" than normal and "less" than they should be.

Paul speaks a sane word of liberation here from such expectations. He teaches, to the contrary, that God gives both the gift of marriage *and* the gift of singleness, and that there are great advantages to the latter. The amount of time and energy a single person can devote to the Lord and to fruitful service, and the freedom and flexibility such a person can have to do the same, is indeed greater than that of the person with a family. This is a point at which the church, however, reinforces society's expectations and paradigms far more than it thinks to support an alternative paradigm. My own experience as a young, single organist and choir director was always to find women in the church eager to draw my attention to one young woman or another, or to support and embrace any young woman I brought to the church.

Now I personally appreciated such women, but that is because I do not believe I received the gift of celibacy. However, where is the support network for those who are called to singleness? Do we view them as specially gifted by God for devotion and service to Christ? Or do we view them as "unfortunates" who fell through the cracks of dating and marriage? Do we think of helping young people discern their calling to singleness or marriage, and actively present both as equally valid and valued stations in the church? I have three sons, and my wife and I have already begun to think about them dating, marrying, and making us grandparents. Would we be equally glad to have one or more remain single, and distinguish himself in bearing spiritual fruit rather than biological fruit? If we are to be faithful to Paul's vision for the church, we will help them realize that their happiness depends not on society's model or our own model for the "family man" or woman, but on discerning God's calling and being faithful to God's vision for our lives.

Living the "As Though Not"

In the middle of this discussion on marriage and singleness, Paul says a few profound words that are meant to bring an "apocalyptic adjustment" to our priorities and our focus as we live our lives in this world. It is so easy for us to get caught up in the affairs of this life, and to have them so completely consume our attention, energy, and time that we fail to nurture what is of lasting significance. Many men and women give as much as sixty to seventy hours per week on the job. People fixated on the qual-

ity of the possessions that surround them routinely mortgage their futures with credit cards and bank loans, condemning themselves to be slaves to their work, since they will have to pay off debt for years and years. Both the pleasures and the vicissitudes of marriage can consume our attention, leaving us with little time or energy for anything spiritual.

Paul warns us that all such concerns belong to a temporary reality, one that will not last. He begs us to awaken afresh to the things of everlasting significance—nurturing our relationship with the Lord, supporting fellow Christians on their spiritual journeys, sharing Jesus with our neighbors and with any in need of hearing. If we remember that work, possessions, even marriages last for this life only, we might attain the "as though not" we need in order to remain free to listen to God, to put God's calling first, to witness with our lives to the life of the world to come.

SHARING THE SCRIPTURE

Preparing Our Hearts

This week's devotional reading is found in 1 John 4:7-16. This familiar passage tells us to "love one another, because love is from God" (4:7). We are to abide in this love, which was so great that God sent Jesus to embody it. How would you describe the love that comes from God? How do you share this love, which we do not have a special name for in English, with others? What affect would truly living in God's love have on our relationships?

Pray that you and the class members will live with the love of God permeating all your relationships.

Preparing Our Minds

Study the background Scripture from 1 Corinthians 7:1-20, 23-40 and the lesson

Scripture, 1 Corinthians 7:2-15. Think about marriage and singleness, both of which are deemed as valid, vital ways of life according to Paul.

Write on newsprint:
❑ information for next week's lesson, found under "Continue the Journey."

Plan a lecture for "Examine Paul's Teachings on Marriage and Singleness," if you choose to do this option.

LEADING THE CLASS

(1) Gather to Learn

❖ Welcome the class members and introduce any guests.

❖ Pray that the students will experience God's presence as they consider how to live in godly relationships with others.

❖ Read aloud these statistics pertaining to the United States, which are found at www.divorcemag.com. The figures are from the year 2002, unless otherwise noted.

■ **Percentage of population that is married**   **59%**
  (down from 62% in 1990, 72% in 1970)
■ **Percentage of population never married**   **24%**
■ **Percentage of the population that is divorced**   **10%**
  (up from 8% in 1990, 6% in 1980)
■ **Percentage of married people who reach their:**
  • 5th anniversary   82%
  • 10th anniversary   65%
  • 15th anniversary   52%
  • 25th anniversary   33%
  • 35th anniversary   20%
  • 50th anniversary   5%
■ **Percentage of the population who had never been married in 1999**
  • **Midwest**   28%
  • **Northeast**   28%
  • **South**   26%
  • **West**   29%
■ **Unmarried couples living together**   **5.5 million**

❖ Invite the class to comment on these statistics. What surprised them? What reasons can they give for some of these numbers?

❖ Read aloud today's focus statement: **Relationships with others are a vital part of life. What kind of relationship is best for us? Focusing on human relationships, Paul gives advice to help Christians discern whether they should marry or stay single.**

(2) Examine Paul's Teachings on Marriage and Singleness

❖ Choose volunteers to read segments of today's passage from 1 Corinthians 7—one reader for verses 2-7; another for verses 8-9; a third for verses 10-11; and a final one for verses 12-15.

❖ Read aloud the second paragraph under 1 Corinthians 7:1-9, 32-40 in Understanding the Scripture to give the class background information on marriage in Paul's time.

❖ Discuss these questions, or answer them yourself in an optional lecture. Check Understanding the Scripture for information.

(1) **What views does Paul express here on marriage?**
(2) **What are his views on singleness?**
(3) **Which does he prefer? Why?**
(4) **Recall that Paul believed that the return of Christ was imminent. How might this belief affect his view of marriage?**
(5) **What are Paul's views on divorce? Why do you agree or disagree with his views?** (Tread carefully here, since some members of the class are likely divorced. Make clear that Paul is not encouraging spouses to remain in abusive relationships or ones marred by adultery.)
(6) **Note that Paul chose to remain single. What dynamics and feelings might come into play when people are single not by choice but because they could not find a suitable partner?**
(7) **If Paul were to review the statistics we discussed earlier in the session, what might his response be?**

❖ Wrap up the discussion by asking class members to comment on any surprises they found in Paul's teachings or any new insights that struck them.

(3) Identify Characteristics of a Life-affirming Relationship

❖ Work with the class to write a broad definition of a life-affirming relationship.

You may want to list just words or phrases on newsprint rather than carefully craft a definition. Do not limit the definition to certain types of relationships, such as husband/wife, parent/child, and so on. Instead, concentrate on facets of any good relationship, such as the ability to communicate well, trust, loyalty, and respect.

❖ Focus for a few moments on marriage. Invite the students to describe examples of good marriages, possibly including their own. How do the partners treat each other? What is the secret to a healthy, long-lasting relationship?

❖ Focus for a few moments on friendships. Solicit the class members' ideas concerning how people of the same or opposite sex have good, wholesome friendships. Identify the traits of such relationships.

(4) Evaluate the Learners' Relationships in Light of What They Have Learned

❖ Distribute paper and pencils. Encourage the students to write about the best relationship they have ever had. How did this relationship reflect what they have learned today? Make clear that they will not be asked to disclose any of the ideas that they will be writing about in this portion of the lesson.

❖ Call time and ask them to write confidentially about a relationship that is currently rocky. Suggest that they identify reasons for the problems in this relationship by drawing on what they have learned today.

❖ Call time again and encourage them to create a plan of action for improving the rocky relationship so that it will be a wholesome, life-affirming one. Assure them that they will not be asked to reveal what they have written.

❖ Conclude this portion of the lesson by challenging the students to act on any discoveries they have made so as to strengthen their relationships. Suggest that if the rocky relationship they have written about is marriage, they may want to seek help from a qualified counselor.

(5) Continue the Journey

❖ Pray that the participants will be more aware of the value of their relationships and treat others with respect and love.

❖ Read aloud this preparation for next week's lesson. You may also want to post it on newsprint for the students to copy. **Prepare for next week's session, "To Eat or Not to Eat," by reading 1 Corinthians 8:1-13, which is both the background and lesson Scripture. Consider these ideas as you study: People need to be aware of how their actions affect others. How can we show consideration to others? Paul urges Christians to live in such a way that we do not cause another to sin.**

❖ Read aloud the following three ideas. Challenge the students to commit themselves to use these activities as a springboard to spiritual growth.

(1) Offer support to someone grappling with issues of marriage and divorce. Encourage this person to seek Christian counseling to get the marriage off to a positive start or to get it back on track.

(2) Do something special this week for a significant person in your life.

(3) Be alert for examples of the media exploiting or cheapening God's good gift of sexuality. Write a letter expressing your concern to a media outlet or sponsor.

❖ Sing or read aloud "When Love Is Found."

❖ Close the session with this benediction, which you may want the class members to echo after you: **Go forth committed to serve, obey, and give as people who have been called to live faithfully in Christian community. Amen.**

UNIT 2: CALLED TO OBEDIENCE

To Eat or Not to Eat

PREVIEWING THE LESSON

Lesson Scripture: 1 Corinthians 8:1-13
Background Scripture: 1 Corinthians 8:1-13
Key Verses: 1 Corinthians 8:8-9

Focus of the Lesson:

People need to be aware of how their actions affect others. How can we show consideration to others? Paul urges Christians to live in such a way that we do not cause another to sin.

Goals for the Learners:

(1) to study Paul's teachings about making life choices based on consideration of the weak.
(2) to identify stumbling blocks the learners encounter.
(3) to demonstrate a desire to live so as not to cause another to sin.

Pronunciation Guide:

Aesculapius (as klee' pee uhs)
Demeter (dih mee' tur}

Supplies:

Bibles, newsprint and marker, paper and pencils, hymnals; optional: dominoes, optional: Bible companions or Bible dictionaries

---

READING THE SCRIPTURE

NRSV
1 Corinthians 8:1-13

¹Now concerning food sacrificed to idols: we know that "all of us possess knowledge." Knowledge puffs up, but love builds up. ²Anyone who claims to know something does not yet have the necessary knowledge; ³but anyone who loves God is known by him.

⁴Hence, as to the eating of food offered to

NIV
1 Corinthians 8:1-13

¹Now about food sacrificed to idols: We know that we all possess knowledge. Knowledge puffs up, but love builds up. ²The man who thinks he knows something does not yet know as he ought to know. ³But the man who loves God is known by God.

⁴So then, about eating food sacrificed to idols: We know that an idol is nothing at all

idols, we know that "no idol in the world really exists," and that "there is no God but one." [5]Indeed, even though there may be so-called gods in heaven or on earth—as in fact there are many gods and many lords—[6]yet for us there is one God, the Father, from whom are all things and for whom we exist, and one Lord, Jesus Christ, through whom are all things and through whom we exist.

[7]It is not everyone, however, who has this knowledge. Since some have become so accustomed to idols until now, they still think of the food they eat as food offered to an idol; and their conscience, being weak, is defiled. [8]**"Food will not bring us close to God." We are no worse off if we do not eat, and no better off if we do. [9]But take care that this liberty of yours does not somehow become a stumbling block to the weak.** [10]For if others see you, who possess knowledge, eating in the temple of an idol, might they not, since their conscience is weak, be encouraged to the point of eating food sacrificed to idols? [11]So by your knowledge those weak believers for whom Christ died are destroyed. [12]But when you thus sin against members of your family, and wound their conscience when it is weak, you sin against Christ. [13]Therefore, if food is a cause of their falling, I will never eat meat, so that I may not cause one of them to fall.

in the world and that there is no God but one. [5]For even if there are so-called gods, whether in heaven or on earth (as indeed there are many "gods" and many "lords"), [6]yet for us there is but one God, the Father, from whom all things came and for whom we live; and there is but one Lord, Jesus Christ, through whom all things came and through whom we live.

[7]But not everyone knows this. Some people are still so accustomed to idols that when they eat such food they think of it as having been sacrificed to an idol, and since their conscience is weak, it is defiled. [8]**But food does not bring us near to God; we are no worse if we do not eat, and no better if we do.**

[9]**Be careful, however, that the exercise of your freedom does not become a stumbling block to the weak.** [10]For if anyone with a weak conscience sees you who have this knowledge eating in an idol's temple, won't he be emboldened to eat what has been sacrificed to idols? [11]So this weak brother, for whom Christ died, is destroyed by your knowledge. [12]When you sin against your brothers in this way and wound their weak conscience, you sin against Christ. [13]Therefore, if what I eat causes my brother to fall into sin, I will never eat meat again, so that I will not cause him to fall.

UNDERSTANDING THE SCRIPTURE

Introduction. Paul begins a lengthy discussion of the relationship of Christians to meats that had come from animals sacrificed to pagan gods (1 Corinthians 8:1–11:1). Paul discusses a variety of settings in which meat "offered to idols" might be consumed. One of these settings is the private home. Meat purchased in the marketplace in Corinth might have come straight from the farm. Sometimes, however, it was purchased from local temples after their sacrifices. Buying meat in the marketplace, then,

one could never be sure whether or not the meat was "tainted" by the spiritual power of an idolatrous ritual. Paul also discusses the public consumption of such meat on the grounds of a pagan temple, whether as part of a public ritual conducted in the temple itself (and the feast that followed) or as part of a private dinner party held in one of the dining rooms adjacent to several of the temples in Corinth, which could be rented out for private affairs.

Corinthian Christians were divided concerning the appropriateness of eating meat that had been sacrificed to an idol. One of the basic prohibitions circulated in the "Apostolic Decree" (see Acts 15) was the prohibition of eating food sacrificed to idols. Gentile converts were to make a clean and complete break with their idolatrous past and with everything that kept them looking back to that past. Some Christians in Corinth, then, were rather scrupulous about avoiding meat that had been involved in a pagan sacrifice, thinking it a violation of their commitment to the new faith and a spiritual danger to themselves.

Another group, however, claimed that, since idols were mere empty vanities concocted by their ancestors who did not know the One God as the converts now did, there could be no harm to eating meats that had been sacrificed in rituals before the idols. This group prided themselves on the "freedom" that their knowledge about the real emptiness of the idol gave them from any superstitious scruples about eating meat without worrying about its origin or about the context in which they ate it. What harm could it do to accept a dinner invitation from a pagan friend to dine in the "fellowship hall," as it were, beside the temple of Demeter or the shrine of Aesculapius? The motivation for doing so was not merely to satisfy one's craving for a good meal, but to maintain one's social, political, and economic connections in the community by continuing to hobnob with their non-Christian networks.

1 Corinthians 8:1-3. Paul begins by reframing the entire debate. The Corinthians were carrying on as if this were an intellectual debate about the nature of the pagan gods, and as if the "knowledge" inherent in the Christian confession of one God and one Lord (8:6) should lead everybody to throw off the shroud of superstition and act in line with the "freedom" party in Corinth. Life in the Christian community, however, is not about "knowledge." It is about "love." Paul would agree with those

Corinthians who said that food was a matter of indifference: One is neither harmed nor benefited by the meat itself. The community, however, is harmed when some members act in line with their knowledge, but not in line with love.

The Corinthians with "knowledge" that "liberated" them from superstition looked down on their sisters and brothers who still had scruples about the negative spiritual power of food offered to idols. They were "puffed up" against their fellow Christians, and the bond of unity was broken. Love, on the other hand, seeks what will best serve and protect one's sister or brother, building them up toward a stronger faith without pushing them into acting against their own consciences or beyond their own spiritual maturity. Paul will return to these themes in 1 Corinthians 13:1, 4. Love embodied a different kind of knowledge—a relational "knowing" of one's sisters and brothers, a knowledge of their limitations, and a willingness to respect where they are in their faith journey. It is by loving that we arrive at the only truly valuable kind of knowledge—being intimate with God, and being recognized by God as God's own.

1 Corinthians 8:4-6. There were indeed "many gods" and "many lords" revered in Corinth, and social, civic, and commerce guild events would always have some "religious" component. The central Jewish creed, that "the LORD is our God, the LORD alone" (Deuteronomy 6:4), was adopted by Christians and extended to include Jesus as the mediator of God's favor. Paul presents Jesus Christ here as the one through whom the earth was formed by God. This creed implied that the gods of the Greeks and Romans were mere shadows with no substance. Paul agrees in principle, but he holds that there is still a real spiritual power behind all false religions that distract people from the one God and one Lord—demonic forces (1 Corinthians 10:14-22). The "knowledge" that the pagan gods are not real does not give a person liberty to continue to associate with pagan religious practices: This would be a prideful and foolish flirtation with demonic influences.

1 Corinthians 8:7-13. The main problem Paul identifies in this situation is that believers who have scruples about eating food that had been sacrificed to idols might be pressured or encouraged to act against their own consciences if they saw their sisters and brothers indulging in dinner parties at the idol's temple. Carried along by the "flow," or shamed by the attitude of the "strong" toward their scruples, they might go to such a dinner party themselves. Later, however, they would wonder if they had sinned, feel "defiled" in their conscience, and thus have their communion with God interrupted by doubts and guilt. The "loving" course of action would be to safeguard the "weak," to make sure that they were never led to act against their own conscience, even if that meant that the "strong" inconvenienced or deprived themselves of something they knew to be morally neutral. If Christ's love for the "weak" was so great that he died on their behalf, is it too great a sacrifice for the "strong" to abstain from some craving, or from some social event, that might tear down the faith of another Christian?

INTERPRETING THE SCRIPTURE

My Rights, My Freedom

The "knowledge" that idols were "nothing" gave certain Christians the freedom to eat the food sacrificed to idols—both in private homes and in the banquet halls of the idols' temples—without fearing for their relationship with God. Paul largely agreed with their theological position, though he would have to warn them against entering any setting where idols would be worshiped. Paul took issue, however, with their attitude of insisting on their right to enjoy the prerogatives that their "knowledge" gave them. Instead of being so concerned with indulging themselves, they ought to have been more concerned with the impact their actions would have on the other Christians around them, especially those who were uncertain about food sacrificed to other gods.

Paul appears to interrupt the topic of what to do about food that had been sacrificed to an idol (chapters 8 and 10) when he talks about his own example in chapter 9. Some see this as a digression defending Paul's apostolic authority. Paul is not, however, changing the subject at all. Rather, he provides a different perspective on the same question by talking about his own use of the freedom he has in Christ. Paul claims certain "liberties" as a result of his position as a messenger of the gospel, especially the right to be supported financially by his converts and to be free of the burden of supporting himself at a trade. Paul, however, does not insist on his rights or on enjoying all the indulgences that belong to him. Rather, he makes it his aim to conduct himself in such a way that best enables his hearers to respond positively to, and grow in, the message about Jesus. If that means abstaining from his right to financial support so as not to give an occasion for stumbling ("Oh, he's just another preacher trying to take advantage of the credulous for his own gain"), then he abstains. If it means observing some basic kosher laws in order to better plant the gospel among Jews, he sets aside the freedom from those laws that he knows is his in Christ. The bottom line is that Paul uses his "freedom" always with a view to helping others come to faith and get better rooted in faith—never with a view to insisting on getting his own way or enjoying what is his by rights.

This is where Paul would challenge us, who are so conscious of our "rights" or our "freedom." Knowing our freedom in Christ, we are invited to consider how we are affecting other believers by our conduct and to voluntarily deny ourselves an indulgence where this would serve to protect the faith of another believer. Paul would not have us say: "No one is going to cramp my style. I know God is OK with my doing this activity, and I don't care what my unenlightened sisters and brothers think about it." On the other hand, Paul would not have us act out of fear for what our sisters and brothers will think of us, abstaining from the activities we know to be all right for us because we want to "look good" in their eyes. This would amount to allowing another person's scruples to destroy our own freedom (1 Corinthians 10:29). The middle road that Paul lays out is motivated by selfless concern and love for the sister or brother, not fear or concern about our appearance or reputation: "Do not seek your own advantage, but that of the other" (10:24; compare 10:33; Philippians 2:3-4).

A Very Modern Problem

The actual situation Paul describes is not that remote from modern Christianity, if we broaden our view to include our sisters and brothers across the globe. A Taiwanese student here found 1 Corinthians 8–10 deeply relevant for the situation of Christians in her homeland, where ancestor worship is an important part not only of private devotion but also of public life. Prayers and offerings to the ancestors played a part in civic festivals and other public functions. This poses a dilemma for Taiwanese Christians. On the one hand, many Christians regard it merely as part of their cultural heritage, and ascribe no religious significance to participating. On the other hand, it involves one in acts of worship directed toward figures other than the one God and the Christ. Many other Christians, then, regard it as part of their

pagan past and a sign of the idolatrous practice of their unconverted fellow citizens. In such a situation, Christians who have scruples about these rites can observe other Christians, who have "knowledge" about the innocence of the rites, participating in these rites (and, incidentally, continue to benefit from "fitting in" to Taiwanese culture). The latter may embolden the former to participate, but with doubts in their minds. At the end of the day, the scrupulous have acted against their own conscience and been "torn down" in their faith.

Becoming Sensitive to Stumbling Blocks

Where do we find analogous situations in Western culture? I was raised Episcopalian, so I have no trouble with light social drinking. However, I work and live among United Methodist and Brethren and Pentecostal sisters and brothers who have religious scruples about the consumption of any alcohol. Others, associating alcohol with their own involvement in a rather colorful past, would regard drinking as a kind of return to their sinful lifestyle—and an act that gave spiritual power over them to the destructive forces that formerly harmed their lives. When I go to the house of some Presbyterian colleagues, I have no problem with their opening wine (whether or not I actually imbibe). But if I invite some friends over who I think might be sensitive on this issue, I will certainly not offer wine or drink any myself. I would never wish by my example or my offer to entice someone into acting against his or her own conscience. Far better to be "inconvenienced" and to limit my own freedom.

Examples like this could be multiplied. I knew a strong Christian in college, a leader in a campus fellowship, who thought nothing of staying overnight at the apartment of his girlfriend. They knew they weren't having sexual relations, and that's all that mattered to them. However, other Christians in the same campus fellowship were being enticed by that example to act against their own consciences, of course going further than the first couple. This led to a useful examination of the relevance of 1 Corinthians 8 as a group. In some circles, joining organizations like the Masons is very popular, and many solid Christians have become involved. However, some Christians are taught to view joining any "secret society" as subverting their loyalty to the family of Christ in the church. Such sisters and brothers need to be safeguarded against defiling their own conscience—not merely encouraged to join.

Paul arranges his life so as to avoid putting impediments in the spiritual journeys of other Christians. He does not prescribe a series of rules to control everyone's behavior and cater to the scruples of the "weak," but he does insist that individual "liberty" in Christ be used with the spiritual good of the other in mind. In the absence of "law" and "rule-based religion," the importance of seeking out the leading of the Spirit in such matters becomes all the more important and fruitful.

SHARING THE SCRIPTURE

Preparing Our Hearts

This week's devotional reading is found in Mark 9:42-48. In his comments on how we are to handle temptations to sin, Jesus said, "If any of you put a stumbling block before one of these little ones who believe in me, it would be better for you if a great millstone were hung around your neck and you were thrown into the sea" (9:42). Jesus certainly minced no words. Yet, many of us set up stumbling blocks for others by the way we act. When have you fallen over a stumbling block in your Christian walk? When have you, perhaps inadvertently, set up a barrier for others? Meditate on these stumbling blocks and ask God for guidance in avoiding them.

Pray that you and the class participants will be careful about your actions and attitudes so as not to cause another to stumble.

Preparing Our Minds

Study the background and lesson Scripture, both of which are found in 1 Corinthians 8:1-13. As you read, think about how your actions affect others.

Write on newsprint:
❏ covenant for "Demonstrate a Desire to

Live so as Not to Cause Another to Sin."
❏ information for next week's lesson, found under "Continue the Journey."

Set up the dominoes prior to class if you plan to do this activity for Gather to Learn.

Gather reference books if you plan to do the optional activity for "Study Paul's Teachings About Making Life Choices Based on Consideration of the Weak." Check each book to be sure the students will be able to find appropriate information there.

Plan the lecture for "Study Paul's Teachings About Making Life Choices Based on Consideration of the Weak" if you choose to do that option.

LEADING THE CLASS

(1) Gather to Learn

❖ Welcome the class members and introduce any guests.

❖ Pray that the adults will be open to the Spirit's word for them today.

❖ **Option:** Stand up dominoes on a table where everyone can see this visual demonstration. The set-up may take a few minutes to do prior to class because you will need to make sure that the dominoes are spaced to fall in turn when the first one is pushed. When the class has gathered, just push the first domino, watch them all fall, and then discuss these questions. If you do not have dominoes set up, invite the class to envision them in their minds and then discuss these questions.

(1) What just happened?

(2) What does this experiment with dominoes suggest about how the action of one person can affect others?

❖ Read aloud today's focus statement: **People need to be aware of how their actions affect others. How can we show consideration to others? Paul urges Christians to live in such a way that we do not cause another to sin.**

(2) Study Paul's Teachings About Making Life Choices Based on Consideration of the Weak

❖ Use the information in "Introduction" in Understanding the Scripture to create a lecture that will set the stage for today's session. Students need to understand the settings in which meat was often eaten in order to understand what is at stake in Paul's argument.

❖ **Option:** Divide the class into groups and provide at least one Bible companion or Bible dictionary for each group, along with paper and pencils for each student. Ask them to search for information on food offered to idols and report back to the whole group.

❖ Choose two volunteers, one to read 1 Corinthians 8:1-6, and the other to read verses 7-13.

❖ Prompt the class to restate Paul's argument in their own words. Write key words and phrases on newsprint. As an option, do this as a lecture based on the material in Understanding the Scripture and the first two paragraphs of "My Rights, My Freedom" in Interpreting the Scripture.

(3) Identify Stumbling Blocks the Learners Encounter

❖ Read aloud the last paragraph of "My Rights, My Freedom" in Interpreting the Scripture.

❖ Move immediately to provide examples of modern stumbling blocks by retelling some of the anecdotes in "Becoming Sensitive to Stumbling Blocks" in Interpreting the Scripture.

❖ Allow a few moments for the students to consider silently the boundaries of their rights and freedom as Christians.

❖ Brainstorm with the students other stumbling blocks that have been thrown before them, or that have set before someone else, even inadvertently. List these ideas on newsprint. As the students speak, they do not have to state whether they set up or confronted a particular barrier. Affirm that in our increasingly secular world, more and more barriers seem to be thrown in the paths of Christians.

❖ Talk about Paul's antidote to such blocks, namely, acting in love and concern for all members of the community so that everyone is built up in the faith.

(1) What does acting in love mean in relation to the stumbling blocks the students have identified?

(2) What actions should you take?

❖ **Option:** The class may want to discuss how they can make reasonable accommodations to their culture without making unacceptable compromises. Perhaps some of the stumbling blocks already identified will be touchpoints for discussion.

(4) Demonstrate a Desire to Live so as Not to Cause Another to Sin

❖ Distribute paper and pencils. Ask the students to think about all that they have learned today and then copy and complete this covenant, which you will write on newsprint.

I,_____, covenant with you, O Lord, and with my brothers and sisters in Christ to live in love and take responsibility for my actions so as not to cause others to sin. To this end, I will . . . .

❖ Ask the participants to stand and read in unison the first sentence and then quietly say before God what it is that they will do to fulfill this covenant.

❖ Suggest that they place the covenant in their Bibles and review it regularly.

(5) Continue the Journey

❖ Pray that the students will act with love, even if that means that they must set aside some actions that they could do in good conscience.

❖ Read aloud this preparation for next week's lesson. You may also want to post it on newsprint for the students to copy. **Prepare for next week's session, "Called to Win," by reading 1 Corinthians 9:24–10:13, which is both the background and lesson Scripture for this session. As you read, focus on these ideas: Many people struggle to follow through with commitments. What is the key to persevering in life and seeing commitments through to the end? Paul says that those who rely on God's strength are the ones who will reach their goal.**

❖ Read aloud the following three ideas. Challenge the students to commit themselves to use these activities as a springboard to spiritual growth.

(1) Be alert for opportunities to act in love by setting aside something you may do in good conscience that might raise questions or doubts for someone else.

(2) Recall that "idol meat" was a hot issue in the early church. Make a list of the hot issues in our day. Write a few words about how you react to each one and how other people of faith may react. If there are differences, what does that suggest that you might do as a matter of loving principle when confronted by these issues?

(3) Consider your own diet. Do you "look down" on people who make different choices? Do you feel that others judge you for your choices? What criteria determine the kinds of foods and beverages you consume? How are these criteria in keeping with the principle of love that is so important to Paul?

❖ Sing or read aloud "Jesus, United by Thy Grace."

❖ Close the session with this benediction, which you may want the class members to echo after you: **Go forth committed to serve, obey, and give as people who have been called to live faithfully in Christian community. Amen.**

UNIT 2: CALLED TO OBEDIENCE
CALLED TO WIN

PREVIEWING THE LESSON

Lesson Scripture: 1 Corinthians 9:24–10:13
Background Scripture: 1 Corinthians 9:24–10:13
Key Verse: 1 Corinthians 9:24

Focus of the Lesson:
Many people struggle to follow through with commitments. What is the key to persevering in life and seeing commitments through to the end? Paul says that those who rely on God's strength are the ones who will reach their goal.

Goals for the Learners:
(1) to review Paul's teaching on the need to persevere in self-discipline.
(2) to illustrate Paul's words with examples from their own lives.
(3) to engage in at least two spiritual disciplines this week.

Pronunciation Guide:
Baal-peor (bay' uhl pee' or)

Supplies:
Bibles, newsprint and marker, paper and pencils, hymnals; optional: video or DVD of athletes in training and appropriate player

---

READING THE SCRIPTURE

NRSV
1 Corinthians 9:24-27

24Do you not know that in a race the runners all compete, but only one receives the prize? Run in such a way that you may win it. 25Athletes exercise self-control in all things; they do it to receive a perishable wreath, but we an imperishable one. 26So I do not run aimlessly, nor do I box as though beating the air; 27but I punish my body and enslave it, so that after proclaiming to others I myself should not be disqualified.

NIV
1 Corinthians 9:24-27

24Do you not know that in a race all the runners run, but only one gets the prize? Run in such a way as to get the prize. 25Everyone who competes in the games goes into strict training. They do it to get a crown that will not last; but we do it to get a crown that will last forever. 26Therefore I do not run like a man running aimlessly; I do not fight like a man beating the air. 27No, I beat my body and make it my slave so that after I

1 Corinthians 10:1-13

¹I do not want you to be unaware, brothers and sisters, that our ancestors were all under the cloud, and all passed through the sea, ²and all were baptized into Moses in the cloud and in the sea, ³and all ate the same spiritual food, ⁴and all drank the same spiritual drink. For they drank from the spiritual rock that followed them, and the rock was Christ. ⁵Nevertheless, God was not pleased with most of them, and they were struck down in the wilderness.

⁶Now these things occurred as examples for us, so that we might not desire evil as they did. ⁷Do not become idolaters as some of them did; as it is written, "The people sat down to eat and drink, and they rose up to play." ⁸We must not indulge in sexual immorality as some of them did, and twenty-three thousand fell in a single day. ⁹We must not put Christ to the test, as some of them did, and were destroyed by serpents. ¹⁰And do not complain as some of them did, and were destroyed by the destroyer. ¹¹These things happened to them to serve as an example, and they were written down to instruct us, on whom the ends of the ages have come. ¹²So if you think you are standing, watch out that you do not fall. ¹³No testing has overtaken you that is not common to everyone. God is faithful, and he will not let you be tested beyond your strength, but with the testing he will also provide the way out so that you may be able to endure it.

have preached to others, I myself will not be disqualified for the prize.

1 Corinthians 10:1-13

¹For I do not want you to be ignorant of the fact, brothers, that our forefathers were all under the cloud and that they all passed through the sea. ²They were all baptized into Moses in the cloud and in the sea. ³They all ate the same spiritual food ⁴and drank the same spiritual drink; for they drank from the spiritual rock that accompanied them, and that rock was Christ. ⁵Nevertheless, God was not pleased with most of them; their bodies were scattered over the desert.

⁶Now these things occurred as examples to keep us from setting our hearts on evil things as they did. ⁷Do not be idolaters, as some of them were; as it is written: "The people sat down to eat and drink and got up to indulge in pagan revelry." ⁸We should not commit sexual immorality, as some of them did—and in one day twenty-three thousand of them died. ⁹We should not test the Lord, as some of them did—and were killed by snakes. ¹⁰And do not grumble, as some of them did—and were killed by the destroying angel.

¹¹These things happened to them as examples and were written down as warnings for us, on whom the fulfillment of the ages has come. ¹²So, if you think you are standing firm, be careful that you don't fall! ¹³No temptation has seized you except what is common to man. And God is faithful; he will not let you be tempted beyond what you can bear. But when you are tempted, he will also provide a way out so that you can stand up under it.

UNDERSTANDING THE SCRIPTURE

1 Corinthians 9:24-27. Athletic images would have been quite meaningful for the Corinthians, who hosted several important athletic competitions for all of Greece in addition to having regular local athletic competitions. They had seen many people put themselves through rigorous training programs requiring effort, discipline, and self-sacrifice merely for the honor of being crowned with a wreath made of olive branches or celery, which would soon wither up. How much more, Paul argues, should they—as he does—exercise self-control, for example in the matter of abstaining from meat sacrificed to an idol if that will help a sister or brother keep running well, in pursuit of honor in heaven that will never fade. Paul shared the view of many philosophers that the real contest involves overcoming not another athlete, but one's own cravings, desires, and weaknesses so that one can grow in virtue.

1 Corinthians 10:1-5. In order to understand 1 Corinthians 10:1-10, we need to keep turning back to stories about the Hebrews' exodus from Egypt and their wanderings in the desert, for in the short space of ten verses Paul points the hearers back to no fewer than eight episodes from Exodus and Numbers as admonitory "examples" for Christians. These would have the force of historical precedents—proofs that the dangers Paul sees facing the Corinthian Christians are in fact real, if they persist in factious, self-indulgent behavior.

The Hebrews leaving Egypt enjoyed God's presence and guidance, as he went before them in a "pillar of cloud" (Exodus 13:21), and enjoyed God's deliverance from slavery as they passed through the waters of the Red Sea, which becomes a favorite symbol for baptism (as does Noah's passage through the waters of the flood in 1 Peter 3:20-21). The manna they ate was called "the bread of angels" in Psalm 78:25, and the water they drank was miraculously provided in the desert, both thus appropriately called "spiritual" sustenance. The Pentateuch only speaks of God miraculously providing water toward the beginning (Exodus 17) and the end (Numbers 20) of their journey. What did the Israelites do for water in between? A tradition arose that the waters that sprang from the rock followed the Israelites through the desert to supply them. Paul reflects a development

that suggests that the rock itself followed them, making it even more suitable as a symbol for Christ's presence nourishing God's people.

All of these become "types"—foreshadows—of Christian liturgical experience in baptism and holy communion, and the experience of knowing God's guidance through the Holy Spirit so vividly present in their midst (as was the cloud over Israel). The Hebrews' spiritual experiences, however, did not guarantee their safe passage to the promised land. Rather, after they rebelled against God's command to take the land (Numbers 14), everyone that came out with Moses through the Red Sea (save for Joshua and Caleb) was condemned to wander in the desert until they dropped dead. This serves as a warning to the Corinthian Christians not to presume on their spiritual status and the spiritual power God bestows upon them. Unless accompanied by loyalty to God and by conduct befitting those who follow the selfless, crucified Redeemer they, too, may come to a bad end.

1 Corinthians 10:6-11. Paul uses these examples as a word of caution to those believers who are overly confident in their knowledge, lest their cravings actually tend toward what is sinful, and not merely morally indifferent. Paul specifically has participation in idolatrous rituals in mind, something that the "strong" in Corinth were far too complacent about with their "knowledge" that an idol was nothing. Verse 7, which quotes Exodus 32:6, refers to the golden calf incident, where sexual immorality, eating, and idolatry are closely linked. Verse 8 refers to the incident of Baal-Peor in Numbers 25:1-9, another story in which sexual immorality is joined with going after other gods (the gods of the Moabites). This consistent joining of idolatrous feasts and sexual promiscuity reflects the realities of evening entertainment in Corinth (see also the linking of the two in the Apostolic Decree of Acts 15:28-29 and in Revelation 2:14-15, 20).

Verse 9 recalls Numbers 21:4-6, where the Hebrews grumble about the food that God provided (which one tends to juxtapose with the "fleshpots of Egypt") and against Moses' leadership. Verse 10 conjures up similar stories. The reference here is somewhat vague. Paul may refer to the rebellion against Moses' leadership by Korah and his family, whose cause is then taken up by the people as a whole. This would explain the reference to "the destroyer," since by the intertestamental period the plague in Numbers 16 was attributed to the action of "a fiery angel" punishing the people (see 4 Maccabees 7:11), a tradition of which Paul seems to be aware. However, the incident of complaining in Numbers 11:4-6 might be in view, where the Hebrews complain against Moses and against God's provision of manna, craving the "meat" of Egypt instead. This episode ends with God killing a great number of the Hebrews "while the meat was still between their teeth" (Numbers 11:33). This story would certainly be a relevant warning to the Corinthians whose appetites and social habits were disturbing the unity of the congregation, jeopardizing the spiritual safety of the "weak,"

and involving them too closely in idolatrous settings.

The Corinthian Christians now enjoy the spiritual realities and promises toward which all of sacred history had been moving as its goal and end (hence, "the ends of the ages"), and so must be especially careful to honor those spiritual benefits with diligent pursuit of the congregation's good and with exceptional self-control with regard to all questionable cravings.

1 Corinthians 10:12-13. Paul has come full circle here, first standing alongside the "strong" to help them think about the spiritual good of the "weak," now confronting the "strong" face-to-face about their own spiritual health. Are they so sure that their practices do not harm their walk with the one God? Are they so sure that the idol's temple and its benefits hold no spiritual power over them? Paul makes them re-examine their position, to discern afresh whether they are walking in their "freedom" or into "temptation." Here, the way out from the latter is simply to "flee from the worship of idols" (10:14) rather than flirt with it from a supposedly "safe" distance.

INTERPRETING THE SCRIPTURE

Eyes on the Prize

By drawing an analogy with the kind of intense training and rigorous exercise that went into competing in the Isthmian Games or any of the other athletic events that would have been well known to the Corinthians, Paul calls attention to the level of commitment that is required of those who desire to arrive at the goal for which they began their journey of faith in Christ. That goal involves the discovery of all the spiritual gifts and riches that God has for God's children, progress toward becoming more and more like Jesus in our hearts and

lives, and finally experiencing the life of the world to come and the power of the resurrection.

Paul reminds us, however, that it is not enough simply to be baptized, receive communion, and sit in church. This is an enterprise that will call for discipline, rigor, and commitment every day of our lives. How can we keep focused and keep commitment strong? Paul points first of all to the challenge of self-mastery. The image of beating his body and subduing it refers not to actual mistreatment of the self, such as was practiced by the more radical Stoic and Cynic philosophers and then by Christian ascetics through the centuries. Rather, it refers to the battle for domination within a person between reason and the passions. Paul refuses to allow the passions of the flesh—the appetites or cravings, the emotions, and the like or dislike for certain sensations—to gain the upper hand in his life. Rather, he keeps his life on course by exercising self-control over the passions and "beating" them down so that they never lead him on a detour away from the goal of discipleship.

Spiritual disciplines such as fasting, prayer vigils, and simplicity of life are time-honored and effective means by which Christians have combated the distractions that drain off commitment to the race of faith. All provide opportunities to deprive the cravings of the eyes and the body, weakening their power, for the sake of greater spiritual freedom and connection with God. Another important part of our training is having regular times of solitude with God in prayer and meditation. As God becomes more and more real and personal, and as the joys of knowing God's presence become more and more "felt," our commitment to keep investing in what makes our sisters, brothers, and ourselves grow in Christian maturity increases.

Knowledge or Arrogant Disregard of Spiritual Danger?

Although Paul does seem to agree with the "strong" in Corinth that "no idol in the world really exists" and that there is only one God in the cosmos (8:4), Paul also knows that their boasting in this knowledge betrays their naiveté about spiritual dangers. The warnings in 1 Corinthians 10:1-13 no doubt catch the "strong" off guard, even as they continue to caution the "weak" not to allow the pressures or examples of others lead them to act against their own consciences. Paul will go on in verses 19-20 to point out to those who assumed that an idol is nothing that, in fact, demonic forces surrounded idolatrous rituals, keeping people separated

from the One God and worshiping the symbols of their own fallen way of life.

By attending events where idols were worshiped, the believers were opening themselves up again to those forces that draw people away from God, enticing them with the social networks that they would continue to enjoy, the business and political connections that they would maintain, as well as with the satisfying of the cravings of belly and below. Their "knowledge" might hold true for the meat itself, but it blinded them to the spiritual power of some of the settings where they were eating the meat.

We, too, boast of great stores of "knowledge." We continually hear claims made that we understand the world, nature, biology, and the like so much better than Paul and the other early Christian leaders, with the result that we think ourselves "free" to indulge in many activities against which "superstition" had barred the door in more "medieval" times. When it comes to ethical behavior, we "know better" than our church's social principles or articles of faith, or the Scriptures themselves. It is probably quite relevant that Paul's Old Testament examples focus on religious syncretism, questionable sexual indulgence, and a factious, rebellious spirit, all of which continue to be focal points of contention in the church and potential traps to "strong" and "weak" alike. In all such cases, Paul warns us: Standing on such knowledge, beware lest you fall. Wherever "knowledge" is really just making room for us to indulge our appetites and cravings, we should beware of being led astray as our rationalizations legitimate our gratifying of the passions. There might indeed be spiritual forces of darkness using our pride and our "knowledge" to keep us from experiencing the full freedom of children of God.

Lead Us out of Temptation

Paul is challenging the Corinthian Christians to re-examine the attachments they have to settings where idols are worshiped or honored, as well as their motivations for continuing to associate with their non-Christian neighbors, business associates, and political allies in those settings. Could it be that they have walked into temptation, rather than exercised genuine Christian freedom? Are they chasing after distractions from their journey of faith, rather than walking in line with the Holy Spirit?

One of the greatest challenges to Christian commitment is the presence of other attractions that arouse our cravings and promise to bring satisfaction to our life. These diversions distract us from our race toward maturity in Christ all the more since they are visible, tangible, and everywhere present. They do not have to be "spiritually discerned" (2:14), as do the benefits of remaining close to God; they are everywhere celebrated in media, in pop culture, in the lifestyles of those around us.

The drive for attaining wealth and the enjoyment of creature comforts surrounds Western Christians, and often catches us up into its dragnet. How much time, energy, and desire is taken away from our own pursuit of friendship with God and our helping our families and friends in the faith find deeper roots in God by our succumbing to the temptation of wanting "more," always "more" of the consumer's ideal? Many Christians wrestle with sexual addictions, substance addictions, or performance addictions, tempted to fulfill core longings in sinful ways. Where does slavery of this kind drain away our strength and commitment for living for God, following his Spirit rather than our compulsions?

Paul calls us to self-examination on this point, to see how the temptations of a secular mindset, of gratifying our temporal cravings, have taken hold of our lives. But he does so with words of assurance. Whatever a faithful response to God requires in our life situation, God provides the strength to make that response. And, as another early Christian author reminds us, Jesus walks alongside us as one who "in every respect has been tested as we are, yet without sin" (Hebrews 4:15). Because of his tender love for us, we are emboldened to face our temptations squarely and honestly, knowing that there is no test of our commitment that he would fail to equip us to pass when we call on him for help (Hebrews 2:17-18).

SHARING THE SCRIPTURE

Preparing Our Hearts

This week's devotional reading is found in Hebrews 12:1-12. In this familiar reading that reminds us a "cloud of witnesses" is watching over us, we are encouraged to "run with perseverance the race that is set before us" (12:1). We know the race is difficult, and that some runners will drop out before they reach the finish line. What enables you to keep running the race of the Christian life? How do you remain true to your spiritual commitments? If you find these commitments challenging, what can help you stay on the racecourse? Envision yourself running this race; see yourself victoriously crossing the finish line.

Pray that you and the class members will follow the example of Jesus and stay the course until the end.

Preparing Our Minds

Study the background and lesson Scripture, both of which are found in 1 Corinthians 9:24–10:13. As you read this passage, think about keys to seeing commitments through to the end.

Write on newsprint:
- ❏ list of spiritual disciplines for "Engage in at Least Two Spiritual Disciplines This Week."
- ❏ information for next week's lesson, found under "Continue the Journey."

Set up a VCR or DVD player if you plan to use the option under Gather to Learn.

LEADING THE CLASS

(1) Gather to Learn

❖ Welcome the class members and introduce any guests.

❖ Pray that each one who is present will be challenged by the Spirit to endure in their Christian faith.

❖ Begin a discussion about the teams—any sport, any level of competition—that class members participate in or support. After identifying these teams, talk about what makes them winners. Or, what they need to do, collectively and individually, to overcome their problems so as to become winners.

❖ **Option:** Show a video of athletes in training and continue the discussion by talking about how they train. Focus on effort and commitment, rather than specific training techniques.

❖ Read aloud today's focus statement: **Many people struggle to follow through with commitments. What is the key to persevering in life and seeing commitments through to the end? Paul says that those who rely on God's strength are the ones who will reach their goal.**

(2) Review Paul's Teaching on the Need to Persevere in Self-discipline

❖ Choose a volunteer to read 1 Corinthians 9:24-27. Point out that verse 24 is today's key verse.
- ■ Use information from 9:24-27 in Understanding the Scripture to introduce this passage.
- ■ Read aloud "Eyes on the Prize" in Interpreting the Scripture. Read again the first three sentences of the second paragraph. Invite the students to respond to the question by talking about ways they "keep focused and keep commitment strong."

❖ Select someone to read 1 Corinthians 10:1-13.
- ■ Invite the students to comment on any images in this passage that they find familiar.
- ■ Present a brief lecture using information from Understanding the Scripture to unpack these images. If time permits, have the students turn in their Bibles to the cited references.

(3) Illustrate Paul's Words with Examples from the Learners' Lives

❖ Point out that Paul's words probably caught off guard the "strong," who believe that an idol is really nothing.

❖ List on newsprint idols in our society that the class can identify. (Be sure to include superstars in sports and entertainment, money, possessions, status, position at work, sex, and popularity.)

❖ Talk with the class in general terms about how these idols can interfere with our ability to run the race of the Christian life.

❖ Distribute paper and pencils. Ask the students to respond confidentially to these questions. Those who choose not to write may simply meditate on their answers.
- **(1) Which idols tempt you to swerve away from your commitments to Christ?** (pause)
- **(2) How do you handle such temptations?** (pause)
- **(3) What helps you to get back on track?** (pause)

(4) Engage in at Least Two Spiritual Disciplines This Week

❖ Note that the purpose of spiritual disciplines is to help us become the people that

God wants us to be. These disciplines are not ends in themselves but tools for this task.

❖ Post this list of spiritual disciplines, which you have written prior to the session: *prayer, meditation, worship, devotional Bible reading, labyrinth walking, journaling, fasting, retreat, pilgrimage, simple living.*

❖ Invite the students to add other disciplines to the list.

❖ Encourage everyone to talk about experiences they have had with any of these disciplines.

❖ Ask each student to make a silent commitment to engage in at least two of these disciplines a week.

❖ Conclude this part of the lesson by doing this guided imagery. Ask the students to get comfortable in their seats and close their eyes to envision the scenes that you will read. Be sure to pause long enough for them to become engaged in each portion of this activity.

■ **Imagine yourself as a runner, bicyclist, or swimmer. You are waiting for the gun to sound to begin a very competitive race. What are you thinking right now about your training and your chance for victory?** (pause)

■ **Hear the starter's pistol and feel yourself move away from the starting line. What are your thoughts focused on as you push ahead?** (pause)

■ **See something that distracts you. What is it? How will you refocus your attention?** (pause)

■ **Envision yourself back on course and racing hard. The finish line is now in sight but your body is exhausted. What will empower you to finish, now that you have come this far?** (pause)

■ **Hear the roar of the crowd as you cross the finish line and take a victory lap. Give thanks for winning this victory.** (pause)

(5) Continue the Journey

❖ Conclude the guided imagery by praying that the participants will go forth from class with renewed commitments to run the race of the Christian life in such a way that they are victorious.

❖ Read aloud this preparation for next week's lesson. You may also want to post it on newsprint for the students to copy. **Prepare for next week's session, "All for One," by reading the background and lesson Scripture from 1 Corinthians 12:1-13. Center your thoughts on this focus statement: Everyone has something to contribute to the common good. How should we use our gifts, abilities, and talents? Paul indicates that every believer has received a spiritual gift that can be used to build up the body of Christ.**

❖ Read aloud the following three ideas. Challenge the students to commit themselves to use these activities as a springboard to spiritual growth.

(1) **Learn more about spiritual disciplines by consulting one of the numerous books on this topic that you can find in your local library or bookstore, or browse "spiritual disciplines" on the Internet.**

(2) **Try one spiritual discipline that is unfamiliar to you this week. Evaluate your response to it. Not all disciplines work equally well for each person, so decide if you will continue to use this one or not.**

(3) **Support someone who is suffering the consequences of poor choices. Do whatever you can to help this person get back on the right track.**

❖ Sing or read aloud "Victory in Jesus."

❖ Close the session with this benediction, which you may want the class members to echo after you: **Go forth committed to serve, obey, and give as people who have been called to live faithfully in Christian community. Amen.**

UNIT 2: CALLED TO OBEDIENCE

ALL FOR ONE

PREVIEWING THE LESSON

Lesson Scripture: 1 Corinthians 12:1-13
Background Scripture: 1 Corinthians 12:1-13
Key Verse: 1 Corinthians 12:7

Focus of the Lesson:

Everyone has something to contribute to the common good. How should we use our gifts, abilities, and talents? Paul indicates that every believer has received a spiritual gift that can be used to build up the body of Christ.

Goals for the Learners:

(1) to explore the various spiritual gifts that Paul says are spread among the church's members for the common good.
(2) to identify at least one gift they have received from God.
(3) to commit to using their God-given gifts for the common good.

Pronunciation Guide:

Marcus Aurelius (mar' kes o ree' lee os)
Menius Agrippa (may nee us uh grip' uh)

Supplies:

Bibles, newsprint and marker, paper and pencils, hymnals, craft paper for drawing of human body

READING THE SCRIPTURE

NRSV

1 Corinthians 12:1-13

[1]Now concerning spiritual gifts, brothers and sisters, I do not want you to be uninformed. [2]You know that when you were pagans, you were enticed and led astray to idols that could not speak. [3]Therefore I want you to understand that no one speaking by the Spirit of God ever says "Let Jesus be

NIV

1 Corinthians 12:1-13

[1]Now about spiritual gifts, brothers, I do not want you to be ignorant. [2]You know that when you were pagans, somehow or other you were influenced and led astray to mute idols. [3]Therefore I tell you that no one who is speaking by the Spirit of God says, "Jesus be cursed," and no one can say, "Jesus is Lord," except by the Holy Spirit.

cursed!" and no one can say "Jesus is Lord" except by the Holy Spirit.

⁴Now there are varieties of gifts, but the same Spirit; ⁵and there are varieties of services, but the same Lord; ⁶and there are varieties of activities, but it is the same God who activates all of them in everyone. **⁷To each is given the manifestation of the Spirit for the common good.** ⁸To one is given through the Spirit the utterance of wisdom, and to another the utterance of knowledge according to the same Spirit, ⁹to another faith by the same Spirit, to another gifts of healing by the one Spirit, ¹⁰to another the working of miracles, to another prophecy, to another the discernment of spirits, to another various kinds of tongues, to another the interpretation of tongues. ¹¹All these are activated by one and the same Spirit, who allots to each one individually just as the Spirit chooses.

¹²For just as the body is one and has many members, and all the members of the body, though many, are one body, so it is with Christ. ¹³For in the one Spirit we were all baptized into one body—Jews or Greeks, slaves or free—and we were all made to drink of one Spirit.

⁴There are different kinds of gifts, but the same Spirit. ⁵There are different kinds of service, but the same Lord. ⁶There are different kinds of working, but the same God works all of them in all men.

⁷Now to each one the manifestation of the Spirit is given for the common good. ⁸To one there is given through the Spirit the message of wisdom, to another the message of knowledge by means of the same Spirit, ⁹to another faith by the same Spirit, to another gifts of healing by that one Spirit, ¹⁰to another miraculous powers, to another prophecy, to another distinguishing between spirits, to another speaking in different kinds of tongues, and to still another the interpretation of tongues. ¹¹All these are the work of one and the same Spirit, and he gives them to each one, just as he determines.

¹²The body is a unit, though it is made up of many parts; and though all its parts are many, they form one body. So it is with Christ. ¹³For we were all baptized by one Spirit into one body—whether Jews or Greeks, slave or free—and we were all given the one Spirit to drink.

UNDERSTANDING THE SCRIPTURE

1 Corinthians 12:1-3. The Corinthian Christians no doubt prided themselves on their spiritual endowments. Paul's effusive opening paragraphs in 1 Corinthians greet the church with the image it no doubt had of itself—"not lacking an any spiritual gift" (1:7). However, they are not all using these gifts wisely. Paul sets out here to inform them, to enlighten them in their ignorance, about these gifts that they are wielding, like children who have found a parent's handgun. Paul begins by contrasting the "spirits" that they formerly encountered before their conversion, when they witnessed—and perhaps even experienced—the ecstasy of being possessed by a supernatural being,

with the Spirit that now possesses and manifests its graces in the Christian assembly. Mysterious and impressive spiritual displays (ecstatic speech being a common one) contributed to their being "led astray" to continue in the worship of idols. The phenomena they witnessed, however, were manifestations of other spirits, demons (see 1 Corinthians 10:14-22) involving the pagans in their blasphemies against God and God's Messiah. They have come into a new religious experience, however, upon their conversion to Christ, where it is the Holy Spirit that directs the manifestation of spiritual gifts—and the rules are quite different from what they have come to expect from their education in a culture that used everything, including religious displays, to enhance personal standing and prestige.

1 Corinthians 12:4-7. Paul underscores the importance of the diversity of spiritual gifts. This was rendered necessary by the fact that certain gifts, as a result of their flashier and more visibly "spiritual" nature, tended to be overvalued and overused in the congregation, while other, necessary gifts were being neglected and undervalued. The source of the gifts provides unity ("the same God," "the same Lord," and "the same Spirit"), so that diversity never need threaten our sense of unity and identity (see also 12:12-13), but the variety of the gifts is essential to the functioning of the church. Paul will develop this same point in 1 Corinthians 12:14-19 using the metaphor of the human body, a variety of parts with a variety of functions and "gifts," all of which are essential to the collective functioning of the whole. No member should feel "left out"; each has something critical to contribute for the well-being and complete functioning of the whole.

The Spirit gives these endowments "for the common good" (12:7; see also 14:12). They are not a matter of private spiritual experiences, and certainly not a badge of spirituality by which some in the congregation can promote themselves as "better" than others or more worthy of precedence in the church. Paul underscores their character as "gift" (hence not a cause for boasting; see 1 Corinthians 4:7), as "service" (hence not an opportunity for self-promotion or claiming power and precedence in the congregation), and as the "working" not of individual people, but of God (hence not a source for personal recognition, but another reason to recognize God for God's provisions).

1 Corinthians 12:8-11. Paul lists several kinds of spiritual gifts here. Fundamental to his understanding of these gifts is his conviction that God's Spirit is alive and active and engaged with God's church: The Spirit can be expected to intervene frequently in the life of the church by means of the gifts the Spirit gives each of its members for the good of all. The Spirit can provide much-needed guidance and knowledge for the whole church as it faces particular challenges through those believers that are receptive to the Spirit's voice. "Faith" is here a special gift of seeing and trusting what God is doing beyond the faith that all believers have, connected perhaps with a specific mission or work that God is calling the church to perform. The ability to convey healing or to work some other marvel (perhaps referring to exorcisms), to bring a "word from the Lord" with regard to present or future challenges, to discern when a prophecy is from God or from some other source (see 1 Thessalonians 5:20-22; 1 John 4:1), to speak in strange human or angelic languages, and to interpret what is said in an unknown language are all expected ways by which the Spirit helps the church fulfill its mission and grow into the full stature of Christ. The latter two pairs exemplify the complementary nature of these charismatic endowments: Prophecy requires others to have the gift of discernment; speaking in tongues requires that others have the gift of interpretation or translation. Paul will add several other "gifts" in 12:28—the gifts of leadership (a primary task of leaders being the maintenance of harmony) and providing various kinds of help and service.

Verse 11 underscores again the theme of stewardship. The Spirit decides who will exercise what gift, and the Spirit manifests himself in the gifts. They cannot be interpreted or used as a spirituality ranking within the church (compare 1 Corinthians 4:7).

1 Corinthians 12:12-13. Many ancient authors used the metaphor of the body, a unity composed of many parts of varying status working together for the common good, as an image for the well-functioning political body. Menius Agrippa used this image in a time of civil distress when the economically and politically weaker members became factious and disruptive as a means of stressing that the well-to-do were in fact doing their part to help the whole body, so that the plebeians should keep the peace and harmony of the city intact for the good of all. The image was also applied in less politically manipulative ways by Plato and Marcus Aurelius to underscore the fundamental connectedness between people in a civic body.

Paul also uses this image to teach a particular social body, the Corinthian congregation, that participation in the church is not a matter for pursuing individual profit or advantage at the expense of others. Rather, each Christian finds advantage only as the whole congregation is built up, edified, made stronger in faith, made more secure by mutual love and acts of service. Paul's vision for Christian community, however, is vastly different from Menius Agrippa's vision for Roman community. Rather than urging the weaker members to submit to the stronger, Paul exhorts the more honorable, gifted, and prominent to give attention to "clothing" the weaker members with honor, recognition, and a sense of being valued in the community (see 1 Corinthians 12:22-25).

INTERPRETING THE SCRIPTURE

The Diversity of Spiritual Gifts

Paul's teaching about spiritual gifts is of vital importance to every local congregation, since his basic message is that everyone—*everyone*—has something to contribute that is vital to the church's ability to fulfill its mission. The Spirit wants to work not only through the paid staff or through the more prominent and naturally gifted individuals, but also through every member of the body of Christ.

Natural gifts and abilities are important, and we do not want to undervalue these in any way. However, Paul tells us that there are other modes by which individual Christians can contribute to the life and mission of the Church. "Spiritual" gifts are exactly that—endowments by the Holy Spirit, not talents we have developed through painstaking practice and study. I have devoted myself to the study and practice of organ playing and choral directing, and this is the primary way I have contributed to the life of local congregations. But this is not what Paul has in mind when he speaks of "spiritual" gifts.

Spiritual gifts are manifestations of the Holy Spirit in our midst as a gathered body of believers. They extend beyond our natural abilities, and bring God's abilities to bear on the life of the church, though they often correspond to the tendencies and inclinations of our renewed nature. These tend to be associated with the "charismatic" churches, and one of the great contributions those churches have made to the life of the church universal is to remind us that God moves in ways beyond rational thought and breaks into our lives in ways beyond natural human abilities.

I have been privileged to be associated with several churches (one Episcopal, one United Methodist, one Assemblies of God) where the discovery and exercise of spiritual gifts was supported. In these churches, people receive a "word from the Lord" (a "prophetic utterance") that brings timely knowledge or wisdom or diagnosis, which the church as a whole can then weigh and process. Sometimes it turns out to be a fabrication of the speaker; often it turns out to be a word on target for the spiritual health and direction of the congregation. The gift of "discernment of spirits" assists the church both as it attempts to verify whether or not the Spirit is at work behind a gift and as it attempts to minister to people whose issues may derive from spiritual oppression as well as "natural" sources. The gift of "faith" assists, for example, those who pray for the healing or deliverance of an individual, as well as those who venture into a new mission or outreach. Gifts of leadership and helping are other ways in which the Spirit moves through individuals to assist the church in the discernment, administration, and execution of its mission to individuals, the community, and the larger world.

Many "spiritual gifts inventories" exist to help believers discern the ways in which the Spirit works through them for the good of others. These are readily available in print form as well as online (try a web search for "spiritual gifts inventory" using www.google.com or some other search engine). These will use the vocabulary of 1 Corinthians 12:8-10 as well as the vocabulary of 1 Corinthians 12:28-30 and Romans 12:6-8. Paul's words strongly commend making this a part of your church's "curriculum"—learning how to recognize the prompting of the Spirit, learning the ways in which the Spirit has equipped you in particular circumstances to exercise spiritual gifts, becoming sensitive to and discerning of the ways in which the Spirit manifests gifts through the people around you and through yourself.

The Focal Point of Spiritual Gifts

One of the greatest concerns about "spiritual gifts" is their misuse or abuse. We hear of extravagant and showy displays of "spiritual manifestations" and question the legitimacy of the whole. Or we witness ways in which an individual's or group's pride swells as that entity becomes more "spiritual" than others in the church. I have also experienced the use of "spiritual gifts" to try to manipulate individuals and church leaders. It is important to remember that these concerns are not modern phenomena—they account for a large part of 1 Corinthians as well. Paul was no less concerned than the modern Presbyterian or United Methodist about things "getting out of hand" or about spiritual gifts leading to a kind of spiritual elitism and, ultimately, division in a church. Paul was not prepared, however, to throw out the Spirit with the sinful use of the Spirit.

As an answer to such concerns, Paul emphasizes two focal points for the right use of spiritual gifts. The first is their source, namely God. This has been a theme running throughout 1 Corinthians. Apostles are not focal points for boasting, since God is the one giving all the increase to the crop they plant (3:5-9). All spiritual goods are gifts from God, and therefore not causes for pride or divisive elitism (4:7). To "know" spiritual truths that make one proud and haughty is nothing compared to being "known" by God in loving relationship (8:1-3). So also the person who moves in a spiritual gift can never forget that no virtue or merit of his or her own is behind it, but rather the God whose Spirit disposes as it pleases God (12:7, 11, 18).

The second focus is the purpose of these gifts. They are never given for the sake of advancing personal agendas or feeding self-aggrandizement. Rather, they are given for the strengthening of the whole church and the fulfilling of its mission. The "gifts" are not for the users, but for the whole body of believers who will be benefited by them. The "body" metaphor is very important here. We need to move beyond our model of self and self-interest toward a model of being one part of a well-functioning whole, and putting the interests of that whole first.

Life as a "Body"

Understanding the church as a body, and ourselves individually as component parts of a larger whole, opens up several avenues for growth as communities of faith. The first avenue focuses on the local congregation, as we begin to really look at all of the people around us, and to work with God and with them to help each discover their spiritual gifts and to mobilize each other for ministry. The metaphor teaches us to value one another as God's gifts to us and to the whole church, and to look for ways in which to actualize those gifts that the Spirit wishes to bestow through one another.

Another avenue calls us to look beyond our local church first to other churches in our locality, and to begin to recognize the gifts that each can bring to the church universal as it seeks to fulfill its mission and to address a wide variety of needs and challenges. Each local church tends to have some aspect of Christian worship, nurture, or outreach in which it excels, complementing the gifts and graces of other churches in the community. Only through all of these local "bodies" is the mission of God advanced in a particular community. Growing in an awareness of one's neighboring churches might lead to deeper discoveries concerning the spiritual gifts of one's own church, as well as opening up exciting new ways to learn from one another and reach out to the needs of the community more effectively.

SHARING THE SCRIPTURE

Preparing Our Hearts

This week's devotional reading is found in 1 Corinthians 12:27-31, which concludes the chapter we will study today. Here Paul reminds the people that they are part of the body of Christ. Note the list of offices that God has given to edify the body. Also note that no one person has all of the gifts. Why do you suppose God distributed the gifts among many people, rather than give each person all of the gifts? Think about the gifts that you have been given and how you are—or are not—using them.

Pray that you and the class members will not only discern your spiritual gifts but also commit to using them in ways that benefit the whole church.

Preparing Our Minds

Study the background and lesson Scripture, 1 Corinthians 12:1-13. As you read, recognize that everyone has gifts to share with the church and begin to think about ways in which those gifts can be used.

Write on newsprint:

❑ information for next week's lesson, found under "Continue the Journey."

Use a large sheet of craft or butcher paper to trace the outline of a human body with a pencil or crayon. If you are not artistic, perhaps a child would lie on the paper as a model for you. You need not add features, but cut the body into puzzle pieces. Be sure to have enough pieces for everyone in the class. If the class is extremely large, make several puzzles, but be sure to keep them separate by marking them or using a different color paper for each puzzle.

LEADING THE CLASS

(1) Gather to Learn

❖ Welcome the class members and introduce any guests.

❖ Pray that all who have entered this morning will be blessed by fellowshipping and learning together.

❖ Spread out the human body puzzle pieces on a table, or hang them at random on a wall or bulletin board. See if the class can figure out what this conglomeration of pieces is. When they have guessed, note that you will be assembling the puzzle later in the session. Talk about how important it is that everything in the human body—and the church—fit together properly for maximum effectiveness.

❖ Read aloud today's focus statement: **Everyone has something to contribute to the common good. How should we use our gifts, abilities, and talents? Paul indicates that every believer has received a spiritual gift that can be used to build up the body of Christ.**

(2) Explore the Various Spiritual Gifts That Paul Says Are Spread Among the Church's Members for the Common Good

❖ Select someone to read 1 Corinthians 12:1-13.

❖ Look carefully at verses 4-8. Prompt the students to talk about why they think Paul continues to repeat the word "same." (Note that while Paul recognizes diversity among the gifts, they are all given by the same God for the same purpose: to build up the church.)

❖ Make a list on newsprint of the gifts Paul identifies. Encourage students to call out ideas, using as many translations as possible so as to become familiar with the nuances of meaning.

❖ Discuss these questions with the class.

(1) **Paul insists that God has given each person spiritual gifts to be used for the common good. What happens when people fail to discern or use these gifts?**

(2) **Do you see any evidence of Paul valuing one gift over another? If not, why not? And if not, why then do we in the church seem to appreciate some gifts more than others?**

(3) **Recognizing that spiritual gifts can be misused, how does Paul help people recognize the right use of spiritual gifts?** (See the two focal points—God is the source of all gifts, and the purpose of the

gifts is to build up the church—in "The Focal Point of Spiritual Gifts" in Interpreting the Scripture.)

❖ Use the information in Understanding the Scripture for verses 12-13 to help the learners understand that the image of the many parts of the body working together for the common good was not an idea unique to the church. However, it is a very appropriate image that continues to have meaning in the church today.

(3) Identify at Least One Gift Each Learner Has Received from God

❖ Distribute paper and pencils. Ask each person to write down one or two spiritual gifts that God has entrusted to them. They may want to check 1 Corinthians 12:27-30 and Romans 12:6-8, in addition to the gifts previously listed. They are to sign this paper.

❖ Ask the adults to gather in small groups, preferably with people who know them. Take a few minutes and pass the papers around. Let each person in the group add a gift or two that he or she has discerned in this person. Make sure the papers are returned to their owners.

❖ Let the groups talk about any surprises. Perhaps group members will have discerned in one person gifts he or she did not recognize.

❖ Gather the class together and discuss possible uses for at least some of the gifts. If the gifts were used in the suggested ways, how would the church benefit?

(4) Commit to Using God-given Gifts for the Common Good

❖ Distribute one puzzle piece of the human body to each student present. If you have pieces left over, invite people to take an additional one.

❖ Invite each person to write on the puzzle piece one spiritual gift that he or she will commit to using for the good of the church.

❖ Encourage the students to work together to assemble the puzzle so that they can visualize how these gifts all fit together. Work on a table, if possible, or the floor, a wall, or a bulletin board.

❖ Read the following litany and as you motion with your hand for them to speak, ask the participants to respond (R), **"We give you thanks, O God."**

■ **For each person who has come today to share with us the gift of fellowship and new ideas, (R).**

■ **For the spiritual gifts that you have given us to build up your church, (R).**

■ **For empowering us to use those gifts to complete the work to which you have called us, (R).**

(5) Continue the Journey

❖ Pray that the adults will use their gifts and work together for the common good.

❖ Read aloud this preparation for next week's lesson. You may also want to post it on newsprint for the students to copy. **Prepare for next week's session, "Love Comes First," by reading 1 Corinthians 13. Keep focused on these ideas as you read this very familiar passage, which is both** our background and lesson Scripture: **Everyone needs to feel loved. How can we relate to each other in a spirit of love? Paul indicates that love should underlie the exercise of our spiritual gifts.**

❖ Read aloud the following three ideas. Challenge the students to commit themselves to use these activities as a springboard to spiritual growth.

(1) **Engage in a church activity involving teamwork so as to build up the body of Christ.**

(2) **Thank several people this week who consistently use their gifts for the common good of the church. Consider writing a note, making a phone call, or planning lunch for those you wish to honor.**

(3) **Help a newer Christian to begin to identify his or her spiritual gifts and find ways to use them.**

❖ Sing or read aloud "Christ, from Whom All Blessings Flow."

❖ Close the session with this benediction, which you may want the class members to echo after you: **Go forth committed to serve, obey, and give as people who have been called to live faithfully in Christian community. Amen.**

UNIT 2: CALLED TO OBEDIENCE
LOVE COMES FIRST

PREVIEWING THE LESSON

Lesson Scripture: 1 Corinthians 13
Background Scripture: 1 Corinthians 13
Key Verse: 1 Corinthians 13:13

Focus of the Lesson:
Everyone needs to feel loved. How can we relate to each other in a spirit of love? Paul indicates that love should underlie the exercise of our spiritual gifts.

Goals for the Learners:
(1) to explore Paul's description of the love that exemplifies the greatest expression of the Christian faith.
(2) to describe God's love in action.
(3) to evaluate their treatment of others in light of 1 Corinthians 13.

Pronunciation Guide:
eschatological (es kat uh log' i kuhl)
Peregrinus (per u grin' us)
sine qua non (si ni kwa nan' – Latin, meaning: that which is absolutely essential)

Supplies:
Bibles, newsprint and marker, paper and pencils, hymnals

READING THE SCRIPTURE

NRSV

1 Corinthians 13

[1]If I speak in the tongues of mortals and of angels, but do not have love, I am a noisy gong or a clanging cymbal. [2]And if I have prophetic powers, and understand all mysteries and all knowledge, and if I have all faith, so as to remove mountains, but do not have love, I am nothing. [3]If I give away all my possessions, and if I hand over my body so that I may boast, but do not have love, I gain nothing.

NIV

1 Corinthians 13

[1]If I speak in the tongues of men and of angels, but have not love, I am only a resounding gong or a clanging cymbal. [2]If I have the gift of prophecy and can fathom all mysteries and all knowledge, and if I have a faith that can move mountains, but have not love, I am nothing. [3]If I give all I possess to the poor and surrender my body to the flames, but have not love, I gain nothing.

⁴Love is patient; love is kind; love is not envious or boastful or arrogant ⁵or rude. It does not insist on its own way; it is not irritable or resentful; ⁶it does not rejoice in wrongdoing, but rejoices in the truth. ⁷It bears all things, believes all things, hopes all things, endures all things.

⁸Love never ends. But as for prophecies, they will come to an end; as for tongues, they will cease; as for knowledge, it will come to an end. ⁹For we know only in part, and we prophesy only in part; ¹⁰but when the complete comes, the partial will come to an end. ¹¹When I was a child, I spoke like a child, I thought like a child, I reasoned like a child; when I became an adult, I put an end to childish ways. ¹²For now we see in a mirror, dimly, but then we will see face to face. Now I know only in part; then I will know fully, even as I have been fully known. **¹³And now faith, hope, and love abide, these three; and the greatest of these is love.**

⁴Love is patient, love is kind. It does not envy, it does not boast, it is not proud. ⁵It is not rude, it is not self-seeking, it is not easily angered, it keeps no record of wrongs. ⁶Love does not delight in evil but rejoices with the truth. ⁷It always protects, always trusts, always hopes, always perseveres.

⁸Love never fails. But where there are prophecies, they will cease; where there are tongues, they will be stilled; where there is knowledge, it will pass away. ⁹For we know in part and we prophesy in part, ¹⁰but when perfection comes, the imperfect disappears. ¹¹When I was a child, I talked like a child, I thought like a child, I reasoned like a child. When I became a man, I put childish ways behind me. ¹²Now we see but a poor reflection as in a mirror; then we shall see face to face. Now I know in part; then I shall know fully, even as I am fully known.

¹³And now these three remain: faith, hope and love. But the greatest of these is love.

UNDERSTANDING THE SCRIPTURE

1 Corinthians 13:1-3. Love is the mode in which all spiritual gifts must be used if they are to have any meaning, value, or benefit. Paul lists several of the gifts he introduced in 1 Corinthians 12:8-10: speaking in tongues, prophetic utterance, knowledge, and faith. Without love, the exercise of the flashier, ecstatic gifts like speaking in tongues is nothing more than the noise that accompanies pagan worship (the gong and brass instruments being well-known instruments in pagan rites). Even if these are exercised at an exceptionally high level, and acts of self-sacrifice in the extreme added besides, they are all ultimately worth nothing if they are not exercised or done out of love for Christ and his church. They might indeed bring some temporary notoriety, something that some of the Corinthian Christians were counting on. Even self-

immolation could be an act undertaken with a view to gaining a reputation (as in the case of Lucian's character Peregrinus, an itinerant peddler of philosophies and religions). But no real advantage could be gained by any self-serving use of these spiritual endowments.

1 Corinthians 13:4-7. In the previous chapter, Paul had used the metaphor of the "body," the single, living organism made up of many parts, to describe relationships within the church. In such a system, competition is entirely out of place, but "love" as Paul describes it is necessary to its health, since it promotes harmony. Self-promotion of one part at the expense of others spells disease for the entire organism. Envy by one part of the body at the well-functioning and success of another part runs absolutely contrary to the nature of the body as a single whole, where the joy of one part means joy for the whole and the loss or degradation of one part means loss and degradation for the whole. The metaphor of the body and the virtue of love accord well with the dominant metaphor for the Christian community, namely family. The ethos of kin entailed cooperation, harmony, solidarity, and the sharing of all goods. As the family of God, Christians share in one another's victories and defeats. Christians have nothing to gain by defeating a sister or brother, by putting him or her down, or by working against him or her. That only contributes to everyone's loss.

Such a philosophy runs completely counter to the cultural values in which the Corinthians had been raised, which pitted one person (or one family) against others in a competition for honor, power, and goods. The ethos of "sibling love" called for just the opposite. If one sibling was more gifted, more honored, or more prominent, he or she was urged to downplay those advantages rather than boast about them, and use them to the advantage of the less prominent siblings. Much of what Paul promotes under the heading of "love," then, depends upon each believer's acceptance of the others as part of a single family working together; conversely, living out of "love" toward one another would help make that experience of "family" real to each of its members.

Many of the characteristics of love listed by Paul are precisely targeted at deficiencies in the Corinthians' behavior. For example, while love is not "envious" or "jealous" (a loving person does not set himself or herself in opposition to others, such that one feels compelled to "keep up" with them or "keep ahead" of them), the Corinthians are beset with such strife (see 3:3). Love is not boastful, seeking praise and recognition, rather than seeking the good of others and faithful service to the Lord who bought us— but some Corinthians are. Love is not "arrogant," "puffed up," "inflated" with self-importance, self-promotion, and self-

interest. Paul uses this same term in 4:6 and 8:1 to describe the Corinthians' attitude. In 1 Corinthians 8:1, it is also presented as the opposite of love, which inflates others and is concerned with what is in the best interests of the sister or brother.

Love is "not rude" really in the sense that it "does not act dishonorably" or "disgracefully." More than mere courtesy is being urged here. The same word is used in 1 Corinthians 7:36 to speak of sexual impropriety. Love will not take advantage of another person in any way. Paul writes that love does not seek its own interests, using the same words as he did in Philippians 2:4, where seeking after the interests of others was seen as walking in line with the mind of Christ. This is something that all believers are expected to embody, not simply to stand back and admire in Jesus without imitating this behavior themselves. That love puts up with or "bears all things" calls to mind Paul and his team (1 Corinthians 9:12), who also put up with everything in order not to put a stumbling block in anyone's way. To love is to imitate Paul's attitude insofar as he imitates Christ's attitude (1 Corinthians 11:1).

In some respects, love acts in line with the best virtues of Greco-Roman society (beneficent, seemly); in other respects, Christian love is based on a fundamentally different value system than the competitive quest for honor and precedence in community that marked first-century Mediterranean societies and that continues to be perpetuated in the competitive political and economic systems of our modern world, not to mention the local manifestations of jockeying for "first place."

1 Corinthians 13:8-13. This final paragraph puts spiritual gifts in eschatological (end-time) perspective. Prophecy and knowledge are useful now, because we perceive spiritual realities but dimly and incompletely. We rely on the supplements to our own perception that these gifts bring, but even with these gifts our understanding is partial at best. When we all stand before God, however, our partial experience of God's truth will yield to a perfect and complete understanding, just as our natural childhood with its limited perception yields inexorably to adulthood and, hopefully, maturity. Just as Paul will not boast in the physical attributes that allow some people to put on a good performance, valuing rather that knowledge of God's power made present in weakness that alone can give life to our dead bodies, so Paul will not boast in spiritual endowments that only have value on this side of the last day. Love, which carries through into eternity after faith has become sight and hope possession, is indeed far more excellent.

INTERPRETING THE SCRIPTURE

The Sine Qua Non of Christian Discipleship

What ultimately stands at the center of your spirituality? What motivates your engagement in service to the church and the world? What is at the root of your attitude toward other people? In this chapter, arguably the most famous passage of New Testament Scripture, Paul inexorably points us to love as the only acceptable basis and the necessary condition for meaningful discipleship.

This emphasis is certainly consonant with the driving rhythms of the New Testament. When asked to provide a summary of the Law, to encapsulate the essence of the doing of God's will as revealed in the Torah, Jesus named love—love of God and love of neighbor—as that essence (see Matthew 22:34-40). Paul himself would summarize the fulfilling of the Law as loving one's neighbor (Galatians 5:13-14; Romans 13:8-10). John, of course, also enshrines love at the heart of Christian discipleship when he presents as the "new commandment" of Jesus (that is really the "old commandment," 1 John 2:7-11): "Love one another" (John 15:12, 17; 1 John 3:23; 4:7).

The corollary of these statements, however, is that, without love, there is no fulfilling of God's just requirements of God's people. There is no Christian spirituality or service. As we examine ourselves, it is not enough to say that we have sung in the choir, attended or even led Bible studies, gone on mission trips, supported the church and its outreach with our time, talents, and treasures. All of these mean nothing if we have not done them with love in our hearts for our neighbors, because "service" of any kind can all too easily become "self-serving" without this dimension of love for the other. There is little danger that one can have love without engaging in service insofar as one is able; there is great danger that one can be actively involved in the work of the church without love. The danger is that, after so much investment of oneself, after bringing positive good to others, we ourselves should find that we are disqualified from the prize even after proclaiming it to others (1 Corinthians 9:27). It is imperative, therefore, that we allow the Spirit to perform that greatest of all miracles—the transformation of our cold or selfish hearts into hearts full of love and compassion for those God places around us.

Love in Action

I still remember a sermon preached by a pastor, who was really more of a mentor, about fourteen years ago. He said that if you were to take out the word "love" and replace it with "Christ" in 1 Corinthians 13:4-7, the result would still be a true proclamation. This is fitting, since Jesus has always set the benchmark for love, from the time John the

Elder declared that we know what "love" is by considering Jesus' act in laying down his life for us (1 John 3:16) to the penning of the hymn text "Lord, you show us love's true measure." Imitating Jesus, being conformed to Jesus' mind and heart, which is the essence of Christian discipleship, means walking in love "as Christ loved us and gave himself up for us" (Ephesians 5:2).

Paul's words about love help us to recognize love in action, and help us also recognize where love is non-existent in our hearts, thoughts, and actions as we relate to other people. Keeping these familiar words in our minds can set a watch over our lives, stopping us when we fall short of love and giving us an opportunity to get our hearts "right" before God and toward our neighbor before proceeding any further. Rather than going to a meeting at the church thinking, "I've got to make sure they don't shoot down my proposal," love might check us and change our attitude to: "I hope we all remain centered on God and discern what will be in the best interests of advancing God's will here." Rather than harboring inner resentment with the thoughts, "I don't like all the attention that new family is getting. What about me, after the ways I've been supporting this church's ministry for years?!"—love might prompt us both to be glad for the affirmation the new family is receiving as they begin their journey with this congregation *and* speak honestly about our own needs for affirmation. Rather than thinking little of another Christian because he or she does not seem as gifted or involved, and priding oneself for how well one comes out in comparison, love would cause us to really look at that sister or brother and consider how best to tease out the ways in which the Spirit would use and involve him or her.

Growing Up in Christ

Whole theories of counseling have been based on 1 Corinthians 13:11, focusing on the necessity of leaving behind patterns of behavior or thinking that helped us survive difficult family or other dynamics as a child, but which ultimately hinder us from enjoying full and free relationships in our adult lives. Paul's wisdom has certainly been vindicated by the counseling field, but it extends considerably further as we consider the use to which he puts this maxim of moving on to maturity.

Paul uses this image to establish a relationship between the present time, in which we exercise our natural and spiritual gifts to gain some insight into the ways and will of God, and the future time, when we will stand in God's unmediated presence and "see face to face" and "know fully" (13:11-12). This present time is to the eschatological era as our childhood is to our adulthood. This realization alone should fill our hearts and minds with humility in matters religious and spiritual. We know enough to follow the way to salvation, but we are so far from knowing it "all" that our heated schisms over minute doctrinal and liturgical points can only appear ridiculous when we view them in the full light of God on the other side. Perhaps this is also why Paul stresses harmony and love rather than endorsing factions on the basis of supposed "knowledge" we possess. Our "knowledge" now will be superseded by our face-to-face perception of God then, but the love that holds us together now will hold us together for eternity.

Paul challenges us with this insight to live in line with the ultimate values of our faith confession and eschatology (namely, where all "this"—the world around us, the action of God, the goal of discipleship—is heading). He urges us to allow the ultimate realities to illumine the temporary nature of so much of our reality and our interests, squabbles, and agendas. This single revelation can lead us to immense wisdom in our relationships with one another, our use of spiritual gifts, our investments of our energies and our selves. As we seek what enhances another's relationship with God, what builds up relationships between one another, what embodies appreciation for the gifts each other person is from God to us, we step out of the temporary obsessions that cheapen our lives (for example, power plays, the endless pursuit of "more," evaluation of self and others on the basis of performance and achievements that will not matter for eternity) and into the experience of timeless love and community that connects us with eternity.

SHARING THE SCRIPTURE

Preparing Our Hearts

This week's devotional reading is found in John 3:16-21. "For God so loved the world that he gave his only Son." These words, though so familiar, are almost impossible to comprehend. Can we even begin to imagine a love as great as this? God's gift of love is the root, foundation, and source of our Christian lives. As Christians we are called to follow God's example and love others with abundant love. If God were to rate you on your love for others, what would that rating be? Seek God's guidance about changes that you may need to make.

Pray that you and the class members will act on Paul's belief that love is the greatest expression of Christian faith.

Preparing Our Minds

Study the background and lesson Scripture, the beloved thirteenth chapter of 1 Corinthians. As you study Paul's poetic description of love, consider how we can relate to others in a spirit of love.

Write on newsprint:
❑ information for next week's lesson, found under "Continue the Journey."

Gather identical copies of 1 Corinthians 13 for each student if you want the class to read this passage in unison.

Prepare an optional lecture as suggested under "Explore Paul's Description of the Love That Exemplifies the Greatest Expression of the Christian Faith."

LEADING THE CLASS

(1) Gather to Learn

❖ Welcome the class members and introduce any guests.

❖ Pray that all who have gathered will experience anew God's gift of love and willingly share that love with others.

❖ Brainstorm with the class members the wide variety of meanings that the word "love" can have. They may generate a long list, including: romantic love, parent/child love, sibling love, love of country, love of pets, love of nature, love of a team, and other ways that we use the word "love."

❖ Note that in some languages, including Greek, different words exist to describe these different expressions of love. Invite the students to comment on whether they believe the single word "love" in English helps to broaden its meaning or dilutes it. Is it possible than when we use the word "love" people really do not know what we mean because the definition is so imprecise?

❖ Read aloud today's focus statement: **Everyone needs to feel loved. How can we relate to each other in a spirit of love? Paul indicates that love should underlie the exercise of our spiritual gifts.**

(2) Explore Paul's Description of the Love That Exemplifies the Greatest Expression of the Christian Faith

❖ Choose someone to read aloud 1 Corinthians 13. As an alternative, have copies of the same translation available and ask the entire class to read this extremely familiar chapter in unison.

❖ Divide the class into groups and distribute paper and pencils. Ask each group to write what this chapter means to them. They will need to consider what love is—and isn't. The groups will also want to explore the centrality of love to the Christian life.

❖ Give each group time to report back on its understanding of this passage.

❖ **Option:** Present a lecture based on the Understanding the Scripture portion to help clarify the meaning of chapter 13. You may wish to use this lecture only if you feel it will add to the comments already made by the groups.

❖ Conclude this portion of the lesson by asking the students if they wish to add any ideas to Paul's description. (You will likely find that Paul's points are so timeless and universal that most adults will not have anything to add, but at least provide them with the opportunity to do so.)

(3) Describe God's Love in Action

❖ Read the first vignette and ask the students to talk with a partner or small group about how they would respond to the situation in a manner befitting the love that Paul describes. After allowing a few minutes for discussion, read the second story, and so on.

(1) **You are standing in a long line at the grocery store and your time is limited. A woman with two small children is in line behind you, and one of the children is crying inconsolably. The exasperated mother starts yelling at the child. What do you do?**

(2) **You hear fire engines and realize that a neighbor's house is on fire. You run up the street, breathe a sigh of relief that it is not a friend's house, and then see an older couple you do not know**

being assisted by emergency personnel. What do you do?

(3) **You are approached by a homeless person on a shopping center parking lot who asks if you could spare some change for coffee or a burger. He says he's a disabled veteran and is very hungry. What do you do?**

❖ Gather the class together. Ask the groups to comment on any actions where there was a wide difference of opinion as to what love in action might look like. Obviously, there is no one "right" way to show God's love to others, but you may want to ask a few class members to share the reasoning behind their suggested actions.

(4) Evaluate the Learners' Treatment of Others in Light of 1 Corinthians 13

❖ Distribute paper and pencils. Ask the learners to make a confidential list of individuals or groups (for example, co-workers, other drivers or shoppers) who they encounter on a regular basis. They should write each name on one line. Next to each name or group, the students should rate themselves on a "Love Scale" from one to five, with one being the "least loving" and five being the "most loving."

❖ Ask each student to choose one name or group that rated low and write a few words about how he or she will try to be more loving toward this individual or group.

❖ Provide a few moments for silent prayer and reflection as the adults ask God to help them be more loving.

(5) Continue the Journey

❖ Break the silence by praying that God's love will surround and flow from each one who has come today.

❖ Read aloud this preparation for next week's lesson. You may also want to post it on newsprint for the students to copy. **Prepare for next week's session, "Forgiving and Reconciling," by reading 2 Corinthians 2:5-11 and 7:2-15. Our lesson will focus on chapter 7, verses 2-15. Think about these ideas as you read: Everyone experiences the pain of a broken relationship at some point. How can these relationships be healed and restored? Paul indicates that forgiveness is the key, and he rejoiced in his own reconciliation with the Corinthian church.**

❖ Read aloud the following three ideas. Challenge the students to commit themselves to use these activities as a springboard to spiritual growth.

(1) **Perform some random acts of kindness this week for people you do not know as an expression of God's love for all people.**

(2) **Memorize 1 Corinthians 13:4-7.**

When confronted by a situation that makes you angry or upset, silently repeat these words before you say or do anything.

(3) **Examine the work you do for the church in light of Paul's teachings on love. Do you do what you do as an expression of your love for the God who first loved you? Do you behave lovingly toward others, even when they disagree with your ideas or act rudely? Be alert for ways to show love in the midst of a tense situation.**

❖ Sing or read aloud "The Gift of Love."

❖ Close the session with this benediction, which you may want the class members to echo after you: **Go forth committed to serve, obey, and give as people who have been called to live faithfully in Christian community. Amen.**

UNIT 3: THE SPIRIT OF GIVING

FORGIVING AND RECONCILING

PREVIEWING THE LESSON

Lesson Scripture: 2 Corinthians 7:2-15
Background Scripture: 2 Corinthians 2:5-11; 7:2-15
Key Verse: 2 Corinthians 7:10

Focus of the Lesson:
Everyone experiences the pain of a broken relationship at some point. How can these relationships be healed and restored? Paul indicates that forgiveness is the key, and he rejoiced in his own reconciliation with the Corinthian church.

Goals for the Learners:
(1) to study Paul's instruction concerning forgiveness.
(2) to draw a connection between Paul's teaching and the role of forgiveness in their church relationships.
(3) to offer forgiveness and reconciliation to a specific person.

Pronunciation Guide:
salvific (sal vi' fik)

Supplies:
Bibles, newsprint and marker, paper and pencils, hymnals

READING THE SCRIPTURE

NRSV
2 Corinthians 7:2-15

²Make room in your hearts for us; we have wronged no one, we have corrupted no one, we have taken advantage of no one. ³I do not say this to condemn you, for I said before that you are in our hearts, to die together and to live together. ⁴I often boast about you; I have great pride in you; I am filled with consolation; I am overjoyed in all our affliction.

NIV
2 Corinthians 7:2-15

²Make room for us in your hearts. We have wronged no one, we have corrupted no one, we have exploited no one. ³I do not say this to condemn you; I have said before that you have such a place in our hearts that we would live or die with you. ⁴I have great confidence in you; I take great pride in you. I am greatly encouraged; in all our troubles my joy knows no bounds.

[5]For even when we came into Macedonia, our bodies had no rest, but we were afflicted in every way—disputes without and fears within. [6]But God, who consoles the downcast, consoled us by the arrival of Titus, [7]and not only by his coming, but also by the consolation with which he was consoled about you, as he told us of your longing, your mourning, your zeal for me, so that I rejoiced still more. [8]For even if I made you sorry with my letter, I do not regret it (though I did regret it, for I see that I grieved you with that letter, though only briefly). [9]Now I rejoice, not because you were grieved, but because your grief led to repentance; for you felt a godly grief, so that you were not harmed in any way by us. **[10]For godly grief produces a repentance that leads to salvation and brings no regret, but worldly grief produces death.** [11]For see what earnestness this godly grief has produced in you, what eagerness to clear yourselves, what indignation, what alarm, what longing, what zeal, what punishment! At every point you have proved yourselves guiltless in the matter. [12]So although I wrote to you, it was not on account of the one who did the wrong, nor on account of the one who was wronged, but in order that your zeal for us might be made known to you before God. [13]In this we find comfort.

In addition to our own consolation, we rejoiced still more at the joy of Titus, because his mind has been set at rest by all of you. [14]For if I have been somewhat boastful about you to him, I was not disgraced; but just as everything we said to you was true, so our boasting to Titus has proved true as well. [15]And his heart goes out all the more to you, as he remembers the obedience of all of you, and how you welcomed him with fear and trembling.

[5]For when we came into Macedonia, this body of ours had no rest, but we were harassed at every turn—conflicts on the outside, fears within. [6]But God, who comforts the downcast, comforted us by the coming of Titus, [7]and not only by his coming but also by the comfort you had given him. He told us about your longing for me, your deep sorrow, your ardent concern for me, so that my joy was greater than ever.

[8]Even if I caused you sorrow by my letter, I do not regret it. Though I did regret it—I see that my letter hurt you, but only for a little while—[9]yet now I am happy, not because you were made sorry, but because your sorrow led you to repentance. For you became sorrowful as God intended and so were not harmed in any way by us. **[10]Godly sorrow brings repentance that leads to salvation and leaves no regret, but worldly sorrow brings death.** [11]See what this godly sorrow has produced in you: what earnestness, what eagerness to clear yourselves, what indignation, what alarm, what longing, what concern, what readiness to see justice done. At every point you have proved yourselves to be innocent in this matter. [12]So even though I wrote to you, it was not on account of the one who did the wrong or of the injured party, but rather that before God you could see for yourselves how devoted to us you are. [13]By all this we are encouraged.

In addition to our own encouragement, we were especially delighted to see how happy Titus was, because his spirit has been refreshed by all of you. [14]I had boasted to him about you, and you have not embarrassed me. But just as everything we said to you was true, so our boasting about you to Titus has proved to be true as well. [15]And his affection for you is all the greater when he remembers that you were all obedient, receiving him with fear and trembling.

UNDERSTANDING THE SCRIPTURE

2 Corinthians 2:5-11. Some significant events separate the writing of 1 Corinthians from this passage. Paul made a visit to the Corinthian churches ahead of schedule, on the way to Macedonia (2 Corinthians 1:15-16) rather than on the way back after his visit to Macedonia (examine 1 Corinthians 16:5-7). This surprise visit resulted in a public, painful confrontation with a church member in Corinth. The details are murky, and the antagonist is referred to only in the most veiled terms as "someone," "he/him," and "the one who did the wrong." From the issues Paul raises in 2 Corinthians, it is likely that the "offender" offered a direct assault on Paul's apostolic legitimacy, having been won over by rival Jewish Christian teachers who were trying to undermine Paul's authority and assert their own in Corinth (see 2 Corinthians 3:1; 5:12; 10:12-14; 11:12-15, 21b-23). Paul's own vacillating about his travel plans played right into their hands (see Paul's defense of his actions in this regard in 2 Corinthians 1:15–2:4). More disturbing was the failure of the rest of the church to intervene on Paul's behalf, content to watch the conflict rather than voice any support for Paul. Had Paul lost his spiritual children?

This visit was a "painful visit" that Paul was unwilling to repeat, with the result that he sent a letter, written "with many tears" (2 Corinthians 2:4), to address the problems that he encountered. This letter, now completely and discreetly lost, apparently had good effect, described at the beginning of this week's Scripture. In response to Paul's letter, and no doubt in part to the effective mediation of Titus, who delivered the letter, the "majority" of the congregation (2:6) decided that Paul was being unfairly maligned by the rival teachers and had been unfairly mistreated by the "offender." They took some kind of disciplinary action against this member—the sort of thing they ought to have done on the spot, if their hearts had been truly with Paul during his painful visit. Titus brought word of this to Paul (2 Corinthians 2:12-13; 7:6-7), which both took as a positive sign that the relationship between Paul's team and the Corinthian churches was heading back toward solid ground.

Paul's objective was not to make the church choose Paul over the brother who offended, but to choose Paul over the rival teachers who were promoting themselves based on their human credentials and performance. Now that the church is more clearly moving in that direction, his heart goes out to the "offender." His exclusion or humiliation can no longer serve any positive purpose, now that the Corinthians have responded positively toward Paul. It is time now to restore the "offender" within the church, to extend forgiveness recognizing that he is not an enemy, but a brother for whom Christ died.

The *real* enemy is not the fellow Christian, no matter how grievous the affront, but Satan, who uses such affronts to destroy believers and communities of faith. It is not enough that the church as a whole be won back from following ministers of a false, performance-oriented gospel; the brother who offended must also be restored so that not even one will be lost. Paul gives an excellent example here that winning an argument but losing a brother or sister is not an acceptable conclusion to a church conflict. Such would also be to fall prey to another of the Enemy's strategies for weakening the church. Instead, Paul exhibits forgiveness toward this brother, knowing that this benefits the whole community—for broken relationships hurt the whole community.

2 Corinthians 7:2-7. The lesson jumps from chapter 2 to chapter 7 in order to follow the continuity of the theme of reconciliation. There are many signs that reconciliation, while *in process,* is not yet complete. This passage, with its appeal for the reopening of hearts and denials of allegations of wrongdo-ing (including Paul's mishandling of the col-lection funds), provides several such signs. The skipped material in 2 Corinthians 2:12–7:1 deals with the main issues that pre-cipitated the conflict between Paul and the Corinthians during the painful visit and, with the continued presence of the rival teachers, continued to threaten their relation-ship. These issues centered on Paul's apos-tolic presence, the sorry figure of a man beset by many hardships and not particularly gifted in oratory and "stage presence." Paul must demonstrate that, far from disqualify-ing him as an apostle, all his hardships bene-fit the Corinthians, since he is able to bring to them in their trials the encouragement he learns from God in his trials, and his vulner-ability to his own weakness allows him to discover God's power. He thus has far more to offer the Corinthians, if they would be honest about their own weakness, than other teachers who rely on their personal strengths rather than the strength of God.

Second Corinthians 7:5-7 tells how Titus, coming from delivering the "tearful letter," met up with Paul to give him the encourag-ing news about their response. This is the source of the confidence that Paul shows throughout this passage that things will turn out well in their relationship.

2 Corinthians 7:8-15. Paul wrestles with the fact that he had said some hard-hitting things in the "tearful letter," things that brought a lot of pain to the surface among the Corinthians. It gave him no joy to hurt them, but he does rejoice that God used the letter and the grief to reawaken their love for their founding apostle. God's working of a positive and healthful result made the pain "salvific"—saving, rather than damag-ing.

Paul reveals again his main motive for writing that letter (see 2:9)—it was not to get even with someone who humiliated him in front of the church, but to help the Corinthians rediscover how important Paul was to them, just as he kept before him how important they were to him, not only in this life but for the next as well (7:3). The Corinthians' response has so far confirmed his best hopes for their relationship, and he hopes that the next few steps they take will cement their relationship, namely as they resume their part in the collection project Paul is administering for the poor Christians in Judea.

INTERPRETING THE SCRIPTURE

Aware of Satan's Schemes

Paul often points us to unseen, spiritual forces at work behind the visible phenomena in our relationships and surroundings. He believed that behind many "battles" we face (whether within our churches, our personal struggles against sins or weaknesses, or our endeavors to reach out to the world around us) lies the battle of the spiritual forces of darkness against the children of God (see, for example, 1 Corinthians 7:5; 2 Corinthians 12:7; Ephesians 6:10-18; 1 Thessalonians 2:18; 2 Thessalonians 2:9). In many circles it is not fashionable to speak of devils; in others, it is far too fashionable. Wherever one finds one-self in between, there is something vital to be learned from contemplating what Paul saw as the "designs" of the Enemy—the vision that darker forces have for the tearing down of the human soul and the erosion of strong, Christian community, and the subtle or direct strategies by which such a vision is realized.

Many readers will be familiar with C. S. Lewis's book *The Screwtape Letters*, a fictional collection of letters by a senior devil advising an apprentice tempter disclosing an all-too-true picture of the self-centered lies, beliefs, and actions that beset our humanity and hinder us from attaining God's ideal for us. When two Christians are at odds and a rift in the body of Christ has occurred, there is great hope in Hell of it spreading, infecting other Christians. There is hope that the two principal actors will never speak to one another or cooperate or even look kindly upon one another again. As each tries to hold onto his or her "rightness" and avoid honest reconciliation, it is neither party, nor the church, but the Enemy who benefits. But it is not enough that any such conflict be resolved to the justification of the one and the shaming or exclusion of the other. In such a case, the church may appear to have been "restored" by putting an end to the conflict, but, in fact, the church has been weakened by the loss and discouragement of one member, and again the Enemy has a victory. Not winning or losing, but reconciliation is the only acceptable outcome for conflict in the church: Both parties must be brought to the place where each is affirmed in the other's love, and where both are affirmed in the church's love.

Through Tears to Joy

The path to reconciliation can mean passing through some turbulent waters, addressing hard and painful issues together. This was certainly the case for Paul and the churches in Corinth as they wrestled together with their relationship. Either party could have succumbed to a number of temptations. Perhaps the greatest temptation would be to simply walk away from the relationship, treating it as irreparable. Paul had too much invested in the Corinthians to do that, however, and it is likely that they had too much invested in him as well. Each chose to keep investing for the sake of all that God had done through and in each party up to that point.

Another temptation for Paul might have been to go in with a "guns blazing" approach to vindicate himself, beat down the offender, and set everyone straight. A "win-lose" approach, however, also hinders reconciliation. Paul understood this, and models for us what it means to look at the larger picture of the community's well-being, and engage conciliatory strategies for the good of everyone involved.

Effective reconciliation requires courage, for it is much easier (though more destructive and emotionally draining in the long run) simply to avoid addressing conflicts and hurts head-on. Reconciliation requires the willingness on the part of all parties involved to feel "pain" when hurts and offenses are confronted, rather than seeking to put up walls and avoid that necessary pain (for example, through self-justification, through retorting with blaming remarks when confronted, or through avoidance of the issues altogether). This is the "godly grief" that produces repentance, opens up the path to forgiveness, a deeper understanding of one another, and the experience of mutual compassion and connection through reconciliation (7:10).

True reconciliation requires a clear and pure purpose, for example, the restoration of relationships rather than putting someone down. It requires a pure motivation, for example, a desire to see love flow freely again between people rather than a desire to justify oneself and shift the blame to the other party. It also requires a wise strategy. How can the topic be approached in a way, and in a setting, that will be conducive to the healthful results that one desires? Paul thinks carefully about how to proceed, sending a personal letter and Titus, rather than returning himself for another potentially harmful visit. He affirms them wherever possible, and treats them like his dear friends, even while he raises some serious questions about how fully they have understood his gospel (2:14–7:1).

In 2 Corinthians, we also see something of Paul's spirit as he approaches reconciliation. He exhibits confidence in the Corinthians' underlying good will and reliability rather than doubt and suspicion (see 2 Corinthians 7:4, 12, 14, 16). He approaches them as people who, deep down, want the same thing that he does for their relationship and are willing to take the necessary steps to get there. By extending this "grace" and approaching the Corinthians with a wide heart expecting the best from them, he facilitates the very thing he seeks.

The Responsibilities of the Onlookers

The scenario that Paul faced on his painful visit and thereafter challenges us to think about what our role should be when we witness injuries occurring within the body of Christ, or see relationships deteriorating. At first, the Corinthian believers embodied what, I believe, is the most standard approach to watching a conflict—to sit back and watch from a safe distance, without getting involved in the least. How much better would it have been for all concerned, had other Christians stood up at the time, interposed themselves between the "offender" and Paul, and worked with both parties to help get the real issues out on the table, and to deal with them in a loving manner that did

not break down relationships? Paul would not have gone away feeling defeated and abandoned by the church he founded at such great cost to himself; the offender would not have encountered such harsh discipline later after the Corinthians finally decided to take a stand; Paul and Titus might have been able to devote a lot of energy, attention, time, and resources to new outreach ministries.

Other responses are, of course, possible. Onlookers might start to take sides, argue amongst themselves, and allow a breach between two people to widen and include more and more of the church. Or, they might simply grumble and slander one party or another. The point is that anything less than active involvement in facilitating reconciliation between believers who are at odds contributes to the problem rather than its solution. Throughout the New Testament, we are encouraged to "butt into other believers' business" in ways that are supportive of positive, faithful, loving outcomes. We are thus to be a healing resource for one another as members of the larger family of God.

SHARING THE SCRIPTURE

Preparing Our Hearts

This week's devotional reading is found in Matthew 18:21-35. Here Jesus responds to Peter's question concerning forgiveness by telling the parable of the unforgiving servant. With whom in this story do you identify? Which character are you most like? Which are you least like? Ponder how you are similar to and different than Peter. Do you want to limit forgiveness, or are you willing to continue to forgive over and over? Does there come a point, perhaps if abuse is involved, that one needs to forgive and step away from the other person?

Pray that you and the class members will repent of words and actions that have caused relationships to rupture.

Preparing Our Minds

Study the background Scripture from 2 Corinthians 2:5-11 and 7:2-15. The lesson Scripture is 2 Corinthians 7:2-15. As you prepare this lesson, consider Paul's teachings on how relationships can be healed and restored.

Write on newsprint:
❏ information for next week's lesson, found under "Continue the Journey."

Plan the suggested lecture under "Study Paul's Instruction Concerning Forgiveness," if you choose to use this option.

LEADING THE CLASS

(1) Gather to Learn

❖ Welcome the class members and introduce any guests.

❖ Pray that class members will recognize that part of the spirit of giving entails offering forgiveness and reconciliation.

❖ Read aloud this excerpt submitted to www.forgiving.org by a pastor. **As a pastor of many churches over a twenty-four–year period, I have encountered every conceivable attack from "church people" imaginable. Most of them are from my acceptance of all races into a "white" church because Jesus loves them and I do too. Why do we spend so much time in this world placing people in different categories and races? Do we not realize that we are all one under God and he made us to be who we are? ... I've had to forgive many people throughout the years and may I say, "unforgiveness robs one of life and the real pursuit of happiness." I've had to deal as a mediator between families as they fought for their parents' property after their deaths. I've seen hatred so ingrained between family members that one said, "I would kill my brother if he walked into my yard at this moment." The gospel story of Jesus Christ is all about forgiveness. . . . I love all people and I have come to realize that forgiving is a release and a freedom that God has given us to exercise and prosper from.**

❖ Solicit reactions to this story. What does it say about forgiveness? What does it say about the church?

❖ Read aloud today's focus statement: **Everyone experiences the pain of a broken relationship at some point. How can these relationships be healed and restored? Paul indicates that forgiveness is the key, and he rejoiced in his own reconciliation with the Corinthian church.**

(2) Study Paul's Instruction Concerning Forgiveness

❖ Provide background for today's lesson by reading the information for 2 Corinthians 2:5-11 in Understanding the Scripture. If time permits, you may want to read the Scripture passage aloud.

❖ Choose a volunteer to read 2 Corinthians 7:2-15. Ask the class to envision themselves in a house church in Corinth hearing these words.

❖ Invite the students to respond to Paul's words as if they were Corinthian church members who had known the apostle for several years. Clearly, on a previous "painful visit" an incident had occurred with an individual that had ruptured the relationship between the church and Paul.

❖ Discuss these four questions, or create a lecture answering these questions.

(1) **What options did Paul have to respond to the individual church member who caused him pain?** (See "Through Tears to Joy" in Interpreting the Scripture.)

(2) **Which option did he choose? Why?**

(3) **What options did the church members have to respond to this situation?** (See "The Responsibilities of the Onlookers" in Interpreting the Scripture.)

(4) **How did the church members respond? Why?**

❖ Select six volunteers to role-play the following scenario that has taken place in contemporary churches. Assign the following parts: Mr. Aye, Pastor Arnold, (at least) one church official who sides with Mr. Aye, (at least) one person who sides with Pastor Arnold, and (at least) one person who tries to bring reconciliation to the situation. Read the scene: **One prominent member, Mr. Holy M. Aye, of Community Church had become increasingly dissatisfied with Pastor Arnold's preaching. Mr. Aye used his influence and financial contributions to turn others against Pastor Arnold. At a meeting of the governing body of the church, he lobbied members to withdraw support from Pastor Arnold and together insist that a new minister be appointed. At least one person supported Pastor Arnold, and at least one tried to step back and take a** more objective view so as to find ways to bring about reconciliation.

❖ Invite the students who watched this role-play to comment on which strategies damaged the church and which ones moved the church to reconciliation and wholeness. What other ways of handling the situation could they add? What insights do they now have for handling broken relationships within the church?

(3) Draw a Connection Between Paul's Teaching and the Role of Forgiveness in the Learners' Church Relationships

❖ Note that in 2 Corinthians 7, we glimpse Paul's joy at the church's repentance.

❖ Divide into small groups and provide each with newsprint and a marker. Ask each group to identify one area of conflict that divides the church universal or the churches within your denomination. Brainstorm how this conflict could be resolved with forgiveness so that the church could be reconciled and reunited.

❖ Invite a spokesperson for each group to report back to the class.

(4) Offer Forgiveness and Reconciliation to a Specific Person

❖ Distribute paper and pencils. Provide quiet time for the students to identify and lift in prayer a person with whom they need to be reconciled. If possible, this will be a person within the church.

❖ Ask them to write this person's name on a sheet of paper, which they will keep confidential, and outline a plan of action for approaching this person and trying to heal the relationship by offering and/or asking for forgiveness.

(5) Continue the Journey

❖ Break the silence by praying that the students will reach out with reconciliation and forgiveness to those with whom they have broken relationships, regardless of who is to blame for the estrangement.

❖ Read aloud this preparation for next week's lesson. You may also want to post it on newsprint for the students to copy. **Prepare for next week's session, "Giving Generously," by reading 2 Corinthians 8:1-15, which is the Scripture for both the background and the lesson. Focus on these ideas as you study: People often find it difficult to be generous. How can we learn to be unselfish in our giving? Paul encourages believers to give generously as a response to Jesus' example of total unselfishness. Paul further teaches that we should be generous in spreading the gospel.**

❖ Read aloud the following three ideas. Challenge the students to commit themselves to use these activities as a springboard to spiritual growth.

(1) Identify at least one person that you need to forgive who is either deceased or whose whereabouts are unknown. Since you cannot speak to this person, write a letter offering sincere forgiveness. Such an exercise will help you heal.

(2) Think about your experiences in the church over the years. Have you found forgiveness flows easily among Christians? If not, why? What changes does the church need to make?

(3) Read C.S. Lewis' *The Screwtape Letters.* **Write in your journal what you learn about forgiveness from this classic.**

❖ Sing or read aloud "Forgive Our Sins as We Forgive."

❖ Close the session with this benediction, which you may want the class members to echo after you: **Go forth committed to serve, obey, and give as people who have been called to live faithfully in Christian community. Amen.**

UNIT 3: THE SPIRIT OF GIVING
GIVING GENEROUSLY

PREVIEWING THE LESSON

Lesson Scripture: 2 Corinthians 8:1-15
Background Scripture: 2 Corinthians 8:1-15
Key Verse: 2 Corinthians 8:9

Focus of the Lesson:
People often find it difficult to be generous. How can we learn to be unselfish in our giving? Paul encourages believers to give generously as a response to Jesus' example of total unselfishness. Paul further teaches that we should be generous in spreading the gospel.

Goals for the Learners:
(1) to understand Paul's description of giving, not as a demand, but as a response to Jesus' example of total unselfishness.
(2) to examine their views of giving in light of Paul's exhortation to maintain a fair balance between their abundance and others' needs.
(3) to assess a "fair balance" in their own giving.

Pronunciation Guide:
Macedonian (mas uh doh' nee uhn)
omer (oh' muhr)

Supplies:
Bibles, newsprint and marker, paper and pencils, hymnals

READING THE SCRIPTURE

NRSV
2 Corinthians 8:1-15

¹We want you to know, brothers and sisters, about the grace of God that has been granted to the churches of Macedonia; ²for during a severe ordeal of affliction, their abundant joy and their extreme poverty have overflowed in a wealth of generosity on their part. ³For, as I can testify, they volun-

NIV
2 Corinthians 8:1-15

¹And now, brothers, we want you to know about the grace that God has given the Macedonian churches. ²Out of the most severe trial, their overflowing joy and their extreme poverty welled up in rich generosity. ³For I testify that they gave as much as

tarily gave according to their means, and even beyond their means, [4]begging us earnestly for the privilege of sharing in this ministry to the saints—[5]and this, not merely as we expected; they gave themselves first to the Lord and, by the will of God, to us, [6]so that we might urge Titus that, as he had already made a beginning, so he should also complete this generous undertaking among you. [7]Now as you excel in everything—in faith, in speech, in knowledge, in utmost eagerness, and in our love for you—so we want you to excel also in this generous undertaking.

[8]I do not say this as a command, but I am testing the genuineness of your love against the earnestness of others. [9]**For you know the generous act of our Lord Jesus Christ, that though he was rich, yet for your sakes he became poor, so that by his poverty you might become rich.** [10]And in this matter I am giving my advice: it is appropriate for you who began last year not only to do something but even to desire to do something—[11]now finish doing it, so that your eagerness may be matched by completing it according to your means. [12]For if the eagerness is there, the gift is acceptable according to what one has—not according to what one does not have. [13]I do not mean that there should be relief for others and pressure on you, but it is a question of a fair balance between [14]your present abundance and their need, so that their abundance may be for your need, in order that there may be a fair balance. [15]As it is written,

"The one who had much did not have too much,

and the one who had little did not have too little."

they were able, and even beyond their ability. Entirely on their own, [4]they urgently pleaded with us for the privilege of sharing in this service to the saints. [5]And they did not do as we expected, but they gave themselves first to the Lord and then to us in keeping with God's will. [6]So we urged Titus, since he had earlier made a beginning, to bring also to completion this act of grace on your part. [7]But just as you excel in everything—in faith, in speech, in knowledge, in complete earnestness and in your love for us—see that you also excel in this grace of giving.

[8]I am not commanding you, but I want to test the sincerity of your love by comparing it with the earnestness of others. [9]**For you know the grace of our Lord Jesus Christ, that though he was rich, yet for your sakes he became poor, so that you through his poverty might become rich.**

[10]And here is my advice about what is best for you in this matter: Last year you were the first not only to give but also to have the desire to do so. [11]Now finish the work, so that your eager willingness to do it may be matched by your completion of it, according to your means. [12]For if the willingness is there, the gift is acceptable according to what one has, not according to what he does not have.

[13]Our desire is not that others might be relieved while you are hard pressed, but that there might be equality. [14]At the present time your plenty will supply what they need, so that in turn their plenty will supply what you need. Then there will be equality, [15]as it is written: "He who gathered much did not have too much, and he who gathered little did not have too little."

UNDERSTANDING THE SCRIPTURE

2 Corinthians 8:1-7. In chapters 8 and 9, Paul appeals to the Corinthian Christians to fulfill their commitment to contribute to the collection project that Paul has undertaken for the poor in the Judean churches. This collection is a prominent part of Paul's ministry. Acts appears to speak of a previous, smaller-scale collection sent to the poor in Judea in an earlier period in Paul's life (Acts 11:29-30), but Paul himself has a much grander plan here. Paul had spoken about this collection prior to writing 1 Corinthians, probably during his first, extended stay in that area, and gave detailed instructions about it in 1 Corinthians 16:1-4. He also actively promoted this collection at least in Macedonia (see Romans 15:26 in addition to 2 Corinthians 8:1-6).

Paul considers the collection to be part of his own agreement with the Jerusalem apostles (Galatians 2:10). His zeal to fulfill this obligation reflects not only his compassion for his poorer sisters and brothers, but also his desire to prove himself a reliable partner with those "pillars" in Jerusalem. Even more importantly, the collection project represented, for Paul at least, the unity of the church of Gentiles and Jews, and the harmonious partnership of Paul's largely Gentile Christian mission with the churches in Judea (Romans 15:25-27).

Generosity is a source of recognition and honor for people in the Greco-Roman world. Paul retains this within the church to some extent (but with notable modifications; see 2 Corinthians 9:6-12). Here, Paul honors the Macedonian Christians for their generosity by praising them to the Corinthian congregations (2 Corinthians 8:1-5; 11:9), underscoring their virtuous character by noting that they did not allow their own poverty to hinder their generosity. It is not the size of the gift that matters, but the spirit and love with which it is given in proportion to one's means. The Macedonians exemplified the ideal praised by Seneca in *On Benefits* (1.7.1): At times we feel more indebted to people who have given small gifts from a large heart, who "by their spirit matched the gifts of royalty," who gave what little they had gladly, who beholding our poverty forgot their own (see also Jesus' praise of the widow's gift in Luke 21:1-4).

The Corinthians' renewed participation in this collection project would signify their renewal of partnership with Paul and their restored confidence in him. This is especially important in light of allegations of financial misconduct (see 2 Corinthians 12:16-18, as well as hints in 2 Corinthians 7:2). Paul's refusal to accept patronage from the Corinthian converts, preferring instead to work with his hands and receive occasional support from his partners in Macedonia, had led to suspicion about Paul's finances. If he did not want to make himself a client of the wealthier Corinthians, was his plan to skim off the top of the collection?

The Macedonian Christians take an exemplary approach to giving in a number of ways. Quite strikingly, they regard the opportunity to share their goods with their Judean sisters and brothers not as a burden upon them, but as a favor or "privilege" in which the Macedonian Christians earnestly "begged" Paul to be allowed to participate (2 Corinthians 8:4). They are presented as an example for the Corinthians even more urgently in regard to their approach to the apostle. Just as the Macedonians "gave themselves first to the Lord and . . . to us" (8:5) prior to their participation in the collection, so the Corinthians have been urged to rededicate themselves to God (5:16-21) and give themselves anew to Paul and his team (6:11–7:4). Moving forward with the collection would provide them with a concrete way of showing that they had opened their hearts wide once again toward Paul as well.

2 Corinthians 8:8-12. Early Christian authors frequently call for action as a "proof" of the genuineness of an inner disposition. James is famous for his demand that the genuineness of a person's faith manifest itself in deeds of kindness and mercy (James 2:14-17; 1:26-27). The author of 1 John also calls for love, if it be genuine, to break forth in concrete acts of service and giving toward sisters or brothers in need

(1 John 3:16-18). Paul is no different in this regard (2 Corinthians 8:8).

At the root of these expectations is the example of Jesus, in whose steps Christians are called to follow. Jesus spent his "all" to benefit us (8:9), not only in his crucifixion at the close of his earthly ministry, but, as Paul would elsewhere stress, in his very incarnation (Philippians 2:5-8). Walking as Jesus walked requires the cultivation of a generous heart manifested in generous acts. Paul puts the Corinthians on the defensive here: It is time for them to "make good" on their declarations of intent, so that their inclination to be generous does not turn into yet more empty boasting.

2 Corinthians 8:13-15. Paul quotes Exodus 16:18 in 2 Corinthians 8:15, drawing attention to a little-noticed aspect of the miracle of God's provision of manna in the desert. Each person was to gather one omer of manna. Some Hebrews gathered more than their allotted amount, thinking to hoard a little extra, but when it came time to measure it they found they only had an omer per person. Some were unable to gather a full omer per person, but found, upon measuring it, that they had the full measure. Part of the miraculous provision of God was that everyone should have enough—neither lack nor excess. Paul holds this up as the revelation of God's will for God's provisions for the church now (see further 2 Corinthians 9:6-10). No one should have more than is needed, so that no one need have less than is necessary; rather, each should have enough in the family of God.

When discussing inheritances, Plutarch advised in "On Fraternal Affection" (11-12) that brothers and sisters were supposed to view themselves as guardians of some part of a larger estate held in common by all siblings. They were encouraged not to allow squabbles over money to divide them and break their harmony and unity. Rather, each was to put whatever he or she possessed at the others' disposal as they had need. In adopting "family" as the ruling metaphor for life together in the body of Christ, Paul would expect similar attitudes about property to prevail.

INTERPRETING THE SCRIPTURE

Exemplary Generosity

Paul presents two outstanding examples of the generous spirit we are called to imitate. The first is the Macedonian Christians, who entered into a special kind of relationship with Paul on account of their desire to share what they had with him and his ministry (see 2 Corinthians 11:8-9). These Christians had a unique perspective on stewardship. They were so full from the experience of joy in their relationship with God that they did not hesitate to empty their pockets for the relief of impoverished Christians in Judea even when suffering economic hardship themselves. Their experience of the living God gave them the feeling of sufficiency, perhaps even of being "rich." Moreover, they understood that they were not just shelling out money: They were living out a relationship both with God and with Paul and his team. They "kept" the best part of their gift, namely the knowledge that it bound them together further with Paul, God, and the communion of saints, so that, again, they were enriched by their giving. Finally, they regarded the call for relief for the poor in Judea as an opportunity, and participation as a favor they hoped Paul would grant them. Rather than hear just another "call for money," they saw an opportunity to demonstrate the reality of their faith and their gratitude toward Jesus.

What pastor would not have her heart

strangely warmed to find that, at the outset of a stewardship campaign, her parishioners beg for the privilege of being partners in the ministries and outreach of the church? Yet stewardship remains one of the most difficult aspects of many pastors' ministries. What accounts for the distance between the contemporary experience of so many churches around the subject of stewardship and the attitude and behavior of the Macedonian Christians?

We may feel that our money is our own, gained by our hard work rather than entrusted to us in any real sense by God. We may fear that, if we give too much money away, there may not be enough for us and for our family, either now or later on. We may simply have bought into our own culture so fully that we can no longer discern how much is truly "enough" for our needs, and so we never discern how much can be shared with others without loss to ourselves.

The second example of generosity, of course, is Jesus. Two dynamics are at work as Paul invokes Jesus' act of generosity. First, there is the expectation that Christians will imitate the example of their Lord, specifically in terms of his self-giving love (see, for example, Ephesians 5:1-2; 1 John 3:16-18). Second, as would be evident to the Corinthians but perhaps a bit less evident to us, there is the expectation that Christians will seek opportunities to make a fair return to Jesus for his generosity toward them. In the Greek, the word "grace" is strategically repeated in 8:6, 7, 9 (the words translated as "generous undertaking" and "generous act" in those verses). First-century people well understood that receiving a benefit or gift put the recipient under an obligation of gratitude. They would hear, therefore, the logic in these verses as "I want you to excel in this gift, remembering the debt you owe to Jesus on account of his gift." The fuel for generosity, so well exemplified by the Macedonians, is a fulsome appreciation of the generosity of Jesus. The more we know

how "rich" he has truly made us, and come to feel the fullness and abundance of the life he has opened up for us, the more we will feel able to share our bounty with others, however "rich" we are by secular standards.

"Fair Balance" and the Widening Gap

Paul elevates the ideal of "fair balance" between Christians in terms of access to and enjoyment of material resources. He seeks to bring the ethical ideals of kinship and friendship, where goods are considered to be held "in common" for the relief of any in need, to life in the church. The free flow of material resources among family and friends helped to connect people one to another and create a sense of solidarity and unity. Compare this with the very real division between the "haves" and "have-nots," and the ways in which wealth held by some and need experienced by others create long-lasting and pervasive barriers between people and groups.

As Christians of greater means learn to share with those of lesser means, devoting themselves to making sure that their sisters and brothers do not lack daily necessities, the "us" and "them" mentality created and reinforced by the acquisition and concentration of wealth yields to an experience of the family of God enjoyed both by the givers and the recipients. Both parties are enriched as relationships and partnerships are formed where cold isolation formerly prevailed, and as both parties participate in the prayers and spiritual insights of the other. Moreover, the love and provision of God becomes all the more real to people in need. I remember my grandmother telling me how difficult life was for her widowed mother raising seven children. She would also relate how, one day, when her mother broke down in tears praying to God for help when there was no food for the children, the doorbell rang. Someone had left a bag of groceries, and she blessed the anonymous giver and the God who used him or her to meet their desperate need. Where would the answer to that prayer have been, however, without another person responding to the inner prompting of God?

Paul does not foresee this always being a one-way street. People of means today can be people in need tomorrow. Many of us were brought up with the maxim, "save for a rainy day." According to this worldly advice, we ultimately rely on ourselves— and can only rely on ourselves—for help in time of need. Paul is seeking to nurture a global Christian community wherein everyone looks out for the needs of others, and the best insurance policy against want tomorrow is being generous today, so that when we find ourselves in need someone else will have the opportunity to be generous toward us (2 Corinthians 8:14).

The Message of the Manna

One of the greatest challenges to arrival at what Paul calls "fair balance" is our ability to determine how much is "enough." With so many of our sisters and brothers in Christ throughout the world facing not merely the pain, despair, and difficulties of being poor (which are great enough) but even starvation and death, it becomes all the more urgent that we look closely at how we are living, saving, and spending, and asking whether the standards of living and acquisition we set for ourselves are truly a measure of having "enough" or of flagrant self-indulgence.

The message of the manna is that those who hoard do not find their lives overflowing with abundance. Many people who make six-figure incomes still feel the pressure of being in debt, because their standards of living keep outpacing their incomes. Moreover, people who hoard are impoverished by their own failure to experience the fullness of the family of God and the joys and security of the human community God seeks to form as we share God's bounty. If we are to attain to the "fair balance" for which Paul calls, perhaps we need to consider again the saying, "Live simply, so that others may simply live."

SHARING THE SCRIPTURE

Preparing Our Hearts

This week's devotional reading is found in Luke 20:45–21:4. Here we see a stunning contrast between the behavior of the learned leaders of the temple who want their status to be acknowledged and the behavior of one of society's most vulnerable figures: a poor widow. Instead of receiving money, this woman gives "all she had to live on" (21:4). Her contribution amounted to about 1/64th of a laborer's daily wage. Jesus is not commending the amount that she gave, but rather, the generous spirit with which she offered her gift. While others tossed in much larger sums, they still had ample resources left. This woman had nothing more to give. Where do you see yourself in this story?

Pray that you and your class members will examine yourselves to determine the spirit in which you give.

Preparing Our Minds

Study the background and lesson Scripture by reading 2 Corinthians 8:1-15. As you prepare, think about how we can be generous in our giving.

You may want to look ahead to the next session, which also looks at giving. Bear in mind that today's lesson highlights giving generously; next week's focus is on giving as a witness to one's faith.

Write on newsprint:

❑ information for next week's lesson, found under "Continue the Journey."

Plan the lectures as suggested for "Understand Paul's Description of Giving, Not as a Demand, but as a Response to Jesus' Example of Total Unselfishness."

LEADING THE CLASS

(1) Gather to Learn

❖ Welcome the class members and introduce any guests.

❖ Pray that all who have come today will be receptive to the Spirit's leading in their lives.

❖ Read these stories of generosity, reported on beliefnet, that followed in the wake of the catastrophic tsunami that hit parts of Asia on December 26, 2004.

■ **A group of California surfers, many of whom have surfed on the coasts of Thailand and Indonesia, raised more than $500,000 for the relief effort through an international organization, SurfAid.**

■ **The Vietnamese Buddhist Congregation, located in Mission, near Vancouver, British Columbia, sold their temple and gave the entire proceeds of the $405,000 sale to the Canadian Red Cross.**

■ **The focus of a meeting meant to seek funds for economically depressed Meghalaya, India, turned into what the media called "a rare and generous gesture," when the villagers, who were not affected by the tsunami, decided to give their money to aid the town of Kyndiah.**

❖ Invite the students to respond to these stories by mentioning anything that surprised them, encouraged them, and/or challenged their way of viewing generosity.

❖ Read aloud today's focus statement: **People often find it difficult to be generous. How can we learn to be unselfish in our giving? Paul encourages believers to** give generously as a response to Jesus' example of total unselfishness. Paul further teaches that we should be generous in spreading the gospel.

(2) Understand Paul's Description of Giving, Not as a Demand, but as a Response to Jesus' Example of Total Unselfishness

❖ Choose a volunteer to read 2 Corinthians 8:1-7.

■ Use information in Understanding the Scripture for verses 1-7 and "Exemplary Generosity" in Interpreting the Scripture to create a lecture that helps the adults understand (1) how generosity was viewed in the Greco-Roman world and (2) how the generosity of the Macedonian Christians stands in contrast to the usual cultural approach.

■ Ask the students to envision themselves as members of the Corinthian church and comment on the Macedonian church's efforts.

❖ Select someone to read 2 Corinthians 8:8-15.

■ Use information in Understanding the Scripture for verses 8-15 and " 'Fair Balance' and the Widening Gap" and "The Message of the Manna" in Interpreting the Scripture to create a lecture that encourages the adults to see that (1) Jesus' self-giving is our example and (2) we must consider the needs of others in light of our own abundance.

■ Challenge the students to sum up Paul's teaching in their own words.

(3) Examine the Learners' Views of Giving in Light of Paul's Exhortation to Maintain a Fair Balance Between Their Abundance and Others' Needs

❖ Discuss these questions with the class.

(1) How do Paul's teachings on generous giving challenge our cultural norms?

(2) How can we go about determining what constitutes a "fair balance"?

(3) Look at verses 13-15. How does the story of the manna given to the Israelites in the desert aptly illustrate Paul's point?

❖ Provide a few moments for the learners to reflect on how their understandings of generous giving compare or contrast with those that Paul teaches.

❖ Break the silence by inviting volunteers to share any insights or questions this lesson has raised for them.

(4) Assess a "Fair Balance" in the Learners' Giving

❖ Distribute paper and pencils. Assure the participants that their response to this activity will be known only to God. Ask them to take these steps, which you will read aloud.

■ **Write your annual income.** (pause)

■ **Write an estimate of your necessary expenses, such as mortgage, utilities, medical bills, and so on.** (pause)

■ **Write an estimate of your discretionary spending, that is, things you want, not things you need to have.** (pause)

■ **Write an estimate of the amount you give to agencies that do the work of Christ beyond the church. Think here about programs to aid the poor, sick, or those who are otherwise vulnerable.** (pause)

■ **Write whatever pledge or estimate of giving you made to the church this year.** (pause)

■ **Review all of your figures. Do you honestly believe that your giving is in "fair balance" both with the way you spend the rest of your money and with the needs of others? If not, review your figures and see where you can make changes.**

❖ Close this activity by challenging the students to look through their financial records at home to see how close their estimates are and then take whatever action is needed to bring their giving into "fair balance."

(5) Continue the Journey

❖ Pray that those who have come today will begin, or continue, to give sacrificially of whatever God has entrusted to their care.

❖ Read aloud this preparation for next week's lesson. You may also want to post it on newsprint for the students to copy. **Prepare for next week's session, "Reasons for Giving," by reading 2 Corinthians 9:1-15, especially noting verses 3-15. As you read consider these ideas: People give to causes for a variety of reasons. Why should we give of our money or our time? Paul says we are to give in response to God's generosity.**

❖ Read aloud the following three ideas. Challenge the students to commit themselves to use these activities as a springboard to spiritual growth.

(1) Research several church-related or other non-profit agencies whose causes are in keeping with the gospel of Christ. When you have found at least one whose mission and use of resources reflects sound biblical stewardship, give sacrificially to this program.

(2) Create a plan of giving so that you are intentional about contributing specific dollar amounts or percentages of your income to the church and, if you choose, other organizations.

(3) Hold a yard sale. Donate the proceeds to help others in need.

❖ Sing or read aloud "What Gift Can We Bring."

❖ Close the session with this benediction, which you may want the class members to echo after you: **Go forth committed to serve, obey, and give as people who have been called to live faithfully in Christian community. Amen.**

UNIT 3: THE SPIRIT OF GIVING
REASONS FOR GIVING

PREVIEWING THE LESSON

Lesson Scripture: 2 Corinthians 9:3-15
Background Scripture: 2 Corinthians 9:1-15
Key Verse: 2 Corinthians 9:8

Focus of the Lesson:
People give to causes for a variety of reasons. Why should we give of our money or our time? Paul says we are to give in response to God's generosity.

Goals for the Learners:
(1) to look at how Paul describes the stewardship of money as a response to God's generosity and as a witness to one's faith.
(2) to evaluate their current stewardship of money, time, and talent in light of this passage.
(3) to take steps to bring their stewardship in line with the teachings of this passage.

Supplies:
Bibles, newsprint and marker, paper and pencils, hymnals

READING THE SCRIPTURE

NRSV
2 Corinthians 9:3-15

³But I am sending the brothers in order that our boasting about you may not prove to have been empty in this case, so that you may be ready, as I said you would be; ⁴otherwise, if some Macedonians come with me and find that you are not ready, we would be humiliated—to say nothing of you—in this undertaking. ⁵So I thought it necessary to urge the brothers to go on ahead to you, and arrange in advance for this bountiful gift that you have promised, so that it may be ready as a voluntary gift and not as an extortion.

NIV
2 Corinthians 9:3-15

³But I am sending the brothers in order that our boasting about you in this matter should not prove hollow, but that you may be ready, as I said you would be. ⁴For if any Macedonians come with me and find you unprepared, we—not to say anything about you—would be ashamed of having been so confident. ⁵So I thought it necessary to urge the brothers to visit you in advance and finish the arrangements for the generous gift you had promised. Then it will be ready as a generous gift, not as one grudgingly given.

⁶Remember this: Whoever sows sparingly

[6]The point is this: the one who sows sparingly will also reap sparingly, and the one who sows bountifully will also reap bountifully. [7]Each of you must give as you have made up your mind, not reluctantly or under compulsion, for God loves a cheerful giver. **[8]And God is able to provide you with every blessing in abundance, so that by always having enough of everything, you may share abundantly in every good work.** [9]As it is written,

"He scatters abroad, he gives to the poor;
his righteousness endures forever."

[10]He who supplies seed to the sower and bread for food will supply and multiply your seed for sowing and increase the harvest of your righteousness. [11]You will be enriched in every way for your great generosity, which will produce thanksgiving to God through us; [12]for the rendering of this ministry not only supplies the needs of the saints but also overflows with many thanksgivings to God. [13]Through the testing of this ministry you glorify God by your obedience to the confession of the gospel of Christ and by the generosity of your sharing with them and with all others, [14]while they long for you and pray for you because of the surpassing grace of God that he has given you. [15]Thanks be to God for his indescribable gift!

will also reap sparingly, and whoever sows generously will also reap generously. [7]Each man should give what he has decided in his heart to give, not reluctantly or under compulsion, for God loves a cheerful giver. **[8]And God is able to make all grace abound to you, so that in all things at all times, having all that you need, you will abound in every good work.** [9]As it is written:

"He has scattered abroad his gifts to the poor;
his righteousness endures forever."

[10]Now he who supplies seed to the sower and bread for food will also supply and increase your store of seed and will enlarge the harvest of your righteousness. [11]You will be made rich in every way so that you can be generous on every occasion, and through us your generosity will result in thanksgiving to God.

[12]This service that you perform is not only supplying the needs of God's people but is also overflowing in many expressions of thanks to God. [13]Because of the service by which you have proved yourselves, men will praise God for the obedience that accompanies your confession of the gospel of Christ, and for your generosity in sharing with them and with everyone else. [14]And in their prayers for you their hearts will go out to you, because of the surpassing grace God has given you. [15]Thanks be to God for his indescribable gift!

UNDERSTANDING THE SCRIPTURE

2 Corinthians 9:1-5. Scholars who try to divide 2 Corinthians into multiple letters often also separate chapters 8 and 9 from each other as individual letters. In so doing, however, they miss the remarkably balanced and artful strategy Paul has employed in these chapters when they are read as a unity.

In the beginning of chapter 8, Paul had commended the Macedonian Christians to

the Corinthians as examples of praiseworthy giving, lauding their generosity beyond their means to the proud Corinthians. At the close of chapter 8 (8:24) and the beginning of chapter 9, Paul now turns this around and challenges the Corinthians to establish their honor in the eyes of other Christians, verifying the good words Paul has spoken about them in the hearing of other congregations (especially in Macedonia). Concern for their reputation in the eyes of other cells of the early Christian movement, here notably the Macedonian churches, should help motivate the Corinthian Christians to make good on their promises of showing noble generosity in regard to the collection project. Thanks to Paul's boasting about them, the Corinthians had already gained an honorable reputation within the larger Christian community. Now, however, they had to put their money where Paul's mouth was, or else they would be put to shame, having failed to live up to the reputation Paul had helped to establish on their behalf.

2 Corinthians 9:6-10. To the Corinthians, it was clear enough that God was behind the more obvious spiritual endowments like prophecy, tongues, teaching, and words of knowledge (see Romans 12:6-8; 1 Corinthians 12:4-11). Paul had to remind some of them, at least, that God gave such gifts not for personal aggrandizement but for the strengthening and nurture of the whole community. Stewardship, the ability to give material aid and service to others, is also, however, a gift of God. Indeed, it is a manifestation of God's patronage of the community—God's care for God's people—mediated through its members. God enriches the Corinthian Christians specifically so that they will have the means whereby to supply whatever is wanting in the lives of their sisters and brothers throughout the Christian communion. God supplies all things, so that Christians are called to share as an obedient response to the purpose of the Giver, as those who have been entrusted by God with resources *intended for others.*

This would contrast rather starkly with the model of patronage between human beings, the model that would have been foremost on the minds of the Corinthians who were able and disposed to share their material resources. These people would have been accustomed to regarding their property as their own, and those to whom they gave gifts as obligated to them. Paul,

however, views the sharing of resources among Christians as God's beneficence working itself out through responsive Christians (2 Corinthians 9:8, 10).

Paul is not the only author comparing the giving of gifts to sowing with a view to reaping a harvest. Seneca, author of a veritable textbook on giving and receiving gifts nobly, entitled *On Benefits,* uses it frequently. He urges people to select the recipients of their gifts wisely, since "we do not sow seed in worn out and unproductive soil" (1.1.2); he compares the risk of giving gifts to sowing seed, for there is never the guarantee of a harvest (4.33.1-2); he advises that clients need to be cultivated with constant attention to ensure that the relationship takes hold, like a farmer cultivates the land on which he has sown his seed (2.11.4-5). Paul redirects this cultural advice, however. The harvest that the Corinthians should be most concerned about is not the gratitude or indebtedness of other people, but the harvest of righteousness that shall be accounted to them, which follows upon sowing deeds of charity and kindness among one's larger Christian family.

2 Corinthians 9:11-15. Acts of generosity were perhaps the most prominent means by which local patrons would build up their reputation and their client base. "Giving" established patron-client relationships and the reciprocal obligations that went along with such relationships. By giving to others, patrons, in effect, indebted others to them, since the recipients of gifts and benefactions knew themselves to owe gratitude (respect, loyalty, and service, in the case of those who were unable to reciprocate gifts in kind) to the giver. Paul will not allow giving within the church to become yet another means by which individuals indulge themselves in power plays and self-promotion, using gifts of money, hospitality, and aid to build up their client base. Rather, by transforming patronage into "stewardship," he locates the source of all gifts in God and directs gratitude back toward God (2 Corinthians

9:11b). This is appropriate, since God is ultimately the source of the bounty that has been shared (9:6-10). Those who act generously within the church are still to be honored, but as obedient stewards of God's bounty, and not as power brokers within the church.

An important motive for giving was supplied by Paul's interjection of Christ's generous example, who "though he was rich, yet for your sakes . . . became poor" (8:9). Having reminded them of their own immense debt of gratitude to Jesus and to God for their bounty and self-sacrificing kindness, Paul promotes participation in this relief effort as a means by which they can enact their gratitude, since it will bring honor to their divine benefactor (9:13) and show themselves obedient to his intentions for enriching them in the first place. They are honor-bound to use the riches entrusted to them for God's purposes, namely relieving the needs of the saints.

This relief effort is not merely a "one-way street," however. The Judean Christians reciprocate with prayer on behalf of the Gentile Christians (9:14). Spiritual favors and material favors can be exchanged in the reciprocal relationships between believers and churches, and the latter are no more "real" than the former (see also Romans 1:11-12; 15:26-27; 1 Corinthians 9:11; Galatians 6:6).

INTERPRETING THE SCRIPTURE

Money and Power

By re-envisioning Christian giving as God's provision for the needs of God's whole family—in other words, by transforming patronage into "stewardship"—Paul removes Christian giving from the realm of competition among humans for honor and accumulation of power. This remains a message as relevant today as ever. Much tension within contemporary churches could be relieved if we took to heart Paul's "paradigm shift" for patronage. Those who contribute to the local church do not lay the minister or the congregation under obligation, but are enacting faithfully their service to the God who has entrusted them with a portion of God's bounty for the relief of others. Such people are indeed to be honored on this basis, but as obedient stewards rather than "local patrons." They give not in order to secure a return (usually in the form of power and influence within the local church), but because God has given to them with explicit instructions on how to use the resources.

Such a transformation begins by meditating upon God's generosity toward you, making a careful account of what God has enabled you to do and the ways in which God has preserved you to this day. If we pierce the myth that we have made ourselves what we are by own efforts and begin to discern that what we are, we are by the gift of God, we will move considerably closer to Paul's understanding of God's economy. The next step would be to understand our acts of giving as a response of obedience and gratitude to God—something that nurtures our connection with God rather than enhances our position and power within the church or other settings where we give. Here again we cannot help recalling the Macedonians' attitude that participating in relief efforts was as much a favor granted the givers as a favor done by the givers.

The Attitude of Giving

In 2 Corinthians 9:7b, Paul draws on Proverbs 22:9 (in the Greek translation of the

Old Testament that was current in the first-century churches; this will look different in your English Old Testament, which is based on the Hebrew text), giving us perhaps one of our most familiar stewardship slogans: "God loves a cheerful giver." By reciting this line from Proverbs, Paul begins to interact with, and invites the hearers to call to mind, the body of wisdom texts about giving—the cultural knowledge about giving passed on in the Old Testament.

One important stream of tradition has to do with the connection between righteousness, or justice, and giving. Psalm 37:21, for example, reads: "the righteous are generous and keep giving." Giving is a fruit and a manifestation of a well-formed, just character. It is a reflection of God's beneficence, "who gives to all generously and ungrudgingly" (James 1:5). Paul himself invokes God's example of beneficence as he recites Psalm 112:9 in 2 Corinthians 9:9, again making the connection between giving and righteousness. God's "scattering" of blessings to all, and his particular generosity toward the poor, are manifestations of his "justice" or "righteousness." It is this righteousness of God that Paul wants to see at work among his converts, as Paul makes explicit in the following verse (9:10) by applying Psalm 112:9 to God's work among them. The God celebrated in that psalm supplies the Corinthians with resources by which to reflect God's righteousness in their own acts of kindness and generosity.

Another stream in this wisdom tradition about giving emphasizes that giving never impoverishes the giver, while hoarding or withholding relief never enriches the miser. Psalm 112:5 affirms, "It is well with those who deal generously." The author of Proverbs 11:24-25 observes: "Some give freely, yet grow all the richer; others withhold what is due, and only suffer want. A generous person will be enriched, and one who gives water will get water." Against the modern wisdom of saving for a rainy day, the author of Proverbs concludes that trust-ing in riches (that is, by not giving freely to others, but hoarding for oneself) leads to want, while generous giving (again construed as being "righteous") makes a person flourish (Proverbs 11:28). In this same stream, Paul promises that God will continue to enrich the generous (2 Corinthians 9:8, 11), and not only in terms of economic resources but also in the spiritual wealth of a grateful heart, an experience of fullness, and a deeper connection with both God and the larger community of faith that the giver serves.

God's Purposes for Wealth

We must guard against construing Paul's words at this point, as far too many modern "peddlers of God's word" (2 Corinthians 2:17) preach, as a divine scheme of getting richer ourselves by giving to others. This is a revival of a tenet of pagan religion, *do ut des*—"I give [to you gods] so that you will give [to me]." We cannot give to others in the hope that God will reward us with more wealth to spend on ourselves, any more than we can give to others as a means of justifying the greater amount we keep for ourselves. Any abundance we receive from God is given so that we "may share abundantly in every good work" (9:8), so that our own "harvest of righteousness"—our embodiment of the righteousness of God—may increase.

Why do we (or, if we are retired, did we) work? What purpose drives our labors? Is it to stockpile wealth for our own financial security in the future? Is it to facilitate our acquisition of material goods or our participation in enjoyable (but often expensive) activities? Or is it to be able to have the means to do good for others in need, to support God's work in the world, and to invest in advancing the kingdom of God?

Proving Our Confession

Our actions or omissions of action can either confirm or belie our claim to be followers of Jesus Christ. This is true across a broad spectrum of behaviors and attitudes, but is especially emphasized in matters of sharing or refusing to share possessions, even among other Christians. The author of 1 John questions how our love for God can be genuine when we do not reach out in love toward our sisters and brothers in obvious need (1 John 3:16-18). James asks how our faith can be real or alive at all when our response to a person who lacks food or clothing is merely "Go, be warm, be filled" (see James 2:14-17). Similarly, Paul regards his invitation to the Corinthians to complete their participation in the collection project generously as a test of the genuineness of their love (2 Corinthians 8:8) and of their

"obedience to the confession of the gospel" (9:13—the "testing of this ministry" refers not to the Corinthians' testing of Paul's service, but rather presents the opportunity to minister as a testing of the Corinthians).

Paul's challenge to "put our money where our mouth is," at least as far as our confession of faith is concerned, invites us first to consider carefully what it is we believe about the source and purpose of our money and other resources. It invites us also to ponder how we can make our faith real both to others and to ourselves by our choices of how to use those resources. Such an inquiry can help us discover new depths of meaning in our work and our spending.

SHARING THE SCRIPTURE

Preparing Our Hearts

This week's devotional reading is found in Psalm 37:16-24. Verse 21 states, "the righteous are generous and keep giving." How does this statement apply to you or anyone you know? Are there limits to giving? If so, how do you establish these boundaries? If not, or if these limits are very broad, what motivates you to keep on giving? Write in your spiritual journal some of your own reasons for giving.

Pray that you and the class members will be open to thinking and talking about money, a subject often considered taboo in the church, but which Jesus talked about often.

Preparing Our Minds

Study the background Scripture from 2 Corinthians 9:1-15. Our lesson will delve into verses 3-15. As you encounter this passage, think about why God's people are to give their time, talent, and money.

Look ahead, if you have not already done so, to our new unit for the fall quarter,

which is a survey of the Old Testament highlighting the theme of covenant. Be sure to have copies of *The New International Lesson Annual* for everyone on your teaching team.

Write on newsprint:
❑ list of reasons for giving for the Gather to Learn section, if you choose this option.
❑ information for next week's lesson, found under "Continue the Journey."

Plan a brief review of last week's session, if you choose to do so.

Prepare the lecture for "Look at How Paul Describes the Stewardship of Money as a Response to God's Generosity and as a Witness to One's Faith."

LEADING THE CLASS

(1) Gather to Learn

❖ Welcome the class members and introduce any guests.

❖ Pray that through our Bible study today God's Spirit will teach the participants how to live more faithfully through their giving.

❖ Brainstorm with the class reasons why they believe people give to the church and other agencies or causes that they believe are valuable.

❖ **Option:** List these ideas on newsprint prior to class and discuss them with the group. Invite them to add other ideas. Note that these items are listed in no particular order.

    A. Giving has tax advantages.

    B. Giving sets an example.

    C. Giving makes me feel good.

    D. Giving may have a beneficial impact on my life, such as finding a cure for a disease that I or a loved one may have.

    E. Giving allows me to emulate people I admire who have been generous.

    F. Giving is necessary to meet the budget.

    G. Giving enables me to make a difference in the world.

    H. Giving helps me avoid winding up like Ebenezer Scrooge.

    I. Giving provides me with status and influence.

    J. Giving enables me to respond to the gift God has given me in Jesus Christ.

❖ Provide a few moments for the students to think about their own reasons for giving in light of whichever list you have discussed.

❖ Read aloud today's focus statement: **People give to causes for a variety of reasons. Why should we give of our money or our time? Paul says we are to give in response to God's generosity.**

(2) Look at How Paul Describes the Stewardship of Money as a Response to God's Generosity and as a Witness to One's Faith

❖ **Option:** Since this week's session is very closely connected to the previous one, you may want to review briefly information related to the collection for the Jerusalem church and the Macedonian church's generosity in that endeavor.

❖ Choose a volunteer to read the Scripture lesson from 2 Corinthians 9:3-15.

❖ Present a lecture based on ideas from Understanding the Scripture and Interpreting the Scripture. Be sure to include:

    ■ arguments Paul uses to encourage the members of the Corinthian church to make good on their pledge for the collection to benefit the church in Jerusalem.

    ■ biblical attitudes toward giving: (1) in relation to power; (2) in relation to righteousness; (3) in relation to the giver, who is never impoverished by giving; (4) in relation to God's purposes for wealth.

❖ Conclude this portion of the session by asking the students to comment on how giving demonstrates the faith we confess in Christ.

(3) Evaluate the Learners' Current Stewardship of Money, Time, and Talent in Light of This Passage

❖ Recognize that we are stewards of whatever time, talent, money, or other attributes God has entrusted to us. The owner is actually God, the Creator of all things. This understanding is the foundation for Paul's encouragement for giving. Talk about how this biblical understanding compares and contrasts with the prevalent idea in the United States that people "own" all that they have and, therefore, can make gifts according to their priorities.

❖ Distribute paper and pencils. Read aloud the suggested verses and ask the students to write a response or a question they would like to ask Paul about his teachings on stewardship. Be sure to allow time for the students to think about each verse before moving on to the next one.

■ 2 Corinthians 9:6.

■ 2 Corinthians 9:7.

■ 2 Corinthians 9:8.

■ 2 Corinthians 9:11-12.

■ 2 Corinthians 9:13-15.

❖ Provide "talk back" time for the students to read their responses and raise their questions. You will likely have a fruitful discussion if you pursue the questions the students have raised. Some may deal with the disparity between the "haves" and "have-nots"—aren't the poor blessed by God? Others may deal with the church's role in providing for the poor, just as Paul was urging the Corinthian church to do for those in Jerusalem.

(4) Take Steps to Bring the Learners' Stewardship in Line with the Teachings of This Passage

❖ Post the list of reasons for giving that the class generated or you provided for the Gather to Learn section.

❖ Ask the students to reflect silently on this list. On the back of the paper they have already received, they are to rank their reasons for giving. For example, if "giving makes me feel good," which would be letter C on the list suggested in the lesson, is the first choice, the student would write 1-C. Encourage the students to add any other reasons they may have.

❖ Call time and ask the adults to look at their rankings in light of the teachings in this passage. Read these questions slowly.

(1) **How do your reasons for giving stack up against Paul's teachings?** (pause)

(2) **Do you need to reconsider why you give so as to bring your reasons into line with biblical stewardship?** (pause)

(3) **If so, what steps will you take?** (pause)

(5) Continue the Journey

❖ Pray that all who have gathered will continue to recognize how their giving is a reflection of their relationship to and witness for Christ.

❖ Read aloud this preparation for next week's lesson. You may also want to post it on newsprint for the students to copy. **Prepare for next week's session, "Leaning on Grace," by reading the background and lesson Scripture from 2 Corinthians 12:1-10. As you study, consider these ideas: Many people struggle with difficulties in life. What can help us through the difficulties we encounter? In referring to a deeply spiritual experience that he had, Paul recalls God's promise that God's strength would help him through the difficult times.**

❖ Read aloud the following three ideas. Challenge the students to commit themselves to use these activities as a springboard to spiritual growth.

(1) **Contemplate the biblical meaning of stewardship. How does this idea of being entrusted with things and attributes for the good of all differ from our society's belief that we own everything we have and can use it as we please?**

(2) **Page through your calendar. What do your appointments suggest about your stewardship of time? What changes might you need to make?**

(3) **Contemplate your reasons for giving to the church as you write your check or place your money in an offering envelope.**

❖ Sing or read aloud "Praise God, from Whom All Blessings Flow" or another familiar doxology.

❖ Close the session with this benediction, which you may want the class members to echo after you: **Go forth committed to serve, obey, and give as people who have been called to live faithfully in Christian community. Amen.**

UNIT 3: THE SPIRIT OF GIVING
LEANING ON GRACE

PREVIEWING THE LESSON

Lesson Scripture: 2 Corinthians 12:1-10
Background Scripture: 2 Corinthians 12:1-10
Key Verse: 2 Corinthians 12:9*a*

Focus of the Lesson:
Many people struggle with difficulties in life. What can help us through the difficulties we encounter? In referring to a deeply spiritual experience that he had, Paul recalls God's promise that God's strength would help him through the difficult times.

Goals for the Learners:
(1) to examine Paul's personal example and teaching that Christ provides strength to face life's difficulties.
(2) to recognize God's sufficient grace within their own lives.
(3) to celebrate God's gifts of strength and sufficient grace.

Supplies:
Bibles, newsprint and marker, paper and pencils, hymnals; optional: pictures from magazines showing people in distress

---

READING THE SCRIPTURE

NRSV
2 Corinthians 12:1-10

¹It is necessary to boast; nothing is to be gained by it, but I will go on to visions and revelations of the Lord. ²I know a person in Christ who fourteen years ago was caught up to the third heaven—whether in the body or out of the body I do not know; God knows. ³And I know that such a person—whether in the body or out of the body I do not know; God knows—⁴was caught up into Paradise and heard things that are not to be told, that no mortal is permitted to repeat.

NIV
2 Corinthians 12:1-10

¹I must go on boasting. Although there is nothing to be gained, I will go on to visions and revelations from the Lord. ²I know a man in Christ who fourteen years ago was caught up to the third heaven. Whether it was in the body or out of the body I do not know—God knows. ³And I know that this man—whether in the body or apart from the body I do not know, but God knows—⁴was caught up to paradise. He heard inexpressible things, things that man is not permitted

⁵On behalf of such a one I will boast, but on my own behalf I will not boast, except of my weaknesses. ⁶But if I wish to boast, I will not be a fool, for I will be speaking the truth. But I refrain from it, so that no one may think better of me than what is seen in me or heard from me, ⁷even considering the exceptional character of the revelations. Therefore, to keep me from being too elated, a thorn was given me in the flesh, a messenger of Satan to torment me, to keep me from being too elated. ⁸Three times I appealed to the Lord about this, that it would leave me, **⁹but he said to me, "My grace is sufficient for you, for power is made perfect in weakness."** So, I will boast all the more gladly of my weaknesses, so that the power of Christ may dwell in me. ¹⁰Therefore I am content with weaknesses, insults, hardships, persecutions, and calamities for the sake of Christ; for whenever I am weak, then I am strong.

to tell. ⁵I will boast about a man like that, but I will not boast about myself, except about my weaknesses. ⁶Even if I should choose to boast, I would not be a fool, because I would be speaking the truth. But I refrain, so no one will think more of me than is warranted by what I do or say.

⁷To keep me from becoming conceited because of these surpassingly great revelations, there was given me a thorn in my flesh, a messenger of Satan, to torment me. ⁸Three times I pleaded with the Lord to take it away from me. **⁹But he said to me, "My grace is sufficient for you, for my power is made perfect in weakness."** Therefore I will boast all the more gladly about my weaknesses, so that Christ's power may rest on me. ¹⁰That is why, for Christ's sake, I delight in weaknesses, in insults, in hardships, in persecutions, in difficulties. For when I am weak, then I am strong.

UNDERSTANDING THE SCRIPTURE

2 Corinthians 12:1. As we begin to read this passage, we jump in at the middle of Paul's "answer" to some Jewish Christian teachers that have come to Corinth and made a strong impression on the Christians there. These teachers regard Paul not as their partner, but as their rival, and they have been at work trying to usurp his place in the hearts of the Corinthians so as to promote themselves and extend their influence (2 Corinthians 10:14-15). It is not with their explicit teaching that Paul takes issue, as he does with the rivals in Galatia. Rather, Paul takes issue with their tendency to promote their own legitimacy as God's representatives—and to denigrate Paul's legitimacy as an apostle—by playing up to the performance- and appearance-oriented cultural expectations of "gifted speakers."

These rival teachers promote themselves by comparing themselves with Paul (2 Corinthians 10:12) on the basis of human strengths and worldly qualifications. They criticize Paul, pointing out that his physical appearance and presence do not match the weightiness of his letters when writing from a safe distance (10:10), and accusing him of not being sufficiently spiritual to be a worthy leader (10:2). They pride themselves on their polished performance, their ethnic privilege, and most likely their mystical or ecstatic experiences that distinguish them as "spiritual" and "in touch" with divine realities (11:18, 22-23a; 12:1). Paul regards them as so great a threat to the Corinthians' rootedness in the gospel of the crucified Messiah that he calls their message "a different gospel" presenting "another Jesus" and imparting "a different spirit" (11:4) and calls them "servants" (NIV) or "ministers" (NRSV) of Satan, the deceiver (11:13-15).

By their strategies for self-promotion, these rival teachers reinforce the essence of that ethos Paul had tried to drive out from the Corinthians in 1 Corinthians—competition, comparing and evaluating one person against another, boasting in spiritual or natural gifts and achievements as a tool for one-upmanship in the church. Their "boasting" prompts Paul, very reluctantly, to answer with boasting of his own (2 Corinthians 11:16–12:13), something he knows to be foolish from a divine perspective but somehow necessary to liberate the Corinthians from being too taken with these interlopers. Paul will also use a lot of irony in his boasting as a means of moving the focus back from external strengths to the transforming power of God at work where human strengths are exhausted.

2 Corinthians 12:2-4. Paul matches the rivals' boasts in regard to receiving visions and revelations by narrating one of his own. He follows the conventions of "inoffensive self-praise" by speaking of himself indirectly, as "such a person." This is not a reference to Paul's conversion experience, which appears not to have involved an ecstatic experience of an otherworldly journey, but a slightly later mystical experience. The levels of the heavens are variously numbered in Jewish literature of the period as three, seven, or ten; Paul is probably speaking of the third heaven as the highest tier, God's "Paradise." This vision, however, cannot benefit his hearers, since he cannot repeat the esoteric knowledge he learned there.

2 Corinthians 12:5-7a. Paul does a bit of rhetorical juggling in this passage. On the one hand, he wants the hearers to be aware that he, too, has had exceptional visionary experiences. On the other hand, Paul has matched the rivals' boasts only to throw the criteria that they have been using out of court. The real criteria Paul wants to advance are those that show through his weaknesses, not his strengths (see also 2 Corinthians 11:30). Just prior to our passage, he used this approach to demonstrate the genuineness of his connection with God. Rather than by listing his performance-oriented abilities and achievements like his rival, he set forth how many beatings, insults, and other hardships he endured as evidence of his steadfastness toward Christ in the midst of difficult circumstances. These are the real proofs of personal connection to Jesus that make one worthy to be called his "servant," Paul asserts, in keeping with the conventions of how genuine philosophers "prove" the viability of their way of life. Now Paul will present his "weakness" as the place where genuine, helpful divine revelation came to him—a mystery that he *can* communicate to his hearers.

2 Corinthians 12:7b-10. We are not certain what Paul's "thorn in the flesh" actually was. The fact that Numbers 33:55 and Ezekiel 28:24 use the term "thorn" (notably, "barbs in your eyes and thorns in your sides" in Numbers 33:55) to refer to the unwelcome presence of non-Hebrews remaining in the promised land has suggested that Paul has in mind some person who has caused Paul particular trouble. Presenting this thorn rather actively as a "messenger of Satan" (2 Corinthians 12:7) strengthens this argument. However, scholars tend to favor the view that Paul is referring to some physical malady, all the more as Paul does in fact seem to suffer from some chronic physical ailment—one that would have played into the rivals' hands as another reason to disqualify Paul as a representative of the powerful God. Whether this ailment was related to his vision (suggested on the basis of Galatians 4:13-15) or some other annoying condition that interfered with his ministry cannot be determined.

After praying to God to remove this burden, Paul learned a deeper mystery: God's power is most present in those times and places where we are most aware of our weakness and utter dependence on God. We are put "in touch" with divine power in a way quite different from the model embodied by the rival teachers. When we have come to the end of our resources that is when God can really break through into our lives. That is where we come to know and grow in faith in the "God who raises the dead," and find freedom from the myth of self-reliance (2 Corinthians 1:9). Paul came to regard this "thorn" as a "gift" from God to keep him centered on that spiritual truth. He has found contentment in all distressing circumstances since they have become opportunities for him to know and to reveal the power of Christ to others (4:7-12).

INTERPRETING THE SCRIPTURE

Paul's Incarnational Ministry

In our modern world, we tend to regard every pain, every sickness, every hardship, even every inconvenience as bad things to be avoided at all costs. When we fall into any one of these difficulties, our main agenda is to get out of it as quickly as possible. I often wonder, if being identified as a "Christian" cost us as dearly as it does many of our sisters and brothers across the globe, if we would not quickly abandon that association with Jesus in order to avoid the deprivations that might be imposed upon us.

Paul, however, confronts us as a strange model. He is content to suffer many of those experiences against which we insulate ourselves at all costs (even to the extent of turning our eyes away from, of shutting out of our minds, the many people around us who suffer hunger, homelessness, marginalization, and the like). The Corinthians might easily have preferred leaders who were above all that, who cut a better figure in the public eye. But Paul understood that God was working in him through the experiences of hardship.

Being hard-pressed himself, Paul is not out of touch with the weakness and the distress that beset his converts (2 Corinthians 11:28-29). Sharing fully in the underside of the human condition, he finds the experience to be a source of sympathy, caring, and connection with them. His pattern, unlike that of the rival teachers behind the scenes in Corinth, is very much more akin to the pattern of Jesus, who also did not remain aloof from human suffering. The mystery of the incarnation is that God the Son chose rather to immerse himself in the fullness of human suffering, to experience life as the common person experiences it, to experience hardship and death at their worst, so that no situation we face would ever be beyond his redemptive power. He is a sympathetic and effective redeemer precisely because of the incarnation (see Hebrews 2:17-18; 4:14-16).

More than this, his experience of weakness and distress—his coming to the point where his own resources fail—opens up Paul to the experience of God's encouragement, comfort, and empowerment, which in turn becomes a resource he can offer to the believers in their distress (2 Corinthians 1:3-7; 13:9). How often have you heard about someone who turned her battle with cancer into a ministry to others battling cancer, or about someone whose experience of divorce led him to become effective in reaching out to other persons surviving divorce? Such people have learned the same truth Paul learned again and again in his ministry—that God is present to us in our distress, giving us the strength we need to persevere and making us able to minister more effectively and share God's strength through the experience.

What You See Is What You Get

Paul sets aside his visionary experiences and insists rather that the Corinthians see him as he is and for what he is. He wants them to see him not through the filter of what he might say about his past achievements or experiences, but through their own eyes and ears as he is "today." The advantage of this approach is that the Corinthians can experience Paul himself, and not merely his "projected self," which would obscure both their perception of Paul and their experience of God's power at work in Paul.

To what extent, or in what settings, do we allow others to see us this way? Do we seek to see others this way? If you observe your own speech and the speech of others in social settings, you will often find that we tend to throw out lists of achievements, positions, and credentials at other people as a means of projecting a certain image (and potentially throwing them "off the scent" of any weaknesses and vulnerabilities we might feel). We often want to be known "for something" rather than "what is seen in me or heard from me" *right now.* It is the immediacy of seeing one another as we truly are in the here and now, however, that allows intimacy to grow between people.

It is also when we abandon the "projected self" and allow others to see us for who we are, and look at others for who they are, that God can move in our relationships within the church to bring much needed support and healing to one another. When Kelly and Ron dropped the facade of being a family that "had it together" and began to let fellow Christians know the pain of their hearts, they were able to connect with other believers who had walked through those difficulties themselves and could provide support and guidance on the way to reconciliation through facing some tough issues. When Julian decided not to hide any longer behind his many achievements and accolades, and to allow select Christian brothers to see the pain behind his driven career, they were able together to connect with the healing love of God. Julian was transformed from a rather intimidating success story into a person in whose life God was evident, and

who was approachable by those who needed that touch from God themselves.

Mixed Blessings

Paul's "thorn in the flesh" was no doubt unpleasant—so much so that he called it a "messenger of Satan" (12:7) sent to torment him. Like us, his first instinct was to find a way out of that experience. What he found, however, was that God was content to allow that condition to continue. There are some Christian communities today that, presented with a church member whose prayers went unanswered, would fault him or her for lacking sufficient faith, or even for having some secret sin that kept him or her from being healed. This passage suggests, however, that sometimes God simply says "no," and has another purpose for the unpleasant condition or circumstances.

Some believers manifest the faith to be healed of distressing conditions; others manifest the faith to persevere in love and faithful service in the midst of hardships or distresses that will not be taken away. For the latter, their experience—like Paul's— becomes a testimony to the sincerity and genuineness of their faith in and love for God. God can work either way both for the sake of the individual in distress and for the sake of others with whom God will bring that individual into contact. Very often it is the person who has passed through distress with her faith intact who can bring greater help to another person facing similar distress than can the person who is simply healed of that distressing condition (see 2 Corinthians 1:3-7; 4:11-12).

In Paul's case, the thorn was used to good effect, namely to keep him from becoming puffed up or too confident in his own spiritual virtuosity like his rivals were. Similarly, his every experience of weakness, distress, and hardship became an opportunity for him to decide to remain vulnerable and allow his weaknesses to show precisely so that those around him might have the opportunity to sense and to encounter the power of God that worked in him. He chose to prevent his "clay vessel" from distracting others from or trying to compete for attention with the brilliance of its contents (2 Corinthians 4:7-12). Only thus could he, and can we, bring people into contact with that power of God that will ultimately transcend death, when all human strengths have failed.

SHARING THE SCRIPTURE

Preparing Our Hearts

This week's devotional reading is found in James 4:1-10. Here James writes about the conflicts that result from our friendship with the world, which he believes make us enemies of God. Verse 6 speaks about God giving grace. What does the word "grace" mean to you? Check its meaning. Where have you been especially aware of God's grace in your life? How has grace kept you focused on God, rather than craving the things of this world?

Pray that you and the class members will lean on God's grace, especially when the world and its ways challenge you to make other choices.

Preparing Our Minds

Study the background and lesson Scripture, both of which are found in 2 Corinthians 12:1-10. As you study, think about what can help you to get through the difficulties that you encounter in life.

Write on newsprint:

❏ information for next week's lesson, found under "Continue the Journey."

Prepare the suggested lectures for "Examine Paul's Personal Example and Teaching That Christ Provides Strength to Face Life's Difficulties."

If you plan to invite a speaker for "Recognize God's Sufficient Grace Within the Learners' Lives," be sure to contact this person early in the week to extend the invitation, explain the thrust of the lesson, and give the speaker a time limit.

If you plan to use Option 3 under "Celebrate God's Gifts of Strength and Sufficient Grace," collect some magazine pictures of persons in distress, such as victims of war, natural disaster, or accident.

LEADING THE CLASS

(1) Gather to Learn

❖ Welcome the class members and introduce any guests.

❖ Pray that the members and friends who have come today will experience God's presence in a new and life-changing way.

❖ Challenge the class to brainstorm as many difficulties in life as they can in two minutes. Write their ideas on newsprint.

❖ Encourage the adults to talk with the class, or in groups, about any of the listed difficulties that they have personally encountered by answering these questions.

(1) How did you get through this problem?

(2) What difference did your relationship with Christ make as you encountered and moved through this difficulty?

❖ Read aloud today's focus statement: **Many people struggle with difficulties in life. What can help us through the difficulties we encounter? In referring to a deeply spiritual experience that he had, Paul recalls God's promise that God's strength would help him through the difficult times.**

(2) Examine Paul's Personal Example and Teaching That Christ Provides Strength to Face Life's Difficulties

❖ Ask a volunteer to read the first part of today's passage, 2 Corinthians 12:1-7*a* (end with "revelations").

■ Use information from Understanding the Scripture to help the class delve into (1) Paul's rivals, and (2) Paul's revelations.

■ Allow the students time to talk about Paul's mystical experiences. What questions would they want to ask Paul about them? How do these experiences potentially counter charges by Paul's rivals?

❖ Select someone to read 2 Corinthians 1:7*b*-10.

■ Use information from Understanding the Scripture to suggest possibilities for Paul's "thorn."

■ Read the following: **Paul is a model for us of one who endures hardships, including a "thorn" that distresses him to the point that he calls it "a messenger of Satan" (12:7). Some modern churchgoers would say that Paul could be healed if he had enough faith, and yet he accepts the fact that healing is not going to occur and this "thorn" will be with him. Instead of complaining, he proclaims that God's grace is sufficient for him. His weakness becomes a strength that God can use. How do you react to Paul's attitude toward his suffering? Is this a model that you can emulate? Why or why not?**

(3) Recognize God's Sufficient Grace Within the Learners' Lives

❖ **Option:** Invite someone to speak to the class about his or her experience with the power of Christ "made perfect in weakness" (12:9) in his or her own life. Set in advance a time for this person to speak, and a time for the class to ask questions, if the guest would feel comfortable in fielding them. Here are some ideas.

■ Ask a class member who has coped with serious medical challenges to speak with the group.

■ Invite a church member willing to share his or her experience of God's presence in a serious family crisis.

■ Contact a member of the community who has suffered due to a natural catastrophe, faced oppression perhaps in another country, or survived a Holocaust experience.

❖ Encourage volunteers from within the class to speak about their own experiences with God's grace in times of weakness. If you divide into small groups, more people will have an opportunity to share their stories.

❖ Prompt the students to name and discuss biblical characters who serve as models of faith for them in the midst of suffering and difficult situations. Some of these characters include: Moses, Job, Esther, and John the Baptist.

❖ Conclude this part of the session by asking the class members to read in unison today's key verse, 2 Corinthians 12:9*a*.

(4) Celebrate God's Gifts of Strength and Sufficient Grace

❖ Distribute paper and pencils. Do one of the following options.

Option 1: Encourage the participants to write a poem, psalm, or litany of thanksgiving for the gifts of strength and sufficient grace that the learners have received in time of need.

Option 2: Distribute hymnals. Ask the adults to page through and write the titles of hymns that lift them up when they face serious challenges. Suggest that they write a few comments about how the hymn(s) they have selected remind them of God's gracious presence.

Option 3: Distribute magazine pictures showing persons in distress. Invite the students to each select a picture and then use their imaginations to write a story to accompany it. Somehow the story should illustrate how people respond gratefully to God's grace and strength in time of need.

❖ Provide time for those who wish to do so to report back by retelling or reading what they have written.

(5) Continue the Journey

❖ Pray that the students will recognize God's sufficient grace in their lives, regardless of what is happening.

❖ Read aloud this preparation for next week's lesson. You may also want to post it on newsprint for the students to copy. **Prepare for next week's session, "Finding Security," by reading background from Genesis 9:1-17 and focusing on verses 1-15. Keep these ideas in mind as you prepare for this first lesson of the fall quarter in a unit entitled "In Covenant with God": We all long for some sense of security. What can we trust as being sound and secure? God promised all creation never to send another flood, and the rainbow serves as a reminder that God is keeping this promise.**

❖ Read aloud the following three ideas. Challenge the students to commit themselves to use these activities as a springboard to spiritual growth.

(1) Think about a "thorn" that exists in your life. Is it a physical infirmity, a difficult family member, a high-stress work situation? Make a conscious effort to repeat "God's grace is sufficient for me," adapted from today's key verse, when you feel pressures mounting as you deal with this problem.

(2) Contemplate and/or write in your spiritual journal about how God's gracious strength has carried you in times of weakness. Give thanks to God for this gift of grace.

(3) Tell someone else about the grace of God you have experienced and invite this person to experience that gift.

❖ Sing or read aloud "Praise, My Soul, the King of Heaven."

❖ Close the session with this benediction, which you may want the class members to echo after you: **Go forth committed to serve, obey, and give as people who have been called to live faithfully in Christian community. Amen.**

SAYING HELLO AND GOOD-BYE

The Preacher reminds us, "For everything there is a season, and a time for every matter under heaven" (Ecclesiastes 3:1). These words describe the circle of life. We are always coming and going, greeting others and then, eventually, parting company. In this article we will explore examples of people saying hello or good-bye, as recorded in selected sessions from our weekly lessons. Then we will consider how we as a class and as individuals can be more intentional in our welcoming and leave-taking with one another.

Biblical Greetings and Farewells

Advent is the season of the liturgical year set aside to prepare anew for the arrival of Emmanuel, God with us, and also to look ahead to his return in glory. The promises of the Suffering Servant Songs of Isaiah and Mary's Magnificat in Luke 2, which we will study in December, point us in the direction of the One whose coming will change the world—and us. If we spend time putting our lives in spiritual order, we will be ready to greet the coming Messiah as the King of kings and Lord of lords. We will be truly ready to welcome Jesus with all the praise, honor, and glory due him. Like the shepherds who first heard the good news from the angels, we will drop everything to rush and meet the newborn Savior. Also like the shepherds, we will eagerly tell others about Jesus.

Going out to greet others and tell the good news becomes a major theme of the rest of the New Testament. It is certainly the focus of Acts, which we will study in the fall quarter. In Acts 2, the followers of Jesus, who had huddled together behind closed doors in a home in Jerusalem, experienced a dramatic, life-changing event when the Holy Spirit fell upon them. It was time to say good-bye to life as disciples and take up the dynamic ministry of being "witnesses in Jerusalem, in all Judea and Samaria, and to the ends of the earth" (Acts 1:8). These believers would need to step out boldly in faith to do the work that the risen Christ had appointed for them. As the story of Acts continues, we find Peter, John, Philip, Priscilla, Aquila, Paul, and many others being led to people and places they likely would not have chosen on their own. These dedicated witnesses understood that they had been sent by God to preach the good news of the in-breaking reign of God. Their mission involved meeting and greeting people who lived in different cultures and worshiped different gods. Their task, though critically important, was not easy. Those sent by God had to learn how to reach others with the gospel, and then move on—sometimes being forcibly ejected from a city because of local opposition to their message—to begin again elsewhere with courage and enthusiasm. As they traveled and fulfilled their calling, they surely began to understand the meaning of Jesus' words, "If any want to become my followers, let them deny themselves and take up their cross daily and follow me" (Luke 9:23).

Paul, perhaps more than any other, understood the cruciform life. We see evidence of this understanding not only in Acts but also in 1 and 2 Corinthians, which we will focus on during the summer, and in 1 and 2 Timothy and Titus, which we will explore in January and February. A zealous Pharisee, Paul had thought he was doing God's will by persecuting Jesus' followers. After a spectacular greeting by the risen Christ while on the Damascus road,

Paul encountered God's truth and began to live passionately for Christ. He suffered persecution from many quarters, both without and within the church. Second Timothy 4, for example, records that even Paul's friends and supporters deserted him at his "first defense"; only God came to his rescue. Even in Corinth, where Paul lived for a year and a half after establishing a congregation, the apostle and his ministry were deeply hurt by the divisions within this church and especially by one who offended him. Although we do not know the exact nature of this offense, Paul was so grieved that he decided not to make another "painful visit" to the Corinthian church. He did, however, write to them in tears, asking them to forgive the one who had harmed him.

In another episode, prior to his departure for Jerusalem, Paul called together the elders at Ephesus for a poignant good-bye. He shared with these colleagues the response he expected to receive there: "I am on my way to Jerusalem, not knowing what will happen to me there, except that the Holy Spirit testifies to me in every city that imprisonment and persecutions are waiting for me" (Acts 20:22-23). And yet, Paul willingly went, even knowing that he would be greeted with hostility and physical suffering. Prior to his departure, "there was much weeping among them all; they embraced Paul and kissed him, grieving especially because of what he had said, that they would not see him again" (Acts 20:37-38).

Death always seems to us to be the final good-bye. We can hardly begin to imagine Job's suffering as he heard about the death of his children when the home of their eldest brother collapsed on them while they were dining. What had Job said to each one the last time that he saw them? He had no idea that his children would all predecease him and was certainly unprepared for their untimely deaths. In contrast, the disciples did realize that they had said their final good-bye to Jesus as he was arrested, tried, and found guilty of a crime punishable by crucifixion. Good Friday—and Jesus' death—were quite real and horrifying. But Easter morning came and the women found him alive—resurrected by the power of God! Fear swept over them and they fled, according to Mark 16, "for terror and amazement had seized them" (16:8). How could death, the great chasm, suddenly be bridged? How could good-bye be transformed into hello? How could Jesus, who had been crucified, show himself to his followers, "appearing to them during forty days and speaking about the kingdom of God" (Acts 1:3), and command them to remain in Jerusalem until they received the promised Holy Spirit? How could they set off to be his witnesses as he had instructed in Acts 1:8? Yet, they did go and proclaim the mighty deeds of God, and through their message others were drawn to Christ. The Christian community began to be formed, and all who chose to follow Christ were greeted and welcomed into this fellowship.

Bidding Welcome

Just as biblical people did, we too greet new people, walk along with them for a finite time, and then must part company. We do this on a small scale each week at the beginning of the session as we welcome class members, their guests, and others who have chosen to join with us for the day. While some may be truly visitors, passing through our community as they travel, other newcomers may be seeking a church home. Will they find in us people who joyfully extend hospitality and a warm welcome? As we conclude our session, we say good-bye by repeating a benediction that we learn during the course of each quarter. We affirm each other as we go forth to serve God. Inherent in the benediction is the promise that we will again say hello to resume our fellowship and study together.

Beyond these small weekly rituals, are there other ways that we can be more intentional about saying hello and good-bye to people who cross our paths, particularly those with whom we journey for some period of time in the church? Most definitely! Let's consider some of them.

"Hi, my name is . . . and I'm so glad to see you this morning. I don't believe I know your name." Such a simple greeting, but one that can have a real impact on whether or not someone feels at home. Perhaps you have visited a church that you later described as "cold." Most often when we say that, we are not referring to the temperature but to the fact that no one took a moment to welcome us and find out who we are. Some people in large-membership churches worry that a personal introduction may be embarrassing if the other individual is already a member. Such worry seems more like an excuse, especially if the greeting is carefully worded. While it is true that many visitors do not want to be asked to stand before the congregation to introduce themselves, most people appreciate a personal greeting.

That greeting can be further extended by offering a small gift, such as a votive candle or visitor's pin. Some churches keep homemade pies in the freezer to give to visitors. Others send a church member with a warm loaf of bread that Sunday afternoon to thank a family for visiting. A follow-up visit, call, or letter from someone in the class or church at large can really let visitors know that their presence was noticed, appreciated, and desired again.

A mentor can also help people to feel at home. Just as Paul mentored Timothy, we can serve as role models and one-on-one teachers for those who are new to the faith—or just to our church. Simple acts of kindness, such as sharing a Bible or hymnal, can help someone assimilate quickly. Mentors are also needed to help newcomers discern and employ their spiritual gifts, as Paul wrote about in 1 Corinthians 12. Being available to chat, even if you do not know all the answers (who does?), can also signal a warm greeting and openness to a long-term relationship. Perhaps your class would consider designating people who would serve as mentors for visitors and newcomers.

We sometimes forget that a new clergyperson needs to be welcomed into our midst as much as new members do. This pastor likely uprooted a family to come to our church. A service of installation followed by a luncheon or reception is important, but we also need to welcome this minister in other ways. We should look for strengths that will help our congregation move forward, and encourage the pastor to use them. We should avoid the comparisons and factionalism that plagued the church in Corinth. This pastor is continuing the planting-and-watering process that others have begun. Thank the pastor for coming, invite him or her to dinner, send a small gift, say a word of heartfelt praise, or in some other way let this new leader know that he or she is welcome and appreciated.

Taking Leave

People come and go in our lives. And so it is with the church. Newcomers move into the community, but faithful members also move away. A business transfer, a need to move elsewhere to care for a family member, or retirement prompt folk to leave "home." How do we say good-bye? Some classes or churches have a reception where folk can gather around the table to say good-bye and tell those who are leaving what their presence has meant. *The United Methodist Book of Worship* includes a more formal recognition, "An Order of Farewell to Church Members," designed to bid a public good-bye in the context of a worship service to members moving to another community.

Churches also have special-recognition services to say good-bye to a pastor as he or she leaves for a new church or retirement. Like the Ephesian elders who wept as Paul left, we too often shed many tears when a beloved pastor who has baptized our children, married us, buried our loved ones, and pointed us in the direction of spiritual maturity moves on. A meaningful service and reception can begin to help us accept the reality of this change and prepare for a new pastor to come among us.

Sometimes we must take leave of a church building. A building whose walls hold many cherished memories must be torn down to make way for a newer space that will move the congregation's ministry into the future. Or changes in the landscape of the community place our building in the path of an oncoming highway. A natural disaster may strike our sanctuary and, even if the sanctuary is rebuilt and rededicated, it never seems the same to us. Or, a congregation may dwindle in size to the extent that it needs to merge with another congregation, thus closing the doors of one building forever. While The United Methodist Church, and likely others as well, have rituals for leaving a building, it is still hard for us to come to grips with saying good-bye to a sacred space that has held such important, personal meaning for us. Church members need time to grieve the loss of this very special place and give thanks for its role in their lives so that they can look ahead to new spaces where future memories will be created. If your church is facing such a situation, consider providing class time to allow the members to voice their feelings and share memories with one another.

We turn now to the ultimate leave-taking: death. Sometimes we know that a beloved one is seriously ill. While the interval between a diagnosis and death is always unknown, we can use whatever time we have to let this person know how much she or he is valued and has contributed to our life. Encourage the class members to make a phone call, send a card or flowers, visit if the sick one is able to receive company, or give the caregiver some respite time. We go to funeral homes to pay our respects, but our good-byes must be said long before the hearse arrives. In fact, we need to live each day as if Christ will be returning at any moment. Such an attitude will help us to live mindfully, ready to say a good word and perform an act of kindness. We need not, indeed should not, wait until the eleventh hour to say "I love you" or "My life would never have been as wonderful if you had not been part of it," or "I'm sorry; please forgive me." Such daily words enable us to look back on whatever time we have had together without regretting things done and things left undone. This way of living is especially helpful in coping with a sudden, unexpected death where a formal good-bye was not possible.

As appropriate opportunities arise, remind the Sunday school class members that each one of us can help those we love by preparing for death while we are still healthy and of sound mind. We can talk over with our family, pastor, and close friends our wishes regarding end-of-life issues such as resuscitation and heroic measures to extend life. We can have a properly prepared and executed last will. We can leave plans for a funeral or memorial service, so that our loved ones need not wonder what we would have preferred. We can also prepare written instructions regarding organ donation and the disposal of our bodily remains by means of burial, cremation, or donation of our body for scientific research. We can ensure that insurance, investment, and other financial matters are in good order. Such proactive planning is a blessing to survivors who are grieving and vulnerable. By tying up loose ends and making realistic preparations for those we will leave behind, we give them the gift of a final good-bye that allows them time and space to grieve the profound loss of our earthly company and contemplate the joyous hello when we meet again.

POSSIBLE CHRONOLOGY OF THE LIFE OF PAUL

Although Paul dominates much of the New Testament, we really cannot accurately date most of his ministry. Acts provides information about where Paul traveled, but not exactly when. Since Luke's account in Acts does not always square with comments Paul makes in his own letters, we cannot be absolutely sure of his itinerary and schedule.

Interestingly, Acts makes no mention of Paul's letter-writing activity, the means by which we best know Paul. Thirteen letters in the New Testament are attributed to him, but these too are undated. Scholars do agree that Paul wrote 1 Thessalonians, 1 Corinthians, 2 Corinthians, Philippians, Philemon, Galatians, and Romans. Second Thessalonians, Colossians, and Ephesians cannot be said with certainty to have been written by Paul himself. Many commentators believe that although 1 and 2 Timothy and Titus reflect some of Paul's concerns, these letters were likely written by his followers long after his death.

The chronology presented here, adapted from a United Methodist website, appears quite reasonable, but you and/or the students may find others with different information. Likely your class will not want to trace scholarly arguments supporting or refuting particular dates, so use this chart simply as a guide.

Date	Paul's Location	Events	Letter(s) Written
10-31	Paul is born and grows up in Tarsus; son of a Roman citizen; ancestors are of "tribe of Benjamin"	Becomes a zealous Pharisee	
31/33	Jerusalem	Persecutes Christians	
33/35		Called by God to be a preacher to the Gentiles	
35/38	Arabia and Damascus	Worked as missionary but Aretas expelled him	
37/38	Jerusalem	Met briefly with Peter and James	

After 37/38	Cilicia, Syria, maybe Greece	Missionary work	
47/50			1 Thessalonians
50/51	Corinth	Brought before Gallio, proconsul who refused to hear case of the Jews against Paul	
49/51	Jerusalem	Council meeting	
52/57	Asia Minor and Greece	Missionary work	Galatians, Philippians, Philemon, 1 and 2 Corinthians
56/57	Corinth		Romans
57/58	Jerusalem	Brings money he has collected from churches; arrested and imprisoned at Caesarea for two years	
59/60	Sea journey to Rome		
62	Rome	Imprisoned and executed	

SUGGESTED CLASS MISSIONS PROJECTS

Many of the lessons in this year's studies relate to missions. Perhaps your congregation is one of the many churches that sponsors missionaries or missions projects. If so, you may already have a missionary or project that you support financially and/or with hands-on work. However, if your class does not, consider designating a project or agency. Here are some suggestions.

Most denominations have a group devoted to relief efforts. In The United Methodist Church, for example, UMCOR (United Methodist Committee on Relief) springs into action when catastrophes strike. As their website, http://gbgm-umc.org/umcor, states, "UMCOR is the not-for-profit international humanitarian aid organization of The United Methodist Church, active in many parts of the world bringing hope, providing relief from hunger and disasters, and teaching peace." For more information about how you can contribute to projects, contact UMCOR by writing to them at General Board of Global Ministries, Room 330, 475 Riverside Drive, New York, NY 10115, or calling 212-870-3816.

The annual CROP walk is a well-known, ecumenical event in numerous communities. According to the CROP website, http://www.churchworldservice.org/CROP, their "community-based fund raising events raise money for local hunger-fighting agencies as well as the international relief and development efforts of Church World Service." Class members may be encouraged to participate in the community walk and raise pledges from sponsors and/or donate money to this worthwhile project.

If your class leans more toward political advocacy, check out Bread for the World at http://www.bread.org, or contact them by mail at 50 F Street, NW, Suite 500, Washington, DC 20001, or by phone at 202-639-9400 or 800-82-BREAD. "Bread for the World is a nationwide Christian citizens movement seeking justice for the world's hungry people by lobbying our nation's decision makers. [Bread for the World Institute] seeks justice for hungry people by engaging in research and education on policies related to hunger and development." You may wish to participate in their annual Offering of Letters.

Challenge the class to perform some hands-on ministry at a local shelter or soup kitchen.

Any class can sponsor a food drive to collect non-perishable items for hungry people. The church may distribute such food on its own, but churches in many locations unite to create a central food pantry or other non-profit agency where people who need food can get it.

The Society of Saint Andrew "is an ecumenical Christian ministry dedicated to meeting both spiritual and physical hungers. [They] feed the hungry all year long by saving fresh produce that would otherwise go to waste and giving it to the needy." The society sponsors three programs: the Potato Project, the Gleaning Network, and Harvest of Hope. Class members can contribute financially, participate in gleaning, and/or attend informational seminars. For more information, contact http://www.endhunger.org/index1.htm.

Consider building a home with the internationally acclaimed non-profit, Habitat for Humanity. Families who live in substandard housing are selected to put sweat equity into a home and then purchase it from Habitat at an affordable price, without having to pay interest. This ecumenical group works on the principles of biblical economics.

Plan a trip with a volunteer agency such as Volunteers in Mission, http://gbgm-umc.org/vim, to build or repair homes or other important community structures. Teams from local churches work together on these projects in economically depressed areas and/or places devastated by natural catastrophes. Volunteers usually raise money to provide their own transportation.

If the age range of your class members is mostly fifty to ninety-nine years of age, consider a trip with Primetimers by contacting Primetimers Program, Mission Volunteers Office, GBGM, 475 Riverside Dr., Suite 330, New York, NY 10115, or calling 1-877-882-4724. According to the website, http://gbgm-umc.org/vim/features/primepro.htm, "Primetimers experiences offer older adults opportunities for educational forums, cross-cultural exposure, faith-filled reflection, and greater exposure to the work of The United Methodist Church and the church universal." According to the website, as much as 60 percent of the Primetimers experience is expected to be spent in educational settings, with the remainder of time used in Christian service; a typical Volunteers in Mission experience consists of working 70 percent of the time, with the remainder to learn, sightsee, and rest.

You might also want to check with your pastor about mission service for those who can devote months, a year, or more to such activities. Remind the students that missions encompasses not only sharing the good news verbally but also tending the sick, feeding the hungry, teaching, doing agricultural work, engineering, and many other opportunities for committed Christians to use their "secular" skills to build up the body of Christ.

Jesus said, "The harvest is plentiful, but the laborers are few" (Matthew 9:37). Encourage your class members to make a commitment to labor in some field of missions by sacrificially giving of their time, talent, and/or financial resources.

INDEX OF BACKGROUND SCRIPTURES, 2005–2006